Complementary Methods
for Research in Education

Complementary Methods
for Research in Education

Edited by
Richard M. Jaeger

American Educational
Research Association
Washington, DC

American Educational Research Association
1230 17th Street, NW
Washington, DC 20036
202-223-9485

ISBN: 0-935302-08-5 (paper)
0-935302-09-3 (cloth)

Library of Congress Catalog Card Number 88-070121

Printed in the United States of America

Contents

Preface

The etiology of this book is complex and tortuous. It began as a set of scripts for an audio tape series entitled *Alternative Methodologies in Educational Research*. The series was prepared under the sponsorship of the Committee on Research Training of the American Educational Research Association. Members of the Committee recognized the existence of many high-quality textbooks on methods of educational research intended for use in graduate-level instruction. Nevertheless, they concluded that a series of audio tapes, each devoted to a single method of disciplined inquiry in education and accompanied by supplementary materials in print form, might significantly enlarge the set of resources available to instructors and students in introductory educational research courses. The success of the audio tape series, first published in 1978, resulted in a number of requests from members of the Association for a textbook that was based on the tape scripts. Each author of a tape agreed to revise and update his script, to transform it into a chapter that was suitable for visual (rather than auditory) presentation, and to select and introduce one or more "readings" from the educational research literature that exemplified sound application of the research method discussed in his chapter.

One deficiency often found in existing educational research textbooks is their overemphasis on quantitative research methods, to the exclusion or neglect of methods that emphasize verbal portrayals of findings or observational techniques, and methods based on naturalistic inquiry. Most available textbooks treat quantitative research procedures quite thoroughly; experimental methods, correlational procedures, quasi-experimental methods, and other procedures that are grounded in psychology and, to some degree, sociology, receive considerable emphasis. Survey research procedures and historical inquiry methods are also addressed in many basic texts, but with comparative superficiality.

One objective of the original audio tape series, and of this book as well, was to provide a more balanced presentation of the wide variety of approaches to disciplined inquiry that could be brought to bear on problems in education. In particular, it was desired to give appropriate emphasis to case study methods, ethnographic methods, philosophical inquiry methods, historical inquiry procedures, and survey methods beside more traditionally emphasized experimental and quasi-experimental/correlational approaches to educational research.

In his chapter on the nature of disciplined inquiry in education, Lee Shulman advances the readily confirmed hypothesis that choice of a method of inquiry involves more than determination of the way in which a given research question will be answered. To a great degree, it also determines the nature of the research question that will be asked. Ethnographic researchers and experimental researchers, for example, ask very different research questions. If students are exposed only to more quantitatively grounded researchers and research questions, they will lose more than knowledge of a set of research techniques, or a particular approach to research. They will fail to learn about the wide range of topics and questions for inquiry typically posed by those who engage in naturalistic inquiry. Moreover, they will never consider alternatives to the logical positivist philosophy of science that forms the foundation of classical quantitative inquiry methods.

In a period when inquiry in education lends itself to a richly diverse collection of methods and techniques, it is virtually impossible for a single individual to develop expertise in each. If one or two authors were to attempt to develop a text on educational research methods with the breadth and depth provided here, the task would be formidable indeed. Fortunately, the American Educational Research Association was able to call on accomplished and recognized specialists in each of the research methods represented in the book. Gene V Glass, author of the chapter on quasi-experimental procedures, has published widely on those methods; in particular, he was senior author of a book on time-series analysis, the principal focus of his chapter. Carl F. Kaestle is a historian as well as an educator, and is the author of several volumes on the history of education, the methodological focus of his chapter. Andrew C. Porter, author of the chapter on experimental research methods, has made extensive contributions to the journal literature on the statistics of education, including the development of methods for analyzing data collected in experiments in which measurement is less than perfectly reliable. Michael Scriven, author of the chapter on philosophical inquiry methods in education, has been a prodigious contributor both to the philosophical literature and to the literature of educational evaluation. A number of books as well as dozens of journal articles must be counted among his contributions. Lee S. Shulman prepared the initial chapter of this volume, on the nature of disciplined inquiry in education. Given Shulman's research in such diverse arenas as educational psychology, the education of teachers, curriculum theory, and medical education, it is fitting that he attempt to encapsulate the commonalities and contrasts among diverse methods of inquiry in education. Robert Stake, author of the chapter on case study methods, is best known, perhaps, for his fundamental work in the theory of educational evaluation. Recently, he codirected a study of education in the sciences in public schools throughout the United States that is reported in a collection of eleven case studies of science education in eleven different school systems. Harry F. Wolcott, who prepared the chapter on ethnographic methods in educational research, is both an anthropologist and an educational researcher. His published works include ethnographies of several peoples, with a focus on the role of education in those cultures. I wrote the chapter on survey research methods in education. I have directed a number of nationwide survey research studies and am the author of a book on sampling methods for research in education and the social sciences.

Each of the audio tape scripts that underlie the chapters of this book was subjected to "blind" review by at least two specialists in the method of educational research it addressed, was pilot tested with at least one group of students studying educational research methodology, and was modified on the basis of specialists' and students' recommendations and students' performances on a short test of comprehension of the relevant subject matter.

This book expands upon the audio tape series on which it is based in a significant way. Each author has identified one or more research papers, book chapters, or essays that exemplify high-quality application of the research method that is the subject of his chapter. These "readings" form companion pieces to the primary papers in this book, and each is introduced by a short section that explains why the author deems it an exemplary work.

This book has benefitted substantially from the varied contribution of many colleagues. I would like to express my appreciation to Peter Airasian, John Christian Busch, Geraldine Clifford, Frederick Erickson, Bruce Hall, John Hills, Kenneth Hopkins, James Impara, Thomas Knapp, Ray Rist, Todd Rogers, Richard Shavelson, George Spindler, David Tyack, and James Wardrop for assisting in the review of one or more of the original tapescripts. Cynthia Cole provided substantial editorial assistance and many helpful suggestions on the overall organization of the book. I would also like to thank several hundred graduate students in education and the social sciences at the University of North Carolina-Greensboro, Virginia Polytechnic Institute and State University, and the University of Wisconsin-Madison for their careful and thoughtful responses to tapescripts and study materials, and for a wealth of suggestions on how to improve the pedagogical value of the text.

Richard M. Jaeger
Greensboro, North Carolina

A Note to Instructors

This book, the audio tapes that compose the series entitled *Alternative Methodologies in Educational Research,* and the *Study Guide* that accompanies the tape series provide an integrated set of instructional materials for courses that include the study of educational research methods. All of these materials were designed for use in graduate-level courses on the methodology of educational research. Because the materials are modular, they can be used in many ways, and their usefulness transcends courses devoted solely to the study of research methodology.

Beyond the introductory section on the nature of disciplined inquiry in education, the remaining sections of this book are virtually independent. Therefore, selected portions of the book could be used in courses devoted to specific methods of research or to specific research perspectives—such as qualitative inquiry methods. In addition, the book provides a set of readings on educational research that could be used independently of the chapters on method.

Each of the audio tapes in the series *Alternative Methodologies in Educational Research* mirrors one of the sections on method contained in this book. It is thus possible to have students reinforce their reading by listening to the same authors describe the features of a methodological approach, using somewhat different language. The *Study Guide* that accompanies the audio tape series contains one section for each audio tape, and is available either as an entire manuscript or in individual modules associated with each tape.

Each section of the *Study Guide* contains a detailed topic outline of the material presented in its associated audio tape. Each section also contains a set of study questions and an annotated bibliography to the literature introduced by its associated tape. Some *Study Guide* sections contain exercises, short examples of specific research methods applied to real or fictitious problems, illustrative published materials, and in one section (quasi-experimental research methods), graphical material that is essential to understanding the associated audio tape.

The audio tapes and corresponding *Study Guide* sections are available either individually or as a complete series from:

Publications Sales
American Educational Research Association
Alternative Methodologies Tape Series
1230 17th Street, NW
Washington, DC 20036

Some Thoughts on Ways to Use These Materials

This book and the associated audio tape series could be used either to structure an entire course, or to enrich units devoted to particular methods contained in a course with some other principal focus—such as a graduate course in educational psychology or a graduate course on the sociology of education.

If you decide to use this book as your primary text in a course on educational research methods, you might want to supplement your lectures by playing the associated audio tapes during your class. You could interrupt the audio tapes as necessary, to emphasize and direct a discussion of key points. You could also use the exemplary readings in this book as a focus for discussion of the application of various research methods.

You might want to place the audio tape series in your institution's library or media center, and have students listen to the tapes outside of class. You could ask students to prepare answers to selected study questions in this book or the *Study Guide* for discussion during your class, or as homework assignments, to be submitted to you for review and grading.

Another approach to the use of these materials would be to treat the audio tape series as a voluntary reference source that students could use on their own in your institution's library or media center. You could then use this book either as a primary or supplementary text. Rather than playing the audio tapes during your class or using them for assigned listening, you could make the tapes and the *Study Guide* available to students whose optimum learning modality is auditory rather than visual, or to students whose prior research background requires them to supplement your assigned work.

Even if you choose to play the audio tapes during your class, you might want to place them in your institution's library or media center so that students can hear them again. Having the opportunity to listen to the tapes at their own pace, with the ability to start and stop the tapes, or to review specific sections, would enhance the learning of many students. Materials listed in the bibliographies at the end of each chapter on method in this book and in the *Study Guide* could be placed in the reserve section of your institution's library to ensure ready access by interested students, even if you do not assign additional readings from these lists.

A Note to Students

The materials contained in this book and an associated series of audio tapes entitled *Alternative Methodologies in Educational Research* have been designed to provide you with an efficient, interesting, and painless introduction to powerful and widely used methods of inquiry in education. Following are some hints on ways you can use these materials most effectively.

1. If you are using this book as a text in a course on research methods in education, ask your instructor to place the *Alternative Methodologies in Educational Research* audio tape series in your institution's library or media center. The chapters on method contained in this book were developed from scripts used in these audio tapes, and the tapes present the essential ideas in the chapters from a slightly different perspective.

2. A *Study Guide* accompanies the audio tape series and contains a section that corresponds to each tape. Each section of the *Study Guide* contains a detailed outline of its corresponding tape designed to help you understand what you are about to hear when you listen to the tape. Prior to reading a chapter in this book that introduces a method of inquiry, you might want to listen to the corresponding audio tape, so as to gain some advance knowledge of the key ideas in the chapter. If you choose to study in this way, review the content outline in the *Study Guide* before you listen to the associated tape. Then as you listen to the tape, follow along on the outline, to keep in mind where you've been and where you're going next. You'll find that the outline will help focus your attention on the most important concepts presented in the tape and contained in the chapter. It will aid your recall as well.

3. You will find a series of study questions at the end of each chapter on method in this book, and in each *Study Guide* section. Try to answer these questions shortly after you finish reading a chapter or listening to the corresponding audio tape, regardless of whether your instructor assigns them. The questions will help you assess what you know, what you should ask your instructor, and what you should try to remember. You might also find the study questions helpful when you are reviewing key concepts prior to an examination.

4. Each section in this book and each section of the *Study Guide* contains an annotated bibliography of important references on a method of disciplined inquiry in education. Use these references to supplement what you learn from the examples provided in this book, in the audio tapes, and in the *Study Guide*. Most of the bibliographies contain specific suggestions on what to read first and what to read after you know a bit more about the method of inquiry discussed in the chapter or on the tape. In all cases, the bibliographies divide references among

introductory sources, advanced sources, and sources that treat special topics within a methodological area. You can do a better job of learning almost any subject if you expose yourself to the views and ideas of several authors. Therefore, set a personal goal of reading at least two sources in the bibliographies provided at the end of each chapter on a method of inquiry.

5. Following each paper in this book that introduces a method of inquiry, you will find one or more selections from the educational research literature. These selections illustrate at least one use of the method you have just studied. They are preceded by a brief introduction in which the author tells you why the selection is important and what you should look for when you read it. When you read these introductions, be sure to take note of the most important points you should learn from the selections that follow.

6. In some sections of the *Study Guide* you will find actual problems that you can complete. These problems are designed to give you first-hand experience in applying the concepts introduced on the associated audio tape or in the corresponding section of this book. Try to work the problems while the information you have gained from this book or the audio tape is fresh in your mind. You can profitably return to the problems and your solutions when you are reviewing for examinations.

7. If you use the audio tapes in the *Alternative Methodologies in Educational Research* series as a supplement to your reading, encourage your instructor to place the tapes in a location that will allow you to listen to them at your own pace, and to start and stop the tapes as you wish. Then listen to the tapes in "bite-size chunks" rather than all at once. After you have listened to the material corresponding to a major section of the outline provided in the *Study Guide*, stop the tape, think about what you've just heard, and write down any questions you'd like to discuss with your instructor. Then listen to the next section.

8. The section of the *Study Guide* that accompanies the audio tape on quasi-experimental research methods, entitled "Quasi-Experimental Research Methods: Time Series Experiments," contains graphical material that you must have in view while you listen to the tape. If you do not have ths material in front of you, much of the tape will make no sense at all. So ask for the *Study Guide* when you get the quasi-experimental methods tape.

9. Researchers who use methods that involve collection and analysis of numerical information—such as experimental methods, quasi-experimental methods, and survey methods—often hold a fundamentally different philosophic view of the nature of truth and reality than do researchers who make use of naturalistic methods—such as case study methods, ethnographic methods, and historical methods. So choice of a method of inquiry by a professional researcher might reflect far more than mere selection of a technique. Ask your instructor to describe this distinction, and to introduce you to the philosophies of science that underlie disciplined inquiry in education and the social sciences.

Section I
The Nature of Disciplined Inquiry
in Education

Disciplines of Inquiry
in Education: An Overview

Lee S. Shulman
Stanford University

Few works in the English language are as rich as Shakespeare's *Hamlet*. One phrase is of particular interest. Hamlet is in deep grief and despair over the recent death of his father, King of Denmark. In his melancholy he has been acting rather strangely, and many have called him mad. Yet Polonius observes of Hamlet, "Though this be madness, yet there is method in it."

What does Shakespeare wish to convey with this phrase? How can the apparent lack of coherence or sanity of Hamlet's behavior be characterized by method? To assert that something has method is to claim that there is an order, a regularity, obscure though it may be, which underlies an apparent disorder, thus rendering it meaningful. Method is the attribute which distinguishes *research* activity from mere observation and speculation.

When adversaries argue about the nature of the world or the best approach to some particular human endeavor, we typically find ourselves evaluating their respective claims by examining the methods they use to reach their conclusions. There are few subjects that generate as much passion among scientists as arguments over method. This is not surprising, since scholars who agree on matters of method can pursue research questions in a parallel fashion and then argue over the results of their respective investigations. However, if they do not agree even on some matters of research method, then their findings are likely to be incommensurable. There will be no way to properly compare one inquiry with the other. It is for this reason that major controversies in educational research so frequently focus on problems of research method. What is the role of research methodology in educational research? How can we tell proper from improper uses of research methods? To answer these questions, we must turn to a central concept in educational research methodology—disciplined inquiry.

This material was prepared while the author was a Fellow at the Center for Advanced Study in the Behavioral Sciences. I am grateful for financial support provided by the National Institute of Mental Health (National Research Service Award 2 T32 MH 14581-04) and the Spencer Foundation.

Method and Disciplined Inquiry

Educational researchers are typically eager to distinguish their work from other forms of discourse which, for them, cannot lay claim to being research. Take for example the following statement from the preface of Cremin's (1961) prize-winning history of American progressive education, *The Transformation of the School.*

> There is currently afoot a simple story of the rise of progressive education, one that has fed mercilessly on the fears of anxious parents and the hostilities of suspicious conservatives. In it John Dewey, somewhat in the fashion of Abou Ben Adhem, awakes one night with a new vision of the American school: the vision is progressive education. Over the years, with the help of a dedicated group of crafty professional lieutenants at Teachers College, Columbia University, he is able to foist the vision on an unsuspecting American people. The story usually ends with a plea for the exorcising of this devil from our midst and a return to the ways of the fathers. This kind of morality play has always been an influential brand of American political rhetoric, used by reformers and conservatives alike. But it should never be confused with history! (p. vii)

Cremin forcefully draws the distinction between doing history and engaging in political rhetoric. Clearly, he claims, the results of the two forms of discourse must be treated with different degrees of respect and credibility. "Real history" should be given far greater credence than mere political rhetoric. How is one to distinguish between the two? I would suggest that, while the difference is not entirely a matter of method, the historian would distinguish his work from that of the rhetorician by the ways observations are collected, evidence is marshalled, arguments are drawn, and opportunities are afforded for replication, verification, and refutation.

When we speak of research, we speak of a family of methods which share the characteristics of *disciplined inquiry.* Cronbach and Suppes (1969) attempted to define disciplined inquiry a number of years ago in a monograph prepared with the collaboration of their colleagues in the National Academy of Education. Here are some of the definitions of disciplined inquiry they suggest:

> Disciplined inquiry has a quality that distinguishes it from other sources of opinion and belief. The disciplined inquiry is conducted and reported in such a way that the argument can be painstakingly examined. The report does not depend for its appeal on the eloquence of the writer or on any surface plausibility. (p. 15)

Hence, perhaps, a major difference between disciplined inquiry and political rhetoric is that disciplined inquiry does not depend on eloquence or surface plausibility alone. Cronbach and Suppes continue:

> Whatever the character of a study, if it is disciplined the investigator has anticipated the traditional questions that are pertinent. He institutes control at each step of information collection and reasoning to avoid the sources of error to which these questions refer. If the errors cannot be eliminated he takes them into account by discussing the margin for error in his conclusions. Thus, the report of a disciplined inquiry has a texture that displays the raw materials entering the argument and the logical processes by which they were compressed and rearranged to make the conclusion credible. (pp. 15–16)

That definition of disciplined inquiry could be misconstrued to imply that the appropriate application of research methods in education always leads to a sterile, ritualized, and narrowly conceived form of investigation. This is not the case. As Cronbach and Suppes observe subsequently.

> Disciplined inquiry does not necessarily follow well established, formal procedures. Some of the most excellent inquiry is free-ranging and speculative in its initial stages, trying what might seem to be bizarre combinations of ideas and procedures, or restlessly casting about for ideas. (p. 16)

What is important about disciplined inquiry is that its data, arguments, and reasoning be capable of withstanding careful scrutiny by another member of the scientific community.

If it is clear what constitutes disciplined inquiry and there is little disagreement regarding the need for research methods to be consistent with the standards of disciplined inquiries, why should this field be so filled with controversy? There are several reasons.

First, scientific inquiries cannot involve mere recitation of the "facts of the case." Indeed, inquiry demands the selection of a particular set of observations or facts from among the nearly infinite universe of conceivable observations. Just as in a court of law the legal adversaries may disagree profoundly about the relevance of a piece of evidence or the warrant to be given to the conclusions drawn from each other's reasoning, so in disciplined inquiry in education there is often lack of consensus about the grounds, the starting points, for chains of reasoning.

There is another, even more serious source of disagreements about method. Disciplined inquiry not only refers to the ordered, regular, or principled nature of investigation, it also refers to the disciplines themselves which serve as the sources for the principles of regularity or canons of evidence employed by the investigator. What distinguishes disciplines from one another is the manner in which they formulate their questions, how they define the content of their domains and organize that content conceptually, and the principles of discovery and verification that constitute the ground rules for creating and testing knowledge in their fields. These principles are different in the different disciplines.

A major reason why research methodology in education is such an exciting area is that education is not itself a discipline. Indeed, *education is a field of study,* a locus containing phenomena, events, institutions, problems, persons, and processes, which themselves constitute the raw material for inquiries of many kinds. The perspectives and procedures of many disciplines can be brought to bear on the questions arising from and inherent in education as a field of study. As each of these disciplinary perspectives is brought to bear on the field of education, it brings with it its own set of concepts, methods, and procedures, often modifying them to fit the phenomena or problems of education. Such modifications, however, can rarely violate the principles defining those disciplines from which the methods were drawn.

Applications of Research Methods: Some Examples

It is important to recognize that differences in method are not merely alternative ways of reaching the same end or answering the same questions. What distinguishes methods from one another, usually by virtue of their contrasting disciplinary roots, is not only the procedures they employ, but the very types of questions they tend to raise. This point might be best understood if I take an area of educational inquiry and describe how questions would be asked and studies conducted from the perspectives of different forms of disciplined inquiry in that field of study. Each of the examples I draw will be credible pieces of research; that is, forms of disciplined inquiry. This experience will illustrate the variety of forms of research method that can be employed in a disciplined manner in the same domain of inquiry.

One of the most important areas of educational research is the study of reading. In these days of "back to basics" in education, there is no basic more basic than reading. Millions of dollars and the time of thousands of individual investigators are invested in research to help us understand more about the teaching and learning of reading. Research is conducted in order to become smarter about certain matters, in this case, the teaching and learning of reading. What do we wish to know? What kinds of questions ought we to ask about language, reading, and learning? What kinds of reading research are possible and what can we learn from each?

One reasonable question is, "What makes some people successful readers and others unsuccessful?" How can you predict which sorts of people are going to have difficulty learning to read, in order, perhaps, to institute preventive measures before serious damage has been done? In this sort of research, one would collect a variety of measures on individuals, including measures of their performance on a number of tasks, their demographic or personal characteristics, aspects of their backgrounds, and anything else that could conceivably assist in accurate prediction of the likelihood of reading difficulty or failure. An investigator would then employ the techniques of correlation and regression to investigate the relationships between those predictors and sets of useful outcome measures of reading performance for students of various ages. Correlation is a statistical procedure used to determine whether two variables are related, or how much they are related. The approach would be quantitative and would involve no intervention or manipulation other than that required to administer the instruments needed to collect the necessary data. In general, correlational research attempts to describe the relationships among naturally occurring variables or phenomena, *without* attempting to change them.

Another investigator might now say, "I'm not really interested in predicting reading failure. I want to identify the best possible methods for teaching reading to all youngsters, irrespective of their backgrounds or aptitudes." Such an individual is unlikely to be satisfied with research methods that correlate attributes of individuals with concurrent or subsequent reading performance. This individual will be inclined to design experimental studies. Individuals or groups are systematically assigned to contrasting methods of reading instruction. The effects of these contrasting methods are then compared by testing the reading performance of those who have been taught. This approach involves experimental methods which contrast strikingly with those of correlational research. Naturally, there are times when the degree of control over the assignment of individuals or groups to treatments is not as great as may be theoretically desirable.

We may, for example, wish to contrast two schools which are using very different reading programs. Since pupils were not originally assigned to those schools at random, this cannot be considered a "true" experiment. In such cases we see researchers use other methods which attempt to identify which treatment was best without the benefits of random assignment. These are often called "quasi-experimental" procedures. Like "near beer," they are not the real thing, but they can come close.

Yet another investigator may say that neither predicting reading failure nor identifying the best methods of teaching reading constitute the questions of interest for him. Instead his questions may be. "What is the general level of reading performance across different age, sex, social or ethnic groups in the population?" "Where do the most significant areas of reading success and failure occur?" "What are the reading habits of particular groups in the general population?" This investigation will best be conducted through a variety of survey techniques measuring reading performance or questioning reading practices. The work of the National Assessment of Educational Progress and the International Education Association's studies of crossnational achievement exemplify this approach. Once again, different procedures are employed to ask different questions and to solve different problems.

In the cases I have described thus far, the significant questions concern how well or how much reading ability has been gained or developed. Thus there are comparisons between alternative methods of teaching reading or among different individuals or cohorts of students learning to read. Quite another sort of question can be asked about reading. There are many times when we wish to know not how many or how well, but simply how. How is reading instruction carried on? What are the experiences and perceptions of teachers and students as they engage in the teaching and learning of reading? What is the underlying or explicit system of rules by which this complex activity is accomplished?

Although at first blush this might seem a much less powerful form of question than the quantitative questions which precede it, this is not necessarily the case. Some of the most important and influential investigations in the history of social science have been of that form. Perhaps an example can illustrate that point.

When Binet and Simon were asked to develop a better method for identifying the children in the public schools of Paris who could profit from special education programs, they responded by creating the individual intelligence test. The goal of their research and development was to improve the precision with which one could measure the differences in intellectual ability among persons.

Nearly 20 years later, a young Swiss associate of Simon, Jean Piaget, became intrigued with a very different sort of question about human intelligence. He asked, "What does intelligence look like and how does it develop?" He was most concerned with the common elements characterizing the intellectual performance of all individuals at a given stage of development, rather than the levels of performance that distinguished among them. He was attempting to answer questions about shared regularities rather than measuring systematic differences.

Similarly, an individual interested in investigating the game of golf may decide to focus on differences in performance among golfers. What distinguishes good golfers from poor golfers? The study can be conducted experimentally, through contrasting alternative methods of training golfers. It can be accomplished correlationally by examining the attributes of poorly- and well-scoring golfers through use of everything from videotape analyses to measures of age, experience, and social characteristics. But a very different question would be, "How does one play the game of golf?" What are the functional rules of the game? In this case the investigator is interested in understanding the common elements or regularities shared by all golfers, whether they are national champions or weekend duffers.

To continue these examples about reading, there are investigators attempting to understand how reading instruction is accomplished in the classroom in general. They tend to use the methods of case study as they document or portray the everyday experiences of teachers and students in the teaching and learning of reading. In much case study work, there is a general assumption that American public schools are very similar to one another as institutions. Therefore, individual experiences of learning to read will not be enormously different from one setting to another. In other case study work, the assumption may be that "average" reading development does not exist. These researchers wish to document the dramatic diversity among individuals in the rate, sequence, and character of their development of reading competence.

These studies are likely to focus on only one classroom or school, a small number of them at most. Depending on the orientation of the researcher, the portrayals could emphasize the social character of learning to read in a classroom group, the intellectual and emotional experiences of individual children struggling to master the intricacies of reading, or even the manner in which individual children acquire the implicit rules for turn taking and status attainment in the classroom. Data gathering can include detailed prose descriptions written longhand on yellow pads, videotaping classroom episodes and analyzing their contents exhaustively, interviewing teachers and students to discover their reactions, perceptions, or expectations in classrooms, and collecting examples of work produced by teachers and students for careful review and interpretation.

The disciplines from which these methods draw their rules of discovery and verification are typically anthropology, ethology, linguistics, or particular subfields of sociology, such as symbolic interaction. These contrast sharply with the disciplinary roots of the more quantitative approaches, predominantly psychology, agriculture, genetics, and such quantitative branches of sociology as demography.

A philosopher approaching the problem of research in reading might raise yet another set of questions. He or she might examine the kinds of inquiry just described and observe that the *concept* of reading has not been adequately defined. What does it mean to be able to read? Do we denote by the term "reading" the ability to recognize the correspondence between visible symbols and sounds in isolation, mere word identification? Do we imply the ability to comprehend written prose, and, if so, at what level of sophistication or subtlety?

For example, does someone who knows how to read have the ability to detect the difference between assertion and irony in a prose passage? Analysis of the meaning of the reading process affects the kinds of tests and measurements of reading achievement that are constructed. What we choose to define as reading will be important whether pursuing predictive studies of reading failure, experimental studies of reading instructional methods, or general surveys of reading performance. A philosopher would conduct inquiries into the nature of the reading process that would entail quite different research procedures from those of the other investigators. These analytic procedures would be disciplined by the rules of evidence proper to philosophy.

Similarly, questions of what distinguishes readers from nonreaders can be approached historically. As soon as someone attempts to answer the question "What proportion of the U.S. population is illiterate?" the ambiguity of the definition of "literacy" becomes apparent. How well must a person read and write to be considered literate? How has that definition changed for societies with contrasting economic systems, religious orientations, sex role prescriptions, or social class hierarchies? A careful historical analysis can help account for both the conditions that foster increased literacy among members of a society, and the possible consequences of illiteracy for those members.

I have attempted in the examples just presented to illustrate the variety of ways in which types of research method can be applied to a topic of inquiry in education—reading instruction. Moreover, I have tried to indicate that the alternative methods not only approach the doing of research differently, but, by and large, ask different questions, and hence, generate quite different answers. This is hardly surprising and surely not disturbing. The need for a multiplicity of methods was recognized centuries ago, perhaps most eloquently by Aristotle, who, in the introduction to his treatise *De Anima (On the Soul)*, observed,

> It might be supposed that there was some single method of inquiry applicable to all objects whose essential nature we are endeavoring to ascertain . . . in that case what we should seek for would be this unique method. But if there is no single and general method for solving the question of essence, our task becomes still more difficult: in the case of each different subject we shall have to determine the appropriate process of investigation. (*Ethics*. I:1) (McKeon, pp. 145–146)

Generalizability of Research

However different the objects of investigation and the goals of inquiry, there are certain problems shared by all research methods. These problems include the *generalizability* of findings: that is, the degree to which findings derived from one context or under one set of conditions may be assumed to apply in other settings or under other conditions. Although there may be disclaimers from some research practitioners, all researchers strive for some degree of generalizability for their results. They are rarely content to have the research they have conducted generate understanding that is relevant only to the particular cases that were observed. There are several forms of generalization. The most frequently discussed is generalization from the particular sample of individuals who are tested, taught, or observed in a given study to some larger population of individuals or groups of which they are said to be representative. For example, if we conduct a study of reading comprehension with third graders in Philadelphia, can we generalize our results to third graders all over the country? Or must we limit our generalizations to children of certain social and economic backgrounds, ability levels, and the like?

The second form of generalization is from the particular tasks or settings in which a piece of work is conducted to that population of tasks or settings that the research situation is claimed to represent. For example, we may contrast phonics and whole-word approaches to reading instruction using two particular sets of books or methods. If we find one approach consistently superior, can we generalize these findings to *all* phonics and whole-word methods? Or must we limit our generalizations to those particular teaching materials alone?

While both types of generalizability are important, much more has been written about the first kind, generalizability across people, than about the second, generalizability across situations. We shall see that the two have certain elements in common. In classical statistics, the argument was made that if one samples randomly from a population in making certain measurements or conducting certain experiments, inferences can then properly be drawn to the entire population from which the random sample was taken. Unfortunately, it is rarely the case that investigators truly sample randomly from a total population to which they might ultimately wish to generalize. A truly random sample is one in which each individual in the population has an equal chance of appearing. In a now classic paper, Cornfield and Tukey (1956) have argued that this is never the case. Indeed, we sample as best we can and then make a case for the subsequent claims of generalizability. To use their metaphor, we must then build an inferential bridge between the particular groups of people whom we studied directly in our research and those other groups concerning whom we wish to generalize. We do so by documenting as comprehensively as necessary the characteristics of the individuals whom we have studied and the procedures we have used. Then, the reader can examine our documentation and critically evaluate whether our claims of generalizability are warranted. More specifically, the reader must judge whether the findings we report for the individuals whom we have studied should be considered applicable to any other group of individuals regarding whom our reader might be interested.

Cornfield and Tukey's concept of bridge building extends fruitfully to other aspects of generalization as well. When we report on a setting or a task we must be equally careful to document in detail its characteristics so that readers who are as concerned about the generalizability of our task characteristics as they are the generalizability of our sample can make the appropriate inferences.

Finally, we can now see that those who perform case studies are confronted with a problem of generalizability that is not different in kind from that confronted by their quantitative colleagues. To claim that one is conducting a case study requires that an answer be provided to the question. "What is this a case of?" Not every description is a case study. It may be a description of a singular individual or event. To claim that something is a case study is to assert that it is a member of a family of individuals or events of which it is in some sense representative. In much the same way that the reader of a quantitative study must build his Cornfield-Tukey bridge to evaluate whether the results of that study are relevant to certain other situations, so the critical reader of a case study must examine whether an inferential bridge can be built between this case and other cases of interest to the reader.

Controversy over Methods: Experimental Versus Correlation

One of the best known examples of a controversy over method was explicated by Cronbach (1957) in his now classic paper, "The Two Disciplines of Scientific Psychology." Cronbach observed that the field of psychology had divided early into two major streams—the correlational and the experimental. Both these streams share what Cronbach calls the "job of science," which is to ask questions of nature. A discipline, he observes, is a method of asking questions and testing answers to determine whether those answers are sound. Correlational psychology is *not* a form of research that uses only one statistical technique—namely, correlation. Those researchers who are deemed correlationists are interested in studying nature as it is, in studying the natural correlations occurring in nature. They are committed to understanding the functional relationships between variations in one set of events or characteristics and variations in another. Thus, they may ask about the relationship between income and achievement, or between the number of physicians per thousand population and infant mortality, or between phases of the moon and the behavior of tides on earth. They see nature presenting itself for inspection and the role of the scientist that of identifying which of the variations that nature presents are associated with other processes or outcomes.

In contrast, experimentalists are interested, as Cronbach observes, only in the variation they themselves create. The experimental method is one in which scientists change conditions in order to observe the consequences of those changes. They are interested in understanding how nature is put together, not through inspecting nature as it is, but through introducing modifications or changes in nature in order to better understand the consequences of those changes for subsequent states. They argue that only through the systematic study of planned modifications can we distinguish causal relationships between events or characteristics from mere chance co-occurrences. Thus, for example, foot size and vocabulary are correlated in the general population, but that does not mean that large feet cause larger word knowledge (or vice versa). It merely reflects the larger vocabulary size of older (hence, bigger) people relative to children.

All too frequently ignored is the intersection of research methods with the underlying theoretical, political, or social purposes of the research being conducted. As I indicated earlier in this paper, research methods are not merely different ways of achieving the same end. They carry with them different ways of asking questions and often different commitments to educational and social ideologies. We can observe this intersection of ideology and method in considering the historical roots of correlational and experimental approaches.

In the scientific world of later 19th-century England, the work of Charles Darwin on the origin of the species commanded special attention. Central to his evolutionary theory was the principle of natural selection—nature selects for ultimate survival those species or subspecies that are best adapted to the conditions confronting them. "Survival of the fittest" is a phrase used to describe the process by which individuals and species adapt to variations in environmental conditions in order to survive. The "struggle for life" favors those whose structure and behavior are adaptive to the challenges of their environment and are thus more likely to produce offspring who flourish.

This view of human evolution as a struggle for survival had a substantial impact on prevailing views of society. Buttressed by the centrality of competition and the free market to the economic thinking of 19th-century England, a movement called "Social Darwinism" developed. Social Darwinists viewed members of a society as struggling for rewards and undergoing "selection" based on their talents or merits.

Francis Galton, a cousin of Darwin, observed that it was important to study those variations in human abilities and performance contributing most significantly to successful adaptation. He thus began systematically studying those human attributes contributing most to social effectiveness. He assumed those characteristics were enduring traits, unlikely to undergo change. His research was broad indeed, ranging from studies of what he viewed as hereditary genius to investigation of the efficacy of prayer. His research was characteristic of what we now call correlational studies. He developed early forms of the statistical methods which currently underlie correlational research.

Galton's work is historically linked to the brand of social theory that came to be known as Conservative Darwinism (Cremin, 1961). Conservative Darwinists attempted to develop better means for identifying those members of the society who were most likely to adapt successfully and to provide opportunities to those individuals, whatever their social class or family background, to receive education and other perquisites from the society. They constituted the forerunners of the modern testing movement, which can be seen as a way of applying correlational psychology to the problem of identifying the fittest in the society and providing them opportunities for social mobility and leadership.

The testing movement thus began as an attempt to divorce the ability of individuals from their social backgrounds through basing economic and social mobility on performance rather than on patrimony. Ironically, those who now oppose the testing movement base their opposition on the argument that tests merely support and amplify existing social class and ethnic differences.

Opposition to this application of Darwinism to social research developed quickly. Scientists and social reformers questioned the assumption that existing individual or group differences were durable or necessary *by nature*. Indeed, they claimed that such differences were typically historical or social artifacts created by political inequalities. The role of the educator, they asserted, was not merely to develop better ways of identifying the variations already occurring in nature in order to select individuals who are most competent. Instead, the responsibility of the educator was to identify those interventions in nature that would lead to more successful adaptation and survival for the largest number of human beings. Thus, while survival of the fittest remained the watchword, the responsibility of the educator was to increase the proportion of individuals in the world who are fit, and the responsibility of the educational researcher was to experiment with alternative methods of rendering individuals more fit, more adaptable, than they might otherwise have become. This group was known historically as Reform Darwinists, and their political philosophy is implicit in many applications of experimental methods to educational research.

The goal of the correlationist thus became to understand and exploit the natural and, presumably, enduring variations among individuals, while that of the experimentalist was to create conditions to reduce those variations.

This example of how the two major streams in scientific psychology are ultimately rooted in distinctive political or social commitments is *not* meant to leave you with the impression that these two alternatives must always remain sharply contrasted and never integrated. Indeed, many researchers have devoted their careers to identifying research methods capable of transcending the contrast between experimental and correlational methods. That is a topic, however, that goes far beyond the proper subject of this discussion.

Thus, although Hippocrates was correlating and Galileo experimenting centuries before Darwin, these two strategies of research took on distinctly new ideological implications in the hands of competing Darwinists. In our day, the values commitment implicit in the choice of method is often unrecognized, even by the investigators themselves. This makes it even more dangerous to treat methodological issues without an understanding or concern for the specific substantive questions being asked. One of the enduring problems in research methodology has been the tendency to treat selection of method as primarily a technical question not associated with the underlying theoretical or substantive rationale of the research to be conducted.

Selecting the method most appropriate for a particular disciplined inquiry is one of the most important and difficult responsibilities of a researcher. The choice requires an act of judgment, grounded in both knowledge of methodology and the substantive area of the investigation.

Quantitative and Qualitative Methods

In looking at the differences between quantitative research methods and those typically dubbed qualitative, such as case study or ethnography, we find another type of political or social contrast that is of interest. Quantitative methods, whether correlational or experimental, require large and approximately random samples of individuals. Quantitative approaches require that sampling of both individuals and situations be conducted in order to maximize the generalizability of the findings to the widest possible population. In so doing they tend to sample from individuals and settings *as they are,* rather than *as they might be,* though this may be an overstatement for the experimental approach.

In contrast, it is intriguing to examine the types of setting frequently studied by qualitative researchers. For example, studies of open classrooms, free schools, or other radical educational innovations are often conducted using case studies or ethnographic methods. In these studies the researcher is attempting to portray the workings of circumstances that differ dramatically from what typically presents itself in the "natural" functioning of our society and our educational systems. It is as if the researcher is attempting to document with vivid characterizations that nature need not be the way it typically is. The researcher is attempting to communicate that we can create settings far different from those we may discover through random sampling. Moreover, those settings can be both sensible and rule governed.

Often, qualitative researchers studying unusual educational settings accuse quantitative researchers attempting to characterize education more generally, as committed to maintaining the educational status quo. Qualitative researchers, in contrast, are often committed to demonstrating the viability of truly alternative educational approaches.

I do not want to draw these contrasts too starkly. Obviously, many studies of broader educational questions are conducted using qualitative methods, such as some of the more striking investigations of school desegregation, or evaluations of special programs. Conversely, many experimental studies of educational change, such as those conducted in the National Follow-Through experiment, are attempts to introduce significant new approaches to the practices of contemporary education. Here again, however, I have been trying to draw attention to the intricate ways in which the multiplicity of methods we have available in educational research present us, not merely with an enormous technical challenge, but rather with the opportunity to investigate an impressive variety of questions from a rich set of alternative social and political perspectives.

Choosing Among Methods

It is interesting that the most frequently employed educational research methods, and therefore those with the greatest current respectability, are the quantitative methods of experimental, correlational, quasi-experimental, and survey research. Their disciplinary roots are in agriculture, genetics, and other studies of heredity, and actuarial studies of life expectancies conducted two centuries ago in the service of insurance companies. They not only share fairly long traditions in education, but also carry with them the prestige of quantifiable precision. Through the application of modern statistical methods, researchers can estimate the likelihood and size of errors in estimates of the state of nature more precisely than is usually possible in approaches deriving from anthropology, history, or philosophy. Should we tend to use the more traditional methods because we understand them better and they have a longer track record? John Stuart Mill argued:

If there are some subjects on which the results obtained have finally received the unanimous assent of all who have attended to the proof, and others which . . . have never succeeded in establishing any considerable body of truths, so as to be beyond denial or doubt; it is by generalizing the methods successfully followed by the former enquiries and adapting them to the latter, that we may hope to remove this blot on the face of science.

Yet an equally brilliant British philosopher of the next century, Alfred North Whitehead, was far less certain that well-developed and understood methods were always likely to be superior. He observed:

Some of the major disasters of mankind have been produced by the narrowness of men with a good methodology . . . to set limits to speculation is treason to the future.

If we are not always well advised to choose the methods that have been used the longest and that we understand best, what of choosing methods on the grounds of precision, on the grounds that some methods provide us a much better base for knowing exactly how much we know and how much is likely to be error? Here again, we are advised to focus first on our problem and its characteristics before we rush to select the appropriate method. We can again hark back to Aristotle, who made this famous point about precision in the *Ethics:*

Our discussion will be adequate if it has as much clearness as the subject matter admits of, for precision is not to be sought for alike in all discussion, any more than in all the products of crafts. . . . For it is the mark of an educated man to look for precision in each class of things just as far as the nature of the subject admits; it is evidently equally foolish to accept probable reasoning from a mathematician and to demand from a rhetorician scientific proofs. (*Ethics,* I: 3) (McKeon, pp. 309–310)

We must avoid becoming educational researchers slavishly committed to some particular method. The image of the little boy who has just received a hammer for a birthday present and suddenly finds that the entire world looks to him like a variety of nails, is too painfully familiar to be tolerated. We must first understand our problem, and decide what questions we are asking, then select the mode of *disciplined inquiry* most appropriate to those questions. If the proper methods are highly quantitative and objective, fine. If they are more subjective or qualitative, we can use them responsibly as well.

The anthropologist Geertz (1973) probably put it best when he said,

I have never been impressed by the argument that, as complete objectivity is impossible in these matters (as, of course, it is) one might as well let one's sentiments run loose. As Robert Solow has remarked, that is like saying that as a perfectly aseptic environment is impossible, one might as well conduct surgery in a sewer. (p. 30)

Geertz also observed, as Wolcott cites in his discussion of ethnographic research methods elsewhere in this volume, "You don't have to know everything to understand something."

Summary

Let me summarize the important points I have tried to make in this introductory discussion of research methodology. What distinguishes research from other forms of human discourse is the application of research methods. When we conduct educational research we make the claim that there *is* method to our madness. Educational research methods are forms of disciplined inquiry. They are disciplined in that they follow sets of rules and principles for pursuing investigations. They are also disciplined in another sense. They have emerged from underlying social or natural science disciplines which have well-developed canons of discovery and verification for making and testing truth claims in their fields. Education itself is not a discipline, but rather a field of study on which we bring to bear the various forms of disciplined inquiry which we have been discussing.

Each of these forms of inquiry asks different questions or has different ways of asking educational research questions. I have tried to illustrate some of the questions characteristic of major forms of educational research methodology. I have also tried to indicate the ways in which the selection of research method is frequently related to theoretical or ideological commitments of the investigator.[1] (Parenthetically, the possibilities of doing certain kinds of social research change as the political and social mood of a society evolves. For example, the notion of randomly assigning individuals to contrasting experimental treatment groups may seem far less acceptable as research strategy in these days of legislation requiring informed consent and protection of human subjects. Can we continue to practice experimental social and educational research and still abide by the law of the land that requires informed consent of all participants in research?)

Finally, each of the examples of research methodology discussed must in some fashion deal with questions of precision and generalizability, although the standards and criteria for these will vary from one form of disciplined inquiry to another.

The neophyte educational researcher, when confronted with this imposing array of alternative research methodologies, may be tempted to throw up his or her hands in despair and say, "What can I possibly do to become competent in this field?" I can suggest several answers. First, attempt to become skilled and experienced in at least two forms of research methodology. Facility in only one strikes me as somewhat dangerous, the equivalent of a methodological "Johnny One-Note." Second, be fully aware of the rich variety of methods that comprise the family of disciplined inquiry in educational research. Recognize that the most effective programs of educational research are likely to be characterized by what Merton (1975), the distinguished sociologist, or Schwab (1969), the eminent philosopher of education, have called applications of "disciplined eclectic." The best research programs will reflect intelligent deployment of a diversity of research methods applied to their appropriate research questions. Finally, do not limit your education to methodology alone, for only in combining substantive knowledge and methodological competence will you become a well-rounded, effective educational researcher. Here, once again, an insight of Aristotle's is relevant.

> Now each man judges well the things he knows, and of these he is a good judge. And so the man who has been educated in a subject is a good judge of that subject,

and the man who has received an all-round education is a good judge in general. (*Ethics.* I:3) (McKeon, p. 310)

Remember, selection of appropriate methods is an act of *judgment*.

A variety of methods comprise educational research: historical, philosophical, case studies, ethnographic field studies, experiments, quasi-experiments, surveys. Each is demanding and rigorous and follows disciplined rules or procedures. Taken together these approaches build a methodological mosaic that is the most exciting current field of applied social research—the study of education.

Note

[1]For a particularly instructive example of this principle in the history of education, see the following reading by Tyack.

References

Aristotle. (1947). *De anima (On the soul)*. In R. McKeon (Ed.), *Introduction to Aristotle*. New York: Modern Library.

Aristotle. (1947). *Nicomachean ethics.* In R. McKeon (Ed.), *Introduction to Aristotle*. New York: Modern Library.

Cornfield, J., & Tukey, J. W. (1956). Average values of mean squares in factorials. *Annals of Mathematical Statistics, 27,* 907–959.

Cremin. L. A. (1961). *The transformation of the school.* New York: Vintage Books.

Cronbach, L. J. (1957). The two disciplines of scientific psychology, *American Psychologist, 12,* 671–684.

Cronbach, L. J., & Suppes, P. (Eds.). (1969). *Research for tomorrow's schools: Disciplined inquiry for education.* New York: MacMillan.

Geertz. C. (1973). Thick description. In C. Geertz (Ed.), *The interpretation of cultures.* New York: Basic Books.

Merton, R. K. (1975). Structural analysis in sociology. In P. Blau (Ed.), *Approaches to the study of social structure.* New York: Free Press.

Schwab, J. J. (1969). The practical: A language for curriculum. *School Review, 78,* 1–23. [Reprinted in Schwab, J. J. (1978). *Science, curriculum and liberal education* (pp. 287–321). Chicago: University of Chicago Press.]

Tyack, D. (1976). Ways of seeing. An essay on the history of compulsory schooling. *Harvard Educational Review, 46,* 355–389.

Suggestions for Further Reading

Following are some suggested readings on research methods and the impact of disciplined inquiry in education; each will broaden and deepen your insights on how research on education is conducted and how it shapes the field.

Cronbach, L. J., & Suppes, P. (Eds.). (1969). *Research for tomorrow's schools: Disciplined inquiry for education*. New York: MacMillan.   This is a report of a special committee of the National Academy of Education. It includes a detailed discussion of disciplined inquiry, a number of historical case studies of educational research programs, and a set of policy recommendations.

Denzin, N. K. (1978). *The research act: A theoretical introduction to sociological methods* (2nd ed.). New York: McGraw-Hill.   A sound introduction to the "qualitative" approaches to social research.

Geertz, C. (1973). Thick description. In C. Geertz, *The interpretation of cultures*. New York: Basic Books.   A most eloquent and influential account of the sorts of description practiced by the cultural anthropologist.

Kerlinger, F. N. (1973). *Foundations of behavioral research* (2nd ed.). New York: Holt, Rinehart and Winston.   A now-classic statement of the rationale and methods for quantitative studies in the social sciences and education.

Schwab, J. J. (1979). *Science, curriculum & liberal education*. Chicago: University of Chicago Press.   In this volume of collected papers, Schwab's essays "What do scientists do?" and his series of three contributions on "The practical" are most germane to the present topics.

Suppes, P. (Ed.). (1978). *Impact of research on education: Some case studies*. Washington, D.C.: National Academy of Education.   A set of historical case studies involving areas as diverse as vocabulary and word-frequency research, intelligence testing, and the influences of Freud, Skinner, and Piaget. A paperback edition of the case study summaries is also available.

Study Questions

1. Think of a specific example of controversy involving competing claims for educational approaches, e.g., the fairness of intelligence tests, admissions standards for professional schools, free schools vs. traditional education, modern math vs. traditional math, etc. How would you study the problem in a *disciplined inquiry*? What examples of non-disciplined inquiry can you recall or construct as applied to that same problem?

2. How would you apply each of the methods described in this paper to (a) reading research, and (b) other fields of study in education?

3. Outline a program of research on reading that effectively *combines* several of the methods described in this chapter as distinct alternatives, e.g., experimental, correlational, case study, historical.

4. In your own words, what does it mean to generalize from a sample of individuals to some larger population? From a particular research task to a larger domain of tasks? Give an example of each in the following areas of research: ability testing, effectiveness of instructional methods, and development of computational skills.

5. "Some of the major disasters of mankind have been produced by the narrowness of men with a good methodology." What do you think Whitehead meant by that observation? Do you agree? Can you think of any examples? What can we do to prevent the disasters attributable to narrowness about methodology, however good?

6. What are the principal features that distinguish disciplined inquiry methods from other ways of asserting truth or plausibility?

7. Two types of generalizability are discussed in this paper—generalizing from a sample of persons to a population of persons, and generalizing from a research context to a population of contexts. Do these two types of generalizability present problems of similar difficulty? In the methods of inquiry familiar to you, do researchers handle these two types of generalizability similarly?

8. Quantitative and qualitative inquiry methods are obviously distinguished by their relative emphasis on numerical data. Is this the principal difference between them? What other features distinguish quantitative from qualitative modes of inquiry?

9. If you had a specific research problem in mind, what factors would you consider in choosing a method of disciplined inquiry to apply to the problem? If you had a general area of research in mind, but not a specific problem, do you think that choice of an inquiry method would influence your selection of a research problem? Why or why not?

10. You are advised in this paper to "become familiar with more than one method of disciplined inquiry." Why is this a good suggestion? What might you gain from becoming skilled in several methods? What might you lose if you have skills in only one method?

Reading

Introduction
Ways of Seeing, Ways of Knowing

Lee S. Shulman

Ways of Seeing is a paper that must be read at several levels, for it carries multiple messages. It is, first, an essay on the history of compulsory schooling in America. But it is an uncommon essay, for it does not array its data in accordance with a single explanation for the phenomena described. Indeed, it is not only a piece of history, but an essay in historiography, that branch of knowledge that deals with the methods of historical investigation and inference. In it, Tyack attempts to make transparent the most important stage of historical research, which is not the collection of evidence but the offering of explanation. Historical facts become historical evidence only when placed in a framework of explanation, a way of seeing without which facts are mute, incapable of "speaking for themselves."

This aspect of Tyack's essay makes it the ideal companion for our opening paper, "Disciplines of Inquiry in Education." The messages are parallel, even congruent. Tyack argues for the insufficiency of any single perspective in providing explanations for historical data. Similarly, I state that educational research must necessarily draw upon multiple disciplinary perspectives in its efforts to understand and improve educational practice.

Why does historiography present such a lovely analog for the world of educational research *writ large*? History, more than most other disciplines, is a hybrid, a methodological home for a wide variety of approaches, techniques, and modes of inquiry. Among all the disciplines, it has resisted categorization. Some consider history part of the social sciences; others count it among the humanities. Some historians focus their efforts on the conflicts among nations; others attend to the domestic battles within a family or a particular school. Some historians count, measure, and analyze the resulting numbers; others describe, narrate, and interpret personal meanings. Most able historians do some of each, counting and describing, measuring and interpreting. We find in history, as we do in educational research, a methodological mosaic.

Tyack begins his essay with a telling quote from Kenneth Burke who observed that "a way of seeing is always a way of not seeing." He informs us that historians, like scholars in most other fields, typically make their reputations through adherence to a single line of argument. Nevertheless, he suggests, "it seems useful to entertain alternative modes of explanation as a way of avoiding the reductionism that selects evidence to fit a particular thesis. Using different lenses to view the same phenomenon may seem irresponsibly playful to a true believer in any one interpretation, but at least it offers the possibility of self-correction. . . ."

Tyack proceeds to illustrate his point with a presentation of the basic data on changes in compulsory attendance legislation in the United States during the 19th and 20th centuries and associated statistics on school attendance during those same periods. The "facts" are apparently clear. But what do they mean? Why did state after state pass such legislation? Why were more and more youngsters attending public schools? If the answer seems obvious to many of us (it certainly did to me before reading the essay), it is only because we have failed to consider alternative explanations.

Tyack then shows how at least five different kinds of explanation can be advanced to account for the phenomenon of compulsory schooling. They are not mutually exclusive, but they are certainly distinctive. Each accounts for the facts, more or less. None accounts for all. Each emerges from a different disciplinary or ideological framework. These frameworks call for contrasting definitions of the problem, of the units of analysis, and of the adequacy of an explanation.

Tyack's analysis thus calls our attention to the significance of both units of analysis and universe of discourse as essential elements in any attempt to use educational research as the basis for description, explanation, planning, or prediction. What should be described? What are the "natural units"?

It may be useful to think of an analogy from biology. One can argue that the natural starting point for biological inquiry and explanation is the individual cell, for it is the building block of all other forms of life or biological structures. To explain any biological phenomenon, therefore, should require that the biologist relate structures and functions to their underlying cellular components. To understand how living systems function, therefore, is to explain how cells aggregate to form organs, organ systems, and organisms. Thus biological explanation draws from below, from biochemistry, biophysics, and the like.

Alternatively, it can be asserted that the organism itself, that entity capable of independent existence and functioning—whether composed of one cell or millions—is the proper unit of analysis. Starting from the organism, one would then seek explanations of how individual organs function to enable the organism's activities, how they are organized into systems, and how equilibrium among and within those systems is maintained. Biological explanation would focus on asking how the parts of intact organisms are themselves organized into functioning wholes.

Finally, though by no means exhaustively, one could argue that neither cells nor organisms are adequate as units of inquiry, for each is no more than a part of an even larger natural whole, which is the community or ecosystem. It is as impossible to understand the workings of any individual organism independent of its ecosystem as it is impossible to define the functions of a cell independent of the organized system of organs to which it contributes.

In a similar fashion, Tyack notes on page xx, historians differ over the units of inquiry and the forms of explanation.

> Those arguing for the political construction of education emphasize the role of the state. . . .The ethnocultural interpretation posits religious-ethnic differences as a motive force. . . .The organizational synthesis stresses the role of the new middle class. . . .Human capital theorists focus on the family as a decision unit in calculating the costs and benefits. . . .Marxists see class struggle as the source of the dialectic that produces historical change. Each interpretation, in turn, directs attention to certain kinds of evidence which can confirm or disprove its assertions of causation. . . .
>
> The models deal with social reality on quite different levels: the individual or the family, the ethnocultural group, the large organization, and the structure of political or economic power in the society as a whole.

"Ways of Seeing" illustrates with great clarity the manner in which these alternative frameworks are brought to bear on a given body of data. While advocating the use of multiple perspectives by individual scholars, Tyack also warns against the dangers of unbridled eclecticism, in which every imaginable explanation is thrown together. Research in education requires judgment and selectivity grounded in broad understanding, certainly broader than can be provided by any single explanatory perspective. Ways of seeing are ways of knowing and of not knowing. And knowing well is knowing in more than a single way.

Ways of Seeing: An Essay on the History of Compulsory Schooling

DAVID B. TYACK

Stanford University

In this essay the author describes the rise of compulsory schooling in the United States and then views this phenomenon through five different explanatory models. The first two are largely political, revealing compulsory schooling as a form of political construction and as an outgrowth of ethnocultural conflict. Noting the rise of educational bureaucracies, the author next offers an organizational interpretation as a third way of viewing compulsory schooling. The last two models are largely economic: one depicts the growth in schooling as an investment in human capital, and the other, using a Marxian approach, shows compulsory schooling to be a means of reproducing the class structure of American society. In conclusion, Professor Tyack observes that alternative ways of seeing not only draw on different kinds of evidence, but also depict different levels of social reality and so aid us in gaining a wider and more accurate perception of the past.

I should warn you that what you are about to read is not a bulletproof, airtight, unsinkable monograph. It is an *essay* in the root sense of the word: a trial of some ideas. Kenneth Burke wrote that "a way of seeing is always a way of not seeing."[1] In our specialized age people are taught and paid to have tunnel vision—and such specialization has many benefits. Socialization within the academic disciplines focuses inquiry: economists explain events in economic terms, sociologists in sociological ways, psychologists by their own theories. Splintering even occurs within

[1] Kenneth Burke, *Permanence and Change* (New York: New Republic, 1935), p. 70.

Harvard Educational Review Vol. 46 No. 3 August 1976

fields; Freudians and behaviorists, for example, see the world through quite different lenses.[2]

Historians tend to be eclectic more often than people in other disciplines, but they often make their reputations by developing a single line of argument. The frontier was the major shaping force in American history, Turner tells us. Status anxiety is the key to the progressive leaders, Hofstadter argues. Economic interests are the figure in the historical carpet, Beard claims. Other historians make their reputations by attacking Turner, Hofstadter, or Beard.[3] And so it goes.

Historiography normally is retrospective, telling us in what diverse ways scholars have explained events like the American Civil War. What I propose to do here is a kind of prospective historiography. I am impressed with the value of explicitly stated theories of interpretation but also struck by the value of discovering anomalies which any one theory does not explain. Thus, it seems useful to entertain alternative modes of explanation as a way of avoiding the reductionism that selects evidence to fit a particular thesis. Using different lenses to view the same phenomenon may seem irresponsibly playful to a true believer in any one interpretation, but at least it offers the possibility of self-correction without undue damage to an author's self-esteem.[4]

The topic of compulsory schooling lends itself to sharply different valuations, as the cartoons in figures 1 and 2 suggest. Earlier students of compulsion, like Forest Ensign and Ellwood Cubberley, regarded universal attendance as necessary for social progress and portrayed the passage and implementation of compulsory laws as the product of noble leaders playing their role in a long evolution of democracy.[5] Standing firmly on "the structure of civilization," as in figure 1, leaders used the mechanism of schooling to raise "American Social and Economic Life." In recent years radical critics have offered a quite different view of compulsory schooling. Figure 2 visually represents some of the elements of this revised interpretation. The school offers different and unequal treatments based on the race, sex, and class of incoming students. Compartmentalized internally, it produces a segmented labor force incapable of perceiving common interest. Rather than liberating the individual, the school programs him or her so as to guarantee the profits of the invisible rulers of the system. The school is thus an imposition that

---

[2] Everett C. Hughes, *Men and Their Work* (Glencoe, Ill.: Free Press, 1958).
[3] Herbert Bass, ed., *The State of American History* (Chicago: Quadrangle Books, 1970).
[4] Edward N. Saveth, ed., *American History and the Social Sciences* (New York: Free Press, 1964).
[5] Forest C. Ensign, *Compulsory School Attendance and Child Labor* (Iowa City, Iowa: Athens Press, 1921); Ellwood P. Cubberley, *Changing Conceptions of Education* (Boston: Houghton Mifflin, 1909).

FIGURE 1

Source: Edgar Mendenhall, *The City School Board Member and His Task* (Pittsburgh, Kans.: College Inn Books, 1929), frontispiece.

FIGURE 2

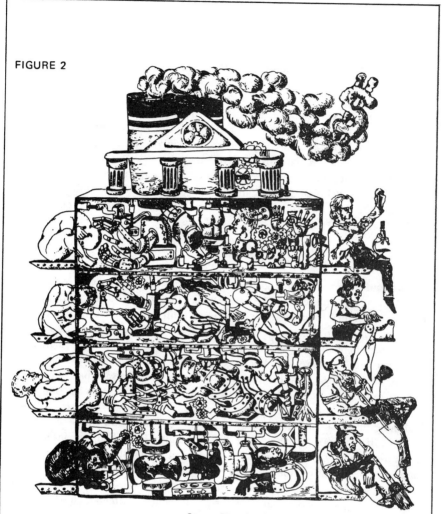

Source: Diane Lasch, *Leviathan*, 1, No. 3 (June 1969), 12.

dehumanizes the student and perpetuates social stratification.[6] Such differing valuations as these necessarily influence explanatory frameworks and policy discussion.

In this intentionally open-ended essay, I first sketch what I take to be the phe-

---

[6] A sampling of radical views can be found in writings of Paul Goodman, Ivan Illich, Michael Katz, and Samuel Bowles and Herbert Gintis (the last two are discussed below in the "Marxian Analysis" section).

nomena of compulsory schooling that the theories should explain. Then I examine two sets of interpretations, political and economic, which I find initially plausible. Some of the explanations are complementary, some contradictory; some explain certain events well but not others. Although each discussion is brief, I have tried to state the theories fairly, believing it not very useful to shoot down interpretations like ducks in a shooting gallery, only to bring out the *right* one (mine) at the end. But naturally I have interpretive preferences. Therefore, I intend to indicate what I see as flaws in the theories and anomalies they may not explain. In my conclusion, I do not attempt to reconcile the various interpretations in any definitive way, but instead suggest what we can learn from such comparative explorations.

What Needs to Be Explained?

At this point in my reading, I see two major phases in the history of compulsory school attendance in the United States. During the first, which lasted from mid-nineteenth century to about 1890, Americans built a broad base of elementary schooling which attracted ever-growing numbers of children. Most states passed compulsory-attendance legislation during these years, but generally these laws were unenforced and probably unenforceable. The notion of compulsion appears to have aroused ideological dispute at this time, but few persons paid serious attention to the organizational apparatus necessary to compel students into classrooms. Therefore, this phase might be called the *symbolic* stage. The second phase, beginning shortly before the turn of the twentieth century, might be called the *bureaucratic* stage. During this era of American education, school systems grew in size and complexity, new techniques of bureaucratic control emerged, ideological conflict over compulsion diminished, strong laws were passed, and school officials developed sophisticated techniques to bring truants into schools. By the 1920s and 1930s increasing numbers of states were requiring youth to attend high school, and by the 1950s secondary-school attendance had become so customary that school-leavers were routinely seen as "dropouts."[7]

Even before the common-school crusade of the mid-nineteenth century and before any compulsory laws, Americans were probably in the vanguard in literacy and mass schooling among the peoples of the world. Although methods of support and control of schools were heterogeneous in most communities before 1830, enrollment rates and literacy were very high—at least among whites. Public-school

---

[7] For a more detailed explication of this phasing, see my study *The One Best System: A History of American Urban Education* (Cambridge, Mass.: Harvard Univ. Press, 1974).

TABLE 1

Selected Educational Statistics for the United States, 1840–1890

	1840	1850	1860	1870	1880	1890
Enrollment rates of persons aged 5–19, in percentage (a)	37	42	49	60	58	64
Percentage of enrolled pupils attending daily (b)	–	–	–	59	62	64
Average length of school term, in days (b)	–	–	–	132	130	134
Percentage of population 10 years and older illiterate (c)	25–30	23	20	20	17	13

Sources: a) John K. Folger and Charles B. Nam, *Education of the American Population* (Washington, D.C.: GPO, 1967), chs. 1,4.

b) W. Vance Grant and C. George Lind, *Digest of Educational Statistics*, 1974 ed. (Washington, D.C.: GPO, 1975), p. 34.

c) Folger and Nam, *Education*, pp. 113-114.

advocates persuaded Americans to translate their generalized faith in education into support of a particular institution, the common school. Between 1850 and 1890 public expenditures for schools jumped from about $7 million to $147 million. Funds spent on public schools increased from 47 percent of total educational expenditures to 79 percent during those years.[8] Table 1 indicates both the high initial commitment to schooling and the gradual increase in attendance and decline in illiteracy.[9]

Educational statistics and data on literacy during the nineteenth century are notoriously unreliable, but table 1 at least suggests the magnitude of change. The aggregated national data, however, mask very important variations in attendance and literacy by region (the South lagged far behind the rest of the nation); by ethnicity (commonly forbidden to read under slavery, Blacks were about 90 percent illiterate in 1870; and foreign-born adult whites were considerably less liter-

[8] Albert Fishlow, "Levels of Nineteenth-Century Investment in Education," *Journal of Economic History*, 26 (1966), 418–24; Albert Fishlow, "The American Common School Revival: Fact or Fancy?" in *Industrialism in Two Systems: Essays in Honor of Alexander Gerschenkron*, ed. Henry Rosovsky (New York: Wiley, 1966), pp. 40–67.

[9] John K. Folger and Charles B. Nam, *Education of the American Population* (Washington, D.C.: GPO, 1967), chs. 1, 4; W. Vance Grant and C. George Lind, *Digest of Educational Statistics*, 1974 ed. (Washington, D.C.: GPO, 1975).

ate than native-born); and by other factors such as social class and urban or rural residence. Furthermore, the use of the broad age range of five to nineteen (common for both census and Office of Education statistics) hides variations in attendance at different age levels in different kinds of communities. In the industrial states, for example, children tended to start school earlier and to leave earlier than in farm states. In a census sample of both kinds of states, however, eight or nine out of ten children attended school from ten to fourteen. Finally, the percentages obscured the magnitude of the sevenfold absolute growth in enrollment from 1840 to 1890; in the latter year, over fourteen million children were in school. By the close of the nineteenth century the typical child could expect to attend school for five years, according to United States Commissioner of Education William T. Harris; Harris and many others regarded this as a triumph, and indeed by then the United States led the world in its provision for mass education.[10]

These changes in attendance and literacy before roughly 1890 took place with minimal coercion by the states—despite the fact that by then twenty-seven legislatures had passed compulsory-attendance laws. A survey in 1889 revealed that in all but a handful of states and individual cities the laws were dead letters. Indeed, in several cases state superintendents of education said that responsible local officials did not even know that there was such legislation.[11] Educators were often ambivalent about enforcement of compulsory-attendance laws. Often they did not want the unwilling pupils whom coercion would bring into classrooms. In many communities, especially big cities, schools did not have enough seats even for children who wanted to go to school. And many citizens regarded compulsion as an un-American invasion of parental rights. Except in a few states like Connecticut and Massachusetts, provisions for enforcement were quite inadequate.[12]

Phase two of the history of compulsory schooling, the bureaucratic stage, built on the base of achievement laid down during the symbolic stage. The basically simple structure of the common school became much more elaborate, however, and mass education came to encompass the secondary school as well, as indicated by table 2.

Public attitudes toward compulsory schooling appeared to become more positive in the years after 1890. This was true even in the South, which had previously

10 Folger and Nam, pp. 25, 3, 211–68; William T. Harris, "Elementary Education," in *Monographs on Education in the United States*, ed. Nicholas M. Butler (Albany, N.Y.: J. B. Lyon, 1900), pp. 79–139.

11 United States Commissioner of Education, "Compulsory Attendance Laws in the United States," *Report for 1888–1889*, I (Washington, D.C.: GPO, 1889), ch. 18, pp. 470–531.

12 Mary J. Herrick, *The Chicago Schools: A Social and Political History* (Beverly Hills, Calif.: Sage, 1971), p. 58; John D. Philbrick, *City School Systems in the United States*, U.S. Bureau of Education, Circular of Information, No. 1 (Washington, D.C.: GPO, 1885), pp. 154–55.

TABLE 2

Selected Educational Statistics for the United States, 1900–1950

	1900	1910	1920	1930	1940	1950
Enrollment rates of persons aged 5–19, in percentage (a)	72	74	78	82	84	83
Percentage of enrolled pupils attending daily (a)	69	72	75	83	87	89
Percentage of total enrollment in high schools (a)	3	5	10	17	26	23
High School graduates as percentage of population 17 years old (b)	6	9	17	29	51	59
Percentage of population 10 years and older illiterate (c)	11	8	6	4	3	3
Estimates of educational attainment, in years (d)	–	8.1	8.2	8.4	8.6	9.3

Sources: a) W. Vance Grant and C. George Lind, *Digest of Educational Statistics,* 1974 ed. (Washington, D.C.: GPO, 1975), p. 34.
b) United States Bureau of the Census, *Historical Statistics of the United States: Colonial Times to 1957* (Washington, D.C.: GPO, 1960), p. 207.
c) John K. Folger and Charles B. Nam, *Education of the American Population* (Washington, D.C.: GPO, 1967), p. 114.
d) Folger and Nam, *Education,* p. 132.

resisted such legislation. States passed new laws with provisions for effective enforcement, including requirements for censuses to determine how many children there were, attendance officers, elaborate "pupil accounting," and often state financing of schools in proportion to average daily attendance. Age limits were gradually extended upwards, especially under the impact of the labor surplus in the Depression, until by the mid-1930s youths were typically required to attend school until age sixteen.

Early in the century the great majority of teenagers in school were lumped in the upper grades of the elementary school as a result of the frequent practice of forcing children to repeat grades. In the 1920s and 1930s, however, the practice of "social promotion"—that is, keeping age groups together—took hold, and the percentage of teenagers in high schools increased sharply. The increasing numbers of children compelled to attend schools, in turn, helped to transform the structure and curriculum of schooling. Of course, there were still many children who escaped the net of the truant officer, many who were denied equality of educational opportunity: an estimated two million children aged six to fifteen were not in any school in 1940. But during the twentieth century universal elementary and secondary schooling gradually was accepted as a common goal and approached a common reality.[13]

Over the long perspective of the last century and a half, both phases of compulsory school attendance may be seen as part of significant shifts in the functions of families and the status of children and youth. Households in American industrial cities became more like units of consumption than of production. Indeed, Frank Musgrove contends that the passage of compulsory-school legislation in England "finally signalized the triumph of public over private influences as formative in social life and individual development; in particular, it tardily recognized the obsolescence of the educative family, its inadequacy in modern society in child care and training."[14] Advocates of compulsory schooling often argued that families—or at least some families, like those of the poor or foreign-born—were failing to carry out their traditional functions of moral and vocational training. Immigrant children in crowded cities, reformers complained, were leading disorderly lives, schooled by the street and their peers more than by Christian nurture in the home. Much of the drive for compulsory schooling reflected an animus against parents considered incompetent to train their children. Often combining fear of social unrest with humanitarian zeal, reformers used the powers of the state to intervene in families and to create alternative institutions of socialization.

Laws compelling school attendance were only part of an elaborate and massive transformation in the legal and social rules governing children.[15] Children and youth came to be seen as individuals with categorical needs: as patients requiring specialized medical care; as "delinquents" needing particular treatment in the courts; and as students deserving elaborately differentiated schooling. Specific adults came to be designated as responsible for aiding parents in the complex tasks of child care: teachers, truant officers, counselors, scout leaders, and pediatricians, for example—not to mention Captain Kangaroo. Formerly regarded as a central

13 United States Bureau of the Census, *Historical Statistics of the United States: Colonial Times to 1957* (Washington, D.C.: GPO, 1960), pp. 207, 215; John K. Norton and Eugene S. Lawler, *Unfinished Business in American Education: An Inventory of Public School Expenditures in the United States* (Washington, D.C.: American Council on Education, 1946); Newton Edwards, *Equal Educational Opportunity for Youth* (Washington, D.C.: American Council on Education, 1939), p. 152.

14 Frank Musgrove, "The Decline of the Educative Family," *Universities Quarterly*, 14 (1960), p. 377.

15 John W. Meyer and Joane P. Nagel, "The Changing Status of Childhood," paper presented at the Annual Meeting of the Society for the Study of Social Problems, San Francisco, Calif., 1975.

function of the family, education came finally to be regarded as synonymous with schooling. The common query "Why aren't you in school?" signified that attendance in school had become the normal career of the young.[16]

Political Dimensions of Compulsory Attendance

Only government can compel parents to send their children to school. In legally compelling school attendance, the democratic state not only coerces behavior but also legitimizes majority values, as Michael S. Katz has argued.[17] Thus, sooner or later, any historian investigating compulsory school attendance logically needs to attend to political processes.

In recent years, however, few historians of American education have paid close attention either to the politics of control of schools or to the nature of political socialization in schools. Echoing Horace Mann's concern for social cohesion as well as social justice, R. Freeman Butts has suggested that both radical historians (stressing imposition by economic elites) and "culturist" historians (broadening the definition of education to include all "habitats of knowledge") have somewhat neglected the political functions of public schooling in both national and international contexts—what he calls civism.[18] Such neglect did not characterize much of the earlier work in the history of education, which like writings in other branches of history, had a marked political and indeed nationalistic flavor. Among political sociologists, the emergence of new nations has also aroused interest in the political construction of education.

I begin, then, with an examination of a broad interpretive framework which stresses education as a means of incorporating people into a nation-state and legitimizing the status of "citizen" and "leader." After noting difficulties in relating these notions to the loosely organized political system of the United States, I proceed to a rather different form of analysis—namely, one which seeks to interpret the passage of compulsory-schooling laws as a species of ethnocultural conflict. This explanation appears to fit phase one far better than phase two. To interpret phase two I draw upon what one historian has called "the organizational synthesis," an approach that seeks to explain political and social changes during the progressive era in terms of the growing importance of large-scale bureaucratic organizations and the attempt to resolve political issues by administrative means.

[16] Robert H. Bremner, ed., *Children and Youth in America: A Documentary History*, I–II (Cambridge, Mass.: Harvard Univ. Press, 1970–71).
[17] Michael S. Katz, "The Concepts of Compulsory Education and Compulsory Schooling: A Philosophical Inquiry," Diss. Stanford Univ., Palo Alto, Calif., 1974.
[18] R. Freeman Butts, "Public Education and Political Community," *History of Education Quarterly*, 14 (1974), 165–83.

The Political Construction of Education

It is natural in the Watergate era to agree with Dr. Johnson that "patriotism is the last refuge of the scoundrel" and to suspect that nationalistic rhetoric about schooling disguises real motives. Yet I am struck by the range of ideology and class among persons in the United States who justified compulsory public education on explicitly political grounds. If the patriots were scoundrels, there were many of them in assorted walks of life. Moreover, nationalism has been associated with compulsory attendance not in the United States alone but also in European nations during the nineteenth century and in scores of developing nations today. In 1951 UNESCO sponsored a series of monographs on compulsory education around the globe; the organization assumed that all United Nations members agreed on "the general principle of the necessity of instituting systems of compulsory, free and universal education in all countries."[19]

How can one construe the political construction of education? Why does schooling seem so important to the modern state? In their essay, "Education and Political Development," John W. Meyer and Richard Rubinson have argued that modern national educational systems in effect create and legitimate citizens. New nations are commonly composed of families and individuals who identify with regions, religions, ethnic groups, tribes, or interest groups. Such persons rarely think of themselves as either participants in or subjects of the state. Indeed, the whole notion of universal citizenship might seem to them fanciful and implausible. Meyer and Rubinson argue that the central political purpose of universal education is precisely to create citizens and legitimize the state. Families in potentially divisive subgroups turn over their children to state schools to learn a common language, a national history, and an ideology that incorporates them as citizens into the broader entity called the state. The point is not that this new compulsory political socialization is actually successful in accomplishing its cognitive or affective tasks, but simply that the institutional process is designed to create a new category of personnel—citizens. Similarly, advanced education may create and legitimate elites. People who formerly ruled by hereditary right or other kinds of ascriptive privilege may still wield power, but the rituals of higher state education turn them into legitimate "civil servants." As states expand their control over new sectors of society, state schooling gives an apparently rational and modern justification for new social rules that replace the older ones based on regional, ethnic, religious, or family loyalties. By these means, education helps to institutionalize the authority of the state.[20]

[19] Australian National Commission for UNESCO, *Compulsory Education in Australia* (Paris: UNESCO, 1951), preface.

[20] John W. Meyer and Richard Rubinson, "Education and Political Development," in *Review of Research in Education*, III, ed. Fred Kerlinger (Itasca, Ill.: F. E. Peacock, 1975), 134–62.

It is a complicated argument. Let me illustrate with historical examples from American, French, and Prussian experience. After the American Revolution, numerous theorists like Thomas Jefferson, Benjamin Rush, and Noah Webster argued that without a transformed educational system the old pre-Revolutionary attitudes and relationships would prevail in the new nation. Rush said that a new, uniform state system should turn children into "republican machines." Webster called for an "Association of American Patriots for the Formation of an American Character," strove to promote uniformity of language, and wrote a "Federal Catechism" to teach republican principles to school children. Jefferson wanted to create state primary schools to make loyal citizens of the young. In addition, many early theorists wanted a national university to prepare and legitimate elites for leadership.[21] Similarly, French writers on education after the 1789 Revolution advocated a universal state system that would teach all French citizens to read and would give them pride in their country's history and political institutions. In both cases education was regarded as an instrument deliberately used to create a new status, to turn people with diverse loyalties into citizens of a new entity—the republican state.

The use of schooling as a means of incorporating people into the nation-state was not limited to liberal regimes, however. Compulsory schooling also served militant nationalism in conservative Prussia during the nineteenth century by attaching people to the centralized and corporate state. Victor Cousin observed in his report on Prussian education that the parental duty to send children to school "is so national, so rooted in all the legal and moral habits of the country, that it is expressed by a single word, *Schulpflichtigkeit* [school duty, or school obligation]. It corresponds to another word, similarly formed and similarly sanctioned by public opinion, *Dienstpflichtigkeit* [service obligation, that is military service]."[22]

To some degree the political construction of education I have sketched here does fit the development of compulsory schooling in the United States. As mentioned above, post-revolutionary writers on education stressed the need to use schools to transform colonials into citizens. Repeating their arguments, Horace Mann contended that common schools would imbue the rising generation with traits of character and loyalties required for self-government. Waves of immigration intensified concern over the incorporation of new groups into the polity. For a time the federal government took an active interest in schooling ex-slaves so that they,

[21] David Tyack, *Turning Points in American Educational History* (Waltham, Mass.: Blaisdell, 1967), pp. 83–119.
[22] Cousins, as quoted in Edward Reisner, *Nationalism and Education Since 1789: A Social and Political History of Modern Education* (New York: Macmillan, 1922), p. 134; ch. 2.

too, might become proper citizens like their foreign-born fellow compatriots.[23] The national government even used schooling as a way to shape people conquered in war into the predetermined mold of republican citizenship: witness the fate of Native American children torn from their parents and sent to boarding schools, the dispatch of American teachers to Puerto Rico and the Philippines after the Spanish-American war, and the attempts to democratize Germany and Japan after World War II.[24] Even the Japanese-Americans "relocated" during World War II were subjected to deliberate resocialization in the camps' public schools.[25]

Clearly, Americans had enormous faith in the power of schooling to transform all kinds of people—even "enemies"—into citizens. The process of entry into the status of citizenship was rather like baptism; like the sprinkling of water on the head of a child in an approved church, schooling was a ritual process that acquired political significance because people believed in it. Characteristically, Americans intensified their attempts at political socialization in schools whenever they perceived a weakening of loyalties (as in World War I), or an infusion of strangers (as in peak times of immigration), or a spreading of subversive ideas (whether by Jesuits or Wobblies or Communists). Interest in compulsory attendance seems to correlate well with such periods of concern.[26]

There are problems, however, with applying this conception of the political construction of education to the United States. The ideas of the revolutionary theorists were not put into practice in their lifetime, for example. One could argue that early Americans learned to be citizens by participating in public life rather than by schooling and indeed, that they had in effect been American "citizens" even before the Revolution. Before the common-school crusade, educational institutions tended to reflect differences of religion, ethnicity, and social class—precisely the sorts of competing loyalties presumably detrimental to national unification. Furthermore, in the federated network of local, state, and national governments, it was by no means clear what "the state" really was. Although many advocates of compulsion turned to Prussia for evidence on how the state could incorporate

---

23 William Edward Burghardt DuBois, *Black Reconstruction in America, an Essay toward a History of the Part which Black Folk Played in the Attempt to Reconstruct Democracy in America, 1860–1880* (Cleveland, Ohio: World Pub., 1964), pp. 637–69.

24 John Morgan Oates, *Schoolbooks and Krags: The United States Army in the Philippines, 1898–1902* (Westport, Conn.: Greenwood Press, 1973).

25 Charles Wollenberg, *All Deliberate Speed: Segregation and Exclusion in California Schools, 1855–1975* (Berkeley: Univ. of California Press, forthcoming), ch. 3.

26 Howard K. Beale, *A History of Freedom of Teaching in American Schools* (New York: Charles Scribner's Sons, 1941); John W. Meyer, "Theories of the Effects of Education on Civil Participation in Developing Societies," unpublished paper, Dept. of Sociology, Stanford Univ., Palo Alto, Calif., May 1972.

the young into schools for the public good, opposition to centralization of state power was strong throughout the nineteenth century. The ritualized patriotism of Fourth-of-July orations and school textbooks was popular, but actual attempts to coerce parents to send their children to school were often seen as un-American and no business of the state. Prussian concepts of duty to the state sharply contrasted with nineteenth-century American beliefs in individualism and laissez-faire government. Different groups in American society tended to express different points of view about using the state to reinforce certain values and to sanction others.[27] I will explore this point in the next section on ethnocultural politics.

During most of the nineteenth century, the apparatus of federal and state control of education was exceedingly weak. Although leaders from Horace Mann forward talked of the virtues of centralization and standardization in state systems, state departments of education were miniscule and had few powers. In 1890 the median size of state departments of education, including the superintendent, was two persons. At that time there was one state education official in the United States for every one hundred thousand pupils. One pedagogical czar with effective sanctions and rewards might have controlled such masses, but state departments of education prior to the turn of the twentieth century rarely had strong or even clear-cut powers.[28] Federal control was even weaker, although some reformers dreamed of massive federal aid and extended powers for the Office of Education. In effect, the United States Commissioner of Education was a glorified collector of statistics—and often ineffectual even in that role. An individual like Henry Barnard or William T. Harris might lend intellectual authority to the position, but the Office itself probably had trivial influence on American schools.[29] De facto, most control of schools lay with local school boards.

So the theory of the political construction of education is powerfully suggestive, but the American historical experience raises certain anomalies. Most Americans during the early national period apparently felt no need to legitimize citizenship through formal state schooling, although that idea began to take hold by mid-nineteenth century. Until the end of the century there was considerable opposition to centralized state power, both in theory and in practice. Thus it is difficult to envisage *the state* during either period as legitimizing individuals as citizens through education or effectively extending its jurisdiction into other parts of society like the family.

Much of this changed in the era beginning roughly in 1890, as the notion of the

[27] Merle Curti, *The Roots of American Loyalty* (New York: Columbia Univ. Press, 1946).
[28] Department of Superintendence, NEA, *Educational Leadership: Progress and Possibilities* (Washington, D.C.: NEA, 1933), p. 246, ch. 11.
[29] Donald Warren, *To Enforce Education: A History of the Founding Years of the United States Office of Education* (Detroit: Wayne State Univ. Press, 1974).

state as an agency of social and economic reform and control took hold and an "organizational revolution" began. Thus it seems useful to supplement the broad theory of the political construction of education with two other interpretations that give a more focused perspective on the two phases of compulsion.

Ethnocultural Politics in Compulsory-School Legislation during the Nineteenth Century

During the nineteenth century Americans differed significantly in their views of citizenship and the legitimate domain of state action, including compulsory-attendance legislation. A number of interpreters of the political contests of the period have argued that these cleavages followed ethnic and religious lines. In a perceptive essay on this ethnocultural school of interpretation, James Wright notes that these historians dissent from both the economic class-conflict model of Charles Beard and the consensus model that emerged after World War II. The ethnocultural historians, he says, do not argue

> . . . a simplistic model in which ward heelers appeal to ethnic, religious, or racial prejudices and loyalties in order to divert attention from "real" economic issues. Rather, the real issues of politics have been those most significant relative to life style and values: prohibition, public funding or control of sectarian schools, sabbatarian laws, woman suffrage, and efforts to hasten or retard ethnic assimilation.[30]

Richard Jensen points out that religious congregations, often divided along ethnic lines, were very important in shaping political attitudes and behavior in the Midwest. Such sectarian groups provided not only contrasting world views but also face-to-face communities that reinforced them. Like Paul Kleppner, Jensen has identified two primary religious persuasions that directly influenced political expression. One was represented by the *pietistic* sects—groups like the Baptists and Methodists that had experienced great growth as a result of the evangelical awakenings of the century—which tended to reject church hierarchy and ritual and insist that right belief should result in upright behavior. Seeing sin in the world, as represented by breaking the Sabbath or drinking alcohol, for example, the pietists sought to change society and thereby, as Kleppner explains, "to *conserve* their value system and to restore the norms it preserved." The *liturgicals*, by contrast, believed that salvation came from right belief and from the preservation of the particular orthodoxies represented in the creeds and sacraments of the church. Liturgicals like Roman Catholics and Lutherans of certain synods tended to see morality as the preserve not of the state but of the church, the family, and the

---

30 James Wright, "The Ethnocultural Model of Voting: A Behavioral and Historical Critique," *American Behavioral Scientist*, 16 (1973), p. 655.

parochial school. According to both Kleppner and Jensen, the Republican Party tended to attract the pietists, the Democratic Party the liturgicals. By and large, the Republicans supported a "crusading moralism" for a single standard of behavior, while the Democrats spoke for a "counter-crusading pluralism."[31]

These politically important religious distinctions cut across ethnic lines. Although old-stock Americans tended to be pietistic and Republican, the Irish Catholics to be liturgical and Democratic, for example, other ethnic groups, like the Germans, split into different camps. *The* immigrant vote was a fiction based on nativistic fear; canny politicians knew better. Furthermore, this kind of status-group politics needs to be distinguished from the theory of the politics of status anxiety or status discrepancy that was advanced by political scientists and by Richard Hofstadter in the 1950s. Status groups asserting themselves through the political process during the nineteenth century rarely saw themselves on the skids socially. Rather than regarding ethnocultural politics as in some sense pathological, it is quite as accurate to describe it as the positive assertion of groups that believed in their own values and life styles and sought to extend their group boundaries and influence.[32]

The politics of "crusading moralism" and "counter-crusading pluralism" often focused on issues like temperance or Sabbath observance and frequently resulted in blue laws, which, like dead-letter compulsory-attendance legislation, were often more symbolic assertions than implementable decisions. Republican politicians often winked at breaches of the laws where it was politically astute to do so. It was one thing to enforce prohibition in a town where the only public drinker was the town Democrat, and quite another to do so in German wards of Milwaukee. Laws which stamped the pietistic foot and said "Be like me" might satisfy symbolically without alienating dissenters by active enforcement.[33]

Were nineteenth-century compulsory-school-attendance laws of that character largely passed by Republican pietists? I don't know, but the hypothesis seems worth testing by evidence; perhaps by the political composition of the state legislatures that passed such laws and by values expressed in textbooks. For now, the interpretation seems plausible. Evangelical ministers were at the forefront of the common-school crusade as the frontier moved westward, and ministers like Josiah Strong saw the school as a bulwark of the evangelical campaign to save the cities.

[31] Richard Jensen, *The Winning of the Midwest: Social and Political Conflict, 1888–1896* (Chicago: Univ. of Chicago Press, 1971), pp. 63–66, xv; Paul Kleppner, *The Cross of Culture: A Social Analysis of Midwestern Politics, 1850–1900* (New York: Free Press, 1970), pp. 71–74.
[32] John W. Meyer and James G. Roth, "A Reinterpretation of American Status Politics," *Pacific Sociological Review*, 13 (1970), 95–102; Joseph R. Gusfield, *Symbolic Crusade: Status Politics and the American Temperance Movement* (Urbana, Ill.: Univ. of Illinois Press, 1963), chs. 1, 6, 7.
[33] Jensen, p. 122.

Public schooling was widely publicized as the creation of "our Puritan, New England forefathers." Pietists saw themselves not as an interest group but as representatives of true American values. People who wanted compulsory-attendance laws were presumably already sending their children to school; by branding the nonconforming parent as illegal or deviant, they thereby strengthened the norms of their own group (the explanation follows what can be called the tongue-clucking theory of the function of crime).[34]

Much of the rhetoric of compulsory schooling lends itself to this ethnocultural interpretation and further refines the theory of the political construction of education. In 1891 superintendents in the National Education Association (NEA) passed a resolution favoring compulsory education. The resolution's preamble stated that "in our free Republic the State is merely the expression of the people's will, and not an external governmental force." The NEA statement sounds quite different than the notion of a strong central state creating citizens through schooling, as in the view explored above. Why then, did the state have to compel citizens to send their children to school? Because compulsion created liberty.[35]

The assumptions behind this Orwellian paradox become more clear when one reads accounts of the discussions of compulsion which took place that year in the National Council of Education, the prestigious think tank of the NEA. A committee had just reported to the Council that the idle and vicious were filling the jails of the nation, corrupt men were getting the ballot, and "foreign influence has begun a system of colonization with a purpose of preserving foreign languages and traditions and proportionately of destroying distinctive Americanism. It has made alliance with religion. . . ." The committee was really saying that there were two classes of citizens, us and them. Said an educator in the audience: "The report assumes that when the people established this government they had a certain standard of intelligence and morality; and that an intelligent and moral people will conform to the requirements of good citizenship." Things have changed, he observed: "People have come here who are not entitled to freedom in the same sense as those who established this government." The question was whether to raise these inferior newcomers to the standards of the Anglo-Saxon forefathers or to "lower this idea of intelligence and morality to the standard of that class" of new immigrants from southern and eastern Europe. Republican liberty depended on a homogeneity of virtue and knowledge that only compulsion could create in

---

[34] Timothy L. Smith, "Protestant Schooling and American Nationality," *Journal of American History*, 53 (1967), 679–95; David B. Tyack, "Onward Christian Soldiers: Religion in the American Common School," in *History and Education*, ed. Paul Nash (New York: Random House, 1970), pp. 212–55.

[35] J. K. Richards, *Compulsory Education in Ohio: Brief for Defendent in Error in the Supreme Court of Ohio, Patrick F. Quigley v. The State of Ohio* (Columbus, Ohio: Westbote, 1892), p. 23.

the new generation. Almost without exception native-born and Protestant, NEA leaders in the nineteenth century took naturally to the notion that real citizens were those who fit the pietist mold.[36]

In 1871, in a speech on the "New Departure of the Republican Party," Republican Senator Henry Wilson linked compulsory schooling to nativist and Protestant principles. Pointing out that the Fifteenth Amendment had expanded suffrage to include Blacks and that unrestricted immigration was flooding the nation with millions "from Europe with all the disqualifications of their early training," he argued for an educational system that would transform "the emigrant, the freedman, and the operative" into proper citizens in accord with the "desirable traits of New England and the American character."[37] An editorial in the *Catholic World* promptly attacked Wilson for wanting compulsory schooling to mold all "into one homogeneous people, after what may be called the New England Evangelical type. Neither his politics nor his philanthropy can tolerate any diversity of ranks, conditions, race, belief, or worship."[38]

Evidence of ethnic and religious bias abounds in the arguments about compulsory schooling throughout the nineteenth century. In the 1920s bias surfaced again in Oregon when the Ku Klux Klan and its allies passed a law that sought to outlaw private schooling. Two compulsory-schooling laws in Illinois and in Wisconsin in 1889 aroused fierce opposition from liturgical groups, especially German Catholics and Lutherans, because of their provisions that private schools teach in the English language and that they be approved by boards of public education. In both states Democrats derided the laws as instances of Republican paternalism and hostility to pluralism; defeated Republicans learned to disavow spokesmen who believed that extremism in defense of virtue is no vice. After the disastrous votes in 1892, one Republican wrote to a friend that "defeat was inevitable. The school law did it—a silly, sentimental and damned useless abstraction, foisted upon us by a self-righteous demagogue."[39] Both Kleppner and Jensen see these contests over compulsory instruction in English as classic examples of ethnocultural politics.[40]

These Illinois and Wisconsin conflicts may, however, be exceptional cases; other states passed similar laws requiring English-language instruction and state ac-

---

[36] National Education Association, *Journal of Addresses and Proceedings, 1891* (Topeka: Kansas Pub. House, 1891), pp. 295, 298, 393–403.

[37] Henry Wilson, "New Departure of the Republican Party," *Atlantic Monthly*, 27 (1871), 11–14.

[38] Editorial, *Catholic World*, 13 (1871), 3–4; John Whitney Evans, "Catholics and the Blair Education Bill," *Catholic Historical Review*, 46 (1960), 273–98.

[39] Jensen, pp. 122, 129.

[40] Kleppner, pp. 169–70.

creditation without such contests erupting. It is possible that there was bipartisan support for the ineffectual state laws passed before 1890 and that widespread belief in public education made consensus politics the wisest course. The South, which lagged in compulsory legislation, had few immigrants and few Catholics; its population was native-born and evangelical with a vengeance. How well does an ethnocultural hypothesis fit the South? Is the educational politics of race substantially different from white ethnocultural politics? Only careful state-by-state analysis can test the theory that ethnocultural politics was a key factor in compulsory-attendance legislation during the nineteenth century. But where there is the smoke of ethnocultural rhetoric it is plausible to seek political fires.[41]

In any case, the high point of ethnocultural politics of compulsory education was probably the nineteenth century. The assumption persisted into the twentieth century that there were *real* citizens—those with the right heredity and principles —who needed to shape others to their own image. But at the turn of the century attention shifted to efficient organizational means for compelling school attendance.

From Politics to Administration:
An Organizational Interpretation

Despite some notable exceptions, open ethnocultural strife in school politics appears to have subsided during phase two of compulsory attendance. Many of the decisions that once had been made in the give-and-take of pluralistic politics now shifted to administrators within the system. At the turn of the century a powerful and largely successful movement centralized control of city schools in small boards of education elected at large rather than by ward. Furthermore, state departments of education grew in size and influence and led in the consolidation of rural schools and the enforcement of uniform educational standards. Advocates of these new forms of governance argued that education should be taken out of politics and that most decisions were best made by experts. Government by administrative experts was, of course, a form of politics under another name: decisions about who got what in the public allocation of scarce resources were simply shifted to a new arena. The line between public and private organizations became blurred as proponents of centralization urged that school systems adopt the corporate model of governance. As decision-making power shifted to superintendents and their staffs, the number of specialists and administrators ballooned. School systems grew in size, added tiers of officials, and became segmented into functional divisions:

---

[41] Horace Mann Bond has given us a brilliant analysis of how the politics of race mixed with the politics of competing economic groups in his *Negro Education in Alabama: A Study in Cotton and Steel* (Washington, D.C.: Associated Pub., 1939).

elementary, junior high, and high schools; vocational programs of several kinds; classes for the handicapped; counseling services; research and testing bureaus; and many other departments.[42]

The new provisions for compulsory schooling reflected these bureaucratic technologies. In city schools, in particular, large attendance departments were divided into supervisors, field workers, and clerks. Attendance experts developed the school census, elaborate forms for reporting attendance, manuals on "child accounting," and civil-service requirements for employment. By 1911 attendance officers were numerous and self-conscious enough to start their own national professional organization. Schools developed not only new ways of finding children and getting them into school, but also new institutions or programs to cope with the unwilling students whom truant officers brought to their doors: parental schools, day-long truant schools, disciplinary classes, ungraded classes, and a host of specialized curricular tracks. Local officials gathered data by the file full to aid in planning a rational expansion and functional specialization of the schools. Doctoral dissertations and other "scientific" studies analyzed existing patterns of attendance and promoted the new methods.[43]

Surely one can find examples of these new techniques and institutional adaptations prior to phase two, but what I find striking is the very rapid increase in the machinery of compulsion and the structural differentiation of the schools in the years after 1890. A new method of inquiry called "educational science" helped educators to gather and process information so that they could not only describe quantitatively what was going on in schools, but also forecast and plan. In national organizations these new functional specialists shared ideas and strategies of change. Older local perspectives gradually gave way to more cosmopolitan ways of thinking. The new hierarchical, differentiated bureaucracies seemed to many to be a superb instrument for continuous adaptation of the schools to diverse social conditions and needs. Theoretically at least, issues of religion or ethnicity were irrelevant to decision making in such bureaucracies, as were parochial tastes or local prejudices.[44]

Samuel Hays sees the rise of large-scale organizations and functional groups as characteristic of many sectors of American society during the twentieth century. He points out that the new technical systems defined what were problems and used

---

[42] Marvin Lazerson, *Origins of the Urban Public School: Public Education in Massachusetts, 1870–1915* (Cambridge, Mass.: Harvard Univ. Press, 1971), chs. 5–9; Joseph M. Cronin, *The Control of Urban Schools: Perspectives on the Power of Educational Reformers* (New York: Free Press, 1973).

[43] Frank V. Bermejo, *The School Attendance Service in American Cities* (Menasha, Wis.: George Banta Pub., 1924).

[44] Tyack, *One Best System*, part 4.

particular means for solving them. "Reason, science, and technology are not inert processes by which men discover, communicate, and apply facts disinterestedly and without passion, but means through which, through systems, some men organize and control the lives of other men according to their particular conceptions as to what is preferable." He argues that the rapid growth of empirical inquiry—normally called "science"—has enabled people in organizations to plan future courses of action. This differentiates these new technical systems from earlier bureaucracies. Not only did these new methods change decision making within organizations, but functional specialists like educators, engineers, or doctors banded together in organizations to influence the larger environment collectively as interest groups.[45]

How does this vision of organizational change help explain the enactment and implementation of compulsory schooling? John Higham has observed that "the distinctive feature of the period from 1898 to 1918 is not the preeminence of democratic ideals or of bureaucratic techniques, but rather a fertile amalgamation of the two. An extraordinary quickening of ideology occurred in the very midst of a dazzling elaboration of technical systems."[46] Robert Wiebe, likewise, sees the essence of progressivism as "the ambition of the new middle class to fulfill its destiny through bureaucratic means."[47] Thus one might interpret the passage of child-labor legislation and effective compulsory-attendance laws as the work of functional groups and national reform associations that combined ideological commitment with bureaucratic sophistication. These groups knew how to create enforcement systems that would actually work, and they followed up on their results. Active in this way were such groups as educators (who increasingly came to the forefront in compulsory-schooling campaigns), labor unions, the National Child Labor Committee, and elite educational associations (like the Philadelphia Public Education Association) with cosmopolitan connections and outlooks.[48]

In his essay, "The Emerging Organizational Synthesis in Modern American History," Louis Galambos says that historians of this persuasion believe

> . . . that some of the most (if not the single most) important changes which have taken place in modern America have centered about a shift from small-scale, informal, locally or regionally oriented groups to large-scale, national, formal or-

[45] Samuel Hays, "The New Organizational Society," in *Building the Organizational Society: Essays on Associational Activity in Modern America*, ed. Jerry Israel (New York: Free Press, 1972), pp. 2–3, 6–8.

[46] John Higham, "Hanging Together: Divergent Unities in American History," *Journal of American History*, 61 (1974), p. 24.

[47] Robert Wiebe, *The Search for Order, 1877–1920* (New York: Hill & Wang, 1967), p. 166.

[48] Walter Trattner, *Crusade for the Children: A History of the National Child Labor Committee and Child Labor Reform in America* (Chicago: Quadrangle Books, 1970).

ganizations . . . characterized by a bureaucratic structure of authority. This shift in organization cuts across the traditional boundaries of political, economic, and social history.[49]

This interpretation has called attention to the fact that large-scale organizations deeply influence the lives of most Americans, and to a degree it has explained how. There is somewhat less agreement among historians as to *why* this shift has taken place or how to assess the human consequences. Most historians would agree that the rise of complex organizations relates in some fashion to new technology, new forms of empirical inquiry, and institutional innovations designed to cope with size and scope of functions. Economic historians like Thomas Cochran, Alfred Chandler, and Fritz Redlich have described how business firms changed from small, local enterprises (often owned and run by a single family) to vast and diversified multi-tier bureaucracies in order to cope with problems of growth of markets, complexity of production, and widening spans of control.[50] Raymond Callahan and others have shown how educational administrators consciously emulated these new business corporations.[51]

Although the new organizational approach in history may provide a useful focus for the study of compulsory attendance, especially in the years after 1890, the interpretation is not without flaws. It may not be sound to generalize urban experience to the educational system as a whole; bureaucratization was probably neither rapid nor systemic throughout American schools, but gradual and spreading from certain centers like drops of gas on water. The conceptualization of an organizational revolution is also somewhat rudimentary at this point, leading to the same dangers of misplaced concreteness one finds in the use of concepts like "modernization" and "urbanization." It is very important not to portray this kind of organizational change as an inevitable process. Some people helped to plan the changes and benefited from them, others did not; some results were intended, others were not. Schools are rarely so politically neutral as they portray themselves. One virtue of the economic interpretations to which we now turn is that they provide models of behavior that help to explain the interests or motivations of people who acted collectively in organizations.[52]

[49] Louis Galambos, "The Emerging Organizational Synthesis in Modern American History," *Business History Review*, 44 (1970), p. 280.

[50] Thomas C. Cochran, *Business in American Life: A History* (New York: McGraw-Hill, 1972), chs. 9, 16; Alfred D. Chandler, Jr., and Fritz Redlich, "Recent Developments in American Business Administration and Their Conceptualization," *Business History Review*, 35 (1961), 1–31.

[51] Raymond E. Callahan, *Education and the Cult of Efficiency* (Chicago: Univ. of Chicago Press, 1962).

[52] For some of these criticisms of the "organizational synthesis" I am indebted to Wayne Hobson's unpublished manuscript, "Social Change and the Organizational Society," Stanford Univ., Palo Alto, Calif., 1975.

Two Economic Interpretations of School Attendance

It is misleading, of course, to attempt to separate economic interpretations too sharply from political ones. In the three variants of political models sketched above, issues of economic class are present even where, as in ethnocultural conflict, they may not be salient. Both of the economic interpretations I examine also involve political action. Not surprisingly, however, economic historians tend to focus on economic variables, and it is useful to see how far this kind of analysis carries us in interpreting school attendance.

Two contrasting views seem most relevant: human-capital theory and a Marxian model. Both have precursors in nineteenth-century educational thought, but both have received closest scholarly attention during the last generation. Both are related to political interpretations in the broad sense in which Thomas Cochran says that the economic order shaped the political order: "On the fundamental level the goals and values of a business-oriented culture established the rules of the game: how men were expected to act, what they strove for, and what qualities or achievements were rewarded."[53] Naturally, economic interpretations may differ in what they take to be the basic driving forces in historical events, and such is the case in the two models I explore.

Human-Capital Theory and School Attendance

Mary Jean Bowman has described the notion of investment in human beings "as something of a revolution in economic thought." The notion of investigating the connection between resources spent on increasing the competence of workers and increased productivity and earnings was not entirely new, of course, but experience after World War II showed that "physical capital worked its miracles only in lands where there were many qualified men who knew how to use it (the Marshall Plan countries and Japan)." Economists interested in economic growth then began to analyze the effects of "human capital" on development and discovered that education appeared to have considerable explanatory power.[54]

Work on investment in human beings moved from general studies of the contribution of schooling to economic growth in whole societies to analyses of the rates of return of formal education to individuals. Economists treated the micro-decision making of individuals or families about schooling as a form of rational cost-benefit analysis. They developed increasingly sophisticated ways to estimate rates of return on investment in education by including not only the direct costs of schooling

53 Cochran, p. 304.
54 Mary Jean Bowman, "The Human Investment Revolution in Economic Thought," *Sociology of Education*, 39 (1966), 113, 117; Berry R. Chiswick, "Minimum Schooling Legislation and the Cross-Sectional Distribution of Income," *Economic Journal*, 315 (1969), 495–507.

but also the value of foregone earnings and the costs of maintaining students as dependents. Albert Fishlow, for example, has calculated that during the nineteenth century the "opportunity costs" paid by parents about equalled the sums paid by the public to support all levels of the educational system. Despite disagreements over specific rates of return, most economists agree that schooling does have significant impact on growth and earnings.[55]

Although economists have only recently honed the theory of human investment, similar notions have been current in educational circles for a long time. An idea circulating among educators for over a century has been that schooling created economic benefits for the society as a whole through greater productivity and for individuals through greater earnings. The first influential advocate of this view in the United States was Horace Mann, Secretary of the Board of Education of Massachusetts, who devoted his *Fifth Annual Report* in 1842 chiefly to this theme. In his report Mann presented an economic justification for greater investment in schooling, but his arguments were soon picked up as justification for compulsory school attendance. As Maris Vinovskis has observed, Mann actually preferred to advocate education by noneconomic arguments—the role of schools in moral or civic development, for example. But in his fifth year as Secretary, when his work was under political attack in the legislature and when a depression was forcing government to retrench, Mann decided that the time had come to show thrifty Yankees that education was a good investment. He argued that education not only produced good character and multiplied knowledge "but that it is also the most prolific parent of material riches." As proof he adduced the replies of businessmen to his questionnaire asking about the differences between educated and uneducated workers. What his study lacked in objectivity and scientific rigor it made up in evangelical enthusiasm; Mann concluded that money spent on primary schooling gave an aggregate rate of return to society of about 50 percent. He claimed that education enabled people to become rational decision makers by "comprehending the connections of a long train of events and seeing the end from the beginning." In addition to instilling this orientation toward the future—perhaps of most benefit to entrepreneurs—schooling made workers punctual, industrious, frugal, and too rational to cause trouble for their employers.[56]

Although Mann's evidence was largely impressionistic, his questionnaire highly biased, and his conclusions suspect for those reasons, his report was welcome ammunition to school reformers across the country. The New York legislature printed

[55] Bowman, 118-19; Fishlow, "Levels of Investment," p. 426; Marc Blaug, *An Introduction to the Economics of Education* (London: Penguin, 1972), chs. 1-3.

[56] Maris Vinovskis, "Horace Mann on the Economic Productivity of Education," *New England Quarterly*, 43 (1970), 562, 550-71.

and distributed eighteen thousand copies; Boston businessmen applauded him for proving that the common school was not only "a nursery of souls, but a mine of riches"; and a leading educator said in 1863 that Mann's report probably did "more than all other publications written within the past twenty-five years to convince capitalists of the value of elementary instruction as a means of increasing the value of labor."[57] In 1870 the United States Commissioner of Education surveyed employers and workingmen and reported results similar to those of Mann.[58] A committee of the United States Senate which took testimony on "the relations between labor and capital" in the mid-1880s found that businessmen and employees across the nation tended to agree that schooling increases the productivity and predictability of workers.[59] So fixed had this view become by the twentieth century—reflecting dozens of rate-of-return studies at the turn of the century—that a high school debaters' manual on compulsory schooling listed these as standard arguments for the affirmative:

> Education is the only guarantee of the prosperity of every individual in the State. Education will pay in dollars and cents.
> The education of the State and the wealth of the State bear a constant ratio, one increasing with the other.[60]

As human-capital theory has developed in recent years, economists have applied models of decision theory to the development of compulsory schooling in the nineteenth century. Generally they have focused upon individuals or their families and assumed that they make rational calculations of their presumed future benefits. For example, in their essay "Compulsory Schooling Legislation: An Economic Analysis of Law and Social Change in the Nineteenth Century," William Landes and Lewis Solmon adopted as their "theory of the determinants of schooling levels" the model that an individual "would maximize his wealth by investing in schooling until the marginal rate of return equaled marginal cost (expressed as an interest rate)."[61] They found that in 1880 there was a higher investment in schooling in states that had compulsory-attendance laws than in those that did not.

---

57 Vinovskis, p. 570.

58 United States Commissioner of Education, *Report for 1870* (Washington, D.C.: GPO, 1870), pp. 447–67.

59 United States Senate, *Report of the Committee of the Senate upon the Relations between Labor and Capital and Testimony Taken by the Committee* (Washington, D.C.: GPO, 1885), II, 789–90, 795–96, and IV, 504–5, 729–30.

60 John S. Patton, ed., "Selected Arguments, Bibliographies, Etc., for the Use of the Virginia High School and Athletic League," *University of Virginia Record, Extension Series,* I (1915), 103–104.

61 William Landes and Lewis Solmon, "Compulsory Schooling Legislation: An Economic Analysis of Law and Social Change in the Nineteenth Century," *Journal of Economic History,* 32 (1972), 58–59.

But by also examining levels of schooling in 1870, when only two states had laws, they discovered that the states which passed laws during the 1870s had already achieved high levels of investment in public education prior to enactment of compulsory legislation. They concluded that compulsory-education laws did not much influence the supply and demand curves and were

> . . . not the cause of the higher schooling levels observed in 1880 in states with laws. Instead, these laws appear merely to have formalized what was already an observed fact; namely, that the vast majority of school-age persons had already been obtaining a level of schooling equal to or greater than what was to be later specified by statute.[62]

In other words, the legislation merely applauded the decisions of families who had concluded that schooling paid off for their children. But this does not explain why parents had to be forced by law to send children to school. In another article, Solmon admits that variation in state support for schooling "might reflect politics rather than individual market decisions, but even these are worked out in the 'political market place' and presumably reflect the tastes of the 'typical' individual."[63]

Why, then, pass the laws? Landes and Solmon argue that on the demand side, educators wanted "legislation that compels persons to purchase their product" (the laws did appear to increase the number of days the schools were open); and law may have had external benefits "to members of the community since it is a way of giving formal recognition to the community's achievement in committing more resources to schooling."[64] With regard to supply, since schooling was already widely available and most parents were sending their children anyway, the cost of passing the laws was minimal in light of the presumed gains.

Albert Fishlow reaches similar conclusions in his study of investment in education during the nineteenth century. He notes a rapid rise of spending on human capital in the industrialized nations of the United States, England, France, and Germany. But in contrast with the key role of the central state in Europe, Fishlow says, American investment arose from a local consensus on the value of education: "Under such circumstances, the educational commitment was a matter of course from parents to children rather than from community to schools."[65] Most parents, he argues, made the calculation that education was worth the price, both in public outlays and in private opportunity costs. But there were some families that did

---

[62] Landes and Solmon, 77–78.
[63] Lewis Solmon, "Opportunity Costs and Models of Schooling in the Nineteenth Century," *Southern Economic Journal*, 37 (1970), 72.
[64] Landes and Solmon, pp. 87–88.
[65] Fishlow, "Levels of Investment," pp. 435–36.

not make this decision, and Fishlow argues that "the entire history of compulsory-schooling legislation and of child-labor legislation is usefully viewed as social intervention to prevent present opportunity costs from having weight in the educational decision."[66]

The actual opportunity costs differed sharply between rural and urban communities and between richer and poorer families. Schools in farm areas could adjust the academic calendar to match the need for child labor in agriculture, thus nearly eliminating the need to forego the earnings of children. In cities, by contrast, work opportunities were generally not seasonal, and compulsory attendance effectively barred children from adding substantially to family income. In addition, the poor did not have the same opportunity to invest in their children as did middle- and upper-income families, since they could not generally borrow capital against their children's presumed higher future income. Thus the very large private contribution to schooling through the opportunity costs was a source of major educational inequality—one recognized, incidentally, by truant officers, judges, and other officials who confronted the problems of compulsory attendance firsthand.[67]

How convincing is the human-investment paradigm in explaining the history of school attendance? On the surface it appears to require quite a stretch of the imagination to envisage families actually making the complex calculations of future benefit embodied in some of the models of economists. But, as Mary Jean Bowman writes, "the economist is not concerned, as is the psychologist, with explaining individual behavior per se. If people behave *as if* they were economically rational, that is quite enough, provided we are dealing with multiple decision units."[68] The decision-making model is of course a conscious simplification, omitting factors of public welfare or intrinsic pleasure that probably do affect choice. If one defines as voluntary that school attendance which is unconstrained by law (in the absence of law, or beyond legally required years, or in communities where laws were unpublicized or unenforced), it does appear that voluntary attendance was influenced in part by the prospect of future economic advantage, for families always had competing demands on their incomes. And the evidence is quite convincing that compulsory laws were passed in states where most citizens were already investing in schooling up to the point required by law. A powerful recurring argument for compulsion was that taxpayers could realize the full return on their large investment only if free schooling reached all the children; the presumption was that children who were out of school needed education the most and would

---

[66] Fishlow, p. 427.
[67] Fishlow, p. 426; Solmon, 68–72.
[68] Bowman, p. 120.

become an economic burden to the community if left uneducated. Hence there was a social benefit in investing in all children as human capital. Thus far the human-capital theory seems fruitful.

The kind of decision making assumed by this theory requires, I believe, at least some awareness of the economic benefits of education. Did nineteenth-century Americans, in fact, link schooling with economic success? In this century we have become accustomed to thinking of schools as sorters, as institutions that help to determine the occupational destiny of students. Increasingly, not only the professions but many other jobs as well have come to require educational credentials or prescribed levels of schooling even for entry-level positions.[69] Not only is this screening function of schools embodied in specific institutional arrangements, like high-school counseling programs, but it has also become common knowledge in the population at large. In 1973, 76 percent of respondents in a Gallup poll said they thought education was "extremely important" to "one's future success."[70]

There is little evidence, however, that citizens in the nineteenth century thought this way about schooling. Rhetoric about the purposes of education emphasized socialization for civic responsibility and moral character far more than as an investment in personal economic advancement. Indeed, there is some counter-evidence that businessmen, for one group, were actually hostile to the notion of education beyond the confines of the common school.[71] The arguments of Horace Mann and his early successors stressed not so much *individual* earnings as *aggregate* productivity and the workmanlike traits such as reliability and punctuality. The most influential spokesmen for nineteenth-century educators—people like William T. Harris—did stress a general socialization for work, but they tended to see success as the result of later behavior in the marketplace. Harris estimated that as late as 1898, the average person attended school for only five years. Out of one hundred students in all levels of education, ninety-five were in elementary, four were in secondary, and only one was in higher education.[72] Furthermore, family incomes were much lower in the nineteenth century than in mid-twentieth, and the structure of the labor force was far different. The percentage of the population engaged in agriculture dropped from 37.5 in 1900 to 6.3 in 1960, while the

[69] Ivar E. Berg, *Education and Jobs: The Great Training Robbery* (New York: Praeger, 1970).

[70] Stanley Elam, ed., *The Gallup Polls of Attitudes towards Education, 1969–1973* (Bloomington, Ind.: Phi Delta Kappa, 1973), p. 169.

[71] Irwin Wyllie, *The Self-made Man in America* (New Brunswick, N.J.: Rutgers Univ. Press, 1954), ch. 3; Cochran, pp. 174–76.

[72] Harris, 3–4, 54; Selwyn Troen, *The Public and the Schools: Shaping the St. Louis System, 1838–1920* (Columbia: Univ. of Missouri Press, 1975), ch. 6.

percentage in white-collar occupations rose from 17.6 to 43.5 in those years.[73] It is likely, then, that motives other than future rate of return on educational investments in individuals were more significant during the nineteenth century than in the twentieth. The micro-decision-making paradigm of human capital better explains our more recent history, when disposable family income has substantially risen, when parents are better educated and more capable of calculating future benefits, and when schooling has become far more important in sorting people into occupational niches.[74]

A Marxian Analysis

"We are led to reject the individual choice model as the basis for a theory of the supply of educational services," Samuel Bowles and Herbert Gintis have written.

> The model is not wrong—individuals and families do make choices, and may even make educational choices roughly as described by the human capital theorists. We reject the individual choice framework because it is so superficial as to be virtually irrelevant to the task of understanding why we have the kinds of schools and the amount of schooling that we do.[75]

Why superficial? Because the individual choice model provides only a partial interpretation of production, treats the firm "as a black box," and offers no useful insight into the basic question of how the capitalist class structure has been reproduced. The perpetuation of great inequalities of wealth and income over the past century and the development of schools as social institutions have not resulted simply from an aggregation of individual choices, Bowles and Gintis argue; rather, schooling has served to perpetuate the hierarchical social relations of capitalist production. In their view, society is not a marketplace of individuals maximizing their advantages but a class structure in which power is unequally divided. It may appear that the American educational system has developed in accord with "the relatively uncoordinated 'investment' decisions of individuals and groups as mediated by local school boards," but in actuality these "pluralistic" accommodations have taken place in response to changes in production "governed by the pursuit

[73] United States Bureau of the Census, *Historical Statistics of the United States* (Washington, D.C.: GPO, 1960), pp. 67–78.

[74] In "Education and the Corporate Order," *Socialist Revolution*, 2 (1972), p. 51, David K. Cohen and Marvin Lazerson point out that the "tendency to use market criteria in evaluating education flowered around the turn of the century"; for a survey of such studies, see A. Caswell Ellis, "The Money Value of Education," U.S. Bureau of Education, *Bulletin No. 22* (Washington, D.C.: GPO, 1917).

[75] Samuel Bowles and Herbert Gintis, "The Problem with Human Capital Theory—A Marxist Critique," *American Economic Review*, 65 (1975), 78.

of profit and privilege by those elements of the capitalist class which dominate the dynamic sectors of the economy." By setting boundaries of decision—establishing the rules of the game—the capitalist class determines the range of acceptable choice in a manner that strengthens and legitimizes its position.[76]

Bowles and Gintis are primarily interested in the consequences of the system of schooling rather than in the conscious motives of elites or school leaders. The important question is whether the outcomes of formal education have supported capitalism—for example, through differential training of workers and employers in ways that maintain the social division of labor. From this point of view, if Mann were a saint and yet his system of education perpetuated injustice because it supported exploitative relations of production, then the case for radical change would be all the stronger.

In developing their model of economic and educational change, Gintis and Bowles do not treat compulsory attendance in detail, but one can easily extrapolate an interpretation of compulsion from their theory. Their explanation has two major components. First, they account for educational reform periods, which shaped ideology and structure, as accommodations to contradictions engendered by capital accumulation and the incorporation of new groups into the wage-labor force. Second, they seek to demonstrate how the educational system has served capitalist objectives of achieving technical efficiency, control, and legitimacy.

"The capitalist economy and bicycle riding have this in common," they argue: "forward motion is essential to stability." As capital accumulates and new workers are drawn into expanded enterprises, potential conflict arises. Bowles and Gintis say that the contradictions inherent in this process gave rise to the common-school movement during the mid-nineteenth century, a time of labor militancy as the wage-labor force expanded and inequality increased. Such contradictions, they believe, also gave rise to the progressive movement at the turn of the twentieth century—a period of conflict between big business and big labor. Social discord stemmed from the integration of immigrant and rural labor into the industrial system. During these times, they argue, workers demanded more education, and "progressive elements in the capitalist class" acceded to the demands only insofar as they could adapt the school to their own purposes. Bowles and Gintis see educational development, then, "as an outcome of class conflict, not class domination." Workers won schooling for their children, but by controlling decision making in education and "suppressing anti-capitalist alternatives," the ruling class maintained the social relations of production while ameliorating conditions and dampening conflict. In this view, schooling has been a crucial tool for perpetuat-

[76] Bowles and Gintis, p. 75.

ing the capitalist system amid rapid economic change. Periodically, when the schools ceased to correspond with the structure of production, major shifts in the scope and structure of education took place, dominated in the final analysis by the class that set the agendas of decision.[77]

How did schools meet the capitalist objectives of technical efficiency, control, and legitimacy? Gintis and Bowles claim that the social relations of the school closely matched the needs of the hierarchical relations of production. The school prepared individuals differentially—in skills, traits of personality, credentials, self-concepts, and behavior—for performance in different roles in the economic hierarchy. This differentiation was congruent with social definitions of race, sex, and class. Thus, for example, when structures of production were relatively simple, schools concentrated on such qualities as punctuality, obedience to authority, and willingness to work for extrinsic rewards—all of which were useful in shaping a disciplined labor force for industry or commerce. As economic organizations became larger and more complex and the labor force increasingly segmented in level and function, schooling in turn grew more differentiated. This segmentation, coupled with differential treatment based on race and sex, helped to splinter employees into separate groups and to blind them to their common interest as workers. Schooling increasingly selected those who would get the good jobs; the rhetoric of equality of opportunity through education rationalized unequal incomes and status and legitimized the system. "The predominant economic function of schools," Bowles and Gintis observe, was "not the production or identification of cognitive abilities but the accreditation of future workers as well as the selection and generation of noncognitive personality attributes rewarded by the economic system."[78] As the work of different classes differed, so did the pattern of socialization in schools.

Just as Mann prefigured some of the human-capital theory, earlier Marxian theorists anticipated some of the Bowles–Gintis model, but they tended to see the laboring class as a more continuously active agent in educational change and capitalists as more hostile to public education. In 1883, for example, Adolph Douai, as a representative of the Socialistic Labor Party of the United States, presented a Marxist perspective on schooling to the United States Senate committee on the

[77] Samuel Bowles and Herbert Gintis, "Capitalism and Education in the United States," *Socialist Revolution*, 5 (1975), 111, 116–18.

[78] Samuel Bowles and Herbert Gintis, "The Contradictions of Liberal Educational Reform," in *Work, Technology, and Education*, ed. Walter Feinberg and Henry Rosemont, Jr. (Urbana, Ill.: Univ. of Illinois Press, 1975), pp. 124, 133; I have cited these essays by Bowles and Gintis because the more complete version of their analysis was not available at the time of writing. Now, see *Schooling in Capitalist America: Educational Reform and the Contradictions of Economic Life* (New York: Basic Books, 1976), esp. chs. 2, 4, 5, 7, and 9.

relations between labor and capital.[79] Half a century later, in the midst of the Great Depression, Rex David wrote a Marxian pamphlet on *Schools and the Crisis*.[80] Both strongly urged the creation of free and compulsory education for all young people; both stressed the opposition of capitalists to expanded educational opportunity; both saw teachers and other intellectual workers mostly as servants of vested interests but believed that educators could become an important means of spreading the light for socialism. For them as for a number of progressive labor historians, the working class was normally the dominant part of the coalition pushing for equality, and the ruling class was frequently hostile.

The interpretation of these earlier Marxists differs in emphasis from but does not directly contradict the Bowles-Gintis theory of educational change. Bowles and Gintis develop a more explicit model of how an apparently liberal educational system played a crucial part in reproducing unequal distribution of wealth and hierarchical relations of production. They further argue that owners and employers were not part of an undifferentiated group of capitalists but that the schooling reforms were engineered by those who controlled the leading sectors of the economy—exemplified by the corporate leaders at the turn of the century who sought to stabilize and rationalize the economy and supporting social institutions.[81]

Bowles and Gintis offer a general model of capitalist education rather than a specific interpretation of compulsory attendance. Thus what follows is my own extrapolation from their writing. Since they say that the "impetus for educational reform and expansion was provided by the growing class consciousness and political militancy of working people," presumably worker groups were advocates of universal attendance, perhaps aided by "progressive elements in the capitalist class." According to the theory that entry of new groups into the wage-labor force prompted demands for education, one might predict that the compulsory-education laws would appear first where the wage-labor force was growing most rapidly. At the same time, the ineffectiveness of these laws during the nineteenth century might be interpreted in part as a sign of ambivalence toward universal education among capitalists themselves (some might have preferred cheap child labor to the labor of schooled youth or adults, for example). On the other hand, phase two, the period of effective laws and increasing bureaucratization, might reflect growing capitalist consensus on the value of differentiated schooling in producing a segmented labor force for increasingly complex social relations of production. Indeed, the correspondence of the structure and processes of the schools with those

[79] Douai's testimony is in United States Senate, *Report on Labor and Capital*, II, 702–43.
[80] Rex David, *Schools and the Crisis* (New York: Labor Research Assoc., 1934).
[81] Bowles and Gintis, "Contradictions."

of the work place is precisely the point of the analysis; changes in the latter drive the former.[82]

The Marxian model sketched here is to a degree congruent with both the general theory of the political construction of education and the organizational snythesis. It suggests, however, that the capitalist class, as the ruling class, defines the production of citizens through education according to its own interests in the political economy. It adds to the organizational synthesis an explanation of why the large organization became dominant: capitalists had concentrated their ownership and power. It does not deny the choice model of human-capital theory, but it declares that the choices have been set within a capitalist zone of tolerance; further, it adds the notions of class conflict and reproduction of social structure.

The Bowles-Gintis analysis addresses important questions and poses a clear, explicit model. In my view, however, this kind of class analysis does not sufficiently explain the motive force of religious and ethnic differences in political and social life, especially within the working class. It tends to downplay important variations among employers' attitudes toward child labor and the different forms of education. The older Marxist view here has some substance; as Thomas Cochran and others have documented, many businessmen were opposed to extension of educational opportunity. The wage-labor hypothesis does not help us to understand widespread provision of schooling and numerous compulsory-schooling laws in communities and states in which the family farm was the predominant mode of production. As class analysis becomes further refined, however, it promises to add much to our understanding of both the continuities in social structure and the dynamics of economic and educational change.[83]

Conclusion

So what does one learn from exploring alternative ways of seeing compulsory schooling? Should one simply add them all together, like the observations of the blind men feeling an elephant, and say that the reality is in fact accessible only through multiple modes of analysis, that each mode is helpful but partial? Do some explanations fit only a particular time or place? To what degree are the interpretations mutually exclusive, and to what degree do they overlap? How might

82 Bowles and Gintis, "Capitalism," pp. 118, 126–33.
83 On ethnic and religious dimensions to school politics see Troen, chs. 2–4; Diane Ravitch, *The Great School Wars, New York City, 1805–1973: A History of the Public Schools as Battlefield of Social Change* (New York: Basic Books, 1974), chs. 3–7. As Solmon and Fishlow indicate (see references in footnote 67 above), enrollments in rural schools in many parts of the nation were higher than in industrialized areas; almost two-thirds of the states that passed compulsory-schooling legislation prior to 1890 were overwhelmingly rural in the distribution of population.

one test the assumptions and assertions of each by empirical investigation? Would any kind of factual testing be likely to change the mind of a person committed to a particular way of seeing or to a particular purpose?

The different kinds of interpretations do call attention to different actors, motives, and evidence, and in this sense one could say that the historian interested in all the phenomena of compulsory schooling might simply add together the various sets of observations. Those arguing for the political construction of education emphasize the role of the state and stress the importance of incorporating a heterogeneous populace into a unified state citizenry. The ethnocultural interpretation posits religious-ethnic differences as a motive force in political actions. The organizational synthesis stresses the role of the new middle class in changing the nature of American life through the creation of large organizations that dominate political and economic activities. Human-capital theorists focus on the family as a decision unit in calculating the costs and benefits of schooling. Finally, the Marxists see class struggle as the source of the dialectic that produces historical change. Each interpretation, in turn, directs attention to certain kinds of evidence which can confirm or disprove its assertions of causation: growth of new state rules and apparatus, religious differences expressed in political conflict, the rise of large organizations and related ideologies, the individual and social rates of return on schooling, and changes in the social relations of production and of schooling.[84]

There are problems with simple additive eclecticism, however. Some interpretations do fit certain times and places better than others, as we have seen. More fundamentally, the models deal with social reality on quite different levels: the individual or the family, the ethnocultural group, the large organization, and the structure of political or economic power in the society as a whole. Scholars advancing such interpretations often have quite different conceptions of what drives social change and hence quite different notions of appropriate policy. Some may concentrate on changing the individual, others on improving the functioning of organizations, and still others on radically restructuring the society. Ultimately, one is likely to adopt a framework of interpretation that matches one's perception of reality and purpose in writing, and thus simple eclecticism may lead to blurring of vision and confusion of purpose.

To argue that one should not mix interpretations promiscuously does not mean that it is unwise to confront alternative conceptualizations or to attempt to integrate them into a more complex understanding of social reality. This, in turn, may make historians more conscious of the ways in which theories and empirical re-

[84] Charles M. Dollar and Richard J. Jensen, *Historian's Guide to Statistics* (New York: Holt, Rinehart and Winston, 1971), chs. 1–2.

search interact with one another, so that an anomalous piece of evidence may call a theory into question and a new mode of explanation may be generated.[85] One of my purposes in this essay has been to extend the boundaries of discussion about the history of American education. I have become convinced that much of the recent work in the field—my own included—has used causal models too implicitly. It has also tended to constrict the range of value judgments. Was schooling "imposed" by elites on an unwilling working class, for example, or was John Dewey a servant of corporate capitalism? Entertaining explicit alternative models and probing their value assumptions may help historians to gain a more complex and accurate perception of the past and a greater awareness of the ambiguous relationship between outcome and intent—both of the actors in history and of the historians who attempt to recreate their lives.[86]

[85] Martin Rein, *Social Science and Public Policy* (London: Penguin, 1976); Henry Levin, "Education, Life Chances, and the Courts: The Role of Social Science Evidence," *Law and Contemporary Problems*, 39 (1975), 217–40.
[86] Robert K. Merton, "The Bearing of Sociological Theory on Empirical Research," and "The Bearing of Empirical Research on Sociological Theory," in *Readings in the Philosophy of the Social Sciences*, ed. May Brodbeck (New York: Macmillan, 1968), pp. 465–85.

Section II
Historical Methods in Educational Research

Recent Methodological Developments in the History of American Education

Carl F. Kaestle
University of Wisconsin at Madison

Historians often observe that their discipline is both science and art. When they say that history is a science, they mean that historians follow certain common procedures of investigation and argument, a fact which allows them to agree on some generalizations about the past even though individual historians' values and their understanding of human nature may differ. In many cases they can agree simply because the evidence is ample and clear, and because they agree on the ground rules. Factual statements like "Horace Mann was born in 1796" cause little debate as long as we are talking about the same Horace Mann and as long as the surviving records are not contradictory. More complex statements can also be verified and may attract wide agreement among historians. Examples are such statements as the following: "The average white fertility rate declined in America between 1800 and 1860," or "Most leading American educators in 1840 believed that public schooling would reduce crime."

However, the rules of investigation and analysis help us less and less as we attempt to make broader generalizations about the past, or make judgments about its relation to the present, and this is part of what we mean when we say that history is also an art. Consider such statements as: "Slavery destroyed the black family," or "Schooling was a major avenue for the social mobility of immigrants." These claims are immensely difficult to study because the relevant facts are complicated and because they involve problems of definition and value judgments. The process of making such historical generalizations is not merely inductive; one cannot simply add up all the little facts and make them into statements about larger structures and processes. Generalization remains an act of creative interpretation, involving the historian's values, interests, and training. Although the evidence establishes some limits, writing history remains subjective to a considerable degree.

The history of education shares the methodological problems of the field of history in general. There is no single, definable method of inquiry, and important historical generalizations are rarely beyond dispute. Rather they are the result of an interaction between fragmentary evidence and the values and experiences of the historian. History is a challenging and creative interaction, part science, part art.

It is important for educators to understand this problematic nature of historical methodology because historical statements about education abound far beyond textbooks or required history courses in schools of education. Beliefs about the historical role of schooling in America are encountered every day as arguments for educational policies. For example, in the great debates about urban school decentralization in the 1960s, advocates of decentralization argued that centralization was a device by which social elites in the early 20th century had gained control of urban education, protected the social structure, and tried to impose their particular values on public school children. The decentralizers argued that centralization had been an undemocratic means of social control, and therefore it deserved to be reversed. Opponents of decentralization claimed that it would lead to inefficiency and corruption. Besides, they said, a common, uniform school system had been a successful tool in creating a cohesive, democratic society in America. They too cited history as their authority. Behind these contending positions was a mass of complex evidence and conflicting values. The historian has no magic formula to tell you which analysis is correct.

The uncertain nature of historical generalization has been particularly apparent in the history of American education during the past 15 or 20 years. During this period the traditional methods and assumptions of historians of American education came increasingly under attack. The controversy has led to fresh insights, new questions and, more than ever, a heightened sense of the precariousness of historical generalizations.

The Traditional Framework

Current methodological issues in the history of American education are best understood in the light of the assumptions and conclusions of traditional American educational historians. Until the 1950s most writers of educational history shared two basic assumptions: first, that the history of education was concerned centrally, indeed, almost exclusively, with the history of public school systems; and second, that state-regulated, free, tax-supported, universal schooling was a good thing. These assumptions were rarely questioned, partly because many educational historians performed a dual role as educational administrators or professors of education, and therefore they had a vested interest in seeing public schooling in a good light. But also there was widespread popular agreement that public schooling was an unquestionably positive American institution.

There were several unstated corollaries to these assumptions, and they provided the framework—what some might call the paradigm—for research in educational history. Four elements in this paradigm helped determine methodology and occasioned later criticism. The first has to do with the focus on schooling. Because they tended to equate education with schooling, traditional historians rated the educational well-being and enlightenment of earlier societies by assessing how much formal schooling there was, and to what extent it was organized under state control. Because their view of historical development was dominated by their present conception of desirable educational policy, they spent much effort trying to explain the lack of enthusiasm for state-regulated schooling prior to the 1830s, and they underestimated the importance of the family, the workplace, the churches, and other educational agencies in pre-industrial society.

Related to this problem of focus is the problem of intent. Traditional historians of education saw those who favored state-regulated school systems as enlightened leaders working for the common good; they portrayed people who opposed educational reform as ignorant, misled, or selfish. The attribution of human motivation is a very difficult methodological problem in historical writing; it involves careful comparison of public and private statements, if they are available; it requires the historian to distinguish as clearly as possible between the intent and the consequences of actions; and it requires us to separate, if we can, our attempt to determine the historical actor's personal motivation from our own moral judgments on the effects of an event or a policy. Moral judgments may be timeless, but the historical actor's motivation must be understood in the context of the social values and scientific knowledge of the day. The value bias of most traditional educational historians prejudiced them against recognizing self-interest on the part of school reformers or legitimate, principled objection on the part of the opponents. On the other hand, some recent so-called "revisionist" historians have simply reversed the bias, making school reformers the villains and their opponents the heroes. Either value bias tends to collapse the complexity of educational history and to side-step methodological problems in determining intent.

A third corollary of the assumption that state schooling was a good thing is the equating of growth with progress. Methodologically this prompted historians to glory in numerical growth, often without controlling for parallel population growth or monetary inflation, and without taking seriously the differential educational opportunities of different groups. The tendency is seen equally in the traditional history of Roman Catholic schooling in America, which is largely a chronicle of increasing schools, children, and budgets.

A fourth corollary of the goodness theme is the focus on leadership and organization rather than on the educational behavior and attitudes of ordinary people. The methodological implication of this focus on the governors rather than on the clients of schooling is to give central attention to public records created by elites rather than attempting to tease out of scanty evidence some inkling of the educational lives of the inarticulate, as recent social historians of education have been attempting to do.

The great majority of books and doctoral dissertations written prior to 1950 in the field of the history of American education adhered to this paradigm, one focusing on the progressive and beneficial evolution of public school systems. There were some notable exceptions, and even within the paradigm many excellent legal, institutional, and intellectual studies were written. Nevertheless, the traditional framework had outlived its usefulness by the late 1950s and early 1960s, when it came under attack.

Two Strands of Revision

The two major strands of revision in the history of American education resulted from distinct critiques of the major tenets of the traditional paradigm:

that is, that the history of education is essentially the history of schooling, and second, that state-regulated schooling was benign and desirable. The first critique broadened the focus of educational history to look at various agencies of instruction other than schools; it has yielded its finest fruits in the works of Bernard Bailyn and Lawrence Cremin on the colonial period of American history, when schooling was much less important than it is today in the transmission of knowledge. It remains to be seen whether this broader focus can be applied successfully to the history of education in more recent periods. It will be more difficult to construct a coherent account of all the ways children learn in 20th-century society. Merely broadening our definition of education to include every aspect of socialization would leave the historian of education hopelessly adrift; each historian must therefore now decide carefully what definition of education lurks in his or her work, and this must depend upon what questions are being asked. If one is asking questions about how children acquire skills and beliefs in a society, then the definition of education must be quite broad indeed. If, on the other hand, we are asking questions about the origins of state policy toward education, we can legitimately focus on schooling, because past policymakers, like past historians, have equated schooling with education. Society as a whole educates in many ways; but the *state* educates through schools.

There has been a second, quite different, strand of revision in recent educational history, one which has caused considerable commotion among educators. Some revisionists have questioned the assumptions that state-regulated schooling has been generated by democratic and humanitarian impulses and that it has resulted in democratic opportunity. Their work has emphasized variously the exploitative nature of capitalism and how schools relate to it, the culturally abusive nature of mainstream values asserted by the schools, and the negative aspects of increasingly bureaucratic school systems. This reversal of ideological perspective on the development of school systems has not always resulted in methodologically sophisticated work, although as a whole the works labelled "radical revisionism" have raised important questions about the gloomier aspects of our educational system and have made some persuasive statements about our educational failures. Since this chapter is about methodology, not ideology, this is not the place to argue the merits of the radical view of school history.

Quantitative Methods

Recently, a small number of educational historians of diverse ideological persuasions have been pursuing a more methodological sort of revision. Their methods and their subject matter may help answer some of the questions raised by the radicals. These quantitative social historians have adopted the most substantial and problematic recent methodological innovations. Their work responds to two aspects of the inadequate traditional framework summarized above: a naive use of numerical data and a focus on the leaders rather than on the clients of educational institutions. Recent social historians of education have taken these problems as their starting point. They have adopted techniques from sociology and statistics to map out in some detail patterns of school attendance, years of schooling, school expenditures, voter characteristics on school issues, and other educational variables, correlating them with family and community characteristics and trying to chart changes over time. Much of this work would have been impossible 20 years ago. It has been made possible by the development of computer programs for social scientists and by the availability of microfilmed sources of information, such as the manuscript federal censuses of the 19th century. The inspiration and the models have been provided by European historical demographers and by other American social historians, who have been charting changing family structures, mobility patterns, wealth distribution, and other phenomena that affect common people. The new emphasis on parents and children in educational history also parallels similar emphases in other fields of educational research: sociologists are studying outcomes of schooling, lawyers are studying students' rights, and philosophers are studying the ethics of child-adult relations.

Hopefully, the complex description provided by quantitative historical studies will help us learn about educational supply and demand in the past, about the role of schooling in different types of communities, about the different school experiences of different social groups, and about the impact of schooling on later life in different historical periods. The great virtue of quantitative educational history is that it gets us in touch with the realities of schooling in the past; it gives us a way to start doing history from the bottom up, as it were, and a way to compare popular behavioral patterns with the opinions and policies of educational leaders. However, the quantitative social historian of education also faces problems, problems so numerous and frustrating that they cause some researchers to shun the techniques altogether. Others feel compelled by questions that demand quantitative answers, and they are groping toward a more adequate descriptive social history of American education, and toward theories that will help explain the patterns they are discovering.

Here is a short list of some of the problems they encounter. First, statistics and computers are unfamiliar, indeed alien, to many historians. Even for those who learn the techniques, the work is still very time consuming and expensive. Experts are constantly devising improved and more arcane statistical techniques. Social historians have trailed along behind sociologists and economists, picking and choosing the techniques that seem most appropriate. Some have moved from simple cross-tabulations and graphs into multiple regression and its various offspring. For example, a two-way cross-tabulation might display geographical regions (Northeast, Southeast, Midwest, etc.) in the left column and average years of school completed (0 to 4, 5 to 8, 9 to 11, high school grad, etc.) from left to right. This would be an appropriate and straightforward way to compare the regions' average school attainment rates. However, before speculating about the causes of differences among the regions we would want to look at such factors as per capita income, occupational structure, and degree of urbanization. Multiple regression is a mathematical procedure that allows one to assess the relative predictive association of several selected factors on one variable, such as school attainment. Multiple regression is, however, complex and time consuming, and it still leaves us the problem of interpreting the observed patterns of association. If a social historian can solve the problems of time, money, and expertise involved in quantitative work, he or she will then have to worry about the audience for whom the work is intended. Most readers of history balk at simple tables; but statistical adequacy demands detailed documentation and detailed presentation of results. This creates problems of style. Methodological sophistication is not worth much if you cannot reach the audience you wish to reach, and it is difficult to serve both a technical audience and a general audience in the same work.

As serious as these matters of training and style are, there are more substantive methodological problems in quantitative educational history. First, the data are crude and incomplete. Often the available school records and population censuses are ambiguous on crucial matters. Often they failed to ask the questions that interest us most now. Most of the data are cross-sectional; they provide only a snapshot of a group at a given moment. But education is a process, and many important questions about educational careers, or the influence of education on people's lives, can be answered only by data that trace individuals over time. Similarly, questions about the role of education in economic development require comparable aggregate data over time. Some historians have taken up this challenge and have developed longitudinal files by linking data from different sources, but that task is prodigious, and the attrition rate in studies of individuals (the cases lost by geographical mobility, death, and the ambiguity of common names) is so great as to render many conclusions dubious. More commonly, historians have tried to infer process from cross-sectional data. For example, they have estimated the average years of schooling completed among different social groups by calculating the average school entry and school leaving ages of the different groups in a single sample year; or they have made inferences about the impact of industrialization on communities' educational practices by comparing communities at different stages of industrialization in a given year. Although the questions in these cases are about processes, in neither case do the data trace individual children or communities over time. The logical and methodological problems of inferring processes from static information are serious, and they constitute an important problem in quantitative history today.

Even within legitimate cross-sectional analysis—that is, in pursuing questions about a population at a given moment—there can be a conflict between statistical adequacy and conceptual adequacy. Because research funds are limited and historical data are sparse, historians often work with small samples. Statisticians tell us that we need fairly large samples in order to be confident that the relationships we observe are not just random variation. If the results are not statistically significant, we cannot generalize from our sample to a larger population. In order to attain statistically significant results, we are sometimes tempted to collapse categories that should remain distinct. For example, if we are trying to relate ethnic background and teenage school attendance while controlling for parental occupation, we may decide to combine immigrant groups with quite different cultural and economic features, in order to achieve statistically significant comparisons between children of immigrants and nonimmigrants. But we risk misunderstanding the experience of distinct groups if we lump, for example, Poles, Italians, and Irish together. The best solution to this dilemma is to provide the reader with the significant statistics for the grossly aggregated categories, as well as the descriptively useful information about the smaller subcategories, and then ponder the meaning of both sorts of analysis. Here again, though, there are problems of space limits and the risk of presenting a tedious amount of information.

There are many other problems in this new area of research in educational history. For instance, it is difficult to know how conscientiously the data were reported in the first place, or what individual and institutional biases may have affected the results. Caution on this matter is reinforced when we find substantial contradictions between different sources that claim to measure the same variable in the same population. It is also difficult to create time series on educational variables like attendance, teachers' salaries, educational expenditures, or length of school year, because often the items were defined differently in different periods or omitted altogether. Even when ample and reliable quantitative information is available, it generally tells us about behavior and structure—numbers of children in school, the size of institutions, data on expenditures, votes on educational issues, and similar matters. The challenge for social historians in the coming decades is to find data, methods, and concepts that will link up behavior with belief, structure with ideas.

Despite these many problems, however, some impressive work is beginning to emerge, work which helps to locate the history of American education more solidly in the context of social structure and economic development. It is hardly a time for methodological self-congratulation, but neither is it a time for despair. One of the important by-products of quantitative work in educational history has been to sustain the methodological self-consciousness that began with the critiques of the traditional paradigm nearly 20 years ago. When the historian does not take methodology for granted, and when his or her methodology is critically scrutinized by other researchers, and when historians are constantly searching for new sources of evidence and techniques of analysis, better work will result.

Not all questions are linked to quantitative research, nor is the history of education now subsumed as a branch of social history. It is important to remember that history of education is still vitally concerned with the history of educational ideas. Much good work remains to be done on leadership and on curriculum, on the intellectual and institutional history of education in America. The excitement of the last 20 years has not resulted in a new single methodology, nor in a new, broadly accepted interpretation of educational history. However, the collapse of the old consensus has caused educational historians to explore new questions, discard old assumptions, try new techniques, and attempt to meet more rigorous standards of evidence and argument.

Theory and History

Many great social theorists, including Karl Marx, Max Weber, Emile Durkheim, Ferdinand Tönnies, and Talcott Parsons, wrote about history. Contemporary theorists from disciplines as diverse as sociology, linguistics, anthropology, philosophy, and statistics also do work that is relevant to historical study. Historians, however, differ in the amount of importance they give to theory, about whether they should attempt to test general theories with historical data, or about whether historians should get involved with theories at all.

There are several reasons why historians should read about theory and think about its relationship to their work. Because historical writing is selective and interpretive, it is necessarily guided by the individual historian's sense of what is important, where to find meaning, and how social change and human motivation work. The answers arise partly from the materials, of course. Although history is not *merely* inductive, it is *partly* inductive. The answers also lie, however, in an individual historian's temperament, convictions, hunches, and theories, whether explicit or implicit. By paying attention to the best theoretical work in related disciplines, historians can better identify their informal, personal theories. More important, they can shape their understanding of human experience by learning from other disciplines. Finally, historical work can reflect back in important ways on social theories, confirming, refuting, or modifying various theoretical statements.

A historian need not, therefore, adopt an entire theoretical system in order to profit from theoretical work in other disciplines. Some excellent work has been done from rigorous and systematic theoretical viewpoints, but most historians use theory incidentally and selectively. An excellent example of an educational historian using theories in an eclectic but explicit way is David Tyack's essay "Ways of Seeing," which is reprinted in Section I of this volume.

Theory has many implications for historical methodology, too numerous to cover in this chapter. Theories may influence what sort of evidence we look for, what sort of evidence we will accept, and what sort of arguments we will make from the evidence. For example, if one accepts the Marxist theorem that an individual's relationship to the means of production is crucial to his experience, one will make a concerted effort to determine historical actors' class status and class consciousness, and one will make class a prominent part of the explanation of historical events. If one accepts anthropologist Clifford Geertz's theory that ritualistic or even apparently trivial everyday behavior can symbolize the deeper meaning of a culture, one will devote much attention to developing an interpretation that moves from observed behavior to cultural meaning. Whether a historian accepts a large theoretical system, uses theory incidentally, or resists the mixing of theory and historical writing, each should be conversant with major theoretical positions in related disciplines and self-conscious about their possible relevance for historical methodology.

Conclusion: Some Fundamental Methodological Concerns

This chapter closes with four key problems to watch for when assessing arguments about the history of education, problems that have been highlighted by recent work in the social history of education but which are also pertinent to other approaches.

The first problem is the confusion of correlations and causes, a problem particularly salient in quantitative work, but certainly not unique to it. To demonstrate that two phenomena occur together systematically is not, of course, to prove that one causes the other, but historians as well as social scientists are constantly tempted into this kind of argument. For example, Irish families in 19th-century urban America sent their children to school less often and for fewer years, on the average, than many other groups. This does not, however, demonstrate that "Irishness" (whatever that is) caused low school attendance. First we must ask whether Irish immigrants also tended to be poor, because it might be poverty that caused low attendance. Then we would need to control for family structures, religion, and other factors. If, in the end, we satisfied ourselves that controlling for all the factors we could measure, Irish status was independently associated with low school attendance, we still would not yet have established a causal relationship. We would have to investigate, and speculate on, *why* and *how* being Irish affected school attendance. Correlations are just concerned with proximate occurrence; causality is about how things *work,* and correlations don't tell us much about how things work. Because human motivation is often multiple and vague and because society is not very much like a clock, historians must exercise great caution in moving from systematic statistical associations to assertions of causality.

The second problem to which critical readers must give close attention is the problem of defining key terms. We can subdivide the problem of definition into two common pitfalls: vagueness and presentism. As an example of vagueness, the notion that industrialization caused educational reform is a commonplace in educational history. However, the statement has almost no analytical value until we specify what is meant by the umbrella terms "industrialization" and "educational reform." In contrast, consider the statement: "The expansion of wage labor in 19th-century communities or regions was followed by an expansion of annual school enrollment." This is much more precise, it has important causal implications, and we can investigate it empirically.

By "presentism" we mean the danger of assuming that terms had their present-day connotations in the past, the fallacy of applying to past developments present-day terms that did not exist or meant something else at the time. A classic example in educational history involves the use of the word "public." In the 18th century a "public" educational institution was one in which children learned collectively, in contrast with private tutorial education, and it was one devoted to education for the public good, as opposed to mere selfish gain. Thus, the colonial colleges, which were controlled by self-perpetuating trustees and financed mainly by tuition, were thoroughly "public" and were called so at the time. In today's terminology they would be called "private," but calling them "private" in historical work greatly muddies our understanding of 18th-century society. Avoiding presentism thus means paying close attention to the etymology of key terms, and it is an absolute must in good history.

A third problem that critical consumers of educational history should keep in mind is the distinction between evidence of ideas about how people *should* behave, and evidence of how ordinary people *in fact* behaved. Too often we lack the latter evidence of behavior and let prescriptive evidence stand in its place; that is, we assume that people did as they were told. The methodological dilemma is posed by the following problem: If the legislative bodies of a society constantly passed rules requiring school attendance, is it evidence that people of that society valued schooling highly, expressing this value in their legislation, or is it evidence that people in that society did not value schoolgoing much, thus alarming its leaders into coercive efforts? To answer the question we need to know something about who makes the rules and about school attendance patterns by different groups. Here is a more specific example. There was widespread agreement among professional educators and physicians beginning in the late 1830s in the northeastern part of the United States that school attendance by very young children was unwise, even dangerous to their health, as well as being a nuisance to teachers. Parents were constantly urged to keep their children under 5 or 6 at home. This campaign continued throughout the 1840s and 1850s. To infer from this that children normally began school at age 5 or 6 during these decades, however, would be incorrect. Parents resisted the conventional expertise. As we now know from analysis of manuscript censuses and statistical school reports, they persisted in sending 3- and 4-year-old children to school, for reasons we can only guess, until they were coerced into keeping them home by local regulations on age of school entry in the 1850s and 1860s. Only then did the average age of entry rise substantially. Here, then, is an example of the lag between elite opinion and popular behavior. Child-rearing manuals may not cause or even reflect actual child-rearing practices; and exhortations about educational policies often fall on deaf ears.

The fourth and final problem has to do with the distinction between intent and consequences. No matter how wise our educational leaders have been, their powers of foresight have rarely equalled the historians' powers of hindsight. We know how things turned out, which is an inherent advantage in historical analysis, but it is also a problem. The problem lies in the danger of assuming that the historical actors could have (and *should* have) foreseen the full consequences of their ideas and of the institutions they shaped. It is undoubtedly true that many of the consequences of educational leadership have been precisely as the leaders intended; it does not follow, however, that we can infer intent from consequences. The fact that large bureaucracies are effective instruments of racial discrimination does not necessarily mean that their creators had a racist intent. The fact that schooling has done an unimpressive job in reducing crime does not mean that school reformers who touted it for that purpose were hypocrites. We cannot infer intent from consequences. We need direct evidence of intent at the time an act occurred.

No historian can completely transcend or resolve the four problems, but each must recognize the problems and the associated methodological challenges when trying to make meaningful generalizations about our educational past and to sort out the tremendous array of diverse and conflicting views that are presently circulating. Historians have always been scavengers. Since history involves all human experience and thought, historians have constantly raided other disciplines for new techniques of analysis and for new insights into society and human nature. This helps explain why there is no single methodology in history, and why historians love their craft so much: because it is so complex and so all-encompassing. Recent trends in the history of American education—the effort to see education as broader than schooling, the effort to see school systems in the context of social and economic development, and the effort to study popular attitudes and behavior as well as the history of elite intentions and actions—these trends have greatly accelerated the borrowing process in this historical subfield. Historians of education have reached out and become involved in the history of the family, of childhood, and of reform institutions, for example, in addition to deepening their traditional commitment to economic and political history as a context for educational development. They have also explored recent work in sociology, anthropology, psychology, and statistics for new techniques and helpful theories.

Because this period of exploration and revision has resulted in diverse eclectic methodologies, because no new methodological or ideological consensus has emerged—in short, because there is no successful paradigm in educational history today—it is all the more important that each reader of educational history be critically alert and independent.

Suggestions for Further Reading

Methodology and Historiography

Bailyn, B. (1960). *Education in the forming of American society*. Chapel Hill: University of North Carolina Press.

Best, J. H. (1983). *Historical inquiry in education: A research agenda*. Washington: American Educational Research Association.

Berkhofer, R. F. (1969). *A behavioral approach to historical analysis*. New York: Macmillan.

Butterfield, H. (1931). *The Whig interpretation of history*. London: Bell.

Cohen, S. (1976). The history of the history of American education, 1900–1976: The uses of the past. *Harvard Educational Review, 46*, 298–330.

Cremin, L. A. (1965). *The wonderful world of Ellwood Patterson Cubberley: An essay on the historiography of American education*. New York: Teachers College Bureau of Publications.

Graff, H. (1977). The new math: Quantification, the new history, and the history of education. *Urban Education, 2*, 403–439.

Hughes, H. S. (1964). *History as science and art*. New York: Harper & Row.

Kaestle, C. (1982). Ideology and American educational history. *History of Education Quarterly, 22*, 123–137.

Warren, D. R. (Ed.). (1978). *History, education, and public policy*. Berkeley: McCutchan.

Contrasting Interpretations of American Educational History

Cremin, L. A. (1964). *The transformation of the school: Progressivism in American education*. New York: Alfred Knopf.

Cremin, L. A. (1980). *American education: The national experience, 1783–1876*. New York: Harper & Row.

Cubberley, E. P. (1934). *Public education in the United States* (rev. ed.). Boston: Houghton-Mifflin.

Kaestle, C. F. (1983). *Pillars of the republic: Common schools and American society: 1780–1860*. New York: Hill & Wang.

Kaestle, C. F., & Vinovskis, M. A. (1980). *Education and social change in nineteenth-century Massachusetts*. New York: Cambridge University Press.

Karier, C. J., Violas, P., & Spring, J. (1973). *Roots of crisis: American education in the twentieth century*. Chicago: Rand McNally.

Katz, M. B. (1968). *The irony of early school reform: Educational innovation in mid-nineteenth century Massachusetts*. Cambridge: Harvard University Press.

Katz, M. B. (1975). *Class, bureaucracy & schools* (expanded ed.) New York: Praeger.

Lazerson, M. (1971). *Origins of the urban school: Public education in Massachusetts, 1870–1915*. Cambridge: Harvard University Press.

Ravitch, D. (1974). *The great school wars: New York City, 1800–1968*. New York: Basic Books.
Spring, J. H. (1972). *Education and the rise of the corporate state*. Boston: Beacon Press.
Tyack, D. B. (1974). *The one best system: A history of American urban education*. Cambridge: Harvard University Press.

Study Questions

1. What is meant by the statement, "Any history of education is partly art and partly science"?

2. Is the history of American education the same thing as the history of schooling in the United States?

3. In reporting history, must a historian necessarily impose his or her moral values, or can history be totally objective?

4. Explain the role of traditional assumptions in the history of American education.

5. Describe the "problem of intent" in historical approach.

6. Give examples of research questions that would: a) properly allow an educational historian to focus only on the schools, and b) require that education be examined both in and out of schools.

7. Do quantitative research methods, including statistical analyses, have any role in historical research? Why or why not?

8. Is there a single methodology of historical inquiry in education, or are there many different methods? Support your conclusion with examples.

9. Describe the "correlation problem" that is present in both historical and quasi-experimental research.

10. What is the meaning of the term "presentism"?

11. Can historical actions usually be inferred from historical statements of intent? Can you think of examples to support your conclusion?

12. Can conclusions on intent safely be inferred from historical evidence on outcomes or consequences? Can you give an example?

Exercise for Class Discussion: The History of Education Game

Introduction

Below you will find two historical scenarios with some fragmentary evidence. The scenarios are fictional, but they are similar to situations historians have tried to analyze recently. One is deliberately arranged to be more ambiguous than the other. The game is to decide: what generalizations might I make on the issues posed, and how would I argue these generalizations from the evidence? Second, what questions can I *not* answer with any confidence from the evidence presented, and what kinds of further evidence would I need before I could answer them? (You might wish to poke around local school archives or research libraries to find out whether such evidence does in fact exist.) The game does not recreate what a historian actually does, but for discussion purposes it should raise some of the same issues historians have faced in similar situations.

The Scenarios

A. Roman Catholics and the Public Schools in Metropolis

Metropolis in 1840 was a large eastern seaport with a high percentage of Roman Catholic immigrants in its population. We are interested in the attitudes of its Catholic citizens toward schooling, and in particular, whether they preferred Catholic parish schools over public schools and, if there were no Catholic schools in their vicinity of the city, whether they preferred public schools to none.

Item 1. The bishop of Metropolis diocese argued repeatedly that Catholic parents could not and would not send their children to the godless public schools. In the absence of sufficient parish schools, he said, large numbers of Catholic children were roaming the streets.

Item 2. Protestant charity workers often commented that street kids and delinquents were disproportionately Catholic and immigrant.

Item 3. The local Catholic newspaper, which sometimes took positions opposed to the clergy, argued that immigrant Catholic parents should send their children to public schools to learn English and become good Americans.

Item 4. Ward school reports, complaining of the bad effects of newly created Catholic parish schools, often reported attendance figures comparing the enrollments at public schools before and after the opening of Catholic schools. Typical of such reports is the following:

Table 1. *Metropolis public schools attendance figures: Ward 3, School No. 15*

Time	Boys	Girls	Total
Before St. Mary's School opened	186	170	356
After St. Mary's School opened	120	110	230

Item 5. In arguments with the public school officials, Catholic spokesmen documented numerous instances of derogatory attitudes toward Roman Catholicism in public school textbooks.

If we take these items to be typical, what can you conclude about Catholics' attitudes about having their children attend public and parochial schools? How sure can you be? What other information would be most valuable?

B. The High School Controversy in Milltown

Milltown was a small textile manufacturing town in the middle-Atlantic states. For some time in the 1840s the local school board had been saying that the community needed a public high school, to be located in the center of town, instead of relying on private academies or sending children to the high schools of larger neighboring towns. In 1851 the issue came to a townwide vote, the results of which were recorded in the town meeting minutes.

Item 1. For years the school board had been criticizing wealthy people who sent their children to private schools, saying that they harmed the public school system and withheld their support for greater public school expenditures.

Item 2. The *Milltown Working Man's Advocate* urged all working-class voters to support the high school, arguing that public schooling was one of the crucial avenues of opportunity in America.

Item 3. At a town meeting, however, a factory worker complained that the new school would burden him with taxes even though his children, who needed to work in their teenage years, would not be able to use it.

Item 4. The voting lists, summarized by ward and occupational group, were as follows:

Table 2. *Milltown high school vote*

Occupational group	Center ward Total vote	Center ward Yes n	Center ward Yes %	Outer ward A Total vote	Outer ward A Yes n	Outer ward A Yes %	Outer ward B Total vote	Outer ward B Yes n	Outer ward B Yes %	All wards combined Total vote	All wards combined Yes n	All wards combined Yes %
Merchants and manufacturers	78	47	60	22	10	45	11	5	48	111	62	56
Lower white-collar workers	55	39	71	10	6	60	8	3	63	73	48	66
Skilled workers	110	69	63	32	17	54	27	14	52	169	100	59
Unskilled workers	275	124	45	120	50	42	67	27	40	462	201	44
Farmers	15	12	80	87	36	41	108	42	39	210	88	42
Totals	533	289	54	271	119	44	221	91	41	1025	499	49

From these items, what can you say about why the high school vote lost? Does the occupational information given in Item 4 suggest that social class was the crucial factor? What other factors might have been involved?

Discuss your answers before turning to my brief comments on the scenarios.

Comments on the Scenarios

A. Roman Catholics in Metropolis

The bishop was expressing the church's point of view, that public school attendance threatened the faith of Catholic children (Item 1). This belief may have been shared by many Catholic parents, but more evidence would be needed than is cited here. Protestant charity workers and various officials (Item 2) often commented on the high rate of delinquency and crime among immigrants and/or Catholics. Some prejudice may be involved in these opinions, but statistics not cited here tend to support them. However, high rates of crime and delinquency may have resulted from immigrant Catholics' low income status and poor housing. It does not tell us much about parents' attitudes toward the schooling of young children, although it may suggest what the alternatives were for some older children. The advocacy of public schooling by the Catholic newspaper (Item 3) is interesting, because it shows a diversity of opinion among Catholics whose views have been recorded. Parents were faced with conflicting advice. Those who decided to ignore the bishop's advice and send their kids to public schools could find some support for their decision. The statistical information in Item 4 supports this possibility. To the extent that the attendance report is typical, one can conclude that substantial numbers of Catholic parents preferred Catholic schools to public schools, but that lacking Catholic schools they preferred public schools to none at all. Of course, the real bias of the public schools against Catholics (Item 5), as well as the clergy's opposition to public schooling, was probably troubling to many Catholics and probably acted as a deterrent to attendance by some children, as well as creating enthusiasm for the creation of Catholic schools. Still, the quantitative evidence suggests that many Catholic parents wanted schooling for their children, even if it was public schooling.

B. Milltown High School

The evidence here is more ambiguous. Item 1 suggests that wealthy people may have opposed the public high school because they sent their children to private schools, but the evidence is not direct. Two possibilities are suggested about working families lower in the social scale: that they supported the high school as a possible avenue of advancement for their children (Item 2), or that they opposed it because they would have to pay for it while more privileged people's kids used it (Item 3). In fact, there is considerable evidence that both of these attitudes existed among mid-19th-century workingmen. The statistics on the vote (Item 4) do not completely clarify the class issue, even if we use occupational status as an indicator of social class. Looking at the totals by occupational groups for all wards combined, we see that the greatest support came from lower white-collar workers, a small "middle-class" group, and the next greatest support came from skilled workers, also a middling occupational status. But the merchants and manufacturers were not far behind, and among unskilled laborers and farmers a substantial minority also voted for the high school. One could conclude that the middling occupational groups were the most enthusiastic about the high school and that opposition among unskilled workers and farmers accounted for its downfall, perhaps for the reason suggested in Item 3. When we look at the statistics by ward, however, another factor—distance from the town center—becomes clear. Among all occupational groups, residents of the outer wards were more opposed to the high school than residents of the center ward. Farmers, heavily concentrated in the outer wards, voted heavily against the high school, even though that category included men of quite different income levels. Distance still mattered in the mid-19th century. The outer wards may have had strong traditions of neighborhood control, and may have been resentful of townwide institutions. Also, within a given occupation, those with higher incomes and those who were more receptive to educational innovations may have tended to live in the center ward. More evidence would be necessary to make such arguments, however. The evidence in this scenario is more ambiguous than in Scenario A.

In both cases, you surely found many issues to discuss beyond the few raised here. I hope the scenarios have suggested that historical reasoning is not only difficult, but worth the challenge.

Reading

Introduction
A Historiographical Turning Point: Bernard Bailyn's
Education in the Forming of American Society

Carl F. Kaestle

In 1956 a group of scholars convened at Chatham, Massachusetts, to consider "The Role of Education in American History." They concluded that much historical writing about education had been done by authors trained outside of academic history departments, often professors at schools of education committed to a positive judgment on public schooling and a narrowly institutional definition of their subject matter. The committee concluded that history of education as a field should become more involved in the methods and concerns of American historians in general. One member of the group, Bernard Bailyn, soon had an occasion to implement this point of view. A colonial historian trained in the Harvard History Department, Bailyn was at the time teaching the history of American education at Harvard's Graduate School of Education. He was thus ideally situated to assess the relationship between existing histories of education and historical scholarship more generally. This assessment became a book when the Institute for Early American History and Culture at Williamsburg asked Bailyn to write an extended essay on needs and opportunities for study in the history of education in early America. The result was *Education in the Forming of American Society*, which appeared in 1960. The book included two essays. The first, entitled "An Interpretation," included a historiographical critique of the field as well as a hypothetical essay demonstrating the explanatory power of a broader definition of education. The second part of the book was a bibliographical essay that sketched out a broader subject matter for educational historians to ponder.

In the excerpt that follows, from the first essay, Bailyn considers the shared educational functions of family, church, school, and workplace, the impact of the colonial environment on these institutions, and how they changed over time. Defining education not just as schooling but as "the entire process by which a culture transmits itself across the generations," Bailyn explored the central educational roles of the family, the church, and the apprenticeship.

Readers may profitably contemplate how such a perspective could be applied to 20th-century developments. What new institutions and settings have loomed important in the range of children's educational experiences? How has the configuration of educational institutions changed during the 20th century? What tensions have contributed to such shifts, or resulted from them? Also, consider the problem that Bailyn's very broad definition of education poses for students of education in a culturally diverse, technological society.

Bailyn announced that his interpretive essay was hypothetical and warned that it "may well prove to be wrong or misleading." In the subsequent years of exciting research on the colonial family, much of which was stimulated by Bailyn's book, scholars have revised his emphasis on a shift from an extended English family to a nuclear colonial American family. The nuclear family, it seems, was more often the norm in both the premigration English situation and in the colonial settlements. Although the new world environment had not transformed the structure of the family, however, colonial American conditions did change its functions. Bailyn's concept of education as a "configuration of educational processes" has been a major contribution to the field. Furthermore, his insight that in the face of social change people gradually transferred educational functions from one institution to another broadened the analytical framework for understanding schooling and society. Beyond his impact on educational historians as specialists, Bailyn's essay contains a subtle model of social change, one that has withstood the test of time and further research. In Bailyn's explanation, people make unintended and temporary changes in traditional institutions and assumptions when they are confronted with a changed environment or a new set of social relations; only later do these temporary adjustments become rationalized and worked into new institutional configurations.

Although Bailyn's essay is not methodological in a technical sense, it still stands today as the most concise and original statement of a point of view that turned the history of education in new directions. With its broader definition and scope, it prompted subsequent scholars to ask new questions, seek new methods, and gain new insights.

An Interpretation

WHEN THE SPONSORS
of this conference invited me to prepare a paper on the
needs and opportunities for study in the early history of
American education, they hoped that I would be able to
present in some coherent form a survey of the writing that
now exists in that area and a number of recommendations
for further work, including a list of specific topics for
papers, monographs, and surveys. At least that is what I
understood them to have in mind and what in fact my
predecessors in these Institute Conferences have done with
excellent results. But when I attempted to follow these
directions I found myself confronted with a peculiar problem. The field of study with which I was concerned, unlike
the history of science, law, or Indian-white relations, has not
suffered from neglect, which firm direction and energetic

Bailyn, Bernard. *Education in the Forming of American Society: Needs and Opportunity for Study.* New York, W.W. Norton, 1960, pp. 3–49. Reproduced by permission.

research might repair, but from the opposite, from an excess of writing along certain lines and an almost undue clarity of direction. The number of books and articles on the schools and colleges of the colonial period, on methods of teaching, on the curriculum, school books, and teachers is astonishingly large; and since at least the end of the nineteenth century the lines of interpretation and the framework of ideas have been unmistakable. And yet, for all of this, the role of education in American history is obscure. We have almost no historical leverage on the problems of American education. The facts, or at least a great quantity of them, are there, but they lie inert; they form no significant pattern.

What is needed, it seems to me, is not so much a projecting of new studies as a critique of the old and, more important, an attempt to bring the available facts into relation with a general understanding of the course of American development. I would like, therefore, to depart somewhat from the usual procedure of this Needs and Opportunities series and approach the subject of education in a round-about way. I would like to start backwards, and begin by tracing back to its origins the path that led to the present interpretation and to consider certain implications of that view. I would like then to suggest an alternative approach and follow it out as far as I am able towards a general statement of the place of education in the forming of American society. It will be a statement at least two of whose limitations can be known in advance. It will not be comprehensive in the sense of touching on all aspects of education in early American history. It will, instead, deal with one theme only, though a theme of preeminent importance, basic, I believe, to an understanding of the larger history. Further, since it will not fall into the familiar categories it will of necessity be based on scattered and incompletely assembled evidence. It will be a hypothesis, in other words, an essay in hypothetical history. Like all such projections it may well prove to be wrong or misleading. But if so, its purpose will nevertheless have been served by eliciting the contrary proof, which, too, will tell a different and I think a more useful kind of story about education than those we are accustomed to hear.

It is only when this much has been accomplished, when the knot of our present entanglements in the history of education has been at least loosened and when the lines of a different interpretation have been suggested, that I wish to turn to the specific needs and opportunities for study in the early history of American education. For I would like to center that discussion, which will be found in a separate bibliographical essay, on the themes stated in the general interpretation.

I

It is not a difficult task to trace back to its origins the present interpretation of education in American history, for its leading characteristic is its separateness as a branch of history, its detachment from the main stream of historical research, writing, and teaching. It is a distinct tributary, and it leads directly back to a particular juncture at the end of the nineteenth century. The turning point may be marked by the completion in 1900 of two notable books. Edward Eggleston's *Transit of Civilization* is a remarkably imaginative effort to analyze "the original investment from which has developed Anglo-Saxon culture in America" by probing "the complex states of knowing and thinking, of feeling and passion of the seventeenth-century colonists." The opening words of the book make clear the central position of education in the ambitious sweep of this history:

What are loosely spoken of as national characteristics are probably a result not so much of heredity as of controlling traditions. Seminal ideas received in childhood, standards of feeling and thinking and living handed down from one overlapping generation to another, make the man English or French or German in the rudimentary outfit of his mind.

All the major topics—"mental outfit," medical notions, language, folklore, literature, "weights and measures of conduct," and land and labor—are conceived as phases in the transmission of a civilization. The longest chapter is entitled "The Tradition of Education." The entire book is, in fact, a study in the history of education; for all the crudities of its construction and imbalances of interpretation, it is one of the subtlest and most original books ever written on the subject.

It should have been a seminal work. It should have led to a highly imaginative treatment of the theme of education in American history. But it did not. It was laid aside as an oddity, for it was irrelevant to the interests of the group then firmly shaping the historical study of American education.

For them, the seminal book, marking "an epoch in the conception of educational history in English," was *A History of Education*, written by that "knight-errant of the intellectual life," as his devoted friend William James called him, the exuberant polymath and free-lance educator, Thomas Davidson. His too was a remarkable book, if only for its scope. Davidson starts with "The Rise of Intelligence" when "man first rose above the brute." Then he trots briskly through "ancient Turanian," Semitic, and Aryan education, picks up speed on "civic education" in Judaea, Greece, and Rome, gallops swiftly across Hellenistic, Alexandrian, Patristic, and Muslim education; leaps magnificently over the thorny barriers of scholasticism, the medieval universities, the Renaissance, Reformation, and Counter-Reformation; and then plunges wildly through the remaining five centuries in sixty-four pages flat.

But it was less the range than the purpose and argument of this book that distinguished it in the eyes of an influential group of writers. Its purpose was to dignify a newly self-conscious profession, education, and its argument, a heady distillation of Social Darwinism, was that modern education was a cosmic force leading mankind to a full realization of itself. A few sentences from Davidson's Preface will make clearer than any explanation could the origins of a distinct school of historical writing. "My endeavor," Davidson wrote,

. . . has been to present education as the last and highest form of evolution. . . . By placing education in relation to the whole process of evolution, as its highest form, I have hoped to impart to it a dignity which it could hardly otherwise receive or claim. From many points of view, the educator's profession seems mean and profitless enough, compared with those that make more noise in the world; but when it is recognized to be the highest phase of the world-process, and the teacher to be the chief agent in that process, both it and he assume a very different aspect. Then teaching is seen to be the noblest of professions, and that which ought to call for the highest devotion and enthusiasm.

For Davidson, as for a whole generation of passionate crusaders for professionalism in education, history was not simply the study of the past. It was an arcane science that revealed the intimate relationship between their hitherto despised profession and the destiny of man. The purpose of his *Textbook in the History of Education* (1906), wrote Paul Monroe, Professor of the History of Education at Teachers College, was not merely to supply information and vicarious experience to the student of education, but, more important, to furnish him with "a conception of the meaning, nature, process, and purpose of education that will lift him above the narrow prejudices, the restricted outlook, the foibles, and the petty trials of the average schoolroom, and afford him the fundamentals of an everlasting faith as broad as human nature and as deep as the life of the race."

A subject that could give the neophyte an everlasting faith in his profession clearly deserved a central position in the curriculum. And such a position it duly received. The History of Education came to be taught as an introductory course, a form of initiation, in every normal school, department of education, and teachers college in the country. A subject of such importance could not be left to random development; the story had to be got straight. And so a few of the more imaginative of that energetic and able group of men concerned with mapping the over-all progress of "scientific" education, though not otherwise historians, took over the management of the historical work in education. With great virtuosity they drew up what became the patristic literature of a powerful academic ecclesia.

The development of this historical field took place, consequently, in a special atmosphere of professional purpose.

It grew in almost total isolation from the major influences and shaping minds of twentieth-century historiography; and its isolation proved to be self-intensifying: the more parochial the subject became, the less capable it was of attracting the kinds of scholars who could give it broad relevance and bring it back into the public domain. It soon displayed the exaggeration of weakness and extravagance of emphasis that are the typical results of sustained inbreeding.

The main emphasis and ultimately the main weakness of the history written by the educational missionaries of the turn of the century derived directly from their professional interests. Seeking to demonstrate the immemorial importance and the evolution of theories and procedures of the work in which they were engaged, they directed their attention almost exclusively to the part of the educational process carried on in formal institutions of instruction. They spoke of schools as self-contained entities whose development had followed an inner logic and an innate propulsion. From their own professional work they knew enough of the elaborate involvement of school and society to relate instruction somehow to the environment, but by limiting education to formal instruction they lost the capacity to see it in its full context and hence to assess the variety and magnitude of the burdens it had borne and to judge its historical importance.

But there is more to it than that. The willingness to restrict the history of education to formal instruction reflects not merely the professional concerns of the writers but also certain assumptions about the nature of history itself. To these writers the past was simply the present writ small. It differed from the present in the magnitudes and arrangement of its elements, not in their character. The ingredients of past and present were the same; and they took their task to be the tracing of the careers of the institutions, ideas, or practices they knew so well. They had no capacity for surprise. They lacked the belief, the historian's instinct, that the elements of their world might not have existed at all for others, might in fact have been inconceivable to them, and that the real task is to describe the dawning of ideas and the creation of forms—surprising, strange, and awkward then, however familiar they may have become since—in response to the changing demands of circumstance.

Distortions and short-circuiting of thought inevitably resulted. Persisting in their search for familiarity in an unfamiliar past, they had no choice but to accept crude facsimiles, deceptive cognates. "Public" was perhaps the most important. In their own time it was the "public" aspect of education that most involved their energies and that framed their vision: "public" *vs.* "private," the state as equalizer and guarantor, assuring through tax-supported, free, publicly maintained and publicly controlled schools the level of education that made democracy effective. Men like Ellwood Cubberley, whose formative professional experience was gained as superintendent of public schools in San Francisco and whose major field as an educator of educators was not history but public administration, saw as the main theme in the history of American education the development of public school systems. Cubberley and the others told a dramatic story, of how the delicate seeds of the idea and institutions of "public" education had lived precariously amid religious and other old-fashioned forms of education until nineteenth-century reformers, fighting bigotry and ignorance, cleared the way for their full flowering. The seeds were there at the beginning—though where, exactly, was a matter of considerable controversy. There is no more revealing historical debate than that between George H. Martin, Agent for the Massachusetts State Board of Education, and Andrew S. Draper, New York State Superintendent of Public Instruction, a debate that ran to six articles in leading educational journals between 1891 and 1893. The question they disputed was whether the appearance of public education in seventeenth-century America should be attributed to the Puritans in Massachusetts or the Dutch in New York. Considering the historical materials available at the time, it was an informed discussion. But it missed the point. Public education as it was in the late nineteenth century, and is now, had not grown from known seventeenth-century seeds; it was a new and unexpected genus whose ultimate character could not have been predicted and whose emergence had troubled well-disposed, high-minded people. The modern conception of public education, the very idea of a clean line of separation between "private" and "public," was unknown before the end of the eighteenth century. Its origins are part of a complex story, involving changes in the role of the state as well as in the general institutional character of society. It is elaborately woven into the fabric of early modern history.

Other, similar anachronisms resulted from reading present issues and definitions back into the past. In the telescoping and foreshortening of history that resulted, the past could be differentiated from the present mainly by its primitivism, the rudimentary character of the institutions and ideas whose ultimate development the writers were privileged to know so well. There was about their writing, consequently, a condescension toward the past that exaggerated the quaintness and unreality of the objects they described. The story became serious only when these antiquities, sufficiently displayed, were left behind and the immediate background of present problems was approached. By their failure to see the past as essentially different and to allow apparent similarities to blend naturally into the unfamiliarities of a distant setting, they lost the understanding of origins and of growth which history alone can provide.

How much they lost, how great was the sacrifice of intellectual leverage that resulted from the concentration on formal institutions and from the search for recognizable antecedents, may be seen in their treatment of the colonial and Revolutionary periods. How were they to make sense of this era? Though it comprised two-thirds of the American past, its pedagogical institutions were so few and so evidently pitiful, so bound down by religion and other antiquated concerns, that it was hard to know what to say about them except that they demonstrated by comparison the extent of subsequent progress. Some authors were quite ingenious. One, R. G. Boone, Professor of Pedagogy at Indiana University, suggested as an "interesting historical study" of the colonial period "the abuse of the principle" of free schools. Not that they wasted much time on the subject. Of the fifteen chapters in Cubberley's exceedingly influential text (over 100,000 copies of it have been sold since its publication in 1919), exactly one is devoted to the first two centuries of American history. But at least Cubberley gave his readers fair warning. He called his book *Public Education in the United States,* and since there was neither public education nor the United States before 1776 he was free in effect to ignore everything that happened before and to assume without explanation that political independence is a logical starting point for the history of educational institutions.

Imbalance, quaintness, and jagged discontinuities mark these brief treatments of the colonial period. Mountains were made of religion in the Puritan laws of the 1640's, of the Symmes and Eaton bequests, of hornbooks, dame schools, Corlet, and Cheever. New England carried the burden, with assists from the Quakers, the Society for the Propagation of the Gospel, and "well-to-do planters." Over it all was the "dominance of the religious purpose," properly illustrated by the *Primer*'s alphabetical catechism: "In Adam's Fall/We sinned all." The eighteenth century, lacking even Puritans and the Dutch, was a particular embarrassment, and it was quickly disposed of with remarks about the "waning of the old religious interest," mention of the "rise of the district system," and a few words about some new colleges and an academy. The story lurched and bumped along without apparent purpose or direction. Organization, so clear a reflection of understanding, was primitive when it existed at all. Three "type attitudes" framed Cubberley's colonial material: "compulsory maintenance attitude" (Massachusetts), "parochial-school attitude" (Pennsylvania), and "the pauper school non-state-interference attitude" (Virginia).

It is this casual, inconsequential treatment of the colonial period that is the best measure of the limitations of the history these professional educators wrote and of the school of interpretation, still flourishing, which they founded. Restricting their inquiry to the problems and institutions they knew, they did not recognize, they had no way of understanding, the first, and in some ways the most important, transformation that has overtaken education in America.

This fundamental change, completed before the end of the colonial period and underlying the entire subsequent history of American education, may be seen only when the premises and concerns of the turn-of-the-century educators are laid aside and when one assumes a broader definition of education and a different notion of historical relevance. It becomes apparent when one thinks of education not only as formal pedagogy but as the entire process by which a culture transmits itself across the generations; when one is prepared to see great variations in the role of formal institutions of instruction, to see schools and universities fade into relative insignificance next to other social agencies; when one sees education in its elaborate, intricate involvements with the rest of society, and notes its shifting functions, meanings, and purposes. And it becomes evident also only when one assumes that the past was not incidentally but essentially different from the present; when one seeks as the points of greatest relevance those critical passages of history where elements of our familiar present, still part of an unfamiliar past, begin to disentangle themselves, begin to emerge amid confusion and uncertainty. For these soft, ambiguous moments where the words we use and the institutions we know are notably present but are still enmeshed in older meanings and different purposes—these are the moments of true origination. They reveal in purest form essential features which subsequent events complicate and modify but never completely transform.

The change I have in mind was not unique to America, but like much else of the modern world it appeared here first. It was part of the rapid breakdown of traditional European society in its wilderness setting. In the course of adjustment to a new environment, the pattern of education was destroyed: the elements survived, but their meaning had changed and their functions had been altered. By 1800 education in America was a radically different process from what anyone in the early seventeenth century would have expected. On almost every major point the expectations of the first generation of settlers had been frustrated. These expectations form a necessary background for understanding the transformation of education in colonial America; and therefore before attempting a detailed description of the change I have in mind, I would like to turn to those assumptions, experiences, and ways of thinking of late sixteenth- and early seventeenth-century Englishmen, stressing those features that would be most affected by the American environment.

2

The forms of education assumed by the first generation of settlers in America were a direct inheritance from the medieval past. Serving the needs of a homogeneous, slowly changing rural society, they were largely instinctive and traditional, little articulated and little formalized. The most important agency in the transfer of culture was not formal institutions of instruction or public instruments of communication, but the family; and the character of family life in late sixteenth- and early seventeenth-century England is critical for understanding the history of education in colonial America.

The family familiar to the early colonists was a patrilineal group of extended kinship gathered into a single household. By modern standards it was large. Besides children, who often remained in the home well into maturity, it included a wide range of other dependents: nieces and nephews, cousins, and, except for families at the lowest rung of society, servants in filial discipline. In the Elizabethan family the conjugal unit was only the nucleus of a broad kinship community whose outer edges merged almost imperceptibly into the society at large.

The organization of this group reflected and reinforced the general structure of social authority. Control rested with the male head to whom all others were subordinate. His sanctions were powerful; they were rooted deep in the cultural soil. They rested upon tradition that went back beyond the memory of man; on the instinctive sense of order as hierarchy, whether in the cosmic chain of being or in human society; on the processes of law that reduced the female to perpetual dependency and calibrated a detailed scale of male subordination and servitude; and, above all, on the restrictions of the economy, which made the establishment of independent households a difficult enterprise.

It was these patriarchal kinship communities that shouldered most of the burden of education. They were, in the first place, the primary agencies in the socialization of the child. Not only did the family introduce him to the basic forms of civilized living, but it shaped his attitudes, formed his patterns of behavior, endowed him with manners and morals. It introduced him to the world; and in so doing reinforced the structure of its authority. For the world to the child was an intricate, mysterious contrivance in controlling which untutored skills, raw nature, mere vigor counted for less than knowledge and experience. The child's dependence on his elders was not an arbitrary decree of fate; it was not only biologically but socially functional.

But the family's educational role was not restricted to

elementary socialization. Within these kinship groupings, skills that provided at least the first step in vocational training were taught and practiced. In a great many cases, as among the agricultural laboring population and small tradesmen who together comprised the overwhelming majority of the population, all the vocational instruction necessary for mature life was provided by the family.

The family's role in vocational training was extended and formalized in a most important institution of education, apprenticeship. Apprenticeship was the contractual exchange of vocational training in an atmosphere of family nurture for absolute personal service over a stated period of years. Like other forms of bonded servitude, it was a condition of dependency, a childlike state of legal incompetence, in which the master's role, and responsibilities, was indistinguishable from the father's, and the servant's obligations were as total, as moral, and as personal as the son's. Servants of almost every degree were included within the family, and it was the family's discipline that most directly enforced the condition of bondage. The master's parental concern for his servants, and especially for apprentices, included care for their moral welfare as well as for their material condition. He was expected and required by law to bring them up in good Christian cultivation, and to see to their proper deportment.

What the family left undone by way of informal education the local community most often completed. It did so in entirely natural ways, for so elaborate was the architecture of family organization and so deeply founded was it in the soil of stable, slowly changing village and town communities in which intermarriage among the same groups had taken place generation after generation, that it was at times difficult for the child to know where the family left off and the greater society began. The external community, comprising with the family a continuous world, naturally extended instruction and discipline in work and in the conduct of life. And it introduced the youth in a most significant way to a further discipline, that of government and the state. So extensive and intricate were the community's involvements with the family and yet so important was its function as a public agency that the youth moved naturally and gradually across the border line that separates the personal from the impersonal world of authority.

More explicit in its educational function than either family or community was the church. Aside from its role as formal educator exercised through institutions of pedagogy which it supported and staffed, in its primary purpose of serving the spiritual welfare and guarding the morals of the community it performed other less obvious but not less important educational functions. It furthered the introduction of the child to society by instructing him in the system of thought and imagery which underlay the culture's values and aims. It provided the highest sanctions for the accepted forms of behavior, and brought the child into close relationship with the intangible loyalties, the ethos and highest principles, of the society in which he lived. In this educational role, organized religion had a powerfully unifying influence. Indistinguishable at the parish level from the local community, agent and ward of the state, it served as a mechanism of social integration. In all its functions, and especially in those that may be called educational, its force was centripetal.

Family, community, and church together accounted for

the greater part of the mechanism by which English culture transferred itself across the generations. The instruments of deliberate pedagogy, of explicit, literate education, accounted for a smaller, though indispensable, portion of the process. For all the interest in formal instruction shown in the century after the Reformation in England, and for all the extension of explicitly educational agencies, the span of pedagogy in the entire spectrum of education remained small. The cultural burdens it bore were relatively slight. Formal instruction in elementary and grammar schools, and in the university, was highly utilitarian. Its avowed purpose was the training of the individual for specific social roles. Of the love of letters, knowledge, and science for their own sakes in Elizabethan and Stuart England there was, needless to say, no lack; but the justification for formal education was not phrased in terms of the enrichment of the personality and the satisfactions of knowledge. Literacy had its uses required for the daily tasks of an increasing part of the population. Latin grammar and classical literature, far from being then the cultural ornaments they have since become, were practical subjects of instruction: as necessary for the physician as for the architect, as useful to the local functionary as to the statesman. Even the middle classes, for whom classical education had acquired a special meaning as a symbol of social ascent, justified their interest in grammar school training by reference to its moral and social utility. And the universities' function as professional schools had not been transformed by the influx of sons of gentle and noble families; it had merely been broadened to include training for public responsibility.

The sense of utility that dominated formal education was

related in a significant way to the occupational structure of the society. Despite a considerable amount of occupational mobility, the normal expectation was that the child would develop along familiar lines, that the divergence of his career from that of his parents' and grandparents' would be limited, and that he could proceed with confidence and security along a well-worn path whose turnings and inclines had long been known and could be dealt with by measures specified by tradition.

Whatever their limitations by modern standards, formal institutions of instruction occupied a strategic place in English life, and they therefore fell within the concern of the state. But the role of the state in formal education, though forceful, was indirect. It was exhortatory, empowering, supervisory, regulatory; it was, with rare exceptions, neither initiating nor sustaining. Support for schools and universities was almost universally from private benefaction, usually in the form of land endowments; public taxation was rare and where it existed, local and temporary. The reliable support from endowment funds gave educational institutions above the elementary level a measure of autonomy, an independence from passing influences which allowed them to function conservatively, retarding rather than furthering change in their freedom from all but the most urgent pressures.

Of these characteristics of education as it existed in late sixteenth- and early seventeenth-century England prospective emigrants to America would hardly have been aware, and not simply because they were not habituated to think in such terms. They had little cause to probe the assumptions and circumstances that underlay their culture's self-perpetuation. The rapid expansion of instructional facilities of which they were witness had not sprung from dissatisfaction with the traditional modes of education, but from the opposite, from confidence, from satisfaction, and from the desire and the capacity to deal more fully, in familiar ways, with familiar social needs. The basis of education lay secure within the continuing traditions of an integrated, unified culture. The future might be uncertain, but the uncertainties were limited. Nothing disturbed the confident expectation that the world of the child's maturity would be the same as that of the parents' youth, and that the past would continue to be an effective guide to the future.

3

None of the early settlers in English America, not even those who hoped to create in the New World a utopian improvement on the Old, contemplated changes in this configuration of educational processes, this cluster of assumptions, traditions, and institutions. Yet by the end of the colonial period it had been radically transformed. Education had been dislodged from its ancient position in the social order, wrenched loose from the automatic, instinctive workings of society, and cast as a matter for deliberation into the forefront of consciousness. Its functionings had become problematic and controversial. Many were transferred from informal to formal institutions, from agencies to whose major purpose they had been incidental to those, for the most part schools, to which they were primary. Schools and formal schooling had acquired a new importance. They had assumed cultural burdens they had not borne before. Where there had been deeply ingrained habits, unquestioned tradition, automatic responses, security, and confidence there was now awareness, doubt, formality, will, and decision. The whole range of education had become an instrument of deliberate social purpose.

In many ways the most important changes, and certainly the most dramatic, were those that overtook the family in colonial America. In the course of these changes the family's traditional role as the primary agency of cultural transfer was jeopardized, reduced, and partly superseded.

Disruption and transplantation in alien soil transformed the character of traditional English family life. Severe pressures were felt from the first. Normal procedures were upset by the long and acute discomforts of travel; regular functions were necessarily set aside; the ancient discipline slackened. But once re-established in permanent settlements the colonists moved toward recreating the essential institution in its usual form. In this, despite heroic efforts, they failed. At first they laid their failure to moral disorder; but in time they came to recognize its true source in the intractable circumstances of material life.

To all of the settlers the wilderness was strange and forbidding, full of unexpected problems and enervating hardships. To none was there available reliable lore or reserves of knowledge and experience to draw upon in gaining control over the environment: parents no less than children faced the world afresh. In terms of mere effectiveness, in fact, the young—less bound by prescriptive memories, more adaptable, more vigorous—stood often at advantage. Learning faster, they came to see the world more familiarly, to concede more readily to unexpected necessities, to sense more accurately the phasing of a new life. They and not their parents became the effective guides to a new world, and they thereby gained a strange, anomalous authority difficult to accommodate within the ancient structure of family life.

Other circumstances compounded the disorder. Parental prestige was humbled by involvement in the menial labor necessary for survival; it faded altogether when means of support failed in the terrible "starving periods" and large households were forced to sub-divide and re-form in smaller, self-sufficient units. Desperate efforts to enforce a failing authority by law came to little where the law was vaguely known, where courts were rude and irregular, and where means of enforcement were unreliable when they existed at all. And the ultimate sanction of a restrictive economy failed them: where land was abundant and labor at a premium it took little more to create a household than to maintain one. Material independence was sooner or later available to every energetic adult white male, and few failed to break away when they could. Dependent kin, servants, and sons left the patriarchal household, setting up their own reduced establishments which would never grow to the old proportions.

The response was extraordinary. There is no more poignant, dramatic reading than the seventeenth-century laws and admonitions relating to family life. Those of Massachusetts are deservedly best known: they are most profuse and charged with intense Old Testament passion. But they are not different in kind from the others. Within a decade of their founding all of the colonies passed laws demanding obedience from children and specifying penalties for contempt and abuse. Nothing less than capital punishment, it was ruled in Connecticut and Massachusetts, was the fitting punishment for filial disobedience. Relaxation of discipline was universally condemned, and parents and masters were again and again ordered to fulfill their duties as guardians of civil order. But as the laws and pleas elaborated so too did the problems. If guardians failed, it was finally asked, who would guard the guardians? The famous Massachusetts law of 1679 creating tithingmen as censors extraordinary logically concluded the efforts of two generations to recreate the family as the ordered, hierarchical foundation of an ordered, hierarchical society. By the end of the century the surviving elders of the first generation cried out in fearful contemplation of the future. Knowing no other form than the traditional, they could look forward only to the complete dissolution of the family as the primary element of social order. When that happened, when "the rude son should strike the father dead," they knew the elemental chaos that would result:

> What plagues and what portents, what mutiny,
> What raging of the sea, shaking of earth,
> Commotion in the winds, frights changes horrors,
> Divert and crack, rend and deracinate
> The unity and married calm of states
> Quite from their fixure. Oh, when degree is shak'd,
> Which is the ladder to all high designs,
> The enterprise is sick.

Degree was shak'd, order within the family badly disturbed; but the conclusion was not chaos. It was a different ordering and a different functioning of the basic social grouping than had been known before.

By the middle of the eighteenth century the classic lineaments of the American family as modern sociologists describe them—the "isolation of the conjugal unit," the "maximum of dispersion of the lines of descent," partible inheritances, and multilineal growth—had appeared. The consequences can hardly be exaggerated. Fundamental aspects of social life were affected. In the reduced, nuclear family, thrown back upon itself, traditional gradations in status tended to fall to the level of necessity. Relationships tended more toward achievement than ascription. The status of women rose; marriage, even in the eyes of the law, tended to become a contract between equals. Above all, the development of the child was affected.

What is perhaps the most fundamental consequence to the development of the child, reaching into his personality and his relations with the world, is the most difficult to establish and interpret. It concerns the process of the child's entry into society. As the family contracted towards a nuclear core, as settlement and re-settlement, especially on the frontier, destroyed what remained of stable community relations, and constant mobility and instability kept new ties from strengthening rapidly, the once elaborate interpenetration of family and community dissolved. The border line between them grew sharper; and the passage of the child from family to society lost its ease, its naturalness, and became abrupt, deliberate, and decisive: open to question, concern, and decision. As a consequence of such a translation into the world, the individual acquired an insulation of consciousness which kept him from naked contact and immediate involvement with the social world about him: it heightened his sense of separateness. It shifted the perspective in which he viewed society: he saw it from without rather than from within; from an unfixed position not organically or unalterably secured. The community, and particularly the embodiment of its coercive power, the state, tended to be seen as external, factitious. It did not command his automatic involvement.

There were other, more evident and more easily established consequences of the pressures exerted on the family during these years. Within a remarkably short time after the beginnings of settlement it was realized that the family was failing in its more obvious educational functions. In the early 1640's both Virginia and Massachusetts officially stated their dissatisfactions in the passage of what have since become known as the first American laws concerning education. The famous Massachusetts statute of 1642, prefaced by its sharp condemnation of "the great neglect of many parents and masters in training up their children in learning and labor," was one of a series of expedients aimed at shoring up the weakening structure of family discipline. It not only reminded parents and masters of their duty to provide for the "calling and implyment of their children" and threatened punishment for irresponsibility, but added to this familiar obligation the extraordinary provision that they see also to the children's "ability to read and understand the principles of religion and the capitall lawes of this country." Virginia's exactly contemporaneous law ordering county officials to "take up" children whose parents "are disabled to maintaine and educate them" reflected the same concern, as did the Duke's Laws of New York in 1665.

Such laws, expressing a sudden awareness, a heightened consciousness of what the family had meant in education, of how much of the burden of imparting civilization to the young it had borne, and of what its loss might mean, were only the first of a century-long series of adjustments. Responses to the fear of a brutish decline, to the threat of a permanent disruption of the family's educational mechanisms, and to the rising self-consciousness in education varied according to local circumstance. In New England a high cultural level, an intense Biblicism, concentrated settlements, and thriving town institutions led to a rapid enhancement of the role of formal schooling. The famous succession of laws passed in Massachusetts and Connecticut after 1647 ordering all towns to maintain teaching institutions, fining recalcitrants, stating and restating the urgencies of the situation, expressed more than a traditional concern with schooling, and more even than a Puritan need for literacy. It flowed from the fear of the imminent loss of cultural standards, of the possibility that civilization itself would be "buried in the grave of our fathers." The Puritans quite deliberately transferred the maimed functions of the family to formal instructional institutions, and in so doing not only endowed schools with a new importance but expanded their purpose beyond pragmatic vocationalism toward vaguer but more basic cultural goals.

In the context of the age the stress placed by the Puritans on formal schooling is astonishing. In the end it proved too great to be evenly sustained. The broad stream of enforcing legislation that flows through the statute books of the seventeenth century thinned out in the eighteenth century as isolated rural communities, out of contact, save for some of their Harvard- and Yale-trained ministers, with the high moral and intellectual concerns of the settling generation, allowed the level to sink to local requirement. But the tradition of the early years was never completely lost, and New England carried into the national period a faith in the benefits of formal schooling and a willingness to perpetuate and enrich it that has not yet been dissipated.

In the south the awareness that only by conscious, deliberate effort would the standards of inherited culture be transmitted into the future was hardly less acute, but there the environment and the pattern of settlement presented more difficult problems than in the north. Lacking the reinforcement of effective town and church institutions, the family in the south was even less resistant to pressures and sustained even greater shocks. The response on the part of the settlers, however much lower their intellectual demands may have been than the Puritans', was equally intense. The seventeenth-century records abound with efforts to rescue the children from an incipient savagery. They took many forms: the importation of servant-teachers, the attempt to establish parish or other local schools, repeated injunctions to parents and masters; but the most common were parental bequests in wills providing for the particular education of the surviving child or children. These are often fascinating, luminous documents. Susan English of York, for example, who could not sign her name, left each of her children one heifer, the male issue of which was to be devoted to the child's education. Samuel Fenn ordered his executors to devote the entire increase of his stock of cattle to the "utmost education" which could be found for his children in Virginia, and John Custis left the labor of fourteen slaves for the preliminary education of his grandson in Virginia, adding a special provision for paying for its completion in England.

The extravagance and often the impracticality of such efforts in Virginia suggest a veritable frenzy of parental concern lest they and their children succumb to the savage environment. All their fearfulness for the consequences of transplantation, their awareness of the strangeness of the present and the perils of the future, seems to have become concentrated in the issue of education. Their efforts in the seventeenth century came to little; the frustrations multiplied. But the impetus was never entirely lost. The transforming effect of the early years carried over into the education of later, more benign times. When in the eighteenth century the re-emergence in the south of approximate replicas of Old World family organizations and of stable if scattered communities furnished a new basis for formal education, something of the same broad cultural emphasis notable in New England became noticeable also in these southern institutions.

This whole cluster of developments—the heightening of sensitivity to educational processes as the family's traditional effectiveness declined, the consequent increase in attention to formal education and in the cultural burdens placed upon it—was not confined to the boundaries of the original seventeenth-century settlements. It was a pattern woven of the necessities of life in the colonies, and it repeated itself in every region as the threat of the environment to inherited culture made itself felt.

4

There was beyond this group of developments another area of education affected by changes in family life. Apprenticeship, sharing the fate of other forms of legal servitude but particularly involved with the fortunes of the family, was significantly altered.

Bonded servitude had fallen under severe pressures in the seventeenth century. With labor scarce and the recruitment of servants difficult when possible, the lines of dependency weakened and became confused. Amid a universal outcry against rampaging insubordination, servants, in far stronger bargaining positions than ever before, reduced their obligations by negotiation, by force, or by fraud, and gained their independence with startling speed and in startling numbers. By the eighteenth century, despite valiant efforts by the leaders of society to maintain the ancient forms of subordination, bonded servitude, with its carefully calibrated degrees of dependency, was rapidly being eliminated, drained off at one end into freedom and independent wage labor, and at the other into the new, debased status of chattel slavery. Between them there remained only the involuntary but yet terminal servitude of the children of indigent parents, common only in a few urban centers, and a reduced system of voluntary indenture by which impoverished immigrants repaid the cost of their transportation and native boys learned the rudiments of trade.

These were remnants, but yet vital remnants. Apprenticeship was still a significant institution for the transmission of skills. But the evidence of its decline was as clear in changes in its internal characteristics as it was in its quantitative decrease.

The tendency to reduce the once extensive network of mutual obligations to a few simple strands and to transfer the burden of all but strict vocational training to external, formal agencies of education increased through the years. Officially, legally, the assumption continued that the master stood *in loco parentis*, that his duties included all those of an upright father, and that the obligations of apprentices remained, as sanctified in law and tradition, filial in scope and character. But both sets of obligations were increasingly neglected as both sides responded to the pressures of the situation.

Masters, pressed for workers, increasingly inclined to look upon apprenticeship as a badly needed source of labor, treated it with increasingly pragmatic simplicity. Moral indoctrination, Christian training, and instruction in literacy seemed encumbrances upon a contractual arrangement of limited purpose. Furthermore, the ancient demands appeared increasingly anomalous and burdensome in families where the entire apparatus of authority had been weakened and where the servants involved were often of necessity incompatible outlanders: Germans, Scots, and Irish. The masters did provide the required occupational training, but with increasing frequency they provided little else.

Nor were they commonly urged by the servants to do more. In a situation where full entrance into crafts, trades, and even professions was open to anyone with a modicum of capital, enterprise, and ingenuity, it was for instruction in specific skills, and only for that, that apprentices were in fact dependent upon their masters. To the apprentices too the old obligations were felt to be archaic entanglements: impediments in the path to independence.

The seventeenth-century statutes reveal extravagant efforts made not merely to retain the broad scope of apprenticeship obligations within the structure of the family, but to extend it, to include within it cultural matters dislodged from other areas and threatened with extinction. But the evidences of failure and the displacement of functions are manifest in the records of successive generations. They are voiced in the increasingly shrill laws and legislative pronouncements of the seventeenth century demanding the proper discharge of broad obligations, exhorting, and threatening punishment for failure. One group of masters—those in charge of public wards—was subjected to particular scrutiny and their performance officially deplored. In the colonies as in England children of the poor or of those otherwise considered incompetent were taken up as potential threats to the community and sold to masters pledged to care for them, body and soul, and equip them with a trade before the age of twenty-one. That such masters should have been required by law to look upon their charges as public dependents and provide them with the full range of parental care and training is hardly surprising. But that law after law should have been necessary to remind them of their duties, to spell out the extent of their responsibilities, and to threaten punishment for neglect is not merely evidence of human greed; it is an indication also of the change that had overtaken the entire institution of apprenticeship.

It might be said, however, that apprenticeship of the poor, being involuntary, was unrepresentative of the institution as a whole. But the direction of change in this form of apprenticeship was characteristic of the others. In all, there took place a reduction in the personal, non-vocational obligations that bound master and servant and a transfer of general educational functions to external agencies. With increasing frequency masters assigned their apprentices to teachers for instruction in rudimentary literacy and in whatever other non-vocational matters they had contracted to teach. The process did not stop there. The transfer was institutionalized by the introduction of evening schools which were originally started, Professor Bridenbaugh explains, "to instruct apprentices whose indentures stipulated a certain amount of reading, writing, and ciphering." The

ultimate conclusion was the specific provision in the con-
tracts of apprenticeship not simply that the master provide
for the education of his charge but that he send him to
school for a particular period of each year. Seybolt found
108 indentures in the province of New York alone that contained such provisions. The common wording was that the
apprentice be sent "One Quarter of a Year in Each Year
of said Term to a good Evening School in Order to be well
instructed in reading, writing Accounting and the like."

The number of such schools in the eighteenth century
is remarkable. Exactly how many were started is not
known, but Seybolt published as "typical evening school
curricula" a list of subjects taught in 100 such institutions
between 1723 and 1770. Such numbers cannot be accounted
for by the educational needs of apprentices alone. Serving
all those "confined in Business in the Day-Time," welcom-
ing all the "emulous sons of industry," as one eighteenth-
century advertisement put it, the evening schools satisfied
other needs as well, and they thereby take on a special
importance in the early history of education in America.

What these needs were is perhaps best seen in the educational work of Benjamin Franklin. For in organizing his
famous Junto of printers, scriveners, shoemakers, and join-
ers this ex-apprentice and tradesman was acting upon the
same impulse that led others to turn to the evening schools.
At first glance it seems incredible that he could have succeeded in interesting these workmen in the artificially elevated, self-consciously high-brow questions he proposed
to them in meeting after meeting. They shared, perhaps,
the broad Enlightenment concern with improving the condition of mankind by rethinking and attempting to reshape
institutions, and they may have shared also a genuine delight

in literature. But no group of people, not even Franklin and his hard-working colleagues in self-improvement, is motivated solely by such elevated and aesthetic impulses. Their interest was a practical, realistic response to the problems they faced in adjusting to the conditions of an altered society.

Franklin, whose whole life, Carl Van Doren remarked, was "the Junto . . . enlarged and extended," knew well what these problems were. Like Henry Adams, and for similar reasons, he saw his entire career as a series of problems in education; indeed, with at least as much justification as Adams he might have called his apologia *The Education* . . . . The similarities between the two autobiographers is, in fact, striking. Both were immensely aware and intelligent egotists, skilled writers, who could not possibly withstand the temptation to spread the record of their lives before the world, skillfully editing as they went along to emphasize their apparently opposite conclusions: while Adams ironically sought his justification by proving that he had failed, Franklin, here as always blandly playing life straight, found his by making an object lesson of his success. But however they chose to interpret it, both told essentially the same story. Defeated or triumphant, both had fought the same battle of locating themselves in an unfamiliar world, a world for which by early training and normal expectation they had not been prepared. Both early in life had realized that the past no longer held the key to the present or future, that the knowledge, traditions, and responses of their parents would not suffice for their needs, that they would have to undertake their own education into careers whose patterns were not only indistinct but nonexistent, mere possibilities whose shape they would themselves determine.

It was this sense of an open-ended universe that lies behind everything Franklin wrote about education and hence about the conduct of life. The purpose of schooling was to provide in systematic form what he had extemporized, haphazardly feeling his way. Convinced that the proper aims of education were to train and equip the young for just such a tour of surprises as he had known, he sketched the plans for a revolution in formal instruction. But it was a subtle revolution, too often interpreted as somehow peculiarly "utilitarian." Indeed, he did expect education to be useful, as who did not; but his revolution consisted in the kind of utility he had in mind. He wanted subjects and instruction that trained not for limited goals, not for close-bound, predetermined careers, but for the broadest possible range of enterprise. He had no argument with the classics as such. What he objected to was their monopoly of the higher branches of education which denied the breadth of preparation needed for the open world he saw. He stated his whole philosophy of education in the single sentence with which he concluded his *Idea of the English School*: "Thus instructed youth will come out of this school fitted for learning any business, calling, or profession."

Any business, *any* calling, *any* profession! This was too much of a new thing even for eighteenth-century America, as Franklin himself discovered when he tried to put his ideas into practice. But if traditional, formal institutions had a resistant force of their own, informal ones did not. What Franklin failed to implant upon the curriculum of the Academy and College in Philadelphia, he and many others, responding in lesser degrees, perhaps, and with more limited understanding but with equal spontaneity to the movement of society around them, accepted as the goals of mutual aid and self-instruction. What lay behind the interest in mutual instruction, in informal education of all sorts, and in extemporized institutions like evening schools was the recognition that one's role in life had not been fully cast, that the immediate inheritance did not set the final limits, that opportunities beyond the expectation of birth lay all about and could be reached by effort.

The juntos and the evening schools, the self-improvement efforts of the eighteenth-century tradesmen, were not a passing phenomenon. They reflect the beginnings of a permanent motion within American society by which the continuity between generations was to be repeatedly broken. The automatic transfer of occupational and social role from generation to generation, with all that this means for the confidence, ease, and security with which the child locates himself in society—this transfer of life patterns had already by Franklin's time been so generally disrupted that the exception was becoming the rule. The increasingly common experience was departure from rather than adherence to the inherited pattern. The result was not only heightened expectations but new uncertainties. Responses were no longer automatic but deliberate, not insensibly acquired in childhood as part of the natural order of things, but learned, usually late, as part of a self-conscious quest for appropriate forms of behavior. Learning—the purposeful acquisition not merely of technical skills but of new ways of thinking and behaving—was essential. It was a necessary part of social and vocational as well as purely intellectual life, and if it could not be acquired through existing institutions it would be otherwise found, by adapting what lay at hand, by creating new devices for self-improvement and education.

5

In these ways, as part of alterations in family life, in the nature of servitude, and in the opportunities for careers, major elements in the traditional pattern of education were transformed. Other changes, associated with other adjustments in society, contributed still further to the recasting of education. Organized religion and the forms of group life were directly involved.

Though poorly informed on the details of living in wilderness communities, the planners of settlement in the early seventeenth century made one obvious but far-reaching assumption that involved them directly in a new educational enterprise. They assumed that society in the colonies would be the opposite of homogeneous, that it would contain disparate and probably conflicting groups, and that the differences would center on matters of religion. It was, consequently, as a Christian duty and the high moral justification for their colonizing ventures that they undertook the task of reconciling the differences by converting the native Indians to civilized Christian living. Doubting neither their power nor the necessity to recreate the familiar unity of social life, they launched the first campaign of missionary education in British America.

In view of the later history of Indian-white relations, it is natural to slight the seriousness of their concern with the fate of the natives and to see in it only a bland piety and hypocrisy. But their sincerity is attested by the extent of the efforts they made in the face of continuous discouragement. In Virginia, Maryland, and especially in Massachusetts, the first and most carefully planned efforts in education were directed not at the settlers but at the Indians. The planning of Henrico College and the East India Company School in Virginia, the Indian College at Harvard, and John Eliot's celebrated missionary efforts culminating in the founding of Natick as the first of the "Praying Indian" towns, were only the most notable episodes in a long and eventful series. While the initial impulse lasted, thousands of pounds and immeasurable amounts of effort were expended on attempts to educate the Indians. And even afterwards, when the major responsibility came to rest not with overseas entrepreneurs but with land-hungry settlers, and when as a consequence aggressive hostility succeeded the early missionary zeal, and partial annihilation became the usual first step in the process of conversion, there remained not merely the rhetoric of earlier days but effective pockets of continuing missionary activity among the colonists.

Epic and farce, high tragedy and low comedy, the education and conversion of the Indians was a drama of endless frustration. The English settlers, insensitive, inflexible, and righteous, poured into bewildered savage minds a mysterious brew of theology, morals, and lore. They were atrocious anthropologists, and they failed almost entirely in their efforts to convert the Indians and to lead them in harmony into a unified society.

The original missionary fervor faded in the eighteenth century as the expanding frontier removed the natives from direct contact with the centers of white population, and commercial and military considerations came to dominate relations between the races. But it had left an ineradicable mark on American life. It had introduced the problem of group relations in a society of divergent cultures, and with it a form of action that gave a new dimension to the social role of education. For the self-conscious, deliberate, aggressive use of education, first seen in an improvised but confident missionary campaign, spread throughout an increasingly heterogeneous society and came to be accepted as a normal form of educational effort.

The drift of missionary education away from its extemporized and optimistic beginnings may be seen first in the variety of its applications by the dominant English elements in the population to the problems presented by the smaller, subordinate groups that appeared by the early eighteenth century. For to the English, a remarkably ethnocentric people, the similarities among others often outweighed the differences, and the hopes once held and the methods devised for converting and civilizing the American aborigenes were easily transferred to imported Africans and to a variety of infidels, from "Papists" to Pietists, and even to settlers of English ancestry: defiant sectarians or backsliders into savagery on the wild frontier. By the 1740's it was a natural response of one like Franklin, struck by the strangeness and integrity of the German communities in Pennsylvania, by their lack of familiarity with English liberties and English government, and fearful of alien domination, to turn to missionary education, and to help in organizing the Society for the Propagation of the Gospel to the Germans in America.

But what gave this dynamic use of education its greatest importance and its characteristic form was its position in the emerging pattern of American denominationalism.

In the unstable, highly mobile, and heterogeneous society of eighteenth-century America, sectarian religion became the most important determinant of group life. It was religion under peculiar pressures and influences. So universal and so numerous had sectarian groups become by the eve of the Revolution that not only was an enforced state orthodoxy almost nowhere to be found but it was often impossible to say which groups represented orthodoxy and which groups dissent. All of them, even the established churches, lacked the full sanction of public authority by which to compel allegiance, and all of them faced an equal threat of erosion among those elements of their membership, especially the young, that were infirm in faith and vulnerable to temptation. Persuasion and nurture would have to do what compulsion could more easily have done. Furthermore, in such voluntary religious groupings "Christianity itself," Professor Mead comments, "tends to be conceived primarily as an activity, a movement, which the group is engaged in promoting." It takes a "promotional and propagandistic" attitude to its confession: the "sense of mission forms the center of a denomination's self-conscious life." Schools and colleges were therefore essential: schools to train the young in purity and loyalty; colleges to educate the educators, to produce a proper ministry and mission, and to provide benefits which otherwise would be sought by the ambitious young from proselytizing rivals. Sectarian groups, without regard to the intellectual complexity of their doctrine or to their views on the value of learning to religion, became dynamic elements in the spread of education, spawning schools of all sorts, continuously, competitively, in all their settlements; carrying education into the most remote frontiers. Even their weaknesses contributed: schism, surging upward from uncontrollable sources of division, multiplied their effect.

But their goals in education, always clear, were always limited. Their aims in education were not served by a neutral pedagogy that might develop according to its own inner impulses and the drift of intellectual currents. The education they desired and created was an instrument of deliberate group action. It bore the burden of defining the group, of justifying its existence by promoting the view that its peculiar interpretations and practices conformed more closely "to those of the early Church as pictured in the New Testament than the views and policies of its rivals." And it was by carefully controlled education above all else that denominational leaders hoped to perpetuate the group into future generations.

The members of such groups participated in a continuous enterprise of indoctrination and persuasion, an enterprise aimed no longer at unifying society but only at aiding one group to survive in a world of differing groups. To them the transmission of culture was problematic in the extreme, surrounded by pitfalls, doubts, and difficulties. Education, so central to their purposes, was deliberate, self-conscious, and explicit. The once-automatic process of transfer would continue to operate only by dint of sustained effort. Education was an act of will.

6

Such a view and use of education, dynamic, aggressive, and disputatious, rested upon the assumption that the control of education would remain in the hands of the group itself, that education, once launched, would not attain an institutional autonomy, an independence, that would free it from the initiating purposes. That this assumption proved workable, that the multiplying units of denominational education adhered to the goals of their founders, was to a considerable extent the result of the forms of institutional financing and control that emerged in the course of the seventeenth century.

In these matters as in so many others, there had been no desire on the part of the settlers to alter the traditional forms. Everywhere the original reliance was on private benefaction, and everywhere, in the very first years, donations for schools were made in the familiar manner. In the Massachusetts Bay area, for example, private donations accounted for the founding of schools in nine towns, and the Hopkins bequest, which in England would have been indistinguishable from hundreds of other private gifts for education, underwrote the creation of three grammar schools in Connecticut and western Massachusetts. But it quickly became apparent that such benefactions would not satisfy the needs. Sufficient funds were not forthcoming, and those that appeared failed to produce the expected yield.

To a large extent these difficulties resulted simply from the lack of surplus wealth. But they were compounded by the peculiar problems encountered in the creation of endowments. For even if the funds were available, how were they to be invested so as to provide a steady and reliable income? In real estate, in land, was the obvious answer; and indeed the profitable endowments that did exist in the seventeenth century were largely investments in real estate. But more often than not land endowments failed to produce the traditional revenues, for their yield was expected to flow from tenancy, which, where unclaimed land was the one abundant commodity, failed to develop to any significant extent. Untenanted land could be, and often was, given as endowment, but its profits, if any, obviously lay in the future. When, as in the case of the Company land set aside for Virginia's Henrico College, tenants were deliberately imported and planted on endowment land, they left at the first opportunity and could be replaced only with the greatest difficulty. Even, as in the more highly populated areas of the north, when rents were forthcoming they were often unreliable. Their value fluctuated sharply as continuous crises—gluts and famines, devastations by wind, weather, the seas, and the Indians—shook the fragile economy. Furthermore, a chronic shortage of specie and the necessity to accept payments in kind involved the recipient in an exchange of goods and hence the risks of trade. Finally, inflation in the eighteenth century, especially in New England, reduced the value of all long-term investments.

Strenuous efforts were made to find new and more reliable forms of investment: public utilities, primarily mills and ferries, short-term personal loans, shipping, even commercial ventures were all tried with varying success. In the end none were reliable enough, nor was the capital available for such endowments sufficient, to finance the education desired by the colonists. Other sources of support were clearly necessary.

They were found only in direct and repeated contributions by the community. There was, at first, not only an understandable reluctance to venture beyond the familiar forms of financing but also considerable confusion as to what procedures were proper once such steps were contemplated. In Massachusetts, for example, the pledge of community property for education became common only after laws were passed compelling individuals of supposed wealth to volunteer more generously; and when it was apparent that not even the grant of common town land would be sufficient and that direct taxation would have to be resorted to, the yield from school rates most often was considered to be only temporary supplements to the more familiar endowments and tuition payments.

The solution that emerged by mid-century in New England—the pooling of community resources in the form of general taxation—did not, of course, appear everywhere. But for all the differences, the various forms that developed shared with taxation one all-important characteristic. Everywhere—in the middle colonies and in the south as well as in New England—the support for schools and even colleges came not from the automatic yield from secure investments but from repeated acts of current donation, whether in the form of taxes, or of individual, family, or community gifts. The autonomy that comes from an independent, reliable, self-perpetuating income was everywhere lacking. The economic basis of self-direction in education failed to develop.

It is this common characteristic which taxation shares with the other modes of colonial school financing, and not its "public" aspects, that gives it great importance in the history of American education. Dependent for support upon annual or even less regular gifts, education at all levels during the early formative years came within the direct control, not of those responsible for instruction, but of those who had created and maintained the institutions. When in the eighteenth century a measure of economic maturity made it possible to revert to other, older forms, the tradition of external control was well established. That it remained so, and that consequently American education at all levels, and especially at the highest, has continued to be sensitive to community pressure, delicately reflecting the shifting interests and needs of the founding and sustaining groups—particularly the denominational, but ethnic and geographic as well—is a consequence of the utility of this tradition in the emerging pattern of American group life.

7

All of these elements in the transformation of education, turning on the great axles of society—family, church, community, and the economy—had become clear before the end of the colonial period. Like all else of those early years that form part of the continuity of American history, they passed through the toils of revolution. They were not unaffected by that event. But the effect of the Revolution on education was typical of its generally limited impress upon social institutions. For the Revolution was a social movement only in a special sense. It did not flow from deep sources of social discontent, and its aims were not to recast the ordering of the society that had developed in the earlier years. In education as in so many other spheres of social action, its effects were to free the trends of the colonial period from legal and institutional encumbrances and to confirm them, to formalize them, to give them the sanction of law in a framework of enlightened political thought.

Much more at first had been expected by the leaders of the Revolution. Most of the major statesmen had sweeping schemes for national systems of education and national universities, or other programs by which the new nationalism and its republican spirit might properly be expressed. But the efforts to realize these plans came to nothing. They rose too far above the needs and interests of the scattered, variegated, semi-autonomous communities that comprised the new nation; they placed too concrete a meaning on national life and a national society. The forces shaping education had never been closely related to the higher political organizations; they had, if anything, grown up in deliberate opposition to them. They owed little to political independence.

But they found a fuller meaning and a more secure status as a consequence of the Revolution. The spontaneity of local impulses, the variety of educational forms, and the immediacy of popular control survived the war and political changes and were actively confirmed. The central question was that of the survival of denominational influence, and the issue was never in doubt. Wherever schemes for state systems of education threatened the influence of sectarian groups they were defeated or fell under the control of the denominations. It took Jefferson forty years to create the University of Virginia, and when it opened in 1825 it had acquired religious attributes he had struggled to eliminate. His famous plan for an elaborate system of public schools in Virginia was wrecked on the shoals of apathy and sectarian opposition and never enacted.

Elsewhere it was the same. Typical and particularly important in itself was the fate of the College of Philadelphia. Like another Anglican institution, King's College, it was seized by the state in 1776, its charter confiscated, and its Board of Trustees eliminated. A new state institution was formed by the legislature in its place. But this act of confiscation threatened essential powers of the denominations —all denominations as it was ultimately realized—as well as the stability of business organizations, and it was therefore repeatedly challenged in its legality, at first by the former Provost, William Smith, and his Trustees, later by others in sympathy with them. Struggling before the legislature, the courts, and the Council of Censors to regain their rights, the defenders of the old charter elaborated the implications of the case until they merged with those of another great political and constitutional issue in Pennsylvania, the seizure by the legislature of the charter of the Bank of North America. Both seizures had been made in the name of the People and as part of an effort to eliminate enclaves of special, state-protected privilege. But who were the People? A handful of legislators? Not bankers, not educators whose enterprise would advance the general good? To eliminate all privilege from private groups was, it would seem, tantamount to giving it all to the State. But what was the State in a republican government? Should it have powers against the people themselves? Was not the answer the multiplication rather than the elimination of privilege?

The debate on these questions in the 1780's was one of the most significant of the entire Revolutionary period. Centering on the nature of privilege and the rights of voluntary groups before the state, it probed the meaning of Revolutionary thought and its bearing on American society. The verdict, the first of a series in several states that culminated in the decision of the Supreme Court in the Dartmouth College case thirty years later, in effect restored the old charter of the College and endorsed the right of initiating groups to control what they had created, to gain from the state equal privileges with all other groups and to retain them even against the state itself.

8

Confirmed rather than disturbed by the Revolution, American education passed on into the nineteenth century as it had developed in the colonial period. On almost every major point the original inheritance had been called into question, challenged by circumstance, altered or discarded. A process whose origins lay in the half-instinctive workings of a homogeneous, integrated society was transformed in the jarring multiplicity, the raw economy, and the barren environment of America. No longer instinctive, no longer safe and reliable, the transfer of culture, the whole enterprise of education, had become controversial, conscious, constructed: a matter of decision, will, and effort.

But education not only reflects and adjusts to society; once formed, it turns back upon it and acts upon it. The consequences of this central transformation of education have significantly shaped the development of American society. Two kinds of results have been perhaps most important. First, education in this form has proved in itself to be an agency of rapid social change, a powerful internal accelerator. By responding sensitively to the immediate pressures of society it has released rather than impeded the restless energies and ambitions of groups and individuals. And the fact that so much of the acquisition of culture has taken place away from the direct influence of family elders and so much of it gained either directly from the environment, from the child's contemporaries, or from formal institutions themselves sensitive to social pressures, has helped create a situation where, as Margaret Mead puts it, "children of five have already incorporated into their everyday thinking ideas that most elders will never fully assimilate."

Second, education as it emerged from the colonial period has distinctively shaped the American personality; it has contributed much to the forming of national character. Crèvecoeur's "American, this new man," was not simply the result of "the government, climate, mode of husbandry, customs, and peculiarity of circumstance," nor of the mixture of peoples and the material abundance which the American Farmer also discussed. What was recognized even before the Revolution as typical American individualism, optimism, and enterprise resulted also from the processes of education which tended to isolate the individual, to propel him away from the simple acceptance of a predetermined social role, and to nourish his distrust of authority.

The transformation of education that took place in the colonial period was irreversible. We live with its consequences still.

Section III
Philosophical Inquiry Methods
in Education

Philosophical Inquiry Methods in Education

Michael Scriven
University of Western Australia

Background: The Relation of Philosophy to Education

There has always been a small but sturdy band of distinguished scholars straddling the fields of philosophy and education. In the Western tradition, one thinks immediately of Plato and Rousseau and Dewey who were philosophers first and most famously, and educators later—though it would be more accurate to regard the activities as intertwined. Without any expert historical knowledge it is easy to mention a good many more, from Whitehead and Russell to Suppes and Peters.

Now, why is this scholarly connection between philosophy and education so strong? You cannot run off a string of names of chemists or mathematicians or linguists who have made the same kind of contribution to education. Why not? Why indeed does *philosophy* of education get into many "foundations" courses in schools of education?

The word "philosophy" comes from the Greek and means "love of knowledge"—not just knowledge about any one thing, but knowledge itself, the whole of it. People who care about a very wide range of knowledge are, in that respect, generalists rather than specialists. I think that to a limited extent philosophy still draws in generalists; and people with wide-ranging interests are more likely to contribute to fields other than the one in which they receive their first training. Hence philosophers—more than scientists, who are more prone to specializing—are likely to contribute to fields which are not primary fields of academic research training: to education, for example, and to other subjects.

Parenthetically, it might be noted that mathematics and the sciences themselves have benefited enormously from the work of philosophers; originally, of course, most sciences sprang from philosophical work. It must also be added that much of the academic tradition in philosophy has run in the opposite direction: the subject that should be concerned with all knowledge has frantically tried to make itself into a haven for specialists.

Another reason for the overlap of philosophy and education is that, while educators are concerned with methods for imparting knowledge, philosophers are professionally concerned with the concept of knowledge itself. The entire subdiscipline known as epistemology is concerned simply with that notion. Educators, in looking at teaching methods and theories about how to impart knowledge, naturally want to begin with a sound understanding and definition of knowledge itself; and getting such a definition requires quite an excursion into philosophy. On such excursions one is likely to meet philosophers and interest them in one's special problem. So the connection through a common interest in knowledge is an important one. The same line of argument can be provided with respect to the area of ethics and the aims of life—a key philosophical area, and also one where the educator and the educational theorist are vitally interested in trying to provide direction and proper procedures for the enterprise of education. Thus there are two professional parties involved in many of these problems from education.

Each of these parties—the philosopher and the educator—learns something from the other. The philosopher gets hints about what knowledge is from studying the learning and teaching process, which shows what actually counts as knowledge in the practical context. And the educator picks up suggestions about what knowledge is, but perhaps more importantly, is not, by listening to philosophers make distinctions or clarify the relationships between knowledge, on the one hand, and instincts or attitudes or skills or habits or feelings, on the other; and between learning on the one hand and experiencing or living or changing or trying on the other.

Thus the philosopher analyzes many of the complex concepts which educational researchers study from a scientific or historical point of view. Researchers who are interested in moral education, for example, will first have to get clear about how to define *moral* education, and how to distinguish it from education in manners, conventions (which are not the same as manners), or prudence, or in cognitive knowledge of the content of moral codes. If the researcher becomes interested in, say, multicultural awareness, philosophical analysis can help clarify the basic concept of multicultural awareness itself by sorting out and bringing in other work on such notions as empathy, sympathy, understanding, and *verstehen,* as well as bare knowledge of other cultures.

This paper is intended to document the need for educational researchers to have in their repertoire well-developed skills in conceptual analysis, one crucial part of philosophical expertise, and to explicate some of the methods of conceptual analysis, by example and by description. Finally, it suggests ways to acquire training in these skills.

The Crucial Role of Conceptual Analysis

Many researchers have thought that the first part of their job—analysis of the concepts that are going to be studied—could be done, or could be done better, without any help from philosophers. That path is paved with major disasters. Once in a while such researchers have been lucky, and once in a while they have been sufficiently good at conceptual analysis anyway to be able to do the job themselves. Usually, they simply lack the skills to keep out of trouble and they finish up with definitions that include many things they themselves wanted to exclude, and exclude things they wanted to include. The student, indeed the author of such definitions, is understandably confused by these attempts. But that is not to say that turning to some philosopher when you are doing the philosophical analysis always pays off. Many philosophers have no interest at all in applied conceptual analysis of this kind. Others do it well, but only in some subject-matter areas such as physics or mathematics. Still others have interest but lack the talent. Much the best solution lies in training educational researchers to a reasonable level of competence in conceptual analysis.

It is true that the same might be said about training in historical and historiographical analysis and in the various other methodologies which are discussed in other parts of this book. There really isn't any shortcut to competence in educational research. Rather, more skills are required in educational research than in most subjects, essentially because it is an applied field that involves more component disciplines than most subjects. The attempt, during the middle third of this century, to convert the subject into applied social science has only succeeded in demonstrating that it is more than that, and that applied social science research is itself all too often conceptually ill-founded.

It has been very encouraging in the past few decades to see the number of philosophers who have been doing analytical work in education; not just teaching, but publishing articles and texts. One thinks particularly of R. S. Peters, Israel Scheffler, and D. J. O'Connor, but there are also many others doing work of very high quality. An example of this latter group is Anthony Flew, with his most valuable discussions of the distinction between education and propaganda or brainwashing (see, e.g., Flew, 1972). Nevertheless, it is still the case in the United States (somewhat less so in Canada and Great Britain) that educational researchers' academic preparation is very often devoid of serious training in philosophical analysis.

Educational researchers' courses of study may well have included something called "Philosophy of Ed," usually in the undergraduate curriculum. However, that subject is usually quite different from what we are talking about. It usually comprises a review of normative theories about the ideal form of education. (There are some quite good but entirely independent arguments for including that in every researcher's training.) Only rarely is philosophy of education made into a course in philosophical analysis, and still more rarely is an advanced version of it required for the graduate degree. In its usual form it is really part of the history of thought—the history of extremely general theories about the ideal nature of education, taught in a way analogous to political philosophy.

Using a distinction that emerged in the philosophy of history, we can say that there is a major difference between *speculative* philosophy of education and *analytic* philosophy of education. A course in speculative philosophy of politics, history, or education could surely enlarge the vision and sharpen the thinking of researchers, but it may involve very little explicit training in analysis or analytic techniques. Though it *might* involve such training, and will be a better course if such training is included, there is always a time cost involved in such an inclusion, a cost that translates to a loss of coverage of the desired range of historical or speculative topics.

It is a mistake to argue that every researcher in the subject field X must have extensive training in the philosophy of X, because the philosophy of any subject is a massive subspecialty and the economy of time doesn't really allow coverage of everything of that kind; i.e., everything that is related in some quite serious way to the primary research field. What we do argue here is that basic training in conceptual analysis is absolutely fundamental for researchers in education, for exactly the same reasons that statistical training is fundamental if they intend to do large-scale empirical studies such as survey or experimental work. The difference is only that the need for conceptual analysis applies to every kind of educational research, not just to one subarea.

That it applies to those doing statistical work is obvious from the grotesque blunders that have been and are being made as a result of confusing statistical significance with educational significance. Most studies were—and to a ridiculous extent still are—content to report on significance level as if that somehow guaranteed (was a *sufficient condition* for) educational significance, whereas it is obvious that it is at most an *occasionally necessary* condition for it. What is needed beyond the significance test, to avoid triviality, is an extensive discussion of the relation of the absolute size of the treatment effect, once it has been shown to be more than one could expect by chance, to the needs assessment data (if anyone has bothered to acquire any), and preferably also to comparable data for a number of alternatives. Without this further discussion, a study is always incompetent and its results are usually trivial. The fact that there turns out to be a "highly significant" (e.g., statistically significant at the .0005 level) relationship between watching *Sesame Street* and learning to read is of absolutely zero educational/social/policy significance. The only possible way in which the study that generated such results could be of any serious interest is if it shows that some completely different conditions are met; for example, that the absolute size of the reading achievement gains is substantially larger than the kind of gains obtained from comparably costly/enjoyable alternative procedures, including, but not limited to, standard reading programs. Even more is needed: for example, it must be shown that the size of these gains is large enough to make a *substantial* contribution to the reading skills deficit of those children served. Here is where the needs assessment data come in, along with all sorts of questions that make quantitative researchers nervous, such as how to decide what to count as "substantial," or how to distinguish needs from wants and ideals. These are the inescapable fundamental questions; without answers to them, there is no way to know what research is worth doing, even for intellectual payoffs, let alone socially valuable ones. And they are, of course, philosophical/analytical questions, not statistical/analytical ones.

The substitution of statistical for evaluative criteria of significance is a blunder whose consequences included the trivialization of a very great deal, perhaps most, of educational research in most of this century. And it is a blunder that can be avoided by researchers with serious training in conceptual analysis.

It is not the only blunder of this kind that affects statistical work; the very choice and interpretation of different significance levels, *within their proper field of use*, involves deep and ill-thought-out assumptions, as the literature on "the significance test controversy" amply demonstrates—but few researchers are even familiar with the main points in that literature. When should you pick which significance level? Under what circumstances are none of the usual levels adequate? Can one ever make plausible the move from the rejection of the null hypothesis to the acceptance of a particular explanation? (The latest contributions to this discussion are easily accessible through a keyword search of *Psychological Abstracts*, and perhaps other social science databases via Dialog, Lockheed's online database collection, accessible from your nearest library. An excellent anthology reprinting the original papers of a few years back is *The Significance Test Controversy* [Morrison & Henkel, 1970].)

In the tests and measurement area, a dozen new conceptual problems arise. A list of examples would have to include: the aptitude/achievement distinction (so often rejected on the attractive but conceptually superficial grounds that any measurement of aptitude is a measurement of achievement); the intelligence test controversy; the difficult and shaded distinction between reading and reasoning; the key notion of bias; the Fallacy of Definitional Irresponsibility—the idea that one can define concepts in any way that seems appropriate or convenient. (This last problem will be discussed in a later section of this paper.)

Once we move away from the self-styled "scientific" area of educational research to naturalistic or historical studies or policy studies, the need for conceptual analysis skills becomes even greater. Concepts of causation and explanation, of intention, of meaning, and of valuing become crucial and involve quite sophisticated conceptual analysis. There is no need to wallow in the vast philosophical literature devoted to each of these topics, as long as you know enough of the basic logical analysis to avoid the crucial traps; and exactly that kind of help is what a well-trained philosopher in an education department should be able to provide. And provide at the graduate and faculty level, not just in a review of speculative philosophies of education to the undergraduates.

Explaining the Lack of Training in Conceptual Analysis

All this seems obvious enough. Why is so little of it done? Why do we continue with this deficiency in conceptual-analytic training in virtually all programs for training educational researchers?

One possible explanation for this continued acceptance of deficient preparation is education's search for status as a social science, a search which automatically dooms a program to the essential weaknesses of most social science programs—incompetence in conceptual analysis; overemphasis on mindless data collection, numerical analysis, and the hypothesis-testing model; and eschewal of evaluative investigations. One must therefore ask what it is that misleads both social science graduate programs and educational ones.

All too often, and for no good reason, the social sciences are themselves playing catch-up—in this case, with the physical/biological sciences. They are engaged in their own mistaken search for status. One must, I think, conclude that the villain of the piece is a very simple-minded conception of the nature of science. This leads to trouble in the procedures for training researchers and, consequently, to trouble in the practice of educational research. The error—and of course it is another conceptual error—is that of supposing science to be as it is described in the so-called empiricist tradition. (More accurately, this position should not be called the empiricist tradition, but the neo-positivist conception of science.)

Understanding why so little training in conceptual analysis is offered may be one of the most useful aids to avoiding the same mistake in one's own career choices or in the presuppositions of the training program with which one is associated. The two are closely linked: the same factors that lead to the preparation of conceptually incompetent researchers explain the rash tendency of researchers to rush into building a lifetime of research on a foundation of conceptual sand. You might, for example, build a lifetime of research on the teaching process upon a weak analysis of what teaching itself is. Teaching is, in fact, a very difficult notion to define, and if you decide that you can define it any way you like or if you think it is a very simple notion to analyze, you will finish up doing a great deal of research on a process which is definitely not teaching, and is only related to it in some obscure way. In short, your research will be useless for any practical concerns, such as the improvement of teaching, and for any theoretical concerns since, as you have defined teaching, its relevance to any understanding of the phenomena that people are trying to explain in working on a theory of teaching is not clear. The simpler efforts of this kind involve identifying teaching with didactic presentation or the production of learning or the transfer of information; but the hard parts get us into the distinction between teaching and indoctrinating—the problem of circumscribing the affective component of legitimate teaching. Very little significant work can be done on teaching without a satisfactory analysis of the concept.

False Doctrines About Conceptual Analysis

Two doctrines are often thought, with considerable justification, to be key components of conceptual analysis. One of these is the doctrine that the correct way to define terms in science is to use so-called "operational definitions"—that is, the kind of definition which equates a concept with the results of certain measurements. The laudable idea behind this approach is to ensure that we pin down the meaning of any term we use in a way that will eliminate vagueness and, in particular, to connect the language of science with the operations of science—measurements. Thus the operationalist approach maintains that all concepts should be defined in terms of the measurements (operations) that will be used to determine their presence and magnitude.

The other doctrine is that of linguistic arbitrariness, or, more specifically, one interpretation of it that was referred to above as the Fallacy of Definitional Irresponsibility. That term is here used to refer to the idea that it is "just a matter of convention" how terms are defined. In this view, definitions are *essentially* arbitrary though certainly not capricious. The definition is thoughtfully proposed and appears reasonable to the proposer. However, it is, unlike claims about the connection between, for example, mass and gravity, which is a matter of empirical fact, not something to be settled by definition. You cannot define away the force of gravity that operates between bodies with a finite mass. But it is thought that you *can* define any other concept you like in any way that suits yourself. The combination of these two doctrines offered a neat way to end-run conceptual analysis. After all, if linguistic labels are arbitrary—and they certainly are artifacts (that is, they are merely the product of human endeavor, not part of the original furniture of the world)—we can avoid trying to analyze messy old shopworn concepts, and start afresh. Moreover, we can use the method of operational definition when replacing these old concepts, thereby ensuring a really useful language, one which is unambiguous and tied precisely to scientific measurement.

The social sciences especially were—and still are—impressed with these two doctrines. Since it is the social sciences that constitute the role models for most educational research, it is hardly surprising that conceptual analysis has not been seen as particularly important to educational research and in the training of educational researchers.

But when we look closely at the evidence, the initial plausibility of these two planks in the neopositivist platform begins to evaporate. In the first place, operational definitions turned out to be a great disappointment. It was not so much that one could not create operational definitions of scientific concepts (it is not too hard to make them up) but that nobody cared about them; nobody wanted them; nobody would use them. They were not recognized as helpful or even accurate accounts of existing concepts they were supposed to define, and that hardly gave one any confidence about how they would reflect new concepts. Even Percy Bridgman, the Harvard low-temperature physicist who came up with the whole idea, cooled off on operational definitions considerably. And people in psychology, for example, who tried them out ran into unexpected resistance. Was this just the resistance of conservatism, the inertia of those who had grown up with the untidy old concepts and who were unwilling to drop them for newer, cleaner ones?

At first it seemed as if that might be the trouble; the young Turks of the new movement of operationalism certainly thought so. But gradually we came to realize that the whole approach was based on a fallacy, and that the fallacy was essentially a misinterpretation of the doctrine of linguistic arbitrariness. When you interpret that ambiguous phrase—linguistic arbitrariness—with care, then it turns out that under one interpretation it is true, but on that interpretation it will not support the use of operational definitions. And if you interpret it so as to support them, it turns out that you no longer have a sensible doctrine.

Before I discuss these two interpretations, let me call your attention once more to the fact that we are now doing conceptual analysis. This chapter is not a long-winded historical introduction to some examples; it is an example. And we are not only analyzing the concept of definition itself, which is a key tool in any kind of research and, hence, in educational research, but also looking into the nature of language—in particular, the sense in which it can be said to be arbitrary. That is a key substantive question in understanding language and language learning, which are the vehicles for most education and the subject of a great deal of educational research.

Back to the question of legitimate and illegitimate interpretations of the doctrine of linguistic arbitrariness. Language is arbitrary in the sense that German and Japanese and Spanish, and so on, all do a fine job in communicating ideas, and are totally different. So there is some sense in which the world does not define what language has to be used in describing it; *we* do that defining; we create those languages. Moreover, these languages emerge in their respective cultures entirely as a result of the language building and language learning activities of those societies and individuals, not as a result of some law connecting the local climate or crops or social structure with language forms. Languages are obviously arbitrary in the sense of being conventions rather than laws of nature.

The General Irrelevance of Redefinition

All that, however, is not to say that these languages are *now* arbitrary. They now have very strict rules, and if you take any one term from any one of them and give it a new definition, you will not be speaking that language—just as you will not be playing chess if you say that a castle can move diagonally. There is nothing about the shape of castles that makes it a law of nature that they cannot move diagonally; but what was arbitrary once is no longer so. Of course, you can make up a new chess variant or an entirely new game with the same pieces. Then the crucial question is, why would anybody want to play with you? You say, because it is simpler and cleaner and clearer than chess; it has simpler rules. Who cares? We can always play checkers or dice or hearts, if we want something simpler than chess. But chess players want solutions to chess problems, not to other problems. Language speakers want solutions to the problems they express in their language—and which have equivalent relevance to the problems in questions. Behind the arbitrariness of language there is the reality which they all describe, the reality of sorrow and love and anxiety, of learning and teaching and explaining, the reality which psychology and educational research are trying to understand. Redefinition of these concepts makes no contribution to understanding them. It is as useless a contribution to solving the problems as redefining the moves of chess pieces is to solving chess problems.

For that matter, we could always talk "baby talk"; it is much simpler than "grown-up talk." But why should we? Baby talk lacks the strength to do the job—make the distinctions, name the crucial phenomena—that the adult language does, and why settle for less than that? In educational as in any other kind of research you can always go off into a corner and play your own little game, but your results will have no known connections with the problems of humanity or of researchers trying to understand the phenomena of human behavior. Those are problems in any language, whether it is French, German or Spanish. They are problems about the reality which is reflected in the concepts embedded in every mature language, and redefining those concepts is just a sidetracking exercise.

So the dilemma that faced researchers in the empiricist or positivist tradition was that they could give a nice operational definition of anxiety, for example, as whatever the Taylor scale measured. But then it turned out that the Taylor scale does not discriminate between anxiety and, let us say, hostility. What should we do then? We can say that that proves the Taylor scale is no good, because it does not measure anxiety in the usual sense of that term, or we can say that we have redefined anxiety in terms of the Taylor scale, and what we have just discovered is simply a fact about anxiety in this new sense. This latter strategy, which we might call the "brazen-it-out" strategy, obviously raises the question of why anybody should bother to investigate "Tayloriety"—the Taylor version of anxiety.

Moreover, it raises the second question of why the researcher has confused matters by using the preexisting word instead of a new word, like Tayloriety. If you reply by saying that the scale measures something close to anxiety in the old sense, and that is why you stayed with the old term, you next have to face the problem that you do not know exactly how close it is. In particular, does it get to the heart of the notion, from the point of view of the psychodynamics (and hence psychotherapy), or the understanding of function impairment? For example, you have just discovered one divergence and can hardly deny that there may be many others. Hence it will *never* be clear whether we should treat your results as artificial products of your arbitrary definition, or as real discoveries about anxiety—the concept as we understand it. Who wants to get into that kind of mess? Who wants to spend time on doing research of unknown significance?

The Exceptional Case

There is one move you can make at this point which would save the day. It is a very difficult move to pull off, and only very rarely has it been done; in the educational area, virtually never. Moreover, people do not realize its significance and its difficulty; and they quote examples where it did not work, as if they support the general practice of convenient redefinition of scientific or of everyday terms. They have failed to notice the greater part of the iceberg. In these cases of giving a nice clean definition of some concept that previously existed, the move that saves you from disaster, from doing research which nobody is going to be interested in because they do not know how to interpret the results because you are speaking your own language and not theirs, involves proving that your redefined concept is better than the one it replaces.

What does it mean to say that a concept is a better one? Well, "clearer" and "simpler to apply" are part of what is meant by "better," so the operational definitions have that going for them. But the hard part is the rest of it. The hard part is to show, other things being equal, that the supposedly better concept can, in fact, make the main distinctions that were marked by the previous concept—and that, of course, is where the Taylor scale of anxiety gets into trouble. Tayloriety cannot be distinguished from hostility, but anxiety *can* be distinguished from hostility and, indeed, rather easily. So, Tayloriety cannot be as close to the concept of anxiety as its supporters maintained. It is different in a major and clear way. It would be risky, unnecessarily risky, to bother with it.

When Skinner defined thirst as "the propensity to drink when water is made available," he was offering a nice simple substitute for the prior notion—but not a good substitute, because it is obvious that someone with a gun at his back will drink when not thirsty, and some people with, as they say, a "great thirst" are not interested in water. So you are trying to trade off simplicity for reasonable accuracy in mapping the original concept—a dangerous trade. These two examples, which come from the behaviorist/empiricist/positivist tradition, show you just how crude those trade-offs were. And they turned out, as further instances of their inadequacy emerged—to be *very* poor substitutes for the original notions. People were simply not willing to risk the time investment involved in working on them. That track record is the key reason why someone who cares about evidence in assessing hypotheses—the self-defining feature of the empiricist—must abandon the move for redefinition and turn instead to the hard work of conceptual analysis of the existing concepts.

The people who favored the move towards operationalist redefinitions had had virtually no training in the capacity to analyze the prior concept, so they really had no way in which to make the key test of the superiority of their proposed simplification. They just favored it because it was new and simpler, and they *felt* that the messiness of the old concept was an impediment to research (it was) and probably reflected many confusions of people with unscientific training (it probably did) and hence had no redeeming features—which is where they made their mistake. For the messy concept contains all the subtlety that experience has forced upon it; it reflects the real phenomena, perhaps not clearly but usually rather comprehensively. Since the most important part of science is accurate reflection of reality, this part of the matter cannot be dismissed lightly. So, although some limited trades of simplicity for accuracy are possible, you have to do the homework first—or be very lucky.

As was said before, there have been some cases where this trade-off really is worthwhile, where in fact the redefinition pays off. One of them is of great interest to educational researchers. To define intelligence in terms of the score of an IQ test either does this trick or comes very close to it. It's not an example that educational researchers or psychologists like to be reminded about, and it's not one they have defended with much skill when it came under attack, mainly because they rarely had any understanding of just what the merits of this case were. The key point in the defense of the use of the IQ test as a measure of intelligence—the part that few people know about—is the claim that the IQ score correlates better with the average of the judgments of several experienced teachers of a given pupil than those judgments do with each other. Thus, the key point in the defense of the IQ test is not that it is simpler than the usual rather murky concept of intelligence, not that it provides an operational definition of IQ, not that it is quantitative, but just that it is a better indicator of intelligence than the judgment of the average well-placed evaluator.

Of course, it won't always be better than the judgments of *every* such evaluator; for one thing, that's a standard that is not met by any human evaluator. It's just (allegedly) better in more cases than any identifiable type of human evaluator, and hence, even if there are some evaluators that are better, most people will not have access to them, leaving the test as the only thing that most people can use.

Now if that claim about the IQ test is true—and the recent and well-justified elimination of the relatively few class- or race-contaminated items in many of the standard forms of the IQ test makes it more probable—then it certainly makes most of the distinctions that those teachers (or counselors or consulting psychologists) could consistently make. If the new concept is closer to the average judgment of teachers who know a given individual, than any one of their judgments is to that average, then, of course, any distinctions that they are consistently making will show up in the substitute notion—the IQ definition of intelligence. So, one cannot attack it on the grounds that we used to attack Tayloriety. We will be in a position to meet that challenge. In addition, we have the added simplicity and applicability of a behaviorally defined notion.

No one has so far located a *systematic* error in the IQ definition of intelligence, apart from the aforementioned biases due to the social or racial group of the norming population, some of which have been corrected in revised test forms. Of course, there are scores of *alleged* systematic errors, and since the concept of intelligence is in disrepute, everyone has one or two of these in their conversational repertoire. There is no substantial evidence that these systematic errors have in fact been established. We simply do not have the studies to show there is any systematic superiority of *any* group of expert judges over the test. So here we have a real example of the operational definition representing an improvement—if the key claim quoted above can in fact be supported. In all the debates, virtually no one has seen that this claim *is* the key to the *scientific* part of the issue, and that is what makes clear the lack of training in conceptual analysis.

Now, none of this settles the question of whether one should use IQ tests in schools, and for what purposes. It's perfectly clear that there have been plenty of inappropriate uses of them in the past, sometimes resulting in unfortunate penalties for children. Anyone who thinks that that is a good reason for dropping the use of the tests is sorely in need of training in conceptual analysis; and it is quite possible that 99 percent of the people who have given any thought to this issue in the past decade or two are thus condemned. For the only issue is whether *fewer* children are penalized when the IQ test is used than when it is not used. The original telling argument for school entry examinations was Disraeli's plea that it would introduce some objectivity into a process that was riddled with prejudice and, in particular, in those days in England, anti-Semitism. It's not at all clear that the reversion to teacher-based estimates of capability and performance will reduce the total amount of bias *or* simple error that will be involved in decisions about the placement and treatment of children. And no one seems to be treating this as a matter for investigation; we are too busy expiating our guilt over the biases that were present in the tests to realize that jumping out of frying pans is not a guaranteed optimization strategy.

So redefinition in the social sciences has occasionally been of benefit—but not for reasons that anyone cares to remember when the pressure goes on. Nor are people clear exactly what reasons have to be provided in order to justify redefinition, namely evidence that nothing crucial is being lost in the way of distinctions and subsumptions that are currently important; and that something substantial is being gained in the way of simplification and/or the shedding of confusing implications or blurred distinctions. How does one establish that these conditions apply? Essentially by doing extensive and careful analysis of both the existing and the proposed definition; and to do that requires considerable skill in conceptual analysis.

The Conditions for Redefinition

It can also be said that a number of redefinitions have succeeded in the physical sciences. The most interesting example, perhaps, is the way in which the concept of temperature has been redefined four times in the history of thermodynamics. In some redefinitions, the concept was identified with a new measurement, a fully operational definition. Each redefinition was theoretically fertile, theoretically *interesting,* because each of these redefinitions was involved in a restructuring of the whole science of thermodynamics and the concept of temperature was tied in to the new, basic concepts in each case. These redefinitions were sometimes operational; they were clear; they were theoretically interesting; and they did a very good job of matching the existing concept. They did not match the ultimate preexisting concept of *felt* temperature very well, but they were not meant to; they did match—and indeed surpassed—the existing concept of *real* temperature, which was best judged, prior to the introduction of thermometers, by getting a number of judges to make an estimate of temperature. All of the thermodynamic definitions were immune to the well-known tricks that can be used to yield conflicting accounts of temperature from judges; and in addition each new notion was quantitative, sometimes that is always a bonus though not always the best alternative. Furthermore, the new notion covered a much longer scale range than the preexisting version and it yielded simple general physical laws. In short, the new temperature definition in each case did the IQ trick—it provided a better measure of temperature and lost little if anything.

Now, it is quite important to notice that these definitions of temperature had rather a short life; that is, after a few years or decades they were abandoned completely. How could that be the case, if they were redefined because the new definition was simpler—how could it cease to be simpler?

The new definitions were abandoned because in the light of increasing sophistication in our analysis of temperature phenomena, they came to be seen as unsatisfactory. They came to be seen as not matching the scientific concept of temperature as it was emerging and changing. What that tells you is something about the rest of the iceberg. It tells you that the *true total meaning* of temperature was never encapsulated in the operational definition. It tells you that, in fact, the referee for this whole game was invisible. It was the total linguistic environment of use by scientists and others of the concept of temperature that determined whether each of the so-called operational definitions of temperature was acceptable.

If it had been the sort of operational definition that the empiricists and positivists thought was possible, according to the doctrine of linguistic arbitrariness, then of course it could not possibly have been overthrown. It was simply something that had been made true by definition. However, it turned out *not* to be true by definition, but rather to be just a convenient shorthand. That is what simple definitions of important concepts always turn out to be; they are not really complete encapsulations of the meaning of these terms. They are simply convenient abbreviations for the meaning of them and they survive just as long as those abbreviations are, in fact, reasonably good matches to the total meaning of the concept. Much of that meaning is, in science—not just in physics, but in astronomy and chemistry and electronics—still in the common-sense background. This meaning is steadily developing, perhaps, but still there and not abandoned when the new definition is coined. Changes with one or another science may lead us to change the thermodynamic definition but only as long as we preserve most of the old connections so that we can see that we are really still dealing with essentially the same concept. If you just looked at the definitions, which have almost no common elements, you would think that some radical shift of meaning had occurred; whereas in fact, what has occurred is a tidying up of one corner of the total network of meaning for this concept.

You will notice that these remarks on the development of definitions of terms in the physical sciences give a quite different picture from the "total reconstruction" of meaning proposed by the naive philosophers of science in the empiricist/positivist tradition. They give a picture of a great mass of meaning of these key concepts from which we crystallize out some simple form that serves us well as a substitute for most purposes, but not for the basic purpose of understanding the full meaning of the term. That understanding requires years of learning about all the meaning connections, and without that understanding one cannot come to see whether a new "definition" should be accepted pro tem. In any case, on this picture, it is "minor tinkering" that occurs rather than "total reconstruction."

In any event, such cases are very rare. Where they are most likely to occur is in subject matters where most of the phenomena are new, and hence are not fully covered by the preexisting language of everyday life. That is a fair description of the "hard sciences." It has little to do with the social sciences and less to do with educational research.

There is an additional reason for this that very often applies to educational research. In that area we are often dealing with terms that have a large affective or perceptual component—terms like anxiety or understanding or appreciation or attitude or perception or personal significance. With such terms, measurement using a behavioral test such as the IQ test is not going to capture all of the core of the notion and, indeed, in many cases like that of anxiety, it will not even capture the main core notion. Because so much of education is concerned with psychological states of one kind or another, highly resistant and ultimately irreducible to a purely linguistic explication, much of it cannot reasonably be subjected to simple, conceptual redefinition, as in the case of intelligence.

Conclusions for Educational Research

What follows from all this? It follows that most conceptual analysis in educational research has to be done by analyzing and not by replacing the complex concepts. These concepts are usually not reducible in any plausible way to simpler replacements, and are too important to be disposable in favor of any such replacements. To explain/predict/control the kind of behavior in which we are interested, we must analyze these concepts as much in terms of their subjective component as of their behavioral or objective (as it is sometimes described) component.

How does one do this? We've provided some hints and examples for consideration in the preceding pages. At an introductory level a useful handbook is *An Introduction to the Analysis of Educational Concepts* (1978) by Jonas Soltis. More reading follows this paper, but it may be as well if we mention, right now, one key feature of any successful approach. It is essential that you *limit the amount of analysis to the least amount the job requires.* Do more than that, and you're doing philosophy for its own sake. (*Enjoy* doing more than that, and it's time to change over to philosophy.) Do less, and you'll do worthless research.

Let us take an example from another area for a moment. If you had to give a completely general analysis of the concept of "morally justified" in order to discuss any specific issues in the area of practical ethics, you would never get started. To give a completely general analysis of a very general concept is very, very difficult indeed. Even a "convenient equivalent" is hard to find, especially in philosophy where everything is open to challenge. It is much better to try first to answer the questions: Why do I need this piece of conceptual analysis? At what level of precision? What distinctions am I trying to make? Do I need the wholly general definition, or could I settle for a more limited kind of definition? For example, if I am going to talk about the morality of abortion or the morality of brainwashing or torture, do I really need a completely general definition of morality, or could I get by with a definition which focuses on a specific type of distinction, for example, the distinction between torture and punishment? That would be much easier, and the secret of good conceptual analysis is to try to focus on the area in which you need to do the conceptual clarification before doing it. For example, clarifying the distinction between education and indoctrination is much more manageable than trying to define education (and indoctrination) in the abstract. It's hard enough, but perfectly manageable, and there are excellent discussions of the problem in the literature, by Tony Flew and others; extracts follow this chapter.

Various useful procedures emerge from any study of conceptual clarification and conceptual analysis. One of them is that one should nearly always use what I have called the "method of examples and contrasts," and not the method of explicit definition. That is, you should try to clarify a notion by giving paradigmatic examples; examples which illustrate the core meaning, the most typical use of the term, and examples which illustrate what it is not, when it should not be applied. That approach is a good one, whereas giving an explicit definition which allegedly gives you a string of words that can be substituted for the original concept on all occasions of the use of the original concept turns out to be grossly overambitious. After all, it turned out not to be possible even in the physical sciences in the very cases where it was said to be best illustrated. For example, in Newtonian physics, gravity was defined according to the model of reality held by the physicists of the time. As physics matured, models of reality changed and more phenomena related to gravity became "visible" to the physicist, causing older definitions to give way to new definitions. We really were not giving a definition which encapsulated the total meaning; we were giving a definition which was practical at a certain stage of the development of science. But lots of residual meaning was omitted and not encapsulated in the original, simple definition. The "method of examples and contrasts" is better able to clarify important distinctions that are appropriate for a particular application, while avoiding the risks of oversimplification inherent in "operational" or arbitrary definitions.

Ranging a little further in our quest for methodologies for doing conceptual analysis, we find that the general use of analogies and of evocative language, rather than proofs, axiomatization, and quantification, is our main concern. Conceptual analysis is not mathematics, though it is no less powerful than mathematics—in its own domain, which of course includes establishing the foundation of mathematics (or did you think mathematics could establish its own foundations?).

Let me illustrate that last point briefly by reference to another kind of case where the methodology involves an approach that is rather similar to the one that I am advocating here in talking about philosophical analysis in education. In jurisprudence, that is, in the theory of law—and, indeed, in legal argument in the higher courts at the appeal phase—one does not find very much use of quantification or of the experimental method of hard measurement. One finds a great deal of use of arguments from analogy and the method of examples and contrasts. Once again, when you get to the foundations of a subject, you cannot use the methodology *of* that subject, since you haven't yet established the legitimacy of the subject or the methodology. In the same way, only these comparatively simple and unchallengeable universal tools of conceptual analysis can be used in the conceptual analysis which has to be part of almost any worthwhile project in educational research.

Such subtle arguments from paradigms and analogies are not, therefore, to be thought of in any way as weak sisters (or weak brothers) of hard-core empirical research. They provide the foundations on which any worthwhile empirical research must be based—foundations which if not handled with considerable competence and skill will let down the whole structure that is built on them when we do get into the laboratory or out into the field.

So one needs to develop some skills in managing complex arguments from analogy, particularly with respect to establishing the meaning of the terms involved, and those skills are often best illustrated in legal reasoning cases. (Similes and metaphors are also often used in conceptual analysis.) Much is made to rest on arguments by analogy, and they cannot be converted into deductive reasoning or a mathematical model. These forms of argument are very sophisticated and subtle; they can mislead not only beginners in educational research, but also many senior educational researchers who are beginners in this kind of activity.

Much of educational research is dominated by analogies and metaphors, relatively simple conceptions or pictures that drive the direction of thought and experimentation. At the moment, for example, the analogy between the brain and a computer is a dominant theme in the information-processing approach to educational psychology. In the particular area of moral behavior and training, Kohlberg (1981) has extensively criticized the weaknesses of a dominant metaphor—the "bag of tricks" metaphor—which he feels has controlled and misled research in that area. Kohlberg argues that moral reasoning depends on each individual's underlying world view which evolves over time, yielding internally consistent decisions at each stage, but qualitatively different decisions between stages. This is in contrast to the dominant approach to moral training which involves teaching individuals a set of injunctions—the "bag of tricks." The arguments over IQ have partly been arguments over whether the mind should be seen as consisting of a few general skills or abilities like skill with the driver, the irons, and the putter in the case of a golfer who can use them to play on any course, or whether it is more like the large collection of special and relatively distinctive skills that make up the repertoire of someone who has degrees in math, French, and sociology.

So arguments by analogy are loose—but powerful and inescapable. One must get to exact theories via loose analogies, and in educational research we very rarely get to exact theories.

There are other tricks of the trade in conceptual analysis which are of great importance to educational research—for example, training in making the most plausible generalizations from particular instances of a phenomenon, and in seeing loopholes or counter-examples in generalizations that have been proposed to do just that. No amount of philosophical training in conceptual analysis will substitute for brilliant insights, but it certainly can help in avoiding faulty insights that look brilliant at first. And it can help with getting the best formulation of fairly straightforward generalizations, for these are both logical skills from the analyst's stock in trade. A philosopher trained in conceptual analysis has to critique hundreds of examples of seductive—and often long-believed—but fallacious generalizations or definitions from the history of popular and scientific as well as philosophical thought. And much of philosophical thought is only one step more general in its aims than scientific thought, seeking to provide a theory about very general features of the universe, and about the nature of our species, rather than the special characteristics of the learner or teacher; so the gap is not wide.

Getting Training in Conceptual Analysis

Where do people get the kind of training whose virtues I have been extolling? In any given year there are many universities whose philosophy departments are committed to it, but in a later year, following a power shift within the department, one may find the analytical skills downplayed in favor of the study of Buddhism or "system-building" or "speculative philosophy." The program for graduates and undergraduates may then focus on a different set of skills, if that is what they should be called (I am a skeptic about their legitimacy), skills which do not qualify as being of much use to the educational researcher or prospective researcher. I've mentioned a good introductory book (Soltis, 1978); if you feel that you need something really basic as an introduction to practical conceptual analysis, you might want to look at a book of mine called *Reasoning* (1977), where I set this out for introductory studies at some length. For advanced work, the Soltis book I just mentioned is good, but you might go beyond it by looking up any books by Israel Scheffler and D. J. O'Connor that are available in your local library.

There are other sources for training also, depending on the interests of your local college faculty. For example, causation is a notion that is central in all methodologies in educational research and requires serious and difficult conceptual analysis. Causation is also a key concept within historiography—the study of the methodology of historical studies. It is not usually true that methodological approaches overlap between the history of education and the experimental approach. However, in this case, a great deal can be learned from the historian who has been trained in conceptual analysis, if your history department has one. The historian rarely has the luxury of large numbers of experiments, never has control groups, and often cannot inspect or interview the people being studied. As a result, historians have developed much more sophisticated techniques for study of the single case than are commonly found in mainline educational research. (These, of course, depend on a conceptual analysis of the concept of causation, the kind of analysis we have been stressing here.)

Not just historical studies, but contemporary ones where no manipulation is allowable—the "ethnographic" studies—depend on refinements of causal analysis. These are now common in anthropology and linguistics, for example. Mainline educational researchers often view ethnographic or case-study approaches with considerable suspicion. When you start talking about what such studies prove, you are, of course, talking about the *philosophical* question of legitimate inferences from them, a question that cannot be reduced to quantitative notions since they are not, in fact, quantitative disciplines. Thus, we come back to philosophy as a source of training once more.

Back to Philosophy

These questions about what the ethnographic and case study approaches prove that is of general interest immediately raise the general question of the payoff from educational research. Is educational research worth doing? And that, of course, although it is partly a question of the economics of education, is *also* a philosophical question because the payoff from education is surely partly in terms of quality of life, the value of a positive attitude towards self. These are, of course, philosophical matters. Look at the catalog descriptions of ethics courses or "philosophy of the social sciences" courses to see whether the instructor shows interest in such questions. This kind of philosophical question is not just a question of conceptual analysis; it is what people sometimes call a "substantive" philosophical question. But I consider that term prejudicial, so we will call it "issue- (or problem-) centered" in contrast to conceptual analysis. The study of such issue-centered questions is fundamental to your development as an educational researcher, and can provide an essential basis for deciding the "what" of your research pursuits. Such study is not a substitute for learning to do conceptual analysis, but a necessary complement if you are to bring the richness of philosophy to bear on your educational inquiry.

References

Flew, A. (1972). Indoctrination and doctrines. In I. A. Snook (Ed.), *Concepts of indoctrination: Philosophical essays*. Boston: Routledge & Keegan Paul.

Kohlberg, L. (1981). *The philosophy of moral development* (Vol. 1). San Francisco: Harper and Row.

Morrison, D. E., & Henkel, R. E. (Eds.). (1970). *The significance test controversy: A reader*. Hawthorne, NY: De Gruyter Aldine.

Scriven, M. (1977). *Reasoning*. New York: McGraw-Hill.

Soltis, J. (1978). *An introduction to the analysis of educational concepts* (2d ed.). Reading, MA: Addison Wesley.

Suggestions for Further Reading

Peter, R.S. (1973). *The philosophy of education*. Oxford: Oxford University Press. This anthology, edited by one of the best philosophers of education, covers both conceptual analysis and normative issues like the general problem of the justification of education. Some of the main concepts analyzed here include teaching, learning, quality in education, the work/labor/education distinctions, all of educational relevance. It's an excellent set of examples of several authors doing just the kind of thing that most educational researchers need to do more carefully and seriously than they now do.

Thompson, K. (1972). *Education and philosophy: A practical approach*. New York: Blackwell.   This inexpensive paperback, in the series "Blackwell's Practical Guides for Teachers," is a single-author philosophical excursion from philosophy *into* education. Its great virtue is the use of the classroom-related examples.

Soltis, J. (1978). *An introduction to the analysis of educational concepts* (2d ed.). Reading, MA: Addison Wesley.   This book is wholly devoted to the critical process. It's easily available, inexpensive, comprehensive, and actually worth reading twice (as the author suggests on p. 106), an undertaking facilitated by its commendable brevity. If you want to put a toe in the water of conceptual analysis, this book will be your best choice; but remember that the other books are necessary in order to avoid any inclination to think of the area as having a monolithic and uncontroversial structure. This is still philosophy, not mathematics; which is not to say that there are no right answers, only that they are not, for the most part, Yes or No answers.

Study Questions

1. There is a close association between philosophy and education in the history of thought. Plato, Rousseau, Dewey, and Russell all contributed to both fields. Name (discover) four other philosophers of note whose contribution to education has been substantial—two of them from the 20th century.

2. Philosophy has other contributions to make to education besides its analytic techniques, e.g., in its substantive results about alternative possible foundations for ethics, which bear on the content of moral education. Give another example of a substantive area in philosophy where the results bear on education, e.g., in terms of curriculum content.

3. People often think anyone can do conceptual analysis without training. On the contrary, even very distinguished researchers make blunders that invalidate large slices of their work; e.g., much work on teaching identifies it with the transfer of knowledge (which omits the transfer of attitudes). Teaching cannot be defined as the transfer of knowledge *and* attitudes either, for two very, very important reasons. Can you work out what they are?

4. The idea that a test may be better than the judges whose judgment the test is built to match is at first sight a little paradoxical, unless you are pretty familiar with the testing and measurement literature. Another extremely important example is provided by multiple-choice tests used to measure essay-writing ability. It is often said of certain such tests that they are *better* measures of essay-writing ability than an essay-writing test. How can this make sense?

5. Suppose you wanted to do some useful research on college teaching. Where would (a) conceptual analysis and (b) other philosophical questions come into your overall research plan?

6. An earlier study question asked for two reasons why teaching can't be identified with the transfer of knowledge and attitudes. The first reason is that such transfer also occurs during brainwashing which is not part of what you'd want to include under teaching; and the second reason is that teaching is the name of an activity, one that is not necessarily always completely successful—hence, teaching may be occurring at times when no learning is occurring (hence, no transfer). Maybe those two counter-examples to the proposed definition of teaching do not wholly persuade you. They are very carefully chosen so as not to be too easy or obvious—but they are correct. If you don't think so, you flunked the first question in the Scriven Conceptual Analysis Test (SCAT). You should read the anthology *Concepts of Indoctrination: Philosophical Essays* edited by I. A. Snook, and either concede and explain your error or publish a refuta-

tion of the SCAT, which of course is wholly unconnected with any empirical validation data. (That's the great charm of conceptual analysis; but also the great trap for would-be players.)

The remainder of Section III of this book provides additional study questions and associated readings which will further clarify and apply the concepts discussed in this chapter.

Readings

Introduction
Further Exercises in Philosophical Inquiry Methods

Michael Scriven

This part of Section III is an attempt to bridge the gap between the preceding paper and free-ranging reading in the area of conceptual analysis in educational research. What we offer begins with some further examples of doing philosophical (conceptual) analysis on educational concepts, following the procedures already outlined. Then we go on to look at some distinguished authors dealing with other examples. Among these examples, we go from the simpler to the (philosophically) more sophisticated. Finally, we suggest examples of important issues to which you can apply the techniques you have learned.

First let's try applying some of the procedures covered in the preceding paper to a new case or two.

1. What does the term "handicapped" mean, as it is now used in educational circles? (Remember, you have three possible approaches; a full translation, examples, and contrasts.) How does your answer compare with the dictionary definition? Is this a case where one of the fallacies about redefining concepts is involved? What could be one of the costs of redefinition here? Are those costs serious?

2. What does the term "exceptional" mean, as it is now used in educational jargon? Answer in this case the same questions as in Question 1. Additionally, explain how "handicapped" is related to "exceptional."

3. Included in my paper was one very controversial example, the example of the IQ test. It was argued that, given the truth of one particular claim, the test is an example of how redefinition of concepts in education can sometimes work. The question naturally arises: Is that argument sound? Good analytic technique suggests we should break down these very abstract or "head-on" questions by posing more manageable questions that seem to be crucial to answering the more general one. Let's approach this general question using the following chain of questions:

a. Is it possible that what an IQ test tests is not the same for the black youngster as for the child of white middle-class parents? Let's approach *that* question, which is at least one stage more specific, with the following questions:

   1. Can you say in *general terms* what it is that might be different about the concept of intelligence that would be detected by an IQ test on a black child, by contrast with what intelligence would be detected in a white child?

   2. Can you give *an example* that illustrates your point?

   b. What technique(s) of conceptual analysis, discussed in my paper, have you just exhibited?

   c. Let's look at the views of someone who has a completely different position from that espoused in my paper. The first reading in this section is a chapter from Howard Gardner's famous book, *Frames of Mind: The Theory of Multiple Intelligences.* He proposes seven models or types of intelligence. After completing the reading, discuss the view that a child prodigy in music is intelligent.

   d. Gardner's chapter is an example of a distinguished psychologist doing conceptual analysis. Are you persuaded that he has made the best possible analysis of the concept of intelligence? (This chapter was criticized by some reviewers, and in the introduction to the paperback edition from which we are reprinting this material, Gardner provides an interesting discussion of some aspects of the definitional question and some criticisms of the first edition. You might find that interesting follow-up reading.)

   e. Suppose that IQ is, as many educational psychologists maintain, a completely inadequate measurement of intelligence. What effect does that have on the argument given in my paper? In particular, does it mean that the conceptual analysis is more or less important than is argued there?

4. The second reading in this section is *The Language of Education* by the eminent Harvard philosopher of education, Israel Scheffler.

   a. In the first segment, pp. 167–68, Scheffler illustrates well how the concepts we analyze are part of life, part of a larger context which depends in part on how our analysis comes out, and on which our analysis should also depend. (We have made the point in terms of the doctrine of definitional irresponsibility.) Can you illustrate his point using proposed redefinitions of the term democracy?

   b. In the second segment, pp. 168–73, Scheffler shows how important it is not to treat everything as if it is intended to be literally true. (In fact, the next chapter of his book is called "Educational Metaphors.") Give your own example of two apparently contradictory assertions about the nature of life or education or ethics. Show how they are in fact reconcilable.

5. We now come to the issue of education versus indoctrination, to which I referred previously. It is a very important issue, since the right of parochial and fundamentalist schools in this country to be tolerated or supported indirectly (via tax exemptions) is at stake. Are those schools offering the basic education to which every citizen is entitled, or indoctrination of the kind that we disapprove of in authoritarian societies? The issue deeply concerns parents who won-

der how to treat the education of their children in spiritual values. The essay we reproduce from the anthology *Concepts of Indoctrination: Philosophical Essays* is by the editor, I.A. Snook; and although it makes some reference to other contributions to the volume, you need not have read those other contributions to make sense of Snook's remarks. You will notice that he uses several of the techniques that we have already discussed.

After reading the excerpt reproduced here, do you find that Snook persuades you? Give a brief summary of an argument based on one analysis of indoctrination that might be given for closing all religious schools. Give the case against it. (You should go back and look at the other essays in this volume if you possibly can; it provides an unusually good example of hard-hitting debate in conceptual analysis.)

6. Select one or more of the following concepts—in the sense that they are relevant to education—as the topic for a short essay on alternative ways in which each could be defined, and how these definitions might appeal to different people. Which of the definitions would be justified? Why isn't that an arbitrary decision? Why does it matter which way the definition is set up?

   a. sex education
   b. professional teacher
   c. mature or responsible
   d. pornography
   e. patriotism

What Is
an Intelligence?

I HAVE now set the stage for an introduction of the intelligences. My review of earlier studies of intelligence and cognition has suggested the existence of a number of different intellectual strengths, or competences, each of which may have its own developmental history. The review of recent work in neurobiology has again suggested the presence of areas in the brain that correspond, at least roughly, to certain forms of cognition; and these same studies imply a neural organization that proves hospitable to the notion of different modes of information processing. At least in the fields of psychology and neurobiology, the *Zeitgeist* appears primed for the identification of several human intellectual competences.

But science can never proceed completely inductively. We might conduct every conceivable psychological test and experiment, or ferret out all the neuroanatomical wiring that we desired, and still not have identified the sought after human intelligences. We confront here a question not of the certainty of knowledge but, rather, of how knowledge is attained at all. It is necessary to advance a hypothesis, or a theory, and then to test it. Only as the theory's strengths—and limitations—become known will the plausibility of the original postulation become evident.

Nor does science ever yield a completely correct and final answer. There is progress and regress, fit and lack of fit, but never the discovery of the Rosetta stone, the single key to a set of interlocking issues. This has been true at the most sophisticated levels of physics and

Gardner, Howard. *Frames of Mind: The Theory of Multiple Intelligences.* New York, Basic Books, 1983, pp. 59–70. Reproduced by permission.

chemistry. It is all the more true—one might say, it is all too true—in the social and behavioral sciences.

And so it becomes necessary to say, once and for all, that there is not, and there can never be, a single irrefutable and universally accepted list of human intelligences. There will never be a master list of three, seven, or three hundred intelligences which can be endorsed by all investigators. We may come closer to this goal if we stick to only one level of analysis (say, neurophysiology) or one goal (say, prediction of success at a technical university); but if we are striving for a decisive theory of the range of human intelligence, we can expect never to complete our search.

Why, then, proceed along this precarious path at all? Because there is a need for a better classification of human intellectual competences than we have now; because there is much recent evidence emerging from scientific research, cross-cultural observations, and educational study which stands in need of review and organization; and perhaps above all, because it seems within our grasp to come up with a list of intellectual strengths which will prove useful for a wide range of researchers and practitioners and will enable them (and *us*) to communicate more effectively about this curiously seductive entity called the intellect. In other words, the synthesis that we seek can never be all things for all people, but it holds promise of providing some things for many interested parties.

Before moving on to the intellectual competences themselves, we must consider two topics. First of all, what are the prerequisites for an intelligence: that is, what are the general desiderata to which a set of intellectual skills ought to conform before that set is worth consideration in the master list of intellectual competences? Second, what are the actual criteria by which we can judge whether a candidate competence, which has passed the "first cut" ought to be invited to join our charmed circle of intelligences? As part and parcel of the list of criteria, it is also important to indicate those factors that suggest we are on the wrong track: that a skill that had appeared as a possible intellectual competence does not qualify; or that a skill that seems very important is being missed by our approach.

Prerequisites of an Intelligence

To my mind, a human intellectual competence must entail a set of skills of problem solving—enabling the individual *to resolve genuine problems or difficulties* that he or she encounters and, when appropriate, to create an effective product—and must also entail the potential for *finding or creating problems*—thereby laying the groundwork for the acquisition of new knowledge. These prerequisites represent my effort to focus on those intellectual strengths that prove of some importance within a cultural context. At the same time, I recognize that the ideal of what is valued will differ markedly, sometimes even radically, across human cultures, within the creation of new products or posing of new questions being of relatively little importance in some settings.

The prerequisites are a way of ensuring that a human intelligence must be genuinely useful and important, at least in certain cultural settings. This criterion alone may disqualify certain capacities that, on other grounds, would meet the criteria that I am about to set. For instance, the ability to recognize faces is a capacity that seems to be relatively autonomous and to be represented in a specific area of the human nervous system. Moreover, it exhibits its own developmental history. And yet, to my knowledge, while severe difficulties in recognizing faces might pose embarrassment for some individuals, this ability does not seem highly valued by cultures. Nor are there ready opportunities for problem finding in the domain of face recognition. Acute use of sensory systems is another obvious candidate for a human intelligence. And when it comes to keen gustatory or olfactory senses, these abilities have little special value across cultures. (I concede that people more involved than I in the culinary life might disagree with this assessment!)

Other abilities that are certainly central in human intercourse also do not qualify. For instance, the abilities used by a scientist, a religious leader, or a politician are of great importance. Yet, because these cultural roles can (by hypothesis) be broken down into collections of particular intellectual competences, they do not themselves qualify as intelligences. From the opposite end of analysis, many skills tested for perennially by psychologists—ranging from recall of nonsense syllables to production of unusual associations—fail to qualify, for they emerge as the contrivances of an experimenter rather than as skills valued by a culture.

There have, of course, been many efforts to nominate and detail essential intelligences, ranging from the medieval trivium and quadrivium to the psychologist Larry Gross's list of five modes of communication (lexical, social-gestural, iconic, logico-mathematical, and musical), the philosopher Paul Hirst's list of seven forms of knowledge (mathematics, physical sciences, interpersonal understanding, religion, literature and the fine arts, morals, and philosophy). On an *a priori* basis, there is nothing wrong with these classifications; and, indeed, they may prove critical for certain purposes. The very difficulty with these lists, however, is that they are *a priori*—an effort by a reflective individual (or a culture) to devise meaningful distinctions among types of knowledge. What I am calling for here are sets of intelligences which meet certain biological and psychological specifications. In the end, the search for an empirically grounded set of faculties may fail; and then we may have to rely once more on *a priori* schemes, such as Hirst's. But the effort should be made to find a firmer foundation for our favorite faculties.

I do not insist that the list of intelligences presented here be exhaustive. I would be astonished if it were. Yet, at the same time, there is something awry about a list that leaves glaring and obvious gaps, or one that fails to generate the vast majority of roles and skills valued by human cultures. Thus, a prerequisite for a theory of multiple intelligences, as a whole, is that it captures a reasonably complete gamut of the kinds of abilities valued by human cultures. We must account for the skills of a shaman and a psychoanalyst as well as of a yogi and a saint.

Criteria of an Intelligence

So much, then, for the prerequisites of this undertaking and onward to criteria, or "signs." Here, I outline those considerations that have weighed most heavily in the present effort, those desiderata on which I have come to rely in an effort to nominate a set of intelligences which seems general and genuinely useful. The very use of the word *signs* signals that this undertaking must be provisional: I do not include something merely because it exhibits one or two of the signs, nor do I exclude a candidate intelligence just because it fails to qualify on each and every account. Rather, the effort is to sample as widely as possible among the various criteria and to include within the ranks of the chosen intelligences those candidates that fare the best. Following the suggestive model of the computer scientist Oliver Selfridge, we might think of these signs as a group of demons, each of which will holler when an intelligence resonates with that demon's "demand characteristics." When enough demons holler, an intelligence is included; when enough of them withhold approbation, the intelligence is, if regrettably, banished from consideration.

Ultimately, it would certainly be desirable to have an algorithm for the selection of an intelligence, such that any trained researcher could determine whether a candidate intelligence met the appropriate criteria. At present, however, it must be admitted that the selection (or rejection) of a candidate intelligence is reminiscent more of an artistic judgment than of a scientific assessment. Borrowing a concept from statistics, one might think of the procedure as a kind of "subjective" factor analysis. Where my procedure does take a scientific turn is in the making public of the grounds for the judgment, so that other investigators can review the evidence and draw their own conclusions.

Here then, in unordered fashion, are the eight "signs" of an intelligence:

POTENTIAL ISOLATION BY BRAIN DAMAGE

To the extent that a particular faculty can be destroyed, or *spared* in isolation, as a result of brain damage, its relative autonomy from other human faculties seems likely. In what follows I rely to a considerable degree on evidence from neuropsychology and, in particular, on that highly revealing experiment in nature—a lesion to a specific area of the brain. The consequences of such brain injury may well constitute the single most instructive line of evidence regarding those distinctive abilities or computations that lie at the core of a human intelligence.

THE EXISTENCE OF IDIOTS SAVANTS, PRODIGIES, AND OTHER EXCEPTIONAL INDIVIDUALS

Second only to brain damage in its persuasiveness is the discovery of an individual who exhibits a highly uneven profile of abilities and deficits. In the case of the prodigy, we encounter an individual who is extremely precocious in one (or, occasionally, more than one) area of human competence. In the case of the *idiot savant* (and other retarded or exceptional individuals, including autistic children), we behold the unique sparing of one particular human ability against a background of mediocre or highly retarded human performances in other domains. Once again, the existence of these populations allows us to observe the human intelligence in relative—even splendid—isolation. To the extent that the condition of the prodigy or the *idiot savant* can be linked to genetic factors, or (through various kinds of non-invasive investigative methods) to specific neural regions, the claim upon a specific intelligence is enhanced. At the same time, the selective absence of an intellectual skill—as may characterize autistic children or youngsters with learning disabilities—provides a confirmation-by-negation of a certain intelligence.

AN IDENTIFIABLE CORE OPERATION OR SET OF OPERATIONS

Central to my notion of an intelligence is the existence of *one or more* basic information-processing operations or mechanisms, which can deal with specific kinds of input. One might go so far as to define a human intelligence as a neural mechanism or computational system which is genetically programmed to be activated or "triggered" by certain kinds of internally or externally presented information. Examples would include sensitivity to pitch relations as one core of musical intelligence, or the ability to imitate movement by others as one core of bodily intelligence.

Given this definition, it becomes crucial to be able to identify these core operations, to locate their neural substrate, and to prove that these "cores" are indeed separate. Simulation on a computer is one promising way of establishing that a core operation exists and can in fact give rise to various intellectual performances. Identification of core operations is at this point still largely a matter of guesswork, but it is no less important on that account. Correlatively, resistance to the detection of core operations is a clue that something is amiss: one may be encountering an amalgam which calls for decomposition in terms of its own constituent intelligences.

A DISTINCTIVE DEVELOPMENTAL HISTORY, ALONG WITH A DEFINABLE SET OF EXPERT "END-STATE" PERFORMANCES

An intelligence should have an identifiable developmental history, through which normal as well as gifted individuals pass in the course of ontogeny. To be sure, the intelligence will not develop in isolation, except in an unusual person; and so it becomes necessary to focus on those roles or situations where the intelligence occupies a central place. In addition, it should prove possible to identify disparate levels of expertise in the development of an intelligence, ranging from the universal beginnings through which every novice passes, to exceedingly high levels of competence, which may be visible only in individuals with unusual talent and/or special forms of training. There may well be distinct critical periods in the developmental history, as well as identifiable milestones, linked either to training or to physical maturation. Identification of the developmental history of the intelligence, and analysis of its susceptibility to modification and training, is of the highest import for educational practitioners.

AN EVOLUTIONARY HISTORY AND EVOLUTIONARY PLAUSIBILITY

All species display areas of intelligence (and ignorance), and human beings are no exception. The roots of our current intelligences reach back millions of years in the history of the species. A specific intelligence becomes more plausible to the extent that one can locate its evolutionary antecedents, including capacities (like bird song or primate social organization) that are shared with other organisms; one must also be on the lookout for specific computational abilities which appear to operate in isolation in other species but have become yoked with one another in human beings. (For example, discrete aspects of musical intelligence may well appear in several species but are only joined in human beings.) Periods of rapid growth in human prehistory, mutations that may have conferred special advantages upon a given population, as well as evolutionary paths that did not flourish, are all grist for a student of multiple intelligences. Yet it must be stressed that this is an area where sheer speculation is especially tempting, and firm facts especially elusive.

SUPPORT FROM EXPERIMENTAL PSYCHOLOGICAL TASKS

Many paradigms favored in experimental psychology illuminate the operation of candidate intelligences. Using the methods of the cognitive psychologist, one can, for example, study details of linguistic or spatial processing with exemplary specificity. The relative autonomy of an intelligence can also be investigated. Especially suggestive are studies of tasks that interfere (or fail to interfere) with one another; tasks that transfer (and those that do not) across different contexts; and the identification of forms of memory, attention, or perception that may be peculiar to one kind of input. Such experimental tests can provide convincing support for the claim that particular abilities are (or are not) manifestations of the same intelligences. To the extent that various specific computational mechanisms—or procedural systems—work together smoothly, experimental psychology can also help demonstrate the ways in which modular or domain-specific abilities may interact in the execution of complex tasks.

SUPPORT FROM PSYCHOMETRIC FINDINGS

Outcomes of psychological experiments provide one source of information relevant to intelligences; the outcomes of standard tests (like I.Q. tests) provide another clue. While the tradition of intelligence testing has not emerged as the hero of my earlier discussion, it is clearly relevant to my pursuit here. To the extent that the tasks that purportedly assess one intelligence correlate highly with one another, and less highly with those that purportedly assess other intelligences, my formulation enhances its credibility. To the extent that psychometric results prove unfriendly to my proposed constellation of intelligences, there is cause for concern. It must be noted, however, that intelligence tests do not always test what they are claimed to test. Thus many tasks actually involve the use of more than their targeted ability, while many other tasks can be solved using a variety of means (for example, certain analogies or matrices may be completed by exploiting linguistic, logical, and/or spatial capacities). Also, the stress on paper-and-pencil methods often precludes the proper test of certain abilities, especially those involving active manipulation of the environment or interaction with other individuals. Hence, interpretation of psychometric findings is not always a straightforward matter.

SUSCEPTIBILITY TO ENCODING IN A SYMBOL SYSTEM

Much of human representation and communication of knowledge takes place via symbol systems—culturally contrived systems of meaning which capture important forms of information. Language, picturing, mathematics are but three of the symbol systems that have become important the world over for human survival and human productivity. In my view, one of the features that makes a raw computational capacity useful (and exploitable) by human beings is its susceptibility to marshaling by a cultural symbol system. Viewed from an opposite perspective, symbol systems may have evolved *just in those cases* where there exists a computational capacity ripe for harnessing by the culture. While it may be possible for an intelligence to proceed without its own special symbol system, or without some other culturally devised arena, a primary characteristic of human intelligence may well be its "natural" gravitation toward embodiment in a symbolic system.

These, then, are criteria by which a candidate intelligence can be judged. They will be drawn on repeatedly, as appropriate, in each of the substantive chapters that follows. It is germane here to remark on certain considerations that might cause one to rule out an otherwise plausible candidate intelligence.

Delimiting the Concept of an Intelligence

One group of candidate intelligences includes those that are dictated by common parlance. It may seem, for example, that the *capacity to process auditory sequences* is a strong candidate for an intelligence; indeed, many experimentalists and psychometrians have nominated this capacity. However, studies of the effects of brain damage have repeatedly documented that musical and linguistic strings are processed in different ways and can be compromised by different lesions. Thus, despite the surface appeal of such a skill, it seems preferable not to regard it as a separate intelligence. Other abilities frequently commented upon in specific individuals—for example, remarkable common sense or intuition—might seem to exhibit such signs as "prodigiousness." In this case, however, the categorization seems insufficiently examined. More careful analysis reveals discrete forms of intuition, common sense, or shrewdness in various intellectual domains; intuition in social matters predicts little about intuition in the mechanical or musical realm. Again, a superficially appealing candidate does not qualify.

It is, of course, possible that our list of intelligences is adequate as a baseline of core intellectual abilities, but that certain more general abilities may override, or otherwise regulate, the core intelligences. Among candidates that have frequently been mentioned are a "sense of self," which derives from one's peculiar blend of intelligences; an "executive capacity," which deploys specific intelligences for specific ends; and a synthesizing ability, which draws together conclusions residing in several specific intellectual domains. Beyond challenge, these are important phenomena, which demand to be considered, if not explained. Such discussion, however, is a task best left until later when, having introduced the specific intelligences, I initiate a critique of my own in chapter 11. On the other hand, the question of how specific intelligences come to be linked, supplemented, or balanced to carry out more complex, culturally relevant tasks, is one of the utmost importance, to which I shall devote attention at several points in this book.

Once one has set forth the criteria or signs most crucial for the identification of an intelligence, it is important to state as well what intelligences are *not*. To begin with, intelligences are not equivalent to sensory systems. In no case is an intelligence completely dependent upon a single sensory system, nor has any sensory system been immortalized as an intelligence. The intelligences are by their very nature capable of realization (at least, in part) through more than one sensory system.

Intelligences should be thought of as entities at a certain level of generality, broader than highly specific computational mechanisms (like line detection) while narrower than the most general capacities, like analysis, synthesis, or a sense of self (if any of these can be shown to exist apart from combinations of specific intelligences). Yet it is in the very nature of intelligences that each operates according to its own procedures and has its own biological bases. It is thus a mistake to try to compare intelligences on all particulars; each must be thought of as its own system with its own rules. Here a biological analogy may be useful. Even though the eye, the heart, and the kidneys are all bodily organs, it is a mistake to try to compare these organs in every particular: the same restraint should be observed in the case of intelligences.

Intelligences are not to be thought of in evaluative terms. While the word *intelligence* has in our culture a positive connotation, there is no reason to think that an intelligence must necessarily be put to good purposes. In fact, one can use one's logical-mathematical, linguistic, or personal intelligences for highly nefarious purposes.

Intelligences are best thought of apart from particular programs of action. Of course, intelligences are most readily observed when they are being exploited to carry out one or another program of action. Yet the possession of an intelligence is most accurately thought of as *a potential*: an individual in possession of an intelligence can be said to have no circumstance that prevents him from using that intelligence. Whether he chooses to do so (and to what end he may put that intelligence) fall outside the purview of this book. (See notes to page 68.)

In the study of skills and abilities, it is customary to honor a distinction between *know-how* (tacit knowledge of how to execute something) and *know-that* (propositional knowledge about the actual set of procedures involved in execution). Thus, many of us know how to ride a bicycle but lack the propositional knowledge of how that behavior is carried out. In contrast, many of us have propositional knowledge about how to make a soufflé without knowing how to carry this task through to successful completion. While I hesitate to glorify this rough-and-ready distinction, it is helpful to think of the various intelligences chiefly as *sets of know-how*—procedures for doing things. In fact, a concern with propositional knowledge about intelligences seems to be a particular option followed in some cultures, while of little or no interest in many others.

Conclusion

These remarks and cautionary notes should help to place in proper perspective the various descriptions of specific intelligences which constitute the next part of this book. Naturally, in a book reviewing a whole spectrum of intelligences, it is not possible to devote sufficient attention to any specific one. Indeed, even to treat a single intellectual competence—like language—with sufficient seriousness would require at least one lengthy volume. The most that I can hope to accomplish here is to provide a feeling for each specific intelligence; to convey something of its core operations, to suggest how it unfolds and proceeds at its highest levels, to touch upon its developmental trajectory, and to suggest something of its neurological organization. I shall rely heavily on a few central examples and knowledgeable "guides" in each area and can only offer my impression (and my hope!) that most of the pivotal points could have been equally well conveyed by many other examples or guides. Similarly, I will depend on a few key cultural "roles," each of which utilizes several intelligences but can properly be said to highlight the particular intelligence under study. Some notion of the wider data base on which I am drawing, and of the sources relevant for a fuller inquiry into each intelligence, can be gained from a study of the references for each chapter. But I am painfully aware that a convincing case for each of the candidate intelligences remains the task for other days and other volumes.

A final, crucial point before I turn to the intelligences themselves. There is a universal human temptation to give credence to a word to which we have become attached, perhaps because it has helped us to understand a situation better. As noted at the beginning of this book, *intelligence* is such a word; we use it so often that we have come to believe in its existence, as a genuine tangible, measurable entity, rather than as a convenient way of labeling some phenomena that may (but may well not) exist.

This risk of reification is grave in a work of exposition, especially in one that attempts to introduce novel scientific concepts. I, and sympathetic readers, will be likely to think—and to fall into the habit of saying—that we here behold the "linguistic intelligence," the "interpersonal intelligence," or the "spatial intelligence" at work, and that's that. But it's not. These intelligences are fictions—at most, useful fictions—for discussing processes and abilities that (like all of life) are continuous with one another; Nature brooks no sharp discontinuities of the sort proposed here. Our intelligences are being separately defined and described strictly in order to illuminate scientific issues and to tackle pressing practical problems. It is permissible to lapse into the sin of reifying *so long as we remain aware that this is what we are doing*. And so, as we turn our attention to the specific intelligences, I must repeat that they exist not as physically verifiable entities but only as potentially useful scientific constructs. Since it is language, however, that has led us to (and will continue to dip us into) this morass, it is perhaps fitting to begin the discussion of the particular intelligences by considering the unique powers of the word.

End of reading from Howard Gardner

Education, like art, literature, and other phases of social life, has changing styles and problems in response to changing conditions. These conditions require decisions governing our practical orientation to them. Such decisions may be embodied in revision of our principles of action or our definitions of relevant terms or both. In the making of new definitions for such purposes, there is no special insight into meanings that tells us how revisions and extensions are to be made. Not an inspection of the uniquely real meanings of terms (if this were possible) is here relevant, but an investigation in the light of our commitments, of the practical alternatives open to us as well as of alternative ways of putting desired decisions into effect.

The way in which this point is often overlooked in professional writings on education may be illustrated by the following description of a new program for secondary schooling:

"The curriculum was organized around four sorts of activities, story projects, hand projects, play projects, and excursion projects; opportunity was provided for continuing evaluation of activities, and such evaluation was directed by pupils. The organization of this school program proceeded naturally from the belief that the fundamental meaning of the concept of education is to help boys and girls to active participation in the world around them."

The issue is here put in terms of fundamental meanings. But, in fact, what is at stake? Clear cases of the concept 'education' as embodied in usage prior to the advent of modern innovations did not include cases where play and excursions as well as pupils' continuing evaluation characterized the educational program. But some of the clear cases, like the present example, did involve special institutions, overall direction by adults, evaluation of achievement, and so forth. The present educational innovation, as a matter of fact, is both sufficiently like and sufficiently unlike clear past instances to constitute a borderline case.

To propose an educational reform along the lines of the above passage is to say that such a procedure ought to be tried under the aegis of the schools. The proposal may thus be said to assimilate the borderline case to the past clear cases, leaving intact all those principles of action formulating our positive orientation to educational

Scheffler, Israel. *The Language of Education*. Springfield, IL, Charles C Thomas, 1960, pp. 32–33, 41–46. Reproduced by permission.

endeavor. The stated definition tries to do just that by, in effect, dwelling on the resemblances, i.e., on the common aim to help boys and girls to active participation in the world around them. It would, however, be easy to concoct alternative definitions that built on the differences, segregating the new reform from previous clear cases of 'education.' The issue, in short, is one of practice, and needs evaluation in terms of our preferences and commitments as well as in terms of expected effects. What is to be done with respect to this proposed educational reform is thus our practical responsibility and cannot be decided by inspection of the concept of 'education.'

*   *   *   *

One important corollary is that doctrines that contradict each other as literal statements may nevertheless, in their practical purport, represent abstractly compatible emphases which may, to be sure, vary independently in relevance and moral warrant from context to context. That is, there may be no cause for supposing that we have an irreconcilable conflict of practical proposals of which we must flatly reject at least one. This point may be illustrated by considering a statement that has acquired the typical status of a slogan in education, the statement that there can be no teaching without learning. As there can be no selling without buying, so there can be no teaching without learning. A recent writer[20] has argued against this statement, asking us to consider as a counter-example the case of a teacher who has tried his best to teach his pupils a certain lesson but has failed to get them to learn it. Shall we say that such a man has not, in fact, been teaching, has not earned

20. Broudy, H. S. *Building a Philosophy of Education.* Englewood Cliffs, N. J., Prentice-Hall, Inc., 1954, p. 14. Broudy writes, "Many educators rather glibly pronounce the dictum: 'If there is no learning, there is no teaching.' This is a way of speaking because no educator really believes it to be true, or if he did he would in all honesty refuse to take most of his salary. There is a difference between successful teaching and unsuccessful teaching, just as there is a difference between successful surgery and unsuccessful surgery . . . To teach is deliberately to try to promote certain learnings. When other factors intrude to prevent such learnings, the teaching fails. Sometimes the factors are in the teacher; sometimes in the pupil; sometimes in the very air both breathe, but as long as the effort was there, there was teaching."

his pay, has not fulfilled his responsibility? Surely this case shows that there can be teaching without learning.

If we take the two statements, "There can be no teaching without learning," and "There can be teaching without learning," simply as literal doctrines, we must agree that they are contradictory. Further, we must agree that the counterexample produced against the first of these statements is effective in showing it to be false. If we have an actual case before us of teaching without learning, then we must reject the doctrine that denies the existence of such cases. The counterexample does, moreover, represent a real case of teaching without learning. Here, in short, does seem to be a flat contradiction between two statements, one of which is wrong.

It is, furthermore, easy to see why the statement, "There can be no teaching without learning," sounds so plausible as a literal doctrine, though it is in fact false. For though in some uses of the verb 'to teach' it does not imply success, in others it does. We have already noted the difference between asking, "What have you been teaching him?" ("What have you been trying to get him to learn?") and "What have you taught him?" ("What have you been successful in teaching him?"). The first question, we may say, contains an "intentional" use of the verb, while the second contains a "success" use.[21] It is clear that if the pupil I have been teaching has in fact not learned anything, I may reply to the second question (but not to the first) by saying, "Nothing." For the second question, that is, unless my pupil has learned something, I cannot say I have taught him anything, i.e., there can (here and in all "success" uses) indeed be no teaching without learning.

Some further illustrations may be helpful, especially since the distinction between "success" and "intentional" uses is important and will recur in later discussions. Clearly, if I have been teaching my nephew how to catch a baseball, he may still not have learned, and may in fact never learn, how to catch a baseball. I have, of course, been trying to get him to learn how to catch a baseball, but I need not have succeeded. Generally, then, we may say that the schema "X has been teaching Y how to . . ." does not

21. I am indebted to the treatment of achievement words in Ryle, G.: *The Concept of Mind*. London, Hutchinson's University Library, 1949. See also Anscombe, G.E.M.: *Intention*. Oxford, Basil Blackwell, 1957.

imply success. Suppose, however, that I have taught my nephew how to catch a baseball. If I have indeed taught him, then he must, in fact, have learned how. Were I to say, "Today I taught him how to catch a baseball but he hasn't learned and never will," I would normally be thought to be saying something puzzling. We may, then, say that the schema "X taught Y how to . . ." does imply success. This schema represents a "success" use of 'to teach' whereas the earlier schema does not, representing rather an "intentional" use of the verb.

It should be noted, incidentally, that not every use of the simple past tense of the verb implies success, though the above "success" schema contains such a form. It is, for example, true that some teachers taught mathematics last year to some students who learned nothing of mathematics. It should further be noticed that "success" uses of the verb 'to teach' do not eliminate distinctions of relative proficiency. To have been successful in teaching implies no more than that students have learned in relevant ways, not that they have become masters. We may ask rhetorically, in traffic, "Who taught *him* to drive?" suggesting that, though he has learned, he is not very good at it. It is minimal achievement, sufficient to warrant us in saying that learning has occurred at all, that is normally implied by "success" uses of the verb 'to teach.'

Finally, we should make note of the fact that 'to teach' is not exceptional in having both "success" and "intentional" uses. Indeed, many verbs relating to action have both uses inasmuch as what is done is often described in terms of trying to reach a goal, the attainment of which defines the success of the try. To say a man is building a house does not mean he has succeeded or ever will. He is, of course, doing something with a certain intention and certain hopes and beliefs; he is, in short, trying to bring it about or make it true that there be a house built by himself. It may, further, be normally understood that what he is doing in this attempt is reasonably considered effective. But from the fact that someone is building a house it cannot be inferred that there is (or will be) some house built by him. He may have been building ("intentional" use) until the flood came and wiped away his work, and he then never completed the job. He may thus never have built ("success" use) the house that he had been building ("intentional" use). Or, better, there may never exist any house built ("success" use) by him, though he has, in fact, been house-building ("intentional" use).

If now, with respect to the verb 'to teach,' we recognise that it has both "intentional" and "success" uses, we see that for the latter uses, there can, indeed, be no teaching without learning. If one's examples are all drawn from such uses, the doctrine that there can be no teaching without learning seems entirely plausible. Nevertheless, the general way in which it is expressed leaves the doctrine open to falsification through a single counterexample, such as has been discussed above. Thus we return, after a long digression, to the conclusion we reached earlier: taken as literal doctrines, the statements, "There can be no teaching without learning," and "There can be teaching without learning" are contradictory, hence irreconcilable, and it is the first statement, moreover, that must be rejected.

If, however, we examine the practical purport of these two statements, it becomes clear that, though their practical emphases are not equally relevant and warranted in every context, neither are they opposed as exclusive alternatives. Rather, they relate to different practical aims that are perfectly compatible. The practical purport of the statement "There can be no teaching without learning" is closely related to that of the slogan "We teach children, not subjects," that is, to turn the attention of the teacher toward the child. But we have here a distinctive emphasis on the child's learning as the intended *result* of teaching, the point being to improve the effectiveness of teaching by referring it to its actual as compared with its intended results. This emphasis hardly strikes anyone today as being either very original or very controversial. It seems rather taken for granted in quite prosaic contexts. Imagine someone saying to a soap manufacturer, "Look here, you'd really do a better job if you systematically studied your product and tried to improve it. You can't really call yourself a soap manufacturer unless you produce good soap, and you can't do that unless you look at what you're turning out and make sure that it is up to par." Such a little speech would seem rather out of place in our consumer-oriented world. Soap makers are looking at their products anyway (not, perhaps, always to make better soap, but at least to make soap more attractive to buyers). No soap maker supposes that, apart from their contribution to his final product, his manufacturing processes have any intrinsic value.

But teachers often have supposed something dangerously like this. They often assume that, apart from their effects on students, their teaching in just the way they habitually do has intrinsic value, and is therefore self-justifying. Instead of achieving attainable improvements through deliberate effort, they thus tend to deny that any improvements are needed or possible so long as they continue to teach as before. When such educational inertia is widespread, as it seemed to many observers to be when our slogan gained currency, the practical purport of the slogan may seem urgent, indeed, revolutionary. To speak, moreover, of teaching as selling and of learning as buying, to suggest that teaching be compared with business methods improvable by reference to effects on the consumer, was to signal strikingly the intent to support reform of teaching.

In part because such reform has become widespread, the practical purport of our slogan appears to many current observers irrelevant or less warranted. Indeed, it has seemed to such observers that the pendulum has in many places swung too far in the direction of orientation to the child's world and preoccupation with the effects of teaching on this world. The schools have, in some respects, been described as too much concerned with their consumers. Teachers, feeling the weight of each student's adjustment and personality conflicts resting on their tired shoulders, have in many instances tried to do too much—to become parents, counselors, and pals as well as teachers. They have, (understandably, given such aspirations coupled with the emphasis on consequences) felt harried and guilty at not being able to do all that their charges require, accepting meanwhile the responsibility for all failures in learning upon themselves.[22]

If someone should want to help the morale of such teachers, he would hardly keep repeating the old message under the new conditions. Rather, he would want to say, "Stop feeling guilty, give up your attempts at omnipotence, stop paying so much attention to the inner problems and motivations of your students. Do your very

22. See Freud, A.: The rôle of the teacher, *Harvard Educational Review*, 22:229, (Fall) 1952, and Riesman, D.: Teachers amid changing expectations, *Harvard Educational Review*, 24:106, (Spring) 1954.

best in teaching your subject and testing your students and when you've done that, relax with an easy conscience." This represents just the practical purport of the statement, "There *can* be teaching without learning." It is this emphasis which seems to many current writers relevant and warranted in the present situation.

Both emphases, however,—that of the present statement and that of its opposite—are abstractly compatible in spite of the fact that they may be unequally relevant or warranted in specific educational contexts. It is, thus, possible to hold (and, indeed, to urge) that teaching ought to be appraised and modified in the light of its effects on learners, and at the same time to believe (and to stress) that there are limits to what the teacher can do, with the best will in the world: whatever he does, he may still fail to achieve the desired learning on the part of his pupils.

In given situations, however, it may be considered more important to maintain the teacher's morale by stressing the limits of his responsibility than to try to improve teaching by stressing the need to examine effects. Whether we say "Try to improve!" or "Don't worry, you've done your best!" is indeed, in this way, a function of the context. But these emphases are not, in general, irreconcilable, nor do they require a flat rejection of the one or the other. They may, in fact, occur together and they may alternate in urgency. To sum up, when slogans are taken literally, they deserve literal criticism. We need, independently however, to evaluate their practical purport in reference to their changing contexts, as well as the parent doctrines from which they have sprung. We must, moreover, avoid assuming that when slogans are in literal contradiction to each other, they represent practical proposals that are in irreconcilable conflict.

Indoctrination and moral responsibility

I 2

I. A. Snook

As has been indicated in the previous sections, there are three main candidates for the criterion of indoctrination. These are intention, method, content, or a combination of two or more of them. Without recounting the various arguments and counter-arguments, it can be said that any attempt to isolate the essence of indoctrination must take account of the following cases.

1. Cases which are clearly indoctrination:

   a. Teaching an ideology as if it were the only possible one with any claim to rationality.
   b. Teaching, as if they are certain, propositions the teacher knows are uncertain.
   c. Teaching propositions which are false and known by the teacher to be false.

2. Cases which may seem like indoctrination, but which are not since they are unavoidable:

   a. Teaching young children correct behavior.
   b. Teaching facts (e.g., the tables) by rote.
   c. Influencing the child unconsciously in certain directions.

3. Problematic cases:

   a. Inculcating doctrines believed by the teacher to be certain, but which are substantially disputed.
   b. Teaching any subject, e.g., chemistry, without due concern for understanding.

If method is taken as the criterion then all cases under 1 are accounted for, since each seems to require some degree of method control. It fails, however, to discriminate in 2a and 2b since a non-rational method is often used, and yet one would not want to call it indoctrination necessarily. Of the problem cases, method rules out some cases only of 3a, those in which this is done without adequate discussion or consideration of alternatives. However, because the teacher believes his doctrines to be certain he may have no fear of considering opposing doctrines since they, in his view, cannot stand the tests of reason as his can. Further, on this criterion it becomes impossible to indoctrinate if the teacher uses discussion or the prob-

Snook, I.A.. *Concepts of Indoctrination: Philosophical Essays*. Boston, Routledge & Kegan Paul, 1972, pp. 152–161. Reproduced by permission.

lem-solving method. The second type of problematic case becomes a clear case of indoctrination. This led the Progressivists to eschew rote-learning. On this criterion, the harassed Latin teacher becomes an indoctrinator along with the political ideologist who is consciously forming the minds of children. Method is an inadequate criterion, since indoctrination loses its bad connotation and there is no further way of distinguishing 'good' indoctrination from 'bad'.

There are two senses in which content is taken by those who would use it as the distinguishing mark. Flew holds that for 'indoctrination' to be an appropriate term, the content must be an ideology or intimately connected to an ideology.[1] This rules out 1b and 1c as indoctrination unless some further condition is fulfilled. Cases under 2 are ruled out reasonably well unless the behavior reinforced is linked to some doctrine. The first type of problematic case becomes a clear case of indoctrination while the second is clearly not. If content is understood merely as beliefs which are either false or not known to be true, cases under 1 are taken care of. If any propositions are appealed to such as 'that makes God sad' or 'that leads to bad effects later', 2a becomes problematic, 3a is indoctrination, and 3b not. However, the notion of content is itself vague. If dealing with uncertain content is indoctrination, the philosopher of religion is indoctrinating as much as the teacher of religion. If one adds 'as if certain', method has been introduced.

If content and method are linked, the case becomes more tenable, but not completely; for it means that no matter how the teacher teaches nor how illiberal his aim, he cannot indoctrinate propositions which are certain. The argument then shifts to what is certainty: an epistemological question of great complexity. There is nothing to distinguish a science teacher deliberately making children rigid in their thinking from a busy teacher who cannot stop to discuss every scientific assumption.

If aim and content are joined, all cases of obvious indoctrination are accounted for, but again, the illiberal scientist is excused along with the harassed teacher. If aim is linked with method, the religious or political indoctrinator is excused provided he adopts a 'democratic' method. To hold that aim, content, and method are required would provide a sufficient condition but not a necessary one; for it rules out the illiberal scientist on grounds of content, and a clever political or religious indoctrinator on grounds of method.

As has been hinted from time to time, I believe that only intention can serve as an adequate criterion for distinguishing indoctrination from education, and attempts to link intention conceptually with another factor such as content or method will destroy the delicate balance. White came close to solving the problem. He defines indoctrination in terms of the intention that 'the child should believe that "p" is true, in such a way that nothing will shake this belief'.[2] Rightly understood, this formulation might be adequate. It is, however, open to misunderstanding.

1. As it reads, it seems to imply that a teacher of mathematics is an indoctrinator. White makes no provision for showing that normally we would not want to say that.

2. White's examples deal with beliefs that are either false (and known by the agent to be false) or doubtful. He makes no allowance for the application of 'indoctrination' to the teaching of knowledge that is certain, nor to the teaching of falsehoods not known by the agent to be false. These two criticisms seem to be in opposition, but it is in the tension between them that one of the main problems of indoctrination lies. For what has to be allowed for is the conceptual possibility of indoctrinating true and certain belief and the unwillingness we feel to brand as an indoctrinator one who teaches anything 'in such a way that nothing will shake this belief'.

I suggest that the following provides a necessary and sufficient condition for indoctrination: *A person indoctrinates P (a proposition or set of propositions) if he teaches with the intention that the pupil or pupils believe P regardless of the evidence.* Before demonstrating that this formula will distinguish education from indoctrination and take care of the doubtful cases in an intellectually satisfying manner, it is necessary to clarify the meaning of two terms contained in it: 'teaches' and 'intention'.

There is an ambiguity about 'teaching' which is important in the analysis of 'indoctrination'. This ambiguity can be best shown by a comparison of the two terms. We can say that a small child teaches his mother that the ancient Greeks worshiped Zeus; we would not say that the child indoctrinated his mother with this belief or any other, regardless of the manner in which the teaching was done. A college student might conceivably teach his professor some proposition the latter had not known; yet we are not inclined to say that the student indoctrinated his professor, no matter what sort of proposition was involved. Secondly, we can say that on Tuesday afternoon at 3:00 P.M. I taught the class the difference between 'uninterested' and 'disinterested'; 'indoctrination' seems to resist such close specification as to time.

These differences arise, I would suggest, from the fact that 'teach' can refer to any intentional handing on of information, but that its other use and indeed its main use is a narrower one. In this sense it implies that the person teaching has a position of some authority over the recipient. This authority may arise from any number of factors of which the following are most common: the agent is older than the pupil; he is possessed of wider general experience; he has some physical control over the pupil (e.g., a gaoler); he is possessed of some official status (e.g., a teacher in a school system); he has some prestige which inclines people to listen to him at least on certain matters (e.g., a doctor or lawyer).

Apart from this authority aspect, 'teach' in this sense suggests activities which are extended over a period of time rather than isolated instances. The noun 'teacher' captures this sense better than the verb: hence, we would not say that the child was his mother's teacher nor the student the professor's teacher simply because each taught something to the other. Of course, 'teacher' is not restricted to its institutional sense and applied only to those who are officially designated teachers in a school or university. They are included, of course, but the meaning is not restricted to them. 'Indoctrination' is related to this narrower sense of 'teaching'. As a task word it implies some degree of authority-control and performance extended over a period of time. In the formula given above, 'teaches' is to be understood in this sense.

'Intention' is a very difficult word to analyze. It is used in many different contexts, each of which has its own problems. As used here it is concerned with moral criticism: only if there is the intention to impart beliefs regardless of the evidence do we apply the term 'indoctrination'. This context helps to specify more closely the meaning of 'intention', or more accurately 'with the intention'. For 'teaching' itself suggests that the activities are intentional. 'Indoctrination' implies, I have argued, that this teaching is carried out with the particular intention that the pupil believe the propositions regardless of the evidence.

In the context of moral responsibility, 'intention' has three possible connotations: (1) What is desired; (2) What is foreseen as likely or inevitable; (3) What is foreseeable. My use is meant to include (1) and (2), but to exclude (3). Thus I argue that a person engaged in teaching can be accused of indoctrination if he:

1. Intends (desires) to indoctrinate.
   Or
2. Intends (desires) his pupils to hold beliefs regardless of the evidence.
   Or
3. Foresees that as a result of his teaching such a result is likely or inevitable (provided, of course, the results are within his control).

Since, in everyday usage, intention is sometimes restricted to what is desired, it is necessary to defend the view taken here.

The issue and its practical implications can be brought out by a consideration of two theories. Hart has pointed out that legal theory makes no distinction between the desired and the foreseen.[3] If a person intends (desires) to escape from prison by blasting the wall and knows that his action will kill a guard, he is guilty of murder of the guard. He killed him intentionally even though he did not desire his death. On the other hand, Roman Catholic moral theology makes a distinction. The best-known example concerns the mother-child issue. If the surgeon directly kills the child to save the mother's life, he is guilty of murder. If, however, he removes a cancer knowing that the child will die in the process, he is not guilty. Jonathan Bennett has argued that such a distinction is quite indefensible: each case is on exactly the same grounds, morally.[4] For the key factor, in the Catholic view, is the intention. If this is regarded as what is foreseen, the death of the child is foreseen equally in both cases; if defined as what is inevitable, death is equally inevitable in each case; if defined as what is desired the death of the child is desired in neither case. Any difference rests on the temporal distance between the events (expressed in terms of cause and effect); time should be morally irrelevant, for if it is not, the fisherman who poisons a reservoir serving a city is less guilty than the man who shoots his wife.

It may be true that if a person is typing and incidentally disturbing a neighbour, it is odd to say that he intends to disturb the neighbour. If asked what he is doing he will say he is typing, and the answer specifies his intention. Nevertheless, when the consequences are such that some harm is caused, and the person knew that the harm would be caused, it can be said that he intentionally caused the harm. True, any action has many consequences, and it is strange to suggest that the agent intended them all. As I write, I am using a typewriter and thereby helping the IBM company to make a profit; it seems odd to say I intend to help IBM or that I intentionally help IBM. However, when one of the consequences is one which is capable of moral appraisal, it is not so strange to speak of intentionally bringing it about. By comparison with the previous example, consider the case of a pacifist who realizes that his support of Company X helps the company to make money and produce more weapons for destruction. It has been the force of my argument that the results of indoctrination are such that they are a matter for moral concern and that to act with the knowledge that they will follow is to act intentionally and so render the agent liable to moral criticism.

It is also necessary to justify the exclusion of the foreseeable from the criteria of indoctrination. If what is foreseeable is often sufficient to ascribe responsibility, by what right do I exclude it here? In an earlier draft I was in fact inclined to include it: a teacher would thus be liable to the charge of indoctrination if it was foreseeable that his methods would lead to beliefs regardless of the evidence. It was pointed out, however, that the result of this was that no matter how liberal the aim of the teacher, nor how unforeseen the consequences, the teacher could be accused of indoctrination if a pupil came to hold beliefs regardless of the evidence and this was in some way foreseeable. It was easy to see that this result is absurd; not so easy to locate the error which led to it. It now seems to me that the reason is as follows. In ordinary circumstances we do hold people responsible for the foreseeable: if someone fires a gun in the city and injures another, the fact that he neither desired nor foresaw this outcome does not excuse. To reasonable men it is foreseeable. However, particular hazards are involved in some undertakings. A soldier on the front line runs the continual risk of killing a comrade rather than an enemy. In such circumstances he may be held responsible if he intended (desired) to do so or foresaw it as likely yet within his control. Apart from these circumstances any such killing might be foreseeable by some bystander, just as in the case of firing the gun in the city. But to hold the soldier liable for all such accidents would be to render him incapable of doing his job: killing the enemy.

Teachers are specifically concerned with ideas, beliefs, facts, propositions: their job is to impart knowledge. It is a hazard of such an occupation that some pupils will hold beliefs regardless of the evidence, and to an outsider such results will often be in some sense foreseeable. To hold the teacher guilty of indoctrination in these cases would stultify his whole work. It would be safer for him to impart no knowledge and so avoid any suspicion of indoctrination.

For this reason I have rejected the foreseeable as a criterion of indoctrination. For the term to be applied, the result (holding beliefs regardless of the evidence) must come from teaching in which this result was desired or clearly foreseen by the teacher.

Some writers on intention have stressed that the agent is *prima facie* the best qualified judge of what he is doing.[5] In ordinary cases this may be so. But it is not true in cases in which a moral criticism is written into the words being applied. 'Indoctrination' is one of a family of such words. Consider, for example: murdering, lying, stealing, wasting time, being unfaithful. In each of these cases the agent *might* apply the term to himself, but this is not typical. 'I killed her', says the broken hearted lover; 'you murdered her', says the police officer. 'I gave my excuse', says the school boy; 'you lied', says the teacher. 'I am resting', says the office girl; 'you are wasting time', says her employer. 'I'm having a fling', says the fickle husband; 'you are being unfaithful', says his frank friend. In each pair, the observer statement is not a contradiction of the agent's statement. Each is a description of sorts, the observer merely adding a moral criticism to the description of the act. It is similar with indoctrination. A person conceivably could claim 'I am indoctrinating him', but normally he would not. Indoctrination must be intentional, then, but the intention need not be one to indoctrinate, in the sense that the person would answer 'indoctrinating' when asked what he was doing. However, he must intend something and normally that would be to teach. This brings out the connection between teaching and indoctrination. It is pointless to talk of indoctrinating unless the agent is doing something which could correctly be described as teaching, (normally teaching *that* rather than teaching *to*). This rules out chance happenings and events over which the agent has no control and limits the application of the term to events we would describe as teaching.

This analysis of indoctrination must now be related to the cases mentioned above. Those cases, it will be recalled, were:

1. Cases which are clearly indoctrination:

a. Teaching an ideology as if it were the only possible one with any claim to rationality.
b. Teaching, as if they are certain, propositions the teacher knows are uncertain.
c. Teaching propositions which are false and known by the teacher to be false.

2. Cases which may seem like indoctrination but which are not since they are necessary to education:

a. Teaching young children correct behavior.
b. Teaching facts (e.g., tables) by rote.
c. Influencing the child unconsciously in certain directions.

3. Problematic cases:

a. Inculcating beliefs believed by the teacher to be certain, but which are substantially disputed.
b. Teaching any subject (e.g., chemistry) without due concern for understanding.

On the criterion outlined above all cases under 1 are covered: the teacher intends fixed beliefs and intends them normally in the strong sense of desiring such beliefs. If he denies such an intention he need only be shown that it is an area of dispute and his method must lead to fixed beliefs; once alerted, he can foresee this outcome. His attitude to one who rejects these beliefs will be instructive too; if he is not intending to fix beliefs he will be pleased, not sorry, when a pupil for solid reasons (even solid reasons which the teacher does not accept) rejects his view. If such rejection is seen as a betrayal of all he has taught, he has been indoctrinating.

Case 2a is excluded if the teacher sincerely desires that the child exercise his critical faculties in disputed areas and provides the best reasons he can when these become acceptable to the child. Since there is little chance of the tables impairing the judgment of the child, 2b is excluded: there is no consequence liable to be reviewed morally and intention does not arise as an issue. Case 2c is ruled out since unconscious acts are not intentional in the first stage, and the consequences cannot therefore be intentional either.

Case 3a is a case of indoctrination provided the teacher knows that the beliefs are substantially disputed. Case 3b might be indoctrination if there were positive intent to make the child incapable of further appraisal of the subject or if irrational methods were so consistently used as to lead to a contempt for the evidence. The charge could always be defeated by showing, first, there was no positive intention, which may be done by showing the absence of any motive for doing this. If the critic can point to a motive (e.g., the theory of chemistry being taught was part of an ideology to which the teacher subscribes), further reference to method may be required to determine intent.[6] Secondly, in the main, rational methods were being used even though they were not in evidence all the time. The same line of defense would be open to the busy teacher drilling verbs or setting material for a test; the overall intention is the key. That is, the person accused can rebut the charge by showing that fixed beliefs were neither desired nor foreseen.

In this way there is provision both for a distinction of content on the grounds of whether fixed beliefs are more or less appropriate, and also for the realization, currently being stressed, that an unduly dogmatic view even of an exact science can warp thought: 'Let [a body of knowledge] be taught in such a way that the student learns what substantive structures gave rise to the chosen body of knowledge, what the strengths and limitations of these structures are, and what some of the alternatives are which give rise to alternative bodies of knowledge.'[7]

The positing of intention as the key to indoctrination has been attacked by Crittenden on the grounds that 'in order to justify our claim about the indoctrinator's intention we would have to shift to a discussion of the general nature of inquiry and the prescriptions it contains for methods of teaching and learning.'[8] Indeed we would, to *justify* our claim, but I am not concerned about how we would in practice make the charge of indoctrination stick but about what is meant by the charge. It is one thing to determine what constitutes murder, another to show that a certain person committed it. I believe that the notion of intention I have outlined is involved in the *concept* of indoctrination in a way that content and method, important as they are, are not.

In another place Crittenden says that in applying the criterion of aims, Hare moves into method.[9] He does, too, but again this is done in *applying* the criterion to cases. It seems to me inevitable that as soon as we try to apply the criterion we will be involved in a discussion of content, method, and what Crittenden calls 'the criteria of the methods of inquiry'. But this is a different matter from the analysis of the concept of indoctrination—it is with this that the various writers have been mainly concerned.

In summarizing, it can be said that 'indoctrination' is a term used to condemn some teaching; it is dependent on the intentional bringing about of undesirable states of mind of a specified sort. An active desire to bring this about is a sufficient condition for its application to a style of teaching even if the agent should fail in his task: 'indoctrination' is both a task and an achievement word. Such a desire is not necessary, however, if it is foreseen that such states of mind are likely as a result of what is being done. Even in the latter case, some action must be intentional in the first sense of desired or willed: a person cannot be accused of indoctrinating if he is not doing anything intentional at all. One cannot indoctrinate simply by omission or default. A person's silence in the face of a child's misbehavior cannot be termed indoctrination simply because it leads the child to think that such behavior is acceptable. Similarly, a parent cannot be accused of indoctrination because he neglects to give some information a child should have. One can be held responsible for such omissions, but 'indoctrination' is not an appropriate term for them.

Intentions, then, are paramount, but method and content are important. For it is from a consideration of method that an observer can often detect the intention to indoctrinate. He can point out the likely results and argue that since method is under the teacher's control such results are intentional. Content is important, for not all content is equally susceptible of indoctrination since not all is equally liable to disproof or doubt. Hence, drill in French verbs is less likely to arouse the charge of indoctrination than drill in patriotic sentiments or catechetical responses. The first is much less likely to result in 'belief regardless of evidence', than the latter two. Ideologies, stressed by Flew, are not essential to the term. Nor are they to be regarded as methods, as White suggested. Indoctrination as a process requires explanation; ideologies often explain by furnishing the motive. They do not excuse but explain the action.

As White showed, other motives are possible, e.g., a bet, a psychological or pedagogical experiment. It is because we can rarely find a motive for indoctrinating mathematics that we tend to exclude such activities from indoctrination. I have argued that the concept can include them, but a motive is needed to explain them.

Notes

1 [Paper 6 in this volume—ed.]
2 White, p. 120. [this volume].
3 This comparison was made by Professor H. L. A. Hart in a lecture at the University of Illinois in 1966.
4 Jonathan Bennett, 'Whatever the Consequences', *Analysis*, 26, January 1966, pp. 83–102.
5 'If intentions identify the actions, the reverse is also true. For example, if someone asks me what I am doing, the *description* I give of my act identifies the *intention*'. T. F. Daveney, 'Intention and Cause', *Analysis*, 27, October 1966, p. 24.
6 An interesting example of these criteria in operation is furnished by a recent case. The administration of Adelphi University hired a sociology professor, knowing that he had strong Marxist sympathies. He was later dismissed when it found that Marx was the only reading prescribed for any of his courses, his examinations covered only polemical questions. and he announced his intention of continuing to teach in this manner. Compare this case with two hypothetical cases: (1) A Marxist professor who gave fair consideration to other theorists. (2) A professor, with no Marxist leanings, who also restricted his readings to Marx. See 'Academic Freedom and Tenure: Adelphi University', *AAUP Bulletin*, 53, September 1967, pp. 278–91.
7 J. J. Schwab, 'Structures of the Disciplines: Meanings and Slogans', in J. M. Rich, ed., *Readings in the Philosophy of Education*, Belmont, Calif.: Wadsworth, 1966, p. 258.
8 Brian S. Crittenden, p. 147 [this volume].
9 *ibid.*, p. 147.

Section IV
Ethnographic Research in Education

Ethnographic Research in Education

Harry F. Wolcott
University of Oregon

Cultural anthropologists conducting ethnographic research describe their activities with a modest phrase: they say they are "doing fieldwork." Several years ago anthropologist Rosalie Wax (1971) took that very phrase, *Doing Fieldwork*, for the title of a fine account of her research experiences and some lessons she wanted to draw for future fieldworkers. It has not always been fashionable among anthropologists to concern themselves with methodological issues per se, but in the past two decades they have become both more self-conscious and more explicit about their research.

In recent years, ethnographic research has also been acknowledged, and to some extent even welcomed, as an alternative research strategy for inquiring into education. It is hard to imagine that ethnography will ever wring educational research from the iron grip of the statistical methodologists, but it is comforting to note the current receptivity among educators to other ways of asking and other ways of looking. Today one often hears educators discussing "ethnography" or the "ethnographic approach." The fact that educators use terms like ethnography and ethnographic approach does not, of course, assure that they have a clear sense of how ethnographers conduct their research or what ethnographic research shares in common with related approaches like participant observation studies, field studies, or case studies.

Let me illustrate how educators use the term without necessarily understanding it. One large-scale, federally funded educational project completed in the 1970s made it possible to employ a number of full-time "on-site" researchers to live in rural communities in order to document change processes in the schools and to study school-community interaction. Not all the researchers involved in the project were anthropologists, but the anthropologists among them—trained observers schooled in ethnographic techniques—were inclined to refer to their research as fieldwork and to describe their efforts as ethnography.

After living somewhat apprehensively under the watchful gaze of his resident 24-hours-a-day, 365-days-a-year ethnographer, the superintendent of schools in one of those rural communities received a preliminary copy of a report that had been prepared by the researcher. The superintendent's subsequent reaction, I'm told, was to note with a sigh of relief, "The stuff's okay. It's just pure anthropology."

In fact, the report he read was essentially history—an overview of the community's founding and early days. But I think it instructive to realize that the superintendent had been in association with a full-time anthropologist/ethnographer for months and months, knew that the project would include a major effort in descriptive research, and still had but the faintest idea of what to expect in the completed account. Something of a mystique does surround fieldwork—for insiders as well as outsiders to the process—and I intend here to explore the basis for that mystique. I will not entirely dispel it, but I want to suggest that the *real* mystique surrounding ethnography, as any experienced ethnographer will attest, is not in doing fieldwork but in subsequently organizing and analyzing the information one gathers and in preparing the account that brings the ethnographic process to a close.

Ethnography as Both Process and Product

Ethnography refers both to the research *process* and to the customary *product* of that effort—the written ethnographic account. Essentially I will limit this discussion to describing the research techniques anthropologists use in doing fieldwork. That is a sufficient task for me as author of a chapter, but it is not sufficient to make an ethnographer out of an interested reader. The necessary next stop is to embark on a program of extended reading in cultural anthropology, giving particular attention to ethnographic accounts and examining how different ethnographers have conceptualized and written about different cultural systems. The references and annotated materials accompanying this chapter include a number of such studies. If possible, one should also enroll in anthropology classes in order not only to learn about the field but to appreciate the range of interests and perspectives extant among anthropologists themselves.

Ethnography means, literally, a picture of the "way of life" of some identifiable group of people. Conceivably, those people could be any culture-bearing group, in any time and place. In times past, the group was usually a small, intact, essentially self-sufficient social unit, and it was always a group notably "strange" to the observer. The anthropologist's purpose as ethnographer was to learn about, record, and ultimately portray the culture of this other group. Anthropologists always study human behavior in terms of cultural context. Particular individuals, customs, institutions, or events are of anthropological interest as they relate to a generalized description of the life-way of a socially interacting group. Yet culture itself is always an abstraction, regardless of whether one is referring to Culture in general or to the culture of a specific social group.

Here, I recognize, would be the proper place to provide a crisp definition of culture, yet I am hesitant to do so. The arguments concerning the definition of culture, what one anthropologist refers to as "this undifferentiated and diffuse variable," continue to comprise a critical part of the ongoing dialog among anthropologists. To what extent, for example, does culture consist of what people *actually* do, what they *say* they do, what they say they *should* do, or to *meanings* they assign to such behavior? Does culture make prisoners of us or free us from a mind-boggling number of daily decisions? Does culture emanate from our minds, our hearts, or our stomachs; from our ancestors, our totems, or our deities? And if someone really devised a culture-free test, could we ever find a culture-free individual to take or to interpret it?

In terms of understanding the ethnographer's task, I draw attention to one relatively recent definition of culture that I have found instructive, a definition proposed by anthropologist Ward Goodenough (1976):

> The culture of any society is made up of the concepts, beliefs, and principles of action and organization that an ethnographer has found could be attributed successfully to the members of that society in the context of his dealings with them. (p. 5).

The appeal of this definition for me lies in Goodenough's notion that the ethnographer "attributes" culture to a society. That idea serves as a reminder of a number of critical points. First, the ultimate test of ethnography resides in the adequacy of its explanation rather than in the power of its method. Second, culture cannot be observed; it can only be inferred. Third, the preoccupation with culture per se, discerning its components and their interrelationships in any particular society in order to make explicit statements about them, is the professional task ethnographers have chosen for themselves.

Without ordinarily having to go so far as to try to make it all explicit or to try to obtain as comprehensive and "holistic" a view as the ethnographer might seek, all human beings are similarly occupied with trying to discern and to act appropriately within the framework of the macro- and micro-cultural systems in which they operate as members of particular societies. We all have to figure out and become competent in numerous microcultural systems and in at least one macro-cultural system (cf. Goodenough, 1976). Everyone, anthropologists included, does it out of necessity; ethnographers also do it as part of their professional commitment. Ordinarily an outsider to the group being studied, the ethnographer tries harder to know more about the cultural system he or she is studying than any individual who is a natural participant in it, at once advantaged by the outsider's broad and analytical perspective but, by reason of that same detachment, unlikely ever totally to comprehend the insider's point of view. The ethnographer walks a fine line. With too much distance and perspective, one is labeled aloof, remote, insensitive, superficial; with too much familiarity, empathy, and identification, one is suspected of having "gone native." Successful ethnographers resolve that tension between involvement and detachment (see Powdermaker, 1966); others go home early.

In my opportunities for ethnographic research—inquiries into the social behavior of particular culture-bearing groups of people—I have most often been in modern, industrial settings and never, anywhere in the world, have I met anyone "primitive." Yet I confess that whenever I conjure up an image of an ideal ethnographer, I always envision him or her pulling a canoe up on a beach and stepping into the center of a small group of huts among lightly clad villagers in an exotic tropical setting. This imagery is not entirely a figment of my imagination, for it was in conducting research among exotic, or at least unfamiliar, peoples that anthropology got its start and anthropologists built their discipline.

Anthropologists have only recently begun to examine how their earlier traditions and experiences in exotic and numerically manageable settings both limit and expand the range of work they might do now and in the future (see, for example, Messerschmidt, 1981).

My old-fashioned image of the ethnographer-at-work evidences still more elements that contribute to a fieldwork mystique and that continue to exert an influence in contemporary settings. The exotic continues to have its appeal, not only for the romantic notions involved but for the fact that one's capabilities for observing, recording, and analyzing what Malinowski (1922/1961) referred to as the "imponderabilia of actual life" are presumed to be enhanced in unfamiliar settings.

I should not pass over that point too quickly. When we talk about ethnographic research in schools, we face the problem of trying to conduct observations *as though* we were in a strange new setting, one with which we actually have been in more or less continuous contact since about the age of six. Anthropologists continue to debate whether cross-cultural experience should be a prerequisite for conducting ethnographically oriented research in schools.

Note that I pictured my ideal ethnographer traveling alone. I might have included a spouse or field assistant, but I definitely do not picture a team of researchers or technical assistants. My image also assumes that the anthropologist is there to stay—to become, for a while, part of the village scenery rather than to remain only long enough to have each villager fill in a questionnaire, submit to a brief interview, or complete a few test items. Tradition even informs the expectation of how long my ideal ethnographer should remain in the field: at least one year. That is not to say that all ethnographic studies are of 12 months' duration; rather, in the absence of other determinants, one is advised to remain at least long enough to see a full cycle of activity, a set of events usually played out in the course of a calendar year.

Note also that my image of ethnographic research is an image of people. The ethnographer is the research instrument, the villagers are the population. That instrument—the anthropologist in person—has been faulted time and time again for being biased, inattentive, ethnocentric, partial, forgetful, overly subject to infection and disease, incapable of attending to everything at once, easily distracted, simultaneously too involved and too detached—the list goes on and on. Be that as it may, what better instrument could we ever devise for observing and understanding human behavior?

If we could actually step into my dream and inquire of my image ethnographer how she or he planned to carry out fieldwork in a newly-arrived-at-setting, it might be disconcerting to hear a somewhat ambiguous response posing a number of possible ideas but suggesting a certain hesitancy about pursuing any one of them to the exclusion of the others. I doubt that an old-fashioned ethnographer would be the least bit embarrassed to confess that after doing some mapping and a village census, she or he wasn't sure just what would be attended to next. Such tentativeness not only allows the ethnographer to move into settings where one cannot frame hypotheses in advance but also reflects the open style that most (not all) ethnographers prefer for initiating fieldwork. That tentativeness is not intended to create a mystique, but to those comfortable only with hypothesis testing, an encounter with someone equally intrigued by discovering instead what the hypotheses *are* can be an unsettling experience. The hardest question for the ethnographer is not so difficult for researchers of other bents: What is it that you look at when you conduct your research? The answer is, of course, "It depends."

What one looks at and writes about depends on the nature of the problem that sends one into the field in the first place; on the personality of the ethnographer; on the course of events during fieldwork; on the process of sorting, analyzing, and writing that transforms the fieldwork experience into the completed account; and on expectations for the final account, including how and where it is to be circulated and what its intended audiences and purposes are. The mystique surrounding ethnography is associated with being in the field because we all harbor romantic ideas of "going off to spend a year with the natives." It is easy to lose sight of the ethnographer's ultimate responsibility to return home and to prepare an account intended to enhance our common human understanding.

Nonetheless, what anthropologists ordinarily do in the course of their fieldwork, regardless of whether their field site is an island in the Pacific Ocean or a classroom in the intermediate wing of the local elementary school, provides us with a way of looking at ethnographic research in action. So let me turn to a point-by-point examination of the customary research techniques of the anthropologist doing fieldwork.

Ethnographic Research Techniques

The most noteworthy thing about ethnographic research techniques is their lack of noteworthiness. No particular research technique is associated exclusively with anthropology. Furthermore, there is no guarantee that one will produce ethnography by using a variety of these techniques. I can make that statement even more emphatically: There is no way one could ever hope to produce an ethnography simply by employing many, or even all, of the research techniques that ethnographers use. Ethnography, as Frederick Erickson (1977) has reminded us, us *not* a reporting process guided by a specific set of techniques. It is an inquiry process carried out by human beings and guided by a point of view that derives from experience in the research setting and from the knowledge of prior anthropological research.

Unlike prevailing tradition in educational research, a preoccupation with method is not sufficient to validate ethnographic research. Ethnographic significance is derived socially, not statistically, from discerning how ordinary people in particular settings make sense of the experience of their everyday lives. As anthropologist Clifford Geertz (1968) has observed, "Anthropological interpretations must be tested against the material they are designed to interpret; it is not their origins that recommend them" (p. vii).

None of the field research techniques that I am about to describe, including ethnography's mainstay, "participant observation," is all that powerful or special. The anthropologist's trade secret, freely disclosed, is that he or she would never for a minute rely solely on a single observation, a single instrument, a single approach. The strength of fieldwork lies in its "triangulation," obtaining information in many ways rather than relying solely on one. Anthropologist Pertti Pelto has described this as the "multi-instrument approach." The anthropologist himself is the research instrument, but in his information gathering he utilizes observations made through an extended period of time, from multiple sources of data, and employing multiple techniques for finding out, for cross-checking, or for ferreting out varying perspectives on complex issues and events. By being on the scene, the anthropologist not only is afforded continual opportunity to ask questions but also has the opportunity to learn which questions to ask.

There is no standard approach even for enumerating the most commonly employed fieldwork practices. The list that I present is adapted from a discussion by authors Pertti and Gretel Pelto in their text *Anthropological Research: The Structure of Inquiry* (1978). My adaptation of the Peltos' list is designed to emphasize two major strategies in fieldwork: participant-observation and interviewing. Many anthropologists summarize fieldwork practice by referring only to those two terms, and some insist that "participant-observation" says it all.

In that sense, participant-observation causes some confusion. Like the term ethnography, it has come to have two meanings. Sometimes it refers to the particular technique of being a participant-observer, one of the important ways anthropologists obtain information. Collectively it can also refer to *all* the techniques that comprise fieldwork, and thus it serves as a synonym for fieldwork itself. Here I use it in the former, more restricted sense—participant-observation as a particular technique.

The review of research techniques that follows is organized into four sections representing four basic research strategies. Each strategy is illustrated by a familiar set of techniques and could be expanded to include still others. The four strategies include the two critical ones already noted—*participant-observation* and *interviewing*—augmented by two others, *use of written sources* and *analysis or collection of nonwritten sources*. Taken together, these four categories are sufficiently inclusive to encompass virtually everything ethnographers do to acquire information.

I should warn that approaching the topic of field techniques this way is better adapted to writing about fieldwork than to doing it. When one is in the field, matters of sequence and sensitivity in using different techniques can be far more important than the choice of them. Problems of "gaining entrée and maintaining rapport," coupled with the absolutely endless task of note writing, account for a good portion of the fieldworker's attention and energy. In the "bush," such everyday concerns as potable water, food purchase and preparation, sanitation, or even a reliable way to receive and send mail, may take precedence over all else. Whatever the contemporary equivalents of those seemingly romantic problems, I call attention here to the techniques themselves, not to how and when one uses them or how information learned through these techniques is subsequently processed. Those facets require one to *think* like an anthropologist, not just to act like one. I have limited this discussion to what fieldworkers do, rather than to how they think about and interpret the information they get. Some important contrasts with more conventional educational research approaches will be apparent in this discussion and will provide the opportunity for summary remarks following the outline of techniques.

Participant-Observation

Participant-observation is such an integral part of fieldwork that some anthropologists might not think to include it in compiling a list of explicit techniques. I know that other anthropologists are appalled when they find colleagues appearing to reify the obvious fact that, as circumstances permit, their research strategy includes their presence among members of a group they are studying. We should be circumspect in describing participant-observation as a formal research technique and recognize ambiguity and contradictions in this seemingly simple solution to pursuing ethnographic research (cf. Martin, 1966/1968). Obviously, we are all participant-observers in virtually everything we do, yet we do not all claim to be ethnographers. We are ethnographic observers when we are attending to the cultural context of the behavior we are engaging in or observing, and when we are looking for those mutually understood sets of expectations and explanations that enable us to interpret what is occurring and what meanings are probably being attributed by others present.

I think it is fair to ask anyone who claims title as a participant-observer to provide a fuller description about how each facet—participant, observer, and the precarious nexus between them—is to be played out in an actual research setting. As it turns out, each facet is intertwined with a host of conditions, many of which are quite beyond the control of the ethnographer. Even if we could assume that every ethnographer was equally capable of getting as involved as he or she wanted, and of always having an exquisite sense of just how involved that should be, there are other constraints on the extent to which one can engage in or observe human social behavior. And schools, like other formal institutions, impose rather strict constraints on how anyone—insider or outsider alike—may participate in them. When outsiders come to school as interested observers, it is pretty hard to distinguish among a social scientist, a professor of education, a parent, or a teacher visiting from another school. Schools offer few role options, but one role that is well structured is observer-visitor. Most studies conducted in schools as "participant-observer" research are really "observer" studies augmented by an occasional chance to talk briefly with students or teachers (Khleif, 1974).

If taking a more active role than "observer" seems warranted in conducting ethnographic research in schools, I should point out that there are costs as well as benefits. In my own initiation to fieldwork (Wolcott, 1967), occupying the role of teacher in a cross-cultural classroom may have made a genuine participant-observer study possible, but it also diverted from my research effort the energy that full-time teaching demands. Richard King (1967, 1974) and Gerry

Rosenfeld (1971) are two other researchers whose ethnographic studies are from the teacher's perspective. More recently, Sylvia Hart (1982) found that by volunteering as a classroom aide she achieved an optimum balance between opportunities to participate and to observe in studying the social organization of one school's reading program. A few anthropologists have attempted to take the role of the student in the classroom (e.g., Burnett, 1969; Spindler & Spindler, 1982). It always amuses me to think of that huge George Spindler, a major contributor to anthropology and education, sitting at his third-grade desk in a German village. But it is worth noting that of the relatively few accounts obtained from the perspective of either the teacher or the student as participant-observer, the researchers who have conducted them represent several disciplinary interests—sociology (e.g., Everhart, 1983; McPherson, 1972), social psychology (e.g., Smith & Geoffrey, 1968), education (e.g., Cusick, 1973)—rather than only anthropology.

For my own purposes I have found it useful to make distinctions among different participant-observer styles to take into account whether the researcher has (and is able to use) the opportunity to be an *active participant,* is (or eventually becomes) a *privileged observer,* or is at best a *limited observer.* Regardless of ethnographic pedigree or prior experience, most fieldworkers in schools are privileged observers, not active participants. In some settings, the ethnographer must be satisfied with the role of limited observer; in such cases, other field techniques assume great importance. (I might note here that I think the role of active participant has been underutilized in educational research. I encourage those pursuing ethnographic approaches to give careful consideration to opportunities for being active participants rather than passive observers. In traditional fieldwork, one really had no choice.)

Interviewing

Interviewing comprises the second major category of fieldwork techniques. Again I point out that the same techniques I mention here in association with ethnography are also used by sociologists, social psychologists, collection agencies, psychiatrists, and the CIA. The only distinction the ethnographer would be sure to draw is between his cherished and respected (and sometimes paid) informant and someone else's subjects or (sometimes paid) informers.

I will briefly introduce seven specific types of interview used by anthropologists: key-informant interview, life history interview, structured or formal interview, informal interview, questionnaire, projective techniques, and—primarily because we are considering school-related research—standardized tests and related measurement techniques.

One should recognize, of course, that I use the category "Interviewing" in a very broad sense. How else can I consider the collecting of life history data, conducting a structured interview, and administering an IQ test to be a common set of activities? I include as an interview activity anything that the fieldworker does that intrudes upon the natural setting and is done with the conscious intent of obtaining particular information directly from one's subjects.

In the participant-observer role, ethnographers let the field setting parade before them. In the interviewer role, ethnographers take a critical step in research that can never be reversed—they ask. And regardless of whether they ask you the sum of nine plus eight, what you "see" in a set of printed cards or drawings, or to tell your life story, they have imposed some structure upon the setting. In that sense, ethnographers are like other field researchers. But they are also different, in at least two ways. First, they are less likely to put too much faith in any one instrument, set of answers, or techniques. And second, they are more likely to be concerned with the suitability of the technique in a *particular* setting than with the standardization of the technique across different populations. Ethnographers are more likely to prepare a questionnaire after coming to know a setting well rather than beginning a study by using a questionnaire already constructed (or mailing it in lieu of ever visiting at all). Or, given some highly standardized instrument like an intelligence test, they might even try "destandardizing" it, as Richard King (1967) did with Indian pupils in the Yukon Territory when he set out to see whether his pupils couldn't literally get smarter every week through practice and instruction in how to take standardized tests.

The idea of *key-informant interviewing,* the most purely "anthropological" of any of the techniques under discussion here, flies quite in the face of a prevailing notion in education research that truth resides only in large numbers. Anthropologists are so fond of their special term "informant" that they are inclined to refer to all their subjects that way. But informant has a special meaning—it refers to an individual in whom one invests a disproportionate amount of time because that individual appears to be particularly well informed, articulate, approachable, or available. For the anthropological linguist, one key informant is as large a sample as one needs to work out the basic grammar of an unknown language. Ethnographers do not usually rely that heavily on a single informant, but unwittingly or not, I suspect that most fieldworkers rely on a few individuals to a far greater extent than their accounts imply. Inscriptions in completed ethnographies attest to the contribution informants have made to the doing of ethnography (see also Casagrande, 1960).

Researchers using ethnographic techniques in schools have not made extended use of key informants in studies of contemporary education. My hunch is that most of us feel so well versed about what goes on in schools that we become our own key informant in school research. I refer to this approach as "ethnography-minus-one" (Wolcott, 1984). The phrase ethnography-minus-one serves notice that in school-related studies it is often the researcher who is telling us what everything means (and perhaps even how things *should be*) rather than allowing those in the setting to give *their* vision of *their* world (cf. Malinowski, 1961). This is another of the problems we face in doing descriptive research in settings already familiar, where our subjects are *us* rather than *them.*

The *life history* or biographical approach, while not uniquely anthropological, is uniquely suited to anthropology because it helps to convey how the social context that is of such importance to the ethnographer gets played out in the lives of specific individuals. Life history also helps anthropologists get a feeling for how things were before they arrived on the scene and for how people view or choose to portray their own lives (see, for example, Langness & Frank, 1981). Given pervasive anthropological interests in how things change and how they stay the same, attention to life history adds a critical historical dimension to the ethnographic account at the same time that it provides focus on somebody rather than on everybody.

As I have come to understand the extent to which personal ambitions of educators exert a driving force in American education, I have been thinking about the possibility of adapting a life history approach to help us learn more about the impact of personal careers on the dynamics of public education. Alternatively, looking at the "life history" of educational innovations, projects, fads, or movements provides an opportunity for discerning pervasive "patterns" in educator behavior (see, for example, Wolcott, 1977).

I contrast *structured formal interviews* with *informal interviews,* the next two techniques I wish to introduce, in order to emphasize that being in the field provides the ethnographer with almost unlimited opportunity to talk informally with subjects. Informal interviewing—that is, interviewing that does not make use of a fixed sequence of predetermined questions—is possible because the ethnographer is the research instrument. Ranging as it does from casual conversation to direct questioning, informal interviewing usually proves more important than structured interviewing in an extended study (see also Agar, 1980). It is my impression that being on the scene also facilitates getting information from people reluctant to provide a structured interview but willing to talk casually to a neutral but interested listener. I have found that people often will grant a lengthy face-to-face interview although they may insist they are too busy to fill out a questionnaire.

I include *questionnaires* to point out that "relatively systematic" procedures popular among some researchers may also be used by ethnographers, particularly when they are working in settings with sophisticated, literate, and busy people from whom some base-line census data might be helpful, warranted, and perhaps all one can hope to get. But I have seen anthropologists register surprise when colleagues claim that mass survey techniques comprise part of their customary field procedures. I think that most anthropologists would feel obliged to explain why they employed such techniques in a particular setting, just as researchers of other orientations might feel an obligation to explain why they did not use them on a particular occasion. In collecting census data or genealogical data, or in following the formal eliciting techniques of the so-called "new" ethnography or "ethnoscience" approaches, ethnographers follow procedures that are entirely systematic—but they utilize them because they deem them appropriate for understanding the case at hand rather than to sprinkle their findings with ritual doses of scientific legitimacy.

It is important to remember that, unlike most research reported by educators or psychologists, the ethnographer never intends to base a study on the findings of only one technique, one instrument, or one brief encounter. Take a look at the appendices anthropologists include with their studies. They do not ordinarily provide copies of questionnaires or interview schedules; instead, they provide additional information about their subjects: maps; household composition; glossaries; descriptions of ceremonies, songs, chants, magic; maybe a report about the fieldwork experience; but not a copy of a mailed questionnaire form and the accompanying cover letter.

I have included *projective techniques* in this listing more to record an era in fieldwork than to describe customary practice, particularly if the topic brings to mind such standbys as the use of Rorschach Ink Blot cards or pictures from the Thematic Apperception Test. Ever in search of a unifying theory of humankind, anthropologists were intrigued by the psychoanalytic interpretations of the Freudians; in the 1930s and 1940s it was common for anthropologists not only to use projective tests and to cast their observations in psychoanalytic terminology but also to undergo psychoanalysis before venturing into the field. Those interests permeate much of the ethnography recorded in that period. Not many ethnographers today could produce a set of Rorschach cards, although anthropologists continue to share interests with psychologists and psychiatrists. However, given the diversity that the fieldworker confronts, there is obvious appeal in using any technique that can be administered to everyone alike. George and Louise Spindler continue to report success with their Instrumental Activities Inventory, a set of culture-specific drawings used to elicit comments from young respondents about the kind of activities in which they expect to engage, ranging in choice from traditional/rural to modern/urban (Spindler & Spindler, 1965, 1982).

The final type of interview activity I include here, *standardized tests and other measurement techniques,* serves as a reminder that any fieldworker may use virtually any kind of test as a way of eliciting information. For all the obvious attractions of obtaining quantifiable data so well known to educational researchers, however, I should point out that fieldworkers are often reluctant to use such materials themselves and may object vigorously to being required to administer tests or questionnaires selected or devised by others in connection with a large-scale research project. As educators, we are inclined to forget how intrusive test-taking can be and how different it is to test *in* school, where evaluation is a way of life, and to test in populations *out* of school. Anyone who has listened to an adult describe the trauma associated with having to take a driving test (or even the written examination required to obtain a driver's license) after years of not taking tests is reminded how tests can frighten and alienate.

I have not forgotten the experience of a colleague who wished to obtain some test-like data early in the course of his first fieldwork. He began by making a house-to-house census in the village where he was conducting research. While collecting that information, he also decided to explore the sociometrics of villager interaction and their perceptions of personal power and influence. Because he was residing in the village, was accepted by the villagers, and had requested their cooperation through both formal and informal channels, they dutifully answered his questions about private and personal judgements. But, once having complied, for the next three months no one volunteered further information on *any* topic. Only slowly did he regain the rapport he once had and then lost. Questioning can be rude work. Ethnography is not intended to be rude business. Persistent, maybe, but not rude.

Use of Written Resources

In order to emphasize the importance of historical documents and public records in ethnographic research, I use the term *archives* to refer specifically to one type of written sources and use a broad catch-all term, *other written documents,* to include everything else. The importance of archival materials in ethnographic research may reflect the close link between colonial administrations and the early development of both British and American anthropology. In any case, it is important to note that anthropologists use all kinds of written records; they do not limit themselves to what is available in libraries.

Like historians, ethnographers find primary documents of all sorts—letters and diaries, for example—of great value. In working with populations that include school-age children, ethnographers have sometimes sponsored essay contests to encourage young people to write of their experiences (e.g., Kileff & Kileff, 1970). I have already mentioned fieldwork of my own in which I found that assuming the duties of village teacher seemed to hamper my opportunity for interaction. I was so busy keeping school that I often had little idea of what was going on in the village. Eventually, I discovered that the problem had a compensating side. My customary classroom practice of having students write in class every day was providing not only a daily account of village events but the extra bonus of the students' own views of those events as given in the seclusion of written rather than spoken comments. Furthermore, the youngsters chronicling the events were at an age when they moved easily throughout the village, more easily than I could and far more easily than did their circumspect elders. My only hesitancy in relating this episode is that it took me so long to realize how valuable my students' written accounts were in my efforts to learn about village life.

Analysis or Collection of Nonwritten Sources

Far too many "data-gathering" procedures are designed with an overriding concern for getting data that are manageable, codable, punchable. To date, ethnographers seem impressed by what computers can do but they are not so intimidated that they have begun to think like them. They still collect their information in a variety of forms, rather than with an eye to the degrees of freedom afforded by a punchcard or computer program. Perhaps that is why some anthropologists have an expressed preference for the term "fieldwork" rather than for the phrase "data gathering."

It is hard to envision a scene in which colleagues eagerly assemble to see what a quantitatively oriented researcher has brought back to the office after an intense interlude of data gathering. It is hard to imagine an ethnographer who would not have collected pictures, maps, or examples of local handiwork, even if the field site was a nearby classroom. The wall adornments of anthropologists' offices and homes display the results of compulsive collecting. But the use of nonwritten sources is primarily for examination and illustration, not ornamentation, and the linguist with his tapes, or the ethnographer with his photographs, films, or artifacts, finds such primary materials invaluable in analysis and write-up, as well as in later testing the adequacy of his developing descriptions and explanations.

I trust I have provided sufficient examples of this fourth and last major category, nonwritten sources, to make the case for the importance of *maps, photographs and film, artifacts,* and *video and audio tapes,* in pursuing ethnographic research. These are virtually indispensable aids in all fieldwork. The use of photography, particularly in ethnographic filmmaking, has received special attention (J. Collier & M. Collier, 1986; Heider, 1976) and has been applied effectively in classroom research, particularly for examining nonverbal communication (J. Collier, 1973; M. Collier, 1979; Erickson & Wilson, 1982).

The subject of mapping brings me full circle to participant-observation, for one of the first things the ethnographer is advised to do in a new field setting is to make a map. Just think how interesting it would be to teachers, and how natural an activity for an ethnographer, to prepare a map of a school and schoolground, to plot how different categories of people at the school move through its space, and to probe reasons they might offer to explain how things happen to be used or placed as they are. Is that the principal's car or a handicapped employee's car in the specially marked parking space? Why is the nurse's office so near the front office? Do nurses usually have offices? If the principal is the instructional leader of the school, why is the Instructional Materials Center so far from his or her office? How do new students learn about "territory" in the school? Under what circumstances can certain territory be invaded? You see how quickly one thing can lead to another—and how a knowledge of the setting and the people in it helps one get a sense of which questions to ask, of whom, when, and in what manner.

Preparing the Written Account

As I have noted, for me the real mystique of ethnography is in the process of transforming the field experience into a completed account. Rosalie Wax (1971) wisely counsels would-be ethnographers to allow at least as much time for analyzing and writing as one plans to spend in the field. I can only underscore that time for analyzing and writing should be reckoned in equivalents of "uninterrupted days." Fair warning is hereby given that the time commitment is great in terms of customary expectations for research in education. My own fieldwork-based doctoral dissertation added two years to my graduate program in education and anthropology—one full year in research, a second full year to write it up.

It is in the write-up, rather than in the fieldwork, that the materials become ethnographic. What human beings do and say is not psychological, sociological, anthropological, or what have you. Those disciplinary dimensions come from the structures we impose on what we see and understand. It is in the ethnographer's pulling together of the whole fieldwork experience, an activity informed by the observations and writings of other anthropologists, that the material takes ethnographic shape as both description of what is going on among a particular social group and a cultural interpretation of how that behavior "makes sense" to those involved (see Wolcott, 1985). As the term ethnography has caught on in educational research, I think astute observers who have produced excellent descriptive accounts have frequently been tempted to tack on the label ethnography as though it were synonymous with observation itself (see Wolcott, 1980). Let me emphasize again that one might utilize all the field research techniques I have described and not come up with ethnography, while an anthropologist might possibly employ none of the customary field research techniques and still produce an ethnographic account (or at least a satisfactory ethnographic reconstruction).

I should also note that not every cultural anthropologist cares that much about producing ethnography. Some are more theoretically or philosophically inclined. These days some have become interested in method, the analysis of other people's data, or computer solutions to classic anthropological problems. The more action-oriented look for ways to make better use of the huge corpus of data already available. One journal in the field of cultural anthropology (*American Ethnologist*) went so far as specifically to exclude descriptive ethnographic studies from its purview during its first 5 years of publication. Nevertheless, descriptive ethnographic accounts are the building blocks of the discipline of cultural anthropology, just as fieldwork itself is the *sine qua non* of the cultural anthropologist.

Only recently—since about the mid 1960s—have anthropologists given much explicit attention to their research approach. Even less attention has been directed to the difficult business of organizing and writing, other than to repeat well-worn maxims that fieldwork amounts to naught if the notes are not transformed into an ethnographic account, to advise neophyte fieldworkers to begin writing early (preferably to complete a first draft while still in the field), and to acknowledge, more with awe than with instruction, when an occasional ethnographer seems to have made a literary as well as a scholarly contribution. Critical attention to ethnographies as texts has only begun (Marcus & Cushman, 1982; Marcus & Fischer, 1986).

For the beginning writer of a descriptive account, I can offer a few suggestions that have proven useful in my own work and in guiding the work of others. First, I suggest that every effort be made to couple the writing task to ongoing fieldwork. It is splendid indeed if one is able to follow the advice to prepare a first draft while fieldwork is still in progress. In attempting to set down in writing what you understand, you become most acutely aware of what you do *not* understand and can recognize "gaps" in the data while time remains to make further inquiry. But lacking the time, practice, or perspective required for drafting a full account, one can nonetheless begin to "think" in chapters, sections, or expanded outlines, and thus keep tuned to the difficult task sometimes dismissed as simply "writing up one's notes."

Wherever and whenever the task of writing begins, a second bit of advice is to begin at a relatively "easy" place where you are well informed and know (or should know!) what you are talking about. One good starting point is to describe your fieldwork: where you went and what you did. That material may subsequently become part of your first chapter, or an appendix, or a separate, publishable paper. Another good starting point is to begin with the descriptive portion of the account, resisting any temptation to begin making inferences or interpretation but simply telling the story of what happened. Not only will this help to satisfy the anthropological preference for providing a high ratio of information to explanation (Smith, 1964), but it also invites your reader into the interpretive act because he or she shares access to your primary sources. Description and interpretation need not be so dramatically separated in the final account (i.e., treated as separate chapters), but I think it a valuable exercise for someone new to descriptive writing to begin by preparing an "objective" account as free as possible from one's own inferences and preferences.

My next bit of advice might seem to have come from a short course on writing, but I came upon it in the instructions for assembling a wheelbarrow: Make sure all parts are correctly in place before tightening. There is a certain fluidity in developing an ethnographic account. Problem and interpretation remain in flux and in turn influence decisions about what must be included or may be deleted from the descriptive narrative. In that sense, ethnographic accounts can be *finished* but they are never really *completed*.

Finally, let me offer the advice here that I frequently give to my students and colleagues: I would not be inclined to use the term "ethnography" in my title or to lay claim to be providing ethnography in my written account unless I was quite certain that I wanted and needed to make that claim. That point goes beyond merely finding an appropriate title, and I will turn to it in concluding this discussion.

"Doing Ethnography" Versus "Borrowing Ethnographic Techniques"

Armed with a list of fieldwork techniques such as those reviewed above, and duly cautioned about the critical complementary tasks involved in the subsequent write-up, is a neophyte researcher ready to start "doing" ethnography? I think not. Let me repeat reservations noted earlier and then attempt to provide a perspective on ethnographic research.

First, none of these fieldwork techniques is exclusive to anthropology, so no single one, including participant-observation, guarantees that the results will be ethnographic.

Second, although one can be reasonably certain that the anthropologist will use several techniques, there is no magic formula. Anthropologists conduct their studies of human social behavior by watching and by asking. When you stop to think about it, most of us have been doing those two things, and for basically the same reasons—to acquire cultural knowledge—since we first were able to watch and, subsequently, to ask. Our continued practice in that regard is scant basis for thinking that we will suddenly start producing ethnography instead of merely continuing to act appropriately. At the same time, here is a gentle reminder to all researchers. In learning to become functioning human beings, we ourselves have relied on numerous sources, numerous techniques, and ample time for attending to multiple significant facets in our lives, not just to a few that were easy to understand or that satisfied rigorous statistical tests.

I think a certain reserve is warranted in educational research when we claim to be "doing ethnography" yet restrict our research arena solely to schools. The anthropologist conducting research in educational settings would expect to attend to a broad cultural context, but educational researchers do not ordinarily attempt to produce ethnographies or even "micro-ethnographies" per se. Rather than make the claim that they are doing ethnography, when that is neither what they are doing nor what they intend to do, I think educational researchers are well advised to display some modesty in noting in their research how they may at times avail themselves of several techniques for getting their information, how their approach may have been influenced by the characteristic long-term thoroughness of the fieldworker, or how their perspective or analysis may have been informed at least in part by relevant prior work in anthropology. I think it useful to distinguish between anthropologically informed researchers who *do ethnography* and educational researchers who frequently *draw upon ethnographic approaches* in doing descriptive studies.

It is not the techniques employed that make a study ethnographic, but neither is it necessarily what one looks at; the critical element is in interpreting what one has seen. In research among pupils in classrooms and in other learning environments—work generated out of ethnographic interests—a few ethnographically oriented researchers have been looking at smaller units of behavior, such as classroom teaching and learning styles, or at the classroom "participant structures" through which teachers arrange opportunities for verbal interaction (Philips, 1972). They are developing an ever-increasing capacity for examining fine detail—for example, in repeated viewings of filmed or videotaped segments of classroom behavior. But they are also embedding their analysis in cultural context. (See Wolcott, 1982, for a discussion of "styles" of descriptive research.)

We know we do not need to describe everything. We seek to identify those dimensions critical to our understanding of human social behavior and then to describe them exceedingly well. With his pithy phrase, "It is not necessary to know everything in order to understand something," anthropologist Geertz (1973, p. 20) reminds us that we may make headway through modest increments.

I am distressed when I hear educators lament that we have made no progress toward providing *an* ethnography of schooling, but I am also concerned when I hear others imply that we will someday complete *the* ethnography of schooling. The task of description, and thus the potential for ethnography, is endless. We need to look for those purposes in education to which ethnographic research seems best suited, an issue that continues to excite much discussion in the field of anthropology and education.

I think ethnography is well suited to answering the question, "What is going on here?" That is, anthropologically, a question of behaviors and, especially, a question of meanings. Such inquiry proceeds best under conditions where there will be time to find out, and where there is reason to believe that knowing "what-things-mean-to-those-involved" could conceivably make a difference. It also requires some understanding of how one particular instance, or event, or case, or individual, described in careful detail, is not only unique but also shares characteristics in common with other instances or events or cases or individuals. The ethnographer looks for the generic in the specific, following a "natural history" approach that seeks to understand classes of events through the careful examination of specific ones. Geertz (1973) reminds us that there is no ascent to truth without a descent to cases.

The ethnographer, like other social scientists, is concerned with the issue of "representativeness" but approaches that problem differently, by seeking to locate the particular case under study among other cases. The question, as Margaret Mead once noted, is not "Is this case representative?" but rather, "What is this case representative of?" You conduct your research where you can, with whatever available key informant or classroom or family or village best satisfies your research criteria, and then you undertake to learn how that one is similar to, and different from, others of its type.

The ethnographer's concern is always for context. One's focus moves constantly between figure and ground—like a zoom lens on a camera—to catch the fine detail of what individuals are doing and to keep a perspective on the context of that behavior. To illustrate: An ethnographer assisting in educational program evaluation ought to be looking not only at the program under review but at the underlying ethos of evaluation as well. What meaning does evaluation have for different groups or individuals? How do certain people become evaluators of others? Who, in turn, evaluates them? Or, in studying cases of conscious efforts to introduce educational change, ethnographers ought to be looking at the "donors" of change as well as at the recipients or targets of it. Frederick Erickson has posed a question that guides much current ethnographic research in classrooms: What do teachers and children have to know in order to do what they are doing?

The Role of Ethnographic Research in Education

Will ethnographic research become a potent force in shaping the course of formal education? I would like to tell you that it will, since it is the kind of research that most interests me. But I am pessimistic. I don't believe that educational research of any type has yet had great impact on educational practice, and descriptive research portraying how things really are does not seem to capture the imagination of those impatient to make them different.

In and of themselves, ethnographic accounts do not point the way to policy decisions; they do not give clues as to what should be done differently, nor do they suggest how best to proceed. Ethnographic attention tends to focus on how things are and how they got that way, while educators are preoccupied with what education can become. Educators tend to be action-oriented, but ethnography does not point out the lessons to be gained or the action that should be taken. Worse still, anyone who takes the time to read a descriptive account will probably realize that the complexity of the setting or problem at hand has been increased rather than decreased.

We have not yet found or created a strong constituency of informed consumers who have realistic expectations about ethnographic research in education. Perhaps that is where you can help. Let me conclude with three recommendations for how you might simultaneously benefit from and participate in furthering the use of ethnographic approaches in educational research.

First, expand your reading in professional education to include descriptive studies. Like the linguist who can amaze you by explicating rules of your own language that you never knew you knew, ethnographers' accounts of education should have a ring of authenticity to you as a native member of the group being described. And they ought to help you better understand the central process in which you are engaged both professionally and personally: human learning. If they do not, speak out regarding how, in your perception, observers are missing the point about what is going on or what teachers are trying to accomplish. It is not too unlikely that even in trying to explicate the difference between what observers see and what teachers try to do, you will begin to understand the important and useful distinction between what we do and what we say we do, between culture "on the ground" and culture as a system of mutual expectations about what ought to be.

Second, become familiar with the variety of field techniques described here and watch for instances where a multi-instrument approach would be preferable to relying on only one source of information. You might even watch yourself in action as teacher or administrator and ask whether, in your own professional circumstances, you tend to place too much reliance on too few ways of finding out. It is a ready trap for practitioner and researcher alike.

Third, take a cue from the ethnographer and develop a keener appreciation for context in educational research. Whether reading the research reports of others or trying to understand a setting in which you yourself are a participant, keep probing for more, rather than fewer, factors that may be involved. Researchers have a tendency (and, realistically, an obligation) to oversimplify, to make things manageable, to reduce the complexity of the events they seek to explain. Ethnographers are not entirely free from this tendency; if they were, they would not set out to reduce accounts of human social behavior to a certain number of printed pages or a reel of film. But they remain constantly aware of complexity and context. There are no such things as unwanted findings or irrelevant circumstances in ethnographic research. I wonder if it is the characteristic researcher inattention to broader contexts that makes educational research appear so irrelevant to its practitioners. If so, the ethnographic concern for context may be the most important contribution this approach can make.

References

Agar, M. H. (1980). *The professional stranger: An informal introduction to ethnography.* New York: Academic Press.

Burnett, J. H. (1969). Ceremony, rites, and economy in the student system of an American high school. *Human Organization, 28*(1), 1–9.

Casagrande, J. B. (1960). *In the company of man.* New York: Harper and Brothers.

Collier, J., Jr. (1973). *Alaskan Eskimo education: A film analysis of cultural confrontation in the schools.* New York: Holt, Rinehart and Winston.

Collier, J., Jr., & Collier, M. (1986). *Visual anthropology: Photography as a research method.* Albuquerque: University of New Mexico Press.

Collier, M. (1979). *A film study of classrooms in western Alaska.* Fairbanks, AK: Center for Cross-Cultural Studies.

Cusick, P. A. (1973). *Inside high school: The student's world.* New York: Holt, Rinehart and Winston.

Erickson, F. (1977). Some approaches to inquiry in school-community ethnography. *Anthropology and Education Quarterly, 8*(2), 58–69.

Erickson, F., & Wilson, J. (1982). *Sights and sounds of life in schools: A resource guide to film and videotape for research and education* (Research Series No. 125). East Lansing: Michigan State University Institute for Research on Teaching.

Everhart, R. B. (1983). *Reading, writing and resistance: Adolescence and labor in a junior high school.* Boston: Routeledge and Kegan Paul.

Geertz, C. (1968). *Islam observed.* Chicago: University of Chicago Press.

Geertz, C. (1973). Thick description. In C. Geertz, *The interpretation of cultures.* New York: Basic Books.

Goodenough, W. H. (1976). Multiculturalism as the normal human experience. *Anthropology and Education Quarterly, 7*(4), 4–7.

Hart, S. (1982). Analyzing the social organization for reading in one elementary school. In G. Spindler (Ed.), *Doing the ethnography of schooling: Educational anthropology in action.* New York: Holt, Rinehart and Winston.

Heider, K. G. (1976). *Ethnographic film.* Austin, Texas: University of Texas Press.

Khleif, B. B. (1974). Issues in anthropological fieldwork in schools. In G. D. Spindler (Ed.), *Education and cultural process.* New York: Holt, Rinehart and Winston.

Kileff, C., & Kileff, P. (Eds.). (1970). *Shona customs: Essays by African writers.* Gwelo, Rhodesia (Zimbabwe): Mambo Press.

King, A. R. (1967). *The school at Mopass: A problem of identity.* New York: Holt, Rinehart and Winston.

King, A. R. (1974). The teacher as a participant-observer: A case study. In G. D. Spindler (Ed.), *Education and cultural process: Toward an anthropology of education.* New York: Holt, Rinehart and Winston.

Langness, L. L., & Frank, G. (1981). *Lives: An anthropological approach to biography.* Novato, CA: Chandler and Sharp Publishers.

Malinowski, B. (1961). *Argonauts of the western Pacific.* New York: E. P. Dutton and Co. (Original work published 1922)

Marcus, G. E., & Cushman, D. (1982). Ethnographies as texts. *Annual Review of Anthropology, 11*, 25–69.

Marcus, G. E., & Fischer, M. (1986). *Anthropology as cultural critique.* Chicago: University of Chicago Press.

Martin, M. (1966/1968). Understanding and participant observation in cultural and social anthropology. *Boston studies in the philosophy of science, IV,* 303–330.

McPherson, G. H. (1972). *Small town teacher.* Cambridge, MA: Harvard University Press.

Messerschmidt, D. A. (Ed). (1981). *Anthropologists at home in North America: Methods and issues in the study of one's own society.* New York: Cambridge University Press.

Pelto, P. J., & Pelto, G. H. (1978). *Anthropological research: The structure of inquiry* (2d ed.). New York: Cambridge University Press.

Philips, S. U. (1972). Participant structures and communicative competence: Warm Springs children in community and classroom. In C. Cazden, V. P. John, & D. Hymes (Eds.), *Functions of language in the classroom*. New York: Teachers College Press. (Reprinted 1985 by Waveland Press)

Powdermaker, H. (1966). *Stranger and friend: The way of an anthropologist*. New York: W. W. Norton.

Rosenfeld, G. (1971). *"Shut those thick lips!": A study of slum school failure*. New York: Holt, Rinehart and Winston.

Smith, A. G. (1964). The Dionysian innovation. *American Anthropologist, 66*, 251–265.

Smith, L. M., & Geoffrey, W. (1968). *The complexities of an urban classroom*. New York: Holt, Rinehart and Winston.

Spindler, G. D., & Spindler, L. (1965). The Instrumental Activities Inventory: A technique for the study of the psychology of acculturation. *Southwestern Journal of Anthropology, 21*, 1–23

Spindler, G. D., & Spindler, L. (1982). Roger Harker and Schonhausen: From the familiar to the strange and back again. In G. Spindler (Ed.), *Doing the ethnography of schooling: Educational anthropology in action*. New York: Holt, Rinehart and Winston.

Wax, R. H. (1971). *Doing fieldwork: Warnings and advice*. Chicago: University of Chicago Press.

Wolcott, H. F. (1967). *A Kwakiutl village and school*. New York: Holt, Rinehart and Winston. (Reprinted 1984 by Waveland Press)

Wolcott, H. F. (1977). *Teachers versus technocrats: An educational innovation in anthropological perspective*. Eugene, OR: Center for Educational Policy and Management, University of Oregon.

Wolcott, H. F. (1980). How to look like an anthropologist without being one. *Practicing Anthropology, 3*(1), 6–7, 56–59.

Wolcott, H. F. (1982). Differing styles of on-site research, or, "If it isn't ethnography, what is it?" *Review Journal of Philosophy and Social Science, 7*(1,2), 154–169.

Wolcott, H. F. (1984). Ethnographers sans ethnography: The evaluation compromise. In D. M. Fetterman (Ed.), *Ethnography in educational evaluation*. Beverly Hills, CA: Sage Publications.

Wolcott, H. F. (1985). On ethnographic intent. *Educational Administration Quarterly, 21*(3), 187–203. (Republished in G. & L. Spindler, Eds., *Interpretive ethnography of education: At home and abroad*. Hillsdale, NJ: Lawrence Erlbaum Associates, 1987, pp. 37–57.)

Suggestions for Further Reading

Just as the ethnographer attends both to what people do and to what people say they do, a student can learn about ethnographic research both by reading the accounts produced by ethnographers and by reading what ethnographers say they do or how they advise others to go about their research. The references suggested here for further study distinguish between ethnography dealing specifically with education and ethnography in more traditional settings.

Ethnographic Studies of Formal Educational Settings: Bibliographies, Edited Collections, and Series

Burnett, J. H. (1974). *Anthropology and education: An annotated bibliographic guide*. New Haven, CT: Human Relations Area Files Press.

Roberts, J. I., & Akinsanya, S. K. (Eds.). (1976). *Schooling in the cultural context: Anthropological studies of education*. New York: David McKay Company.

Rosenstiel, A. (1977). *Education and anthropology: An annotated bibliography*. New York: Garland Publishing Company.

Spindler, G. D., & Spindler, L. (Eds.). *Case studies in education and culture*. New York: Holt, Rinehart and Winston.   This series contains 16 titles, each published as a separate monograph. Although no longer in print, the studies are widely available in libraries, and several have been reissued by Waveland Press, P.O. Box 400, Prospect Heights, IL 60070. The following titles may be of particular interest:

Collier, J., Jr. (1973). *Alaska Eskimo education*.

Hostetler, J., & Huntington, G. (1971). *Children in Amish society*.

Jocano, F. L. (1969). *Growing up in a Philippine barrio*.

King, A. R. (1967). *The school at Mopass*.

Rosenfeld, G. (1971). *"Shut those thick lips!": A study of slum school failure*. (Reissued by Waveland Press, 1983.)

Singleton, J. (1967). *Nichu: A Japanese school*. (Reissued 1982 by Irvington Publishers, 551 5th Avenue, New York, NY 10176)

Warren, R. L. (1967). *Education in Rebhausen*.

Wolcott, H. F. (1967). *A Kwakiutl village and school*. (Reissued by Waveland Press, 1984)

Wolcott, H. F. (1973). *The man in the principal's office: An ethnography*. (Reissued by Waveland Press, 1984, with update)

Spindler, G. D. (Ed.). (1982). *Doing the ethnography of schooling: Educational anthropology in action*. New York: Holt, Rinehart and Winston.

Spindler, G. D. (Ed.). (1987). *Education and cultural process: Anthropological approaches*. Prospect Heights, IL: Waveland Press.

Spindler, G., & Spindler, L. (1987). *Interpretive ethnography of education: At home and abroad*. Hillsdale, NJ: Lawrence Erlbaum Associates.

Statements About Using an Ethnographic Approach in Educational Research

Bogdan, R. C., & Biklen, S. K. (1982). *Qualitative research for education: An introduction to theory and methods.* Boston: Allyn and Bacon.

Cassell, J. (1978). *A fieldwork manual for studying desegregated schools.* Washington, D.C., National Institute of Education.   This manual, with its valuable bibliography compiled by Murray Wax, is useful to anyone interested in ethnography in education, not just to those inquiring into desegregated schools.

Erickson, F. (1977). Some approaches to inquiry in school-community ethnography. *Anthropology and Education Quarterly, 8*(2), 58–69.

Erickson, F. (1984). What makes school ethnography "ethnographic?" *Anthropology and Education Quarterly, 15*(1), 51–66.

Erickson, F., & Wilson, J. (1982). *Sights and sounds of life in schools: A resource guide to film and videotape for research and education.* (Research Series No. 125). East Lansing: Michigan State University Institute for Research on Teaching.

Smith, L. M. (1957). The micro-ethnography of the classroom. *Psychology in the Schools, 4,* 216–221.

Smith, L. M. (1982). Ethnography. In *Encyclopedia of educational research* (5th ed.). New York: Macmillan Free Press.

Wolcott, H. F. (1975). Criteria for an ethnographic approach to research in schools. *Human Organization, 34*(2), 111–127.

Wolcott, H. F. (1981). Confession of a "trained" observer. In T. S. Popkewitz & B. Robert Tabachnick (Eds.), *The study of schooling: Field based methodologies in educational research and evaluation.* New York: Praeger.

Wolcott, H. F. (1985). On ethnographic intent. *Educational Administration Quarterly, 21*(3), 187–203.

Anthropological Accounts About Ethnographic Research in General

Agar, M. H. (1980). *The professional stranger: An informal introduction to ethnography.* New York: Academic Press.   The style, the emphasis on interview data, and the attention to early stages in fieldwork make this a valuable introductory book.

Bowen, E. S. (1954). *Return to laughter.* New York: Harper and Brothers.   This is one of the earliest personal accounts of fieldwork experience.

Cesara, M. (1982). *Reflections of a woman anthropologist: No hiding place.* New York: Academic Press.

Geertz, C. (1973). Thick description: Toward an interpretative theory of culture. In C. Geertz, *The interpretation of cultures.* New York: Basic Books.

Heider, K. G. (1976). *Ethnographic film.* Austin: University of Texas Press.

Kimball, S. T., & Partridge, W. L. (1979). *The craft of community study: Fieldwork dialogues.* Gainesville: University Presses of Florida.

Langness, L. L., & Frank, G. (1981). *Lives: An anthropological approach to biography.* Novato, CA: Chandler and Sharp.

Marcus, G. E., & Clifford, J. (1985). The making of anthropological texts: A preliminary report. *Current Anthropology, 26*(2), 267–271.

Marcus, G. E., & Fischer, M. (1986). *Anthropology as cultural critique.* Chicago: University of Chicago Press.

Naroll, R., & Cohen, R. (1970). *A handbook of method in cultural anthropology.* New York: Natural History Press. (Also in paperback edition, Columbia University Press, 1973)

Pelto, P. J., & Pelto, G. H. (1978). *Anthropological research: The structure of inquiry* (2d ed.). New York: Cambridge University Press.   These authors present a point-by-point discussion of each of the techniques described in the chapter.

Powdermaker, H. (1966). *Stranger and friend: The way of an anthropologist*. New York: W. W. Norton.

Spindler, G. D., & Spindler, L. (Eds.). (1965 ff.). *Studies in anthropological method*. New York: Holt, Rinehart and Winston.   This series contains 15 monographs describing particular facets of fieldwork or relating the ethnographer's experiences during a particular study. The series is long out of print, but copies can usually be found in social science libraries.

Spindler, G. D. (Ed.). (1970). *Being an anthropologist: Fieldwork in eleven cultures*. New York: Holt, Rinehart and Winston.

Spradley, J. P., & McCurdy, D. W. (1972). *The cultural experience: Ethnography in complex society*. Chicago: Science Research Associates.   This little classic presents a short introduction to the "New Ethnography" followed by 12 beginning ethnographies conducted by Spradley and McCurdy's undergraduate students using that approach.

Wax, R. H. (1971). *Doing fieldwork: Warnings and advice*. Chicago: University of Chicago Press.

An Ethnographic Sampler

(Original date of publication is given but most of these classics are available in paperback editions. Mead and Turnbull are good authors to read first.)

Firth, Raymond: *We, the Tikopia* (1936).

Malinowski, Bronislaw: *Argonauts of the western Pacific* (1922).

Mead, Margaret: *Coming of age in Samoa* (1927); *Growing up in New Guinea* (1930).

Simmons, Leo (Ed.): *Sun chief: The autobiography of a Hopi Indian* (1942).

Thomas, Elizabeth M.: *The harmless people* (1958).

Turnbull, Colin: *The forest people: A study of the pygmies of the Congo* (1961); *Wayward servants: The two worlds of the African pygmies* (1965). (See also *The Mbuti pygmies: Change and adaptation*. New York: Holt, Rinehart and Winston, 1983).

Contemporary Ethnography

Edgerton, R. B. (1967). *The cloak of competence: Stigma in the lives of the mentally retarded*. Berkeley: University of California Press.

Estroff, S. E. (1981). *Making it crazy: An ethnography of psychiatric patients in an American community*. Berkeley: University of California Press.

Messerschmidt, D. A. (Ed.). (1981). *Anthropologists at home in North America: Methods and issues in the study of one's own society*. New York: Cambridge University Press.

Ogbu, J. (1974). *The next generation: An ethnography of education in an urban neighborhood*. New York: Academic Press.

Taylor, C. (1970). *In horizontal orbit: Hospitals and the cult of efficiency*. New York: Holt, Rinehart and Winston.

Suggested General Reading for Learning About the Field of Cultural Anthropology

Benedict, R. (1934). *Patterns of culture*.   Always available in paperback editions, this best-seller gives an excellent portrayal of cultural diversity although its anthropology is dated.

Geertz, C. (1973). *The interpretation of cultures*. New York: Basic Books.   To a collection of his previously published articles Clifford Geertz added a brilliant introductory essay that makes this book a "must."

Keesing, R. M. (1981). *Cultural anthropology: A contemporary perspective* (2d ed.). New York: Holt, Rinehart and Winston.   Virtually any introductory text or collection of readings in cultural anthropology provides a good introduction to the field. Keesing's book is cited here as an especially good example of a single-author text that has undergone several revisions.

Kluckhohn, C. (1949). *Mirror for man*.   Like Benedict's *Patterns of culture*, this book's timelessness has been proven through repeated printings.

The Forum

The study materials noted above offer the interested student an opportunity to become more familiar with ethnography by reading widely among readily available materials. In addition, there are several national organizations whose members include individuals with particular interests in ethnographic research and whose annual meetings and journals provide a forum for scholarly exchange. Attendance at their meetings or inspection of their journals is an excellent way to learn about current issues, find others who share interest in a specific problem, or begin an active organizational involvement. Details about subscriptions and memberships may be obtained by writing to the addresses listed.

Council on Anthropology and Education, 1703 New Hampshire Avenue, NW, Washington, DC, 20009. (Publication: *Anthropology and Education Quarterly*).

American Educational Research Association, 1230 17th Street, NW, Washington, DC, 20036. (Association publications: *American Educational Research Journal; Educational Researcher; Review of Educational Research*).

Society for Applied Anthropology, P.O. Box 24083, Oklahoma City, OK 73124-0083. (Publications: *Human Organization, Practicing Anthropology*).

Study Questions
(Prepared by Editor Richard M. Jaeger)

1. What are the differences, if any, between the role of hypotheses in ethnographic research and in more quantitative research methods, such as experimental research or correlational research?

2. Is it correct to say that in ethnographic research, in contrast to other research methods in education, decisions on the collection of specific data evolve, rather than being prespecified?

3. Discuss the role of "triangulation" or the "multi-instrument approach" in ethnographic research. Give an example of the way you might employ triangulation in an educational research study.

4. If you were to attempt to develop an ethnographic account of a third-grade class over the period of an entire school year, what roles might allow you to be a participant-observer? What are some possible advantages and limitations for each role?

5. What types of interviewing techniques might be employed in ethnographic research in education? Give an example of how life history interviews might be used in an ethnographic study of a school system.

6. Survey research is usually considered a separate research method. Is it therefore appropriate for an ethnographic researcher to use survey techniques? In using survey research methods, is an ethnographer stepping outside of his/her role and abandoning ethnography?

7. Could an ethnographer use standardized tests in gathering information about third-grade students? If so, would the ethnographer be likely to use the tests in the same way they are used by a school system's director of testing? How would these two uses of standardized tests likely differ?

8. Are "key informants" critical in doing ethnographic research on a school system in the United States? Discuss the relative usefulness of key informants in studying U.S. school systems and Japanese school systems, assuming *you* were attempting to do the research.

9. We usually think of ethnographic research as an attempt to portray a culture in its present-day totality. If this is correct, can historical records, whether formal or informal, play a role in developing an ethnography? Can you give an example of the way historical documents might be used in ethnography? Can you give an example of the way historical documents might be used in ethnographic research in education?

10. Discuss the statement "The ethnographer looks for the generic in the specific, following a 'natural history' approach that seeks to understand classes of events through the careful examination of specific ones." How does this approach differ from that of other educational research methods?

When to Use an Ethnographic Approach:
Three Case Examples

Here are three "somewhat hypothetical" cases in which an ethnographic approach might be considered in conducting research. Examine each case from two points of view, first from the perspective of the person who has responsibility for the project, second from the perspective of someone capable of doing ethnographic research who has been invited to work with the project. (Note that these cases all involve formal projects. The assumption is that people who do ethnographic research without special funding are free to define their own problems. The place to examine ethnographic appropriateness, therefore, is where the ethnographer is asked to provide research services for someone else.)

Case One deals with the design and implementation of a new accountability package called Output Analysis Technology System (OATS). The funding agency that has supported the development of the system wants to know what happens when it is implemented in school districts. A team of educational researchers has already identified a number of variables that will be monitored. Now project staff wonder if an on-the-scene ethnographer might be able to monitor the implementation from a quite different perspective and assure that in the event they have not identified the important variables some backup information will still be available about what did in fact happen. As project director, does this seem like a good idea? As ethnographer, are you interested in watching educators "sow their OATS?"

Case Two deals with a modest tryout of a new set of materials for teaching reading to Indian pupils. The project is called Education Through Honoring New-world Indian Cultures (ETHNIC) and was designed to "meet the needs" of Indian pupils by giving them specially designed reading materials that deal with Indian themes and Indian people. Developers of the program want to know of its acceptance and recognize that because of its cross-cultural basis an anthropologist ought to be helpful. As project director, do you agree? As ethnographer, do you want to "go ETHNIC?"

Case Three occurs in the very school district in which you live. Responding to pressure from parents and teachers alike, the school superintendent agreed three years ago that one junior high school in the district could become an alternative school open to all students or staff within the school system interested in a less traditional and more "creative" approach to schooling. The nucleus of teachers most interested in the idea of the school, somewhat antagonized by the school system's procedures for evaluating new programs, specified that the new school and program ("FAR OUT") would not be subjected to customary evaluation procedures. Now the no-longer-so-new-school is getting mixed reviews, and conservative board members insist that some evaluation must be made. The idea of employing an ethnographer was suggested by the school staff, and the superintendent must decide whether to carry out that idea. And how about you as a candidate for carrying out the study? Should you take a FAR OUT assignment?

* * *

From the perspective of a project administrator who must make the decision about whether to include an ethnographic component on a large-scale research project and whether to hire an ethnographer, your answers to the above questions, like mine, are probably related to broader issues rather than solely to ethnographic concerns. The case for using ethnography in each example might be based on a genuine wish to find out what is really going on, to study some part of the system in great detail, or to "cover your bets" by including an on-the-scene observer who can help in the interpretation of other systematic data, provide interim feedback, and assure that there will be some kind of findings even if more systematic procedures fail because the wrong variables were identified in the first place.

On the other hand, it is not unlikely that you already know what you want to measure. In the reading program, for example, if you really intend to use reading achievement scores anyway, or if you've already decided to scuttle the FAR OUT school because the clamor for alternative schools seems to have passed—then all that careful descriptive information the ethnographer can provide is just window dressing gained at rather great costs in time and even in money. (Ethnographic research isn't all that expensive—its basic costs are the salary of the researcher and some essential back-up secretarial help—but we are still looking at a minimum of several months' time.)

In terms of their special ethnographic appeal, my own responses about accepting the assignments are: Case One, YES; Case Two, NO; Case Three, MAYBE. Let me caution, however, that I am expressing personal as well as professional preferences. If I were an unemployed ethnographer I might accept any of the tasks. I could easily rationalize that decision, since *virtually any setting has ethnographic potential*. Thus any of these settings provides an opportunity to learn about schools. I see no conflict in contracting to look at elements of particular interest to the sponsors and attending at the same time to the broader context that especially interests me. Furthermore, any opportunity to conduct ethnographic research is an opportunity to demonstrate to educational researchers of other persuasions what this approach can accomplish and how it complements (and sometimes seriously questions) more familiar approaches to understanding schools.

Case One, calling for an ethnographic account of the implementation of Project OATS, has several attractions: an opportunity to watch educators do something that they ordinarily do (introduce change as a way to improve things), over an extended period of time, with research conducted in concert with other researchers whose work will provide an invaluable baseline. Since it is rather difficult to watch an innovation actually being implemented, I would begin the fieldwork by asking people what they saw happening and how they felt about it. In at least some ways Project OATS will be like other projects, and studying it in close detail in ethnographic perspective ought also to enable me to look at the social organization of educators and the dynamics of how that organization simultaneously attempts to change and manages to remain stable.[1]

Case Two, in spite of its cross-cultural concern, does not interest me. It would have been of considerable interest if the people designing the material had invited ethnographic input when they were first discussing what to do to improve reading progress for children of a particular ethnic group, a question embedded in the vastly complex and ethnographically intriguing problems of educating in cross-cultural settings. However, the kind of information wanted at this point in the project can be quickly and easily obtained through conventional achievement testing. If supplementary data are really wanted about "acceptance" of the new materials (why do I feel suspicious that it probably is not?), such information can quickly and easily be obtained through a questionnaire or survey. I see this proposal as a quick study of change. In my opinion, ethnography is far better suited to long-term studies of how things are. The setting is right but in this hypothetical case—and in the two real cases rather similar to this in which I was in fact asked to serve as consultant—the ethnographic potential was recognized too little and too late.

Case Three may seem like a "shoo-in" for ethnographic research. I know of several ethnographically oriented educational researchers who have accepted assignments to observe and write about alternative schools. An unusual opportunity for extended ethnographic study of innovative education was made possible by the huge nationally sponsored Experimental Schools program from 1972 to 1977, and ethnographic accounts from that project are still being completed. I would be tempted to take such an assignment myself. It would be fascinating to discern what parts of the traditional educational structure were changed and what parts remained the same in a so-called alternative program. But I also share with some ethnographers of schools a concern for whether ethnography, which grows out of a tradition and interest in *understanding* rather than *judging* human behavior, should become associated with evaluative processes in education. Thus my FAR OUT problem is that the intent of the ethnographic effort appears to be related *only* to evaluation. My feeling is that school researchers are already quite competent at doing evaluation. If evaluators wish to draw upon a wider repertoire of techniques in conducting their evaluation studies, fieldworkers should encourage and assist them. But my ethnographic bias makes me want to look at that evaluative process, not become part of it. When the anthropologist gets immersed in that process, who will be able to step back and look at the process itself?

Evaluation in education seems to me to be a two-edged sword. Becoming program evaluation specialists in education may be good for individual ethnographers, but it may be bad (fatal?) for the future of ethnography as a research approach that stresses understanding existing systems. The issue has been the basis of an interesting dialog in recent years. From an ethnographic point of view, it is an issue on the balance between participation and observation in field-work, a problem nicely epitomized in a perennial question posed by fieldwork-ers: "How native should one go?" The judgments required in program evalua-tion are usually the very judgments that ethnographers have insisted they do *not* make in their descriptions of human social behavior and human meanings. How educators themselves determine that some teachers are "more teacher," some students are "more student," or some schools are "more school" than others— that is the ethnographic question!

Note

[1] In fact, I have conducted ethnographic research in a project similar to OATS. My original assignment was to do a brief study of the last few months of a field test of a new project. Instead, and quite unexpectedly, I ended up conducting fieldwork intermittently over the next three years and studying the process of "de-implementation" as well as the process of implementation. Fieldwork plus writing extended through a period of 4½ years instead of 6 months as originally planned. The results of that experience were reported in a monograph entitled *Teachers Versus Technocrats: An Educational Innovation in Anthropological Perspective,* by Harry F. Wolcott. The monograph was published by the Center for Educational Policy and Management, University of Oregon, Eugene, OR, 1977.

Reading

Introduction
A Case Study Using an Ethnographic Approach

Harry F. Wolcott

Doctoral students invited to read earlier drafts of the preceding material and familiar with my strongly held and frequently stated position that there is a quantum jump from *borrowing a fieldwork technique or two* to *doing ethnography* have asked why I devoted so much of the chapter to explicating those techniques.

My answer is that in addressing an audience of educational researchers I assumed that in spite of my insistence that fieldwork techniques do not lead directly to ethnography, nonetheless these techniques are of great interest to them. Techniques are also amenable to discussions such as this. They can be described with some specificity, they can be organized into lists convenient for orderly presentation, and they can be grouped into manageable clusters that convey the basic fieldwork strategies (participant-observation and interviewing) without losing sight of the importance of multiple ways of finding out, of triangulation. With techniques adequately in tow, and fieldwork properly demystified, I can proceed to develop what is for me (but not necessarily for my readers) the critical issue: The essence of ethnography derives from its anthropological concern for cultural interpretation rather than for how one looks or even what one looks at (see Wolcott, 1987a). Ultimately, the research techniques are not all that important, but they do provide a convenient and, for educational researchers, a familiar way to begin the exploration of an alternative approach to the study of education. Therefore, I introduced the topic of ethnographic research by describing fieldwork techniques.

In selecting a case to *illustrate* ethnographic research in education, I am better able to dramatize how description and interpretation, rather than preoccupation with research "procedures," are the core of the ethnographic enterprise. In the self-contained case study that follows, with the exception of a brief reference to "months of informal conversations and many hours of formal interviews" and the ethnographer's admission of working with heavy hand in excerpting and reorganizing the material according to some dominant themes, there is no mention at all of fieldwork. The case consists of a great deal of information, most of it in a key informant's own words, and a conscious and explicit effort on the ethnographer's part to examine the account from a cultural perspective.

A *cross-cultural* perspective, on the other hand, may seem conspicuous by its absence in the example selected. If that is not quite by design, at least it allows me to make an important point about cultural interpretation. Pushing serendipity to its limits, the ethnographer of this study—myself—was working literally as well as figuratively in his own backyard. I had not sought out my informant (nor had he sought me out) but, like all humans, he had a story to tell, and I was interested in hearing it. We each had personal and complex motives but achieved some common purposes in the telling and listening. The cultural perspective for the interpretation draws on the distinction that anthropologists (and sometimes others) make between *schooling* and *education,* the two processes seen in the even broader context of *enculturation,* how each of us acquires the basic cultural orientation that will influence a lifetime of thoughts and actions.

Although I insist that my students direct their earliest formal attempts in ethnographic interviewing (if, indeed, there really is something properly called an ethnographic interview, rather than an ethnographic interpretation of one) toward people of cultural backgrounds markedly different from their own, eventually, like me, they must try to draw upon their cultural perspective for unveiling patterns of social behavior among those most like themselves. The cultural perspective so critical to ethnography derives in large measure from insight gained in cross-cultural settings, but *every* setting has a cultural perspective if one chooses to examine it. Further, and a point frequently overlooked by educational researchers, the mere fact of being in a cross-cultural setting does not perforce mean that research conducted in that setting will reveal dimensions of culture.

Another reason for selecting this study for illustration is to show what *one* researcher can do through extended interviewing with *one* informant and subsequently organizing the material for a journal-length article in terms of its relevance for some particular focus. Although the case does not presume to be ethnography, it does reflect an ethnographic way of looking. Under the circumstances, it is as ethnographic as it needs to be.

The article was originally commissioned as a think-piece intended to bring an anthropological perspective to the problem of defining educational adequacy (so that, American style, we could subsequently attach a dollar amount to the concept and determine how well school districts and states "measure up"). I reinterpreted the original assignment to create an opportunity to use case study data in examining the notion of educational adequacy itself. From the beginning, the research was problem-focused and highly specific—a partial life history of one young man—but the context was broad (holistic), the perspective cultural.

The heavy reliance on interview data in the completed account is another conscious element in my selecting it here as something of a model. Particularly when we conduct our research in settings familiar to us, or where we see only a portion of the lives of the people we are studying—two conditions that usually obtain in our research in schools—I think we are well advised to let our informants speak for themselves before we impose our interpretations on them.

At the constant risk of presenting too much data (and sometimes being accused of offering too little interpretation), I always strive to provide sufficient information not only to illustrate the basis for my interpretation but also to give readers an adequate basis for reaching independent interpretations of their own. Long after I submit a final draft for a report or publication, I continue to mull over my interpretations, realizing, in the way that Clifford Geertz (1973) characterizes a chronic problem in ethnography, that I still haven't quite gotten it right. Readers willing to engage themselves with case data collected by someone else ought to have sufficient information at hand to warrant that engagement, and toward that end ethnographers need always to remain aware of the difference between trying to be convincing in presenting their interpretations and trying to prove them. The ethnographer's goal is interpretation, not proof; by its very choice of subject matter, ethnography is necessarily ambiguous, just as it is necessarily incomplete.

I should note of this case study that I do not recall anything I had written earlier that prompted more response from early readers to "jump in," either to quarrel with my interpretation, to extend it, or to suggest an altogether different definition of the problem or different perspective on what "society" ought to do about it. To be able to provoke that response makes me feel I have performed the descriptive task well even while I continue to wrestle with the interpretation.

Pointing the way to responsible social action, however, is quite another responsibility, and one that goes beyond ethnography. To go even as far as I do here in raising policy issues in my concluding remarks I must switch roles so that the educator and reformer in me can question what might be done differently or "better." Ethnographers are not denied the right to offer judgments, opinions, and advice—provided there is no confusion about their stepping out of the ethnographer role before rendering such judgements. The reader will have to discern whether the boundaries between description and interpretation, and between interpretation and recommendation, appear to be adequately marked.

Finally, I selected this particular example because it demonstrates the ethnographer's concern for "complex specificness" even in addressing a topic as global as educational adequacy. That specificness is achieved through the natural history approach I described earlier, an approach that "seeks to understand classes of events through the careful examination of specific ones." Through the vehicle of an abbreviated life history related by one 20-year-old, I have tried to provide an account that brings a perspective to issues of broad social significance, including academic achievement, school drop-outs, youth unemployment, provision of welfare services, delinquency, and educative opportunity and responsibility beyond the period of formal schooling. But those are abstractions employed by social scientists, policy makers, and educators. The case relates the specific form in which such abstractions revealed themselves in everyday reality as one American youth experienced and perceived it.

This AERA book has been a long time in the making. At the time I needed to select an illustrative case, the study had just been published. I welcomed another opportunity to present the message of its *content* before a broader audience of educators at the same time that I felt its almost conspicuous absence of method relayed an implicit message about *process* to educational researchers. During this long interim, I wrote something of a sequel to the account that appears here (Wolcott, 1987b). This sequel, published in a collection of materials further illustrating qualitative approaches in educational research, is far more conjectural than the one that follows here and therefore does not serve well as a model for neophyte fieldworkers. Taken with this account, however, I think the more recent article provides an illustration of the ethnographer's efforts at cultural interpretation. Events subsequent to that writing echo Geertz's admonishments that I still have not quite gotten it right.

References

Geertz, C. (1973). Thick description. In C. Geertz, *The interpretation of cultures*. New York: Basic Books.

Wolcott, H. F. (1987a). On ethnographic intent. In G. Spindler & L. Spindler (Eds.), *Interpretive ethnography of education: At home and abroad* (pp. 37–57). Hillsdale, NJ: Lawrence Erlbaum Associates.

Wolcott, H. F. (1987b). Life's not working: Cultural alternatives to career alternatives. In G. W. Noblit & W. T. Pink (Eds.), *Schooling in social context: Qualitative studies*. Norwood, NJ: Ablex Publishing Co.

Adequate Schools and Inadequate Education: The Life History of a Sneaky Kid

Harry F. Wolcott

"I guess if you're going to be here, I need to know something about you, where you're from, and what kind of trouble you are in," I said to the lad, trying not to reveal my uncertainty, surprise, and dismay at his uninvited presence until I could learn more about his circumstances. It wasn't much of an introduction, but it marked the beginning of a dialog that lasted almost two years from that moment. Brad (a pseudonym, although as he noted, using his real name wouldn't really matter, since "no one knows who I am anyway") tersely stated his full name, the fact that his parents had "split up" and his mother was remarried and living in southern California, the local address of his father, and that he was not at present in any trouble because he wasn't "that stupid." He also volunteered that he had spent time in the state's correctional facility for boys, but quickly added, "It wasn't really my fault."

It was not our meeting itself that was a surprise; it was that Brad already had been living at this remote corner of my steep and heavily wooded 20-acre home-site on the outskirts of town for almost five weeks. In that time he had managed to build a 10-foot × 12-foot cabin made of newly cut sapling logs and roofed with plywood paneling. A couple of weeks earlier, I had stumbled across his original campsite, but I assumed it had been made by some youngster enjoying a bivouac en route to hiking a nearby ridge that afforded a fine view, a popular day hike for townspeople and occasional overnight adventure for kids. I also found a saw, but thought it had been left by a recent surveying party. Brad had been watching me at the time and later admitted cursing to himself for being careless in leaving tools about.

I did not realize I now had both a new cabin and an unofficial tenant until a neighbor reported that his 8-year-old son claimed not only to have seen but to have spoken to a "hobo" while wandering through my woods. The "hobo" turned out to be the then 19-year-old youth, of medium build and slightly stoop-shouldered, standing opposite me. And it is his story that I am about to relate.

As intrigued and involved as I eventually became with Brad and his story, my

Copyright by the Council on Anthropology and Education, 1983. Reprinted by permission from the *Anthropology and Education Quarterly, 14* (1), 3–32, with minor revision.

purpose in providing this account transcends the individual case even though I will tie my remarks closely to it. That purpose is related to my professional interest in anthropology and education and, particularly, in cultural acquisition, drawing upon anthropology both for approach and for perspective in looking at educational issues (see Wolcott, 1982). There is no shortage of case study materials about alienated youth.[1] Attention here will be drawn particularly to educationally relevant aspects of this case. Brad's story underscores and dramatizes the critical distinction that anthropologists make between *schooling* and *education* and raises questions about our efforts at education for young people beyond the purview of the schools.[2] Adequate schools may be necessary but they are not sufficient to insure an adequate education.

At first impression, Brad's strategy for coping with his life seemed as bold, resourceful, and even romantic, as was his building of a cabin. Faced with jobs he did not want to do (he abhors dishwashing, yet that seemed to be the only work he felt certain he could get, because "those jobs are always open") and expenses he could not afford (renting an apartment, buying and operating a motorcycle), he had chosen to change his lifestyle radically by reducing his cash needs to a minimum. What he could not afford, he would try to do without.

Never before had he done the things he now set out to do. He had never lived in the woods (though he had gone camping), never built a log house (though he had occasionally helped his father in light construction), never thought about a personal inventory of essential items. He had identified the cabin site, hidden from view but with a commanding view of its own, during one of his endless and solitary explorations of streets, roads, and paths in and around the city. The location was near a section of the city where he once lived as a child. He went deep into a densely wooded area, entering from the east and failing to realize how close he had come to my house on the county road around the west side of the ridge. But he knew he had to be near town. He needed to be where, one way or another, he could pick up the things essential to his anticipated lifestyle. He did not need much, but what he did need—hammer, saw, nails, sleeping bag, stove, cooking utensils, flashlight and lantern, pants and shoes, containers for carrying and storing water—he scrounged, stole, or, occasionally and reluctantly, purchased.

Brad displayed few qualities that would earn him the title of outdoorsman. His tools and equipment often were mislaid or neglected. He proved terrible at tying knots. He cut trees unnecessarily and turned his own trails into slippery troughs of mud. In spite of occasional references to himself as "Jungle Boy," he was basically a city boy making whatever accommodation was necessary to survive inexpensively. His fuel and food came from town; he was totally dependent on the city even though he could not afford to live in it. If his menu gradually became more like that of the woodsman (potatoes, onions, pancakes, melted cheese sandwiches, eggs, soup, canned tuna, powdered milk, and powdered orange juice) it was because he realized that these items could almost stretch $70-worth of food stamps into a month's ration of food. He washed and dried his clothes in coin-operated machines at night at a nearby apartment house complex. His battery-operated radio played almost constantly, and he became even more cabin-bound watching a small battery-operated TV set purchased for him by his mother during a brief visit, their first in over two years.

It was not Brad's wont to take leisurely walks in the woods, spend time enjoying sunsets, or listen to bird calls. He brought what he could find (and carry up steep, narrow trails) of his urban environment with him. Though not very sociable, he calculatingly mismanaged his purchases so that on many days he "had to" bicycle two miles each way to his favorite store to get a pack of cigarettes and perhaps buy a can of beer or "smoke a joint" in a nearby park. Town was the only direction he traveled. Yet almost without exception he returned to his cabin each evening, usually before darkness made the trip hazardous on an unlit bike. The security of having literally created a place all his own lent a critical element of stability to his life. He was proud of what he had built, even though he acknowledged that, were he starting over, his cabin would be "bigger and better in every way." His dreams for improving it never ceased.

For a while he envisioned building a tree house high in a giant Douglas fir nearby. A fearless tree-climber, he attached a high pulley and cable swing so he could trim branches and hoist construction materials. The tree house idea occupied his thoughts for weeks. During that time, few improvements were made on the cabin. The idea of being virtually inaccessible high in a tree proved more appealing than practical, however, and eventually he gave it up, brought his tools back to the cabin, and began work in earnest on improvements that included cutting out a section of wall and adding a lean-to bunk bed. The cable was removed from the tree house site and found its permanent place as a hillside swing with a breathtaking arc amongst the treetops on the slope below. Swinging was a literal as well as figurative high for him; pausing to rest between turns at the strenuous exercise, he volunteered the only positive comment I ever heard him make regarding the future: "I'll still swing like this whem I'm 60."

In brief glimpses, other people's lives often appear idyllic. Brad's "Robinson Crusoe" life had many appealing qualities. He seemed to have freed himself of the trappings of the Establishment, what he saw as a curiously roundabout and unappealing system that required him to take a job he hated in order to earn enough to provide transportation to and from work and money for the rent of some cheap place where he would rather not live. He had seen his father work hard, dream even harder, and yet, in Brad's opinion, "get nowhere." Brad was trying to figure out for himself what he wanted in life and whether it was really worth the effort.

I found it hard to argue on behalf of what some menial job would get him. I heard quite well his argument that, lacking in skill or experience, he would probably have to do work at once physically harder and lower paying than most jobs today. He could be an indefatigable worker, but I think he felt some anxiety about being able to "keep up" on jobs requiring hours of continuous hard physical labor. An earlier and short-lived job as a tree planter had convinced him that hard work does not insure success.

A glimpse into Brad's daily life does not dispel the romantic view of his existence. He arose when he wanted and retired when he wanted (although, with the cold, dark, and perennial dampness of the Northwest's winters, and with little to do, he spent so much time "in the sack" that getting to sleep became a constantly compounding problem). He could eat when he chose and cook or not as mood—and a rather sparse cupboard—dictated. Food and cigarette needs dominated his schedule of trips to town. A trip to the store, or to see about food stamps (in effect he had no address, so he went to the Welfare Office in person) or to secure other supplies (a tire for the bicycle, fuel for lanterns or the stove, hardware items for the cabin) occurred once or twice a week. Dirty clothes were washed regularly. And if there was no needed trip, he was free to decide—quite consciously, though rather impulsively, I think—how to spend the day.

Although the cabin was sometimes untidy and utensils were seldom washed before they were to be used again, Brad kept his person and his clothes clean. He brushed his teeth regularly. He never went to town without "showering" or at least washing his face and hair. In warm weather he underscored the nymph-like nature of his existence by remaining almost, or totally, unclad in the seclusion of his immediate cabin area, though he was excruciatingly self-conscious in public settings. His preference for privacy was highlighted by recollections of his distress at regimented public showering "on procedures" at reform school, and such experience had made options like joining the armed services something he insisted he would only do if he had to. Brad was, at first glance, a free spirit. He regarded himself that way, too: "I do what I want."

The Cultural Context of a Free Spirit

There is no absolute set of things to be wanted or ways to fill one's days and dreams, just as there is no absolute set of things to be learned (cf. Wallace, 1961b, p. 38). What people learn or want or do or dream about is embedded in particular macro- and micro-cultural systems.

Brad was aware of many things in his "culture" that he felt he could do without, including—up to a point—seeking much involvement within his society, seeming to heed its expectations, or depending on its resources. But he was accustomed to technological innovations and had been reared in a society where everyone appeared, at least to him, to have everything they needed. Although he saw himself as living figuratively, as well as literally, at the edge of society, he was still society's child. He was free to insist, "I do what I want," but he was not free to do what he wanted. What he had learned to want was a function of his culture, and he drew narrowly and rather predictably from the cultural repertoire of the very society from which he believed he was extricating himself.

Brad needed to cook. An open fire is slow and quite impractical on a rainy day. One needs a camp stove in order to cook inside a cabin. And fuel. And then a better stove. Cold water is all right for washing hands, but it can be a bit too bracing for washing one's hair or torso, especially when outside with the wind blowing. One needs a bigger pan to heat water for bathing. Soap and shampoo. A towel. A new razor. A mirror. A bigger mirror. Foam rubber mattress. A chair. A chaise longue.

One needs something to look at and listen to. Magazines are a brief diversion, but rock music is essential. One needs a radio. Flashlight batteries are expensive for continual radio listening; a radio operated by an automobile battery would be a better source—and could power a better radio. An automobile battery needs to be recharged. Carrying a battery to town is awkward, and constantly having to pay for battery charges is expensive. As well as access to a power supply (in my carport), one needs a battery charger. No, this one is rated too low; a bigger one is needed. Luckily not a harsh winter, but a wet one. The dirt floor gets muddy; a wood floor would be better. The roof leaks; a heavier grade of plywood and stronger tarpaulin to place over it are required. The sleeping bag rips where it got wet; a replacement is necessary. Shoes wear out from constant use on the trails; clothes get worn or torn. Flashlights and batteries wear out. Cigarettes (or tobacco), matches, eggs, bread, Tang, Crisco, pancake flour, syrup—supplies get low. An occasional steak helps vary the austere diet.

One needs transportation. A bicycle is essential, as are spare parts to keep it in repair. Now a minor accident: the bicycle is wrecked. No money to buy a new one. Brad "hypes" himself up and sets out to find a replacement. Buy one? "When they're so easy to get? No way!"

The Life History of a Sneaky Kid

Here is the place to let Brad relay something of his life and how he had tried to make sense of, and come to grips with, the world about him.

Ideally, in relating a life history through an ethnographic autobiography, informants tell their stories almost entirely in their own words (cf. classics such as Leo Simmons' *Sun Chief* (1942), or Oscar Lewis' *Children of Sanchez* (1961); see also Brandes, 1982). There should be a high ratio of information to explanation in a life story; sometimes there is no explanation or explicit interpretation at all. Time, space, and purpose require me to proceed more directly. I have worked with a heavy hand in reorganizing material and selecting the most cogent excerpts from months of informal conversations and many hours of formal interviews that Brad volunteered for this purpose.[3]

I have given particular attention to aspects of Brad's story that illustrate the two major points of this paper: that education consists of more than schooling, and that we give little systematic attention to the course of a young person's education once out of school. For these purposes I have dwelt more on social concerns than on personal or psychological ones. Brad had some personal "hang-ups," focused largely on his acceptance of his body and a preoccupation with sexual fantasy as yet unfulfilled, *Portnoy's Complaint* personified. In time (or, more candidly, not quite in time, before he sank unexpectedly into a mood of utter despair and abruptly announced he was "hitting the road" because he saw no future where he was), I realized he had some deep-seated emotional hang-ups as well, but my concern in this paper is with Brad as a social rather than a psychological being, and thus with personality-in-culture rather than with personality per se.

"In the Chute"

A speaker at the American Correctional Association meetings in 1981 was reported in the national press to have used the phrase "in the chute" to describe individuals whose lives seem headed for prison even though they have not yet arrived there: "People who are in the chute, so to speak, and heading toward us, are beginning that movement down in infancy."

Brad was not yet "in the chute." It is not inevitable that he end up in trouble, but he could. Excerpts from his life story suggest how things point that way. Here he recalls a chain of events that started at age 10 with what proved a traumatic event in his life, his parents' divorce:

On the Loose. "After my parents got divorced, I was living with my dad. I had quite a bit of freedom. My dad wasn't around. If I didn't want to go to school, I just didn't go. Everybody who knows me now says, 'That guy had the world's record for ditching school.' My dad was at work all day and there was no one to watch me. I was pretty wild. My dad took me to a counseling center at the university; they told me I was 'winning the battles but losing the war.'

"After my dad got remarried, I had no freedom any more. I had a new mother to watch me. I got mad at her a couple of times, so I moved in with her parents. I went to seventh grade for a while and got pretty good grades. Then I went to southern California to visit my mother. When my dad said he'd have to 'make some arrangements' before I could return, I just stayed there. But I got into a hassle with my stepdad, and I ditched some classes, and suddenly I was on a bus back to Oregon.

"My father had separated again and I moved into some little apartment with him. He wanted me to go to another school, but I said, 'Forget it, man, I'm not going to another school. I'm tired of school.' So I'd just lay around the house, stay up all night, sleep all day.

"Finally I told my mom I'd be a 'good boy,' and she let me move back to southern California. But I got in another hassle with my stepdad. I ran out of the house and stayed with some friends for a few months, but then the police got in a hassle with me and they said I'd have to go back with my dad or they were going to send me to a correctional institution. The next thing you know, I was back on the bus."

Getting Busted. "By then my dad had remarried again. I wasn't ready for another family. I stayed about two days, then I left. I figured any place was better than living there. But they got pissed at me because I kept coming back [breaking into the house] for food, so they called the cops on me. Running away from them, I broke my foot and had to go to the hospital. Then I got sent to reform school. They had a charge against me [contraband], but I think the real reason was that I didn't have any place to go. I was in reform school for eight months."

Second-Rate Jobs and Second-Rate Apartments. "I finally played their 'baby game' and got out of reform school. Then they sent me to a halfway house in Portland. I got a job, made some money, got a motorcycle, moved to another place, then that job ended. I got another job with a church-going plumber for awhile, but I got fired. Then I came back and worked for my dad, but there wasn't nothing to do, and I got in some family hassles, so I got a few jobs and lived in some cheap apartments.

"For awhile I was a bum down at the Mission. I'd get something to eat, then I'd go sleep under a truck. My sleeping bag was all I had. I knew winter was coming and I'd have to do something. I saw a guy I knew and he said 'Hey, I've got a place if you'd like to crash out until you get something going.' So I went there and got a job for about four months washing dishes. Then my mom came up from California to visit and found me an apartment. God, how I hated that place, with people right on the other side of those thin walls who know you're all alone and never have any visitors or anything. I quit washing dishes; they cut me down to such low hours I wasn't making any money anyway. So I just hibernated for the winter."

A New Life. "When the rent ran out, I picked up my sleeping bag and the stuff I had and headed for the hills at the edge of town. I found a place that looked like no one had been there for awhile, and I set up a tarp for shelter. I decided to take my time and build a place for myself, because I wasn't doing anything anyway. I just kept working on it. I've been here a year and a half now. I've done some odd jobs, but mostly I live on food stamps.

"I used to think about doing something like this when I lived in Portland. I read a book called *How to Live in the Woods on Pennies a Day*. I even tried staying out in the woods a couple of times, but I didn't know exactly what to do. I wasn't thinking about a cabin then. All I knew was that I needed some place to get out of the wind and some place to keep dry. I saw this piece of level ground and knew that if I had tools and nails I could probably put up some walls. As I went along I just figured out what I would need.

"I put up four posts and started dragging logs around till the walls were built. There were plenty of trees around. It took about a week to get the walls. I slept in a wet sleeping bag for a couple of nights, cause I didn't have a roof. The first roof was some pieces of paneling that I carried up from some kids' tree fort. I had a dirt floor but I knew I'd have to have a wood floor some day. I knew about plaster because I had worked with it before, so I smeared some on the walls. All that I really needed at first was nails. I got other stuff I needed from new houses being built nearby."

'Picking Up' What Was Needed. "I got around town quite a bit. Any place where there might be something, I'd take a look. If I found anything that I needed, I'd pick it up and take it home. I just started a collection: sleeping bag, radio, plywood for the roof, windows, a stove, lanterns, tools, clothes, water containers, boots. If you took away everything that's stolen, there wouldn't be much left here. Like the saw. I just walked into a store, grabbed it, put a piece of cloth around it to hide it, and walked out.

"Before I got food stamps, I'd go to the store with my backpack, fill it with steaks and expensive canned food, and just walk out. If anybody saw me, I'd wave at them and keep walking. I didn't have much to lose, I figured. The closest I ever got to being stopped, I had two six-packs of beer and some cooked chicken. The guy in the store had seen me there before. I just waved, but he said, 'Stop right there.' I ran out and grabbed my bike, but he was right behind me. I knew the only thing I could do was drop the merchandise and get out of there with my skin and my bike, and that's what I did. He didn't chase me; he just picked up the bag and shook his head at me."

The Bicycle Thief. "We lived in the country for about three years while I was growing up. Moving back into town was kinda different. I went pretty wild after moving to town. Me and another kid did a lot of crazy stuff, getting into places and taking things. I'd stay out all night just looking in people's garages. I'd get lots of stuff. My room had all kinds of junk in it. That's when I was living with my dad, and he didn't really notice. He still has an electric pencil sharpener I stole out of a church. He never knew where I got it.

"Instead of going to school, I'd stay home and work on bikes. We used to steal bikes all the time. We'd get cool frames and put all the hot parts on them. I've stolen lots of bikes—maybe around 50. But I probably shouldn't have never stolen about half of them, they were such junk. I just needed them for transportation."

Being Sneaky. I've always been kind of sneaky, I guess. That's just the way I am. I can't say why. My mom says that when I was a small kid I was always doing something sneaky. Not always—but I *could* be that way. I guess I'm still that way, but it's not exactly the same. It's just the way you think about things.

"I don't like to be sneaky about something I could get in trouble for. But I like to walk quietly so no one will see me. I could get in trouble for something like sneaking in somebody's backyard and taking a roto-tiller. I did that once. I sold the engine.

"I guess being sneaky means I always try to get away with something. There doesn't have to be any big reason. I used to tell the kid I was hanging around with, "I don't steal stuff because I need it. I just like to do it for some excitement."

"Last year I went 'jockey-boxing' with some guys who hang around at the park. That's when you get into people's glove compartments. It was a pretty dead night. One guy wanted a car stereo. He had his tools and everything. So we all took off on bicycles, five of us. I was sort of tagging along and watching them—I didn't really do it. They got into a couple of cars. They got a battery vacuum cleaner and a couple of little things. You go to apartment houses where there's lots of cars and you find the unlocked ones and everybody grabs a car and jumps in and starts scrounging through.

"I've gone through glove compartments before and I probably will again some day if I see a car sitting somewhere just abandoned. But I'm not into it for fun anymore, and it doesn't pay unless you do a lot. Mostly young guys do it.

"I'm still mostly the same, though. I'll take a roll of tape or something from the supermarket. Just stick it in my pants. Or if I saw a knife that was easy to take. That's about it. Oh, I sneak into some nearby apartments to wash my clothes. I pay for the machines, but they are really for the tenants, not for me. And I'll sneak through the woods with a piece of plywood for the cabin."

I Don't Have to Steal, But. . . . "I'm not what you'd call a super thief, but I will steal. A super thief makes his living at it; I just get by. I don't have to steal, but it sure makes life a hell of a lot easier. I've always known people who steal stuff. It's no big deal. If you really want something, you have to go around looking for it. I guess I could teach you how to break into your neighbor's house, if you want to. There's lots of ways—just look for a way to get in. It's not that hard to do. I don't know what you'd call it. Risky? Crazy?

"I can be honest. Being honest means that you don't do anything to people that you don't know. I don't like to totally screw somebody. But I'll screw 'em a little bit. You could walk into somebody's garage and take everything they have—maybe $5,000 worth of stuff. Or you could just walk in and grab a chain saw. It's not my main hobby to go around looking for stuff to steal. I might see something, but I wouldn't go out of my way for it."

Breaking and Entering. "I remember busting into my second-grade classroom. I went back to the schoolground on the weekend with another kid. We were just looking around outside and I said, 'Hey, look at that fire escape door—you could pull it open with a knife.' We pulled it open and I went in and I took some money and three or four little cars and a couple of pens. There wasn't anything of value, but the guy with me stocked up on all the pens he could find. We got in trouble for it. That was the first time I broke in anywhere. I don't know why I did it. Maybe too many television shows. I just did it because I could see that you could do it.

"And I've gotten into churches and stores. I've broken into apartment house recreation rooms a lot, crawling through the windows. And I've broken into a house before.

"I went in one house through the garage door, got inside, and scrounged around the whole house. God, there was so much stuff in that house. I munched a cake, took some liquor, took some cameras. Another time I thought there was nobody home at one house, and I went around to the bathroom window, punched in the screen, and made a really good jump to the inside. I walked in the house real quietly. Then I heard somebody walk out the front door, so I split. I didn't have nothin' then; I was looking for anything I could find. I just wanted to go scrounging through drawers to find some money.

"If I ever needed something that bad again and it was total chaos [i.e., desperation], I could do it, and I would. It's not my way of life, but I'd steal before I'd ever beg."

Inching Closer to the Chute. "Just before I started living at the cabin, I kept having it on my mind that I needed some money and could rob a store. It seemed like a pretty easy way to get some cash, but I guess it wasn't a very good idea. I had a B-B gun. I could have walked in there like a little Mafia, shot the gun a few times, and said, 'If you don't want those in your face, better give me the money.' There were a couple of stores I was thinking of doing it to.

"I was standing outside one store for about two hours. I just kept thinking about going in there. All of a sudden this cop pulls into the parking lot and kinda checks me out. I thought, 'Oh, fuck, if that cop came over here and searched me and found this gun, I'd be shit.' So as soon as he split, I left. And after thinking about it for so long.

"But another time, I really did it. I went into one of those little fast food stores. I had this hood over my head with a little mouth hole. I said to the clerk, 'Open the register.' And she said, 'What! Are you serious?' I knew she wasn't going to open it, and she knew I wasn't about to shoot her. So then I started pushing all the buttons on the cash register, but I didn't know which ones to push. And she came up and pulled the key. Then someone pulled up in front of the store and the signal bell went 'ding, ding.' So I booked.

"Another time I thought about going into a store and telling this cashier to grab the cash tray and pull it out and hand it to me. Or else I was going to wait till near closing time when they go by with a full tray of 20-dollar bills and grab it. Or go into a restaurant right after closing time, like on a Saturday night or something, and just take the whole till. I was going to buy a motorcycle with that. All I needed was $400 to get one.

"If I was ever that hurting, I could probably do it if I had to. It's still a possibility, and it would sure be nice to have some cash. But you wouldn't get much from a little store anyway. I'd be more likely just to walk in and grab a case of beer."

I'm Not Going to Get Caught. "I can't straighten out my old bike after that little accident I had the other day, and that means I need another bike. I'll try to find one to steal—that's the easiest way to get one. I should be able to find one for free, and very soon, instead of having to work and spend all that money, money that would be better off spent other places, like reinstating my driver's license.

"The way I do it, I go out in nice neighborhoods and walk around on people's streets and look for open garages, like maybe they just went to the store or to work and didn't close the door. I walk on streets that aren't main streets. Someone might spot me looking around at all these bikes, but even if somebody says something, they can't do anything to you. The cops might come up and question me, but nothing could happen.

"Now, if I was caught on a hot bike . . . but that's almost impossible. If I was caught, they'd probably take me downtown and I'd sit there awhile until I went to court, and who knows what they'd do. Maybe give me six months. They'd keep me right there at the jail. But it's worth the risk, because I'm not going to get caught. I did it too many times. I know it's easy.

"Even if I worked, the only thing I'd be able to buy is an old Schwinn 10-speed. The bike I'm going to get will be brand new. Maybe a Peugeot or a Raleigh. A $400 bike at least. It might not be brand new, but if I could find a way, I'd get a $600 bike, the best one I could find. And I'll do whatever I have to, so no one will recognize it."

Home Is the Hunter. "I think this will be the last 'bike hunting' trip I'll ever go on . . . probably. I said it *might* be the last one. I could probably do one more. When I get to be 24 or 25, I doubt that I'll be walking around looking for bikes. But, if I was 25 and I saw a nice bike and I was in bad shape and really needed it, I'd get it. I'm not going to steal anything I don't need. Unless it's just sitting there and I can't help it, it's so easy. I'm not really corrupt, but I'm not 'innocent' any more. I can be trusted, to some people." ["Can I trust you?" I asked. "Yeah. Pretty much. I dunno. When it comes to small stuff. . . ."]

Growing Up. "When I was growing up, I was always doing something, but it wasn't that bad. My parents never did take any privileges away or give me another chance. Anytime I did something in California, my mother and stepdad just said, 'Back to Oregon.' They didn't threaten, they just did it. My mom could have figured out something better than sending me back to Oregon all the time. She could have taken away privileges, or made me work around the house. And in Oregon, my dad could have figured a better way than throwing me out of the house. Bad times for me were getting in a hassle with my parents. Then I wouldn't have no place to go, no money or nothin'. That happened with all of them at different times."

[By my count, including a time when Brad lived with his mother at her sister's home, and when he lived with one stepmother's parents for awhile, he was reared in six families. That fact seemed not particularly disconcerting to him, but the abruptness of being dispatched among them was.]

"The last time I got kicked out in California, I moved back to Oregon, but I only stayed in the house a couple of days. My stepmom and my dad started telling me I wasn't going to smoke pot any more, I would have to go to school, I was going to have to stop smoking cigarettes, and other shit like that. And I didn't like anything about that fucking house. Another reason is that my dad said I couldn't have a motorcycle. So I split. I just hung around town, sleeping anywhere I could find. I ripped off a quilt and slept out on a baseball field for awhile. I stayed in different places for a couple of weeks. Then I got busted, got sent to reform school, then I got some work and the first thing I did was buy a motorcycle. I was riding without a license or insurance for awhile. Even after I got a license, I kept getting tickets, so finally my license got suspended, and my dad took the motorcycle and sold it to pay for the tickets.

"If I had kids, I would just be a closer family. I would be with them more and show that you love them. You could talk to your kids more. And if they do something wrong, you don't go crazy and lose your temper or something."

Getting Paid for Dropping Out. "I've earned some money at odd jobs since I came here, but mostly I live on food stamps. I knew that if I wasn't working and was out of money, food stamps were there. I've been doing it for quite awhile. When I was at the Mission I had food stamps. A guy I worked with once told me, all I had to do was go down there and tell 'em you're broke, that's what it's there for. I haven't really tried looking for a job. Food stamps are a lot easier. And I'd just be taking a job away from someone who needs it more. Now that I've figured out the kinds of things to buy, I can just about get by each month on $70 for food. If I couldn't get food stamps, I'd get a job. I guess food stamps are society's way of paying me to drop out."

Hiding Out from Life. "So now I've got this cabin fixed up and it really works good for me. This is better than any apartment I've ever had.

"I guess by living up here I'm sorta hiding out from life. At least I'm hiding from the life I had before I came up here. That's for sure. The life of a dumpy apartment and a cut-rate job. This is a different way of life.

"This place works a lot for me. What would I have been doing for the year and a half in town compared to a year and a half up here? Like, all the work I've done here, none of it has gone for some landlord's pocketbook. I should be able to stay here until I get a good job.

"I like living like this. I think I'd like to be able to know how to live, away from electricity and all that."

The romantic Robinson Crusoe aspects of a young man carving out a life in the wilderness, what his mother referred to as "living on a mountaintop in Oregon," is diminished by this fuller account of Brad's lifestyle. Brad would work if he "had to," but he had found that for a while—measured perhaps in years rather than weeks—he did not have to. If he was not hiding out from life, he had at least broken out of what he saw as the futility of holding a cut-rate job in order to live a cut-rate existence.

Brad kept a low profile that served double duty. He had a strong aversion to being "looked at" in settings where he felt he did not "blend in," and his somewhat remote cabin protected him from the eyes of all strangers—including the law. His cabin became his fortress; he expressed concern that he himself might be "ripped off." On sunny weekends, with the likelihood of hikers passing through the woods, he tended to stay near the cabin, with an eye to protecting his motley, but nonetheless precious, collection of tools and utensils, bicycles and parts, and personal belongings. He sometimes padlocked the cabin (though it easily could have been broken into) and always locked his bike when in town if he was going to be any distance from it. Had he been ripped off, he would hardly have called the police to help recover his stolen items; few were his in the first place.

Technically he was not in trouble with the law. To some extent the law exerted a constraining influence on him. In his view, to get caught was the worst thing that could happen to him and would have been "stupid" on his part. That tended to circumscribe both the frequency and extent of the illicit activities in which he engaged. But the law also menaced him as a down-and-outer and as a relatively powerless kid, a kid without resources. The law works on a cash basis. Working for me, Brad earned and saved enough money to purchase an engine for his bicycle in order to circumvent his earlier problems with the motorcycle, only to discover via a traffic violation of over $300 (reduced to $90 with the conventional plea, "Guilty, with explanation") that a bicycle with an engine on it is deemed a motorized vehicle, and that he was required by law to have a valid operator's license (his was still suspended), a license for the vehicle, and insurance. To make himself "legal," he needed about $175 and would continue to face high semiannual insurance premiums. In his way of thinking, that expense got him "nothing"; he preferred to take his chances. Traffic fines were actually a major budget item for him, but his argument remained the same, "I won't get caught again."

Margaret Mead once commented that most Americans would agree the "worst" thing a child can do is to steal (MacNeil & Glover, 1959). As a "sneaky kid," Brad had already been stealing stuff—little stuff, mostly—for more than half his lifetime. He seemed to me to be approaching the moment when he would have to decide whether to dismiss his stealing as a phase of growing up and doing "crazy things" (jockey-boxing, breaking into the classroom on weekends, petty shoplifting, stealing bicycles) or to step into the "chute" by joining the big leagues. With mask and gun, he had already faced the chute head-on. That event might have ended otherwise, had not someone called his bluff. With the occurrence of repeated traffic fines, the courts themselves could conceivably precipitate for him a desperate need for quick and easy money.

World View: 'Getting My Life Together'

The material presented thus far lends ample support for Brad's depiction of himself as a "sneaky kid" with a number of antisocial and unsociable traits. In the last 10 of his 20 years, Brad's antics often had resulted in trouble ("hassles") and had paved the way for more trouble than actually had befallen him. (In that regard, it is ironic that being sent to reform school, though on the technically serious charge of "Supplying contraband" coupled with "Harassment," was, in his opinion, more a consequence of having "nowhere else to go" than of the offenses themselves.)

From mainstream society's point of view, Brad's story would seem to reflect the enculturation process going awry, a young person growing apart from, rather than a part of, the appropriate social system. Brad did not behave "properly" on certain critical dimensions (e.g., respect for other people's property, earning his way), and therefore his almost exemplary behavior on other dimensions (his lack of pretense, his cleanliness, and, particularly, his resourcefulness and self-reliance) was apt to be overlooked. He was not a social asset, and he seemed destined for trouble.

Yet in both word and deed (and here is the advantage of knowing him for two years, rather than depending solely on formal interviews), Brad repeatedly demonstrated how he was more "insider" than "outsider" to the society he felt was paying him to drop out. In numerous ways he revealed a personal world view not so far out of step with society after all. Adrift though he may have been, he was not without social bearings. The odds may have been against him, but they were not stacked. This was not a "minority" kid fighting the immediate peril of the ghetto, nor a weak kid, nor a dumb kid, nor an unattractive kid, nor a kid who had not, at some prior time in his life, felt the security of family. Indeed, somewhere along the way he learned to value security so highly that his pursuit of it provided him an overriding sense of purpose.

Both Brad's parents had worked all their adult lives and, judging from statements I personally heard them make, took pride in their efforts. If, as Brad sized it up, they were "not really rich," they were at least comfortable. Perhaps from Brad's point of view they had paid too high a price for what they had or had given up too much to attain it, but they are the embodiment of the American working class. As Brad expressed it, "My dad's worked all his life so he can sit at a desk and not hold a screwdriver any more. But he just works! He never seems to have any fun."

Absolutely no one, including anthropologists who devote careers to the task, ever learns the totality of a culture; conversely, no one, including the most marginal or socially isolated of humans, ever escapes the deep imprint of macro- and micro-cultural systems in which he or she is reared as a member of a family, a community, and a nation. Evidence of that cultural imprinting abounds in Brad's words and actions. I have combed his words and found evidence that in examining his world view one can find glimmers of hope, if only he does not "get caught doing something stupid" or in some unexpected way get revisited by his past. Though he occasionally makes some deliberate, unsanctioned responses, Brad appears well aware of the "cultural meanings" of his behavior (cf. Wallace 1961a, p. 135).

If Brad does "make it," it will be largely because of the cultural imprinting of values instilled at some time in that same past. Let me here make the point to which I will return in conclusion: There was no constructive force working effectively on Brad's behalf to guide, direct, encourage, or assist him. He had no sponsor, no support system, virtually no social network. The agencies poised to respond to him will act when and if he makes a mistake and gets caught. He cannot get help without first getting into trouble. The only social agency that exerted a positive educative influence on him was an indirect consequence of the mixed blessing of food stamps that kept him from having to steal groceries but made it unnecessary for him to work. He had learned to spend his allotment wisely in order to make it last the month.

The following excerpts, selected topically, suggest the extent to which Brad already had acquired a sense of middle-class morality and an ethos of working to achieve material success. They point, as well, to loose strands that remain someday to be woven together if he is to be bound more securely to the Establishment.

A Job—That's All That Makes You Middle Class. "A job is all that makes you middle class. If I'm going to have a job, I've got to have a bike that works, I've got to have a roof, I've got to have my clothes washed. And I'd probably need rain gear, too. You can't go into any job in clothes that look like you just came out of a mud hut.

"Even though I've worked for a while at lots of different things, I guess you could say that I've never really held a job. I've worked for my dad a while—altogether about a year, off and on. I helped him wire houses and do other things in light construction. I scraped paint for a while for one company. I worked for a graveyard for about eight months, for a plumber a while, and I planted trees for a while.

"I wouldn't want to have to put up with a lot of people on a job that didn't make me much money. Like at a check-out counter—that's too many people. I don't want to be in front of that many people. I don't want to be a known part of the community. I don't mind having a job, but I don't like a job where everyone sees you do it. Working with a small crew would be best—the same gang every day. I'd like a job where I'm out and moving. Anything that's not cleaning up after somebody else, where you're not locked up and doing the same thing over and over, and where you can use your head a little, as well as your back.

"My mother said, 'If you had a little job right now, you'd be in heaven.' Yeah, some cash wouldn't hurt, but then I'd have to subtract the $70 I wouldn't get in food stamps, and there might not be a whole hell of a lot left. So I'm living in the hills and I'm not workin'. No car, either. So no girl friend right now. No big deal.

"If I did have a job, the hardest thing about it would be showing up on time and getting home. Living out here makes a long way to go for any job I might get.

"If you get your life together, it means you don't have to worry so much. You have a little more security. That's what everybody wants. Money: a regular job. A car. You can't have your life together without those two things.

"My life is far better than it was. I've got a place to live and no big problems or worries. I don't worry about where I'm going to sleep or about food. I've got a bike. Got some pot—my home-grown plants are enough now, so I don't have to worry about it, even though it's not very high class. But you've got to have a car to get to work in the morning and to get home. I can go on living this way, but I can't have a car if I'm going to do it.

"Sometimes my mom sends me clothes, or shampoo, or stuff like that. But if

I had a job, I wouldn't need that. She'll help me with a car someday, if she ever thinks I'm financially responsible."

Building My Own Life. "I'm not in a big hurry with my life. If I can't do super-good, I'll do good enough. I don't think I'll have any big career.

"Maybe in a way I'll always be kind of a survivalist. But I would like to be prepared for when I get to be 50 or 60—if I make it that far—so that I wouldn't need Social Security. I get my food stamps, so I guess I'd have to say I'm part of The Establishment. A job would get me more into it.

"Over a period of time I've learned what food to buy and what food not to buy, how to live inexpensively. I get powdered milk, eggs, dry foods in bulk, and stuff like that. Food costs me about $80 per month. I could live on $100 a month for food, cigarettes, fuel, and a few little extras, but not very many, like buying nails, or a window, or parts for a bike. But I don't really need anything. I've got just about everything I need. Except there is a few things more.

"I might stay here a couple of years, unless something drastically comes up. Like, if a beautiful woman says she has a house in town, that would do it, but if not for that, it isn't very likely. I'll have to build my own life.

"I wouldn't mind working. I wouldn't mind driving a street-sweeper or something like that, or to buy a $30,000 or $60,000 piece of equipment, and just make money doing stuff for people. You see people all over who have cool jobs. Maybe they just do something around the house like take out washing machines, or they own something or know how to do something that's not really hard labor but it's skilled labor.

"But living this way is a good start for me. I don't have to work my life away just to survive. I can work a little bit, and survive, and do something else."

Being by Myself. "At this time of my life it's not really too good to team up with somebody. I've got to get my life together before I can worry about just going out and having a beer or a good time.

"Being by myself doesn't make all that much difference. I guess that I'm sorta a loner. Maybe people say I'm a hermit, but it's not like I live 20 miles out in nowhere.

"I don't want to be alone all my life. I'd like to go camping with somebody on the weekend. Have a car and a cooler of beer and a raft or something. It's nice to have friends to do that with. If I had a car and stuff, I'm sure I could get a few people to go. Without a car, man, shit. . . ."

Friends. "A friend is someone you could trust, I suppose. I've had close friends, but I don't have any now. But I have some 'medium' friends. I guess that's anybody who'd smoke a joint with me. And you see some people walking down the street or going to a store or to a pay phone. You just say, 'Hi, what's going on?'

"I know lots of people. Especially from reform school. I've already seen some. They're not friends, though; they're just people you might see to say hello and ask them what they've been up to and ask them how long they did in jail.

"The first time I met one guy I know now, I was pushing my bike and I had my backpack and some beer and I was drinking a beer. I'd never seen him before. He said, 'Hey, wanna smoke a joint?' I said, 'Sure.' So I gave him a couple of beers and we smoked some pot and started talking. I told him I lived up in the hills. I see him around every now and then. He's known me for a year and I talk to him sometimes and joke around. He's sort of a friend.

"I had a few friends in southern California, but by the time I left there I wasn't too happy with them. I guess my best friend was Tom. I used to ride skateboard with him all day. His older brother used to get pot for us. That's when I think I learned to ride the very best. We always used to try to beat each other out in whatever we did. I was better than him in some things and after a while he got better than me in a couple of things. But I think I was always a little bit more crazier than he was—a little bit wilder on the board."

I've Been More Places and Done More Things. "I've lived in a lot of different places. Like going to California. Living out in the country. Living different places in town. Dealing with people. Living at the reform school. Living in Portland. Living here.

"I've definitely had more experiences than some of the people I went to school with, and I've had my ears opened more than they have. In *some* things, I'm wiser than other kids my age.

"I saw a guy a few weeks ago who is the same age as me. He lived in a house behind us when I was in fifth grade. He still lives with his parents in the same place. I think about what he's been doing the last nine years and what I've been doing the last nine years and it's a big difference. He went to high school. Now he works in a gas station, has a motorcycle, and works on his truck. I guess that's all right for him, so long as he's mellow with his parents. That way he can afford a motorcycle.

"But you've got what you've got. It doesn't make any difference what anybody else has. You can't wish you're somebody else. There's no point in it."

Some Personal Standards. "In the summer I clean up every day. When it starts cooling down, I dunno; sometimes if it's cold, I just wash my head and under my arms. Last winter I'd get a really good shower at least every three days and get by otherwise. But I always wash up before going to town if I'm dirty. I don't want to look like I live in a cabin.

"I don't really care what people on the street think of me. But somebody who knows me, I wouldn't want them to dislike me for any reason.

"And I wouldn't steal from anybody that knew me, if they knew that I took something or had any idea that I might have took it. Whether I liked them or not. I wouldn't steal from anybody I liked, or I thought they were pretty cool. I only steal from people I don't know.

"I don't like stealing from somebody you would really hurt. But anybody that owns a house and three cars and a boat—they're not hurtin'. It's the Law of the Jungle—occasionally people get burned. A lot of people don't, though.

As long as they've got fences and they keep all their stuff locked up and don't leave anything laying around, they're all right. The way I see it, 'If you snooze, you lose.'

"If you say you'll do something, you should do it. That's the way people should operate. It pisses me off when somebody doesn't do it. Like, you tell somebody you're going to meet them somewhere, and they don't show up. But giving my word depends on how big of a deal it is; if it's pretty small, it would be no big deal.

"Sure, stealing is immoral. I don't like to screw somebody up for no good reason. But my morals can drop whenever I want.

"I went to Sunday School for a while and to a church kindergarten. I guess I heard all the big lessons—you get the felt board and they pin all the stuff on 'em and cut out all the paper figures: Jesus, Moses. But our family doesn't really think about religion a whole lot. They're moral to a point but they're not fanatics. It's too much to ask. I'd rather go to hell. But any little kid knows what's right and wrong."

Moderation: Getting Close Enough, Going 'Medium' Fast. "One of my friend's older brothers in southern California was a crazy fucker. He'd get these really potent peyote buttons and grind them up and put them in chocolate milkshakes. One time they decided to go out to the runways where the jets were coming in, cause they knew somebody who did it before. Planes were coming in continually on that runway. They'd go out there laying right underneath the skid marks, just right under the planes. I never would get that close. Just being out there, after jumping the fence and walking clear out to the runway, is close enough. I never did lie on the runway. . . .

"On the skateboard, I just go medium fast. . . .

"The fun part of skiing is knowing when to slow down. . . .

"When those guys went jockey-boxing, I didn't actually do it with them. I just was tagging along. . . .

"Robbing a store seemed like a pretty easy way to get some cash, but I guess it wasn't a very good idea. . . .

"I don't know why I didn't get into drugs more. I smoke pot, but I've never really cared to take downers and uppers or to shoot up. I don't really need that much. . . .

"I like to smoke pot, but I don't think of myself as a pothead. A pothead is somebody who is totally stoned all day long on really good pot, really burned out all the time. I smoke a joint, then smoke a cigarette, and I get high. I just like to catch a buzz. . . .

"If you really get burnt out your brain's dead. You can get burned out on anything if you do it too much. I don't do it enough to make it a problem. If you take acid you never know who's made it or exactly what's in it. I've taken it before and gotten pretty fried. I don't know if it was bad acid but it wasn't a very good experience. . . .

"Sometimes when I want to be mellow, I just don't say anything. I just shut up. Or somebody can mellow out after a day at work—you come home, smoke a joint, drink a beer—you just sort of melt. . . ."

Putting It All Together. "Anything you've ever heard, you just remember and put it all together the best you can. That's good enough for me."

Formal Schooling

I knew little of Brad's schooling when I began systematically to collect life history data from him. By his account he had often been "slow" or "behind the rest of the class." He could read, but he faltered on "big words." He could write, but his spelling and punctuation were not very good. He had trouble recalling number sequences and basic arithmetic facts. ("Lack of practice," he insisted.) In one junior high school he had been placed in "an EH [educationally handicapped] class with the other stonies." As he recalled, "I don't know if I felt I was special or not, but I didn't like those big classes."

Measures of IQ or scholastic achievement did not really matter any more. Brad was well aware of his capacities and limitations. How far he was once "below average" or "behind" in his schoolwork had become, as it always had been, purely academic. Schooling for him was over; he was out.

Formal schooling aside, for practical purposes Brad could read, he could write, he could do simple arithmetic. The only book he "requisitioned" for his cabin was a dictionary. That alone was incredible; even more incredibly, he occasionally labored through it to find a word—no easy task when the alphabet had to be recited aloud in order to locate an entry.

Schooling had played a part in Brad's life, but not the vital part educators like it to play. In 10 years he enrolled in eight schools in two states, ranging from early years at a small country school to a final eight months at a state reformatory, and including attendance at urban elementary, junior high, and senior high schools. I traced his attendance record where he boasted having "the world's record for ditching school." Perhaps it was not the world's record, but following his mid-year enrollment in grade 5 he maintained 77 percent attendance for that year and 46 percent attendance in grade 6 the year following. He changed schools during the academic year at least once in grades 4, 5, and 6, as well as beginning the term in a new school four different years: "I guess I was in school a lot, but I was always in a different school."

In Brad's assessment, school "did what it's supposed to do. . . . You gotta learn to read." He laid no blame, noting only that "Maybe school could of did better." He acknowledged that *he* might have done better, too:

"I was just never that interested in school. If I knew I had to do something, I'd try a little bit. I could probably have tried harder."

The earliest school experience he could recall was in a church-sponsored kindergarten. Hearing Brad use objectionable language, the teacher threatened to wash his mouth with soap. At the next occasion when the children were washing their hands, he stuck a bar of soap in his mouth: "I showed the kids around me, 'Hey, no big deal, having soap in your mouth.'"

He recalled first grade as a time when "I learned my ABCs and everything. It was kind of neat." Apparently his enthusiasm for schooling stopped there. He could think of no particular class or teacher that he especially liked. His recollection of events associated with subsequent grades involved changes of schools, getting into trouble for his classroom behavior, or skipping school altogether. As early as fourth grade he remembered difficulty "keeping up" with classmates.

By his own assessment Brad did "OK" in school, but he recalled excelling only once, an art project in clay that was put on display and that his mother still kept. During grade 7 his attendance improved and, for one brief term, so did his grades, but he was not really engaged with what was going on and he felt lost in the large classes:

"In those big classes, like, you sit around in a big horseshoe, and you've got a seat four rows back, with just one teacher. Like English class, I'd get there at 9:00 in the morning and put my head down and I'd sleep through the whole class. It was boring, man.

"Another class they tried to get me in was typing. I tried for a little while, but I wasn't even getting close to passing, so I just gave up."

Brad's public schooling ended in southern California. When he got shunted back to Oregon, he did not enroll in school again, although after being "busted" schooling was his principal activity during eight months in reform school. He felt that he had attended "a couple of pretty good schools" in southern California during grades 8, 9, and, briefly, 10, but, as usual, the times he remembered were times spent out of class, not in it:

"By the end of school, I was cutting out a lot. Like, I didn't need PE. Look at this kid—he's been riding bicycles and skateboards all day all his life. I didn't need no PE. I don't need to go out in the sun and play games. I wasn't interested in sports. So I'd go get stoned. I'd take a walk during that class, go kick back in an orange grove, maybe eat an orange, get high, smoke a cigarette, and by the time I'd walk back, it was time for another class. I did it for a long time and never got caught. Anyhow, then I switched schools."

Brad felt that his lack of academic progress cost him extra time in reform school, "So I started to speed up and do the stuff and then I got out." In his assessment, "I was doing 9th-grade work. I probably did some 10th- and 11th-grade stuff, but not a lot."

Although young people seldom return to public schools after serving "time," I asked Brad to identify the grade levels to which he might have been assigned had he gone back to school.

"For math, if I went back, I'd just be getting into 10th grade. In reading, I'd be a senior or better. Spelling would be about 8th grade. I can spell good enough. Handwriting, well, you just write the way you write. My writing isn't that bad if I work on it. I don't worry about that much."

On the other hand, he did recognize limitations in his command of basic school skills. He had "kind of forgotten" the multiplication facts, and he was pretty rusty on subtracting and recalling the alphabet. To be a good speller, he once mused, you've got to "do it a lot," but at reform school he did only "a little bit." His awareness of these limitations is revealed in a letter intended for his mother but later abandoned in favor of a cheerier style:

> Hi
> if I sit hear and stair
> at this pieac of paper
> eny longer ill go crazy
> I dont think im scaird
> of witing just dont like
> to remind myself I
> need improvment. its
> raining alot past
> few days but its warm
> 'n dry inside. . . .

Reading was the school skill at which Brad felt most proficient, and his confidence was not shaken by the fact that some words were difficult for him. He said he did not enjoy reading, but he spent hours poring over instruction manuals. My impression was that although his oral reading was halting, he had good reading comprehension. That was also his assessment. When, at his father's insistence, he briefly entertained the idea of joining the Army, Brad had first to take the G.E.D. exam (for his high school General Equivalency Diploma) and then take a test for the Army. He felt he passed "pretty high" on the Army test and on some parts of the G.E.D., "like reading and a couple of other ones" he felt he did "super, super good."

Brad once observed philosophically, "The people in college today are probably the ones who didn't sleep when I was in English class." At the same time, school was a closed chapter in his life. Other than to acknowledge that he "might have tried harder," however, he expressed no regrets over school as an opportunity missed. Anticipating that his lack of school skills would prove a barrier to enrollment in any technical training program, he could not imagine ever returning to the classroom. And, like most school leavers, he could not think of anything that might have been done that would have kept him in school.[4]

Adequate Schools and Inadequate Education: An Interpretation

It might be socially "desirable" if Brad could read better, write better, do arithmetic better, spell better. With better spelling skills, he would "stare" rather than "stair" at a blank page and perhaps feel less self-conscious about needing "improvment." Considering that he devoted some (although certainly not exclusive) attention to schooling for 10 of his 20 years, he does not do these things very well.

On the other hand, that he can do them as well as he does might also be regarded as a tribute to the public schools. Brad's level of school achievement may be disappointing, but it is not inadequate. He is literate. He did get "something" out of school. True, his performance at the 3 Rs could be more polished, but the importance of his proficiency with such amenities pales before problems of greater social consequence. Brad's schooling has stopped, but his learning continues apace. Exerting some positive, constructive influence on that learning as it pertains to Brad's enculturation into society presents society's current challenge. That challenge has not been taken up.

Schools can affect the rate and level of academic achievement, but they do not set the course of students' lives. Schools are expediters for many, but they do not and cannot "reach" all, even though they may ever so briefly touch them. Schooling is not everyone's cup of tea. As Brad put it, "I've always liked learning. I just didn't like school."

Learning—in the broad enculturative sense of coming to understand what one needs to know to be competent in the roles one may expect to fulfill in society, rather than in the narrow sense of learning-done-at-school—is an ongoing process in which each human engages throughout a lifetime. In Brad's case, the direction that process was taking seemed to reflect all too well what he felt society expected of him: Nothing. He was left largely to his own resources to make sense of his world and create his own life (cf. Mann, 1982, p. 343). He endeavored quite self-consciously to "figure things out," but his resolutions often put him at odds with society; what appeared as inevitable conclusions to him were neither inevitable nor necessarily appropriate in terms of community norms.

Maybe we cannot reach him; surely we cannot reach everyone like him. But I was astounded to realize that no systematic, constructive effort was being exerted to influence the present course of Brad's life. No agency offered help, or direction, or concern, and neither did any of the "institutions" that ordinarily touch our lives: family, school, work, peer group. If it is naive to regard these influences as invariably positive and constructive, our interactions with them do, nonetheless, contribute to our sense of social "self." Brad was, for the most part, out of touch with them all.

If Brad is able to "get his life together," it will have to be almost entirely through his own effort. Perhaps his personal style as a loner helped buffer him from peer influences that seemed to me, as a wary adult, as likely to get him into trouble as to guide him on the straight and narrow; that he could find time and space "on a mountaintop in Oregon" rather than on a beach or under a freeway in southern California seemed to me to give him an advantage over his fellow "street people." His lifestyle was not overly complicated by urban trappings or the quickened pace of city life. He was not crowded or pushed. At the same time, he could neither escape the influence of material wants and creature comforts so prevalent in the society in which he lives nor deny a deeply felt need to connect with someone, somewhere. Seeming loner that he often appeared, even Brad could acknowledge, "There must be a group that I would fit in somewhere in this town."

He had learned to "hunt and gather" for his necessities in the aisles of supermarkets, in neighborhood garages, and at residential building sites. He conceded that stealing was wrong, but, among his priorities, necessity (broadly defined to allow for some luxuries as well) took precedence over conformity. He saw "no alternative" for getting the things he felt he needed but could not afford. Still, he took only what he considered necessary, not everything he could get his hands on. He was not, nor did he see himself ever becoming, a "super thief."

I do not see how society can "teach" Brad not to be sneaky or to shoplift or to steal. Most families try to do that. His family wasn't entirely successful, though more of the message seems to have gotten through than one might at first assume.[5] In that regard I find useful the distinction between deviant *acts* and deviant *persons* as suggested by anthropologist Robert Edgerton (1978). In spite of occasional deviant acts, Brad's statements reveal his underlying enculturation into the prevailing ethos of mainstream American society. He was well aware of the meanings of his acts to others; as he noted, "Any little kid knows what's right and wrong." Although he prided himself on the cunning necessary to survive his "hard life" by whatever means necessary, he staunchly defended his behavior—"I couldn't get by without stealing stuff"—as well as himself: "I am not that rotten of a kid!"

There was a foundation on which to build, but there was neither external help, nor support, nor a modicum of encouragement shaping that process. Was schooling "an" opportunity in Brad's life, or is it the only directed opportunity he gets? It seems to me there might, and should, be a more concerted effort to exert a positive influence to provide him with reasonable and realistic routes of access back into the cultural mainstream. To have any effect, however, such efforts would have to be in the form of increasing the options available to him, rather than trying to "shove" him in some particular direction; he has already heard the lectures about good citizenship.

The community's best strategy would seem to be to assure that *opportunities* exist for a person like Brad to satisfy more of his wants in socially acceptable ways. Fear of getting caught isn't much of a deterrent to someone who thinks he's "too smart" to get caught. Armed robbery is already within the realm of things Brad could, and might, do. With an attitude toward behaviors like shoplifting, "ripping things off," burglary, operating a vehicle with a suspended license, or even his preoccupation with obtaining an adequate supply of "pot," that "just about everybody—or at least everybody my age—does it," he can too easily find himself "in the chute" without realizing that everybody isn't there after all. Having gotten out of mainstream society, he does not see a way back in. Nor is he convinced it is worth the effort to try.

It is convenient—and an old American pastime—to place blame on the schools. Questions concerning educational adequacy, when directed toward the schools, invite that kind of blame-setting by relating the present inadequacies of youth to prior inadequacies of the schools (see Levin, 1983). Employing the anthropologist's distinction between schooling and education encourages us to review the full range of efforts the community makes to exert a positive educative influence on our lives, not only during the school years but in the post-school years as well.[6] The problems Brad now poses for society are not a consequence of inadequate schooling. They dramatize the risk we take by restricting our vision of collective educational responsibility to what can be done in school.

One hears arguments that today's youth vacillate between extremes of taking what they want or expecting everything to be handed to them on a silver platter. One finds a bit of both in Brad's dreams of pulling off a robbery or suddenly finding himself owning and operating a $60,000 piece of machinery, as well as in his reluctance to do work like dishwashing that entails cleaning up after others and where everyone can watch you perform a menial job.

But I wonder if young people like Brad really believe that society "owes" them something? Perhaps that is an expression of frustration at failing to see how to *begin* to accumulate resources of their own comparable to what they perceive "everyone else" already has. A willingness to defer gratification must come more easily to those who not only have agonized during the deferment but have eventually realized some long-awaited reward. Nothing Brad had ever done had worked out that well—at least prior to his effort to build both a new cabin and a new lifestyle. He had virtually no sense of deferred gratification. With him, everything was "now or never."

In a society so materialistic as ours, opportunity is realized essentially with money rather than "school" or "work." To Brad, money represented security and he had limited access to it. That is why food stamps, in an annual amount less than $900, figured so importantly to him. His use of the stamps has left me wondering whether it might be possible to design some governmental agency that would calculatedly confront individuals like Brad in an educative way.

But the educative value of a welfare dole is limited, and, as Brad discovered, the power of the dole-givers and their labyrinth of regulations is ultimate. The stamps made a better consumer of him (buying generic brands, buying large quantities, buying staples), but he realized that the first $70 of any month's take-home pay would be money he would otherwise have received free from the food stamp program. To "earn" his stamps, he had to remain poor.[7] Had he found the second-rate job he so dreaded, part of his earnings would simply have replaced the dole, his other expenses (transportation, clothes, maybe a second-rate apartment) would have increased dramatically, and he would have again been trapped in a second-rate life. Until his food stamps were summarily cancelled for two months, after he failed to participate in a ritual midwinter job search during a period of staggering recession and regional unemployment, he did not aggressively seek work. When he finally realized he was destitute and began in earnest to look for work, 38 days passed before he even got turned down for a job! He put in many hours at painting and yard clean-up for me (although he refused to equate working for me with "real work") and reverted to "ripping off" items he felt he needed but could not afford.

I invited Brad's thoughts on what might be done to help people like him. His idea, other than a dream of finding "just the right job" (never fully specified) without ever going to look for it, was of a "day work" program wherein anyone who needed money could appear at a given time, do a day's work, and promptly receive a day's pay. I'm sure Brad's thoughts turned to the end of the day when each worker would receive a pay envelope, while I wondered what one would do with a motley pick-up crew that wouldn't inadvertently make mockery of work itself. Yet implicit in his notion are at least two critical points.

First is a notion of a right to work: If (when) one is willing, one should be able to work and, if in dire need, be paid immediately in cash. Brad found no such right in his life. Although he had been able to find—but not hold—a number of jobs in the past, now he heard only "No Help Wanted" and read only "Not Presently Taking Applications." He was not entirely without social conscience when he observed that if he found a job he would only be taking it away from someone who needed it more. Brad did not really need a job. And, as he had begun to "figure out," no one really needed him. Maybe he was right; maybe $70 in food stamps was society's way of paying him to drop out.

Second is a notion of an overly structured wage and hour system that effectively prices most unskilled and inexperienced workers like Brad out of the job market and requires a full-time commitment from the few it accepts. Brad's material needs were slight. He could have preserved the best elements in his carefree lifestyle by working part time. However, the labor market does not ordinarily offer such options except for its own convenience. Either you want a job or you do not want a job. But work for its own sake cast no spell over Brad; he did not look to employment for satisfaction, for meaningful involvement, or for achieving self respect. Money was the only reason one worked.[8]

School provides opportunity and access for some youth; employment provides it for others. Neither school nor work presently exerted an influence on Brad. He was beyond school, and steady employment was beyond him. Without the effective support of family or friends, and without the involvement of school or work, he was left to his own devices. In his own words, he could not see a way to win and he did not have anything to lose. From mainstream society's point of view, we would be better off if he did.

After so carefully making provision for Brad's schooling, society now leaves his continuing education to chance, and we are indeed taking our chances. But educative adequacy in the lives of young people like Brad is not an issue of schooling. Schools provided him one institutional opportunity; they no longer reached him, and no other agency was trying. His next institutional "opportunity," like his last one, may be custodial. If it is, we all lose; Brad will not be the only one who will have to pay.[9]

Summary

"The important thing about the anthropologist's findings," writes Clifford Geertz (1973), one of anthropology's more articulate spokesmen, "is their complex specificness, their circumstantiality" (p. 23). Whatever issue anthropologists address, they characteristically begin an account and look for illustration through real events or cases bounded in time and circumstance. The effective story should be "specific and circumstantial," but its relevance in a broader context should be apparent. The story should make a point that transcends its modest origins. The case must be particular, but the implications broad.

Following that tradition, I have related a specific and circumstantial life story to illustrate the necessity of regarding education as more than just schooling and of pointing out how little we attend to that broader concern. That may seem a roundabout way to address so complex an issue, but it is a way to bring an anthropological perspective to the problem.

Brad's story is unique, but his is not an isolated case. He is one among thousands of young people who simply "drift away." His uninvited presence on my 20-acre sanctuary, in search of sanctuary for himself, brought me into contact with a type of youth I do not meet as a college professor. He piqued my anthropological interest with a world view in many ways strikingly similar to mine but a set of coping strategies strikingly different. It is easy for people like me to think of people like Brad as someone else's problem, but, for a moment that lingered out to two years, he quite literally brought the problem home to me. I do not find ready answers even in his particular case; I am certainly not ready to say what might, can, or must be done in some broader context.

Little is to be gained from laying blame at the feet of Brad's parents or his teachers, and to do so is to ignore indications of repeated, if not necessarily effective, efforts to help and guide him. Though our extended conversations may have been enlightening to Brad, as they surely were to me, my more direct efforts to help seemed to go awry. At the end, he departed almost as unexpectedly as he had arrived. I am not sure what I think "society" can accomplish for an amorphous "them" when my own well-intended efforts with just one youth seemed only to demonstrate to him that I had my life "together" (his term) in a manner virtually unattainable for himself. The easiest course is to blame Brad, but to do so is to abandon hope and a sense of collective responsibility.

The only certainty I feel is that it is in our common interest to seek ways to provide opportunities intended to exert a continuing and constructive educational influence on the lives of young people like Brad. I do not know whether Brad can or will allow himself to be reached effectively or in time. I do know that from his perspective he saw neither attractive opportunities nor sources of potential help; by his own assessment, he simply did not matter. He was not free of his society but he had become disconnected from it. Once adrift, nothing seemed to beckon or guide him back.

Because we tend to equate education with schooling, we are inclined to look to the past and ask where the schools went wrong. Brad's story, in which school played only a minor role, serves as a reminder of the importance of other educative influences in our lives. It also points out how little systematic attention we give to discerning what those influences are or how we might better use them to augment, complement, and otherwise underwrite the massive efforts we direct at youth during their in-school years. In that broad perspective, our efforts at *education* appear woefully inadequate in spite of the remarkable accomplishments of our schools. Until I found Brad living in my backyard, however, the problem remained essentially abstract. Now it has confronted me with the "complex specificness" of one young human life.

Notes

Acknowledgements. A portion of the work on which this article is based was performed pursuant to Contract No. NIE-P-81-0271 of the National Institute of Education dealing with issues of educational adequacy under the School Finance Project. Data collection and interpretation are, however, the responsibility of the author. Appreciation is expressed to W. W. Charters, Jr., Stanley Elam, Barbara Harrison, Bryce Johnson, Malcolm McFee, and Esther O. Tron, as well as to "Brad," for critical reading and helpful suggestions with early drafts of this paper.

1. If I found any surprise in reviewing the literature, it was in discovering some remarkable similarities between Brad's story and the ground-breaking classic first published half a century ago, Clifford Shaw's *The Jack-Roller: A Delinquent Boy's Own Story* (1930).

2. Meyer Fortes, writing in 1938, noted the firmly established axiom that "education in the widest sense is the process by which the cultural heritage is transmitted from generation to generation, and that schooling is therefore only part of it" (p. 5). Melville Herskovits (1948) subsequently introduced the encompassing term *enculturation* for referring to education in Fortes' "widest sense," but he retained the term *education*, suggesting that it be restricted to "its ethnological sense of directed learning," in turn distinct from and more encompassing than *schooling*, defined as "that aspect of education carried out by specialists" (p. 311; see also Wallace, 1961b).

3. I have been careful to observe the few conditions Brad imposed on my use of the information; he, in turn, was paid for time spent interviewing and for later checking the written account, and early drafts were informed by his comments. That is not to imply that he was entirely satisfied with my portrayal or my interpretation, but he was satisfied that what I reported was accurate. If only to please me, he even commented that he hoped his story might "help people understand."

4. See, for example, the *Oregon Early School Leavers Study* (Oregon Department of Education, 1980), in which only one third of the young people interviewed responded that "something might have been done to affect their decision to quit public secondary school" (p. 16).

5. Brad expressed only resentment toward his father, but his mother's efforts to provide a positive influence on him were often mentioned. When Brad introduced us, after proudly showing her the cabin during her brief but long-anticipated visit, I asked whether she felt she could exert a guiding influence over him living 1,000 miles away. "We've always been a thousand miles apart," she replied, "even when we were under the same roof."

On a different occasion, responding to Brad's announcement that he needed to "find" another bicycle, I asked, "What would your mother think about you stealing a bike? That it's dumb; that it's smart?"

"Neither," he replied. "She'd just think that I must have needed it. She wouldn't say anything. She doesn't lecture me about things like that. But she used to cut out every-thing they printed in the paper about 'pot' and put it on my walls and she'd talk about brain damage."

6. Although the distinction between education and schooling is sometimes acknowl-edged, it is not necessarily regarded as having much significance, at least for understand-ing contemporary society. To illustrate, note in the following excerpt how educator/economist Henry Levin, addressing the topic *Education and Work* (1982), at once rec-ognizes the distinction between education and schooling but bows to what he describes as the "convention" of equating them:

> Although the term education is sometimes used interchangeably with schooling, it is important to note that schooling is not the only form of education. However, schooling represents such a dominant aspect of education in modern societies that the convention of equating education and schooling in the advanced industrialized societies will also be adopted here (p. 1).

7. The irony of the implications and consequences when *not* working is prerequisite to maintaining a steady income is nicely spelled out in Estroff, 1981. See especially Chapter 6, "Subsistence Strategies: Employment, Unemployment, and Professional Dis-ability."

8. Paul Willis (1980) notes in his study of working-class youth that it is this "reign of cash" that precipitates their contact with the world of work (p. 39). As one of his informants explained, "Money is life." Brad's mother expressed a similar view: "Money, not love, makes the world go round."

9. For a grim scenario, including some discomforting parallels and similarities, see Mailer, 1979. The protagonist of Mailer's "true life novel" makes special note of the impact of reform school on his life (Chapter 22). Brad did not reveal the extent of the impact on his own life of the same reform school, but he did include it specifically in his brief inventory of significant "experiences." Similarities noted earlier between Brad's ac-count and Shaw's *The Jack-Roller* (1930) seem less pronounced in a subsequently pub-lished follow-up, *The Jack-Roller at Seventy* (Snodgrass, 1982).

References

Brandes, S. (1980). Ethnographic autobiographies in American anthropology. In E. A. Hoebel, R. Currier, & S. Kaiser (Eds.), *Crisis in anthropology: View from Spring Hill, 1980*. New York: Garland Publishing Company.

Edgerton, R. (1978). The study of deviance—Marginal man or everyman? In G. D. Spindler (Ed.), *The making of psychological anthropology*. Berkeley: University of Cali-fornia Press.

Estroff, S. E. (1981). *Making it crazy: An ethnography of psychiatric clients in an American community*. Berkeley: University of California Press.

Fortes, M. (1938). *Social and psychological aspects of education in Taleland*. Supplement to *Africa, 11*(4).

Geertz, C. (1973). *The interpretation of cultures*. New York: Basic Books.

Herskovits, M. J. (1948). *Man and his works: the science of cultural anthropology*. New York: Alfred A. Knopf.

Levin, H. M. (1982). *Education and work*. Program Report No. 82-B8. Palo Alto, CA: Institute for Research on Educational Finance and Governance, Stanford University.

Levin, H. M. (1983). Youth unemployment and its educational consequences. *Educa-tional Evaluation and Policy Analysis, 5*(2), 231–247.

Lewis, O. (1961). *Children of Sanchez: Autobiography of a Mexican family.* New York: Random House.

MacNeil, I., & Glover, G. (Producers). (1959). *Four families* (Film narrated by Ian MacNeil and Margaret Mead). National Film Board of Canada.

Mailer, N. (1979). *The executioner's song.* New York: Warner Books.

Mann, D. (1982). Chasing the American dream: Jobs, schools, and employment training programs in New York State. *Teachers College Record, 83*(3), 341–376.

Oregon Department of Education. (1980). *Oregon early school leavers study.* Salem: Author.

Shaw, C. R. (1930). *The jack-roller: A delinquent boy's own story.* University of Chicago Press.

Simmons, L. (Ed.). (1942). *Sun Chief: The autobiography of a Hopi Indian.* New Haven: Yale University Press.

Snodgrass, J. (Ed.). (1982). *The jack-roller at seventy: A fifty-year follow-up.* Lexington, MA: D. C. Heath & Company.

Wallace, A. F. C. (1961a). The psychic unity of human groups. In B. Kaplan (Ed.), *Studying personality cross-culturally.* Evanston, IL: Row Peterson and Company.

Wallace, A. F. C. (1961b). Schools in revolutionary and conservative societies. In F. C. Gruber (Ed.), *Anthropology and education.* Philadelphia: University of Pennsylvania Press.

Willis, P. E. (1980). *Learning to labour: How working class kids get working class jobs.* Hampshire, England: Gower Publishing Co. (Originally published 1977).

Wolcott, H. F. (1982). The anthropology of learning. *Anthropology and Education Quarterly, 13*(2), 83–108.

Section V
Case Study Methods in Educational Research

Case Study Methods in Educational Research: Seeking Sweet Water

Robert E. Stake
University of Illinois

This paper was originally a tape presentation for AERA's "Alternative Methodologies in Educational Research." It is now presented in written form in its entirety, though edited for written presentation.

It is a hypothetical dialog in which I discuss case study methods with my colleagues and students. Together we explore the vast expanses of the case study methodology, "seeking sweet water" for educational research. We speak of the relevance of the case study approach while confronting the objections to this method of research.

Included in the dialog are ideas drawn from several case studies. Full information about the case studies is included in the reference list for this paper; however, before beginning to read, you will want to know who is participating in this dialog: Howard Becker, sociologist, Northwestern University; Charles Brauner, philosopher, University of British Columbia; David Hamilton, educational researcher, Glasgow University; Louis Smith, educational ethnographer, Washington University of St. Louis; and Bernadine Stake, educational researcher, University of Illinois.

Following the dialog are suggestions for further reading and a bibliography, study questions, a set of guidelines for doing a field-observation case study, and an additional exercise on locating common errors in written observation reports.

Student A: Case study? Case study? Why, that's the report of a child with problems, isn't it?

Student B: Well, a case study is what you do if you want to emphasize the affective domain—and you can't measure it.

Student C: A case study is what you call a study, in case, in case you don't have anything else to call it.

Stake: People have different notions as to what a case study is. The term "case study" belongs to medicine, social work, urban planning, plant pathology. It belongs to science and to social service. It belongs to all of us.

Together we will look into the increasing popularity of the case study in education, and also into the continuing objections that many researchers have to the case study method of research.

The biggest complaint I hear about educational research these days is that it always seems to find nonsignificant differences. Case studies are not going to help there. I sometimes hear complaints that even if we were to find significant differences, the research would not be directly relevant to the problems of education. Now this is a place where case studies can help. A case study that portrays an educational problem in all its personal and social complexity is a precious discovery.

I am reminded of the search by the first American pioneers to the West. Finding drinking water for humans and livestock was a precious discovery. Even if it was granuled with brown or green, they happily called it "sweet water."

Let's consider the preparation of one of the best case studies in our literature, an evaluation report by Lou Smith and Paul Pohland (1974) called "Educational Technology and the Rural Highlands."

Smith: The computer-assisted-instruction (CAI) program that we studied in the Rural Highlands was a broadly based attempt to change the achievement of the students in this important basic skill [arithmetic]. One facet of the integration of the computer-aided instruction with the classroom work was the relationships among the drills, what went on at the terminals and the regular classroom work. One general observation we made was that the relationships seemed minimal.

For instance, reading from my notes, on the 17th of November when we were there,

> I made a specific point of checking with two of the [first grade] girls about where they were currently in their math lessons. I wondered then how closely the drills that they were taking corresponded to what they were doing in class. Apparently it is not very close. Ruth told me that the day's classroom lesson was on "writing mathematical sentences." The drills, however, were all simple addition and subtraction problems.

Later in the school year this issue was examined again. For instance, on April 2 we have in our notes:

> I also asked Edith about the relationship between the materials she had on the teletype and what they were doing in class. The conversation ran as follows:
>   Observer: Are you doing multiplication in class?
>   Edith: We're doing fractions.
> I also asked Dick.
>   Observer: Is it (the drill) anything like what you're doing in class?
> His answer was a very emphatic "no!"

We searched our notes and records for factors that seemed to be involved in creating this situation. Several came to mind: (a) the approximately six-week delay in starting the CAI program, the computer-assisted instruction program, seemed very critical; (b) there were frequent system breakdowns, that is, the physical structure of the system, the teletypes, the telephone lines, the computers, the terminals had difficulties; and (c) few teachers appeared to be aware of or chose to exercise the option of reassigning "units" to the children once they were placed in the program. In this sense it was a broadly based, complex, systemic set of causes.

Stake: It is apparent that Smith and Pohland were trying in this case study to acquaint us, their readers, with the teaching and learning system in that arithmetic class. They were not just writing a natural history, and not just telling us that there are "real, live human beings" in that classroom. Smith and Pohland were working on a conceptual structure, building up an understanding, perhaps as would an author of a TV documentary or a biographer telling a story of one person's life; drawing some conclusions, yet leaving room for readers or listeners to make up their own minds. One issue in Smith and Pohland's conceptual structure was the difference between the arithmetic being taught by the computer and the arithmetic regularly taught by the teacher without the computer.

Of course, all research methods emphasize a conceptual structure. Sometimes researchers talk about hypotheses, sometimes about theories, sometimes about educational objectives. All of these are conceptual structures—so the case study is not unique just because it is organized around a conceptual structure. And to be sure, different case study researchers use very different kinds of conceptual structure.

Let's see if we can get at the principal difference between the case study and other educational research studies. Here is a definition of case study by Lou Smith.

Smith: The definition of a case study is certainly not unambiguous. Somehow the term "bounded system" usually comes to mind—that is, the study of a bounded system. The crux of the definition is having some conception of the unity or totality of a system with some kind of outlines or boundaries.

For instance, take a child with learning disabilities as the bounded system. You have an individual pupil, in a particular circumstance, with a particular problem. There are observable behaviors. There are speculations—sometimes I call them foreshadowed problems. What the researcher looks for are the systematic connections among the observable behaviors, speculations, causes, and treatments. What the study covers depends partly on what you are trying to do. The unity of the system depends partly on what you want to find out.

In our work we've been much more interested in finding out how systems work over time. But emphasis on time is a sub-issue. It seems like it's critical for teachers, principals, and actors in the situation. The key notion is that you've got some kind of entity, a case, a kind of unity. A part of that unity may be perceived and studied in a delimited case study.

Stake: Here is a textbook definition from a sociology research-methods book by Goode and Hatt (1952):

The case study then is not a specific technique; it is a way of organizing social data so as to preserve the unitary character of the social object being studied. (p. 331)

So the principal difference between case studies and other research studies is that the focus of attention is the case, not the whole population of cases. In most other studies, researchers search for an understanding that ignores the uniqueness of individual cases and generalizes beyond particular instances. They search for what is common, pervasive, and lawful. In the case study, there may be or may not be an ultimate interest in the generalizable. For the time being, the search is for an understanding of the particular case, in its idiosyncracy, in its complexity.

The principal difference is not one of method. It is true that most case studies in education today use anthropological or sociological field methods. Case study researchers commonly make carefully planned observations in natural settings and use interviews, qualitative analysis, and narrative reports. In another section of this book, Harry Wolcott lists ways ethnographers make observations and keep records. Many case study researchers use these methods, but they don't *have* to. Some case studies are highly impersonal and statistical.

On almost every campus we find a special kind of statistical case study, an institutional research study. It may show up as an annual report to the board of trustees. The student body is described in terms of age, area of specialization, and home town or country. The faculty is described in the aggregate, too, in terms of rank, sex, members of minority races, degrees held, publications authored. The budget and endowment trends are also reported. Though seldom named as such, this statistical description is a case study, too.

Case studies are special because they have a different focus. The case study focuses on a bounded system, whether a single actor, a single classroom, a single institution, or a single enterprise—usually under natural conditions—so as to understand it in its own habitat.

What is being studied is the case. The case is something deemed worthy of close watch. It has character, it has a totality, it has boundaries. It is not something we want to represent by a score. It is not something we want to represent only by an array of scores. It is a complex, dynamic system. We want to understand its complexity. Lou Smith used a fancy name, bounded system, to indicate that we are going to try to figure out what complex things go on within that system. The case study tells a story about a bounded system.

Student A: But how does the researcher know *which* story to tell?

Stake: There are many different stories to be told. The fact that different case study researchers tell different stories is sometimes said to indicate that case study findings lack validity. But of course, different researchers have different conceptualizations of the problem and set different boundaries for the case.

Such differences are common to historians, to astronomers, to experimentalists, to any community of researchers, using any research method.

Which story to tell? That's a difficult question. The ideas change even during the course of the study. Howard Becker (1961) tells of first having a "developmental perspective" as he undertook work at the University of Kansas School of Medicine, but later shifting to another orientation.

Let's consider what Howard Becker meant by a "developmental perspective," and his shift in orientation.

Becker: We began our study with a concern about what happens to medical students as they move through medical school. This concern receded as we became more and more preoccupied with what went on in the school itself and, particularly, with the problem of the level and direction of academic effort of medical students. Nevertheless, there are some things we can say about how medical students change and develop as they go through school.

What happens to students as a result of their schooling? One view is that they are socialized into a professional role. Mary Jean Huntington (1957) has shown that medical students are more likely, with each succeeding year in school, to say that they thought of themselves as a doctor rather than as a student on the occasion of their last contact with a patient. She interprets this to mean that medical students gradually develop a professional self-image in the course of their medical training.

We have not found this framework useful in analyzing our data on the Kansas medical students. We have already seen in earlier chapters that the Kansas students do not take on a professional role while they are students, largely because the system they operate in does not allow them to do so. They are not doctors, and the recurring experiences of being denied responsibility make it perfectly clear to them that they are not. Though they may occasionally, in fantasy, play at being doctors, they never mistake their fantasies for the fact, for they know that until they have graduated and are licensed they will not be allowed to act as doctors.

Stake: *Boys in White* (Becker, 1961) is not the story of a medical student, or several medical students. It is the story of the medical student experience at one medical school. What happens when the student goes home for Christmas or what happens in the dean's office turned out to be outside the boundaries.

Lou Smith's case study of computer-aided arithmetic instruction in a rural school is not a collection of stories about children or teachers or teletype machines. It is a naturalistic study of teaching and learning in one setting. The case is the arithmetic class. It is highly personalized because teaching and learning are highly personalized. The case study here honors people because people are so important in a teaching-learning situation. The system boundaries are not the skins of people, but are the boundaries around a particular experience.

Smith: Such a bounded system can be an individual system or a social system, and it is the latter that we have been interested in over the years.

In our work we've been finding out how systems (school systems, teacher-learner systems, curriculum development systems) work over time.

In *Boys in White*, Howard Becker and his colleagues traced part of the career history of the medical student, but they were more interested in structures of instruction at a particular time. So their boundaries were different from ours.

What is inside the boundaries of those systems depends on what you want to find out, but also on those unexpected things that turn out over time to be related to what you want to find out.

Stake: To carry out most case studies you set the boundaries, and then you search out certain issues or themes. You have to set the boundaries again and maybe again as you come to know the case better.

The people who set the boundaries and authenticate themes are not only the researchers but all those who care about the system. That includes teachers at the scene, and it includes the readers of the case study. Certain things belong to the case, according to their expectations—so that boundaries and themes are set partly by those people anywhere who are interested in the case.

Most researchers only gradually come to realize which issues are best to build the story around. One cannot deal with the totality of anything. Some strong claims have been made for the case study as dealing with the "complete" story. Of course a case study doesn't tell the whole story. But it does deal with the unity of the case, the unity of the experience, in ways other research methods do not.

Here is what Goode and Hatt (1952) said:

> First the wholeness of any object, whether physical, biological, or social, is an intellectual construct. Concretely, there are no limits which define any process or object. Every variable ultimately links with any other. As theoretical biology has pointed out, from some points of view even the living animal (child studying arithmetic) is a construct—and the point at which the animal stops and the environment begins is arbitrarily defined.
>
> From this point of view we see that it is difficult to state at what point it is profitable to stop gathering data about the object so delimited. As has been noted before, an infinite number of observations may be made about even the dullest or most unimportant person. Consequently, neither the case study nor any other approach can be characterized as *the* analysis of the individual in all his uniqueness. The point at which data are adequate must be determined by the research problem itself. (p. 332)

So that leaves us with a pretty loose definition, that the case study is a study of a "bounded system," emphasizing the unity and wholeness of that system, but confining the attention to those aspects that are relevant to the research problem at the time.

Both Lou Smith and Howard Becker observe and interview many persons in preparation for their analyses and reporting. Some case study researchers are inclined to stick with a single person, family, or classroom—for example, Oscar Lewis' *Children of Sanchez* (1961). Another example we will consider is Bernadine Stake's (1977) case study of a fourth-grade class learning arithmetic with the help of the PLATO instructional system.

One thing common to all authors and users of case studies is the search for patterns. All researchers are interested in regularity, consistency. Even in the most unique of persons, even in the most unique curricula, even in the most unique of bond referendum campaigns, there are certain patterns. The researcher is seeking "sweet water," water safe to drink, sustaining, refreshing—patterns of meaning.

The patterns may emerge as a contingency, one thing consistently coexisting with another. The pattern may show up as a repeated sequence of action. Can we think of examples?

Student C: Whenever the child started to cry, the teacher became busy with other children.

Stake: The pattern may emerge as a classification.

Student C: The teacher's attention to reward-systems was constant; she was, those days, the "specialist in behavior modification."

Stake: It is important to become acquainted with the literature using case study methodology. Following this paper is the complete text of one of the exemplary studies in the case study tradition. It is an evaluation study of an orientation week written by philosopher Charles Brauner (1974). He called it "The First Probe." Take some time now to read the first three paragraphs of the study. Take notes if you want to. Try to discover the bounded system, some of the issues, and emerging patterns.

Now that you have had a chance to become acquainted with a case study, what was Brauner's bounded system?

Student A: The Department of Architecture's orientation session.

Stake: O.K. And what do you suppose the issues were?

Student C: Brauner was probably asking, "Does exposing the new class to deprivation and the unexpected change their attitude toward the field of architecture?"

Stake: I'm sure that was one of the issues or foreshadowing questions. Could you identify at least one pattern?

Student C: There were patterns of behavior that caused the staff to call the students the "hoarders," the "sharers," etc.

Student B: And there was a pattern of unwillingness by the students to believe there was no food.

Stake: Two good patterns, and there were others, of course.

The powerful writing in Brauner's case study gives the reader some of the feeling of unexpected deprivation, the disgust and the anger of those young students. The typologizing of people and experience makes the account easily understood. The patterns of events, such as regression to primitive behavior in moments of stress, are patterns easily recognized.

Sweet water! It is dramatic. Usually a case study will not be theatrical like Britannia Beach; more often, it will feature the drama of answering the phone, opening the mail. Drama of the commonplace. We should not over-romanticize our research topics. But it is deceitful to understate them.

Entertainment is not the purpose of such case study research, of course. In making it vivid, and even to create suspense, the researcher appeals, I believe, to more than one way of knowing things, to more than one episte-mology. The writer appeals to one's emotions, but beyond that, at the same time, provides a vicarious cognitive experience. This vicarious experience may be more easily integrated into a reader's existing experience than a quantitative record is. The question can be raised: Do we come to understand an educational experience better by drawing heavily on personal experiences, or by attending to formal statements of relationship?

In giving the reader vicarious experience, Brauner helps readers extend their own experience, to add new to old. Does empathic understanding enable the reader to realize the complexity of an architecture student's need for questioning common living patterns? The UBC faculty wanted the student to have a fresh view of the stress of living conditions. This case study writer saw the best way to convey that goal was to tell it as it happened.

That orientation week for architecture students was unique. It isn't expected that readers will want to plan such a week. Yet, the description may be useful to them. Readers know that they arrive at general understandings of things partly through experience in individual events.

In my own writing I sometimes talk about "naturalistic generalization." I think of this "way of knowing" as very important, for researchers and for others. We all, of course, also arrive at understandings through experimentation and induction, through what is commonly called "scientific generalization." It is not terribly important to decide which is more important. There are ample needs for both modes of acquired understanding.

Most case studies contribute more to naturalistic generalization than to scientific generalization. But however they are useful, I believe, they are more useful when careful thought is given to the boundaries of the case, the issues, and the patterns that illustrate the issues.

Student B: How important is it for the case to be representative?

Stake: Many people criticize case study research because there is too little indication of the degree to which the case is representative of other cases. Usually it is left to the reader to decide. Of course, it is easy to argue that a sample of "size one" is never typical of anything, except itself.

For some research purposes, it will be essential that the "cases examined" be representative of some population of cases. Presumably, a case could be so unique that it might be unwise to consider any finding as true of other cases. However, both MacDonald and Walker have operated on the premise that the unique case helps us understand the more typical cases.

Whether or not a case should be representative of other cases depends on the purposes of the research. It would be presumptuous to dismiss all findings as invalid because the case was not demonstrably representative. Some findings—for the purposes some readers have—do not depend on the notion of generalizing to a population of cases.

Sometimes a researcher wants to find out how just one thing works—for example, how a new writing skills program is working. Another researcher might want to find out how the program would work under other circumstances. Now for that researcher, it would be more important that the case be representative. So it depends on the purposes.

Sometimes the case may not be representative, but an important decision to be made might be typical and worth the attention of many readers. A lovely example of the use of a case study for helping understand a decision is David Hamilton's (1976) "The Case of the Missing Chairs." The question was whether or not, in a new primary school with open classrooms, to provide one chair for every child, or fewer chairs. A trivial question? Not in terms of cost, and not in terms of instructional method. Here is Hamilton's explanation.

Hamilton: In 1973 the plans for the new lower primary building had reached the state where a seating level had to be decided. Consensus among the staff was difficult to achieve since individual members reacted differently to the idea that seating levels might be reduced below one chair per child.

To resolve this issue, the headmaster of the school was asked to act as an arbitrator. By his decision the seating level was duly fixed at 60 percent. In principle this action closed the debate. In practice, however, the teachers were left with a possible alternative: if the designated seating level proved inadequate, it could still be "topped up" with infant-sized furniture left over from the old buildings. The flexibility of this arrangement became apparent when some of the ordered furniture failed to arrive in time for the opening of the new building. The old tables and chairs were immediately pressed into service and, in a complete reversal of the original intention, were "topped up" by the new furniture as it arrived. Eventually a surplus of chairs was created—which meant that the teachers could operate their own seating policies. Some chose the figure of 60 percent while others retained at least one chair for each child.

This arrangement did not last for very long. Within a term all the teachers had built up their seating levels to at least 100 percent. The "topping up," however, did not herald a return to class teaching. Quite the reverse: it marked a recognition that an adequate supply of chairs was necessary to the individualized and balanced curriculum that the case study teachers were trying to implement. Thus, despite a certain sense of public failure among the teachers who tried to work with a reduced provision, the intervening experience had taught them a great deal about the relationship between teaching methods and seating requirements.

Stake: It is not surprising that case study research can be used to aid in the understanding and resolution of a local problem. But the Hamilton study is illuminative for teachers and administrators of primary schools in many countries.

Researchers of all kinds, even those doing the most basic of research and abstract studies, are at times drawn to careful scrutiny of the individual case. Julian Stanley once wrote in a personal letter to me, "When I want to find out something important for myself I often use the case study approach."

Stake: And it is not just during early exploration, as some authors imply, that case study methods are appropriate. During middle and final stages as well, competent researchers turn to careful scrutiny of the individual case.

Student C: I think it is time someone pointed out that knowledge based on personal experience is not trustworthy. Good research needs skeptical thinking and systematic replication.

Stake: You're right, research does need skeptical thinking and systematic replication. Some case study researchers, Becker and Smith, for example, are good at both. What is missing in case study work is automatic, built-in cautiousness, such as you have in statistical testing of the null hypothesis.

Student C: I think it's too likely that a reader of case study research will over-interpret the findings, presuming them to be relevant where they are not.

Stake: Yes, it's likely some readers will read too much into the report. But others will reject relevant findings on false grounds. Some city school principals, for example, almost automatically reject findings from rural settings. There will be errors of both kinds.

We might raise the question, "How much of the burden of being skeptical should be borne by the researcher?" If researchers are too cautious, readers may not find out about emerging insights. Is it not possible for the researcher to assume too large a share of the burden, by refusing to draw in the experience of the reader?

The case study researcher does not guarantee that the reader will have an equal share in the interpretation, but it is common for responsibility to be shared between case study researcher and reader.

Student A: Then that is one of the reasons case study research is becoming more popular?

Stake: Possibly so. But I think it is more a matter of relevance than power. Case studies are still considered not quite legitimate in many places. And they do not seem to have the political "clout" that a statistical study has, particularly in a time of confrontation.

I think that it is naturalistic research that is becoming more popular, the careful study of human activity in its natural and complex state. The fact that case studies are commonly used in naturalistic research is making it appear that case studies are becoming more popular.

And I think it is a matter of increased realization of how we, the teachers, and the teachers of teachers, learn. Of how all experienced people learn.

School people, and researchers as well, have long been dubious about the relevance of much educational research. In recent years many felt misled by curriculum reform, programmed instruction, and by evaluation. Some see the shortcomings of these technological developments as evidence that educational research has not been effective. They are pleased with something more easily understood—and more submissive to their own interpretations.

Student B: What about the criticism that case study findings lack validity?

Stake: Many case studies do have insufficient validity for the purposes of a particular researcher or school official. We should note that validity depends on the use to which the findings are put.

A case study is valid to the reader to whom it gives an accurate and useful representation of the bounded system. Accuracy of observing and reporting is not a matter of everyone seeing and reporting the same thing. Observers have different vantage points. Scenes change. Some observations can be validated by going back and observing from the same point of view. And some good observations cannot be validated at all. Researchers look for ways of directly and indirectly confirming their observations, and readers of case studies participate in the effort to understand the validity of the observations.

Readers have different uses for research reports. One reader expects an exact facsimile of the "real thing." Another reader is attending to a new type of problem that had not previously been apparent. The validity of the report is different for each, according to the meaning the reader gives to it. Validity depends on purposes and points of view. To some people, this sounds hopelessly relativistic, but it is consistent with Lee Cronbach's (1971) respected definition of test validity in the second edition of *Educational Measurement*.

One of the primary ways of increasing validity is by triangulation. The idea comes from sociology (and, further back, from navigation at sea). The technique is one of trying to arrive at the same meaning by at least three independent approaches. Naturally a finding that has been triangulated with several independent data-holdings is usually more credible than one that has not.

One of the issues in Bernadine Stake's (1977) case study of PLATO learning with the computerized instructional system was whether or not children continued to be motivated to work on arithmetic lessons at the terminal. In her report she said:

> Children by then had been using PLATO for six months. They continued to be fascinated and involved with the tasks on it, even in these extraordinary circumstances. Ms. Hamilton [the teacher] encouraged children to be actively engaged in all their activities in any part of the classroom. It was easier to accomplish at the PLATO terminals. The interviews with Ms. Hamilton, classroom observations, and the Teacher's Log substantiate this claim. Ms. Hamilton said, "The children really concentrate on the lessons while at the terminal. They often were so engaged that they would not talk to other children or me while they were working." She said, "It is one-half hour of the day when I knew each child was being instructed." Other teachers who used PLATO also testified to the power of PLATO to help keep children on task. (p. 22)
>
> Ted was an example of a child who was not interested in ordinary school tasks. He wandered about the room and didn't work, and even cried and stamped his foot when asked to finish assignments. At the PLATO terminal he was consistently attentive to the tasks. (p. 23)
>
> Sara finished the "fives" easily. PLATO informed her that she was ready for the "sixes." Sara turned to me and said, "I don't know the sixes and I don't want to know them." I knew that most children her age were working on the sixes so I asked her if she didn't want to try them. She said she did not want to. Not listening, PLATO presented her next problem: 5×6. Sara worked it even though she had said she wasn't going to. Her answer was correct. She clapped her hands and seemed happy with herself. (p. 29)
>
> Teacher's Log: April 12–16. Sara has really done an outstanding job. It was so difficult to get her to complete any math at the beginning of the year. In fact it was often necessary to have her work near me to accomplish her daily tasks. She really seems to enjoy math now. (p. 47)

Stake: A success story is always nice to hear, but the "sweet water" in this story comes from triangulation. From direct observation, from interview, from the teacher's log, and from additional sources, the researcher drew evidence for the one conclusion, that the on-task behavior of the pupils was high and remained high throughout the year.

Time doesn't allow us to consider difficulties in gaining access to the classroom, or the problems of intrusiveness into personal affairs, or the great expense of the naturalistic case study.

Student A: Well, sometimes it will be worth it, to get a much better understanding of the case—whatever it is.

Student B: While it would be easier to learn how to do it if there were only one way to do a case study, the strength of case study research is in using lots of different methods to triangulate the findings.

Student C: Many times case studies shouldn't be accepted for scientific generalization—they may help us establish the limits of such generalization, but mostly they will help us to understand what's happening inside that case, that bounded system.

References

Becker, H. S., Geer, B., Hughes, E., & Strauss, A. (1961). *Boys in white: Student culture in medical school.* Chicago: University of Chicago Press.

Brauner, C. (1974). The first probe. In *Four evaluation examples: Anthropological, economic, narrative, and portrayal, AERA monograph series on curriculum evaluation, no. 7* (pp. 77–98). Chicago: Rand McNally.

Cronbach, L. (1971). Test validation. In R. L. Thorndike (Ed.), *Educational measurement* (2d ed.). Washington, DC: American Council on Education.

Goode, W. J., & Hatt, P. K. (1952). *Methods in social research.* New York: McGraw-Hill.

Hamilton, D. (1976). The case of the missing chairs. In D. Hamilton, *In search of structure: Essays from an open plan school.* Edinburgh: Scottish Council for Research in Education.

Huntington, M. J. (1957). The development of a professional self-image. In R. K. Merton, G. Reader, and P. L. Kendall (Eds.), *The student-physician* (pp. 179–187). Cambridge, MA: Harvard University Press.

Lewis, O. (1961). *The children of Sanchez.* New York: Random House.

Smith, L., & Pohland, P. (1974). Education, technology, and the rural highlands. In *Four evaluation examples: Anthropological, economic, narrative, and portrayal, AERA monograph series on curriculum evaluation, no. 7* (pp. 5–54). Chicago: Rand McNally.

Stake, B. E. (1977). *PLATO—Fourth grade mathematics.* Unpublished doctoral dissertation, University of Illinois, Champaign-Urbana.

Suggestions for Further Reading

You may want to consider additional study materials, or you may want to consider some specific steps for doing case study.

In this section I include guidelines suitable for some case studies. Another set of guidelines appears starting on page 205 of Norman Denzin's book, *The Research Act*. This methods book is to be found in most sociology department libraries. A worthwhile exercise is the careful comparison of these two sets of guidelines.

I also present an exercise which requires you to locate a number of errors that are common when observers write up their observations.

In the bibliography below, I provide a list of references for further reading. For the student desiring to know much more about the techniques of field research, the best reading probably is Schatzman and Strauss (1973). For the student who would like to examine a multiple case study project, Stake's and Easley's *Case Studies in Science Education* presents 11 separate researchers in 11 places investigating the teaching and learning of science in grades K–12 in the United States in 1976, with an assimilation of issues across sites and a discussion of the methodological problems in that project.

Fieldwork Overview

Bogdan, R. C., & Biklen, S. K. (1982). *Qualititative research for education: An introduction to theory and methods*. Boston: Allyn and Bacon, Inc.

Denzin, N. (1970). *The research act*. Chicago: Aldine.

Erickson, F. (1986). Qualitative methods in research on teaching. In M. C. Wittrock (Ed.), *Handbook of research on teaching* (3rd ed.). New York: Macmillan.

Guba, E., & Lincoln, Y. (1981). *Effective evaluation*. San Francisco: Jossey-Bass.

Nisbet, J., & Watt, J. (1978). *Case study*. Rediguide 26. Nottingham: Nottingham University School of Education.

Schatzman, L., & Strauss, A. (1973). *Field research: Strategies for a natural sociology*. Englewood Cliffs, NJ: Prentice Hall.

Simons, H. (Ed.). (1980). *Toward a science of the singular*. Occasional Publication 10. Norwich, England: Centre for Applied Research in Education, University of East Anglia.

Stake, R. E. (1978). The case study method in social inquiry. *Educational Researcher*, 7(2), 5–8.

Stake, R. E. (1985). Case study. In J. Nisbet (Ed.), *World yearbook of education 1984/85*.

Stenhouse, L. (1985). A note on case study and educational practice. In R. G. Burgess (Ed.), *Field methods in the study of education*. London: Falmer Press.

Wolcott, H. (1976). Criteria for an ethnographic approach to research in schools. In

J. T. Roberts & S. K. Akinsanya (Eds.), *Schooling in the cultural context*. New York: David McKay Company.

Yin, R. K. (1984). *Case study research design: Design and methods*. Applied Social Research Methods Series, Vol. 5. Beverly Hills, CA: Sage.

Epistemological Foundation

Campbell, D. T. (1975). Degrees of freedom and the case study. *Comparative Political Studies, 8*, 178–193.

Campbell, D. T., & Fiske, D. W. (1959). Convergent and discriminant validation by the multitrait-multimethod matrix. *Psychological Bulletin, 56*, 81–105.

Geertz, C. (1983). *Local knowledge*. New York: Basic Books.

Glaser, B. G., & Strauss, A. (1967). *The discovery of grounded theory: Strategies for qualitative research*. Chicago: Aldine Press.

Rist, R. C. (1980). Blitzkrieg ethnography: On the transformation of a method into a movement. *Educational Researcher, 9* (2), 8–10.

Scriven, M. (1972). Objectivity and subjectivity in educational research. In H. Dunkel (Ed.), *Philosophical redirection of educational research*. Chicago: National Society for the Study of Education.

Smith, J. K., & Heshusius, L. (1986). Closing down the conversation: The end of the quantitative-qualitative debate among educational inquirers. *Educational Researcher, 15*(1), 4–12.

Smith, L. M. (1978). An evolving logic of participant observation, educational ethnography and other case studies. In L. Shulman (Ed.), *Review of research in education* (pp. 316–377). Chicago: Peacock.

Spindler, G. (Ed). (1963). *Education and culture*. New York: Holt, Rinehart & Winston.

Stake, R. E., & Trumbull, D. (1982). Naturalistic generalizations. In *Review Journal of Philosophy & Social Science, VII*, No. 1 & 2.

Wehlage, G. (1978, November). *The purpose of generalization in field study research*. Paper presented at conference on "The Study of Schooling: Field-Based Methodologies in Educational Research," Racine, WI.

Access, Entry, Ethics

Adelman, C. (1985). Who are you? Some problems of ethnographic culture shock. In R. G. Burgess (Ed.), *Field methods in the study of education*. London: Falmer Press.

Geer, B. (1967). First days in the field. In P. Hammond (Ed.), *Sociologists at work*. New York: Doubleday.

Paddock, S. C., & Packard, J. S. (1981). On the conduct of site relations in educational research. *Educational Researcher, 10* (3), 14–17.

Rainwater, L., & Pittman, D. (1969). Ethical problems in studying a politically sensitive and deviant community. In G. J. McCall & J. L. Simmons (Eds.), *Issues in participant observation*. Reading, MA: Addison-Wesley.

Scott, W. R. (1963). Field work in a formal organization: Some dilemmas in the role of observer. *Human Organization, 22*, 162–168.

Walker, R. (1974). The conduct of educational case study: Ethics, theory and procedures. In B. MacDonald (Ed.), *SAFARI: Innovation, evaluation, research and the problem of control*. Norwich, England: Centre for Applied Research in Education, University of East Anglia.

Data Collection

Brandt, R. M. (1972). *Studying behavior in natural settings*. New York: Holt.
Burgess, R. G. (Ed.). (1985). *Field methods in the study of education*. London: Falmer Press.
Mishler, E. G. (1986). *Research interviewing*. Cambridge, MA: Harvard University Press.
Rist, R. C. (1975). Ethnographic techniques and the study of an urban school. *Urban Education, 10* (1).
Vaughn, W., & Faber, E. (1952). Field methods and techniques: The systematic observation of kindergarten children. *Human Organization, 11*, 33–36.

Data Analysis

Becker, H. S. (1969). Problems of proof and inference in participant observation. In G. J. McCall & J. L. Simmons (Eds.), *Issues in participant observation*. Reading, MA: Addison-Wesley.
Hill-Burnett, J. (1973). Event description and analysis in the microethnography of urban classrooms. In F. A. Ianni & E. Storey (Eds.), *Cultural relevance and educational issues: Readings in anthropology and education*. Boston: Little, Brown and Co.
Lebar, F. M. (1970). Coding ethnographic materials. In R. Naroll & R. Cohen (Eds.), *Method in cultural anthropology*. Garden City, NY: The Natural History Press.
Miles, M. B., & Huberman, A. M. (1984). *Qualitative data analysis: A sourcebook of new methods*. Beverly Hills, CA: Sage.
Zelditch, M. (1969). Some methodological problems of field studies. In G. J. McCall & J. F. Simmons (Eds.), *Issues in participant observation*. Reading, MA: Addison-Wesley.

Exemplary Studies

Becker, H. S., Geer, B., Hughes, E., & Strauss, A. (1961). *Boys in white: Student culture in medical school*. Chicago: University of Chicago Press.
Brauner, C. (1974). The first probe. *AERA monograph series no. 7: Four evaluation examples*. Chicago: Rand McNally.
Burgess, R. G. (Ed.).(1984). *The research process in educational settings: Ten case studies*. London: Falmer Press.
Coles, R. (1967). *Children of crisis*. New York: Dell Publishing Co.
Cusick, P. A. (1973). *Inside high school: The student's world*. New York: Holt, Rinehart and Winston.
Edgerton, R. B. (1967). *The cloak of competence*. Berkeley: University of California Press.
Hamilton, D. (1975). *Big science, small school*. Edinburgh: Scottish Council for Research in Education.
Jackson, P. (1968). *Life in classrooms*. New York: Holt, Rinehart and Winston.
Jenkins, D. (1984). Chocolate cream soldiers: Sponsorship, ethnography, and sectarianism. In R. G. Burgess (Ed.), *The research process in educational settings: Ten case studies*. London: Falmer Press.
Lacey, C. (1970). *Hightown grammar—The school as a social system*. Manchester: The University Press.
MacDonald, B., et al. (1982). *Bread and dreams*. CARE Occasional Publication 12. Norwich, England: University of East Anglia.
Ogbu, J. (1974). *The next generation: An ethnography of education in an urban neighborhood* (pp. 11–20). New York: Academic Press.
Peshkin, A. (1978). *Growing up American*. Chicago: University of Chicago Press.

Peshkin, A. (1986). *God's choice*. Chicago: University of Chicago Press.

Shipman, M. D., Bolam, D., & Jenkins, D. (1974). *Inside a curriculum project: A case study in the process of curriculum change*. London: Methuen.

Smith, L. & Geoffrey, W. (1969). *The complexities of the urban classroom*. New York: Holt, Rinehart and Winston.

Smith, L., & Pohland, P. (1974). Education, technology, and the rural highlands. *AERA monograph series on curriculum evaluation, no. 7*. Chicago: Rand McNally.

Stake, R. E. (1984). An Illinois pair: A case study of school art in Champaign and Decatur. In M. Day et al., *Art history, art criticism, and art production*. Santa Monica, CA: Rand Corporation.

Stake, R. E. (1986). *Quieting reform*. Urbana-Champaign: University of Illinois Press.

Stake, R. E., & Easley, J. (Eds.). (1978). *Case studies in science education*. Urbana: University of Illinois, CIRCE.

Stenhouse, L. (1984). Library access, library use and user education in academic sixth forms: An autobiographical account. In R. G. Burgess (Ed.), *The research process in educational settings: Ten case studies*. London: Falmer Press.

Tikunoff, W., Berliner, D. C., & Rist, R. C. (1975). *An ethnographic study of the forty classrooms of the Beginning Teachers Evaluation Study: A known sample*. Technical Report #75-10-10-5. San Francisco: Far West Regional Laboratory.

Study Questions

1. Are case studies used solely in education, or are they widespread?

2. Is a case study distinguished from other methods of educational research solely by the techniques it employs?

3. What role does conceptualization play in case study research? Is a case study merely a verbatim report of observations?

4. What characteristics define a case study?

5. What is meant by a "case" in case study research? What role does the case play in defining the research?

6. Are the focus of a case study and the set of issues it addresses always determined before the study begins? Is this one way in which case study research differs from some other educational research methods?

7. What is meant by "naturalistic generalization?" How does naturalistic generalization differ, if at all, from scientific generalization?

8. Is representativeness necessary if a case study is to have value? Support your answer.

9. Can you refute the assertion that case studies are unscientific because they are totally subjective?

10. What is wrong with the statement "Case studies cannot be validated."?

One Set of Guidelines for Doing a Field-Observation Case Study

1. Anticipation

Review or discover what is expected at the outset in the way of a case study.
Consider the questions, hypotheses, or issues already raised.
Read some of the case study literature, both methodological and exemplary.
Look for one or more case studies possibly to use as a model.
Identify the "case." Was it prescribed, selected to represent, or mere convenience?
Define the boundaries of the case (or cases), as they appear in advance.
Anticipate key problems, events, attributes, spaces, persons, vital signs.
Consider possible audiences for preliminary and final reportings.
Form initial plan of action, including definition of role of observer on site.

2. First Visit (?)

Arrange preliminary access, negotiate plan of action, arrange regular access.
Write a formal agreement indicating obligations for observer and for host.
Refine access rules with people involved, including union, PTA, officials, etc.
Discuss real or potential costs to hosts, including opportunity costs.
Discuss arrangements for maintaining confidentiality of data, sources, reports.
Discuss need for persons to review drafts to validate observations, descriptions.
Discuss publicity to be given during and following the study.
Identify information and services, if any, to be offered hosts.
Revise plan of action, observer's role, case boundaries, issues, as needed.

3. Further Preparation for Observation

Make preliminary observations of activities. Use other sites for try-outs?
Allocate resources to alternative spaces, persons, methods, issues, phases, etc.
Identify informants and sources of particular data.
Select or develop instruments or standardized procedures, if any.
Work out record-keeping system, files, tapes; coding system; protected storage.
Rework priorities for attributes, problems, events, audiences, etc.

4. Further Development of Conceptualization

Reconsider issues or other theoretical structure to guide the data gathering.
Learn what audience members know, what they want to come to understand.

Sketch plans for final report and dissemination of findings.
Identify the possible "multiple realities," how people see things differently.
Allocate attention to different viewpoints, conceptualizations.

5. Gather Data, Validate Data

Make observations, interview, debrief informants, gather logs, use surveys, etc.
Keep records of inquiry arrangements and activities.
Select vignettes, special testimonies, illustrations.
Classify raw data; begin interpretations.
As needed, redefine issues, case boundaries; renegotiate arrangements with hosts.
Gather additional data, replicating or triangulating, to validate key observations.

6. Analysis of Data

Review raw data under various possible interpretations.
Search for patterns of data, whether or not indicated by the issues.
Seek linkages between program arrangements, activities, and outcomes.
Draw tentative conclusions, organize according to issues, organize final report.
Review data, gather new data, deliberately seek disconfirmation of findings.

7. Providing Audience Opportunity for Understanding

Describe extensively the setting within which the activity occurred.
Consider the report as a story; look for ways in which the story is incomplete.
Draft reports and produce materials for audience use.
Try them out on representative members of audience groups.
Help reader discern typicality and relevance of situation as base for generalization.
Describe methods of investigation and theoretical constructs used.
Revise and disseminate reports and materials. Talk to people.

And Some General Advice

There are always too many ways to spend case study research time. It should help delimit the study and allocate time to decide whether it is really the case or some problems or issues occurring there and elsewhere that is the target of the study. If that *particular case* is the target of interest, one should consider how to deal with issues vital to the case but of little interest to the investigator.

Classrooms and other school spaces are the living spaces of people. Most, by definition, are public, but private by common law. Observation studies can be an unwarranted intrusion into the privacy of people. Seldom should the researcher presume to be the guardian of rationality, efficiency, and morality.

The reader seeking understanding of the case or the issues is usually not very interested in the methods of the study, perhaps not sufficiently so. The researcher has an obligation to indicate the methods used and the choices made, but these statements should not be so placed as to obstruct the reader's effort to understand the substantive findings.

The reader who wants to challenge the findings is likely to say that the case study was subjective, arbitrary, nonrepresentative, and inconclusive. Which is probably true, but the study is not thus invalidated. The counter to these charges, if strong efforts to produce a valid study have occurred, is a good description of the methodological and conceptual reasoning that took place, including efforts at verification and disconfirmation.

Additional Exercise

This exercise is rather difficult. A short vignette has been written to include at least six errors common when observers write up their observations. Comments on the errors are presented, after the vignette. See how many errors you can spot.

Mr. Science

Sometimes when we think about a "Mr. Science type" of teacher we think of TV's Mr. Wizard, or the Galloping Gourmet, or Jacob Bronowsky, one who commands attention by his personality and seeming flawlessness in handling the subject matter. Mr. Fellswoop wasn't that. The klieg lights in his classroom at Fetische High School were on the students, not on the teacher. About 25 juniors and seniors were enrolled in his anatomy class. Mr. Fellswoop stood behind them, all facing the chalkboard scribbled with the language of the muscles.

Mr. F: Let's start with deep peroneal nerves. *(Another team of four students, four husky boys, goes to the front tables, faces the class.)* Okay, Bill, you've shown us the kind of quarterback you are. Now tell us about peroneal nerves. The deep peroneal nerve has been cut; there's function in one leg. What loss of muscular function is expected? Can this person come into your classroom? How would you expect the deformity or problem to be exhibited?

Bill: OK. He would lose 100% of his dorsal flexion and about 80-90% of his inversion. So as he came in he wouldn't be able to raise his toe. When he walked he'd come and he'd walk like this *(demonstrates down aisle)*. He wouldn't be able to raise his toe, so he'd just drag it along. It might go out a little.

Mr. F: What remaining muscles innervated by other nerves can be trained to do some of the lost function?

Bill: *(using notes)* Well, first of all the muscles that are going to be lost when you lose the deep peroneal nerve are the tibialus anterior, the extensor digitorum longus, the peroneus tertius, the extensor hallucis longus, and extensor digitorum brevis. To make up for those muscles which were lost the tibialis posterior would take over and the flexor hallucis longus and the flexor digitorum longus and they would be generated by the posterior tibial. . . .

Mr. F: Take over in what respect?

Bill: They would bring back the dorsal flexion and the loss of inversion. They would compensate for what is gone but they would bring back, y'know, only 10-15% of it.

Mr. F: . . . of the dorsal flexion?

Bill: . . . of the inversion.

Mr. F: Oh, OK. How about dorsal flexion? Any of those that could be trained?

Bill: No.

Mr. F: Good. Phillip, describe therapy exercise in anatomical and in layman terms to strengthen the remaining muscles.

Phil: *(Guiltily)* I didn't have time to work on that.

Mr. F: A championship team's tight end? How about you, Kent?

Kent: OK. There's so much lost that there's nothing you can do for dorsal flexion.

The rest of the class paid attention, laughing at Kent's primitive efforts to draw a foot, some hoping their turn would be put off a day.
How could any bunch of "with-it" California youngsters be turned on by muscles of the foot? Fellswoop was right when he said "what the students do in science depends mostly on what you expect them to do." He allowed that this was not an unusual class; though the course was an elective, most of the kids were pretty bright, and most were thinking a lot about nurses' training, football injuries, artistic drawing, or something that personalized such antiseptic learning.
Fellswoop expected them to "produce," to recognize a bone from any angle, to answer Naming questions without a second's delay, to write research reports from personally gathered data and with reference to professional journals and other reports of recent scientific studies. He did not expect them to be perfect. He only asked for what he knew they could do. He expected hard work, verbal response rate, and ideographic verisimilitude. He had a reputation—most students knew what they were getting into. And afterwards, at least, they too passed the word that it was a good, tough course. Fellswoop got where he was because he never considered that less than their full effort would be adequate.

Questionable Aspects of the Observer's Writing

1. False names should often be used to protect the privacy of persons and schools. Names such as Fellswoop and Fetische are too suggestive. It might be that the teacher here did take sweeping action, and the school might have been overly attuned to fads; but—Shakespeare notwithstanding—vivifying the nomenclature is not a proper way for researchers to inform the readers.

2. The writer ascribes a feeling of guilt to Phillip. It seems an unwarranted and unhelpful interpretation. Even if in some other way Phillip had revealed feelings of guilt, a more behavioral description would be preferred. Perhaps "haltingly."

3. In the next line the writer reveals that this is a school having a championship football team and that it was the tight end who didn't do his anatomy assignment. These terms could have been part of the false cover the writer devised, but true identification marks like these often show through.

4. In the next to last paragraph the writer passes judgment unnecessarily on a statement the teacher made.

5. In the final paragraph the writer introduces technical constructs which have not been defined. Even if they had been defined they would unnecessarily mystify readers. Citing technical terms in the dialog about muscles is different. That actually happened.

6. To terminate the vignette, the writer draws a conclusion—for which no evidence has been presented.

7. The writing throughout is perhaps too flowery, perhaps making it less comprehensible than it should be.

8. In a short vignette there is not much chance to indicate the observer's efforts to triangulate. Validation of the observations might show up in other parts of the report. Although data from classroom observation and teacher interview are indicated here, only in a very broad way might they be considered corroborations of each other, as presented.

Reading

Introduction
Analyzing the Case Study

Robert E. Stake

This section contains the entire text of "The First Probe," a case study written by Charles Brauner. This vivid account of a presession workshop for newly enrolled architecture students at the University of British Columbia is an excellent case study for further analysis.

As you read the article, consider who might find the material useful. The potential audience could include faculty at other schools of architecture, faculty at experimental educational institutions, faculty at traditional educational institutions, students in general, students in architecture, funding agencies, or researchers studying higher education. Are you able to determine from the content, style, or organization of the material which of these audiences might be intended? Try to imagine the points of view of several potential audiences. The outline of the "bounded system" might vary for each audience, yielding a variety of case studies. An important question for any case study researcher is, "Why would they want it?" The answer to this question is critical in shaping the system boundaries. For example, if Brauner had prepared a report for the President of the University of British Columbia, would you expect it to be different? If so, in what ways?

Another consideration is the degree to which the reader believes in the accuracy of the case study report. If the reader is to understand and evaluate the conclusions drawn by the researcher, the report must provide accurate and complete supporting data. It is possible that some readers might find certain aspects of the Brauner report hard to believe. Does it appear that Brauner did any extra work on those less credible parts? If so, how well do you think his efforts succeeded?

As part of the assurance of credibility, many researchers believe that raw data should be presented along with the interpretations, giving readers a chance to make their own interpretations. Brauner's observations are in a narrative format without quotes, and he explicitly states that the account is based on 3-month-old memory unaided by a contemporaneous diary. Do you feel that Brauner provided sufficient uninterpreted observations to back up his conclusions?

Credibility is enhanced when case study researchers confirm the accuracy of their observations. We do not know whether Brauner asked any of the participants to correct misstatements or misinterpretations in this report. Do you spot any findings that probably should have been confirmed by those who were there?

Asking participants for confirmation presents additional dilemmas. There may be large discrepancies between participant and observer perceptions; or a participant may believe that the researcher has no right to report certain information about the participant, even if it is accurate. How do you feel about the desirability of getting confirmation from participants? How should discrepancies in viewpoint be resolved? Who ultimately decides what material can be used and what principles should guide that decision? Which events described in "The First Probe" are most subject to being questioned on these grounds?

The final issue in establishing the credibility of a case study report is that of completeness. Triangulation has been mentioned as an important way of verifying conclusions. As you read "The First Probe," try to decide what more, if anything, you would like to know about the workshop described. How would that additional information be obtained? Would observations be the best way to get that additional information? Why or why not?

3. The First Probe

Charles J. Brauner
University of British Columbia

Rain and mystery opened and closed the presession workshop for students entering architecture at the University of British Columbia. Foul weather and wonder about what was to come provided the only obvious threads linking three weeks of activities that ran from foraging to feast, Spartanism to splendor, privation to saturation. Shrouded in rumors as thick as the clouds overhead, 55 students from all over Canada and several distant countries gathered together for the first time in mid-August on a dock opposite Vancouver's Stanley Park. As college graduates with a common interest in architecture, they had no trouble combining into spontaneous conversation groups.

When the six members of staff arrived, a sense of relief rippled through the crowd as they quieted to hear where they were going. But they were not told. Disappointed, they loaded their camping equipment onto one of the boats and divided into two parties for boarding. All the way out to Horseshoe Bay and up Howe Sound they speculated. After two hours of sailing through thickening fog they no longer knew whether they were traveling north or south. When the boats dropped anchor at a small island a few miles off Britannia Beach they had no idea where they were. Small boats took them to Defense Island in groups of six. Densely forested and guarded by an Indian mask carved in a drift log at the landing, the island was deserted. Three-quarters of a mile long and one-quarter mile wide, with a backbone of rock that ran its length, the island seemed to offer a minimum challenge. By the time the last boat landed, two girls and the main party had a fire going in the opening on the crest. At noon everyone stood around waiting to be fed. Wet, having nothing but what they wore and carried in their

This paper first appeared in the *Architectural Review*, Vol. 146, No. 874, Dec. 1969, pp. 451–56, and was reproduced with minor editing in *Four Evaluation Examples: Anthropological, Economic, Narrative, and Portrayal* (AERA Monograph Series No. 7; Chicago, Rand McNally, 1974, pp. 77–98). It is reproduced here in the latter version, again with permission of the *Architectural Review*.

pockets, but reassured by seeing the staff similarly unequipped, they did not take alarm when the boats sounded their horns and pulled away.

After a half hour of exploration, John Gaitanakis, a codirector, called the students together and explained that the boat would return in 48 hours. Meanwhile, there was no food, no shelter, and no equipment. The time was theirs to use as they saw fit. The first reaction was disbelief. Having found an axe and some nails on a relief tour, a small group insisted other necessities only awaited discovery. The fact that two five-gallon coffee urns of water had been brought ashore from the boats convinced others that food was there for the finding. A general unwillingness to accept the likelihood of deprivation sent everyone on an hour of fruitless searching. Reassembling with nothing new to report, they conjured up their first fears of famine. They all knew that man could do quite well without food so long as he had water, and fresh water was plentiful both from rain and springs. Nevertheless, half a dozen individuals insisted they would succumb to nausea and disability at the very least. Those most fearful set out to forage for edibles. We warned them that a recent red tide had made the shellfish temporarily poisonous; however, the gloom from this blow did not persist. Soon half the group was busy gathering salal berries and toasting sea kelp, the only edibles to be found. By mid-afternoon a dozen self-selected groups were busy building shelters and gathering wood for night fires. By this time, the shelter parties had coalesced into personality groups of three to five, and they remained intact as living units for the rest of the time on the island. Confronted with the basic choice of whether to improve and inhabit existing shelters from half-formed caves to semitunnels formed by overturned trees or to cut and interweave cedar branches, the majority shied away from using the existing natural cover. However, their finished dwellings distinguished them far less than the characteristics that drew them into alliance. To the staff they became known as the hoarders, the sharers, the defilers, the isolates, the raiders, the includers, the excluders, the worriers, the trusters, and the grumblers. Those who found no common cause in personality, location, habitat, or conversation remained around the fire on the crest. Since this cluster-by-default was three times as large as any of the separate living units, their clearing served as a commons ground. A more barren commons would be hard to imagine.

Once fire and rude shelter were assured, the group found absolutely nothing to do but pass time. No game of matchsticks or burning twigs was too trivial. There was not even enough common concern for anyone to do more than note that one of the groups had made off with half the reserve water supply. Efforts to open discussion on why they were there or what they might do proved so fruitless that the dozen who started the talks could not sustain them for half an hour. In the evening a longer chat on "What is architecture" was started. The downpour and darkness were punctuated only by massive tree trunks and widely spaced fires; boredom dictated the effort at conversation. The only thing that sparked interest was the makeup of the staff—two members of the architecture faculty, a visitor from Outward Bound, a specialist in contemporary dance, a sociologist, and an educational philosopher. The thing that seemed to impress the students most was that the staff saw fit to share their discomfort on equal terms, though they had foreknowledge of what was to come. Again, all question about future events went unanswered. When it became clear no profitable discussion would develop, the staff withdrew to the semishelter of a huge cedar tree and bedded down around a fire.

Only four things distinguished the second day: wetter and colder participants, the end of the berries, the building of a raft, the appearance of a boat, and underground fires that threatened to burn the island down. What had been planned as a minimal existence experience turned out to be a "nonexistence." The hope had been that by being freed of cooking, eating, preparation, and clean up—and thus denied the opportunity to lavish time on such mindless occupations—the students might try to make something special of their stay. Instead they spent all their time on the mindless activities left them: buttressing shelters, improving fireplaces, gathering wood. Beyond that, they were determined simply to sit out their time like convicts awaiting parole. Some spent hours just cleaning their fingernails. Even the making of the raft was undertaken with half an eye to floating somewhere to get food. When a boat came in a group tried to signal their need for supplies. Informed that just three weeks before the Provincial Department of Correction had put some hard cases ashore for survival training, those on the boat did not linger. Surviving their fast in good health but low spirits, the groups greeted the last night with huge fires. The fires burned through the ground cover of rotten needles and branches, igniting the dry mulch that coated the ground to a depth of 12 feet in places. A group in a cave on a rock ledge burned themselves out entirely when a covering tree went up in flames and took two more trees with it. Three other groups had runaway fires during the night, and the *"Lord of the Flies"* bunch who took the communal water supply had to use more than 40 buckets of water to damp underground fires that, they insisted, they had under control at all times. When it was time to leave, the staff spent three hours doing nothing but uprooting underground fires that had been left as extinguished. If it had not been for heavy and continuous rain, the island would have become an inferno.

By far the most interesting thing to be seen during the island experience was the students' behavior toward food when it arrived. Before taking us off, the captain of the Columbia landed oranges, apples, and bread. The "marooned" were told that there was enough for each to have a piece of fruit and two slices of bread. The *"Lord of the Flies"* group was the first to the food, followed by several kindred parties. They raided the stores like seasoned pirates. Half the loaves of bread disappeared inside jackets, only because pockets were filled to bursting with fruit. Eight people got more than half the supplies for 61 people. The pattern of resentment among those who went without was remarkable. No one could be heard blaming the gluttons, though they were known to most. The captain became the villain for landing so little provisions, and there was general resentment that they had not been given a feast. Finally annoyance focused on the staff for not anticipating the raiders and deterring them. This settled down to a criticism of a more general nature. Somehow the staff had failed to make the experience meaningful. What happened with the food became symbolic of that failure.

When the boat landed everyone at Brittania Beach, there was a station wagon waiting with enough bread, sliced meat, fruit, cookies, and candy bars for all—or so it seemed. Again the mighty eight plundered the stores. They made sandwiches with more than an inch of meat—not one, but four and six apiece. Even so, the meat and the bread held out. Everyone, except one girl who could hardly eat, overate. The raiders took whole packages of 10 chocolate bars or 36 cookies against future uncertainties. Again, nothing was said. Interesting in itself, what makes it significant is that, except for the girl, no one had suffered severe hunger past the slight pangs of the second day. There was a general feeling of having been physically cleansed.

The unanimous overeating and the special greed of a few seemed more a ritual atonement for failure or a common urge to make up for the empty hours by stuffing their bodies. Overeating by both students and staff remained a characteristic of the group throughout the workshop. A mystery in itself, this hangover from the island cloaked an even deeper feeling. Before going on this trip, several students had known the forest on intimate working terms. Others from cities and foreign countries had heard of it in terms of mixed awe and grandeur. Yet the woods-wise had been as unable to face the challenge of the forest island as the forest unfamiliars. Both had been equally helpless against what neither group had expected to encounter—time. Having brought almost nothing ashore, they found themselves stranded with even less than they imagined. Had they been truly marooned, desperation would have given them common cause that would have filled every moment. Denied even that last resort, they encountered themselves as truly useless. Each one was, harrowingly, alone —only for two days, but that mystery became the yeast that leavened all that followed. However slight, all had suffered a common adversity. However profound, all had faced a common humiliation. In just 48 hours the props of a quarter century of customary daily activity had been knocked flat. They were ready for a new beginning. It was, as it turned out, a workshop of beginnings.

Warmed by cooked food and rations of rum, everyone slept that third night half dry in sleeping bags sheltered by stretches of plastic. Dawn broke clear at 5300 feet, revealing snow-caps surrounding the camp in Garibaldi meadow. Grouped in seven-man teams for the stay on the glacier, some bathed and shaved in mountain streams while others packed for the trip to the top. Rain settled in and efforts to keep dry failed. The question became "Will the weather break long enough for a helicopter to drop in and make 18 lifts from the meadow to the broad back of the glacier?" By mid-afternoon the enveloping mist thinned. Heather, high up the hills, showed magenta against wet grass, as if struggling to serve as tiny beacons. From over the ridge the beat of rotors chopped away at the remaining mist. As sky opened the turbo-jet helicopter swung in, trailing a 55-gallon drum of fuel at the end of a long line. It set the drum between two logs as neatly as a woman might place a vase. The lift was on.

In groups of four and with three additional lifts of 20 backpacks hung in a cargo net beneath the machine, the base camp went to the glacier. The flight up became a personal experience from the moment of lift-off. The machine skimmed off the meadow, circled inside the basin, and darted through a gap in the peaks. The lush Alpine meadow dropped away into rock canyon stripped of vegetation. The helicopter came up to the 500-foot face of the glacier at 120 miles an hour, slipping between clouds and ice like a razor parting tissue. Racing across the frozen ridges of snow that spread all around like a still ocean brought the full fascination of speed up through the glass bubble. As if about to topple over a crest that dropped half a mile, the machine floated into a stall and touched to a stop. Set down at an altitude of 6500 feet, each new arrival looked from the rough crown of encircling peaks into the abyss. A mile across the valley trees disappeared into blue-black on the mountainside. Printed in a solid wash, a stone seemed a clear crystal darkened only by the blue air between. Some students took running slides down steep slopes. Others raced away to the highest ledge they could find. Groups held brief skirmishes in the snow. Still others just sat and looked. Andrew Gruft and two friends experienced in climbing took charge. Safety guidelines were set forth and the prearranged groups were set the task of building shelter. A third of the parties chose to use the snow to their advantage. The rest decided to build their camps on the clear outcropping of rock around the main field. With cooking and shelter under way, half the company set out to use the remaining light to climb by. Curving past blue-green crevasses toward a crest two miles away and 2000 feet above, they strung out like ski troops on maneuvers. Those who stayed behind drank, cooked, joked, built fires from mountain driftwood, improved shelters and attended to idle busywork. Though the rain came back, the mood was as opposite from the island as the surroundings. Although most were cold, wet, getting hungry and tired, no one was bored. The new groupings formed around work, chatter, pranks, and meals. The real chance of a thunder storm on the glacier, rumored to be capable of making experienced climbers panic, held no fear. The known difficulty of climbing down through fog that hid all bearings posed no concern beyond the challenge. The outside chance of severe cold at night worried no one. Where 48 hours on the island had seemed interminable, 36 hours on the glacier seemed no time at all.

Where the dense stand of evergreens reaching up out of sight had hemmed everyone in until each became trapped in some barren patch of self, the broad expanse with nothing on all sides and above became truly timeless. Drawn out from the cramped quarters of self, as vapour must expand in a vacuum, their spirits bubbled to the surface. For the first time there was singing. Who could help but sing on the top of the world? There was play. Joy. Reborn on the glacier while chafing under unexpected discipline, they surged back to life. The island—not the want of food, not the gloom of the forest, not the rain, not the self-inflicted isolation, not the division into camps—had made them old. On the island they behaved like retired folks so old all they had left was to await their final departure. On the glacier they became young again. But the growth they found, like the agedness they settled into when most lost, came from psychological depths none had ever plumbed. Indeed, on the glacier and all through the trip, only a few ever sensed that the territory covered during the workshop paralleled the topography of their spirit. Like animals in a maze, they were much too busy reacting to stimuli to analyze or even to formulate their responses. That would come later.

The climb down the glacier and back to base camp was their first small test of physical endurance. Seven miles over the ice field, down the face, into the valley, and up 4000 feet, they were confronted with the task of covering in each hour what they had flown over in a minute. Sixty-pound backpacks and fog thick enough to limit vision to 50 feet made it a challenge. Divided into three teams of 20 joined by a long stretch of rope, they set out over waist-high ridges of soft snow. The experienced climbers led each unit to the face of the glacier. In a running, tumbling, sliding, skidding free-for-all, each person balanced his pack as best he could and slid down the 45-degree slope as best as he could. Once down in the valley on an unmistakable trail, they were left to make their way up and back to the meadow like draft horses free to find the barn. Those who faced it as a show of strength made it in less than three hours. Others who found it an enjoyable, if demanding, stroll took as long as five hours. Saddled with a pack and confronting an unavoidable two-and-a-half-mile climb up a

20-degree slope, each one had to balance energy against endurance, progress against tedium, interest against fatigue.

Eventually they had to settle down to some common denominator for completing the task. In a narrow, special, private and very physical way, each one had to work out his own "one best means." Some rushed and rested every hundred yards. Others plodded. Many forgot they were climbing at all for as much as a half-mile, caught by the change in perspective as they rose above the valley. A few cursed almost every step. One by one they settled into what Jacques Ellul calls a "technique." They came up against what freedom was left them within the rigid limits of physiological ability and physical conditions. For that brief passage each one worked out his personal style under a special condition of stress. That style told volumes. It was a story that did not take long to tell. Although the style of the others was most apparent and without knowing accurately, fully, or coherently *what* he had exposed, each one sensed that he had exposed himself in some important way. The climb back to the meadow made it clear why certain groups had grown spontaneously on the island and why other combinations of people would not naturally occur. The return from the glacier marked the emergence of an awareness of individual techniques for achieving ends and styles-in-means previously unnoticed.

The new awareness came at the best possible time. Plucked from society and comfort and held in contact with nature for five days, the students were plunged back into the system and surrounded with conveniences. Comfort was a modern motel that provided all facilities and good food and the freedom to roam Port Alberni every evening. Twice each day they would tour a different aspect of the lumber industry. Reborn as social beings, they noticed not only the emperor's nakedness but the alleged cut and fabric of his imaginary gown.

A satrapy of MacMillan Bloedel in the middle of Vancouver Island and left over from an earlier century, Port Alberni is a company town with polluted streams, hepatitis, noxious air, odors that would stun a horse, soot, fumes, loud traffic, periodic layoffs, alcoholism, and treeless hills as side effects of having only one major employer. Yet the effects of industrial technique on the lifestyle of the town were trivial compared to their influence on the men at work. In three days the students saw modern industrial technique at work in fire fighting, paper manufacturing, logging, cutting lumber, and plywood production. Everywhere the most modern equipment stood out as the only evidence of the twentieth century. The two surviving Martin Mars were kept ready as water bombers. The largest planes to see active service in World War II, they pick up 6,000 gallons of water in a 22-second sweep across the surface of a lake.

The pulp and paper mill was as fully automated as possible. Gigantic vats collect, grind, soak, stew, and feed a sticky juice into a block-long oven of drums that press, stretch, dry, bake, and roll up finished newsprint. The nattering of powerful chain saws throughout the forest made a sound as though the whole mountain was host to a swarm of mechanical locusts that would eat it bare. Where the crews had left, the mile-square stands made a cut wheatfield look scraggly. Everything was down. At China Lake the water scooters cut logs from the dumping pools more efficiently than a trained quarter-horse culls a herd. In the sawmill, man-high blades made beams from trees in two cuts. The plywood factory had presses three stories high. Everywhere one technique stood out: Enlarge the machine. Each replacement had been more gigantic than its predecessor. Gradually, the attendant technique became apparent: Rationalize the internal steps of each separate process until that stage is automated. Only then did the discontinuity between gigantic machines begin to make sense. Specialists had automated isolated processes separately, and that separation set the task for human labor. Men did not work so much on, as between, machines. Whenever one complex of machinery finished a set of tasks and another assemblage waited to take it another stage, there was a flurry of human activity. Men rushed pell-mell to fill the gap between two independent mechanical processes.

Unique, specialized, temperamental, costly, and irreplaceable, the machines received irreproachable care. Indeed, the machinery was the only thing unique in any of the operations. The company could no more use a $6 million paper dryer to put out forest fires than it could dry paper with the Hawaii Mars. Only the men were standardized, interchangeable, expendable, indistinguishable, and cheap. . . .

Signs posted everywhere announced the daily lifestyle for workers. Like front line troops, they had learned to live with constant danger. The numbers themselves gave a precise arithmetical index of danger, job by job. They announced that the machinery could not be made man-safe. "No matter what you do the machine will get you. It's just a matter of time." "Look, so and so has escaped injury for 283 days." Yet when you are hurt, "It's your fault." "Men *make* accidents." Whenever anyone was asked about the company's concern for the workers, the safety signs were pointed out. After the second day no one asked. Discussion with management provoked hostility. The very thought that unintended psychological and social contaminants might develop as side effects of company policy came as an unpardonable insult. The safety game stood out as symbolic of a fundamental absurdity. Practical businessmen, regarding themselves as deeply involved in the basic struggle to provide necessary commodities, were prisoners of their own fantasies more than the students had been on the island. Practical laborers committed to bread-and-butter wage earning were more lost than they would have been on the glacier when the fog closed in. Worse, both groups believed they were "communicating." Neither suggested its isolation from the other. A huge industrial complex had grown up between them, and yet it remained invisible. . . .

The result of this mutual blindness was Port Alberni, a peculiar but somehow typical wasteland. For all the devastation of physical resources for the production of commercial exports, they came to little by comparison to the degradation of human resources. The forests, the streams, and the air could still replenish themselves. The people had been used beyond any point of return. Having seen how industrial technique devastates a population, the students went on to follow-up that human devastation in a more advanced stage. Their next stop was Skid Row in downtown Vancouver.

Arriving in the usual downpour, everyone checked into the West Hotel at Carrol and Pender Streets just off Chinatown. With two students to a room at $1.50 each per night, they had the next four days to explore eight square blocks. Before turning them loose, Bud Wood, the codirector, gave each one his $5-a-day allotment of cash. Dressed in boots and camping clothes, with beards and untrimmed hair, they had only manners, speech, and curiosity to separate them from the native inhabitants.

The hotel's bar served as base camp, refresher station, rest home, take-off point, runway, rally ground, and seminar room.

Low-slung, huge, noisy, pillared, blue, black-ceilinged, gilded, mirrored, busy, threadbare, and orderly, the bar catered to a cross-section of the population, two beers at a time. That the patrons were not especially bawdy, frantic, violent, boisterous, or hostile came as a surprise. A gravel-voiced citizen entertained each newcomer with the offer of a diamond from the "crown jewels of Czechoslovakia" smuggled on the last plane out of Prague. A few lads lent themselves to the embraces of an Indian girl happy to give them vivid details of her decline and fall. Others received fatherly advice from pensioners about keeping their cash in a side pocket and not flashing anything bigger than a $2 bill. They saw and heard drunks but found the vast majority quite content to drink well within their budget and limit. After buying a few rounds they found themselves treated in return.

Even before they ventured out on the streets they knew a good deal about the community. Most of all, they knew it was a community. The people they had expected to find broken and in a continuous stupor had a spirit and individuality not to be found in Port Alberni. They reflected, without having heard, Camus' dictum in *The Myth of Sisyphus:* "There is no fate that cannot be surmounted by scorn." These survivors of industrial displacement had many battle scars. Yet herded together in a ghetto left over as an omission in city planning, they retained a certain small measure of independence from commercial-industrial technique. By working little, unsteadily, or not at all, they avoided having to stay in anyone's "good grace." They were, in a most limited way, being themselves. The limitation was that by the time they got there, not much of the "self" was left intact. Contrary to expectation, these people had not given up. They laughed, drank, hoped, fought occasionally, talked endlessly, listened, argued, smiled, dreamed, sang, cried, visited, made friends, and worried. The notable difference was that they had no assigned places in which to do these things. They were "at home" on the street or in an alley, in a bar or a temporary room. They were at home in their bodies instead of in some set space, and it soon became clear that this was not a matter of choice but of necessity.

The architecture students soon noted how little space existed to serve the inhabitants. By day and early evening businessmen came in to open shops for customers who came from outside. Only when the outsiders withdrew and the stores and offices were dark and padlocked did the indigenous facilities stand out. There were small restaurants offering cheap food in quantity for every ethnic group—Greek, Polish, Hungarian, Swedish. Cutting across ethnic lines, bars catered to special social tastes. The mixed couples did not mingle with the transvestites. The solitary drinkers stayed away from the party bars. The hotels and rooming houses polarized around still other groupings. The sailors did not register where the salesmen gathered. Though illegal activities went out to wherever demand promised patronage, each had its center of gravity. Prostitution did not interfere with gambling. Dope peddling did not compete with bootlegging. Once it became clear what the boundaries were, it took just six minutes by actual timing to find a "kit" that someone had stashed for mixing, heating, and injecting heroin. A serious customer never had to wait more than a quarter hour to make contact, whatever might be his needs. Service was far better than the checkout line at any supermarket. Yet the traffic was quite small compared to the size of the population.

Gradually the students grasped one of the basic facts of life on Skid Row. The restaurants, the bars, the streets, the alleys, the porches of tenements, and one very small 30- by 40-foot triangular "park" were the only social centers available. Wherever they might go to sleep, they had to come to one of these places to socialize. This was known and accepted. The great majority did not drink to become convivial, they gathered together to relieve each other's boredom, and rather than cast a man out in the rain because he couldn't afford to buy a drink, someone would order him a beer so he could stay. For a group of people who literally lived in their social centers and only slept or recuperated in their rooms, the guarantee of being welcome was essential. Unfortunately, they had to convert with no help the few facilities left them by an unconcerned city. They had to make social centers out of places least amenable to that function, and they did it with nothing but their own depleted personal resources. However limited, warped, undeveloped, starved, or out of kilter, all they had was their own humanity. Because they brought all of it wherever they went, they were, in their own special way, more wholly and fully present, wherever they went, than most men.

They left nothing behind, kept nothing hidden. Carrying the whole of what was left them as selves, these men often enough exhibited facets of self not customarily seen in public, and that, not the people themselves, was the basis for disapproval. The occupants of Skid Row, the students eventually discovered, lived all too public lives. They did in company what the general public regarded as only fit to be done in private. Urinating and making love, vomiting and sleeping, dressing and tending wounds, taking medicine and resting—all was visible, and those who lived in more compartmentalized ways found such a blend offensive. Having just come away from an island and a glacier where such a blend had been a communal and environmental necessity, the students could accept it quite easily. They were surprised to see that the basic pattern of living on Skid Row differed very little from their own style of camping. The trees had given way to high buildings, the icefield had been replaced by pavement, but the ways of coping with a great deal of time and not very much to do remained the same. Like themselves, these folks were the sole occupants of an island. Their little enclosure was threatened by an ever-rising tide of commercial and industrial development that encroached from all sides. Unlike the students, no one had arranged for their departure on a silent morning.

Later, loaded with camping gear, everyone trudged up a mud road through the rain on Sunday afternoon. All they knew was that they had entered the state of Washington and come to Friday Creek, about 20 miles south of Bellingham. From the distance they heard a Gregorian chant coming through the trees. As they turned a bend they came upon what could have been a Roman ruin. Aged, overlaid with 20-foot high trees growing out of the roof, abounding in symmetrical arches, a circular brick building arched up into a perfect dome. From the inside, the abandoned bee-hive brick kiln curved around and around in layers that drew the eye to the hole on top. Moss and moisture filled the dome with a musty incense. A dozen low arches evenly spaced all around opened to the fading daylight as altars of invitation. The deep tones of the Gregorian chant mixed with the candle light to create a mood of reverence.

Moors coming upon a mosque in an alien land could not have been more awestruck. The chant ceased, and silence admitted the sound of a running stream. As eyes grew more accustomed to the dim light, details became more evident. Throughout, the dome bricks of the kiln were set on edge against each other without mortar. Sounds worked across the dome to drop intact at full volume precisely on their nodal points. The scars of intense heat worked up in carbon streaks as shadows of long-extinguished flames, as if to provide the building with memories. One great room was softly lighted so that the glow faded gradually to a deep claret red. Simple, strong, and so boldly clear in design and construction, it bespoke its very nature. It was as natural as the island forest or the glacier snow. It belonged. Only the rubble of broken brick turned up, scattered, and left by thieves in their search for marketable bricks, and mounds of trash showed the hand of men. That dirty smudge had to be erased. In two days the work parties cleared out all the rubble and rebuilt the floor of the kiln with brick taken from the false roof. They stripped all the growth that threatened to crumble the dome, reinforced it by welding the steel bands holding it together, covered it with clear plastic that waterproofed it, and cleared it of rubble and trash inside and out. Equipped with electricity but not lighted by it, the kiln was ready for use. There was a sense of having restored a monument to its original splendor. It came as a shock to find that the kiln was only 10 years old.

The students, delighted to have a task, did the basic renovation in two days and improved it each day thereafter. As it became the social center, fewer people slept inside. Each day a few new members of the architecture staff arrived. The attendant building provided shelter for sleeping and storage. A catering service supplied hot meals, and a barrel of beer went on tap every evening. With five days left to go, the students felt that finally they had about all they wanted. They had no suspicion that work, shelter, food, and drink was the least of the benefits they were to receive.

The cultural program came on slowly. On the evening of the third day at the kiln they all gathered in the dome at dusk. A solo oboist played an hour of modern music before the beer arrived. After refreshments he came back and discussed the notions of sound, space, harmony, rhythm, atonality, improvisation, and composition underlying the works he had played. He gave an impromptu accompaniment to the reading of an original poem, which was followed by the reading of a chapter from a novel that was being written. A bit startled by the exposure, the students set up a couple of Congo drums and beat their way through half the night until the beer was gone.

Another evening a solo cellist played, talked, joked, and worked her way through a night of music appreciation that extended from Brahms to nursery rhymes by way of viola and violin. The second artist established the pattern of the performances beyond their special cultural merits. The students realized that they were encountering people who had spent most of a lifetime mastering some of the most difficult skills ever undertaken by man, but there was something more. By coming to the students and opening themselves to any questions, they were providing an invitation. In a groping way, the questioning began to focus on what they had to give of themselves and find in themselves to rise to the level of artistry.

The impact of the artists began to show in the students' daytime work. A portion of the floor that had been laid down imperfectly was torn up and redone. Damage to the kiln that had not been noticed was repaired. Shelters, walkways around the adjacent buildings, sheds, a crude drinking station called *"The Plastic Pub"* were all repaired. Even personal care improved. The dam down the creek had a waterfall that became a shower. Some shaved. Without being fastidious the students began to restore themselves back from the dishevelment that had gone unchecked from the island through Skid Row. One day an officer from the Immigration Service arrived. He was under the impression that the community was a religious cult. The fact that the students had turned their hand at building "found sculpture" from machine parts laying all around tended to confirm his suspicion. His concern was very specific. In the most courteous way, he inquired whether there were women present. At that point it came as a shock to everyone to realize that sex differences mattered. After assuring himself that the women were not being held by force or the threat of force, he took a considerable interest in the improvements.

One evening a troupe of three actors from Western Washington University put on a one-act performance drawn from a segment of a poem by Koch. After analyzing and reconstructing their moods, they drew several "volunteers" into the center of the dome and went through a verbal charade called "Coil Supreme." Carrying over into a second keg of beer, the drummers and those who worked over the rented piano partied their way into dawn.

By night and by day the groups worked out their special style and technique. Quite at home with themselves and each other, they played as hard as they worked.

The students sought advice from the staff when it suited them and ignored it on the same basis. The spirit first evidenced on the glacier returned in much amplified strength. None of the gloom or

"Lord of the Flies" position so evident on the island reappeared. Midway through their stay at the kiln they found themselves to be a fully developed and emotionally self-sufficient community. Selves that had remained hidden all that time emerged. Discussion, argument, and debate abounded on everything from adultery to Zen. Life histories were revealed, philosophies exposed, attitudes attacked, values endorsed. Without realizing they were doing anything more than restoring an abandoned kiln and having a good time drinking, they began to make unexamined parts of themselves evident. By bringing them out in the open, they took the first step toward building new selves. Their style became fraternal; they took an interest in each other far beyond the usual. When one lad was refused passage on a bus because of long hair and bare feet it hit them all. When another was caught by the Conservation Officer with two 25-pound salmon he had just killed for a barbecue, he had more volunteer "lawyers" than anyone could use.

Their technique became "stumbling Cartesian." Though not fully aware of the extent to which doubt might reach when nothing was taken for granted, they started along the road. The 17 acres they occupied were no longer an abandoned brick kiln on Friday Creek. It became a modern Benedictine Monastery in which work and meditation mixed with an exploration of the arts and, incidentally, beer. Yet the community was in no danger of becoming a cult. Joined in a common though undefined exploration, they gradually became aware of how different they really were. Fortunately they had learned that they did not have to become ostriches to protect the differences. These were the differences that exposure could cultivate just as the performances of the artists contributed to their special uniqueness.

A recital by the University of British Columbia string quartet brought the collaborative dimension of artistic excellence to the fore. For two hours the dome rang with the sound of strings tuned and played in harmony. After the performance they were surprised to find that the local constabulary and several citizens had come to listen. Having known the place as an abandoned ruin good for several loads of brick and having heard all kinds of stories about the weird rites being performed, the local citizens had trouble believing their eyes and ears. Again and again they marvelled at the transformation and remarked that there had never been anything like the performance anywhere in the area before. The word spread that the Canadians were a breed unknown in those parts—hard working, constructive, fun loving, cultured, friendly, open, creative, intelligent, moral, and somehow too good to be true. Alarmed at what seemed to them the decline and decay of their own youth, they showered the visitors with all the virtues they admired but found lacking. So a counter-myth went around as an antidote to the initial accusations.

The following night many citizens returned and brought friends to hear a basso from the San Francisco Opera and watch his wife do interpretive dancing. Their amazement grew. Promises to preserve the kiln and continue to use and improve it abounded. Men swore to protect it against brick thieves and destruction. Local politicos vowed to use all their influence to further what had been started. Regardless of practical limitations that might keep them from accomplishing their ends, the expression of concern was absolutely genuine. A certain hidden passion for improvement had been touched, and though it might be only an emotional outburst, it represented an awakening. And it augmented the same feeling for preservation and continued use of the facilities that living in and around the kiln had stirred in the students. The guests and the host citizenry who had come to find out what was going on were in perfect accord. Having developed a facility entirely for their own use, the students were able to be fully and wholly themselves in a more expanded and complete sense than would ever be possible for anyone on Skid Row. They could open up into the kiln, the grounds, the countryside, the work, the appreciation, and the sharing without keeping parts of themselves compartmentalized.

In just one week they had put together a whole that exceeded the sum of its parts. Without quite knowing what they were doing, they built themselves a vision. The kiln, the brick laying, the artistic performances, the drinking, the communual living, the geographic isolation, and the continuous discussion were only elements of technique for making it possible. However dim or fleeting, vague or contradictory, spotty or insubstantial, they had caught a glimpse. The glimpse, not the activities, had fired their imaginations. In a hermitage of their own making, they had caught the vision of Shangri-la. They had dabbled on the outskirts of Utopia. However soon they might forget it under the press of ordinary affairs, it would not be lost. They had touched on a new dimension.

Preparation for the last night began in a downpour before dawn.

A pit was dug, coals were laid, a spit was built, and a huge leg of beef was started. All through the day plastic was hung to provide shelter for the guests who would arrive at dusk. Wives, girl friends, local citizens, professors, architects, artists, and scientists were invited from half a dozen places between Seattle and Vancouver. Broken brick was dumped into muddy spots down the road so vehicles would not bog down. A fire was built in the dome to dry it out and a cleanup squad brought the interior and the grounds to their peak of cleanliness. Everyone worked full tilt arranging food, lighting, access, extra accommodations, and special effects. Before the staff withdrew, everyone was told to be in the dome, seated and waiting, by six-thirty. As was customary, the students did not know what they would be waiting for. Not prone to let a mystery go unexamined, they gathered.

The staff drove to a residence in Bellingham to put on Restoration period costumes from the University's drama department. The drive back took them through the town of Alger, about two miles from the kiln. Knowing that a dozen local citizens would be in the crossroads bar, they stopped in. The customers saw a Jesuit priest, a Dominican brother, a nun, two squires in velvet great coats, a buccaneer, an Indian woman in a sari, and a girl in a purple page-boy outfit come in. For the first few minutes they were awestruck. All the men had beards. The women were immaculate. Everyone was barefoot or in hiking boots. Looking from the brown wool of the religious costumes to the blue, purple, and butterscotch velvet greatcoats, they gathered their wits. The owner hurried to get a camera. A couple concluded the costuming had to do with the kiln. Toasts and congratulations were offered from all sides, and the group left to meet several dozen guests who were timing their arrival at the property so everyone could enter together. Principal among the guests was Henry Elder, Director of the University of British Columbia School of Architecture, in the full ceremonial dress of a bishop.

Carrying candles and stepping to a chant, the procession strode up the path, through the trees, and into the dome. All attendants and ladies-in-waiting went to the center and stood around the bishop. The staff members in religious and court dress went around the inside edge and stopped at different low arches. For three-quarters of an hour they performed a one-act existential play that had been written the day before. With lines written on anything that could be concealed, the outer ring looked through their openings to describe different worlds. Each report they gave to the bishop was explained and distorted by his chief administrator. The bishop was asked to decide which world would survive. His answer—that none should survive—was relayed back by the administrator. As each one around the outside blew out his candle, the bishop grew more worried. By extinguishing his aide's candle before all were out, he allowed all the others to relight theirs. The play began with a three minute oration of Pericles' funeral speech in Greek, and ended with the priest chanting a Mass in Latin. All the players withdrew as a soprano sang a soft but bright solo. For several minutes no one spoke.

Just as applause began to ring through the dome half a dozen girls appeared wearing shapely togas and carrying bowls of fruit and jars of wine. Two students in loincloths carried a barbecued leg of beef on their shoulders. More serving girls came in with wicker trays. Loaves of bread—light, dark, french, sour dough —were passed around and everyone broke off what he wanted. Large cheeses—hard and soft, sharp and mild, pungent and creamy—were served. Whole roast chickens were broken apart and passed along; a dozen varieties of salami and platters of beef dripping with natural juices passed from hand to hand. Grapes, nuts, oranges, bananas, plums, and apples were offered. And after every mouthful there was wine—heavy, light, dry, sweet, rosé, Chablis, claret, Zinfandel. Hand to mouth and hand to hand; there was no china or silver to be seen. Each person was his own portable larder with supply stations never more than a few steps away. Eating and drinking in Roman fashion encouraged mobility.

Two drummers set up a wild beat on the tom-toms. Chains formed and circled. The dancing began. Shouts of *olé* mixed with toasts and the room began to rock.

When it seemed the dancing could not get wilder or the chorus louder, a Greek bouzouki band struck out. Beginning with their amplified versions of Western songs evocative of the Mediterranean, they worked into their native music, mixing the Greek strings with Turkish woodwinds. In Zorba fashion, the revelers jumped, whirled, stepped, stooped, sprang up, slapped their heels. Joyfully exhausted, they welcomed the chance to sit and watch when a belly dancer appeared. Beginning with the dance of the veils, she introduced a new motion each time she peeled off a layer. Revealed under the last layer of thinnest gauze, she gyrated seemingly in seven separate directions at once, all the while maintaining a thumping beat with her whole midriff that would have done credit to the girls of Bora Bora. As she went into her last number a young architect burst into the dome clad in nothing but a few vines appropriately draped. In a wild duet of Nature Boy and the Snake of Eden they stimulated the audience into a frenzy of gymnastics it had not known it could even attempt.

Quite beyond themselves, the crowd did not notice the next stage until the strobe lights set out a pattern of flashes that resembled the cannon blasts at the seige of Sevastopol. All motion was frozen in a series of disjointed stills, and the roar of artillery came over the powerful amplifier. A rock-and-roll band of amplified guitars and rim-rattling drums opened a light show. On a parachute held up to the curve of the dome, projectors flashed subliminal images in quick succession and overlay. Color blazed through the smoke and splashed along the silk like dry dust cast by a contemporary Jackson Pollock. The blinding flashes of light slowed the gyrations of the dancers into a slow-motion satire of a Chaplin film. And throughout the dome the ear-splitting roar of the band pressed as thick as an invisible fog suddenly turned harder than steel. Frozen in frantic postures by the flashes of bright and black they were held there motionless by noise so stunning it solidified the very blood in their veins. It was the light, the black, the blindness, the deafness, the start, the stop, the roar, the numbness of Creation. And it went on until dawn.

Somewhere in the rain and the mystery of that night of thoughtless noise, the end came. When they saw the debris by daylight, the workshop was already over. The cleanup was silent. They were going home. Or were they? Something seemed to bar the way. A question? A small doubt? Some wonder? They could not stay, but no one was happy to leave. There was a sense of a vision fading, the trace of a ghost. When would there be another night like the last? Beneath that selfish question, another concern began to stir. Somehow it had been more than just another workshop. Defense Island, Garibaldi Glacier, Port Alberni, Skid Row, and the brick kiln at Friday Creek had been stages in a launching. They had broken away from a tight confinement in a narrowly constricted sense of self. If they were not yet free, at least the bonds of a constraining psychological and social gravity had been weakened. Although they might never find a self-sustaining orbit, they had made a good start. They had begun a first probe toward relevance.

THE MODE

Anyone who has had an adventure and told the tale should have no trouble understanding how or why this account was written. Yet a few details might help. Since no diary was kept, *narrative* accuracy rests entirely on memories three months old. Certainly, some latent *personal* reactions must have been made to seem paramount simply through backward projection at the time of writing. Which ones they are will never be known. Most of the *conjectures* about what might have been learned were efforts to expose the potential inherent in such situations. Once the trip was over, no one was asked to give an account of what he learned. *Normative* judgments were made with the firmness and informality of convictions stated in conversation. Much was made of the *positive* features of people, places, and events. The *negative* aspects of industries, slums, and attitudes were set out in sharp relief. Did some things grow in the telling? Undoubtedly. Hence, it is to be expected that some will view these admissions as unforgivable lapses that render the account worthless. Harsh though it may be, such a verdict could be defended and respected for its grounds. It would be a mistake, however, to take these confessions as a sneak-attack on diaries, clinical records, opinion surveys, questionnaires, interviews, or the analysis and justification of normative judgments. What omissions there are resulted from trying to give an account different in kind from any that rely on such techniques. Overall, this other kind of account seeks to fuse the old to the new. For depth it would restore to the discussion of human problems the reflection so often found in the essays of the eighteenth century. For impact it would create the immediacy of today's reportorial fiction. By working within a framework made of man's most important moods held in constant tension, it may be possible to give expression to that vital *core* of human understandings so lacking in the findings of specialists. A diagram of the crucial moods held in steady tension might make it easier to envision how the core could be conceived (see Figure 3.1). In such an

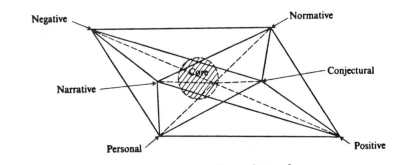

Figure 3.1 Six Crucial Moods

enterprise balance is everything. Yet nowhere can the limits of the moods or the strength of the vectors be stated in advance. To strike the needed balances in the writing, unguided by fixed reference points, is the essence of the literary mode. To find the appropriate posture is to convey an aspect of the human story too often left untold.

Section VI
Survey Methods in Educational Research

Survey Research Methods in Education

Richard M. Jaeger
University of North Carolina at Greensboro

What Is Survey Research?

The purpose of survey research is to describe specific characteristics of a large group of persons, objects, or institutions. For example, a survey researcher might want to know the average length of time all public school teachers in a state had been employed as full-time teachers. Another survey researcher might want information on the attitudes toward school of all high school students in a very large school system. A third researcher might want to investigate the number of dollars spent on the education of each student during the last full school year, by the 2000 largest school systems in the United States. These examples have several characteristics in common: First, the researchers are interested in specific facts that describe a large group. Second, the groups that are of interest are well defined. Third, all the researchers want to know something about the present conditions of a group, rather than something about what would happen if they changed something (such as doubling the tax rate in the 2000 largest school systems, and then determining the effect of the increased revenues on those school systems' expenditures for public education). Fourth, in each example, the most obvious way to secure the desired information would be to ask the right people.

The researcher who wanted to know the average amount of full-time teaching experience of all public school teachers in a particular state could, at least theoretically, ask every public school teacher in the state how long (s)he had been teaching full time. If all of these teachers provided the desired information, calculating the group's average years of full-time teaching experience would be a simple matter, particularly with a computer. But gathering data from all public school teachers in the state would be a waste of time and money if the researcher just wanted to know the average for the entire group. Even in Alaska (the state with the fewest public school teachers), there are about 5000 teachers. And in California, the state with the greatest number of public school teachers, there are over 175,000. Instead of asking every teacher, a more sensible approach would be to choose carefully some of the teachers in the state and ask each of them how long they had been teaching full time. The researcher could then calculate the average length of time the chosen teachers had been teaching full time, and use that figure as an estimate of what would have been found if all public school teachers in the state had been asked.

Some Basic Vocabulary

This example illustrates what is usually done in survey research—that is, collecting data from or about some members of the group that is of interest, rather than collecting data from or about all group members. In fact, we can use the example to introduce some of the most important vocabulary of survey research. The group consisting of all public school teachers in the state is an example of a *population*. In general, a population is any group of persons, objects, or institutions that have at least one characteristic in common. In this case, members of the population are public school teachers, and all are employed in the state that the researcher is investigating. The average length of time all members of the population have been employed full time is an example of a *population parameter*. A population parameter is any numerical value that can be calculated using information on all members of a population, such as the average age of all school buildings in the State of New York, or the total number of students enrolled in the public schools of Los Angeles, or the range of heights of the players on all professional basketball teams in the United States.

The smaller group of teachers that was chosen from the population to provide information on the length of time they had been teaching full time is an example of a *sample*. In survey research, a sample is a part of the population of interest; it is the part used for collection of data. If they are to provide information that is useful in estimating population parameters, samples have to be chosen carefully, according to well-defined rules. We will have more to say about the kinds of rules that are used and the appropriate sizes of samples. Samples that are useful in estimating population parameters are said to be *representative* of the population.

With just a few more definitions, you will know the basic vocabulary of survey research, so stick with it. In our example, once the sample of teachers had been selected, the researcher collected data from each sampled teacher and used those data to calculate the average full-time teaching experience of all teachers in the sample. That average is an example of a *sample statistic*. In general, a sample statistic is any numerical value that is calculated using data from members of a sample. Sample statistics are useful not only to describe the sample that provides data to compute them, but also to serve as estimates of corresponding population parameters. In our example, the average full-time teaching experience of sampled teachers was used as an estimate of what would have been found, had all teachers in the population provided data on their full-time teaching experience.

So a survey is a research study in which data are collected from the members of a sample, for the purpose of estimating one or more population parameters. Using simple English rather than the jargon of survey research, we would say that a survey is a research study in which data are collected from part of a group, for the purpose of describing one or more characteristics of the whole group.

So far we have treated the data collection part of survey research as though it were trivially simple: "If you want to know how many years of full-time teaching experience a public school teacher has, just ask." In truth, different ways of asking would yield different answers to this question. If you called teachers on the phone or asked them face to face, you might get one answer. But if you asked teachers by mailing them a form to complete, you might get another. The way the question was phrased could have a great influence on the types of answers you received. The question seems to be straightforward, but if you think about it, you'll see that it is quite ambiguous. What does full-time teaching mean? Is it defined as teaching at least 4 hours per day, or does some other number of hours per day define the minimum? To be counted as full time, must a person teach every weekday during all weeks that school is in session? Should a semester of student teaching be counted as full-time teaching experience? What about teaching in private schools or nursery schools: Do those experiences count toward full-time teaching experience? To secure data that were comparable, every teacher in the sample would have to be given the same set of rules. If data were collected through telephone calls or face-to-face interviews, the rules could be explained to responding teachers, and specific questions could be answered. For a survey conducted through the mail, the questionnaire would have to carry the burden of clearly explaining the rules. Responding teachers would not have the chance to ask for clarification. Writing clear, unambiguous survey questions is a difficult and time-consuming task, about which we will have more to say later.

In a well-designed survey in which data are collected through interviews, all interviewers are given strict instructions on the questions they are to ask, the order in which questions are to be asked, whether or not they can ask follow-up questions or probe for additional clarification when they do not understand a response, and what they are to tell respondents about the purpose of the survey and the organization that is sponsoring it. The instructions for interviewers and the questions they are to ask are contained in a form called an *interview protocol.*

When data are collected through a mail survey, the instrument that contains the survey questions is called a *questionnaire.* The questionnaire must also contain instructions on how to respond; definitions of terms likely to be unclear to respondents; any necessary instructions on questions that are to be answered by those who fall into one category, but skipped by those who fall into another; and instructions on what to do with the questionnaire once it has been completed.

Whether a survey is conducted using mailed questionnaires or through interviews, a critical objective for the survey researcher is to present all respondents with questions that they interpret and understand in exactly the same way. Perhaps this goal can never be accomplished completely, but strict attention to detail and care in phrasing questions, definitions, and instructions will certainly reduce ambiguity and misunderstanding.

Some Familiar Surveys

Two commercial survey organizations, the Gallup Poll and the Harris Poll, conduct hundreds of surveys every year. The topics of these surveys range from specialized marketing studies for business clients to the annual Gallup Poll on citizens' satisfaction with U.S. public education. Often the results of Harris Poll and Gallup Poll surveys of the general population are reported by the major news services, and appear in newspapers throughout the nation. After reading an article reporting the results of one of these surveys, you might have wondered how reliable conclusions could have been reached on the basis of data provided by a relatively small sample of respondents. Surveys of the general population of U.S. adults, a population that numbers well over 100 million, often report results based on information secured from a sample of only 1500. Although every person sampled must represent over 60,000 persons in the population, the reported survey results are quite reliable. Those who are unfamiliar with sampling methods often assume that they must sample a large proportion of a population (say 10 percent or 25 percent) in order to represent it well. That is true only if the population is very small. When fairly large populations are sampled (e.g., populations with 10,000 or more members), the reliability of sample estimates depends far more on the actual size of the sample than on the proportion of the population that is sampled. Thus 1500 well-selected cases would do about as good a job of representing a population of 100 million or a population of 100 thousand. What matters most is the sample size of 1500 and, of course, choosing those 1500 persons in a way that represents the entire population.

The decennial census of population conducted by the U.S. Bureau of the Census is somewhat like a survey, in that data are compiled from the information reported by individual respondents. However, the census of population is called a census and not a survey, for one important reason. Rather than sampling the population of U.S. residents, the census attempts to collect data from or about everyone in the population. In survey research, a study that involves collection of data from all members of a population is called a *census*, regardless of the nature of the population. The population can be composed of people, institutions, governments, or animals, and the study is still called a census if data are collected for every member of the population.

Exit polls conducted by television news networks during major elections are another kind of survey that might be familiar to you. An exit poll is used to collect information on voters' choices prior to final tabulations of votes, so that election outcomes can be predicted. Exit polls are called *polls* rather than surveys because of the limited amount of information they seek. The questionnaire or interview protocol used in a poll might contain only one or two questions; the instrument used in a survey typically contains many questions on a variety of topics and is far more complex.

Field Studies vs. Experiments

Survey research is part of a larger category of inquiry that social scientists call *field studies*. Another widely used method of social science inquiry is called *experimental research*. Several characteristics distinguish field studies from experimental research, but the defining difference concerns the kinds of actions taken by the researcher. In an experimental study, the researcher *does* something to the subjects or objects of the research, and then attempts to determine the effects of his or her actions. For example, in an experimental study of the effects of curriculum on student achievement, the researcher might assign one group of students to a new, innovative curriculum, and assign another group to a traditional curriculum. The assignment of students would use a process that depended on chance alone in determining which students received which curriculum. At the end of the school year, the researcher would administer the same kind of achievement test to all students, regardless of the curriculum they received, and would regard the groups' average achievement test scores as indicators of the relative effectiveness of the two curricula. In this example the new curriculum was introduced solely to determine its effects on student achievement.

In a field study, the researcher doesn't "do" anything to the objects or subjects of research, except observe them or ask them to provide data. The research consists of collecting data on things or people as they are, without trying to alter anything. In fact, those who conduct field studies often try to be as unobtrusive as possible, to minimize the effect of data collection on the objects or persons being studied. This is certainly the case in survey research. A survey researcher might want to know about teachers' honest attitudes toward their school principals, unaltered by the act of asking. The more intrusive a survey, the lower the chances that it will accurately reflect real conditions.

About the Rest of this Paper

This paper has four major sections, including the one you are now reading. In the next section, you will learn about the essential steps in planning and conducting a survey. That section is a general guide to the sorts of things you would have to think about and do if you were to conduct a survey of your own. The third section is a bit less pragmatic and somewhat more analytical than the second. It contains a discussion of the role of generalization in survey research. It also describes the types of conditions and assumptions that must hold if survey results are to generalize to the population of interest. The fourth section is built around a checklist of things to ask and things to look for when you are reviewing a report on a survey. Although surveys can provide trustworthy and accurate information, many do not. The fourth section will give you some hints on separating the wheat from the chaff.

Following this paper is a guide to additional reading about surveys and survey research. You can use this guide to find helpful books and reports on such specialized issues as questionnaire design or sampling methods, and on more general techniques of survey research.

How to Plan and Conduct a Survey (A Guide to Tasks and Issues)

At first glance, surveys look simple. Just write some questions, ask some people (either directly or by mailing them a questionnaire), count their answers, and write a report. Like most of life, surveys are decidedly more complex at second glance. If you want survey results you can trust, you'll have to exercise a good bit of care. First, you'll have to plan your study thoughtfully and thoroughly. Then you'll have to test your plan. And finally, you'll have to conduct the survey, using every element of your plan and the results of your testing.

There isn't a formula for ensuring a good survey. But years of study and experience have led to guidelines that greatly increase the chances (c.f., Moser & Kalton, 1972; Rossi, Wright & Anderson, 1983). Some of those guidelines will now be described.

Problem Definition

It might be obvious that it pays to figure out what you want to know before you start to gather information. However, many novice survey researchers begin by writing a questionnaire or an interview protocol. They write a few questions that are at the heart of the issue they want to investigate, and then think of other things that would be "nice" to know. Often, the result is a survey instrument that is far from the core of the research problem and laden with trivia that don't address the issues that motivated the survey.

The problem to be investigated must be defined clearly and completely, if the right questions are to be asked and needless questions are to be avoided. The place to start in planning a survey is not with the questions that make up a survey instrument but with basic research questions.

One strategy for defining research questions is to use a hierarchical approach, beginning with the broadest, most general questions, and ending with the most specific. Here's an example.

Suppose you wanted to determine why many public school teachers "burn out" so quickly and leave the profession within a few years. Certainly, many former teachers have reasons for leaving the profession that are personal and situation-specific. But it is also likely that some general factors can be identified. Your survey instrument should be structured around these latter factors.

Without too much thought it is easy to hypothesize several categories of reasons that some teachers leave the profession early. One set of factors might be economic, since teachers are paid very poorly and many have to hold a second job to afford the necessities of life. Other factors might have to do with the conditions of work in the schools. Classes are large, lunch hours are short, and students are often unruly and unappreciative. Yet another set of factors might be teachers' perceived social status. Although teaching was a well-respected profession 20 or 30 years ago, recent surveys have suggested that parents and other citizens have far less regard for public school teachers today.

If these three categories of factors exhausted your interest in the reasons teachers leave the profession early, you might structure your research questions as follows:

I. Do economic factors cause teachers to leave the profession early?
  A. Do teachers leave the profession early because of inadequate yearly income?
    1. Do teachers leave the profession early because their monthly income during the school year is too small?

2. Do teachers leave the profession early because they are not paid during the summer months?

3. Do teachers leave the profession early because their salary forces them to hold a second job during the school year?

4. Do teachers leave the profession early because their lack of income forces them to hold a different job during the summer months?

B. Do teachers leave the profession early because of the structure of their pay scale?

1. Do teachers leave the profession early because the upper limit on their pay scale is too low?

2. Do teachers leave the profession early because their rate of progress on the pay scale is too slow?

C. Do teachers leave the profession early because of inadequate fringe benefits?

1. Do teachers leave the profession early because their health insurance benefits are inadequate?

2. Do teachers leave the profession early because their life insurance benefits are inadequate?

3. Do teachers leave the profession early because their retirement benefits are inadequate?

II. Do working conditions cause teachers to leave the profession early?

A. Do teachers leave the profession early because the physical conditions of their work are unacceptable?

1. Do teachers leave the profession early because of deficiencies in the facilities in which they work?

2. Do teachers leave the profession early because of inadequate teaching materials?

B. Do teachers leave the profession early because of the amount of time their jobs demand?

1. Do teachers leave the profession early because their jobs require them to work during the evening?

2. Do teachers leave the profession early because their jobs require them to work on weekends?

3. Do teachers leave the profession early because of the total amount of time per week their jobs require?

C. Do teachers leave the profession early because of the attitudes and behavior of their students?

1. Do teachers leave the profession early because their students are undisciplined?

2. Do teachers leave the profession early because they perceive their students to be uninterested in learning?

3. Do teachers leave the profession early because they feel that students threaten their safety?

D. Do teachers leave the profession early because of the attitudes and behaviors of their peers and supervisors?

1. Do teachers leave the profession early because of unacceptable attitudes of their fellow teachers?
2. Do teachers leave the profession early because of unacceptable behaviors of their fellow teachers?
3. Do teachers leave the profession early because of unacceptable attitudes of their principals or other supervisors?
4. Do teachers leave the profession early because of unacceptable behaviors of their principals or other supervisors?

E. Do teachers leave the profession early because of the types of activities their jobs demand?
  1. Do teachers leave the profession early because their jobs require excessive custodial work?
  2. Do teachers leave the profession early because their jobs require excessive paper work?

III. Does the perceived social status of teaching cause teachers to leave the profession early?

A. Do teachers leave the profession early because they perceive teaching to be a low-status occupation?
  1. Do teachers leave the profession early because they regard teaching as a powerless occupation?
  2. Do teachers leave the profession early because they feel socially stigmatized?

B. Do teachers leave the profession early because they think others view teaching as a low-status occupation?
  1. Do teachers leave the profession early because they feel that society regards them as powerless?
  2. Do teachers leave the profession early because they feel that society does not consider them to be professionals?

Notice that this hierarchical set of research questions helps to identify large categories of issues, and then to suggest increasingly specific issues within those categories. At the third, most specific level within this illustration, the research questions practically define the content of a questionnaire or interview protocol. With a well-structured set of research questions as a guide, it is easy to determine whether or not a proposed questionnaire item is essential to the purposes of a survey. Since a wealth of experience and dozens of research studies have shown that participation in a survey depends directly on the length of the survey's questionnaire or interview protocol (the shorter the better), it is essential to eliminate all superfluous questions.

Identification of the Target Population

The *target population* of a survey is the group of persons, objects, or institutions that defines the object of the investigation. An essential requirement of survey research is the explicit, unequivocal definition of the target population. In fact, the target population must be defined so well that it is possible to state with certainty whether any given person, object, or institution is or is not a member of that population.

In an earlier example the target population was defined as all public school teachers in a given state. Is this definition "explicit and unequivocal?" You might think so at first, but the boundaries of the population are actually quite fuzzy. What is to be done with administrative personnel, such as principals and assistant principals, who hold valid teaching certificates and teach one course per day? What about substitute teachers who are not regularly employed at a given school? Are part-time teachers to be included? And what about school psychologists and guidance counselors who teach part of the day and provide psychological services or counseling during most of their work time? Are student teachers who happen to be in the schools at the time the survey is conducted to be treated as public school teachers? If these questions are not addressed unequivocally, practices are sure to vary across the schools used to collect data. In some schools administrative personnel will be included in the sample of respondents and in others they will be omitted. The result will be a sample that does not accurately represent any definable population, including the target population. When survey data are analyzed, statements about the target population will not be trustworthy.

In many survey research studies, explicit definition of the target population is difficult. In the example cited above, there might be sound arguments for including or excluding administrative personnel. The final decision should be based on careful consideration of the intended uses of survey results and the research issues that motivated the survey. The factors that affect teachers' decisions to leave the profession early might also apply to administrative personnel who teach part time. In that case, the researchers might want to include such personnel in their survey, as long as part-time administrators were clearly identified. Conversely, the resources available to conduct the survey might not be sufficient for collecting data from administrators as well as classroom teachers, in which case the more restrictive definition of the target population should be used. The essential point here is that *some* decision must be made so as to ensure the consistency of survey results.

Literature Review

Surveys that address previously unresearched topics are extremely rare. It is far more likely that the topic of a current survey has been investigated in several earlier studies.

A review of previous research can be very helpful in planning a new survey. The work of others can suggest modifications or additions to research questions, survey instruments, or plans for analysis of data. Building on the work of others is sound research practice. Often, it can save days of needless work spent rediscovering or reinventing appropriate solutions to common problems.

Sometimes a minor change in the wording of a questionnaire item will facilitate comparison of current findings with those of earlier studies. However, such comparisons must be made cautiously because small differences in the wording of a questionnaire item or protocol question can lead to large differences between distributions of responses. It is also the case that responses to individual questions are context-dependent. Respondents' answers to a question depend not only on the wording of that question, but on the series of questions that preceded it. Identical questions set in different contexts can and do evoke different distributions of response. These facts must be considered when reporting differences between "now" and "then."

There are many good sources of information on past survey research studies. Professional journals in the subject matter of the survey provide an excellent place to begin. With the advent of computerized literature search services, the task of determining what research has been done on a particular topic is far less arduous than in precomputer times. The DIALOG system includes many data bases in the social sciences. Both DIALOG and the ERIC system are available at most academic libraries in the United States. ERIC provides computerized listings of titles and abstracts of articles contained in about 800 professional journals, in addition to information on thousands of papers and reports presented at professional meetings or produced by educational research organizations. It is possible to search the ERIC database for information on precisely delimited topics by specifying unique combinations of key search words. For example, words like PUBLIC SCHOOL, TEACHING, and EMPLOYMENT could be used to request a listing of studies on the employment of public school teachers. DIALOG searches can be organized in much the same way as ERIC searches.

Selection of a Survey Method

Three basic methods of collecting data are available to the survey researcher: mail surveys, telephone surveys, and face-to-face interviews. Selection of a data collection method is a critical decision, since all methods have specific advantages and disadvantages. An extensive review of the issues involved in choosing a data collection method can be found in most texts on survey research, such as Moser and Kalton (1972) or Warwick and Lininger (1975). We will consider only a few examples here.

Mail surveys have the distinct advantage of economy. Since transportation costs are a major expense in most face-to-face interview surveys, mail surveys are almost always less expensive. Telephone interview surveys also eliminate transportation costs, but phone calls are usually more expensive than distribution of questionnaires through the mail, particularly when the survey sample is widely dispersed. In some survey projects, budget restrictions make mail surveys the only feasible choice.

Apart from their economy, many researchers feel that mail surveys have little to recommend them. Past experience has shown that most interview surveys are far more effective in securing the cooperation of respondents than are mail surveys. Without effective procedures to increase survey participation, it is not unusual to find that half the people surveyed by mail fail to return useful questionnaires. Since one can never be sure that the views and characteristics of survey respondents are like those of people who do not respond, it is dangerous to assume that respondents form a representative sample of the target population.

Mail surveys work best when questionnaires are short and simple, and when the topic of the survey can be addressed through a few easily understood questions. Mail survey questionnaires have to be self-explanatory. Whereas an interviewer can ask for clarification if (s)he doesn't understand a respondent's answer, or if the answer is incomplete, the mail survey researcher must live with the respondent's original answer. It is also possible for a respondent to ask an interviewer to clarify a question or define an unfamiliar term. With a mail survey, respondents are on their own. A survey package sent through the mail must clearly tell respondents why they should bother to complete a questionnaire, how they should furnish their answers, what questions they are to answer, and what to do with their questionnaires once they are finished. Unless the survey population consists of a highly educated group, all of this information must be conveyed in simple, jargon-free terms. The range of topics that lend themselves to simple portrayal and communication is clearly limited. Complex issues can be examined through a mail survey only when the survey population is composed of specialists with a common background and a natural interest in the topic.

Telephone interview surveys are usually far less expensive than face-to-face interview surveys, but they have many of the advantages of face-to-face interview surveys. The opportunity to secure additional information when a respondent's answer is either unclear or off the mark is present in both types of survey. In addition, a telephone interviewer can explain the purpose of the survey, why the respondent should participate, and what information is desired. As is true in face-to-face interview surveys, telephone interviews allow questions to be asked one at a time, in the order prescribed by the survey researcher. In a mail survey, the respondent can read through all questions before answering any of them, and can provide answers in any order.

The high costs of transportation often limit the methods that can be used to sample respondents in a face-to-face interview survey. For example, if respondents were widely dispersed throughout the United States, the cost of reaching them could be astronomical. Therefore, it might be necessary to adopt a sampling method that secured clusters of respondents in a few widely dispersed areas. This method of sampling is not as desirable as a scheme that allows each respondent to be selected individually. In a telephone interview survey of national scope, telephone costs are relatively constant, regardless of the geographic distribution of respondents. Thus more attractive sampling methods can be used.

Apart from their costs, face-to-face interview surveys have so many advantages that some survey researchers consider alternative methods to be totally unacceptable. The opportunity to clarify respondents' answers by asking additional questions and to provide information to respondents has already been mentioned. In addition, an interviewer who actually sees the person being interviewed can secure a good bit of information through observation. In social surveys, the type and condition of respondents' housing is often an important factor that can be assessed by looking at neighborhoods and individual dwelling units. By watching body language, an interviewer sometimes can tell whether a respondent understands the question being asked, is willing to respond, and has more to say if encouraged to do so.

Rates of cooperation in face-to-face interview surveys are usually higher than those secured through any other method. It is much easier to hang up the phone or throw a questionnaire in the trash than to refuse to talk to an interviewer who comes to one's home or place of business. A respondent's habits of observing the social conventions of politeness and cooperation are more likely to be followed in face-to-face encounters than in a telephone call or in responding to an unexpected piece of mail.

A distinct advantage of face-to-face interview surveys is the opportunity to identify each person who provides information. In a survey conducted through the mail, it is impossible to tell who completed the questionnaires. For example, a set of questionnaires sent to school principals might well be completed by secretaries, assistant principals, or other school personnel. Even in a telephone interview survey, one cannot be certain that the desired respondents are the persons being interviewed.

All of these factors, in addition to others, must be carefully weighed when a survey method is selected. If the survey budget is tight, questionnaires sent through the mail might be the only feasible method of research. If responses from members of the general population are desired and the research topic is complex or sensitive, a mail survey might be totally inadequate. In such cases, reanalysis of data collected in earlier research studies might be far more informative than gathering new data through a survey.

Secure or Construct a Sampling Frame

In order to select a sample of persons, objects, or institutions, one must have a list from which to sample. Such a list is called a *sampling frame*. Sampling frames are critically important in survey research because they define the *operational population* of a survey. A target population specifies the desires of a survey researcher, but a sampling frame defines reality. Let's consider an example.

A survey researcher might specify as a target population all fourth-grade teachers in Los Angeles, California, whether employed full time or part time. To avoid ambiguity, the researcher might define a fourth-grade teacher as anyone who teaches at least one fourth-grader or any child who would, by virtue of age, be in a fourth-grade classroom if (s)he attended a graded school. In most cities, finding a sampling frame that matched this operational definition of a target population would be difficult, or impossible. Although public school systems in most cities could provide a list of all of their teachers with fourth-grade classes, securing a list of fourth-grade teachers in nonpublic schools would probably be very difficult. In a city the size of Los Angeles, there are hundreds of nonpublic schools that are virtually independent. Although public school authorities might have a list of these schools, they would not be likely to have a list of the schools' teachers. In addition, the researcher's operational definition of a fourth-grade teacher would include independent music teachers, art teachers, and dance teachers, plus teachers in weekend religious schools. Since it would be very difficult to assemble a sampling frame that matched the research-er's target population, some compromises would have to be made. The easiest solution would be to redefine the target population as all public school fourth-grade teachers in Los Angeles. If this was not acceptable, restriction of the target population to fourth-grade teachers affiliated with public and nonpublic day schools in Los Angeles would increase the possibility of assembling a useful sampling frame.

The form in which sampling frames are available is also a major consideration in survey research. A very large list on paper is not nearly as convenient as a list on magnetic tape, a form that can be interpreted by a computer. If a computer-readable sampling frame were available, the computer could be used to sample from the list in ways that might be infeasible if a list on paper had to be sampled by hand.

Sometimes the unavailability of an appropriate sampling frame severely limits the kind of sampling methods that can be used. If a researcher wanted to select a sample of sixth-grade students from the entire state of California, no single agency could provide the necessary sampling frame. Since there are over 1,000 school systems in California, assembling lists of sixth-graders from all school systems in the state would be very time consuming and expensive. In fact, the costs would likely be prohibitive. If a different sampling approach were to be used, a sampling frame of California's sixth-graders might not be needed. The State Department of Education in California has a list of all public schools in the state that enroll sixth-grade students. This list could be used to sample schools from throughout the state, and then sixth-grade students could be se-lected only from sampled schools. Sampling frames of sixth-grade students would still have to be secured from sampled schools, but this would be far less costly than building a list of sixth-graders for the entire state. This sampling method is called *two-stage cluster sampling*. It might require selection of more students than would sampling from a statewide list of California's sixth-graders, but avoiding the costs and time required to assemble one huge sampling frame would be well worth the added data collection burden.

Construct Survey Instruments

All of the careful planning that underlies the development of an effective survey can go for nought if the questions asked—whether in an interview or on a questionnaire that is sent through the mail—are not clear, unambiguous, and appropriate to the survey researcher's purpose. In terms of clarity, the ideal sur-vey question is one that will be interpreted in precisely the same way by every survey respondent. You don't want every respondent to give you the same an-swer, but you do want every respondent to hear or read the same question.

Although there is no science of question writing, survey developers can take advantage of a well-developed and well-tested art in order to move much closer to the ideal of totally unambiguous and readily understood questions. Excellent suggestions on writing questions and constructing survey instruments can be found in a number of books devoted to the topic in whole or in part, including

Babbie (1973), Berdie and Anderson (1974), Moser and Kalton (1972), and Warwick and Lininger (1975). In this brief introduction, only a few principles will be illustrated.

Every survey researcher is faced with the dilemma of what questions to include. Usually the temptation is to ask many questions, since having more information is more appealing than having less. Asking for more than is absolutely needed does have its costs. It is a well-established fact that potential respondents are less willing to participate in a long survey than a short one, whether by interview or by mail. Including questions that aren't essential might cost far more than the extra dollars needed to process the information. To keep your survey free of unnecessary questionnaire items, it is helpful to use the sort of detailed research questions that were illustrated earlier. If an interview question or questionnaire item does not address one or more of the research questions, it should not be asked.

No set of rules will guarantee that your questionnaire items or interview questions will be clear and unambiguous, but several are likely to help. When writing a survey instrument, the people who are to respond to your survey should be kept clearly in mind. If you are surveying the general population, remember that many respondents will have far less education than you do. Keep the vocabulary level of your questions as low as possible, without being insulting. Avoid specialized jargon that is likely to be misunderstood by members of the general population. It is often difficult to remember that the "educationese" used by education professionals (e.g., "tracking," "learning readiness," "achievement motivation," etc.) is a foreign language to many members of the general population. Unless you are preparing a survey for members of the education profession, avoid such terms whenever possible. When there is no alternative to using specialized terms, make sure that they are defined on the survey instrument.

Many authors distinguish between different categories of questions in their guides to survey instrument development. One way of categorizing questions is in terms of the type of information they seek—asking for facts vs. asking for opinions or judgments. Questions can also be classified in terms of their format—whether they ask a respondent to construct an answer (an *open-ended* question such as "How many motion picture films did you see during the last year?"), or to select an answer (a *closed-option* question such as "Did you see any motion pictures last year? __ Yes __ No __ I don't know"). Guides to writing often differ across categories of questions. For example, when writing closed-option questions, one must be certain that all possible answer choices are provided, often including an answer labeled "Other, please specify _____." Use of an answer category that permits a respondent to admit ignorance (e.g., "I don't know") is far better than collecting data that are based on ignorance or, in the case of opinion questions, lack of thought.

When asking questions that require respondents to recall events or other information, it is often helpful to provide reference points or prompts. For example, in a health survey you might want to ask each respondent when they

last visited a physician. You might instruct your interviewers to help their respondents recall by asking, "Was it before Christmas or after Christmas?" or
"Did you visit a physician the last time you were feeling ill? When was that?"
When writing a questionnaire item in which you wanted to know what television programs were watched the previous evening, it would make perfect sense
to stimulate recall by listing all of the possibilities, and asking respondents to
check those they watched. Resulting data would likely be far more accurate than
would responses to the item: "List all television programs you watched last
night," with no aids to recall. Listing alternative answers and having respondents choose those that are correct is fine, provided all of the possibilities have
been listed. The same rule applies when prompts are given. Listing some possibilities and leaving others out is almost certain to bias the answers you will
get. If any possibilities are listed make sure they are exhaustive.

The art of writing questions and developing survey instruments has barely
been introduced in this brief section. Perhaps these few illustrations will provide
some hints on points to consider when you are judging the quality of a survey
instrument, and will inspire you to read some of the suggested references before
you construct your own instruments.

Define a Sampling Plan

Since the data collection costs of a survey are likely to be *the* major budget
item, anything that reduces the amount of data required, without affecting the
quality of the resulting information, should be considered seriously. Choosing
the best possible sampling method is one important way of increasing the efficiency of a survey, thus reducing costs without sacrificing quality or precision.

How much difference can selection of the right sampling procedure make?
In one example involving estimation of the average achievement of the 1200
sixth-grade students in a medium-sized school system, Jaeger (1984) compared
the sample sizes that would be required by 17 different sampling and estimation
procedures. The most efficient procedure (stratified random sampling with op-
timal allocation) required testing only 25 students, and the least efficient procedure (single-stage cluster sampling with unbiased estimation) required testing
1041 students. Thus the least efficient sampling and estimation procedure required testing more than 41 times the number of students needed by the most
efficient procedure! Such dramatic differences won't be found in every survey
application, but differences between the sample sizes required by the most efficient and the least efficient sampling procedures available will usually be noticeable.

An extensive discussion of alternative sampling and estimation procedures is
beyond the scope of this introductory paper, but a few of the possibilities will
be mentioned. *Simple random sampling* is the most fundamental *probability sampling procedure*. Two principles define simple random sampling: First, every element in the population has the same chance of being sampled. Second, selection
of any one element has no influence on the chance that any other element is
selected. There is an inherent fairness in the principles that define simple ran-

dom sampling, since in a population of persons, everyone would have the same chance of being chosen (either initially or after some selections had been made) regardless of who had been chosen already. Simple random sampling is often used as a benchmark when the efficiencies of other sampling procedures are investigated. Some alternative sampling methods have been found to be more efficient than simple random sampling (in the sense that they require the collection of less data to obtain equivalent estimation precision), and others have been found to be less efficient.

One class of sampling methods that is often more efficient than simple random sampling is termed *stratified sampling*. When stratified sampling is used, the population to be sampled is divided into parts (called *subpopulations* or *strata*), and independent samples are selected from each part (called a stratum). The parameter of interest is estimated separately for each stratum, and these estimates are then combined through a weighted averaging procedure. For example, suppose you wanted to know the average height of the 12-year-old children who were enrolled in a particular school, and you didn't want to measure all of them. You could select a sample of the 12-year-olds, and estimate the average height of the population by using the average height of the children in your sample. One way of selecting a sample would be to number all of the 12-year-old children in the population, and then use a table of random numbers (e.g., Rand Corp., 1969) to select the children to be measured. A table of random numbers contains the same proportion of each of the digits 0, 1, 2, 3, 4, 5, 6, 7, 8, and 9, and the arrangement of the digits is totally random (so each digit follows every other digit equally often). Using a table of random numbers ensures that each of the numbered elements in a sampling frame has the same chance of being selected. In our problem, by using a random number table, each of the children in the population would have the same chance of being sampled, and whether or not one child was chosen would not depend at all on whether any other child was chosen. So use of a random number table would meet the requirements of simple random sampling. But suppose you wanted to sample more efficiently. Instead of selecting a simple random sample of 12-year-olds, you could divide your population into a stratum (subpopulation) of boys and a stratum of girls. Since girls typically reach puberty (and therefore have a growth spurt) before boys do, it would not be unusual to find that the stratum of 12-year-old girls had a larger average height than did the stratum of 12-year-old boys. In any case, you would expect the boys and girls to differ noticeably in average height. Since this is the case, if you wanted to estimate the average height of all 12-year-olds regardless of gender, wouldn't it seem sensible to make sure that your sample was balanced in its representation of girls and boys? You could accomplish this through stratified sampling. Once you had divided the population into a stratum of boys and a stratum of girls, you could use a random number table to select a simple random sample from each stratum. You could then estimate the average height of the stratum of girls and the average height of the stratum of boys, using the data from your two simple random samples. The average height of all 12-year-olds would be found by using a formula that appropriately combined the figures for boys and for girls.

Because stratified sampling would ensure that you couldn't select samples that consisted of all boys (who would, on average, be shorter than the population average), or all girls (who would, on average, be taller than the population average), it would eliminate many samples that would do a bad job of estimating the average height of the entire population. This is why stratified sampling is likely to be more efficient than simple random sampling.

In discussing the development of sampling frames, it was noted that the opportunity to use some sampling methods depends on the types of sampling frames that are available. In many survey applications, it is not possible to obtain or construct a sampling frame of the individuals that are of interest; a sampling frame consisting of groups of individuals must be used. An example of this situation, a survey in which estimates were desired for the entire population of sixth-grade students in the public schools of California, was described earlier. In that case, it was suggested that schools with sixth-grade classes be sampled first, followed by selection of sixth-grade students from each of the sampled schools. Since the California State Department of Education has a list of all public schools in the state with sixth-grade classes, an available sampling frame could be used. This type of sampling procedure is known as *cluster sampling*. The schools with sixth-graders are clusters which would provide the groups of sixth-grade students for sampling and measurement. If, when a school was sampled, all sixth-graders in that school were observed or measured, the procedure would be called *single-stage cluster sampling*. If a sample of sixth-graders was selected from each sampled school, the procedure would be called *two-stage cluster sampling*. At the first stage, schools would be sampled, and at the second, sixth-grade students would be sampled.

Depending on how the clusters are chosen and what type of analysis is applied to the data that are collected, the efficiency of cluster sampling can range from very low to very high. Or to put it another way, if you wanted to estimate a population parameter with a given level of precision (e.g., estimate the average height of 12-year-olds to the nearest half inch), you might have to collect much more data, or much less data, using cluster sampling than you would need using simple random sampling. Several of the sampling books in the bibliography at the end of this chapter contain a more detailed discussion of this point.

In summary, when selecting a sampling method, you should choose one that (a) is easy to apply and (b) lets you estimate the parameters you are interested in as precisely as you want, with the smallest possible sample size. Choosing well can make a big difference in the overall cost of your survey.

Designing Field Procedures

The mechanics of collecting data constitute an important part of an effective survey and are termed *field procedures*. In a mail survey, field procedures include mailout of questionnaires, construction and maintenance of records on the distribution of questionnaires, construction and maintenance of records on the receipt of completed questionnaires, and procedures for making repeated requests to people who have not returned completed questionnaires (called *follow-up procedures*). In an interview survey, field procedures include recruitment, training, deployment, and supervision of interviewers, distribution of survey instruments and a schedule of interviews to interviewers, collection of completed survey instruments from interviewers, and rules for making repeated calls on potential respondents who were not available at the time initial calls were made.

If field procedures are not well defined, the quality of a survey will suffer and, in many cases, survey quality cannot be assessed. For example, without a complete list of persons to whom mail survey instruments have been sent, it is not possible to determine the types and proportions of persons who have and have not responded. As a second example, if no rules had been formulated for making repeated calls on potential respondents who were not at home at the time of initial attempts, interviewers would make up their own rules. Since the rules would vary greatly, depending on the tenacity of each interviewer, it would be unlikely that each interviewer would collect data from a comparable sample of respondents. If more tenacious interviewers were assigned to high-income areas while those less apt to make repeated call-backs were assigned to low-income areas, survey results could be biased.

Reduction and Editing of Data

When survey data are collected on questionnaires or through interviews, they are not typically in a form that permits immediate analysis, either by hand or by using a computer. In addition, some of the data collected are inevitably faulty. Some questionnaires or interview protocols are always incomplete. Responses to some questions are usually contradictory or impossible or highly unlikely (e.g., respondents report that they have 25 children or that they were born in 1855).

Prior to analyzing survey data, they must be placed in a form that permits their summarization and interpretation. Since surveys frequently yield large amounts of data, most analyses are conducted with the aid of a computer. In these cases, the data must be available in a form that a computer can process—in a fixed, uniform format, either on magnetic tape, magnetic disk, or punched cards (although the latter form is rapidly becoming obsolete).

The process of transforming data to an analyzable form is called *data reduction*. Data reduction is sometimes a manual process (such as having a clerk read each interview protocol, code the responses into numerical values, and then enter the resulting data in a magnetic disk file by using a computer terminal) and sometimes an automated process (such as using an optical mark sense reader to scan specially prepared mail survey questionnaires. The scanner reads sets of circles or boxes that have been darkened with a number-two pencil, just as an automatic test scoring machine does.). If respondents have provided narrative responses to questions, these must be read by hand and transformed into numerical codes prior to entering the data into a computer file. Although the coding process often can be completed by a clerk, defining the rules for coding is a difficult task that requires the judgment of a professional survey researcher. It is necessary to establish a set of detailed decision rules that will unequivocally accomodate every possible response to every survey question. Each response must fit into one (and only one) category, usually including "miscellaneous" and "does not apply" categories. Collectively, the categories must be exhaustive and must not overlap.

Once data have been reduced to an analyzable form, they must be edited so as to detect and resolve the inevitable errors. A scheme for handling missing data must be developed. Sometimes a respondent who does not provide complete data is eliminated from the data set. In other editing plans, a respondent is not included in analyses involving a variable for which (s)he has not provided data, but is included in all other analyses. Another possibility is to replace missing data with the average of values provided by all other respondents. Certain advantages are associated with each procedure, and deciding which to use requires considerable thought.

Other editing tasks include checking to see whether the responses to any question are impossible or very unlikely. For example, responses to a question on age (in years) would probably be eliminated or checked against other data if they were, in the case of a survey of adults, less than 18 or more than 100. Regardless of the age group sampled, reported ages that were negative would be flagged for review. Erroneous data sometimes are reported by respondents who complete questionnaires, or by interviewers who fill out protocols. In other cases, the reported data are correct but coding clerks have made an error when they entered the data in a computer file. In all of these situations, faulty data must be eliminated prior to aggregation and analysis of survey results in order to avoid the contamination of accurate data.

Although most editing of survey data takes place after the data have been reduced and placed into a computer file, some preliminary editing might be done when the data are in their "raw" form, either on questionnaires or interview protocols. Responses to questions that are particularly critical might be verified for completeness and appropriateness as soon as survey documents are received, so that additional inquiries can be made if necessary.

Regardless of the form and extensiveness of data reduction and editing, these procedures must be planned in detail at the time a survey is designed.

Plans for Analysis of Data

Although it is unlikely that all desirable data analyses can be specified prior to collecting survey data, it is advantageous to specify a set of proposed analyses in great detail. The principal benefit of such detailed plans is their usefulness in determining whether the data to be collected will provide answers to the research questions developed as part of the survey plan.

By preparing a document that links each item on the survey instruments to one or more research questions and one or more proposed analyses, a survey researcher can ensure that the data to be collected are, in fact, needed to answer the proposed research questions. In addition, the linking document can be used to determine that every proposed data analysis is needed to answer a research question and that all of the research questions can be answered using the data to be collected.

Although the statistical procedures used to analyze survey data are becoming increasingly sophisticated, many survey analyses require only the construction of simple tables and graphs. Cross-tabulation, a procedure in which a researcher computes the numbers and percents of cases that simultaneously fall into various categories of two or more variables, is used extensively. Table 1 is an example of a cross-tabulation. This table shows the number and percent of a sample of graduate students who are simultaneously (a) enrolled in various graduate degree programs and (b) currently enrolled in various research methodology courses. The percentages shown in Table 1 are called *row percents*. They represent the percentages of students enrolled in a particular degree program who are currently enrolled in a specified research methodology course. It is also possible to compute the percentage of students enrolled in a particular research methodology course (e.g., a statistics course) who are also enrolled in each degree program. These percents would be called *column percents*. For example, since 100 of the 305 students enrolled in statistics courses are also enrolled in an education program, the column percent for the Education/Statistics cell of the table would be 33. Finally, it is possible to compute *cell percents* for a cross-tabulation. A cell percent is the percent of the total sample that falls into a particular cell (row and column combination) of the table. As an example, 100 of the 500 students in the sample are enrolled in an education program and are currently enrolled in a statistics course. Since 100 is 20 percent of the 500 students in the sample, the cell percent in the upper left-hand cell would be 20.

Although cross-tabulations cannot be completed until survey data have been collected, it is possible to define the form of the cross-tabulations that will be used. Tables that have titles, row headings, and column headings—everything but the data—are called *table shells*. Constructing a complete set of proposed table titles, together with representative table shells, is a useful way to construct a plan for analysis of survey data.

Plans for Reporting Survey Results

A plan for reporting the results of a survey might be considered a final piece of insurance on the consistency of survey objectives and survey outcomes. Both the detailed set of research questions and the plans for analysis of data, described earlier, can be used to plan the reports that are to be prepared from survey results. Major research questions can be used to define the chapters of a report,

TABLE 1. *Number and percent of graduate students, by degree program and type of research methodology course*

| Degree program | Research Methodology Course | | | | | | Total |
| | Statistics | | Ethnography | | Historiography | | |
	n	%	n	%	n	%	
Education	100	50	50	25	50	25	200
Sociology	25	25	50	50	25	25	100
Psychology	180	90	20	10	0	0	200
Total	305	61	120	24	75	15	500

and corresponding table shells can be used to organize the material in the chapters.

In addition to outlining survey reports, a plan for reporting should describe the intended audiences for the reports, and the methods to be used for distributing the reports.

Pilot Survey

A pilot survey is an essential part of any survey research study. Even expert survey researchers cannot predict accurately the effectiveness of survey instruments, plans for distribution and receipt of survey materials, the proportion of a target sample that will participate in a survey, and the time necessary to complete the survey. A pilot survey is used to collect data on all of these points, and more.

Ideally, a pilot survey is the main survey in miniature. To provide required data on the likely success of the main survey, a pilot survey must be planned in detail. The plan should include most of the elements of the main survey, in addition to elements needed to determine the likely pitfalls of the main survey.

Among other things, respondents to a pilot survey are asked whether the questions proposed for the main survey are clear and understandable, whether the instructions for completing survey instruments and providing data are free of ambiguities, and how long it took them to complete the main survey's instruments. An additional questionnaire or interview protocol will have to be developed to secure these essential data.

You might think of a pilot survey as a "dress rehearsal" for the real thing. As a part of that dress rehearsal, the producer, director, and all of the actors and stage hands are responsible for noting exactly what went on, the time needed to run through each act, what worked, what didn't, and why.

Data from a pilot survey are analyzed, just as in the main survey, but with the purpose of determining what must be changed and what can remain as planned.

Revision and Implementation

Components of the main survey, such as instructions, instruments, field procedures, and budget, are revised in accordance with the data provided by the pilot survey. Just like the bones in a skeleton, all of the elements of a survey are connected. If you change one element, everything else must be changed as well. For example, if a questionnaire or interview protocol is revised, it is no longer clear that all of the previously posed research questions will be answerable. And some of the table shells that make up a plan for analysis will surely have to be changed. So modification of survey materials following a pilot survey must include careful attention to the consistency of all survey parts.

Following revision, the plan for the main survey is put into action, and it is at this point that the many benefits of detailed planning become apparent. It would be misleading, however, to suggest that the main survey will be conducted in complete accordance with the plan. More likely, response rates observed for the main survey will differ somewhat from those predicted from the pilot survey. Even the best planning will not allow you to anticipate every problem that will arise when questionnaires are sent through the mail or interviewers are sent into the field. And the presence of real data in the table shells you so carefully developed will undoubtedly suggest new analyses that can shed light on a variety of research questions, some of which were not anticipated when the survey was planned.

But careful planning is the key to sound survey practice. Specifying *why* you want data, *how* you'll collect it, and *what you'll do with it* once you have it, will go a long way toward ensuring the usefulness of the data you collect and avoiding the disappointment of not meeting your real research needs.

The Role of Generalization

Generalization of findings is central to all research but is the very essence of survey research. In survey research, one asks a relatively small number of people to answer a relatively small number of questions and, on the basis of the answers given, draws conclusions about the conditions, attitudes, opinions, or status of a population of persons, objects, institutions, governments, or other entities.

Generalizing from the data collected to the conclusions drawn is an act of faith that can be supported by logic, theory, and sound survey practice. Such generalization can be better understood by considering its component parts, and the assumptions that it demands.

Generalization in survey research is partly statistical and partly substantive. We will discuss *statistical generalization* first. Consider a simple, but fictitious, example. Suppose that you were an inveterate coin flipper, and had a burning desire to know what proportion of the pennies held by a local bank on a particular day would land "heads," were you to flip each coin once. The pennies held by the bank on that day constitute a population, and the proportion that would land heads is an example of a population parameter. You could *calculate* the value of the population parameter if you were willing to work into the night, giving each of the bank's pennies a healthy flip, recording the face that appeared when it landed, and then counting the number of heads that appeared and the number of flips that you made. An alternative that was less physically demanding (and also less demanding of time) would be to select a sample of pennies from the bank's holdings on the day that was of interest, flip each penny in the sample one time, record the number of heads that appeared in those flips, and divide that value by the number of sampled coins. The resulting sample proportion could be used as an *estimate* of what would have been found, if each of the bank's pennies had been flipped.

Now if you took the more sensible and less demanding route to discovering the propensity of the bank's pennies to land heads up, you would have no assurance that the proportion of heads you observed in your sample of flipped pennies would equal the proportion you would have found, had you flipped every penny in the population. Thus the validity of a generalization from the sample of pennies actually flipped to the population of pennies held by the bank on a particular day would be open to question.

Two kinds of statistical error—bias error and random error—threaten the validity of generalizations from a sample statistic to a population parameter. *Bias error* is a form of systematic error, which means that it is predictable. It occurs when the observed sample does not represent the target population. In the penny-flipping example, bias error could occur if the sample of pennies selected for flipping tended to be different from the pennies in the rest of the population in a way that would affect the proportion of heads or tails that appeared when the pennies were flipped. For example, if the sampled pennies tended to be slightly larger in diameter on the side with a tail, that heavier side would probably tend to fall to the bottom, and more heads would appear when the pennies were flipped. In realistic surveys, bias error can arise in many ways. Although pennies cannot refuse to be flipped, people can refuse to be interviewed or to complete questionnaires. Since the people who respond to surveys are very likely to differ from those who refuse or those who cannot be located, high rates of nonresponse can lead to substantial bias error.

Another frequent cause of bias error in surveys is inappropriate or inadequate sampling. Inappropriate sampling occurs when the sampling procedure is flawed by design. The need to use a probability sampling procedure that affords every member of a population the opportunity to enter the sample has already been discussed. Sampling procedures that systematically exclude some members of the target population inevitably lead to bias error. Examples of such procedures include distribution of questionnaires on the quality of education at a meeting of a school's parent-teacher association, when the target population is all parents of students enrolled in the school; and selection of students from elementary schools that are located closest to a district's central office, when the target population is all elementary school students in the district.

Inadequate sampling can occur with the best of sampling designs if the survey is not conducted in accordance with the design. For example, even though potential respondents to an interview survey were selected through simple random sampling, interviewers could fail to secure responses from a large proportion of persons whose jobs required frequent travel or nonstandard working times. Facts about such persons, or their opinions, might well differ systematically from those of respondents who were more accessible.

The second threat to statistical generalization of survey results is *random error*. Random error is inevitable in surveys, but its magnitude can almost always be controlled. Random error occurs because samples are used, and because respondents differ. Therefore the results obtained from one sample almost always differ from those that would have been obtained from another. With most sampling designs, random error can be reduced by taking a larger sample. When samples are large enough, most sample estimates will be fairly close to their corresponding population parameter and statistical generalization will not be threatened by random error. When samples are too small, many sample estimates will differ substantially from their corresponding population parameter, and generalization will be risky.

Valid *substantive generalization* of survey results depends on the satisfaction of a number of assumptions. These assumptions are shown in Figure 1, together with those that must be satisfied to obtain valid statistical generalization.

Construct validity of the survey questions is the first assumption listed under substantive generalization. Construct validity is a complex concept, and this discussion will barely introduce it. To really learn about construct validity, you should read Cronbach and Meehl (1955) and Cronbach (1971). A *construct* can be described as a "constructed variable" that is unobservable. It is a label that is attached to a consistent set of observable behaviors. People are often described in terms of constructs even though constructs cannot be observed. For example, a recent nationwide survey concluded that teachers have a negative attitude toward their jobs. Unlike the teachers' heights, there is no single yardstick the survey researchers could have used to measure teachers' attitudes. Instead, teachers were asked to respond to a set of 20 statements by selecting options ranging from "Strongly Disagree" to "Strongly Agree." The statements included "If I had the opportunity to start my career again, I would choose to be a teacher;" and "I would recommend that today's college students choose teaching as a

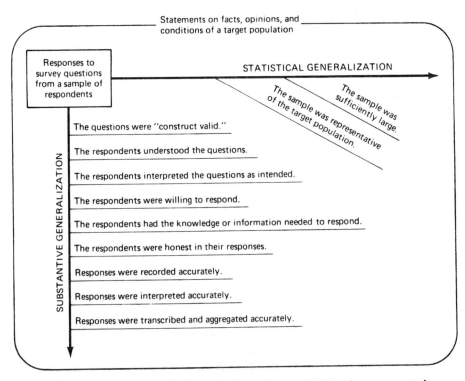

FIGURE 1. *Statistical generalization and substantive generalization in survey research.*
Source: Jaeger (1984). Reprinted by permission.

career." In drawing their conclusions, the researchers who reported the results of this survey generalized *from* teachers' responses to specific statements *to* teachers' positions on the construct "job attitude." In doing so, the researchers assumed that the survey questions they asked measured teachers' attitudes appropriately and adequately, and that the questions were consistent with a body of theory that defines the "job attitude" construct.

The researchers scored teachers' responses to each question from 1 to 5, using 1 for "Strongly Disagree," 3 for "Neither Agree nor Disagree," and 5 for "Strongly Agree." They then summed teachers' scores for the 20 questions to produce an overall score that could range from 20 to 100. The issue of construct validity arises when the researchers define the overall score resulting from this process as a measure of "job attitude," and assume that a higher score represents a more positive job attitude than does a lower score. The validity of this form of substantive generalization can never be "proven," but it must be supported through a careful and extensive set of empirical procedures that are based on a theory that includes job attitude. One type of evidence would show that summed scores on the 20 questions were positively correlated with measures of variables that were expected to be positively related to teachers' job attitudes; e.g., the extent of teachers' voluntary participation in their schools' extracurricular activities. Another type of evidence would show that the average summed score on the 20 questions was higher for teachers who, theoretically, would be expected to have more positive job attitudes than for teachers who, theoretically, would be expected to have less positive job attitudes; e.g., teachers in affluent school systems, compared to teachers in very poor school systems.

Two more assumptions underlying valid substantive generalization are (a) that respondents understood the questions that were asked in the survey, and (b) that the respondents' interpretations of the questions were consistent with those intended by the survey researchers. The act of responding, particularly to closed-option questions, is not a guarantee of understanding. In addition, level of understanding is a critical issue. To assure appropriate substantive generalization of survey results, respondents must have understood the questions posed in the survey, and they must have interpreted those questions just as the survey researchers intended. Even questions that seem unambiguous, such as "Where do you live?" admit such diverse, but plausible, responses as "In the South," "100 Main Street," or "In an apartment." These answers clearly indicate that the respondents were answering what were, to them, three different questions. Aggregations of responses such as these will not support interpretable generalizations.

In addition to understanding what was asked, survey respondents must be willing and able to answer the questions posed to them. For the most part, respondents' willingness can be assessed through their overt cooperation, although specific survey questions (perhaps on highly personal or controversial issues) might tax the willingness of generally cooperative respondents. Ability to respond is not so easily assessed, and is certainly not guaranteed just by obtaining answers to the questions that are asked. Having the ability to respond to a question presumes that respondents know the answer or have the information needed to respond available to them. In face-to-face interview surveys, being confronted with an interviewer who expects an answer provides strong motivation to provide an answer, regardless of ability. And in mail surveys that use closed-option questions, it is easy to select an option without any pertinent knowledge or information.

The issue of ability to respond arises not just with "knowledge" questions, but with "opinion" questions as well. Many opinion questions evoke complex feelings that might not be well understood by respondents. Others stimulate conditional responses that might not fit the format of mailed questionnaires or structured interviews. For example, if asked "Do you favor abortion on demand?", a mailed questionnaire with the options "Yes," "No," and "Don't know" might not allow you to express your true opinion. You might favor abortion on demand under some circumstances, but not others. So the format used to pose survey questions and to record responses might limit the accuracy of your response, and thereby threaten valid generalization of findings.

The dependence of substantive generalization on honesty of response is so transparently obvious that further discussion of the point is unnecessary. Even a small proportion of dishonest responses will poison the well of honest ones to an unknown degree and, in doing so, will distort the meaning of aggregated survey results.

Several seemingly mechanical steps in the survey process can, if handled carelessly, undermine the validity of findings. Any systematic errors in recording responses, or in transcribing and analyzing resulting data, can threaten the generalizability of findings. Occasional errors in recording responses, either on the part of respondents who complete a mailed questionnaire, or on the part of interviewers who record respondents' answers on a protocol, will add to random error but not bias error. This statement presumes that such errors are not systematic in nature. As an example of a *systematic error*, interviewers might fail to use a "No opinion" option in recording answers to opinion questions.

When surveys incorporate open-ended questions, respondents' answers must be interpreted before they are converted to numerically codable data. Valid generalization requires that such interpretations be correct; i.e., that they be consistent with the meanings intended by the respondents.

The list of requirements for valid statistical and substantive generalization of survey results portrayed in Figure 1 is extensive, and might appear impossible to achieve. In reality, perfection is unlikely to be realized in any survey. But sound planning followed by careful application of plans can materially increase the validity of generalizations. Rather than viewing the list in Figure 1 as an insurmountable hurdle, you might consider using it as a framework for survey evaluation. That is the topic of the next section of this paper.

A Short Checklist for Survey Evaluation

So far this paper has provided a step-by-step guide to conducting surveys and a brief treatise on generalization of survey results. This section contains a short checklist that will help you distinguish between a good survey and a poor one. By using the checklist to review a report of survey procedures and findings, you should be able to answer the essential question, "Should I believe the results?"

Of course you will not find that surveys fall into two clearly distinguishable categories labeled "good" and "bad." Some will be exemplars of good practice in their sampling design or instruments, and then fall short in their field procedures. Others will suffer from basic design flaws but show careful application of that design. Still others will be poorly conceptualized and thereby flawed from the outset; no amount of care in operational planning and implementation will compensate for inadequate or inappropriate specification of research questions. The difficult part of survey evaluation is determining the likely effect of a design or implementation flaw on the validity of survey results. Your evaluation skills will develop as you gain greater experience. In the meantime, be a skeptic and a doubter. Here is a set of evaluative questions you can use to focus your inquiry:

1. Does the report contain a list of specific research questions or issues the survey is intended to address?

2. Do the research questions posed by the investigators appropriately and adequately address the topic of the survey; e.g., in a survey on poverty in the United States, does the research include an examination of poverty as a function of race, level of education, and geographic location?

3. Are the research questions posed by the investigators well organized and well structured?

4. Does the report identify the target population to which generalization was desired?

5. Does the report describe available sampling frames?

6. Does the report indicate a close match between the target population and the operational population?

7. Does the report describe the sampling procedures used? Were probability sampling procedures used?

8. Are nonresponse rates reported for the entire survey and for individual questions?

9. Were nonresponse rates low enough to avoid substantial bias errors?

10. Are any analyses of potential sampling bias reported?

11. Are sample sizes sufficient to avoid substantial random errors? Are standard errors of estimate reported?

12. Is the primary mode of data collection (i.e., mailed questionnaires, telephone interviews, face-to-face interviews) consistent with the objectives, complexity, and operational population of the survey?

13. Are survey instruments provided in the report?

14. Are instructions for completing the survey clear and unambiguous?

15. Are questions on instruments clear and unambiguous?

16. Do questions on instruments encourage respondents' honesty in admitting lack of knowledge or uncertainty?

17. Are questions on instruments free from obvious bias, slanting, or "loading"?

18. Was the survey consistent with ethical research practice; e.g., was the anonymity and/or confidentiality of respondents protected?

19. Does the report contain a description of field procedures?

20. Are field procedures adequate and appropriate? Is it likely that major sources of bias error have been avoided?

21. Are data analyses clearly described?

22. Are data analyses appropriate to the purposes of the survey?

23. Did the survey provide answers to the research questions posed by the investigators?

24. Are the researchers' conclusions sound, or are alternative interpretations of findings equally plausible?

25. Does the survey report contain descriptions of deviations from plans for survey implementation and the likely consequences of such deviations?

26. Does the survey report contain an analysis of the quality of the survey?

Don't expect all (or even most) survey reports to measure up on every one of these points. The list of 26 questions defines an ideal that is rarely realized. If you find a survey that falls short on two, three, or even half a dozen of these questions, you might still find its results to be credible and useful. Think of the checklist as a guide to cautions and thoughtful evaluation, not as an inflexible list of essential criteria.

References

Babbie, E. (1973). *Survey research methods*. Belmont, CA: Wadsworth.

Berdie, D., & Anderson, J. (1974). *Questionnaire design and use*. Metuchen, NJ: Scarecrow Press.

Cronbach, L. (1971). Test validation. In R. L. Thorndike (Ed.), *Educational measurement* (2d ed.) (pp. 443–507). Washington, DC: American Council on Education.

Cronbach, L., & Meehl, P. (1955). Construct validity in psychological tests. *Psychological Bulletin, 52*, 281–302.

Jaeger, R. M. (1984). *Sampling in education and the social sciences*. New York: Longman, Inc.

Moser, C., & Kalton, G. (1972). *Survey methods in social investigation* (2d ed.). New York: Basic Books.

Rand Corporation. (1969). *A million random digits with 100,000 normal deviates*. Glencoe, IL: Free Press.

Rossi, P. H., Wright, J. D., & Anderson, A. B. (1983). *Handbook of survey research*. New York: Academic Press.

Warwick, D., & Lininger, C. (1975). *The sample survey: Theory and practice*. New York: McGraw-Hill.

Suggestions for Further Reading

Since governments have counted people at least from Old Testament days, and the history of social surveys dates back to the late 1700s, the existence of a rich literature on survey methods should not be surprising. You can gain useful insights on effective survey research not only from books on methodology, but from reports of high-quality surveys as well. Here are some suggestions for additional reading (adapted, by permission, from Jaeger, R. M., *Sampling in Education and the Social Sciences*. New York: Longman, 1984).

Sources on Method

Two books by E. R. Babbie, *The Practice of Social Research,* and *Practicing Social Research,* both published in 1975 by Wadsworth (Belmont, CA) contain discussions of survey research in the context of other social science research methods. The comparisons Babbie makes provide illuminating contrasts between survey research and other approaches to social science inquiry.

An earlier book by E. R. Babbie, entitled *Survey Research Methods* (Belmont, CA: Wadsworth, 1973), is an elementary text that covers all phases of survey research, from initial survey planning through analysis of data and reporting of results. It is easy to read and does not presume any prior background in survey methods.

A short paperback book by A. Fink and J. Kosecoff, entitled *How to Conduct Surveys: A Step-by-Step Guide* (Beverly Hills, CA: Sage, 1985), provides a brief overview of many of the operational questions that arise when surveys are developed and conducted. Because of its brevity, this book is necessarily superficial (sometimes at the cost of accuracy), but it is easy to read and will at least inform a novice of the range of issues that survey researchers must address.

Two other texts on survey research methods, *The Sample Survey: Theory and Practice,* by D. P. Warwick and C. A. Lininger (New York: McGraw-Hill, 1975) and *Survey Methods in Social Investigation* by C. A. Moser and G. Kalton, 2d ed. (New York: Basic Books, 1972), also cover all phases of survey research. Each is more complete than Babbie's introductory book but requires that the reader be somewhat more sophisticated about research methodology. Moser and Kalton use examples from Great Britain, and many of their terms and writing constructions reflect British language customs, but the richness of detail and breadth of coverage in their book more than compensate for the inconvenience of occasionally novel language.

The *Handbook of Survey Research* (New York: Academic Press, 1983), edited by P. H. Rossi, J. D. Wright, and A. B. Anderson, addresses a very wide range of theoretical and practical issues associated with survey research. Its content ranges from a review of the history and likely future of sample surveys, to theoretical chapters on such topics as sampling and measurement, to very practical chapters on questionnaire construction and item writing, data collection, and mail surveys, to technically demanding chapters on state-of-the-art procedures for analysis of data collected in surveys and statistical procedures that can be used to compensate for missing survey data. Each chapter in the *Handbook* ends with an extensive (usually pre-1981) bibliography on the literature of its topic. The practical chapters in this book can be read with understanding by survey research novices, but those that are more theoretical will be accessible only to persons with extensive knowledge of mathematics and statistics.

The mechanics of questionnaire design, with an emphasis on mail surveys, is well presented in D. Berdie and J. Anderson's *Questionnaire Design and Use* (Metuchen, NJ: Scarecrow Press, 1974). They offer practical hints on increasing the clarity of questionnaires, building respondents' interest, and designing effective letters to introduce a survey.

Years of research on the psychology of interviewing are reflected in the somewhat dated, but still relevant, book by R. L. Kahn and C. F. Cannell entitled *The Dynamics of Interviewing* (New York: Wiley, 1957). The book offers practical guidance on various interviewing techniques and methods, with careful consideration of situational variables, all solidly based on empirical research.

Two books that focus on methods of analyzing survey data are *Elementary Survey Analysis* by J. A. Davis (Englewood Cliffs, NJ: Prentice-Hall, 1971) and *Survey and Opinion Research: Procedures for Processing and Analysis* by J. A. Sondquist and W. C. Dunkelberg (Englewood Cliffs, NJ: Prentice-Hall, 1977). Davis's book is short and, as the title suggests, introductory. In contrast, the Sondquist and Dunkelberg book is more complete and more demanding of the reader. Another more challenging book that provides substantial information on the analysis of data collected in surveys is *An Introduction to Survey Research and Data Analysis* by H. F. Weisberg and B. D. Bowen (San Francisco: W. H. Freeman, 1977).

Reports on Important Educational and Social Surveys

One of the most effective ways to learn about a research method is to study the results of exemplary practice. In the last 15 years, a number of impressive nationwide surveys have been conducted to examine various social institutions and the nature and status of our educational system. Although they are not without fault, these surveys illustrate the application of sound research practice, often on a massive scale. The reports of many of the surveys described below are available in federal government document repositories at college and university libraries throughout the United States.

Equality of Education in the United States. This survey was conducted in 1965–1966 as a result of the Civil Rights Act of 1964. That Act directed the Secretary of Health, Education, and Welfare to report to the Congress, no later than July 4, 1966, on the status of racial isolation in the public schools of the

United States. The survey was directed very broadly at the issue of school segregation and included an attempt to investigate the effects of segregation on the standardized test performance and attitudes of students enrolled in the early elementary grades through the last year of high school. A massive mail survey resulted in data collected from school superintendents, school principals, teachers, and students in every state. Nearly half a million students were surveyed and tested in the study.

One of the objectives of the survey was to provide separate estimates of the degree of school segregation for urban and rural populations in various geographic regions of the nation. In addition, the quality of schooling and the effects of schooling were to be compared for members of various racial groups.

These objectives dictated a complex sampling design that would yield estimates of many different parameters for a number of subpopulations. The design used was two-stage sampling, with counties and metropolitan areas as sampling units in the first stage. Secondary schools were sampled within selected counties and metropolitan areas at the second stage of sampling. All elementary schools that sent a sizable percentage of their students to selected secondary schools were then added to the sample. In all, data were collected from 1170 schools, of which 349 were in metropolitan areas and 821 were rural. Both counties and schools were stratified, so as to ensure a large minority representation in the sample.

The "Coleman Survey," as the study has come to be known, has been criticized for a variety of reasons, including a response rate of 67 to 70 percent. Nonetheless, it is one of the landmark surveys of education in the United States and warrants careful review by any serious student of survey methods. The results of the survey are contained in a large report entitled *Equality of Educational Opportunity* by J. S. Coleman, E. O. Campbell, C. J. Hobson, J. McPartland, A. M. Mood, D. Weinfield, and R. L. York. It is available from the U.S. Government Printing Office, Washington, DC, and can also be obtained from the ERIC Document Reproduction Service under number ED012 275.

National Assessment. The purpose of this continuing survey is to assess changes over time in the educational achievement of four age groups throughout the United States and to produce comparative statistics on these changes for four geographic regions (northeast, southeast, central, and west), two racial groups (white and black), and seven categories of size and type of community, ranging from "main section of a big city" to "extreme rural."

Achievement test exercises in 10 subject areas have been administered for over a decade now to children and young adults, both in and out of schools, in four age groups: 9-year-olds, 13-year-olds, 17-year-olds, and young adults (ages 26–35).

The National Assessment of Educational Progress (NAEP) is so designed that no examinee is required to answer every test question or to complete every exercise. This use of multiple test booklets, coupled with a design for sampling examinees, is known as "multiple matrix sampling."

The design for sampling NAEP examinees in schools includes three stages of sampling. At the first stage, counties or groups of contiguous counties are sampled. At the second stage, both public and nonpublic schools are sampled within selected first-stage sampling units (counties or groups of counties). Finally, at the third stage of sampling, random samples of pupils are selected within each sampled school and pupils are randomly assigned to one of the test booklets. The design for sampling 17-year-olds and young adults who are not in school is equally complex.

The results of National Assessment are reported periodically in newspapers and news magazines. These reports contain statements on the percent of examinees of a particular age group who could successfully perform specific test exercises. In addition, the comparative performances of examinees in various ethnic, geographic, and demographic categories; e.g., white 9-year-olds in large cities vs. white 9-year olds in rural areas, are reported.

You can secure additional information on this study from a report entitled *National Assessment of Educational Progress, General Information Yearbook*, Report No. 03/04-GIY, Washington, DC: National Center for Educational Statistics, U.S. Office of Education, 1974. Summaries of results are contained in various documents published by the Education Commission of the States in Denver, Colorado, including *Three National Assessments of Reading: Changes in Performance, 1979-80* (Report No. 11-R-01), April 1981, and *Mathematical Technical Report: Summary Volume*, 1980. An extensive listing of documents concerning National Assessment (through 1983) can be found in *Selected Publications from the National Assessment of Educational Progress*, a pamphlet that is available from NAEP, Box 2923, Princeton, NJ 08541.

The Gallup Poll. The Gallup organization conducts a large number of surveys for a wide variety of purposes. One such survey provides data for a monthly report on social, political, and economic issues, based on opinions expressed by members of the adult population of the United States living in private households. This survey has been conducted regularly since 1935.

The Gallup Poll is an interview survey. The respondents are selected by using a multistage sampling design in which the nation is divided into geographic regions and categories of community size. Census Bureau data are used to create these strata. A random sample of 320 locations is selected from the geographic and size-of-community strata, so as to ensure balanced coverage of the entire nation. Interviewers in each location are given maps with a randomly selected starting point, and detailed instructions on sampling of respondents from households in their assigned area. The selection procedure is designed to yield a representative sample of the adult (18 years old and older) population living in private households in the United States.

You can find more information on this survey in *The Gallup Report*, a monthly periodical published by the Gallup Poll in Princeton, New Jersey.

Another private polling organization that conducts many surveys of the general population is the Harris Poll. The *Sourcebook of Harris National Surveys* by E. Martin, D. McDuffee, and S. Pressler, published in 1981 by the Institute for Research in Social Science, University of North Carolina at Chapel Hill, contains information on these surveys.

Consumer Surveys. The Survey Research Center, which is part of the Institute for Social Research at the University of Michigan, is one of the leading centers of survey research in the nation. Among the Center's projects is a periodic survey of households in the United States, conducted since 1946, to obtain data on finance-related issues. Members of households are interviewed to obtain information on their attitudes toward personal finance, the economy, and market conditions or prices.

A sample of dwelling units that is representative of the entire nation is selected through a four-stage design. Dwellings are selected from 74 areas in 37 states and the District of Columbia. The United States is first divided into four large geographic regions (northeast, north-central, south, and west). Next, counties and large metropolitan areas are assigned to one of 74 categories (strata) that are balanced on total population. Then these primary categories are divided and subdivided into successively smaller sampling units containing city blocks or clusters of addresses. At the fourth stage of sampling, five to ten small segments are selected from each third-stage sampling unit. Each segment contains four housing units, from which one adult respondent is randomly selected to be interviewed. About 1500 interviews are conducted for each survey.

Additional information on these surveys can be found in *Surveys of Consumers: Contributions to Behavioral Economics,* edited by R. T. Curtin and published in 1969 by the Institute for Social Research at the University of Michigan in Ann Arbor.

The National Longitudinal Study of the High School Class of 1972. A report on this massive survey, written by W. B. Fetters and published by the National Center for Educational Statistics, U.S. Department of Health, Education, and Welfare in 1974, contains a description of the design and results of a longitudinal study of high school students in the United States.

The survey was designed to secure data on the flow of students through the nation's secondary schools and into postsecondary education or part-time and full-time employment. The data were intended to assist in identifying the major points at which adolescents make decisions which affect their educational and occupational choices during the 6- to 8-year period following their departure from high school (as graduates or nongraduates).

Data were collected from over 21,000 seniors in a stratified sample of 1200 high schools, as well as from counselors and principals in these schools. Students reported on their high school experiences, their attitudes and opinions about high school and careers, their plans for the future, and a variety of biographical information. A School Questionnaire, completed by principals or their designates, was used to secure data on each school's grade structure, curriculum, absence rate and dropout rate, racial-ethnic composition, age of buildings, etc. A Counselor Questionnaire was administered to two randomly selected counselors in each sampled school. It was used to secure data on counselors' experience, education, assignments, activities, methods, workloads, and resources.

The initial survey was conducted late in the 1972 school year. Only 87 percent of the initially selected schools agreed to participate, although repeated follow-up surveys resulted in a 94-percent participation rate by students.

One important feature of the survey is its longitudinal design. Students who supplied data during the 1972 survey have been resurveyed periodically, to gain information on their later educational and career choices and experiences. At present, three follow-up surveys have been completed. Various reports, available from the National Center for Education Statistics, U.S. Department of Education, Washington, DC, provide information on the results of these follow-up surveys. A parallel research study of the high school class of 1980, entitled *High School and Beyond,* has also produced a number of reports that are available from the same source.

Study Questions

1. Survey research and experimental research are different in some important ways, yet they share some common characteristics. What would you say is the most important distinction between survey research and experimental research? Can you cite at least one objective that is common to survey research and experimental research?

2. If you want to estimate the characteristics of a population precisely, is it more important that your sample consist of a large proportion of the population, or that your sample be of a particular size?

3. If you wanted to conduct a survey that would yield information on the annual operating budgets of public colleges and universities in the United States, what issues would you consider when you defined your *target population*? Would you want to include two-year community colleges? Would you want to include junior colleges? Would you want to include special-purpose institutions, such as medical and dental schools? Do you think that these issues would affect your results substantially?

4. Suppose you wanted to investigate the attitudes of the general public on the use of domestic animals (such as dogs and cats) in medical research. You might choose to conduct a mail survey, a telephone interview survey, or a face-to-face interview survey. Name at least one advantage and one disadvantage of each of these survey methods, considering your survey objective.

5. If you wanted to estimate the average arithmetic achievement of elementary school pupils in a large school system, do you think stratified random sampling would be better than simple random sampling? In what ways might stratified random sampling be better? What characteristics of the population could you use for stratifying the pupils?

6. Why is it usually necessary to "code" survey data that are collected through interviews? What is meant by "coding?" Suppose that in a household interview survey, the interviewers asked "What is the occupation of the person in this family who earns the largest amount of money?" Do you think it would be necessary to code responses to this question? How might responses to this question be coded?

7. Virtually all textbooks on survey research make a strong case for doing pilot surveys. What are some important questions that can be answered by conducting a pilot survey? In what ways do well-designed and well-conducted pilot surveys reduce the likelihood that a subsequent main survey will avoid major problems?

8. It has been said that statistical generalization of survey results is threatened

by bias error and random error. What is the major difference between these two kinds of error? Describe a survey situation that could result in substantial bias error. Describe a survey situation that could result in substantial random error.

9. What is the essential distinction between substantive generalization and statistical generalization in the interpretation of survey results? Can you think of any survey situations in which either type of generalization would be unnecessary?

10. Suppose you conducted a face-to-face interview survey for the purpose of determining the average household expenditure for food during a given week. What would be the likely impact on the validity of your conclusions if you failed to obtain data from 40 percent of the households you sampled? What type of error would likely result? What type of generalization would be threatened?

Reading

Introduction
A Report of a Survey Research Project in Education

Richard M. Jaeger

This section contains the full text of a report entitled *Use of the Georgia Eighth Grade Criterion-Referenced Test: Reports by Ninth Grade Teachers*, by Helen Suarez DeCasper, dated June 1985. Dr. DeCasper prepared the report at the request of the Georgia Department of Education. It contains the results of her survey of a representative sample of ninth-grade teachers in Georgia's public schools, in which she sought information on the teachers' use of, and opinions about, test results provided by the state department of education.

In many ways, this report exemplifies a large category of surveys concerned with educational issues. Although it examines some research questions that might be classified as "fundamental," the survey would be considered what Cronbach and Suppes (1969) termed "decision-oriented," rather than "conclusion-oriented," research. The information it sought was intended to be put to immediate use by a public agency in evaluating the effectiveness of certain educational policies. To the extent deemed necessary, that agency intended to use the survey's results as a guide to modifying those educational policies.

Surveys concerned with educational issues are very often conducted for the purpose of informing specific policy decisions. Because their results are intentionally limited in generalizability, the reports of such surveys rarely appear in professional educational research journals. More often, the reports are sent only to the agencies that commissioned the surveys, or can be found only in document repositories that are accessible through computerized access services such as ERIC or DIALOG.

Although some of most noteworthy surveys on education (including those listed in the final section of the preceding paper) have spawned numerous papers in professional journals, such papers rarely provide details of the methodology used to conduct the surveys or of the quality of survey results. To critically analyze surveys such as the National Assessment of Educational Progress, you will have to obtain the sometimes massive reports published by the sponsoring agencies, in addition to journal articles that report on specific analyses of survey results.

In evaluating the report that follows, it is suggested that you consider the 26 questions that were listed in the *Short Checklist for Survey Evaluation* provided in the preceding paper. You will find that Dr. DeCasper's report withstands rigorous scrutiny quite well. As is true of most survey research reports, you will not find all of the information that the 26 questions in the *Checklist* demand. But if you look carefully at the main body of the report in addition to the four appendices, you will find most of the answers you seek. For example, the research questions to be addressed by the survey are clearly enumerated, and form the principal structure of the results section of the report. The target population of the survey is well defined, as are the differences between this target population and the operational population provided by available sampling frames.

This beginning list is intended to get you started on a critical reading of the report. Try to determine which of the 26 questions in the *Checklist* can be answered confidently, which can be answered only in part, and which cannot be answered at all. When you finish this task, ask yourself the important questions: Does this report provide the information desired by the researcher and her client? Should I believe the researcher's conclusions? Was the survey successful? What, if anything, could have been done to improve it? Dr. DeCasper's report is unusually clear and complete. You should have little difficulty evaluating the quality of her survey.

Reference

Cronbach, L. J., & Suppes, P. (1969). *Research for tomorrow's schools*. New York: Macmillan.

Use of the Georgia Eighth Grade Criterion-Referenced Test: Reports by Ninth Grade Teachers

Helen Suarez DeCasper

Executive Summary

- Evidence of the usefulness of the Eighth Grade Criterion-Referenced Test reports was obtained from 572 ninth-grade teachers in Georgia public schools. Two-hundred and ninety were language arts or reading teachers, 282 were teachers of mathematics or remedial mathematics.
- These teachers were also asked to comment on the availability of the test report forms.
- The same Georgia educators also provided ratings of two alternative test report forms developed by the investigator.
- The teachers expressed strong support for the report forms.
- From 70 to 80 percent of the teachers responded that the information presented on the Student Report Form and the Student Label was useful to them.
- Teachers rated all of the report forms as 'important' in assisting them in making certain instructional decisions.
- Eighty-four percent of the teachers rated the Alternative Student Report Form as most useful when compared with two of the present forms.
- Ninety-three percent of the teachers rated the Alternative Summary of Student Report Form as useful to crucial to them if prepared for each of their ninth-grade classes at the beginning of the school year.
- Teachers report the CRT scale scores as used with other sources of information for assigning students to classes.
- Teachers rated CRT scores as important when making instructional decisions such as planning instruction, grouping students in class, and remediating or accelerating students.
- Over half of the teachers indicate that they would like assistance in using test results. Language arts teachers expressed the strongest need for such assistance.
- Seventy-three percent of teachers report receiving zero to three hours of instruction in using test results in the last two years.

- Less than 20 percent of the teachers reported that the CRT report forms are *sent* to them.
- From 55 to 70 percent of the teachers reported that the CRT forms are *available* for their use, depending on the form.
- Teachers in schools with no eighth grade find the CRT forms are less accessible to them than teachers in schools with eighth grades.

Introduction

The Georgia Department of Education administers the Student Assessment Program as established by Georgia Board of Education Policy II. Policy II was adopted to implement state legislation passed in 1974 directing the Board to assess the effectiveness of state education programs. In response to this the Criterion-Referenced Tests (CRT) in reading, mathematics and career development were constructed. These tests are designed to measure a core group of basic skills that were identified by Georgia educators as essential to academic progress. Testing of pupils in grades four and eight was begun in Spring, 1976; tests for the first grade were first administered in the 1983–84 school year; and in school year 1982–83 the High School Basic Skills Tests were first administered to tenth graders. The Basic Skills tests measure student competencies in reading, mathematics and problem solving and are among requirements for graduation from Georgia public high schools.

Among the priorities set by Georgia Board of Education in implementing Policy II was the following concerning the reporting of the results of tests to teachers and administrators:

> The program should provide the teachers and administrators in every school basic information for assessing the effectiveness of the principal phases of instruction, both for individual students and for groups of students (Georgia Department of Education, 1983).

In response to this the Department of Education has developed a series of test reports for pupils, parents, teachers, administrators and the public, designed to disseminate individual student, school-wide, system-wide and state-wide results of tests. The test report forms for grades one, four and eight are similar in design, while the Basic Skills Tests reports are of a different format. The test report forms have been designed to provide useful test result information to the particular audiences to which they were aimed.

This is a report of a study which examined how one of those audiences, ninth-grade teachers, uses the test report forms developed for them by the Georgia Department of Education. The report forms selected for study are those based on the results of the eighth grade testing program. This particular level was selected for several reasons. First, since the report forms for eighth grade are similar to those used for the first and fourth grade tests, the results may be generalizable to them. Second, the majority of eighth grade students in Georgia go to a different school in the ninth grade. This may create problems in transmitting the test results from one setting to another. Third, the eighth grade test was revised in 1983 to facilitate the identification of students who need additional help to pass the Basic Skills Tests in the tenth grade. Thus, it is particularly important to determine how and if ninth grade teachers use the information provided on the test reports.

Test Reports Provided for the Eighth-Grade CRT

The test reports and supporting materials are:
1. For individual students:
   • The Individual Student Report
   • The Student Label
2. School-wide reports:
   • Student Achievement Roster
   • Summary of Student Reports
   • Item Analysis Forms
3. Support materials:
   • Teacher's Interpretive Guide
   • Objectives and Assessment Characteristics

Overview of the Study

The study used a survey instrument to address the following research questions:

1. Which of the test report forms are perceived as most useful by ninth grade teachers of language arts, reading, mathematics and remedial mathematics?

2. How useful is the information contained in the two report forms designed specifically for teacher use, the Individual Student Report Form, and the Student Label?

3. Which report forms are sent to teachers, are available for teacher use, or would be helpful to teachers?

4. What are teachers' opinions of the assistance they need or of the assistance that is provided to them in using test results?

5. How useful is the information in the Alternative Individual Student Report Forms A, B, and C for the various instructional decisions teachers make?

6. How do teachers rate the Alternative Summary of Student Report Form?

Method

The Sample

The sample consisted of ninth grade teachers of reading, language arts, remedial mathematics, and mathematics. Ninth grade teachers were selected for the study because the eighth grade CRT is administered in March, and the results and the report forms returned to the schools in May. Eighth grade teachers could use the test results for assessing instruction and curriculum during the past year, and for preparing instructional revisions for the following eighth grade class. However, they would not have enough time to use test information to help individual students.

Ninth grade teachers would be more likely to use the eighth grade CRT results to assess the abilities of these students, and to provide instruction relevant to their needs. They could also use the eighth grade results to help those students who may need additional instruction to prepare them for success on the Basic Skills Tests that will be administered in the tenth grade.

Since test use would most likely differ more between schools than within individual schools, small numbers of teachers were selected from a large percentage of schools with ninth grades throughout the school districts of the state. In order to have teacher representation equivalent to teacher distribution throughout the state, two-stage cluster sampling with the initial stage using sampling with probabilities proportional to size (PPS) was selected. A description of the selection of the sampling frame is located in Appendix D.

The final sampling frame consisted of 800 ninth grade teachers of language arts/reading and mathematics selected from 141 schools in 90 school districts. Eighty-one of the ninety school districts contacted participated in the final survey.

Response Rate: Total Sample

Surveys were sent to 800 teachers, 592 or 74 percent were returned. Twenty of those returned were blank, either because the teacher was no longer at the school or the teacher did not wish to respond.

• The final sample was 572 teachers or 72 percent of those contacted.

Response Rate: Content Areas

Surveys were sent to 400 ninth grade language arts and/or reading teachers and to 400 ninth grade mathematics and/or remedial mathematics teachers. Responses were received from 290 or 73 percent of the language arts/reading teachers and from 282 or 71 percent of the mathematics/remedial mathematics teachers.

The Survey Instrument

Data for this study were collected by a survey questionnaire (see Figure A-1, Appendix A for the survey instrument). The survey was developed by first determining the research questions to be addressed by the study. Second, surveys developed by Goslin and his colleagues (1967) and by the Center for the Study of Evaluation's Test Use Project (Burry, 1981) were studied for ideas about content and format. Third, items were written, shared with colleagues, revised, and shared again. Examples of the survey were sent to Dr. Stan Bernknopf, Coordinator of Student Assessment, Georgia Department of Education for his and his staff's comments and suggestions. A pilot study was conducted when the survey neared its final form.

The Pilot Study

The pilot study was conducted in late August, 1984 with 13 ninth grade teachers of reading/language arts, and 10 teachers of remedial mathematics/ mathematics in two Atlanta, Georgia schools. These were schools that had not been selected for the main study. The teachers were sent an explanatory letter, a survey, and examples of the test report forms. They were asked to complete the survey and to comment about any areas of the survey and accompanying materials that needed clarification or improvement. Their suggestions were incorporated in the final revision of the survey instrument.

Results

Demographic Variables

The sample response rate of 572 is 72 percent of the 800 teachers sampled. One hundred and fifty-five (155) or 27 percent of the sample were males, and 412 or 73 percent were females. Five teachers did not report their sex. The ages of the teachers ranged from 21 years to 64 years, with the mean of 37.7, standard deviation of 9.01 and median of 37.0. Twenty-four teachers did not report their ages.

There were 400 language arts and/or reading teachers and 400 mathematics and/or remedial mathematics teachers contacted. In the final sample, 290 of the teachers teach language arts and/or reading, and 282 teach mathematics and/or remedial mathematics. Over 460 teachers (81%) have either bachelor's or master's degrees as the highest degree (see Table 1).

The degrees were earned in the years 1944 to 1984, with the median year being 1975. The number of years of teaching experience ranged from 1 to 37 with the median number of years of teaching experience at eleven years.

One hundred thirty teachers (24%) reported no course work in statistics, educational research, or measurement in their college programs. The median number of hours in these subjects is 10.00 for all teachers reporting. Over 36 percent of the teachers (207) report that they have received no hours of instruction or assistance in using test results during the last two years (see Table 2).

About one-half of the teachers teach in schools they classify as rural, with one-fourth of the teachers classifying their schools as being urban or suburban areas. About two-thirds of the teachers report that they work in schools with grades nine to twelve with about one-third of the teachers working in schools with both eighth and ninth grades in the same building (see Table 3).

Teachers' Views of Use of Test Reports for Instructional Decisions

One series of questions sought teachers' views of the sources of information used to assign students to classes. Table 4 reports the frequencies and percentages of their responses.

Table 4 indicates that previous grades (88.3%) and teachers' recommendations (87.4%) are most often used as information sources for deciding about assigning students to classes. In addition, 53.1 percent of the teachers use the scale scores of 191 on the reading portion and of 190 on the mathematics portion of the Eighth Grade CRT to make these decisions.

Teachers using the score of 191/Reading and 190/Mathematics were examined with other teacher variables using the chi-square procedure. When exam-

TABLE 1 *Highest degree or certificate earned*

Degree or Certificate	n	%
Bachelor's	243	42.5
Master's	220	38.5
Sixth-year	97	17.0
Doctoral	11	1.9
Missing	1	.2
Total	572	100.0

TABLE 2 *Number of hours receiving instruction in test use in the last two years*

Number of hours	n	%
0 hours	207	36.3
1–3 hours	208	36.4
4–6 hours	84	14.7
7–10 hours	40	7.0
Over 10 hours	32	5.6
Missing	1	.2
Total	572	100.0

TABLE 3 *Number and percentage of teachers in schools organized by grade levels*

Grades	n	%
8–12	133	23.3
9–12	354	62.0
8–9	41	7.2
7–9	29	5.1
Other (7–12)	14	2.4
Missing	1	0.0
Total	572	100.0

TABLE 4 *Sources of information for assigning students to classes*

Source of Information	n	%
Previous Grades	505	88.3
Teachers' Recommendations	500	87.4
Counselors' Recommendations	375	65.6
Score of 191/Reading or 190/Mathematics on 8th grade CRT	304	53.1
Scores on other CRT	66	11.6
Scores on other tests	167	29.2

Note. n for percentages is 572, total number of survey respondents.

ined with setting of school (rural, suburban, urban) the results were significant (see Table C-1, Appendix C).

- Teachers in rural settings are less likely to use the scale scores in assigning students to classes.

When the scale scores are examined with the variable, "are eighth and ninth grades in the same school building?", the results were significant (see Table C-2, Appendix C).

- Schools with no eighth grade are *less* likely to use the scale scores than schools with eighth and ninth grades in the same building.

When the use of the scale score was examined with the number of hours of instruction the teachers had received in using tests and test results, significant results were found (see Table C-3, Appendix C).

- Teachers receiving four or more hours of instruction in test use were more likely to indicate that the scale score was used (65%) than were teachers with less than four hours of instruction (35%).

Teachers were then asked to rate how important they found these sources of information for making three instructional decisions. The following rating scale was used: Not Important (1) to Crucial (5) and Do not Group (remediate or accelerate) (6). The three instructional decisions were, planning instruction at the beginning of the school year, grouping students within the class, and making decisions to provide remediation and acceleration of students. Frequencies for these variables are in Tables C-4 to C-6 in Appendix C. Table 5 reports the means and standard deviations of the judgments teachers made about the importance of each of the sources of information for making the three instructional decisions excluding category 6.

Table 5 indicates that when:

TABLE 5 *Means and standard deviations of importance of particular sources of information for making instructional decisions*

| | Instructional Decisions | | | | | |
| | Planning Instruction | | Grouping Students Within the Class | | Remediate/ Accelerate | |
Sources of Information	Mean	SD	Mean	SD	Mean	SD
Teacher reports	2.795	1.051	2.581	1.068	2.969	1.044
CRT test scores	3.034	1.061	3.055	1.051	3.356	1.040
My experience teaching	3.944	.874	—	—	—	—
Placement test results	—	—	3.067	1.129	3.000	1.115
Results of my tests	—	—	3.333	.976	3.471	.950
My observations	—	—	3.964	.833	3.988	.807

- Teachers were asked the sources of information used most often in planning instruction, teachers rated their teaching experience as the most important source of information. CRT test scores were rated as important.
- When asked about the importance of sources of information in grouping students in class, teachers reported that their own observations were most important. The results of their own tests, placement test results, and CRT test scores were also rated as important.
- When asked about the kinds of information used for making decisions about remediation or acceleration, teachers rated their observations as very important, the results of their tests and CRT test scores as important.

Need for Assistance in Using Test Reports

Teachers were asked if they needed assistance or instruction related to testing and using test results in several applications. They were also asked if such assistance was provided. The frequencies of their responses are listed in Table 6.

In all test-use areas but two—administering tests, and using test results for grouping in my class—

- Fifty to 55 percent of the teachers indicated that they would like to have assistance or instruction related to these areas.

When asked if such instruction and assistance is provided to them, about

- Fifty to 55 percent of the teachers reported that such assistance was avail-

TABLE 6 *Assistance is needed and provided in testing or using test results*

Test Use	I Would Like Assistance		Assistance is Provided	
	n	%	*n*	%
Administering Tests	184	32.2	317	55.4
Analyzing Test Results	315	55.4	323	56.5
Interpreting Test Results to Students	289	50.5	292	51.0
Interpreting Test Results to Parents	297	51.9	296	51.7
Using Test Results for Placement	311	54.4	313	54.7
Using Test Results for Instructional Decisions	295	51.6	255	44.6
Using Test Results for Grouping In My Class	233	40.7	228	39.9
Determining Relationship between the Test Objectives and the Curriculum Guides	313	54.7	259	45.3
Determining Relationship between the Test Objectives and the Text Book Topics	303	53.0	235	41.1

Note. Percentages are based on 572 respondents per question.

able in administering tests, analyzing test results, interpreting test results to students and parents, and using test results for placement.
- Less than half, 40 to 45 percent, of the teachers reported that assistance or instruction is provided for the purpose of using test results for making instructional decisions, using test results for grouping in class, for determining the relationship between the test and the curriculum guide, or for determining the relationship between the test objectives and the textbook topics.

An analysis was performed to determine whether there was a difference in teachers' need for assistance in using test results and the subject taught or whether the eighth grade was in the school (see Tables C-7 to C-11, Appendix C for significant chi-squares).

Significant relationships were found only when the subject taught was language arts and/or reading.

- Language arts teachers indicated the need for assistance with analyzing test results.
- About 60 percent of teachers of language arts indicate they need assistance in interpreting test results to students.
- Sixty-four percent of language arts teachers indicate that they need assistance in using test results for placement.
- Sixty-three percent of language arts teachers express a need for assistance in using tests for instruction.
- Sixty-two percent of language arts teachers, and 58 percent of teachers of both language arts and reading express no need for assistance in using test results in grouping.

Availability of Test Report Forms

The state of Georgia prepares several report forms and interpretive materials for the Eighth Grade Criterion Referenced Tests. Two forms, the Individual Student Form and the Student Achievement Labels, are designed to be used by teachers. Two interpretive manuals are also designed for teacher use, the *Teacher's Interpretive Guide* and the *Objectives and Assessment Characteristics*. The other forms, Student Achievement Roster, Summary of Student Reports, and Item Analysis Forms, are prepared for the school and are sent to the principal, and may also be available for teacher use.

Teachers were asked to answer yes or no if these forms were sent to them, available for their use, and would be useful to them. The sample page used to remind teachers of the forms is given in Figure A-2, Appendix A. Table 7 reports the results of the responses to these questions.

- Less than 20 percent of the teachers reported that the forms were sent to them.
- From 55 to about 70 percent of the teachers reported that all of the forms and interpretive materials were available for their use.

• Between 76 and 85 percent of the teachers reported that the forms and interpretive materials would be helpful to them.

An Examination of Whether Test Reports are Sent to Teachers

A cluster analysis was conducted using SPSSX Quick Cluster procedure to determine whether the groups of teachers responding that the forms were sent to them, or were available to them, or would be helpful to them, were unique in some respect (SPSSX, 1983). The initial cluster analysis for those teachers responding that the forms were sent to them resulted in two clusters.

These two clusters were used in chi-square analyses with several descriptive variables. These demographic variables include: whether eighth and ninth grades are in the same school; the subject taught—reading, language arts, mathematics or remedial mathematics; setting of school—rural, suburban, or urban; the highest degree received and the number of course hours in statistics or measurement earned. Chi squares of both clusters were significant only with the variable that the eighth and ninth grades are in the same school (see Table C-12 and C-13, Appendix C).

• Thus, 65 percent of the teachers, those in schools without eighth grades, responded that they were not sent the Individual Student Form, the Student Achievement Roster, or the Summary of Student Reports.
• 65 percent of teachers in schools with no eighth grade reported that they were not sent the Student Labels, the *Teacher's Interpretive Guide* or the *Objectives and Assessment Characteristics Manual.*

The test report materials in Cluster 2 also showed a significant relationship with teachers of remedial mathematics (see Table C-14, Appendix C).

• Teachers of remedial mathematics reported that they were more likely to be sent the materials in Cluster 3 than were other teachers in the study.

TABLE 7 *Availability of eighth grade CRT report forms and interpretive materials to grade nine teachers*

Name of Form	Availability of Forms					
	Sent To Me		Available For My Use		Would be Helpful to Me	
	n	%	n	%	n	%
Ind. Student Form	103	18.0	446	78.0	463	78.0
Student Ach. Roster	67	11.7	390	68.2	459	80.2
Summary Student Reports	73	12.8	405	70.8	458	80.1
Student Labels	52	9.1	389	68.0	436	76.2
Item Analysis Forms	54	11.2	369	64.5	457	84.9
Teacher Interpret. Guide	44	7.7	336	58.7	475	83.0
Obj/Assess Char.	46	8.0	312	54.5	453	79.2

An Examination of Whether Test Reports are Available to Teachers

Another cluster analysis was conducted for those teachers responding that the forms were available for their use. This procedure resulted in two clusters. The first cluster contained teachers responding that the Individual Student Form, the Student Achievement Roster, the Summary of Student Reports and the Student Labels were available for their use. The second cluster formed contained those teachers responding that the Item Analysis Forms, *Teacher's Interpretive Guide* and the *Objectives and Assessment Characteristics Manual* were available for their use.

These two clusters were used in chi-square analyses with the same descriptive variables used in the previous analysis. Significant relationships were found only between the availability of the forms in Cluster 2: the Item Analysis Form, *Teachers' Interpretive Guide,* and the *Objectives and Assessment Characteristics Manual,* with the variable eighth and ninth grades are in the same school (see Table C-15, Appendix C).

- Teachers in schools with no eighth grades reported (68%) that they did not have the forms available, whereas about 32 percent of teachers in schools with eighth grades reported the forms were not available.

The cluster analyses indicated that there may be significant differences between teachers on the questions of whether a form is sent or available based on the organization of the school, i.e., whether the eighth and ninth grades were in the same administrative unit. To examine this finding in more detail, individual chi-square procedures were performed to examine the relationship between whether a test report form was sent or available to teachers with the variable of whether eighth and ninth grades are in the same administrative unit (see Table C-16 to Table C-22, Appendix C). Table 8 shows the number and percentages of teachers indicating "No," the forms were not sent, in relation to whether the eighth and ninth grades are in the same building.

The results of the individual chi-squares indicate that there was a significant difference between the accessibility of report forms and whether the eighth and ninth grades are in the same building.

- A greater proportion of teachers respond that the Individual Student Form, the Student Label, the Item Analysis Form and the Summary of Student Forms, were not sent to them if they are in schools without eighth grades.
- Similarly, a greater proportion of teachers report that the Item Analysis Form, the Teachers' Interpretive Guide and the *Objectives and Assessment Manual* are not available to them if they are in schools without eighth grades.

Usefulness of Individual Student Test Report Forms

Two of the Georgia CRT report forms are designed specifically to be used by techers in planning instruction, the Individual Student Report Form and the

Individual Student Label. These two forms report a variety of information about a student's results on the mathematics, reading and career development criterion-referenced tests. In order to determine the usefulness of each aspect of these two forms, teachers were asked to respond yes or no to the question, Does the State report the Criterion-Referenced Test scores in a way that facilitates your use of the information? The teachers' "Yes" responses to each aspect of the Individual Student Report Form are reported in Table 9.

Table 9 illustrates that

• Teachers were strong in their support of the information reported in the Individual Student Report Form. Over 60 percent of teachers found every aspect of the form useful.

TABLE 8 *Number and percentage of teachers responding "no", forms not sent or available, by whether grade eight is in the school*

| | School Organization | | | |
| | Grades 8–9 In Same Building | | Grades 8–9 Different Building | |
Form	n	%	n	%
Ind. Stu. Form Sent*	164	28.9	302	53.2
Ind. Stu. Form Avail.	38	6.8	79	14.1
Stud. Ach. Roster Sent	184	32.5	317	55.9
Stud. Ach. Roster Avail.	58	10.3	113	20.1
Summ. St. Report Sent*	178	31.4	317	55.9
Summ. St. Reports Avail.	51	9.1	106	18.9
St. Label Sent*	187	33.2	325	57.7
St. Label Avail.	65	11.6	105	18.8
Item Analysis Sent*	181	32.2	318	56.6
Item Analysis Avail.*	59	10.6	129	23.2
Interpret. Guide Sent	190	33.9	326	58.2
Interpret. Guide Avail.*	70	12.7	148	26.8
Obj/Assmt. Manual Sent	189	33.8	325	58.1
Obj/Assmt. Manual Avail.*	77	13.9	165	29.8

Note. * indicates significant chi-squares.

TABLE 9 *Number and percent of "yes" responses to the usefulness of information of the individual student report form*

| | Usefulness | |
Information	n	%
Scale Score	390	68.2
Cut-Off Score	394	68.9
Listing of Each Objective	450	78.7
No. items answered correctly	427	74.7
No. items needed to pass	436	76.2
Whether student achieved the objective	463	80.9
Listing of areas for additional instruction	441	77.1

Eleven percent of the teachers reported that they could not judge the forms since they did not have them available for use.

Table 10 reports "Yes" responses to the question, Does the State report the Criterion-Referenced Test scores in a way that facilitates your use of the information? The test report form in question here is the Individual Student Label.

- Teachers showed strong support for each component of the Individual Student Label. From 70 to 80 percent of the teachers found the information reported usefully.

Twelve percent of the teachers said they could not make judgments because they had not seen or used the form.

Usefulness of Forms for Instructional Decisions

Teachers were asked to rate how important they found each of the test report forms and materials for the instructional decision situation of planning instruction, grouping, or placement of students in remediation or acceleration. Teachers were asked to rate the forms for each instructional application from Not important (1) to Crucial (5). The instructions for the questions indicated that items should be left blank if a particular form was not available to the teacher. The items left blank were coded Not available (6). See Tables C-23 to C-29, Appendix C for the tables of frequencies of responses for these items. Teachers assigned somewhat similar ratings to each of the forms for the three instructional situations. Examination of the frequencies reflects the similarity of the grouping of responses around the rating 3, with few responses made in the 1 and 5 choices. Table 11 reports the means and standard deviations of the ratings of these items.

The data in Table 11 show that

- The means of the teachers' responses to the importance of various report forms for the three instructional decisions clustered around the rating Important (3).

Teachers' Evaluation of Alternate Individual Student Report Forms

Teachers were asked to consider three report forms, two of which were exactly like report forms used by Georgia, and one of which included additional

TABLE 10 *Usefulness of information on the individual student label*

Information	Usefulness	
	n	%
Skill area into which objectives are grouped	441	77.1
Indicating objective was achieved (*)	456	79.7
Indicating objective was not achieved (−)	445	77.9
Indicating objective was not attempted (N)	414	72.4

information. Report A reported the number of items needed to achieve the objective, the number answered correctly, and whether the objective was achieved or not. Report B reported all of the information of Report A, plus suggestions of areas of additional study. Report C reported all of the information of Report B, plus a reference to teachers of where to look in the *Objectives and Assessment Characteristics* manual for examples of the objective.

Teachers were asked to rank the three reports according to the following scale: Most Useful (1), Next Most Useful (2), Least Useful (3). Table 12 reports the frequencies and percentages of responses.

Table 12 reports that:

• Ninety-three of the teachers found Report A to be the least useful of the test reports.

TABLE 11 *Means and standard deviations of the rating of the importance of each report form for three instructional decisions*

Report Form	Mean	SD
Individual Student Report		
Planning	2.952	1.075
Grouping	3.163	1.047
Remediation/Acceleration	3.365	1.031
Student Achievement Roster		
Planning	3.002	1.101
Grouping	3.090	1.079
Remediation/Acceleration	3.199	1.061
Summary of Student Reports		
Planning	2.895	1.088
Grouping	2.986	1.096
Remediation/Acceleration	3.037	1.087
Student Achievement Labels		
Planning	2.730	1.102
Grouping	2.871	1.096
Remediation/Acceleration	3.037	1.087
Teacher's Interpretive Guide		
Planning	2.864	1.102
Grouping	2.766	1.177
Remediation/Acceleration	2.841	1.186
Objectives and Assessment Characteristics		
Planning	3.005	1.136
Grouping	2.879	1.131
Remediation/Acceleration	3.000	1.146
Item Analysis Form		
Planning	2.826	1.121
Grouping	2.692	1.142
Remediation/Acceleration	2.794	1.150

TABLE 12 *Rankings of the alternative individual student report forms*

	Usefulness					
	Most Useful		Next Most Useful		Least Useful	
Report Form	n	%	n	%	n	%
Report A	15	2.6	13	2.3	529	92.5
Report B	62	11.0	488	85.3	6	1.0
Report C	480	84.1	54	9.8	21	3.9
Missing Cases	15	2.6	15	2.6	15	2.6
TOTAL	572	100.0	572	100.0	572	100.0

- Report B was found to be next most useful by over 85 percent of the teachers.
- Report C was judged to be the most useful by 84 percent of the teachers.

Teachers were then asked to rate the same three reports for their usefulness in seven instructional situations: analyzing test results, interpreting test results to students, interpreting test results to parents, grouping students in class, decisions about remediation, decisions about acceleration, planning instruction, and the overall usefulness of the report. Teachers were asked to rate the usefulness of the reports from 1 to 5 on the following scale: Not Useful (1) to Crucial (5). Tables of frequencies and percentages for the teachers' ratings of each form are given in Tables C-30 to C-32, Appendix C. Table 13 reports the means and standard deviations of these frequencies.

Examining the means for Reports A, B, and C on each of the seven instructional applications of test reports shows a clear trend of

- Lower ratings for Report A, next highest rating for Report B, and highest ratings for Report C on all applications.

The means for all instructional situations for Report A are near to rating 2, Slightly Useful. Those for Report B, are near rating 3, Useful, and those for Report C are near rating 4, Very Useful.

In order to investigate the differences between the means of the three reports, one-way ANOVAs were performed for each instructional application across the three report variables. The SPSSX program MANOVA was used to perform the analyses. Table 14 reports the results of the *F* tests.

As Table 14 indicates, there were significant differences in the ratings teachers assigned to the instructional situations, for each of the three forms. Report A was rated the least useful, Report B, the next most useful, and Report C, most useful for every instructional situation.

This view of the teachers' strong preference for the alternative form with the reference to the *Objectives and Assessment Characteristics* manual was reflected by the teachers' responses to open-ended questions (see Appendix B for a summary of these comments). One person expressed support for Report A, four found

Reports B and C helpful, and twenty-six teachers commented about the usefulness of Report C. An example of the responses teachers made is the following:

> Report C makes the most sense to me as a teacher. I can use the information to explain weaknesses to the student and can review problems to be sure I understand exactly what the objective is testing. Report C is the most useful.

The final question asked teachers to consider an Alternative Summary of Student Report Form. This form would provide a summary to the teacher for students in their ninth grade class on the students' performance on the eighth grade CRT. Teachers were asked to rate the usefulness of this report by selecting the response that best represented their view of the usefulness of the report. The scale used in the question is: Not Useful (1) to Crucial (5).

- Ninety-three percent of the teachers rated the form useful, very useful, or crucial, with the mean being 3.730 and the standard deviation, .784.

About seven percent of the teachers rated the form not useful, or slightly useful.

TABLE 13 *Means and standard deviations of ratings of reports A, B and C for several instructional applications*

Instructional Application	Ratings by Report					
	Report A		Report B		Report C	
	M	SD	M	SD	M	SD
Analyzing Test Results	2.366	.968	3.185	.770	3.758	.810
Interpreting Test Results to students	2.238	.977	3.295	.777	3.844	.833
Interpreting Test Results to parents	2.194	.954	3.298	.773	3.838	.818
Grouping students in class	2.246	.925	3.123	.793	3.712	.911
Decisions about remediation	2.342	.967	3.215	.754	3.801	.835
Decisions about acceleration	2.313	.989	3.134	.805	3.721	.903
Planning instruction	2.224	.959	3.225	.821	3.899	.860
Overall Rating	2.237	.881	3.233	.710	3.874	.808

TABLE 14 *Effects of responses to usefulness of reports A, B, and C, by instructional application*

Variable	F Value (2, 1,124)	Probability of Larger F
Analyzing Test Results	644.1	.000
Interp. Test Results Students	784.3	.000
Interp. Test Results Parents	874.6	.000
Grouping Students	720.8	.000
Remediation	699.3	.000
Acceleration	640.0	.000
Planning Instruction	894.8	.000
Overall Usefulness	968.3	.000

Teachers were given the opportunity to respond to an open-ended question about the usefulness of this form (see Appendix B for a summary of these comments). Seventeen teachers commented that the report form would be helpful to them. An example of such a comment is:

> Summary reports such as the one above would be very helpful. We get 9th graders from the middle school without any information. When you have 155 students it is impossible to study cumulative files before the beginning of school. With such information we could find misplaced students before they are placed in a failing situation.

Summary

Large-scale testing programs, including minimum competency testing, are mandated in over 35 states (Gorth & Perkins, 1979). Although the results of these tests are often used for summative evaluation of schools, school systems, and state departments of education, many educators believe that the results can be used to inform teachers in order to individualize and improve instruction (Rudman et al., 1980). Test publishers have attempted to make test results more useful to teachers by producing narrative test reports to supplement or replace traditional numeric or graphic presentations of results.

The test use literature underscored the need for a study to determine whether high school teachers find the test reports important and useful when making instructional decisions. Most test-use studies have examined elementary teachers' use of test reports, since for many years achievement and criterion-referenced testing was conducted in the elementary grades. With the rise of the minimum competency testing movement, secondary teachers are now finding themselves responsible for preparing students for achievement tests, and are a new audience for the report forms prepared for use with these tests.

This study was conducted to examine how high school teachers use the test report forms and other instructional materials prepared for one such state-mandated testing program, the Georgia State Criterion Referenced Tests.

Major Findings

Teacher Use of Test Reports

Test Results and Other Information Sources

Earlier research has indicated that high school teachers tend to use other sources of information rather than test results when making instructional decisions about students (Goslin, 1967; Yeh, 1980; Salmon-Cox, 1983; Ward, 1982). The other sources most used include their own experience teaching, and the reports of other teachers.

Test Use for Instructional Decision-Making

A series of questions explored teacher use of sources of information in making three instructional decisions: planning at the beginning of the school year, grouping students within the class, and making decisions to remediate or accelerate students. Teachers tended to rate their own experience teaching and their observations of student work as most useful in making these decisions. CRT test scores were also rated as important, as were all of the other sources of information. This supports the earlier research of Shavelson and Stern (1981) that as decision makers, teachers work in a complex environment and must sort through a variety of information before they reach an instructional decision. This suggests that if test information is to be used, it must be presented in a format that is useful to teachers.

Similarly, when teachers were asked to check the sources of information used to assign students to classes, the responses indicated that teachers' recommendations, previous grades, and counselors' recommendations were the most used information sources.

- Fifty-three percent of the teachers indicated the cut-off scaled scores of 191 on the reading CRT and 190 on the mathematics CRT were used.

This scale score is used somewhat as a predictor of success on the Basic Skills Tests. That is, students who score below a cut-off point on the scale scores are identified as students likely to have difficulty passing the Basic Skills Tests.

The use of the CRT scale score was investigated with demographic and teacher variables to see if there were differences in the groups who tended to use this information for assigning students to classes. Significant relationships were found in the following situations:

- Teachers in rural settings reported less use of the scale scores in assigning students to classes.
- Teachers in schools without an eighth grade also were less likely to report the use of the scale score.
- Teachers of remedial mathematics, teachers who teach both remedial mathematics and mathematics, and teachers who teach both language arts and reading report use of the scale score.
- Teachers who reported zero to three hours of test use instruction (36%) are less likely to use the scale score than are teachers receiving four or more hours of instruction.

The scale score may be seen as being representative of the information reported on the individual test report forms, and as such, these results indicate that the use of this information may vary depending on the setting and organization of the school as well as the subject matter taught. For example, a reason teachers in rural schools may be less likely to use this information is that they are often in small districts that may not have the resources to provide training for their teachers in the use of the test results.

These data also indicate that teachers of students in remedial mathematics and reading classes use the scale score more often than teachers of students in mathematics and language arts classes. This indicates that teachers of students in remedial classes may be more aware of the information contained on the individual report forms because of their work with students with academic deficiencies.

That ninth grade teachers in schools without eighth grades use this information less than ninth grade teachers in schools with eighth grades may indicate that school organization contributes to the problem of use of test information.

- The fact that the majority of the teachers surveyed (62%) teach in schools with grades nine to twelve may indicate that there is a problem in transferring information from one school building to another.

Report forms sent directly to the ninth grade schools, or better, to the teachers, may improve these teachers' knowledge of and use of the test results.

Usefulness of Individual Student Report and Student Label

Two Georgia CRT reports are designed specifically for use by teachers, the Individual Student Report and the Student Label. Teachers were asked to respond "Yes" or "No" to the question of how useful each of the components of these reports was in helping them use the test information. Teachers were strong in their support of the format and information presented by these reports (68% to 81% responding "Yes" the components of the reports are useful). Particularly strong support was also expressed for the four test report components of the Student Label (72% to 80% approval).

Teachers were given the opportunity to comment about these reports in an open-ended section. There were no negative comments written about the content or format of these report forms. However, several teachers wrote comments expressing the view that: "I wish these forms were made available to me. I have to pull the permanent record of each of 150 students and record the information off of the label." So, while teachers find the information and its presentation useful, they may find the forms themselves not readily available.

Usefulness of the Existing CRT Report Forms for Instructional Decisions

Teachers rated the importance of each test report form on a scale from Not Important (1) to Crucial (5), for each of three instructional decisions: planning, grouping in class, and remediation or acceleration.

The means for the importance ratings of all report forms for every decision situation were in the 3.0 range (Important), indicating that teachers find the report forms important in making those instructional decisions.

These data, along with the data about the usefulness of the separate components of the Individual Student Report and the Student Labels, indicate that

- Teachers find the information and format of the CRT report forms and manuals useful for instructional decision-making.

However, these data also indicate that a large number of teachers do not see the reports (from 22 percent to 33 percent depending on the report form.) With the differing organizational structures of schools, although forms and manuals are prepared, they are not easily accessible to teachers. This finding indicates the need for attention to the system which links the eighth grade testing and ninth grade test use.

Usefulness of Alternative Report Forms

Teachers were asked to rank then rate the usefulness of each of the three alternative report forms (Reports A, B, and C) for helpfulness in making a number of instructional decisions.

- Report C, the report form developed by the investigator which provides a concrete link between the test results and instruction, was seen as the most useful of the reports for all instructional decisions.

Report C contains information about where in the *Objectives and Assessment Manual* the teacher may go to find information about the objective tested and an example of a test question testing this objective.

Teachers were invited to write comments about these reports (see Appendix B). The comments were generally supportive of Reports C and B. Two typical comments are these: "Report C would help each of us. It could be given to us at the beginning of the year." "Report C was the best because it showed me where to go for help. Maybe all of these forms are available to me, but no one has ever told me they were available. I did not know they existed."

Teachers tend to find the Individual Student Report Form most helpful if it provides the link from testing to instruction that Rudman, et al. (1980) discussed. The information added by the investigator about where to go in the *Objectives and Assessment Characteristics* booklet is readily available to the test publisher, and could be incorporated into the program that produces the test reports. *Objectives and Assessment Characteristics*, however, is reported to be available by only about 56% of the teachers in this study. Therefore, more widespread distribution of this booklet would be needed to make this alternative form useful to teachers.

Usefulness of the Alternative Summary of Student Reports Form

The official Summary of Student Reports form is prepared for every school where the eighth grade CRT is administered. For each objective, it lists all of the students in the school who have not achieved or have not attempted the objective. It is a school-wide report, not a classroom report. The investigator adapted this form to provide the same information but for every relevant class (i.e. reading, language arts, mathematics, or remedial mathematics) for ninth grade teachers.

Over 94 percent of the teachers thought the report was important, very important, or crucial. Written responses were also positive (see Appendix B). For example:

I teach approximately 150 different students every quarter. However helpful test report forms might be, I cannot spend time on them because so many other things are more important. If I had a form (as above) for each of my classes instead of having to pull so many individual records to find the information, that would be very useful.

These data indicate that while teachers generally find the report forms now available useful, they greatly prefer a form that provides more information, such as Report C, for decision-making, or that is sent to them, as is proposed with the alternative Summary of Student Reports form. Teachers' strong preference for the information reported in Report C supports the work of Nisbett and Ross (1980) concerning the importance of presenting information in a format that is highly salient to the decision-maker.

Factors Militating Against Test Use

Teacher Need of Training in Using Test Results

Goslin (1967) and Ward (1980) identified lack of courses and training in measurement and test use as factors related to teachers not using test information. This report found that 23% of teachers had no courses in testing and measurement and 45% had six or fewer hours. Another question addressed the inservice training that was provided to teachers by the school or system. Seventy-three percent reported that they had received three or fewer hours of inservice training in test use in the last two years.

Teachers also report that they would like assistance in using test results. For example, over 50 percent of the teachers indicated they would like assistance in analyzing test results, interpreting test results to students, interpreting test results to parents, using test results for instructional decisions, determining the relationship between the test objectives and the curriculum guide, and determining the relationship between the test objectives and the textbook topics.

Given this expressed need for assistance in using test information by some teachers, and the number of teachers with no courses or training in test use, state testing officials and district test coordinators may want to reconsider the current methods of training teachers in test use. This reconsideration may include developing plans to identify teachers who are most likely to need to use the test information, assessing their ability to interpret test reports, planning traning sessions in test use, and clarification of the report forms themselves, if necessary. This study indicates that teachers of remedial subjects, language arts and those teaching in rural schools may be possible candidates for additional training. Materials like the Test Box (Wanous & Mehrens, 1981) are available to assist school districts in providing training to teachers in the use and interpretation of test scores.

Availability of Test Reports

In another series of questions, teachers were asked about the availability of all of the test report forms and test information examined in this study. Teachers indicated that of the two forms provided expressly for their use, the Individual Student Form and the Student Labels, only 18 percent had the Individual Student Form sent to them, while 78 percent said it was available for their use and would be helpful to them, and only 9.1 percent reported the Student Labels were sent to them, while 68 percent said they were available for their use and 76.2 percent indicated that they would be helpful to them.

Two test manuals have been prepared to inform teachers about the test reports and the testing program, the *Teacher's Interpretive Guide* and the *Objectives and Assessment Characteristics*. About 80 percent of the teachers indicated the manuals would be helpful to them, but only 55 percent of the teachers reported they were available.

Thus, while teachers express strong support for the content and format of the test reports and materials, a large percentage of teachers do not have these materials on hand to use. Swain (1982) reported that teachers used test reports more often when they were sent to them. It may be that the current method of preparing test reports to be filed in students' permanent record folders is better suited to elementary school settings, where teachers may have 25 to 30 students for whom to plan instruction. High school teachers may not have time to gather the test report information together in order to use it with their classes. This may explain why the high school teachers in the Salmon-Cox (1982) study reported that they only went to the permanent record file when they had a student with a particular problem, and they needed more information about the student. In fact, the teachers in this study indicated that they used the information on the test reports more often if they taught students in remedial classes.

The problem of availability of test reports is compounded by the school organization variable examined, that is, whether the eighth and ninth grades are in the same building. A cluster analysis of the forms by whether they were sent, or available showed a greater proportion of teachers reporting that the forms are sent to them when the two grades are in the same building. Also, more ninth grade teachers in schools with eighth grades indicate that the reports are helpful to them than do teachers in schools with grades nine to twelve.

Implications

For Practice

The test forms prepared for use with the Georgia eighth grade CRT are found to be very useful by the teachers in this study. Teachers expressed repeatedly how useful they are and how important the information they present is in making a number of instructional decisions. Other state testing programs may want to examine these forms when developing their narrative and more traditional test report forms.

The study points to the need for improvment of some of the forms to make them more useful to teachers. For example, the Individual Student Report Form could be improved by adding information about resources for helping students who did not achieve the objectives. The Summary of Student Reports would be more useful if it could be prepared for ninth grade classrooms, particularly for schools with the eighth grades in a different building.

As good as a form may be, however, it is not of much value if it is not accessible. A critical problem seems to be that large numbers of ninth grade teachers do not use the report forms. One of the main reasons for this appears to be that they have so many students that they cannot search out this information except under unusual circumstances. The Summary of Student Report forms, sent directly to the classroom teacher, would provide the information in a concise, usable form.

It may not be feasible for the State testing program to prepare individual summary reports of eighth grade results for each ninth grade teacher of language arts, reading, mathematics and remedial mathematics. However, the technology may be available for the computer tapes of these student records to be forwarded to school districts or even schools, with computer programs prepared to assist the districts in printing class lists for teachers. This may be most useful in situations where the eighth and ninth grades are in different buildings.

In addition, a substantial number of teachers in this study have had no research or measurement courses (23.7%), and 36 percent report no instruction in the use of the CRT in the last two years. At the same time, about 50 percent of teachers expressed a need for assistance in using test results. Training, at either the school or system level would inform teachers about the forms and materials available and perhaps increase the use of them.

The report forms for the Georgia Eighth Grade Criterion-Referenced Tests provide important information for use by ninth grade teachers in improving instruction for students. The use of these forms should be encouraged through more direct dissemination of the reports to the teachers, and through additional training in the use of the reports. These improvements should help strengthen the link between testing and instruction.

References

Burry, J. (1981). *Preliminary results of the test use study,* draft report. Los Angeles: University of California, Center for the Study of Evaluation.

Georgia Department of Education. (1983). *Student assessment in Georgia 1982–83: Criterion-referenced tests and basic skills tests contents and results.* Atlanta, GA: Author.

Gorth, W. P., & Perkins, N. R. (1979). *A study of minimum competency testing programs: A report by National Evaluation Systems, Inc.* Washington, DC: National Institute of Education.

Goslin, D. A. (1967). *Teachers and testing.* New York: Russell Sage Foundation.

Jaeger, R. M. (1984). *Sampling in education and the social sciences.* New York: Longman.

Nisbett, R. E., & Ross, L. (1980). *Human inference: Strategies and shortcomings of social judgment.* Englewood Cliffs, NJ: Prentice-Hall.

Rudman, H. C., Kelly, J. L., Wanous, D. S., Mehrens, W. A., Clark, C. M., & Porter, A. C. (1980, January). *Integrating assessment with instruction: A review (1922–1980)* (Contract No. 400–79–0067). Washington, DC: National Institute of Education.

Salmon-Cox, L. (1982, December). *Technical report: Social functions of testing, school building studies.* Pittsburg, PA: University of Pittsburgh, Learning Research and Development Center.

Salmon-Cox, L. (1983, April). *Monitoring achievement in Pittsburgh: The teacher's viewpoint*. Paper presented at the meeting of the American Educational Research Association, Montreal, Canada.

Shavelson, R. J., & Stern, P. (1981). Research on teachers' pedagogical thoughts, judgments, decisions, and behavior. *Review of Educational Research, 51*(4), 455–498.

SPSS-X, Inc. (1983). *SPSS-X User's Guide*. New York: McGraw-Hill Book Company.

Swain, C. L. (1982, December). Using test data effectively. In S. B. Anderson & L. V. Coburn (Eds.), *New directions for testing and measurement: Academic testing and the consumer* (No. 16; pp. 77–86). San Francisco: Jossey Bass.

Wanous, D. S., & Mehrens, W. A. (1981). Helping teachers use information: The data box approach. *Measurement in Education, 12*(4), 1–10.

Ward, J. G. (1980). *Teachers and testing: A survey of knowledge and attitudes*. Washington, DC: American Federation of Teachers Research Department.

Ward, J. G. (1982, December). An overview of the AFT's "Teaching and Testing." In S. B. Anderson & L. V. Coburn (Eds.), *New directions for testing and measurement: Academic testing and the consumer* (No. 16; pp. 47–57). San Francisco: Jossey Bass.

Yeh, J. P. (1980, August). *A reanalysis of test use data* (CSE Report No. 143). Los Angeles: University of California, Center for the Study of Evaluation.

APPENDIX A
Survey Materials

SURVEY OF TESTING PRACTICES
FOR TEACHERS OF GRADE 9 STUDENTS

This survey examines the testing practices of teachers of 9th grade students. Your responses are important in helping to improve the Georgia State Testing Program for **Grade 8**. All responses are anonymous. No respondent will be identifiable. The survey should take about 20 minutes. Thank you for your assistance.

DIRECTIONS: Please fill in the blanks, or circle or check the appropriate response.

1. Sex   M ___ . F ___

2. Age ____ (Years)

3. Grade(s) taught 1984-85 (CIRCLE all that apply)   7   8   9   10   11   12

4. My highest degree/certificate is: (CHECK one) ____ Bachelors ____ Masters ____ Sixth-Year ____ Doctorate

5. Year received ___ ___

6. Number of hours earned in undergraduate or graduate courses in testing, educational research or statistics: _____ (Hours)

7. Number of years you have teaching _____.

8. Courses taught this year (please CHECK all that apply):

   ___ Reading   ____ Remedial Mathematics   Others _____

   ___ English   ___ Mathematics   _____

9. Type of school (please CHECK all that apply):

   ___ 7 - 9   ___ 8 - 9   ____ 8 - 12   ____ 9 - 12

   ___ Other   ____ Urban   ____ Suburban   ____ Rural

INFORMATION SOURCES AND DECISIONS

10. Below are some decisions made in schools. Please CIRCLE yes or no for **all** individuals in your school or district who make these decisions:

	About the curriculum to teach		About assigning students to classes		About accelerating students		About remediating students	
I decide	YES	NO	YES	NO	YES	NO	YES	NO
Teachers' Committees	YES	NO	YES	NO	YES	NO	YES	NO
Counselors	YES	NO	YES	NO	YES	NO	YES	NO
Principals	YES	NO	YES	NO	YES	NO	YES	NO
Curriculum Specialists	YES	NO	YES	NO	YES	NO	YES	NO
Others (List)								

11. What sources of information are used to assign students to classes? Please CHECK all that apply:

   _ Previous grades

   . _ Teachers' Recommendations

   . Counselors' Recommendations

   . A score of 191/Reading or 190/Mathematics on the 8th grade CRT.

   Other scores on the State Criterion Referenced Tests. Describe how used: _____ _____

   ___ ___

   Scores on other tests. Please list the tests below:

   ___ ___

DIRECTIONS: Below are some decision situations. For each situation CIRCLE the number that indicates the importance of each source of information in helping you make a decision.

	Not Important	Slightly Important	Important	Very Important	Crucial
12. Planning instruction at the beginning of the school year:					
a. Other teachers' reports, comments and grades	1	2	3	4	5
b. Students' criterion-referenced test scores	1	2	3	4	5
c. My previous experience teaching	1	2	3	4	5
13. Grouping students within the class:					
a. Other teachers' reports, comments and grades	1	2	3	4	5
b. Students' criterion-referenced test scores	1	2	3	4	5
c. Results of placement tests developed for curriculum use	1	2	3	4	5
d. Results of tests I made up	1	2	3	4	5
e. My own observations of students' classwork	1	2	3	4	5
f. Check here if you do not group students in class _____					
14. Decisions to provide for remediation or acceleration:					
a. Other teachers' reports, comments or grades	1	2	3	4	5
b. Students' criterion-referenced test scores	1	2	3	4	5
c. Results of placement tests developed for curriculum use	1	2	3	4	5
d. Results of tests I make up	1	2	3	4	5
e. My own observations of students' class work	1	2	3	4	5
f. Check here if you do not make such recommendations _____					

Assistance with Test Use

15. Would you like assistance or instruction related to testing and using test results in any of the areas listed below? Have your received assistance in any of these areas? *CIRCLE YES OR NO* in both columns.

	I would like Assistance	Assistance is Provided
a. Administering tests	YES NO	YES NO
b. Analyzing test results	YES NO	YES NO
c. Interpreting test results to students	YES NO	YES NO
d. Interpreting test results to parents	YES NO	YES NO
e. Using test results for placement	YES NO	YES NO
f. Using test results for instructional decisions	YES NO	YES NO
g. Using test results for grouping in my class	YES NO	YES NO
h. Determining the relationship between the test objectives and the topics in the curriculum guides.	YES NO	YES NO
i. Determining the relationship between the test objectives and the text book topics	YES NO	YES NO

COMMENTS _____

_____

16. How many hours have you spent *in the last two years* receiving assistance or instruction related to using test results? Such assistance, for example, could be inservice sessions, committees, and staff meetings. Please *CHECK* the appropriate number of hours:

_____ 0 hours	_____ 4 - 6 hours	_____ 11 - 15 hours
_____ 1 - 3 hours	_____ 7 - 10 hours	_____ 16 or more hours

Criterion Referenced Test Results

17. The State provides several report forms and interpretive materials for the Criterion-Referenced Tests. Indicate below if the report is sent to you, is available for your use, or would be helpful to you. Please *CIRCLE* the appropriate response. (Refer to the separate sheets enclosed, *Examples of Test Report Forms*, for examples of each form).

	Sent to me	Available for my use	Would be helpful to me
Individual Student Form	YES NO	YES NO	YES NO
Student Achievement Roster	YES NO	YES NO	YES NO
Summary of Student Reports	YES NO	YES NO	YES NO
Student Achievement Labels	YES NO	YES NO	YES NO
Item Analysis Forms	YES NO	YES NO	YES NO
Teacher's Interpretive Guide (four page folder)	YES NO	YES NO	YES NO
Objectives & Assessment Characteristics (about 50 pages mimeographed)	YES NO	YES NO	YES NO

Please describe any other type of report that would be useful _____

_____

18. Does the State report the Criterion-Referenced Test scores in a way that facilitates your use of the information?

a. *Individual Student Report Form* for Reading or Mathematics	Useful
1. Scale Score	YES NO
2. Cut-off Scores of 191/reading, 190/mathematics	YES NO
3. Listing of each objective	YES NO
4. Number of items needed to pass objective	YES NO
5. Number of items student answered correctly	YES NO
6. Whether student achieved the objective	YES NO
7. Listing of areas for additional instruction	YES NO

Comments _____

b. *Individual Student Label*	Useful
1. Skill area into which objectives are grouped	YES NO
2. Indicating objective was achieved (*)	YES NO
3. Indicating objective was not achieved (–)	YES NO
4. Indicating objective was not attempted (N)	YES NO

Comments _____

The Use of CRT Test Results for Decision Making

DIRECTIONS: The State provides several report forms and publications for the 8th grade CRT. Indicate below how important each of these form is to you for particular types of decisions you make. Look at the *Examples* pages for examples of the forms. Please *CIRCLE* the appr priate response. *IF A PARTICULAR REPORT FORM IS NOT AVAILABLE TO YOU, PLEASE GO ON THE THE NEXT REPORT FORI*

	Not Important	Slightly Important	Important	Very Important	Crucial
19. The *Individual Student Report Form* is important for making the following instructional decisions:					
a. Planning at the beginning of the school year	1	2	3	4	5
b. Grouping or placement	1	2	3	4	5
c. Remediation or acceleration	1	2	3	4	5
Other Use _____					
20. The *Student Achievement Roster* is important for making these instructional decisions:					
a. Planning at the beginning of the school year	1	2	3	4	5
b. Grouping or placement	1	2	3	4	5
c. Remediation or acceleration	1	2	3	4	5
Other Use _____					
21. The *Summary of Student Reports* is important for making these instructional decisions:					
a. Planning at the beginning of the school year	1	2	3	4	5
b. Grouping or placement	1	2	3	4	5
c. Remediation or acceleration	1	2	3	4	5
Other Use _____					
22. The *Student Achievement Labels* are important for making these instructional decisions:					
a. Planning at the beginning of the school year	1	2	3	4	5
b. Grouping or placement	1	2	3	4	5
c. Remediation or acceleration	1	2	3	4	5
Other Use _____					
23. The *Teacher's Interpretive Guide for Student Reports* is important for making these instructional decisions:					
a. Planning at the beginning of the school year	1	2	3	4	5
b. Grouping or placement	1	2	3	4	5
c. Remediation or acceleration	1	2	3	4	5
Other Use _____					
24. The *Objective and Assessment Characteristics* are important for making these instructional decisions:					
a. Planning at the beginning of the school year	1	2	3	4	5
b. Grouping or placement	1	2	3	4	5
c. Remediation or acceleration	1	2	3	4	5
Other Use _____					
25. The *Item Analysis Form* is important for making these instructional decisions:					
a. Planning at the beginning of the school year	1	2	3	4	5
b. Grouping or placement	1	2	3	4	5
c. Remediation or acceleration	1	2	3	4	5
Other Use _____					

Alternative Individual Student Report Forms

DIRECTIONS: The following questions relate to the kind of information included on a report form for the CRT. Please answer each question regardless of the subject you teach. We are concerned with your evaluation of the *type of information* included on the report form, not the specific subject matter.

Below are examples of reports of a student's performance for Objective 2 of the 8th grade CRT Reading test. Please read each report.

Objective 2: Recognizes explicitly stated main ideas, details, sequences of events and cause and effect relationships.

Report A. 16 or more of 18 items are needed to achieve this objective. 12 were answered correctly. You have not achieved this objective.

Report B. 16 or more of 18 items are needed to achieve this objective. 12 were answered correctly. You have not achieved this objective. You may need help developing a concept of cause and effect. In addition, you may need to know more about recognizing relational words such a *because* or *since* that signal cause and effect.

Report C. 16 or more of 18 items are needed to achieve this objective. 12 were answered correctly. You have not achieved this objective. You may need help developing a concept of cause and effect. In addition, you may need to know more about recognizing relational words such as because or since that signal cause and effect.
Teachers: Refer to pages 10-11 of *Objectives and Assessment Characteristics* for examples for Objective 2.

26. Consider Reports A, B, and C. Give the ranking of 1, 2 or 3 for overall usefulness of each report to you:
1 = Most Useful
2 = Next Most Useful
3 = Least Useful

Report	Ranking
Report A	_____
Report B	_____
Report C	_____

27. Consider Reports A, B, and C again. How useful is each form for the following purposes? *CIRCLE* the number to indicate the usefulness of the report.

	Not Useful	Slightly Useful	Useful	Very Useful	Crucial
Report A					
a. For analyzing test results	1	2	3	4	5
b. For interpreting test results to students	1	2	3	4	5
c. For interpreting test results to parents	1	2	3	4	5
d. For grouping students in class	1	2	3	4	5
e. For decisions about remediation	1	2	3	4	5
f. For decisions about acceleration	1	2	3	4	5
g. For planning instruction	1	2	3	4	5
h. The overall usefulness of the report	1	2	3	4	5
Report B					
a. For analyzing test results	1	2	3	4	5
b. For interpreting test results to students	1	2	3	4	5
c. For interpreting test results to parents	1	2	3	4	5
d. For grouping students in class	1	2	3	4	5
e. For decisions about remediation	1	2	3	4	5
f. For decisions about acceleration	1	2	3	4	5
g. For planning instruction	1	2	3	4	5
h. The overall usefulness of the report	1	2	3	4	5
Report C					
a. For analyzing test results	1	2	3	4	5
b. For interpreting test results to students	1	2	3	4	5
c. For interpreting test results to parents	1	2	3	4	5
d. For grouping students in class	1	2	3	4	5
e. For decisions about remediation	1	2	3	4	5
f. For decisions about acceleration	1	2	3	4	5
g. For planning instruction	1	2	3	4	5
h. The overall usefulness of the report	1	2	3	4	5

Alternative Summary of Student Reports Form

The Spring Eighth Grade CRT testing provides a Summary of Student Reports for each school. It lists the students not achieving or not attempting each objective for each of the tests (see the Examples sheet for a sample of this form).

The following question asks you to consider whether a similar report would be helpful to you as a grade 9 teacher.

Remember, please answer the question regardless of the subject you teach. We are interested in your evaluation of the type of information included on the report form, not the specific subject matter.

28. Below is a report form that summarizes the performance of students in a class on the CRT in Mathematics. Please examine the report.

SUMMARY OF STUDENT REPORTS FOR MRS. GREEN'S PERIOD 1 CLASS
GRADE 8 MATHEMATICS CRT SCORES

OBJECTIVE 1 — Translates forms of rational numbers

HAS NOT ACHIEVED OBJECTIVE

Jenny B. Andrews	Mark W. Bulter	Teresa F. Lewis	Carol D. Scott
John P. Brown	Wendy L. Davis	Gene Morris	Earl Turner

HAS NOT ATTEMPTED OBJECTIVE
Robert P. Brooks   Susan T. Payne

Rate the usefulness of such a form to you, if one were prepared for each of your ninth grade Reading/Language Arts or Mathematics courses at the beginning of the school year. *CIRCLE* the appropriate rating of usefulness.

1		2		3		4		5
Not Useful		Slightly Useful		Useful		Very Useful		Crucial

Review questions 26, 27, 28 above and use the space below to comment about the content and design of the CRT test report forms. What other information, organization of scores, and so on, would be useful to you?

Thank you for your help with this study.

Please place completed survey in the small manila envelope, seal it and mail to your system test coordinator. Thank you.

STUDENT ACHIEVEMENT LABELS FOR ANYTOWN ELEMENTARY   9991234
SPRING 1982   9990002   4

GEORGIA CRITERION-REFERENCED TESTS   GRADE 4

NAME STACY L. STUDENT   TEST DATE   SPRING 1982

READING	LANGUAGE USAGE					WORD RECOGNITION				COMPREHENSION					CLASSI-FICATION		STUDY SKILLS	VOCABULARY			
OBJECTIVE NO.	1	6	7	8	11	20	2	3	4	5	9	12	13	16	17	19	14	15	18	10	TOTAL
*INDICATES ACHIEVEMENT	*	*	*	*	*		*	*	*	*		*	*	*	*	*	*	–	*	*	19

MATHEMATICS	SETS, NUMBERS, NUMERATION		OPERATIONS, PROPERTIES, NUMBER THEORY			RELATIONS, FUNCTIONS		GEOMETRY		MEASUREMENT		PROBABILITY, STATISTICS				
OBJECTIVE NO.	1	2	3	4	5	6	7	8	9	10	11	12	13	14	15	16	17	18	19	20	TOTAL
*INDICATES ACHIEVEMENT	*	*	*	*	*	*	*	*	*	*	*	*	*	*	*	*	*	*	*	*	19

CAREER DEVELOPMENT	SELF-UNDERSTANDING					WORK AND OCCUPATIONS			EDUCATION			DECISION-MAKING				
OBJECTIVE NO.	1	2	3	4	5	6	7	8	9	10	11	12	13	14	15	16	17	18	19	20	TOTAL
*INDICATES ACHIEVEMENT	*	*			*		*		*		*	*			*	*		10

GEORGIA CRITERION-REFERENCED TESTS   GRADE 4

NAME SHANGALEZA T. STUDENT   TEST DATE   SPRING 1982

READING	LANGUAGE USAGE					WORD RECOGNITION				COMPREHENSION					CLASSI-FICATION		STUDY SKILLS	VOCABULARY			
OBJECTIVE NO.	1	6	7	8	11	20	2	3	4	5	9	12	13	16	17	19	14	15	18	10	TOTAL
*INDICATES ACHIEVEMENT	–	*	*	*	–		*	*	*	*		*	*	*	*	*	*	*	*	–	15

MATHEMATICS	SETS, NUMBERS, NUMERATION		OPERATIONS, PROPERTIES, NUMBER THEORY			RELATIONS, FUNCTIONS		GEOMETRY		MEASUREMENT		PROBABILITY, STATISTICS				
OBJECTIVE NO.	1	2	3	4	5	6	7	8	9	10	11	12	13	14	15	16	17	18	19	20	TOTAL
*INDICATES ACHIEVEMENT	*	*	–	–	*	*	–		*	*		–	–		–	–		*	–	*	10

CAREER DEVELOPMENT	SELF-UNDERSTANDING					WORK AND OCCUPATIONS			EDUCATION			DECISION-MAKING				
OBJECTIVE NO.	1	2	3	4	5	6	7	8	9	10	11	12	13	14	15	16	17	18	19	20	TOTAL
*INDICATES ACHIEVEMENT		–	*	–	*		*		*		–			–	*	–		5

GEORGIA CRITERION-REFERENCED TESTS   GRADE 4

NAME RUFUS L. STUDENT   TEST DATE   SPRING 1982

READING	LANGUAGE USAGE					WORD RECOGNITION				COMPREHENSION					CLASSI-FICATION		STUDY SKILLS	VOCABULARY			
OBJECTIVE NO.	1	6	7	8	11	20	2	3	4	5	9	12	13	16	17	19	14	15	18	10	TOTAL
*INDICATES ACHIEVEMENT	*	*	*	*	*	–	*	*	–	*		*	*	*	*	*	*	*	*	*	17

MATHEMATICS	SETS, NUMBERS, NUMERATION		OPERATIONS, PROPERTIES, NUMBER THEORY			RELATIONS, FUNCTIONS		GEOMETRY		MEASUREMENT		PROBABILITY, STATISTICS				
OBJECTIVE NO.	1	2	3	4	5	6	7	8	9	10	11	12	13	14	15	16	17	18	19	20	TOTAL
*INDICATES ACHIEVEMENT	*	*	–	*	*	*		*	*	*		–	–	*		*	*	*	*		14

CAREER DEVELOPMENT	SELF-UNDERSTANDING					WORK AND OCCUPATIONS			EDUCATION			DECISION-MAKING				
OBJECTIVE NO.	1	2	3	4	5	6	7	8	9	10	11	12	13	14	15	16	17	18	19	20	TOTAL
*INDICATES ACHIEVEMENT	*	*			*		–		*		*	*	*			–	*	8

GEORGIA CRITERION-REFERENCED TESTS   GRADE 4

NAME STEPHEN C. STUDENT   TEST DATE   SPRING 1982

READING	LANGUAGE USAGE					WORD RECOGNITION				COMPREHENSION					CLASSI-FICATION		STUDY SKILLS	VOCABULARY			
OBJECTIVE NO.	1	6	7	8	11	20	2	3	4	5	9	12	13	16	17	19	14	15	18	10	TOTAL
*INDICATES ACHIEVEMENT	*	*	*	*	*	*	*	*	*	*		*	*	*	*	*	*	*	*	*	20

MATHEMATICS	SETS, NUMBERS, NUMERATION		OPERATIONS, PROPERTIES, NUMBER THEORY			RELATIONS, FUNCTIONS		GEOMETRY		MEASUREMENT		PROBABILITY, STATISTICS				
OBJECTIVE NO.	1	2	3	4	5	6	7	8	9	10	11	12	13	14	15	16	17	18	19	20	TOTAL
*INDICATES ACHIEVEMENT	*	*	*	–	*	*	*		*	*	*	*	*	–	*	*	*	*	*	–	15

CAREER DEVELOPMENT	SELF-UNDERSTANDING					WORK AND OCCUPATIONS			EDUCATION			DECISION-MAKING				
OBJECTIVE NO.	1	2	3	4	5	6	7	8	9	10	11	12	13	14	15	16	17	18	19	20	TOTAL
*INDICATES ACHIEVEMENT		*	–	–		–		*		–			–		*	–		3

GEORGIA CRITERION-REFERENCED TESTS

SPRING 1982
TESTING DATE

ANYTOWN ELEMENTARY   9991234
SCHOOL NAME AND CODE

9990004 0002
PROCESS NO.

GRADE 4 READING REPORT FOR SHANGALEZA T. STUDENT

Objective 1: Distinguishes between sentence fragments and complete sentences.
SHANGALEZA HAS NOT ACHIEVED OBJECTIVE.
SHE MAY NEED WORK ON RECOGNIZING BASIC SENTENCES.
SHE MAY NEED PRACTICE IDENTIFYING COMPLEX SENTENCE PARTS.

Item No.	37	38	39	72	77
Response	D	C	*	B	C

Objective 2: Identifies sounds of beginning consonants, or two-letter combinations of consonants.
SHANGALEZA HAS ACHIEVED OBJECTIVE.
SHE MAY BE CONFUSING VISUAL AND AUDITORY MATCHING TASKS.

Item No.	4	5	6	7	78
Response	*	*	*	*	C

Objective 3: Identifies the sounds of long vowels and of short vowels in one- and two-syllable words.
SHANGALEZA HAS ACHIEVED OBJECTIVE.

Item No.	32	33	34	35	36
Response	A	*	*	*	A

Objective 4: Identifies number of syllables in a word and divides words into syllables.
SHANGALEZA HAS ACHIEVED OBJECTIVE.

Item No.	30	31	41	42	43
Response	*	A	A	*	*

Objective 5: Identifies sounds that vowels have when they appear before L, W, and R. and distinguishes the soft sounds of C and G.
SHANGALEZA HAS ACHIEVED OBJECTIVE.
SHE MAY NEED PRACTICE WITH HARD AND SOFT SOUNDS OF G.

Item No.	84	85	86	79	80
Response	A	*	*	*	C

Objective 6: Selects the appropriate words such as *here, under, beside, around, above* to indicate position or location.
SHANGALEZA HAS ACHIEVED OBJECTIVE.

Item No.	8	19	68	91
Response	*	*	*	*

Objective 7: Identifies contractions and abbreviations and the words they represent.
SHANGALEZA HAS ACHIEVED OBJECTIVE.

Item No.	9	19	74	75	98
Response	*	*	*	*	*

Objective 8: Selects the appropriate verbs or adjectives which complete sentences.
SHANGALEZA HAS ACHIEVED OBJECTIVE.

Item No.	17	24	25	26	27
Response	*	*	*	*	*

Objective 9: Selects appropriate meaning for the following word endings: S, ES, IES, ING, ED, LY, ER, EST, and Y.
SHANGALEZA HAS NOT ACHIEVED OBJECTIVE.
SHE MAY NEED HELP WITH COMPARATIVE AND SUPERLATIVE FORMS.
SHE MAY NEED HELP IN IDENTIFYING PLURAL FORMS IN CONTEXT.

Item No.	44	68	100	101	102
Response	*	D	*	*	C

Objective 10: Recognizes simple vocabulary words instantly when seen, without having to analyze them in order to pronounce them.
SHANGALEZA HAS NOT ACHIEVED OBJECTIVE.
SHE MAY NEED PRACTICE WITH SIGHT WORDS IN CONTEXT.

Item No.	18	87	88	89
Response	D	*	*	A

Objective 11: Matches symbols and pronouns to the things, ideas, or persons that they represent.
SHANGALEZA HAS NOT ACHIEVED OBJECTIVE.
SHE MAY NEED PRACTICE WITH PRONOUNS AND THEIR REFERENTS.

Item No.	65	66	67	90
Response	C B	A	*	B

Objective 12: Reads short selections and identifies the main idea and supporting details.
SHANGALEZA HAS ACHIEVED OBJECTIVE.
SHE MAY NEED INSTRUCTION IDENTIFYING MAIN IDEA.

Item No.	49	62	63	91
Response	*	C	*	*

Objective 13: Reads short selections and identifies which statements are facts, and which express the writer's opinions.
SHANGALEZA HAS ACHIEVED OBJECTIVE.

Item No.	11	64	69	84	65
Response	A	*	*	*	*

Objective 14: Arranges groups of objects or ideas into simple categories.
SHANGALEZA HAS ACHIEVED OBJECTIVE.

Item No.	20	21	22	70	71
Response	*	*	D	*	*

Objective 15: Arranges words in order, from the most general to the most specific.
SHANGALEZA HAS ACHIEVED OBJECTIVE.

Item No.	29	28	07	88	96
Response	*	A	*	C	D

Objective 16: Reads a simple selection, identifies "heroes," "villains," other main characters, and the setting.
SHANGALEZA HAS ACHIEVED OBJECTIVE.

Item No.	13	90	61	92	63
Response	*	*	*	*	*

Objective 17: Distinguishes between the obvious (literal) and implied (figurative) meanings in simple statements.
SHANGALEZA HAS ACHIEVED OBJECTIVE.

Item No.	10	12	56	61	93	97
Response	*	*	*	*	*	*

Objective 18: Alphabetizes words according to the first two letters, and uses dictionaries and tables of contents to locate specific information.
SHANGALEZA HAS ACHIEVED OBJECTIVE.
SHE MAY NEED HELP ON HOW TO USE TABLES OF CONTENTS.

Item No.	16	76	77	94	96
Response	*	*	A	*	*

Objective 19: Reads and comprehends a simple passage and draws conclusions, recognizes cause-and-effect relationships and/or the sequence of events.
SHANGALEZA HAS ACHIEVED OBJECTIVE.
SHE MAY NEED PRACTICE IDENTIFYING SEQUENCES OF EVENTS.

Item #	1	2	14	42	63	82
Resp.	*	*	*	*	A	*

Objective 20: Recognizes the correct use of basic punctuation marks and recognizes how punctuation can change the meaning of a sentence.
SHANGALEZA HAS NOT ACHIEVED OBJECTIVE.
SHE MAY NEED TO BE TAUGHT THAT SENTENCE MEANING CAN CHANGE WITH THE PLACEMENT OF A COMMA.
SHE MAY NEED HELP IDENTIFYING THE MEANING OF DIRECT QUOTATIONS.

Item No.	3	23	84	98	99
Response	D	D	D	D	B

APPENDIX B
Summary of Written Responses
to Open-Ended Questions

Question 15: Would you like assistance or instruction related to testing and using tests results in any of the areas listed below? Have you received assistance in any of these areas?

1. The counselors, principals and test coordinators offer all of the help needed with scores. (12 responses)

2. I feel competent to make these decisions myself. (2 responses)

3. There is little assistance in analyzing test results. (2 responses)

4. Help is needed in h and i (determining the relationship between test objectives and curriculum topics and between test objectives and textbook topics). (4 responses)

5. The results of the eighth grade CRT are only used by eighth grade counselors to schedule ninth grade classes. (4 responses)

Question 18: Does the State report the Criterion-Referenced Test scores in a way that facilitates your use of the information?

1. I have found the reports to be very helpful. (2 responses)

2. The information is helpful, but I can't find the time to get to the information. (2 responses)

3. I don't look at these unless I have a real problem. (2 responses)

4. These are sent to the counselors; I must go through all of the permanent records to find them. (4 responses)

5. A grade equivalent score would facilitate parents' understanding of the score. (1 response)

6. Use a scale score similar to the BST. (1 response)

Questions 26 and 27: Ranking and rating of Reports A, B, and C:

1. Report C is the most useful of the three reports. (26 responses)

2. Report C would be more useful if it provided information about linking it to textbooks used. (3 responses)

3. The Alternative Summary of Student Report forms would be helpful because it tells at a glance which students need remediation in which objective. (9 responses)

4. The Alternative Summary of Student Report Forms would be helpful at the beginning of the quarter. (7 responses)

General Comments and Concerns:

1. The content and format of the current CRT forms is useful. (16 responses)

2. Having reports sent directly to me, and more instruction in interpreting the scores would be useful. (4 responses)

3. Our high school teachers really need to be more knowledgeable about the CRT. We need more training in its use. (3 responses)

4. It might be helpful to know the areas in which a student has excelled; also the survey mentions acceleration, but little seems to be done in this area with the CRTs. (2 responses)

5. There is nothing wrong with the CRT. The classroom teacher just doesn't have time to concentrate on its development.

6. Overall, the reports are outstanding; we teachers need help in using the results.

7. Ninth grade teachers are not provided this information—8th grade teachers are given the information in the spring. Ninth grade teachers are given a general overview of how the school did in comparison with other schools in the county.

8. We don't have an eighth grade in our school. Most placement decisions for ninth graders are made before they reach us. We sometimes use CRT results to help decide if a student is misplaced and to place him properly.

APPENDIX C
Tables of Data

TABLE C-1 *Chi-square of use of a scale score by setting of a school*

	Setting of School		
Use Scale Score	Urban	Suburban	Rural
Yes	77	98	124
No	64	60	138

Note. $\chi^2(2, N = 561) = 8.683, p = .013$.

TABLE C-2 *Chi-square of use of scale score by grades in school*

	Grades in the School	
Use Scale Score	8–9 Together	8–9 Not Together
Yes	141	162
No	75	189

Note. $\chi^2(1, N = 567) = 18.892, p = .000$.

TABLE C-3 *Chi-square of use of scale score by hours of test use instruction*

	Hours of Instruction				
Use Scale Score	0	1–3	4–6	7–10	Over 10
Yes	90	112	54	26	21
No	114	95	30	14	11

Note. $\chi^2(4, N = 567) = 15.191, p = .0043$.

TABLE C-4 *Information sources important for planning instruction*

Sources of Information	Rating											
	Not Important		Slightly Important		Important		Very Important		Crucial		Not Available	
	n	%	n	%	n	%	n	%	n	%	n	%
Teachers' Reports	69	12.1	146	25.7	212	37.3	110	19.4	29	5.1	2	.4
CRT Scores	59	10.3	84	14.7	248	43.4	127	22.2	47	8.2	5	.9
Experience	11	1.9	16	2.8	120	21.0	270	47.2	153	26.8	1	.2

TABLE C-5 *Information sources important for grouping in class*

Sources of Information	Rating											
	Not Important		Slightly Important		Important		Very Important		Crucial		Do Not Group	
	n	%	n	%	n	%	n	%	n	%	n	%
Teachers' Reports	72	12.6	129	22.6	136	24.0	64	11.3	17	3.0	148	25.9
CRT Scores	35	6.1	79	14.0	163	28.5	104	18.4	34	5.9	149	26.4
Curriculum Tests	51	8.9	60	10.5	155	27.4	112	19.8	39	6.9	149	26.3
My Tests	25	4.4	43	7.5	151	26.7	164	29.0	34	5.9	149	26.3
My Observations	8	1.4	14	2.4	79	13.8	198	35.2	116	20.6	148	26.3

TABLE C-6 *Information sources important for remediation or acceleration*

Sources of Information	Rating											
	Not Important		Slightly Important		Important		Very Important		Crucial		Do Not Remed/ Accel	
	n	%	*n*	%	*n*	%	*n*	%	*n*	%	*n*	%
Teachers' Reports	45	7.9	119	21.1	200	35.5	119	21.1	37	5.6	44	7.8
CRT Scores	29	5.1	53	11.2	193	34.2	164	29.1	71	12.6	44	7.8
Curriculum Tests	53	9.3	62	11.0	180	31.9	167	29.6	57	10.1	45	8.0
My Tests	23	4.1	41	7.2	185	32.6	213	37.6	60	10.6	45	7.9
My Observations	4	.7	13	2.3	109	19.4	253	44.9	141	25.0	43	7.6

TABLE C-7 *Chi-square of need assistance analyzing test results by I teach language arts and/or reading*

Need Assistance	Subject Taught		
	Reading	Language Arts	Both
Yes	18	132	24
No	14	67	31

Note. $\chi^2(2, N = 186) = 9.634, p = .0081$.

TABLE C-8 *Chi-square of need assistance interpreting test results to students by I teach language arts and/or reading*

Need Assistance	Subject Taught		
	Reading	Language Arts	Both
Yes	19	117	22
No	13	81	32

Note. $\chi^2(2, N = 286) = 5.992, p = .0500$.

TABLE C-9 *Chi-Square of need assistance using test results for placement by I teach language arts and/or reading*

Need Assistance	Subject Taught		
	Reading	Language Arts	Both
Yes	15	127	25
No	17	70	30

Note. $\chi^2(2, N = 286) = 8.533, p = .0140$.

TABLE C-10 *Chi-square of need assistance using test results for instruction by I teach language arts and/or reading*

Need Assistance	Subject Taught		
	Reading	Language Arts	Both
Yes	11	126	22
No	21	73	33

Note. $\chi^2(2, N = 286) = 16.061, p = .0003$.

TABLE C-11 *Chi-square of need assistance using test results for grouping by I teach language arts and/or reading*

Need Assistance	Subject Taught		
	Reading	Language Arts	Both
Yes	15	95	16
No	17	104	39

Note. $\chi^2(2, N = 286) = 6.195, p = .0451$.

Table C-12 *Chi-Square of clusters of individual form, achievement roster, summary reports sent to me by eighth grade in school*

	Forms Sent	
Grades	Yes	No
8–9 Together	53	162
8–9 Separate	54	298

Note. $\chi^2(1, N = 567) = 6.961, p = .0083$.

TABLE C-13 *Chi-Square of clusters of student labels, interpretive guide, obj/assessment reports sent to me by eighth grade in school*

	Forms Sent	
Grades	Yes	No
8–9 Together	32	178
8–9 Separate	27	320

Note. $\chi^2(1, N = 557) = 6.914, p = .0085$.

TABLE C-14 *Chi-Square of clusters of student labels, interpretive guide, obj assessment reports sent to me by I teach remedial mathematics*

	Forms Sent	
Remedial Mathematics	Yes	No
Yes	18	82
No	42	415

Note. $\chi^2(1, N = 557) = 5.74004, p = .0166$.

TABLE C-15 *Chi-Square of clusters of item analysis, interpretive guide, obj/assessment reports sent to me by eighth grade in school*

	Forms Sent	
Grades	Yes	No
8–9 Together	139	69
8–9 Separate	149	193

Note. $\chi^2(1, N = 550) = 5.4139, p = .0200$.

TABLE C-16 *Chi-square of individual student form sent to me by grades in school*

	Grades in School	
Form Sent	8 and 9 Together	8 and 9 Not Together
Yes	52	50
No	164	302

Note. $\chi^2(1, N = 568) = 8.19295, p = .0042$.

TABLE C-17 *Chi-square of summary of student reports sent to me by grades in school*

	Grades in School	
Form Sent	8 and 9 Together	8 and 9 Not Together
Yes	37	35
No	178	317

Note. $\chi^2(1, N = 567) = 5.71816, p = .0168$.

TABLE C-18 *Chi-square of student achievement labels sent to me by grades in school*

	Grades in School	
Form Sent	8 and 9 Together	8 and 9 Not Together
Yes	28	23
No	187	325

Note. $\chi^2(1, N = 563) = 5.88094, p = .0153$.

TABLE C-19 *Chi-square of item analysis forms sent to me by grades in school*

	Grades in School	
Form Sent	8 and 9 Together	8 and 9 Not Together
Yes	32	31
No	181	318

Note. $\chi^2(1, N = 562) = 4.41356, p = .0357$.

TABLE C-20 *Chi-square of item analysis forms available to me by grades in school*

	Grades in School	
Form Available	8 and 9 Together	8 and 9 Not Together
Yes	152	217
No	59	129

Note. $\chi^2(1, N = 557) = 4.68461, p = 0.0304$.

TABLE C-21 *Chi-square of teacher's interpretive guide available to me by grades in school*

	Grades in School	
Form Available	8 and 9 Together	8 and 9 Not Together
Yes	139	196
No	70	148

Note. $\chi^2(1, N = 553) = 4.55383, p = 0.0328$.

TABLE C-22 *Chi-square of objectives and assessment characteristics available to me by grades in school*

Form Available	Grades in School	
	8 and 9 Together	8 and 9 Not Together
Yes	133	178
No	77	165

Note. $\chi^2(1, N = 553) = 6.46748, p = 0.0110$.

TABLE C-23 *Rating individual report form for instructional decisions*

	Instructional Decision					
	Planning		Grouping		Remed/Accel	
Rating	n	%	n	%	n	%
Not Important	61	10.7	46	8.1	34	5.9
Slightly Important	72	12.6	51	8.9	41	7.2
Important	210	37.0	203	35.7	177	31.2
Very Important	103	18.1	139	24.5	172	30.3
Crucial	˙34	6.0	41	7.2	56	9.9
Not Available	88	15.5	88	15.5	88	15.5
Missing	4	.7	4	.7	4	.7
TOTAL	572	100.0	572	100.0	572	100.0

TABLE C-24 *Rating student achievement roster for instructional decisions*

	Instructional Decision					
	Planning		Grouping		Remed/Accel	
Rating	n	%	n	%	n	%
Not Important	54	9.5	49	8.6	41	7.2
Slightly Important	63	11.1	52	9.2	46	8.1
Important	166	29.2	165	29.0	159	28.0
Very Important	110	19.4	128	22.5	142	25.0
Crucial	31	5.5	30	5.3	35	6.2
Not Available	144	25.4	144	25.4	144	25.4
Missing	4	.7	4	.7	4	.7
TOTAL	572	100.0	572	100.0	572	100.0

TABLE C-25 *Rating summary student reports for instructional decisions*

| | Instructional Decision | | | | | |
| | Planning | | Grouping | | Remed/Accel | |
Rating	n	%	n	%	n	%
Not Important	65	11.4	58	10.2	52	9.2
Slightly Important	62	10.9	58	10.2	59	10.3
Important	178	31.3	173	30.5	169	29.8
Very Important	103	18.1	112	19.8	119	21.0
Crucial	22	3.9	28	4.9	30	5.3
Not Available	138	24.3	138	24.3	138	24.3
Missing	4	.7	4	.7	4	.7
TOTAL	572	100.0	572	100.0	572	100.0

TABLE C-26 *Rating of student labels for instructional decisions*

| | Instructional Decision | | | | | |
| | Planning | | Grouping | | Remed/Accel | |
Rating	n	%	n	%	n	%
Not Important	76	13.3	68	12.0	61	10.8
Slightly Important	89	15.7	72	12.7	64	11.2
Important	165	29.1	166	29.3	167	29.5
Very Important	84	14.8	106	18.7	119	21.0
Crucial	20	3.5	23	4.1	25	4.4
Not Available	133	23.5	132	23.3	131	23.1
Missing	4	.7	4	.7	4	.7
TOTAL	572	100.0	572	100.0	572	100.0

TABLE C-27 *Rating of teacher's interpretive guide for instructional decisions*

| | Instructional Decision | | | | | |
| | Planning | | Grouping | | Remed/Accel | |
Rating	n	%	n	%	n	%
Not Important	73	12.8	82	14.5	75	13.2
Slightly Important	62	10.8	58	10.2	59	10.4
Important	132	23.2	139	24.5	133	23.5
Very Important	93	16.3	89	15.7	97	17.1
Crucial	31	5.4	21	3.7	25	4.4
Not Available	177	30.9	178	31.4	178	31.4
Missing	4	.7	4	.7	4	.7
TOTAL	572	100.0	572	100.0	572	100.0

TABLE C-28 *Rating of objectives and assessment characteristics for instructional decisions*

| | Instructional Decision | | | | | |
| | Planning | | Grouping | | Remed/Accel | |
Rating	n	%	n	%	n	%
Not Important	53	9.3	62	10.9	53	9.3
Slightly Important	60	10.6	70	12.2	66	11.6
Important	153	26.9	143	25.2	141	24.9
Very Important	96	16.9	98	17.3	102	18.0
Crucial	36	6.3	24	4.2	35	6.2
Not Available	177	30.9	178	31.4	178	31.4
Missing	4	.7	4	.7	4	.7
TOTAL	572	100.0	572	100.0	572	100.0

TABLE C-29 *Rating of item analysis form for instructional decisions*

| | Instructional Decision | | | | | |
| | Planning | | Grouping | | Remed/Accel | |
Rating	n	%	n	%	n	%
Not Important	69	12.2	84	14.8	77	13.6
Slightly Important	65	11.5	74	13.0	64	11.3
Important	156	27.5	144	25.4	148	26.1
Very Important	91	16.0	84	14.8	93	16.4
Crucial	21	3.7	17	3.0	21	3.7
Not Available	165	29.1	165	29.0	165	29.0
Missing	4	.7	4	.7	4	.7
TOTAL	572	100.0	572	100.0	572	100.0

TABLE C-30 *Ratings of usefulness of Report A for instructional decisions*

| | Rating | | | | | | | | | |
| Instructional | Not Useful | | Slightly Useful | | Useful | | Very Useful | | Crucial | |
Decision	n	%	n	%	n	%	n	%	n	%
Analyzing	112	19.9	210	37.3	173	30.7	59	10.5	9	1.6
Interp/Students	135	24.0	231	41.0	135	23.6	52	9.2	10	1.8
Interp/Parents	142	25.2	233	41.4	132	23.4	49	8.6	7	1.2
Grouping	134	23.8	208	37.0	170	30.2	48	8.5	2	.4
Remediation	117	20.8	209	37.2	172	30.6	55	9.8	9	1.6
Acceleration	129	23.0	203	36.1	165	29.4	55	9.8	10	1.7
Planning	142	25.3	212	37.7	155	27.6	46	8.2	7	8.2
Overall Eval.	113	20.1	250	44.5	159	28.3	33	5.9	7	1.2

TABLE C-31 *Ratings of usefulness of Report B for instructional decisions*

Instructional Decision	Rating									
	Not Useful		Slightly Useful		Useful		Very Useful		Crucial	
	n	%	n	%	n	%	n	%	n	%
Analyzing	7	1.2	81	14.4	298	52.9	155	28.5	22	3.9
Interp/Students	7	1.2	62	11.0	280	49.7	186	33.0	28	5.0
Interp/Parents	6	1.1	66	11.7	270	48.0	196	34.8	25	4.4
Grouping	19	3.4	80	14.2	285	50.7	169	30.1	9	1.6
Remediation	9	1.6	72	12.8	283	50.4	185	32.9	13	2.3
Acceleration	17	3.0	86	15.3	275	49.0	171	30.5	12	2.1
Planning	17	3.0	68	12.1	269	48.0	186	33.2	21	3.7
Overall Eval.	7	1.2	59	10.5	303	53.9	182	32.4	11	2.0

Table C-32 *Ratings of Usefulness of Report C for Instructional Decisions*

Instructional Decision	Rating									
	Not Useful		Slightly Useful		Useful		Very Useful		Crucial	
	n	%	n	%	n	%	n	%	n	%
Analyzing	6	1.1	26	4.6	155	27.5	287	51.0	89	15.8
Interp/Students	8	1.4	23	4.1	129	22.9	292	51.9	111	19.7
Interp/Parents	7	1.2	22	3.9	133	23.6	294	52.2	107	19.0
Grouping	17	3.0	30	5.3	145	25.8	276	49.1	94	16.7
Remediation	9	1.6	24	4.3	137	24.3	293	52.0	100	17.8
Acceleration	14	2.5	38	6.8	131	23.3	287	51.1	92	16.4
Planning	11	2.0	21	3.7	110	19.5	293	52.0	128	22.7
Overall Eval.	8	1.4	18	3.2	121	21.5	305	54.3	110	19.6

APPENDIX D
Sampling Methods

The sample consists of ninth grade teachers of reading, language arts, remedial mathematics and mathematics. Ninth grade teachers were selected for the study since the eighth grade CRT is administered in March, and the report forms with the test results are returned to the schools in May. Eighth grade teachers would be able to use the test results to evaluate curriculum and instruction during the past year, and to prepare revisions for the following eighth grade class. There would not be sufficient time remaining in the school year for them to use the test results to provide remediation or review for students in their classes.

Consequently, ninth grade teachers would be those most likely to use the eighth grade CRT results to assess the abilities of these students in order to plan instruction suited to their needs. In addition, the eighth grade CRT results provide useful information to ninth grade teachers concerning those students who may need additional instruction to prepare them for success on the Basic Skills Tests administered in the tenth grade.

The eighth grade CRT tests reading and mathematics. After consultation with the Georgia State mathematics and language arts curriculum coordinators, it was determined that ninth grade teachers of language arts and/or reading were the principal teachers of the content of the Reading CRT. Similarly, ninth grade mathematics and remedial mathematics teachers are the principal teachers of the content tested by the Mathematics CRT. It was decided therefore to survey remedial mathematics, mathematics, language arts and reading teachers to determine their use of test information in their respective fields.

It was assumed that any difference in test use may be greater between schools than within schools, and greater between school districts than within school districts since the emphasis placed on test use by administrators would be similar in the same school or school system. The sample was designed to sample widely throughout the school districts of the state, with small numbers of teachers selected from each school.

The sample selection procedure was designed to select teachers representative of the teacher population throughout the state. This was in order to be able to generalize to teachers in schools that varied on such variables as school organization, size, and metropolitan status. Two stage cluster sampling was selected to meet these goals. The initial stage used sampling with probabilities proportional to size (PPS), the second stage used random sampling (Jaeger, 1984). The sampling frame for the initial stage of sampling was provided by the Division of Standards and Assessment, Office of Planning and Development of the Georgia

Department of Education. It consisted of a list of all schools in Georgia with ninth grades, the districts in which they were located, and the numbers of pupils in the school.

Stage One, Cluster Sampling

Sampling with PPS provides for the numbering of the elements of the sampling frame so that schools with larger student and teacher populations would have a greater probability of being selected than schools with fewer students and teachers. The clusters to be selected in this stage were schools with ninth grades. Twelve schools with less than 25 students were removed from the sampling frame, leaving 353 schools with ninth grades. The schools in this initial sampling frame ranged in size from 50 pupils to 789 pupils. It was decided to select clusters so that a population mean or proportion could be estimated with an error limit of .5. With 353 schools included in the population, this resulted in a requirement of sampling 136 schools. Five additional schools were sampled in case some did not choose to cooperate in the study, bringing the total number of clusters in the first stage to 141.

The first step in two-stage cluster sampling with probability proportional to size was to compute the cumulative number of students in schools with ninth grades. There were 92,332 students in schools with ninth grades in Georgia. A 5-digit number was read from a random number table. The number will lie between 00,000 and 99,999. The selected random number is multiplied by .92332 (the number of elements in the population divided by 100,000). This gives a random number between 0 and 92,332. The school with the same number as drawn from the table was selected for inclusion in the study. The process was repeated until 141 schools were selected.

The 141 schools selected in the first stage represented 90 school districts selected from 174 school districts in the state. Each school district has an appointed district-wide test coordinator who has the responsibility of serving as a liaison between the district and the state student assessment program. The 90 test coordinators for the selected school districts were contacted by Dr. Stan Bernknopf, Coordinator of Student Assessment for the Georgia Department of Education, informed about the project and asked for their cooperation in providing names of ninth grade language arts, reading, remedial mathematics and mathematics teachers for each of the schools selected. Forms were provided for the test coordinators to use at this stage. (See Figure A-1, and Figure A-2, of Appendix A for the letter and form used during this stage of the sampling.) The test coordinators provided names of teachers for all 141 schools selected in the initial sample.

Stage Two, Random Sampling

In the second stage of sampling two groups of teachers were formed. The first group consisted of teachers of language arts and reading and the second group was composed of teachers of remedial mathematics and mathematics. The teachers in the reading/language arts group were assigned consecutive numbers, as were the teachers in the remedial mathematics/mathematics group. There were 704 teachers of reading/language arts in one sampling frame, and 745 teachers of remedial mathematics/mathematics in the other sampling frame. The sex of the teachers in the sampling frames was estimated by examining the names and classifying them as male and female. The breakdown by sex for the language arts/reading sampling frame was 492 female, 102 male, and 110, sex not classifiable. The breakdown by sex for the remedial mathematics/mathematics sampling frame was 445 female, 201 male, and 99, sex not classifiable.

Random sampling was then used to select the final teacher participants in the study.

Sample Size

The data to be collected from the second stage of the sample would be used to make estimates from the data about the proportion of means or teachers making use of a particular report form, or making instructional decisions. It was desired that this estimation be done with a specified level of precision, that is, that the means or proportions be estimated with a low level of error. (The difference between the mean of a specific sample and the population mean, $\bar{y} - \bar{Y}$, is called the error of estimate). It was decided that the error of estimate for this study should be .5. The sample size needed to estimate a population proportion with a probability of .95 of making an error not larger than .5 would require a sample of 200 teachers for each subject group (mathematics/remedial mathematics and language arts/reading). Funds were provided by the Georgia Testing Program, an agency contracted by the Georgia State Board of Education, for sampling 400 teachers per subject.

In summary, two-stage cluster sampling was used with the first stage selecting as clusters schools proportional to the size of the school, and the second stage using random sampling of teachers. It was determined that at least 200 teachers per subject group would be needed to be able to make reliable estimates about the population of teachers to which it was wished to generalize. Since funds were available to sample 400 teachers per subject group, the final sampling frame therefore consisted of 400 ninth grade teachers of language arts/reading and 400 ninth grade teachers of remedial mathematics/mathematics selected from 141 schools in 90 school districts.

Section VII
Comparative Experimental Methods in Educational Research

Comparative Experiments in Educational Research

Andrew C. Porter
Michigan State University

Overview

This introduction to comparative experiments in educational research is organized into four main sections. First, experiments are presented as one formal method for investigating whether or not a specific set of actions causes predictable changes in behavior. Key terms necessary for understanding what experiments are about are defined. In the second section, requirements for arguing cause are considered, and experiments are defined in light of these requirements. Illustrations are provided of both experimental and nonexperimental research, making clear that experiments represent only one form of research.

In the third section, criteria are presented for judging the quality of an experiment. The first criterion concerns the ambiguity in deciding which of several possibilities were the causal factors in an experiment. The criterion is called internal validity. The second criterion, precision, reflects a concern for the accuracy of experimental results. The third criterion is called external validity and reflects the fact that a good experiment provides results that can be generalized for use elsewhere.

Having defined what an experiment is and how to judge its quality, the role of experiments in educational research is considered in the fourth and final section of the paper. Here, the strengths and limitations of experiments are outlined.

Starting With a Question

Much of what educators do they do with the belief that through their actions students will profit in some way. Not surprisingly, therefore, a great deal of educational research is conducted with an eye toward seeing whether beliefs about alternative educational practices are correct. For example, is individualized instruction to be preferred over whole-group instruction? What are the relative advantages among different techniques of teacher questioning? Is it better to place study questions at the front or the back of chapters in a textbook? These questions have in common a concern for choosing among alternative educational practices. If I do this, will the result be better than if I do something else? Experiments represent one formal method for investigating the relative merits of educational practices.

Most experiments begin with just such a broad and general question as which is better, individualized or whole-group instruction. Certainly it would be nice to know the answer to this general question, but unfortunately the question has many interpretations. Each interpretation might result in a different answer. For example, what exactly is meant by individualized instruction? Does it mean students working separately with a common set of materials but at their own pace? Alternatively it could mean each student receives a different set of materials designed to meet the student's particular interests and learning style. And what is meant by whole-group instruction? Are you imagining teacher lectures or are you imagining group discussions? Any of these alternative interpretations would be consistent with the initial question, and the goals of instruction have still to be considered. Are cognitive skills of interest and, if so, in what subject matter area? Some people would be equally interested (or even more interested) in student affect, such as self-concept and how the student feels toward school and learning. Finally, under what conditions are individualized and whole-group instruction to be compared? Is the interest in school learning, or was something else such as military training the context of interest? If the initial general question brought school learning to your mind, what types of teachers and students did you imagine? The point is that a general question about which is preferred among alternative educational practices allows a very large number of interpretations, each of which might lead to a different specific question and so a different answer. If there are different answers depending upon the specific interpretation, then in that sense the general question has no answer.

Hypotheses

Thus, a very important part of experimental research is to take a general question and restate it as one or more of its specific interpretations. The end result of translating a general question into a statement of belief about specific alternative practices is an *hypothesis*. In hypotheses, the alternative practices would represent what is called an independent variable. A variable is simply something that can differ, for example, from student to student, teacher to teacher, or school to school. Since students might be taught by either individualized or by whole-group instruction, those two methods of instruction represent a variable. The goals of the methods of instruction represent what are called dependent variables. In the example about individualized and whole-group instruction, the goal might be to increase reading comprehension. Reading comprehension would then be the dependent variable in the hypothesis. Clearly, reading comprehension differs from student to student, making reading comprehension a variable.

Independent and Dependent Variables

So experiments begin with a general question which is then made into a specific statement of belief called an hypothesis. Two important parts of an hypothesis are the independent variable and the dependent variable. Both the independent and the dependent variables represent characteristics that can be used to describe differences which are of interest, for example, differences among students. The *independent variable* is something that is believed to predict or bring about other differences (e.g., method of instruction). The resulting differences represent the *dependent variable* (e.g., reading comprehension).

Experiments, then, are conducted to check the validity of an hypothesis. For example, it might be hypothesized that:

> Individualized instruction results in better reading comprehension than does whole-group instruction.

Still, the independent variable, type of instruction, and the dependent variable, reading comprehension, need more explicit definition prior to conducting an experiment. The objective is to state an hypothesis that is specific enough that it is either generally true or generally false.

The idea of a statement being either generally true or generally false is very important to experiments. It must be possible to imagine a study which could lead you either to believe more strongly in your original hypothesis or to reject that hypothesis and so come to change your original belief. In short, an hypothesis must be testable. The original question about individualized and whole-group instruction was not directly testable because it was too general. For example, answering the original question would have required considering all different methods of individualized instruction and all different methods of whole group instruction. Similarly, all of the different possible conceptions of reading comprehension would need to be considered.

Population

Even given explicit definitions for the types of instruction and reading comprehension, the hypothesis remains ambiguous as to the conditions for which it is to be true. The validity of the hypothesis may depend on answers to such questions as: What types of students? What types of teachers? In what types of physical arrangements will students be learning? The answers to these and similar questions must be provided before the hypothesis is complete. The answers define what is called the *population* for the hypothesis. A *population*, then, is the collection of instances for which the statement about independent and dependent variables is believed to hold. When an experiment is done to test an hypothesis, then it is done with the intention of concluding that the hypothesis is either true or false for a well-defined population (e.g., all fourth graders in the state of Michigan who are in public schools and who have teachers with three or more years of teaching experience).

You may be thinking that individualized versus whole-group instruction is a positively awful example to select for introducing the concept of experiments in education. After all, doesn't everybody know that individualized instruction is superior to whole-group instruction? But in fact the evidence is contradictory on this general contention, which is exactly the point. It seems to depend on the particulars (see Good and Brophy's *Looking in Classrooms*, 1984, for a summary of this point and supporting research).

Arguing Cause

At a minimum, then, an hypothesis specifies an independent variable, a dependent variable, and a population. But experiments are not appropriate for testing all hypotheses. Experiments are limited to concern for hypotheses about independent variables that cause changes in dependent variables. The important word is "cause." When contrasting individualized and whole-group instruction, the interest is in whether a student will read with better comprehension if he or she is taught with one method rather than the other. In short, does method of instruction *cause* changes in reading comprehension?

Some Necessary Conditions

While philosophers debate the precise meaning of the word cause, there are three conditions that are commonly held as necessary for arguing that an independent variable causes predictable changes in a dependent variable. First, changes in the independent variable must precede in time changes in the dependent variable. Second, the independent and dependent variables must be correlated. *Correlated* simply means that the experimental condition a subject experienced (individualized or whole-group instruction) is useful in predicting the subject's performance on the dependent variable (reading comprehension). This would be the case, for example, if one observed that the average achievement in reading comprehension of students who received individualized instruction was higher than that for students who received whole-group instruction. Third, there must be no plausible third variable that explains why a correlation was found between the independent and dependent variables. The independent variable alone must be the reason that a correlation was found. For example, it should not be the case that brighter students were more likely to receive individualized instruction than they were to receive whole-group instruction, since differences in the brightness of students would then be a plausible third-variable explanation for the correlation observed.

Clearly it is difficult to design and conduct a study which will provide a convincing argument of cause. For example, there are many nonexperimental studies which have found that students who have relatively positive self-concepts of academic ability have also achieved relatively well on cognitive skills in school and vice versa. But these nonexperimental studies leave ambiguous which came first, self-concept or achievement. Even when it seems clear that the independent variable preceded in time differences in the dependent variable, there are an infinity of "third" variables that singly or in combination might have been responsible for a correlation between the independent and dependent variables. To further complicate matters, a lack of correlation can also be due to the effects of "third" variables. For example, many have argued that evaluations conducted to investigate the effects of compensatory education have been biased in that the noncompensatory conditions had the more able students. Since students receiving compensatory education start out behind, they will be doing well just to catch up with students not receiving compensatory education. Some claim, therefore, that evaluations which report no difference between compensatory education and no compensatory education are really evidence in favor of the success of compensatory education (e.g., Campbell & Erlebacher, 1970).

Since a great deal of educational research, not just experiments, is used to support statements of cause, the three conditions for cause just given (i.e., temporal antecedence, correlation of experimental conditions and outcomes, and the lack of plausible alternative explanations) are useful in planning and understanding educational research, regardless of research method. In educational research, even when the word "cause" is not used explicitly, it may still be that cause is the interpretation. This is equally true for the researcher and for the individual readers of a research report. For example, all educational evaluations conducted to assess an innovation, or to aid decisions about which educational practices to prefer, are attempts to establish a causal link between practice and outcomes. Some researchers go out of their way to avoid use of the word cause, because the criteria for arguing cause are so demanding. But many words carry the connotation of cause: produce, create, induce, evoke, elicit, affect, institute, bring about. If cause is of interest, then arguing cause should be one of the explicit goals of the research. The reporting of results and the critiquing of their validity will then be done with both eyes open for plausible alternative explanations of results.

So experiments are done to test hypotheses about causal relationships between independent and dependent variables. But what are experiments and what are they not?

Experiments: A More Formal Definition

The word "experiment" is used a great deal, and in a number of different contexts. For purposes of describing educational research methods, placing some limits on what is meant by an experiment is useful. First, an experiment is comparative. This means that there are at least two different conditions represented by the independent variable, as in the example, individualized versus whole-group instruction. Second, the independent variable is under the direct control of the researcher. For purposes here, then, an experiment is not the study of naturally occurring changes in the independent variable; rather, it is the study of planned changes. In the words of the famous statistician George Box (1966), "To find out what happens to a system when you interfere with it you have to interfere with it (not just passively observe it)." Third, the decision about which subjects will receive which experimental condition is made randomly. Random assignment is a process which gives each subject an equally likely chance of experiencing any one of the experimental conditions under investigation. These three limits are motivated by the three conditions described earlier for establishing cause.

Experiments: An Illustration

An illustration may help. A study was conducted to investigate the accuracy of diagnoses of school psychologists (Frame, Clarizio, & Porter, 1984). Briefly, it was hypothesized that the diagnosis of a learning disabled student depends on the student's race (black/white), socioeconomic status (high/low) and general achievement level of the school which the student attends (high/low). The school psychologists were all from the state of Michigan and were experienced professionals. The experimental task did not involve diagnoses of actual students. Rather, a single student was represented by a file containing the full range of information that school psychologists attempt to collect prior to making a diagnosis. Thus, the main difference between actual practice and the experimental conditions was that instead of working with a child, the school psychologists requested information from the experimenter about a simulated child.

As you have probably concluded, the independent variables of the study were the simulated case's race, socioeconomic status, and school achievement level. As is usually true, there were several dependent variables including the nature of the diagnosis and the extent to which diagnoses among school psychologists were in agreement.

By considering all possible combinations of race, socioeconomic status, and school achievement, eight experimental conditions were created. For example, one such condition was a white student from a family with high socioeconomic status who attends a school where achievement is high. Because a simulated student was used, it was possible to keep all information about the student the same for each of the eight experimental conditions except, of course, the three independent variables. School psychologists were then randomly assigned to diagnose one of the eight simulated students, and their diagnoses were recorded.

Consider again the three requirements placed on experiments. The study was comparative for each of the three independent variables. Each of the independent variables was under the direct control of the researcher. Finally, the decision about which school psychologists would diagnose which experimental conditions was made randomly. The study was an experiment. Incidentally, diagnoses were found to differ according to experimental conditions. For example, school psychologists were less likely to prescribe special class instruction for the black simulated student than for the white simulated student.

To further understand what experiments are, consider some types of research which are not experiments. First, only research studies which are designed to test the validity of statements about independent variables causing changes in dependent variables are candidates for consideration as experiments. This immediately rules out large classes of research studies. For example, studies done to investigate the utility of the Graduate Record Examination for predicting success in graduate school are not experiments. In general, studies which investigate the utility and fairness of criteria used for making decisions about educational opportunities are not experimental studies. Studies with the purpose of describing education as it is are not experiments either, since they lack an interest in causal relationships. A well-known example is the Gallup poll of public opinion about education.

Even research to investigate causal relationships between independent and dependent variables is not always experimental. For example, most research on the effectiveness of alternative teaching strategies has not been experimental, though there are exceptions. The typical study of teaching practices involves testing student achievement in the fall and spring of a school year in several classrooms. During the year observations are made to describe teaching practices. The researcher attempts to relate observed teaching practices (the independent variables) to student gains in achievement (the dependent variables). In this research the independent variables are not under the control of the researcher and there is no random assignment of students to teaching practices. The research is not experimental. Still the interest is in determining what teaching practices result in greatest growth in student achievement, a causal question.

Sometimes studies conducted to investigate the utility of an educational intervention are not experiments. A common method is to test student performance against the goals of an innovation, give the students the innovation, then test the students a second time. For example, the innovation might be some form of computer-aided instruction. While such a study gives the researcher direct control over the independent variable (before innovation versus after innovation), it does not involve random assignment of students to those two conditions. Necessarily, all students are first without the innovation and later all students receive the innovation. An experiment would randomly assign some students to receive the innovation and other students to not receive the innovation.

Three Goals of Experimental Design

Simply being able to distinguish between what is and what is not an experiment is not terribly useful. What is more important, perhaps, is knowing how to assess the strengths and weaknesses of an experiment.

In order to understand the advantages and difficulties of experiments for testing hypotheses about cause/effect relationships, it is useful to understand three goals of experimental design. The first goal is directly related to the interest in cause and is sometimes stated as "an experiment should have internal validity." Consider again the hypothesis that "individualized instruction results in better reading comprehension than does whole-group instruction." To test this hypothesis, a researcher might have some students taught by a particular method of individualized instruction and some other students taught by a particular method of whole-group instruction. Students in both groups would then be given a test of reading comprehension. If method of instruction is the only plausible interpretation for any differences in reading comprehension between the two groups of students in the study, then method of instruction must be the cause of those differences. If the independent variable is the only reasonable explanation for differences in the dependent variable, the study is said to have internal validity.

The second goal of experimental design reflects the possibility that differences among individual students on reading comprehension may be considerable, regardless of the method of instruction used to teach these skills. For example, even if individualized instruction was somewhat better than whole-group instruction, it would be quite likely that several of the best students who received whole-group instruction would have better reading comprehension skills than several of the poorest students who received individualized instruction. Results for these students make more difficult the objective of determining whether whole-group instruction or individualized instruction was better. The second goal of experimental design, then, is to conduct a study in which even small differences caused by the independent variable are measured with sufficient precision that they will not be overlooked, even though they are embedded in relatively large individual differences among subjects. This goal is called precision.

The third goal of experimental design is that valid generalizations can be made from the study. For example, if individualized instruction was superior to whole-group instruction in a particular study, the next question would be: Does the finding generalize to other students, teachers, and conditions? To the extent that the study had external validity, at least some of these desired generalizations would be appropriate.

Thus, when interpreting the results of an experiment, or when designing an experiment, the experiment should be considered from the perspectives of internal validity, precision, and external validity. Each of these three goals is discussed here separately and in greater detail.

Internal Validity

Judging the extent to which you believe an experiment has internal validity is equivalent to deciding the extent to which you believe that at least part of the correlation between the independent and dependent variables was caused by the independent variable. How effective was the design of the experiment in allowing you to rule out explanations, other than the independent variable, for differences between experimental conditions on the dependent variable? Clearly, if the brightest students received individualized instruction and the poorest students received whole-group instruction, a finding in favor of individualized instruction would be suspect.

Confounding Variables

The most important concept of judging the internal validity of an experiment is the concept of confounding variables. A variable is said to be confounded with the independent variable of a study if the two variables are inseparable. In the example above, brightness of student was confounded with method of instruction. Brightness of student is then an explanation for differences between the two groups of students taught by different methods of instruction. Of course, method of instruction is also an explanation, and so the two explanations are confounded. An experiment has internal validity, therefore, to the extent that no variables are confounded with the independent variable.

Random Assignment

As stated previously, a crucial part of the definition of a comparative experiment is that random assignment is used by the experimenter in determining which subjects will experience which experimental condition. The essential idea behind the process of random assignment is that for an initial pool of subjects, each has an equally likely chance of being assigned to any one of the experimental conditions to be compared. Random assignment is, therefore, a way of guarding against confounding variables.

Before considering the strengths and weaknesses of random assignment of subjects to experimental conditions, a brief description of the process is appropriate. Imagine that you have 40 subjects that you wish to randomly assign to one or the other of two experimental conditions. What is needed is a process that gives each of the 40 subjects an equal chance of being assigned a particular experimental condition. One method for random assignment is to use a table of random numbers. The method begins by putting the subjects' names in a list in alphabetical order. A subject can then be represented by a number indicating that subject's position on the list. The table of random numbers has been prepared such that each number has an equally likely chance of having been placed anywhere in the table. The researcher begins reading the table in any row and any column. Reading from the table of random numbers, the first 20 numbers between 1 and 40 indicate the positions of subjects on the list of subjects to be assigned one of the two experimental conditions. The remaining subjects are assigned to the other experimental condition.

In thinking about the value of random assignment in eliminating confounding variables, a few points are worth emphasizing. First, random assignment takes place at the beginning of an experiment and is immediately followed by the experimental conditions. The dependent variable is not observed until the end of the experiment. Thus, for experiments, the independent variable precedes the dependent variable. The temporal antecedence requirement for arguing cause is unambiguously established. In this sense, all experiments include at least three points in time: (a) random assignment, followed by (b) application of experimental conditions, and finally, (c) observation of the dependent variables. Second, randomization is a process of assignment, not a result of assignment. It is virtually impossible to look at the composition of experimental groups created by someone else and from that to judge accurately whether or not they were created randomly. Third, randomization creates comparison groups at the outset of the experiment that differ only by chance on the infinity of possible confounding variables. Randomization not only eliminates confounding variables the researcher may have considered, it also eliminates confounding variables the researcher may have overlooked. This is the real power of random assignment.

The utility of random assignment for controlling confounding variables must, of course, be tempered by the realization that the process is based on chance, and by chance alone, experimental groups will differ at least to some extent. For example, an experiment used to compare individualized and whole-group instruction would begin by identifying a pool of subjects large enough to institute both methods of instruction. If the initial pool for assignment consisted of only two subjects, however, the two groups would differ at the outset of the experiment to the same degree that the two subjects differed (and that might be considerable). In such a case, many characteristics of the two subjects would be totally confounded with the independent variable and would constitute a major threat to the goal of providing a strong statement about cause. If there were four students in the initial pool, the chances would be a little less that the best students would end up in a single group. The more students in the initial pool, the smaller the chance that there will be worrisome differences between experimental groups at the outset of the experiment. Still, chance plays a part in the final results of any experiment.

Assessing the Utility of Random Assignment

Imagine 20 students randomly assigned to receive a version of individualized instruction and 20 students to receive a version of whole-group instruction. One method for delivering the two modes of instruction would be to form two experimental classes of 20 students each and then have one teacher teach the individualized instruction class while another teacher taught the whole-group instruction class. Even if the two teachers were randomly assigned to classes, characteristics of teachers would be confounded with methods of instruction. For most people, this would represent a serious threat to internal validity. One teacher might be more effective, regardless of method of instruction.

One way to unconfound teachers from experimental conditions would be to identify several existing classrooms of students each with a different teacher and then randomly assign classrooms to methods of instruction. Each method would then be represented by several teachers. Of course, the need for several teachers increases the cost of the experiment. You may be wondering, why not have one teacher teach both classrooms? While this would prevent teachers from being confounded with method of instruction, the strategy introduces another confounding variable. If one teacher taught both classrooms, then one classroom would have to be taught first and the other second. Among other difficulties, this confounds both order of presentation and time of day with the independent variable, methods of instruction. The possibilities for confounding variables to enter a design are virtually unlimited.

The internal validity that is gained through random assignment of subjects to experimental conditions is the real strength of experiments, compared to other research methods. Consider again a typical study of teaching practices. Several classrooms and their teachers are recruited, and students are tested on school achievement variables in both fall and spring. The researcher observes teaching practices during the school year and attempts to relate them to student gains in achievement. Useful as these studies may be, they always suffer from the presence of confounding variables. There is always ambiguity in deciding whether or not relationships between teaching practices and student achievement gains are caused by the teaching practices. What confounding variables are you imagining? Probably the first one that came to your mind was student aptitude. The most able students will probably have the biggest achievement gains regardless of the quality of the instruction they receive. There will be a tendency for the teaching behaviors of teachers who have the most able students to appear as though they produced the greatest gains in student achievement.

Teachers of the most able students may have actually employed the most effective teaching methods, or it may simply be that whatever teaching practices were used with the most able students, they would appear to be most effective. There are, of course, many other potentially confounding variables for this nonexperimental design.

The ever-popular pretest/posttest design is yet another context in which to understand the implication of confounding variables. One group of students takes a test on the dependent variable, they then receive an educational innovation, and finally they are tested once more on the dependent variable. The researcher is interested in student gains on the dependent variable and would like to attribute those gains to the innovation. But what are the possibilities for confounding to have occurred between the two times of testing? Campbell and Stanley (1963), in their classic chapter on experimental and quasi-experimental designs, have provided a taxonomy of the types of possible confounding. Students may do better on the second test because they learned from taking the first test; the second test may be different from the first in some way which makes it easier; the students themselves are older and more mature; or during the course of the study the students may have received some experiences (other than the experimental condition) that changed them and improved their performance on the dependent variable.

Experiments are probably the single most effective method for ruling out confounding variables. Experiments are not, however, infallible indicators of the presence or absence of causal relationships. Randomization only starts experimental groups out in the right way. Absence of confounding variables at the beginning of an experiment does not guarantee absence of confounding variables at the end of an experiment. There are plenty of opportunities for important confounding variables to creep into the design while the study is being conducted. Subjects may drop out of the experimental groups at different rates or for different reasons. Observations on the dependent variables may inadvertently result in observers being confounded with experimental conditions, or even reflect experimenter bias. Data can be incorrectly coded in ways that create confounding. In fact, anything that happens systematically during the course of the study and results in different treatment of subjects in one experimental condition from subjects in another must either be a treatment or a confounding variable.

There is no foolproof method for insuring internal validity. Experiments can be a big help, but even experiments differ greatly in their ability to convince. One hopes that as confounding variables are identified (usually in retrospect), their probable effects can be judged either by common sense or from the research literature and in that way be taken into account.

Precision

For an experiment to have internal validity is important, but that alone is not enough. An experiment must also be designed so that if the independent variable does cause differences in the dependent variable, those differences will be detected. In short, the experiment must have precision.

Because of random assignment, chance plays a part in the results of any experiment. Through random assignment there is always the chance that by bad luck all students of a particular type are assigned to the same experimental condition. One way to think about precision is that the more precise an experiment, the less likely it is that the experiment will yield large chance differences between experimental groups.

To better understand this concept of precision, it may be useful to digress a bit and consider the typical ways that results of experiments are reported. At its simplest, an experiment can be thought of as describing the average difference on a dependent variable between two experimental conditions. Thus an experiment might report that, on the average, students who received individualized instruction scored four points higher on a particular test of reading comprehension than did students who received whole-group instruction. Since subjects were randomly assigned to experimental conditions, an important question remains. Is it reasonable to believe that individualized instruction was more effective than whole-group instruction, or should the experimenter conclude that the four-point difference was likely to happen by the chance results of random assignment? Deciding between these two alternative interpretations of the four-point difference is an important aspect of experimental research.

Statistical Significance

The results of an experiment are often reported as "statistically significant" or not. If statistically significant, it means that the researcher decided the difference between experimental conditions did not happen by chance. If not statistically significant, the interpretation is that the study failed to provide evidence of the superiority of one experimental condition over another. There are rules for deciding whether or not the results of an experiment were statistically significant. These rules are called the procedures of inferential statistics.

Briefly, the rules of statistical inference are used by the experimenter to decide for his or her particular study how large the observed difference between experimental conditions must be to be judged statistically significant. Of course, the more certain the experimenter wishes to be that a difference called statistically significant was not due to chance, the larger the required difference must be. Without going into details, the procedures of statistical significance begin with the experimenter stating how willing he or she is to make a mistake when concluding that a true difference does exist. A common criterion is to take a 5% chance of making such a mistake.

Returning to the concept of precision, sometimes experiments result in quite large differences between experimental conditions, and still the rules of statistical inference lead to a decision of no significance. This is a particularly frustrating situation. In one sense, the difference was no larger than might be expected by chance. The researcher is forced to conclude that the independent variable did not affect the dependent variable. The only information gained is that the experiment lacked precision. In fact, this could probably have been predicted without conducting the experiment.

In short, the second goal of experimental design is to cónduct a study such that if a "large difference" is found between experimental conditions, that difference will also be judged by the rules of statistical inference to be significant. ·

Judging the Importance of a Difference

Before considering ways in which the precision of an experiment can be enhanced, a comment on the cavalier use of the term "large difference" is in order. What may be a large difference in the eyes of one person may not be a large difference in the eyes of another. How would you go about deciding what constitutes a large difference in average reading comprehension between individualized and whole-group instruction? Would you consider the four-point difference I mentioned earlier to be large or important if you knew it had been caused by differences in the method of instruction? Of course you can't say. You are probably wondering about the types of items on the test of reading comprehension. You may also be wondering what types of decisions are to be made about school practices based on the four-point difference. You may even be wondering what types of students were involved in the study. Deciding what constitutes large or important differences is a highly personal activity. There is no right or wrong answer.

Saying that a difference found between experimental conditions was statistically significant is not synonomous with saying that a difference was large or important. Using statistical significance as an indication of importance is a common mistake but one that should be avoided. Statistical significance only indicates that a difference was *not* due to the chance consequences of random assignment. A statement of statistical significance leaves completely unanswered the question, how important was the difference that can be attributed to experimental conditions? It is possible to design a study which is so precise that a difference as small as a fraction of a test score point would be judged significant by methods of statistical inference.

Confidence Intervals

While it has been common practice to report the results of an experiment as simply statistically significant or not, many argue that this practice does not go far enough (e.g., Carver, 1978). First, reporting of results as statistically significant or not encourages the confusion that statistical significance implies importance. Second, a researcher is not likely to be satisfied by knowing simply whether or not a difference happened by chance. A researcher will probably want to have some idea about how big the difference was. For these reasons, many researchers prefer to report the size of difference found between experimental conditions and then to indicate that because of random assignment the difference might have been a little higher or a little lower. The procedure of establishing an upper or lower limit on an observed difference between experimental conditions is called building a confidence interval. Confidence intervals represent an alternative to reporting results as simply statistically significant or not.

Basically, the same procedures are used to build confidence intervals as are used to decide whether or not a difference was statistically significant. Returning to the example of a four-point difference between individualized and whole-group instruction, a confidence interval could have indicated that the true difference between instructional methods might be as low as three points or as high as five points. This information indicates that there was a statistically significant difference between methods of instruction and also provides a range of values, three to five, for thinking about how big the difference actually was. Alternatively, had the interval included zero (i.e., no difference between methods), the conclusion would have been that the difference was not statistically significant. Just as deciding on statistical significance requires setting a criterion level for chance errors, so does building a confidence interval. If a researcher were willing to take a 5% chance of mistakenly thinking a difference was real, this same researcher might decide instead to build a 95% confidence interval.

If a confidence interval is used to report the results of an experiment, precision can be thought of in terms of the width of the interval. The narrower the interval, the more precise the experiment. An experiment with perfect precision would yield a confidence interval with no width at all. The interval would be a single point.

Improving Precision

So precision is an important attribute for any experiment to have. Without precision, even an internally valid experiment may fail to detect important differences between experimental conditions and mistakenly leave the impression that the various conditions lead to equivalent results. But how can the precision of an experiment be made acceptable?

The most direct method for increasing the precision of an experiment is to increase the number of subjects assigned to each experimental condition. As indicated earlier, the larger the number of subjects to be randomly assigned, the less likely it is that random assignment will result in unusual groups of subjects. Increasing the number of subjects is often expensive, however, and there are other ways to improve precision.

A straightforward way to make sure that not all of the most able students are assigned to a single experimental condition is first to group students according to aptitude. Then, for each aptitude group of students, randomly assign equal numbers to each experimental condition. This insures that each experimental condition has subjects with similar aptitude levels. The procedure is called blocking and is one way to improve precision.

There are several other ways to improve precision, some of which are quite complicated and technical. For illustration, consider just one more. Clearly, if all subjects for an experiment were identical, random assignment could not result in an unusual composition of experimental groups. Precision would be assured. You are probably saying that identical subjects are an impossibility. In a sense you are right. Still, some researchers have used identical twins as subjects in an attempt to improve precision. My earlier example of an experiment to study the accuracy of school psychologists provides another illustration. In that study school psychologists diagnosed a single simulated student. Using a simulated student increased precision over what it would have been had each psychologist diagnosed a different actual student.

External Validity

The first two goals of experimental design, internal validity and precision, are primarily concerned with interpreting the results of a particular study as it was conducted. But an experiment would have little utility if the results only revealed what was true for that particular study. The third goal of experimental design, then, is to have an experiment from which it is possible to make valid generalizations. The goal is called external validity. The word "external" indicates an interest in concluding that the findings of a particular study have validity beyond or external to that study.

One way to think about external validity is to imagine a particular experiment and then attempt to identify situations in which you believe the results might not apply. To illustrate the point, consider again the experiment to investigate the accuracy of diagnoses provided by school psychologists. The experiment used a simulated learning disabled student to investigate the effects of student race, socioeconomic level, and general level of achievement in the school from which the student came. The school psychologists in the study were all experienced professionals recruited from school districts in the state of Michigan. School psychologists were randomly assigned to diagnose one of the eight versions of the simulated student. To what situations would you be willing to generalize the significant finding from this study that school psychologists were less likely to prescribe special class instruction for the black simulated student? To the extent that you would be unwilling to generalize the result, the experiment lacked external validity for you.

In the words of Bracht and Glass (1968),

> threats to external validity appear to fall into two broad classes: (1) those dealing with generalizations to populations of persons (what population of subjects can be expected to behave in the same way as did the . . . experimental subjects?), and (2) those dealing with the 'environment' of the experiment (under what conditions . . . can the same results be expected?).

In the school psychologist experiment, the subjects were experienced school psychologists from the state of Michigan. While the results may be valid for school psychologists in other states and for inexperienced school psychologists, there is no evidence from the experiment that this is so. Clearly, if generalizations are to be made to other states or to inexperienced school psychologists, the grounds for such generalization would need to be based on information not provided by the experiment.

Random Selection

Depending upon how school psychologists were recruited, it might not even be appropriate to generalize the results of the experiment to all experienced school psychologists in the state of Michigan. Ideally, a list of all experienced school psychologists in the state of Michigan would have been identified. The list would represent the population of school psychologists referred to in the hypotheses for the experiment. Participants in the experiment would then be selected from the list, using a process that gave each person on the list an equally likely chance of being selected and ultimately included in the study. The process is called random selection. Random selection from a well-defined population is ideal, because the process insures, within the limits of chance, that the participants in the study are representative of the population from which they were selected. Had random selection been used to select school psychologists, the results of the study could be straightforwardly generalized to the population of experienced school psychologists in the state of Michigan.

Do not confuse random selection with the earlier concept of random assignment. Random selection and random assignment serve two distinctly different purposes. Random assignment is motivated by internal validity and random selection is motivated by external validity. Random assignment is an essential ingredient of an experiment, but random selection is almost never a part of an experiment's design. Rather, subjects are recruited as best they can be, and this was the case for the experienced school psychologists in the example.

Generalizing Across Subjects

How then should the external validity of the experiment with school psychologists be thought about? Is generalization limited to the subjects immediately involved? More generally, since random selection is rarely used in experiments, are the results of experiments typically limited to the subjects used? Most people answer these questions with a decided "no." People who are willing to generalize from an experiment, however, require a careful description of the subjects. The description defines a hypothetical population to be used for purposes of interpreting results.

We already know that the subjects were experienced school psychologists from the state of Michigan. But clearly we need to know more about these psychologists if we are to generalize the results of the experiment. What was meant by the word experienced? What were the theoretical persuasions of the school psychologists? In general, the more complete the description, the easier it becomes to think about the range of external validity of the experiment. Given a thorough description of the subjects in the experiment on school psychologists, people will differ in their willingness to generalize the results. Some people will conclude that the results are even valid for states other than Michigan.

So the results of an experiment may be valid for types of subjects that were not included in the experiment. There is another way, however, that external validity may be threatened even for the types of subjects used. Imagine that the experienced school psychologists could be categorized into two groups. For example, half the school psychologists may have received their training from one institution and the other half from another institution. School psychologists from both institutions are represented in the study and so, on the surface, it would appear that the results can be generalized to both types of school psychologists. But the results of experiments are reported as averages across all subjects. An experiment can indicate no *average* difference between experimental conditions when in fact there *was* a difference between experimental conditions for each of two types of subjects. This apparent paradox will occur when the difference between experimental conditions was in a different direction for each type of subject. The two differences simply cancel each other when the averages are computed.

Generalizing Across Experimental Conditions

Threats to external validity are not limited, however, to concerns about types of subjects. One must also consider the conditions under which the experiment was conducted.

The school psychologist experiment provides fertile ground for illustrating several ways in which experimental conditions can limit external validity. Remember that school psychologists diagnosed a simulated student that was the same in all eight experimental conditions. Clearly, only one example of learning disability was considered. If the results of the study are to be generalized, one would need to know the nature of that specific example of learning disability. The experiment provides no direct evidence as to whether or not the same results would have been obtained for a different type of learning disability.

The school psychologist experiment is also an example of what might be called a laboratory study. The subjects were not working in their natural environment with a real live student. There is no question but that they realized they were in an experiment, though they were not told the purposes of the experiment. Still, one must at least raise the question of whether or not their behavior in the laboratory setting was representative of how they would behave as psychologists in their school districts. Did the subjects merely respond as they felt they should have responded and not as they would ordinarily? Because they were confronted with only a single student, did they perform their work more carefully than when they are under the pressure of a heavy work schedule? Did the experimenter inadvertently reveal a desired set of responses? Unfortunately, the experiment does not provide answers to these questions. Each of us must decide the answers on our own. The point is that these and similar questions should be raised when judging the external validity of any experiment.

Generalizing Across Outcomes

External validity can also be limited to the extent that results apply for only certain narrowly defined dependent variables. To illustrate this point consider again the example of individualized and whole-group instruction. The dependent variable was reading comprehension, but how reading comprehension was to be measured was not made explicit. Suppose the task for each subject was to read some short paragraphs and then to answer a series of multiple-choice questions. If so, how difficult were the passages to be read? What vocabulary was included in the tasks? What was the nature of the multiple-choice questions? Was the subject also asked to demonstrate reading comprehension of longer passages, perhaps a whole book? What type of book? Was comprehension assessed through an oral examination? Was the subject asked to demonstrate that the information acquired from a passage could also be put to use in solving problems? Reading comprehension can mean many different things. A good experiment would include several definitions of reading comprehension as multiple dependent variables so that external validity could be assessed directly.

Experimental conditions can also lead to unintended results. The method of instruction which promotes greatest gains in reading comprehension might at the same time leave subjects with a distaste for reading. Thus, an experiment should reflect a concern for unintended results by including appropriate dependent variables.

Finally, differences on a dependent variable observed immediately following the experiment may not persevere to later points in time. Education is typically interested in practices which promote sustained effects. It may not be valid to generalize from measures taken immediately at the end of an experiment to what will be true weeks, months, or even years later.

Of course, it is impossible to measure subjects on everything that might be of interest. Nevertheless, one should be cautious about generalizing the results for one dependent variable to what is true for another.

Limitations to Experiments

Now you know what experiments are and how to think about their quality against the three criteria of internal validity, precision, and external validity. What remains to be done is to provide a sense of the role of experiments in educational research.

Among all the methods of educational research, experiments provide the most unimpeachable evidence on whether or not an independent variable causes differences in a dependent variable. The key to the internal validity of experiments lies with random assignment. Without random assignment there will always be variables confounded with the independent variable and which, therefore, offer alternative explanations of results. Explanations of cause have greater ambiguity when random assignment is not used.

But comparative experiments are not the sole methodology of educational research. One obvious reason is that not all educational research is interested in questions about what causes what. Even if cause is of interest, however, research methods other than comparative experiments are frequently used. The reasons for this lie primarily with the nature of the research questions asked.

By definition, experiments involve random assignment to experimental conditions. Thus to conduct any experiment, the researcher must first create experimental conditions. Experiments are anticipatory, not retrospective. Clearly, experiments are not appropriate for investigating the antecedents of an historical event. For example, at this time, experiments cannot be used to investigate the effects of the "new mathematics" curriculum reform. In addition, the researcher must have the authority to randomly assign subjects. Even when an educational event has been anticipated, experiments are not always possible. Imagine that a teacher strike is anticipated in a school district and you are interested in determining the effects of the strike on student achievement, teacher/principal relations, and the like. An experiment would require a comparison of striking teachers and nonstriking teachers, and the comparison would need to be built through randomly assigning teachers (or school districts) to the two conditions. Can you imagine an experimenter having the authority to tell some teachers to strike and others not to strike? Here, the requirements of an experiment are clearly impossible.

In addition to these limitations, there is a third reason why experiments are sometimes not used even when cause is of interest. In an experiment, subjects are not left completely to their own choices. In that sense experiments take subjects out of their natural environment. If research questions concern the everyday practices of professional educators, the utility of experiments must be questioned. As indicated earlier, the very fact that subjects know they are part of an experiment may result in a set of behaviors that would not have happened in a similar but naturally occurring situation.

Finally, experiments necessarily focus on a few selected variables. Because creating experimental conditions and random assignment is difficult to accomplish, the typical experiment investigates the causal effects of only a single independent variable. Even the selection of dependent variables is restricted by the requirement that they be formally observed in a way that is common to all subjects. Experiments attempt to facilitate understanding of a few variables well. Sometimes the goal of educational research is to understand *a* community or *a* school so completely that regardless of the situation, it would be possible to accurately predict the actions of the individuals involved. Anthropologically oriented research of this type requires the consideration of many variables simultaneously. Potentially, many of the variables have causal influences on the behaviors of individuals involved. Experiments do not lend themselves well to answering questions about the several points of view within an educational community.

Using Experiments

Given their strengths and limitations just noted, when are experiments used in educational research? If one defines educational research as that research of potential relevance to improving understanding of the processes of education, then presumably a considerable portion of research conducted in the following disciplines is of interest: psychology, sociology, anthropology, economics, history, philosophy, and political science. Of these disciplines, psychology stands out as the predominant user of comparative experiments.

More clearly within the domain of educational research is the research conducted within an educational context by educators. Much of this research has been conducted with an eye toward developing new programs, curricula, and teacher training procedures. Historically, these efforts have been heavily influenced by psychology, and not so surprisingly they evidence considerable use of comparative experiments. However, there has been a strong tendency to drop the requirement of random assignment. This has resulted in a distinction between true experiments, the topic here, and quasi-experiments, which are comparative studies without random assignment. Educational researchers have been too quick to conclude that random assignment was not possible. The overreliance on nonrandomized quasi-experiments has led to a great many results which leave ambiguous the causal antecedents of behavior.

It is impossible to define the range of educational research questions that might profitably be addressed through experiments. Recent publications in journals devoted primarily to educational research report experimental studies of the effects on achievement of: peer tutoring, teacher questioning techniques, sequencing of instructional material, types of teacher lecture notes, different types of feedback on past achievement, and self-pacing versus instructor pacing. In addition, several recent studies investigated the effects on reading comprehension of positioning of questions in text, organization of prose using semantic, temporal, and random strategies, and different types of pictures to accompany the text. There have been experimental studies of the effects of biracial learning teams on race relations, as well as experimental studies on the effects of achievement and aptitude testing on a variety of dependent variables including teacher expectations for student achievement.

Summary

The term experiment means many different things to many different people. In this chapter the term has been limited to a rather narrow, but useful, definition—an investigation, involving random assignment, of the causal relationship between one or more independent variables and one or more dependent variables. The methodological quality of an experiment should be judged against three standards: (a) internal validity, (b) precision, and (c) external validity. No experiments are perfect according to these criteria. When critiquing an experiment, however, a single flaw should not be sufficient, in and of itself, to discount the results. An attempt should be made to estimate, on the basis of common sense and other research, the likely effect of the flaw. Unless there is reasonable evidence to the contrary, the conclusion of the experiment should be tentatively held as correct.

An experiment is a highly focused investigation, the details of which are specified in advance—this is potentially one of its greatest strengths and one of its greatest weaknesses. The strength is that carefully specified experimental procedures allow rigorous control and provide relatively unambiguous results for a limited set of questions. By concentrating on only a few variables, the difficult measurement problems of each can be given careful attention. The weakness is that the original questions may have been misguided. The method is not well suited for midstudy corrections. Further, the highly focused nature of experiments—which facilitates control and precise measurement—may blind the researcher to recognizing difficulties or findings that might have been obvious with a less structured approach.

This brief introduction to experiments in education has touched on a broad number of issues, including defining, conducting, and interpreting educational experiments. Hopefully you have acquired a slightly better appreciation for what experiments can and cannot accomplish in educational research. Perhaps you will even consider undertaking the study necessary to acquire the skills and knowledge that will enable you to critique and conduct experiments in education.

References

Box, G.E.P. (1966). Use and abuse of regression. *Technometrics, 8,* 625–629.

Bracht, G. H., & Glass, G. V. (1968). The external validity of experiments. *American Educational Research Journal, 5,* 437–474.

Campbell, D. T., & Erlebacher, A. E. (1970). How regression artifacts in quasi-experimental evaluations can mistakenly make compensatory education look harmful. In J. Hellmuth (Ed.), *Disadvantaged child, Vol. 3. Compensatory education: A national debate.* New York: Bruner/Mazul.

Campbell, D. T., & Stanley, J. C. (1963). *Experimental and quasi-experimental designs for research.* Chicago: Rand McNally.

Carver, R. P. (1978, August). The case against statistical significance testing. *Harvard Educational Review, 48* (3), 378–399.

Frame, R. E., Clarizio, H. F., & Porter, A. C. (1984). Diagnostic and prescriptive bias in school psychologists' reports of a learning disabled child. *Journal of Learning Disabilities, 17,* 12–15.

Good, T., & Brophy, J. (1984). *Looking in classrooms* (3rd ed.). New York: Harper and Row.

Suggestions for Further Reading

A great deal has been written which is relevant to acquiring a better understanding of experiments in educational research. Virtually all textbooks designed to provide an introduction to research methods in education contain a chapter on experiments or experimental methodology. The following list contains some of the better known introductions to educational research. I suggest that you read the chapters on experimental research in two or three of them.

Ary, D., Jacobs, C., & Razavieh, A. (1972). *Introduction to research in education.* New York: Holt, Rinehart, and Winston, Inc.

Best, J. W. (1977). *Research in education.* Englewood Cliffs, NJ: Prentice-Hall, Inc.

Borg, W. R., & Gall, M. D. (1971). *Educational research: An introduction.* New York: Longman, Inc.

Englehart, M. D. (1972). *Methods of educational research.* Chicago: Rand McNally Education Series.

Hopkins, C. D. (1976). *Educational research: A structure for inquiry.* Columbus, OH: Charles E. Merrill Publishing Co.

Kerlinger, F. N. (1964). *Foundations of behavioral research.* New York: Holt, Rinehart, and Winston, Inc.

Mouly, G. J. (1970). *Educational research: The art and science of investigation.* Newton, MA: Allyn and Bacon, Inc.

Travers, R. M. W. (1978). *An introduction to educational research.* New York: Macmillan Publishing Company.

Tuckman, B. W. (1978). *Conducting educational research.* New York: Harcourt Brace Jovanovich, Inc.

Wiersma, W. (1969). *Research methods in education.* Philadelphia: J. B. Lippincott Co.

Many textbooks on statistics in psychological or educational research contain chapters or sections which are relevant to the design of educational experiments. Some of these textbooks even contain the words "experimental design" as a part of their title, although, in my opinion, they are more textbooks on statistics than they are textbooks on experimental design. While knowledge of statistics is extremely useful for designing or interpreting educational experiments, there is a separate body of knowledge appropriately labeled experimental design. The following list indicates some statistically oriented textbooks for educational researchers, as well as some of the classics on experimental design. These references will be of interest if you have some background in inferential statistics and if you plan to conduct experiments in the future.

Cochran, W. G., & Cox, G. M. (1957). *Experimental designs* (2d ed.). New York: Wiley.
Dayton, C. M. (1970). *The design of educational experiments.* New York: McGraw-Hill Co.
Fisher, R. A. (1935 and subsequent editions). *Design of experiments.* Edinburgh: Oliver and Boyd.
Kempthorne, O. (1952). *Design and analysis of experiments.* New York: Wiley.
Kirk, R. E. (1968). *Experimental design: Procedures for the behavioral sciences.* Belmont, CA: Wadsworth Publishing Company.
Mendenhall, W. (1968). *Introduction to linear models and the design and analysis of experiments.* Belmont, CA: Wadsworth Publishing Company.

A most important part of becoming familiar with experiments in educational research is to read reports of studies which have used comparative experiments as at least one aspect of their design. The best approach, of course, is to look for examples of experiments that have been conducted in your substantive areas of interest. Following is a partial list of journals relevant to education which typically contain one or more examples of experimental research in each issue. A good exercise would be to select a few issues that seem to be of interest and see if you can identify examples of comparative experiments. For the experiments identified, see if you can judge their quality against the three main goals of experimental design.

American Educational Research Journal
British Journal of Educational Psychology
Child Development
Cognition
Cognitive Psychology
Developmental Psychology
Evaluation Review
Journal of Applied Psychology
Journal of Comparative and Physiological Psychology
Journal of Educational Psychology
The Journal of Educational Research
Journal of Experimental Child
Journal of Experimental Education
Journal of Experimental Psychology: Human Learning
Journal of Genetic Psychology
Journal of Instructional Psychology
Journal for Research in Mathematics Education
Journal of Research in Science Teaching
Journal of Verbal Learning and Verbal Behavior
Psychology in the Schools
The Merrill Palmer Quarterly
Reading Research Quarterly

Study Questions

1. What is an hypothesis and how is an hypothesis used in experimental research?

2. Define the terms independent variable, dependent variable, and population.

3. What is meant by a causal relationship? What are the requirements for arguing cause?

4. What is an experiment? Give an example of an experiment and an example of a study which is not an experiment.

5. State, and define what is meant by, each of the three criteria for judging experimental research.

6. Why are confounding variables of concern to experimenters?

7. What is random assignment and why is it useful?

8. What is meant by a difference being statistically significant? Why is statistical significance not synonymous with importance?

9. State at least two ways to improve the precision of an experiment.

10. What is random selection, how does it differ from random assignment, and why is random selection important?

11. Describe at least three threats to the external validity of an experiment.

12. Give two illustrations of when experiments would be an appropriate research method.

13. Give two illustrations of when experiments would *not* be an appropriate research method.

Reading

Introduction
A Comparative Experiment in Educational Research

Andrew C. Porter

In the following reprint of an article taken from the *American Educational Research Journal,* Gall, Ward, Berliner, Cahen, Winne, Elashoff, and Stanton report findings from two empirical studies. The article illustrates many of the concepts and terms introduced in the preceding chapter. Incidentally, the article also illustrates the facts that educational experiments are sometimes planned, carried out, and reported by a team of researchers and that sometimes educational experiments are supported by federal funds.

Perhaps unfortunately for purposes here, the article illustrates that data from experiments are typically analyzed with fairly sophisticated statistical procedures. If your knowledge of statistics is limited, you may wish to skim the section of the article labeled "data analysis" and pay more attention to the means (averages) reported in Tables 3 and 5 than to the analysis of variance results summarized in Tables 2 and 4.

Clearly, now is not the time and place for a "mini course" on inferential statistics. Still, it may be helpful to know the following:

- "r" refers to a statistic called the correlation coefficient. Briefly, the closer the value of r is to 1.0 (or -1.0), the more nearly two variables being correlated provide the same information about how individuals (subjects) differ.
- Reliability (alpha) indicates the extent to which a variable has been measured with precision (in the sense that if the same subject were measured in the same way again the same results would be found). Reliability can be any value from 0.0 to 1.0 with higher values meaning better reliability.
- Analysis of variance (or analysis of covariance) is one of many techniques used to decide whether means (averages) being compared are enough different from each other to be called statistically significantly different. The "F" statistics reported in the article can take any value from 0.0 to very large numbers. The larger the value of "F," the stronger the evidence

that differences between means being compared are statistically significant.

- Planned comparisons are nothing more than specific comparisons of means (e.g., a contrast of two specific treatments on a particular dependent variable).

While the two studies are of interest in their own right, the purpose here is to illustrate the methodology of comparative experiments. With that in mind, the following may be worth keeping in mind while reading:

1. Like most experiments, the researchers were originally motivated by a general question, "whether the teacher behaviors advocated (by competency-based teacher education) actually promote student learning." The researchers move from there to testable hypotheses, but hypotheses are never explicitly stated. What are the hypotheses tested in "Experiment 1"? What are the independent variables, the dependent variables, the population? Similar questions might be asked for "Experiment 2."

2. Are the hypotheses (or the initial motivating question for that matter) about *causal* relationships of independent variables on dependent variables? In short, are the purposes of the studies consistent with the purposes of comparative experiments?

3. The authors refer to their studies as experiments. Does each of the studies satisfy the requirements of a comparative experiment as presented in the preceding chapter? Where did random assignment enter into the design?

4. Internal validity is one of three main criteria for judging the quality of an experiment. Beyond random assignment, what measures were taken to see that confounding variables did not occur in either study? For example, the Latin Square design is a good illustration of controlling for the problem of order effects (mentioned in the preceding chapter). In the second "experiment," is it possible that difficulty of questions could have been confounded with the four experimental conditions (i.e., varying the percentage of higher cognitive questions)? How might the design have been modified to control for such a possibility?

5. Another criterion for judging the quality of an experiment is precision. Clearly, these two studies had sufficient precision for achieving statistically significant results. Several techniques were used to give the studies good precision. For example, all teachers were required to follow a script and the study was limited to only sixth-grade students. While these design features may have negatively influenced the ability to generalize results, they undoubtedly reduced the possibility for differences in student aptitudes or teacher style to cloud the comparisons of treatment conditions. Can you identify at least one other measure taken by the researchers that likely had a positive effect upon the precision of each study?

6. The authors reported treatment condition means on each dependent variable and tests of statistical significance. They did not report confidence intervals. Do you believe the authors provided sufficient help to the reader to judge for

him or herself whether or not the statistically significant differences among treatment conditions were also important in some educational sense (as opposed to real but trivial differences)?

7. Did the researchers randomly select subjects from well-defined populations? Regardless of your answer, how would you judge the quality of the two studies against the criterion of external validity? One of the strengths of the study was the inclusion of several types of dependent variables (across types of outcomes and across time, to check for retention). Good experiments should contain design features that help test the limits of external validity in just this way. Reports should also describe the research procedures in sufficient detail that the reader can make educated guesses about external validity on other dimensions not explored systematically in the design. Did you feel that the descriptions of students, teachers, and experimental procedures were adequate? In what ways, if any, did the experimental conditions differ from regular school settings?

Also keep in mind while reading the following article that few people understand exactly everything that they read in the report of an experiment, not even seasoned veterans of educational research. Don't dwell on what seems beyond your present grasp. Rather, concentrate on any new understandings of comparative experiment methodology that may occur. Don't be embarrassed if some parts of the article need more than one reading; some parts did for me. Finally, don't be surprised if you spot what appear to be flaws in the studies (beyond those few hinted at already). There is no such thing as a perfect experiment. A flaw in one experiment is simply a motivation for another slightly different experiment. Empirical studies are not meant to stand alone but rather to serve as pieces of a puzzle.

Effects of Questioning Techniques and Recitation on Student Learning[1]

MEREDITH D. GALL
University of Oregon

BEATRICE A. WARD
Far West Laboratory for Educational Research and Development

DAVID C. BERLINER
University of Arizona

LEONARD S. CAHEN
Far West Laboratory for Educational Research and Development

PHILIP H. WINNE
Simon Fraser University

JANET D. ELASHOFF
University of California, Los Angeles

GEORGE C. STANTON
Stanford University

Two experiments were done in which sixth-grade students participated in 10 ecology lessons, each involving reading/viewing of curriculum materials plus a teaching treatment. In Experiment I, four treatments were arranged in three equivalent Latin squares so that each of 12

1. This study was supported by Contract No. NE-C-00-3-0108 given to the Far West Laboratory for Educational Research and Development by the National Institute of Education. The opinions expressed do not necessarily reflect the position or policy of the National Institute of Education, and no official endorsement by the National Institute of Education should be inferred. The authors wish to acknowledge the contributions of Kenneth A. Crown, Robert W. Heath, and Marilyn Madsen to the project.

trained teachers taught each treatment. The treatments varied presence-absence of recitation and presence-absence of probing (a follow-up question to improve a student's initial response) and redirection (asking another student to respond to the question). Experiment II followed the same design, except the treatments varied presence-absence of recitation and percentage of higher cognitive questions (25%, 50%, and 75%) within recitations. Student's information recall, attitudes toward curriculum topics, and ability to respond both in written and oral form to higher cognitive questions were assessed. In both experiments, recitation substantially improved learning, especially information recall and higher cognitive responding. Probing and redirection in Experiment I had no effect on learning. In Experiment II, recitations with 50% higher cognitive questions were unexpectedly the least effective in promoting information recall, relative to recitations with 25% or 75% higher cognitive questions.

Competency-based teacher education is a dominant force in current teacher preparation programs (Gage & Winne, 1975). This approach assumes that skills (competencies) of teaching can be identified; and that if teachers are trained in these skills, their effectiveness will improve. Lists of teaching skills have proliferated, as have programs and materials to train teachers in these skills (Bierly, Clark, Gage, Peterson, & Wessitch, Reference Note 1).

Amidst this surge of activity in competency-based teacher education, there is need to determine empirically whether the teacher behaviors advocated actually promote student learning. Recent reviews of research on teacher effects by Rosenshine (1971) and by Dunkin and Biddle (1974) culled several promising findings, but also suggested that these studies are not sufficient tests of teacher effectiveness on which to base designs for programs in teacher education. Other reviewers (Berliner, 1976; Heath & Nielson, 1974) noted many methodological problems in these studies, including vaguely defined teacher behaviors, undocumented fidelity of treatment, undetermined content validity of student achievement tests, nonrandom assignment of students to treatments, uncontrolled "opportunity to learn" between treatments, unchecked assumptions underlying statistical procedures, and teaching episodes too brief for valid experimentation.

The present experiments investigated whether student learning was affected by three teaching skills (redirection, probing, and higher cognitive questioning) often included in competency-based programs. Both avoided or solved the methodological problems mentioned above.

RELATED LITERATURE

Probing and Redirection. Probing refers to the teacher asking a follow-up or "probing" question to have the student improve the quality of or elaborate an initial answer. Redirection occurs when the teacher calls on another student to respond to a question answered by one student. These actions are hypothesized to promote learning by providing students with practice in organizing their facts and ideas into overt responses and by having responses "shaped" by the teacher or other students.

Rosenshine (1971) identified three correlational studies relating probing and redirection to student achievement. In two studies (Soar, 1966; Spaulding, 1965), these behaviors were claimed to correlate positively with achievement. However, probing and redirection were not correlated directly with student achievement, but factors on which these behaviors loaded were correlated with achievement. Heath and Nielson (1974) criticized this procedure on the basis that factor composites of several teacher behaviors cannot validly represent the degree of correlation of one behavior with a criterion variable.

In the third study (Wright and Nuthall, 1970), frequency of redirection had a positive correlation ($r = .54$) with regressed student achievement scores on a fact-recall test. Asking a probing question at the same or higher cognitive level as the initial question was only slightly correlated with student achievement ($r = .20$). Thus, these few studies, none of which could test causal relations, leave moot the effects of probing and redirection on student learning.

Higher Cognitive Questions. A "higher cognitive" question is characterized by two features described in the *Taxonomy of Educational Objectives: Cognitive Domain* (Bloom, 1956). First it requires the student to state predictions, solutions, explanations, evidence, generalizations, interpretations, or opinions. Second, the answer to the question must not be directly available from the curriculum. Questions that do not meet these criteria are either "fact" questions which require one item of information to be remembered or "multi-fact" questions requiring the recall of several facts. Educators (for example, Sanders, 1966) have theorized that teachers' use of higher cognitive questions stimulates the development of students' cognitive abilities beyond simply memorizing content.

The correlational studies relating cognitive levels of teachers' questions to student learning were reviewed by Rosenshine (1971) and by Dunkin and Biddle (1974). Overall, these studies (Taba, Levine & Elzey, 1964; Taba, 1966; Thompson & Bowers, Reference Note 2; Wright & Nuthall, 1970) show no clear relationship between the frequency with which the teacher uses higher cognitive questions and student achievement.

Winne (Reference Note 3) reviewed 18 experiments which attempted to test the causal relation between teachers' use of higher cognitive questions and student achievement. Of those studies which he judged to be reasonably sound methodologically, only one contrast out of 18 showed that higher cognitive questions lead to improved achievement relative to lower cognitive questions (Buggey, 1971). However, this finding was not replicated in a nearly identical study, by Savage (1972), the only difference being that Buggey studied second graders whereas Savage's study used fifth-grade students. The majority of comparisons among treatment groups, regardless of experimental validity, showed no differences in student achievement as a function of level of teacher questions. But because of frequent doubt about methodology, especially the operational definition of the treatments in these experiments, one cannot be certain of the relation between use of higher cognitive questions and achievement.

EXPERIMENT I

METHOD

Sample

Sixth-grade students from two classrooms in each of six schools participated in the experiment (N = 336). Since reading ability was considered important to the use of curriculum materials prepared for the experiment, students' scores on a state-administered reading test (Comprehensive Tests of Basic Skills, Form Q-Level 2) were obtained. The students' mean score for total reading achievement (vocabulary plus comprehension) was 55.27 (*s.d.* = 16.61), yielding a grade equivalent of 5.2.[2] Students' reading level probably was slightly higher during the experiment, which was conducted six months after the administration of the test.

Twelve teachers from the substitute teacher list of another local school district were recruited to conduct the teaching treatments. Criteria for selection were willingness and capability to conduct the treatments according to the researchers' specifications, as judged by performance in pre-experiment training sessions; possession of a valid teaching credential; and experience with children of upper elementary age. The teachers were aware of the general purpose of the experiments, but were not debriefed about the research hypotheses or rationale for experimental procedures and instrumentation until all data collection in both experiments had been collected.

The students' regular instructors did not participate in the experiment.

Treatments

Experimental Curriculum. All students were provided with identical curriculum materials to equate "opportunity to learn" across treatments. Ecology was selected for the curriculum unit because it was thought that this topic would be perceived favorably by the school district and would appeal to sixth-grade students. The unit included objectives at each level of the *Taxonomy of Educational Objectives: Cognitive Domain* (Bloom, 1956). Also, the unit incorporated a variety of materials to maintain student interest: printed handouts, a game, a film, and two filmstrips.

The experimental lessons extended over ten sessions, one per day, to allow students to acclimate to the treatment and to allow treatment effects to accrue. Each session was approximately 50 minutes, of which approximately 15 minutes were for presentation of pre-teaching curriculum content, 25 minutes for recitation or other treatment, and ten minutes for organizational activities.

2. Grade equivalents obtained from *Examiner's Manual: Comprehensive Tests of Basic Skills.* Monterey, Calif.: McGraw-Hill, 1968, pp. 48-49.

Recitation Treatments. Three of the four treatment groups in each classroom received a recitation for nine of the ten days of the ecology unit. The first day was a warm-up and motivator for all treatment groups.

Sixteen questions were constructed for each of the nine recitations based on that day's curriculum materials. Each recitation included four fact, four multi-fact, and eight higher cognitive questions.

Three recitation treatments were developed from this base of sixteen questions. In the *Probing and Redirection treatment,* each of the four multi-fact and the eight higher cognitive questions were probed and redirected twice. The *No Probing and Redirection treatment* had teachers ask the same 16 questions as before, but no questions were probed or redirected. The *Filler Activity treatment* was identical to the No Probing and Redirection treatment, but added approximately ten minutes of filler activity to each recitation to keep students "on task" but not involved in recitation. These activities included creating crossword puzzles based on ecological terms, writing poetry about the environment, and composing a letter to a politician about ecological concerns. It provided a controlled comparison for the difference in time on task between the Probing and Redirection treatment and the No Probing and Redirection treatment.

An important feature of the recitation treatments was "semi-programmed" teaching in which the teacher followed a script which specified the questions to be asked and their sequence (see also Buggey, 1971; Ryan, 1973). The script is only "semi" programmed because some teacher behaviors are contingent upon student response. For example, the teacher cannot probe a student's response to elicit a rationale if the student is unable to respond at all to the initial question.

An exemplary response was provided for each question to insure that students in all recitation treatments were exposed to the same amount of correct information. If no student gave an acceptable answer to a question, the teacher provided one from this set.

The semi-programmed technique overcomes the flaw in much past research of imprecision in definition of the teaching strategy used by teachers. It also simplifies checking treatment fidelity and constructing content valid posttests which accurately reflect students' "opportunity to learn."

Art Activity Treatment. Students in the Art Activity treatment groups participated in ecology-related art activities. This treatment provided a condition against which the effectiveness of the recitation treatments could be compared and which would be engaging for students. Teachers were instructed not to ask questions of any type during the art activity sessions.

Experimental Design

A Latin square design was used to investigate the effectiveness of the three recitation treatments (Probing and Redirection, No Probing and Redirection, Filler Activity) and the control treatment (Art Activity). This design requires random assignment of treatments to the experimental units within each row and column, with each treatment appearing only once in a row and once in a column. It also assumes no interaction between main effects (classrooms, teachers, and treatments; see Table 1). This is a reasonable assumption here: Since the teachers were trained to follow a prescribed behavior pattern in each treatment, teacher by treatment interactions did not seem likely.

The following procedures were used to create a Latin square design. The twelve classrooms were formed into three sets of four classrooms each. Each set of four classrooms constituted a separate Latin square. Four different teachers were then randomly assigned to each of the three Latin squares. Four groups of students were formed by random assignment from each classroom, each group receiving one treatment. During a given class hour, then, all four of the treatments were administered, each one by a different teacher. Over the course of a school day, each teacher taught a different treatment to four different groups, one from each classroom in the Latin square. To equate treatment groups on male/female composition, boys were randomly assigned to recitation and art activity treatment groups until there were three boys in each group. The same procedure was used to assign three girls to treatments. An example of one of the three Latin squares formed by these procedures is shown in Table 1.

TABLE 1

Example of Latin Square in Experiment I

	Latin Square 1			
	School 1		School 2	
Ecology Teacher	Class 1 (9:20 AM)[a]	Class 2 (10:30 AM)	Class 3 (12:30 PM)	Class 4 (1:30 PM)
1	Probe & Redirect	Filler Activity	No Probe & Redirect	Art Activity
	Boys = 3	Boys = 3	Boys = 3	Boys = 2
	Girls = 3	Girls = 3	Girls = 3	Girls = 4
2	No Probe & Redirect	Art Activity	Probe & Redirect	Filler Activity
	Boys = 3	Boys = 3	Boys = 3	Boys = 3
	Girls = 3	Girls = 3	Girls = 3	Girls = 3
3	Art Activity	Probe & Redirect	Filler Activity	No Probe & Redirect
	Boys = 3	Boys = 3	Boys = 3	Boys = 3
	Girls = 3	Girls = 3	Girls = 3	Girls = 3
4	Filler Activity	No Probe & Redirect	Art Activity	Probe & Redirect
	Boys = 3	Boys = 3	Boys = 2	Boys = 3
	Girls = 3	Girls = 3	Girls = 4	Girls = 3

[a]Approximate time each day for treatment sessions in a particular classroom.

In a few classrooms the procedures could not be used as planned. For example, one classroom was a fifth-sixth grade class with only 17 sixth-graders. The inadequate number of sixth graders were randomly assigned to the recitation treatments only; there was no art activity treatment in this classroom, thus creating a "hole" in the Latin square design.

In classrooms having more than 24 pupils, an alternative form of instruction was provided for the remaining students. Two classrooms, each having 25 pupils, were an exception; the one remaining student was assigned to the Art Activity treatment.

Instruments

The reading ability score from the Comprehensive Tests of Basic Skills was used as a measure of students' reading level and as a possible covariate in the planned analysis of variance.

The Information Test measured students' knowledge of factual information before, immediately after, and three weeks after the curriculum unit (pretest, posttest, and retention test, respectively). The 27 multiple-choice items created from content analysis of curriculum materials and teaching scripts were divided into two subtests. The Intentional Scale contained ten items measuring recall of information covered in the scripted recitation questions. The Incidental Scale measured recall of information *not* covered in recitations but included in the curriculum materials. Differential effects of these two types of test item have been found consistently in research on prose learning (Anderson & Biddle, 1975). Therefore, they were operationalized as separate dependent measures in this study.

It should be noted that the items in the Intentional Scale are "intentional" for the recitation treatments, but "incidental" for the Art Activity treatment since students in the latter treatment did not participate in recitations. Items in the Incidental Scale are "incidental" for all treatments.

The correlation between the two scales of the Information Test, calculated separately for each time of administration, ranged from .24 to .64. Alpha reliability coefficients for the posttest and retention test administrations of the Intentional Scale within each treatment group ranged from .44 to .77, with a median of .71. The alpha coefficients for the Incidental Scale ranged from .60 to .75, with a median of .71.

The Essay Test measured students' ability to give plausible, reasoned, written responses to higher cognitive questions. It was administered before and after the curriculum unit. The 12 essay items were based on the unit, but were different from the higher cognitive questions used in the recitation treatments. This test, and the other free-response measures of higher cognitive processes (Oral Test and Transfer Test), were untimed to allow students sufficient opportunity to organize and communicate their ideas.

The scoring of the Essay Test was in two steps. First, each response was judged to be relevant or not relevant to the question. Second, for the group of relevant responses, each response was scored by trained raters on two scales: a content score reflecting the frequency of plausible predictions, solutions, supported opinions, explanations, and/or inferences; and a logical extension score for the frequency of "because" and "if-then" relationships in the response. The frequency counts were summed across test items to yield total scale scores.

Interrater reliability for the two scales was high. The intraclass coefficient across all pairs of raters was .86 for the Content Scale and .71 for the Logical Extension Scale. The correlation between the two scales was .71 and .57 for the pretest and posttest administrations, respectively.

The Oral Test measured students' ability to give plausible, reasoned, *oral* responses to six higher cognitive questions about the ecology unit. Since the recitation treatments provide students with practice in listening to higher cognitive questions and in giving oral responses to them, a test in the same modalities might reveal treatment effects different than those measured by the paper-and-pencil Essay Test.

The Oral Test was administered individually to each student as a pretest and a posttest. Responses to items were audiotaped for scoring by trained raters on content and logical extension scales. The intraclass coefficient across all pairs of raters was .82 for the Content Scale and .72 for the Logical Extension Scale. The correlation between the two scales was .61 and .66 for the pretest and posttest, respectively.

The Transfer Test, administered as a retention test, assessed whether higher cognitive response skills would transfer to an unstudied but parallel curriculum topic, the problem of human population explosion. It contained nine higher cognitive questions presented in the same format as the Essay Test. Content and logical extension scores were obtained. Interrater reliability was .87 for the Content Scale and .86 for the Logical Extension Scale. The correlation between the two scales was .65.

The Word Association Scale, administered as a pretest and a posttest, measured students' attitude toward six ecological topics examined in the curriculum, e.g., balance of nature and water pollution. Ten bi-polar adjectives, each a 7-point scale, from the evaluative factor of the semantic differential (Osgood, Suci, & Tannenbaum, 1957) were rated for each topic. The scales for four topics were scored so that a positive ecological attitude was represented by a high score. For two topics (air pollution and water pollution), the scoring was reversed so that a high score indicated a negative attitude. Alpha coefficients for the scales ranged from .31 to .96, with a median of .80. Correlations between the six scales generally were low; the median was .20.

Data Analysis

Each dependent variable was examined as a possible controlling covariate in the analysis of variance. For parsimony and ease of interpretation, the most desirable choice for covariate was the pretest paralleling its posttest. When the relevant pretest variable failed to satisfy selection conditions, total reading score was examined as a possible covariate.

Covariance adjustments were not made unless the assumptions for analysis of covariance (see Elashoff, 1969) were justified. These assumptions ideally would be tested within each cell of the Latin square. This approach was precluded since there were only six students in each treatment group. Therefore, the assumptions were tested by examining the regression of individuals' posttest scores on the covariate by pooling classrooms within a single treatment condition. If the test for homogeneity of regression was significant ($p < .05$) or if other assumptions appeared invalid by inspection of scatterplots, the covariance adjustment was not done.

The unit of analysis for each variable was the mean of student scores within each cell of each Latin square. Since students experienced each of the treatments as a social group, the group mean probably is a more appropriate unit of analysis than the individual student score (Peckham, Glass, & Hopkins, 1969).

Each of the main factors of treatment, classroom, teacher, and Latin square was considered as a fixed effect in the analysis of variance or covariance. Since the unit of analysis is the treatment group mean, and only one classroom subgroup is used for each treatment-teacher combination, the within group variance cannot be formed. Thus, the residual term is a pooled estimate of between group variance composed of all the possible interaction terms except the estimable treatment by square interaction. The validity of this analysis rests on the assumption that the unknown interactions are negligible with respect to the identifiable effects.

Two types of "missing" data are present—unequal class sizes and the empty cell for one Art Activity treatment previously discussed. Unequal classes were simply ignored. The missing cell mean was estimated by a full least squares solution where each effect was treated as entering last. Treatment means were calculated from the estimated treatment effects. They are *not* the simple means.

In addition to analysis of the data for overall treatment differences, the following planned comparisons were examined on all dependent variables: Probing and Redirection versus No Probing and Redirection; No Probing and Redirection versus Filler Activity; and the recitation treatments as a whole (Probing and Redirection, No Probing and Redirection, and Filler Activity) versus Art Activity. Each planned comparison had one degree of freedom and was tested for statistical significance using the mean square error term from its analysis of variance or covariance. In the latter case, the comparisons used adjusted cell means.

The significance tests for these planned comparisons for all 16 variables are not independent. Multiple tests like these can show some statistically significant effects even when no real treatment differences exist. Thus, our interpretations are based primarily on the consistency and patterns of differences rather than mere statistical significance.

RESULTS

Fidelity of Treatment

Teachers' adherence to the recitation treatments was checked by audiotaping the three recitations conducted by the teachers on two different days of the ecology unit. Deviations from the script occurred rarely. For example, in the 72 audiotaped recitations there were only three instances in which a teacher asked a scripted question out of order.

Analysis of the audiotapes also revealed high fidelity to the treatment variations. Probing and redirection occurred an average of 25.68 times and 23.67 times, respectively, in each of the Probing and Redirection treatment sessions. In comparison, probing and redirection occurred an average of 2.06 times and .63 times, respectively, in each session of the remaining two recitation treatments (No Probing and Redirection; Filler Activity).

Fidelity of the Art Activity treatment was checked by random observations by the researchers. Teachers followed closely the treatment conditions, including the requirement to avoid use of recitation techniques.

A special concern was that treatment effects might be obscured if students reacted negatively to the experimental conditions. Attitude measures administered after the ecology unit indicated that students generally had positive attitudes to the curriculum, the teacher, treatment group peers, and their particular treatment. Between treatment differences in attitudes were negligible.

Students' attendance during the 10 treatment sessions was recorded. The mean attendance across all treatment groups was 9.14 sessions. Between treatment differences were negligible.

Analysis of Variance

Analysis of variance or covariance for the main effect of treatment (see Table 2) shows statistically significant differences between treatment group means on five of the ten achievement variables. None of the differences between treatment group means on the subscales of the Word Association Scale were statistically significant. Planned comparisons are presented in the next section.

As shown in Table 2, classroom effects were statistically significant for the majority of outcome variables. These results are not noteworthy since they do not affect interpretation of treatment group differences. None of the teacher effects were statistically significant. This was expected, since the teachers were trained to follow behavior patterns carefully defined by the lesson scripts. With the exception of the two scales of the Transfer Test, square and square by treatment effects were negligible.

Planned Comparisons

The planned comparisons show that there was little difference in the effects of the recitation treatments (Probing and Redirection, No Probing and Redirection, and Filler Activity) on outcome variables (Table 3). Exceptions are that the No Probing and Redirection groups achieved a reliably greater score on the Content Scale of the Transfer Test than did the Filler Activity groups. As discussed earlier, this may be a chance finding. In general, these results indicate that teacher use of probing and redirection in recitations does not facilitate knowledge acquisition, higher cognitive responding, or attitudes toward curriculum topics.

TABLE 2
Analysis of Variance Summary for Experiment I Measures of Achievement and Attitude

Dependent Variable	Adjusting Variable	MS error df = 17	F Values for Analysis of Variance Effects				
			Treatment $F_{3,17}$	Class $F_{9,17}$	Teacher $F_{9,17}$	Square $F_{2,17}$	Treatment by Square $F_{6,17}$
Knowledge Variables							
Ecology Information Test:							
Intentional Scale, post	total reading	0.85	5.04*	2.53*	0.46	0.35	0.26
Intentional Scale, delay		1.12	6.90*	3.19*	1.09	2.44	1.73
Incidental Scale, post		2.52	3.07	1.61	1.20	0.06	0.87
Incidental Scale, delay	total reading	2.46	1.06	2.38	0.21	0.61	0.69
Higher Cognitive Variables							
Oral Test.							
Content, post	pre	1.08	6.83*	0.64	0.94	0.62	0.74
Logical Extension, post		1.49	3.05	1.55	1.27	2.12	0.75
Essay Test:							
Content, post	pre	1.92	3.13	3.24*	0.37	2.10	0.53
Logical Extension, post		0.28	5.37*	5.67*	0.75	0.16	1.58
Transfer Test:							
Content, delay	essay pre	1.71	3.42*	3.27*	1.28	8.79*	1.43
Logical Extension, delay		0.26	3.05	5.55*	1.41	11.58*	0.93
Attitudinal Variables							
Word Association Scale:							
Balance of Nature		17.67	0.92	2.11	2.33	1.93	1.90
Ecology		21.16	1.15	2.12	1.47	0.11	0.48
Wolf	pre	32.55	1.30	0.92	0.87	0.10	1.07
Air Pollution		10.59	1.14	1.44	0.45	0.14	0.93
Alligator	pre	27.90	2.24	1.20	0.88	0.28	1.42
Water Pollution	pre	9.58	1.14	0.88	0.59	0.15	1.06

*Significance at the .05 level.

TABLE 3
Experiment I Treatment Means and Planned Comparisons of Measures of Achievement and Attitude

Dependent Variable	Adjusting Variable	Treatment Means				F Values for Planned Comparisons[a]		
		Probe & Redirect	No Probe & Redirect	Filler Activity	Art Activity I	Treatments 1 vs 2	Treatments 2 vs 3	1,2,3 vs 4
		(1)	(2)	(3)	(4)			
Knowledge Variables								
Ecology Information Test:								
Intentional Scale I, post	total reading	5.79	6.00	6.16	4.73	0.30	0.18	14.16*
Intentional Scale I, delay		5.69	5.13	5.73	3.89	1.71	1.97	18.25*
Incidental Scale I, post	total	7.69	7.83	7.02	5.96	0.04	1.56	7.41*
Incidental Scale I, delay	reading	7.00	6.89	6.40	5.93	0.03	0.60	2.90

Higher Cognitive Variables							
Oral Test:							
Content, post	pre	8.41	8.14	7.47	6.55	0.40	2.54	15.24*
Logical Extension, post		2.59	3.33	2.92	2.09	0.28	0.64	7.35*
Essay Test:							
Content, post	pre	10.72	10.58	9.86	9.09	0.06	1.62	6.72*
Logical Extension, post		1.79	1.58	1.40	0.91	1.02	0.66	12.78*
Transfer Test:							
Content, delay	essay pre	8.15	8.09	6.85	6.93	0.01	5.39*	2.67
Logical Extension, delay		1.56	1.55	1.39	0.97	0.00	0.60	8.33*
Attitudinal Variables							
Word Association Scale:							
Balance of Nature		55.62	57.61	57.66	55.52	1.35	0.00	0.91
Ecology		58.41	61.38	61.13	61.34	2.50	0.02	0.40
Wolf	pre	47.27	47.66	45.48	43.30	0.03	0.88	0.91
Air Pollution		60.29	59.35	58.29	58.05	0.50	0.64	1.14
Alligator	pre	52.55	51.62	51.96	47.18	0.19	0.02	6.54*
Water Pollution	pre	59.58	59.39	57.95	57.63	0.02	1.29	1.44

aF$_{1,17}$ for each planned comparison.
*Significance at the .05 level.

The results of the planned comparisons also suggest that time spent in recitation may be of limited importance since there were no significant differences between the No Probing and Redirection treatment and the two recitation treatments which were 10 minutes longer in duration (Probing and Redirection; Filler Activity).

As shown in Table 3, comparisons of the combined recitation treatments with the Art Activity treatment reveal statistically significant differences in 8 of the 10 achievement variables and in 1 of the 5 attitude variables. Thus, the previously identified treatment effects are largely due to the contrast of the combined recitation treatments versus the Art Activity treatment. With one exception, statistically non-significant differences between the recitation treatments and art activity treatment also favored the recitation treatments. Therefore, it appears that use of recitation of the types embodied in the three recitation treatments is effective in promoting knowledge acquisition and retention, higher cognitive response ability (both oral and written), and attitudes toward curriculum topics.

EXPERIMENT II

The major purpose of Experiment II was to compare the effects of recitations which vary the percentage of higher cognitive questions asked by the teacher. Another purpose was to replicate the comparison of recitation teaching treatments versus Art Activity.

METHOD

The methodology of Experiment II repeated, with a few exceptions, the methodology of Experiment I. Experiment II was initiated within a few weeks of completion of the first experiment.

Sample

Twelve sixth-grade classrooms, two in each of six schools, provided 371 students. Students' mean score for total reading achievement on the Comprehensive Tests of Basic Skills was 63.72 (*s.d.* = 14.05), yielding a grade equivalent of 6.2.

The same 12 teachers as in Experiment I were trained to conduct the treatment variations. The students' regular teachers did not participate in the study.

Experimental Design

The same Latin square design of Experiment I was used in this experiment with one exception: all students in a given classroom remaining after six students (three boys and three girls) were randomly assigned to each of three recitation treatments were assigned to the Art Activity treatment. The number of students assigned to this treatment ranged from 9 to 15 students with a mean of 12.9.

The ecology curriculum used in the first experiment was repeated without variation here.

Three recitation treatments and an Art Activity treatment were conducted in Experiment II. Sixteen questions were included in each lesson of the recitation treatments. The questions were varied, however, to create a different percentage of higher cognitive questions (HCQ) in each treatment. In the 25% HCQ treatment, each lesson contained eight fact questions, four multi-fact questions, and four higher cognitive questions. The 50% HCQ treatment (identical to the questions asked in Experiment I) contained the same four multi-fact questions and same four higher cognitive questions as the 25% HCQ treatment. Four additional higher cognitive questions not in the 25% HCQ recitation replaced four of the eight fact questions.

The recitations in the 75% HCQ treatment each included four multi-fact questions and twelve higher cognitive questions. The four multi-fact questions were the same as in the 25% HCQ and 50% HCQ recitations. Of the twelve higher cognitive questions in each recitation four were unique to this treatment; four appeared in this treatment and the 50% HCQ treatment; and four were common to all three of the treatments.

The same "semi-programmed" format of Experiment I also was followed here. Teachers were trained to probe and redirect each multi-fact and higher cognitive question twice in all recitation treatments. This created time differences between treatments, since the number of multi-fact and higher cognitive questions varied across treatments. Filler activities from the Filler Activity treatment of Experiment I were added to each 25% HCQ recitation and each 50% HCQ recitation to equate time on task across the treatments.

The Art Activity treatment was the same as in Experiment I except that the groups generally contained more students.

Instruments

The same instruments and data collection procedures of Experiment I were used again in Experiment II. In this experiment, however, the Information Test items were formed into three scales instead of merely two as before. The Intentional Scale contained eight items which measured recall of information covered in all three recitation treatments. The items in this scale were incidental for the Art Activity treatment. Alpha coefficients, calculated separately within each treatment group for post and for delayed administrations ranged from .50 to .70 with a median of .56.

The 25% HCQ Intentional Scale consisted of seven items which were derived from the fact questions of the 25% HCQ treatment. The items were incidental for the two other recitation treatments and for the Art Activity treatment. Within group alpha coefficients ranged from .38 to .58 with a median of .49.

The Incidental Scale contained ten items which were covered only in the curriculum materials in all four treatments. Within group alpha coefficients ranged from .47 to .71 with a median of .64.

Data Analysis

All of the data analysis procedures were identical to those of Experiment I except that the following planned comparisons on all variables were analyzed: 25% HCQ treatment versus 50% HCQ treatment; 25% HCQ treatment versus 75% HCQ treatment; 50% HCQ treatment versus 75% HCQ treatment; and combined recitation treatments versus Art Activity treatments.

RESULTS

Fidelity of Treatment

Teachers' adherence to the requirements of each treatment were checked using the same procedures as in Experiment I. High level of fidelity of treatment was observed. As expected, use of probing and redirection increased from the 25% HCQ treatment to the 50% HCQ treatment, and again from the 50% HCQ treatment to the 75% HCQ treatment.

As in Experiment I, posttreatment attitudinal measures revealed that students had positive attitudes toward the various features of the treatments. Between treatment differences generally were slight.

The mean attendance of the ten treatment sessions across all treatment sessions was 9.16 sessions. Between treatment differences were negligible.

Analysis of Variance

Table 4 presents the results of the analysis of variance or covariance for each dependent variable. A statistically significant difference between treatment group means was obtained on nine of the twelve achievement variables and on two of the six attitude scales.

The pattern of results for the effects of teacher, square, and treatment by square were similar to Experiment I. Unlike the first experiment, however, there were fewer statistically significant classroom effects. This result may indicate a more homogeneous sample than in Experiment I.

Planned Comparisons

The planned comparisons involving recitation treatment means (see Table 5) show that percentage of higher cognitive questions had a statistically significant influence on the amount of information acquired by students. A consistent pattern of treatment mean scores is depicted in Figure 1 in which a U-curve describes the relation between percentage of higher cognitive questions and achievement on intentional and incidental scales of the Ecology Information Test. In all cases, the 50% HCQ treatment showed considerably lower scores than the other two recitation treatments. The 25% HCQ and 75% HCQ treatment outcomes fall at similar levels for the various subtests. Outcomes for the Art Activity treatment approximate those for the 50% HCQ treatment.

The 25% HCQ treatment was superior to the other two recitation treatments on the 25% HCQ Intentional Scale. This is predictable since these students had the advantage of answering items not covered in the recitations of students in the 50% HCQ and 75% HCQ treatments.

With regard to measures of higher cognitive achievement, students in the 50% HCQ treatment outperformed students in the 75% HCQ treatment on one of the Oral Test measures. They also outscored the 25% HCQ treatment (statistically significant) and the 75% HCQ treatment (approaching statistical significance) on one of the Essay Test measures.

The mean scores of the recitation treatments on the attitude scales were quite similar. Only one of the planned comparisons was statistically significant.

With one exception, the mean scores of students in the combined recitation treatments were statistically greater than those of students in the Art Activity treatment on the Information Test measures. Also, students in the combined recitation treatments statistically outscored students in the Art Activity treatment on three of the six higher cognitive achievement measures. The same trend was observed for the three measures which did not reveal a statistically significant difference.

Planned comparisons involving the attitude measures revealed two significant differences favoring students in the recitation treatments over those in the Art Activity treatment. Differences in scores on the other attitude scales, although not statistically significant, also generally favored the recitation treatments over the Art Activity treatment.

DISCUSSION

The most significant finding of the two experiments is that recitation teaching was more effective in promoting student learning than a nonrecitation instructional experience (art activity) lasting for the same period of time. These results, especially on the incidental subscales for which coverage of content was equal for all groups, strongly show that exposure to the curriculum *plus* teaching is significantly more effective than only exposure to the curriculum.

What student learning outcomes are reliably affected by recitation teaching? The results of both experiments indicate that recitation has a significant positive effect on: (1) acquisition of information about curriculum content; (2) retention of information; (3) ability to listen and respond orally to higher cognitive questions about curriculum content; and (4) ability to respond in writing to higher cognitive questions about curriculum content. The results relating to the Word Association Scale and Transfer Test, although not significant in a statistical sense, are consistent enough to suggest that recitation also promotes (5) positive attitudes toward curriculum content; and (6) transfer of higher cognitive response ability to new curriculum.

Presence or absence of probing and redirection in Experiment I had no effect on student learning. Only one of the many planned comparisons reached statistical significance. This finding has a plausible explanation in the fact that the teachers were scripted so that the quantity of information presented in all treatments was equal. Specifically, regardless of the particular treatment, when students failed to provide an adequate answer the teacher gave the answer. Thus, it may be that when the information presented in lessons is the same, a

TABLE 4
Analysis of Variance Summary for Experiment II Measures of Achievement and Attitude

Dependent Variable	Adjusting Variable	MS error df = 18	F Values for Analysis of Variance Effects				
			Treatment $F_{3,18}$	Class $F_{9,18}$	Teacher $F_{9,18}$	Square $F_{2,18}$	Treatment by square $F_{6,18}$
Knowledge Variables							
Ecology Information Test:							
Intentional Scale, post	total reading	0.33	8.55*	1.42	1.08	0.72	0.69
Intentional Scale, delay	total reading	0.40	12.51*	0.77	0.92	3.85*	0.54
25% Intentional Scale, post	total reading	0.35	9.46*	1.00	0.54	0.48	0.28
25% Intentional Scale, delay	total reading	0.49	5.20*	0.75	0.42	0.54	0.73
Incidental Scale, post	total reading	0.48	7.49*	1.60	0.88	2.37	1.57
Incidental Scale, delay	total reading	0.68	7.30*	1.37	0.49	1.86	0.90

Higher Cognitive Variables							
Oral Test:							
Content, post	pre	1.10	5.53*	0.42	0.73	9.88*	2.12
Logical Extension, post	prc	0.68	4.91*	3.49*	1.19	3.22	1.42
Essay Test:							
Content, post	pre	1.19	8.15*	9.77*	1.35	1.57	0.97
Logical Extension, post		0.71	1.18	2.49*	0.35	0.15	0.34
Transfer Test:							
Content, delay	Ess. Cont. pre	2.29	0.32	1.75	0.34	1.78	0.58
Logical Extension, delay		0.39	0.64	3.33*	1.24	1.03	0.38
Attitudinal Variables							
Word Association Scale:							
Ecology		30.97	0.48	1.14	0.80	1.17	0.79
Balance of Nature		16.51	1.94	0.96	0.79	0.39	1.87
Wolf	pre	10.13	6.33*	0.65	1.55	0.80	1.64
Air Pollution		6.51	0.48	0.34	0.59	1.02	0.57
Alligator	pre	10.62	7.40*	1.84	0.65	0.19	0.81
Water Pollution		6.76	0.53	0.72	0.75	4.21*	1.44

*Significance at the .05 level.

TABLE 5
Experiment II Treatment Means and Planned Comparisons of Measures of Achievement and Attitude

Dependent Variable	Adjusting Variable	Treatment Means				F Values for Planned Comparisons[a]			
		25% HCQ (1)	50% HCQ (2)	75% HCQ (3)	Art Activity (4)	Treatments 1 vs 2	Treatments 2 vs 3	Treatments 1 vs 3	Treatments 1,2,3 vs
Knowledge Variables									
Ecology Information Test:									
Intentional Scale, post	total reading	6.27	5.94	6.29	5.26	2.01	2.21	0.00	22.88*
Intentional Scale, delay	total reading	6.19	5.26	5.85	4.74	13.12*	5.31*	1.73	24.10*
25% Intentional Scale, post	total reading	4.68	3.53	4.01	3.62	22.96*	3.97	7.83*	5.21*
25% Intentional Scale, delay	total reading	4.52	3.56	3.76	3.56	11.59*	0.50	7.30*	2.67
Incidental Scale, post	total reading	5.97	4.92	5.83	5.00	13.66*	10.29*	0.24	6.34*
Incidental Scale, delay	total reading	5.91	4.52	5.34	4.67	17.22*	5.97*	2.91	4.49*
Higher Cognitive Variables									
Oral Test									
Content, post	pre	8.88	8.83	8.42	7.35	0.01	0.96	1.17	15.15*
Logical Extension, post	pre	4.03	3.80	3.10	2.95	0.50	4.30	7.73*	6.39*
Essay Test:									
Content, post	pre	11.58	12.55	11.64	10.36	4.73*	4.11	0.02	18.54*
Logical Extension, post		2.11	2.30	2.03	1.68	1.34	0.62	0.04	2.89
Transfer Test:									
Content, delay	Ess. Cont. pre	8.79	8.99	8.62	8.40	0.10	0.07	0.61	0.61
Logical Extension, delay		1.67	1.73	1.85	1.51	0.07	0.22	0.55	1.37
Attitudinal Variables									
Word Association Scale:									
Ecology		62.49	63.01	64.51	61.91	0.05	0.43	0.79	0.59
Balance of Nature		59.73	59.40	61.41	57.93	0.04	1.48	1.02	4.12
Wolf	pre	57.48	55.74	57.57	52.62	1.81	1.98	0.00	16.46*
Air Pollution		60.21	59.22	59.59	60.27	0.91	0.13	0.35	0.51
Alligator	pre	51.65	49.42	54.61	46.86	2.82	5.74*	0.51	16.15*
Water Pollution		59.91	58.59	59.07	59.15	1.55	0.21	0.62	0.00

[a] $F_{1,18}$ for each planned comparison
*Significance at the .05 level

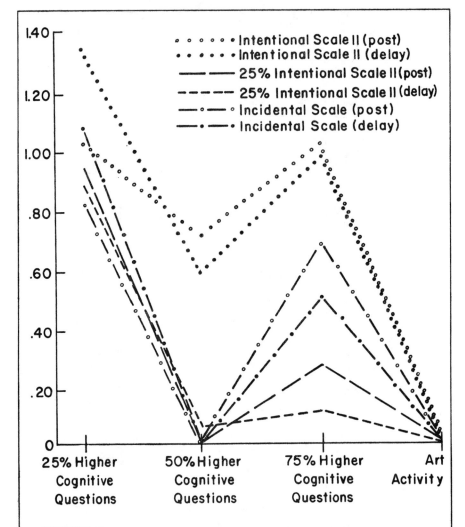

FIGURE 1.
Patterns of Treatment Differences for Information Subtests in Experiment II

Note. Data points on the graph are based on unadjusted treatment means. The three recitation treatment means are expressed on the ordinate as absolute deviations from the art activity treatment means. The latter means serve as a baseline of zero value.

student-centered procedure like probing and redirection is equally as effective as a teacher-centered procedure like having the teacher state the desired response.

In Experiment II the results indicate that variation in the percentage of higher cognitive questions in recitations does affect learning. However, the effects are puzzling. Relative to the 25% HCQ and 75% HCQ treatments, the 50% HCQ treatment was the least effective in promoting knowledge acquisition and retention, but showed a slight trend toward being most effective in promoting higher cognitive performance. Since the recitations of the 50% HCQ treatment did not emphasize either fact or higher cognitive questions, it is possible that students were confused concerning the objective of the recitations—was the objective to rehearse facts, or to think about them? To lessen their sense of confusion, some students may have decided to concentrate on answering teacher higher cognitive questions and ignored the fact questions, thereby causing a decrement in performance on the Information Test.

Generally students in the 25% HCQ treatment outperformed students in the 75% HCQ treatment both on the knowledge acquisition and higher cognitive measures, although the absolute differences between mean scores were small. Contrary to the belief held by many educators, this finding suggests that emphasizing fact questions rather than higher cognitive questions is the more desirable teaching pattern. Further research is needed to determine the effect of more extreme vairations in use of higher cognitive questions—for example, recitations with no higher cognitive questions compared with recitations composed exclusively of these questions.

A secondary problem examined in both experiments tested the hypothesis that recitations promote greater acquisition and retention of curriculum content rehearsed by the recitation questions (intentional learning) than content not rehearsed (incidental learning). In Experiment II this problem was studied by comparing the performance of each treatment group on the post and delayed administrations of the 25% HCQ Intentional Scale. The test items in this scale were intentional for the 25% HCQ treatment and incidental for the other treatments. As predicted, the 25% HCQ treatment groups outperformed the other recitations groups and the art activity groups on this scale, which lends support to the hypothesis.

Another test of the hypothesis was to compare the recitation treatment groups' performance on the Intentional and Incidental Scales of the Information Test. Since the two scales are of different length, an average score per item was computed and used as the basis for comparison. A rough index of comparative item difficulty in the intentional and incidental scales was obtained by comparing the performance of the Art Activity treatment groups on these scales. Since both scales were equally incidental for these groups, any difference in mean item scores between scales should reflect item difficulty rather than intentional/incidental learning effects. No such differences were observed for the Art Activity groups.

Comparisons of average score per item revealed that Experiment I recitation groups performed better on the Intentional Scale than on the Incidental Scale.

No differences were observed among Experiment II recitation groups. It should be noted that students in Experiment II had slightly higher reading ability than students in Experiment I. Perhaps the effect of recitation on intentional versus incidental learning is dependent on this or similar student aptitudes. Further research is needed to test this speculation.

Another question of interest was whether learning gains resulting from recitation teaching would be more pronounced on a modality-consistent measure of higher cognitive response ability (Oral Test) than on a measure involving different modalities (Essay Test). The pre-post gains of the combined recitation treatments on the two tests were compared in both experiments. Every comparison showed a substantially greater gain on the measures of the Oral Test than on the measures of the Essay Test. However, it was not possible to determine empirically whether the items in the two tests were parallel in form and difficulty. Further testing of the hypothesis is needed.

The most noteworthy feature of the research methodology in the two experiments is the use of the semi-programmed teaching episode. These episodes made it possible for the researchers to equate opportunity to learn the curriculum content across the various treatment conditions; to develop content-valid achievement tests; and to verify treatment implementation—all methodological problems which have plagued previous research on teaching. Although the procedure of having teachers conform to a scripted format might seem artificial, in practice it seemed to work well. Raters who listened to audiotapes of the treatment recitations commented that the teachers seemed natural and well organized. The teachers did not object to the format, and appeared able to vary their behavior to conform to the treatment variations. Students' ratings of the recitations generally were positive. The use of this type of teaching episode has potential for future research on teaching techniques and strategies.

Although the experiments were methodologically rigorous, there are some obvious limits to the generalizability of its findings. The experimental recitations were conducted in small groups of only six students instead of a full class, and the teachers taught from scripts developed by the researchers rather than from self-developed lesson plans involving more use of spontaneous questioning techniques. Another limit on generalizability is that only a few treatment variations were examined in the experiments. The effects of probing and redirection were assessed at only one level of higher cognitive questioning (50%) in Experiment I. In the second experiment, however, it was found that this level of higher cognitive questioning was not generalizable in its effectiveness to other levels (i.e., 25% HCQ and 75% HCQ). Moreover, every one of the ten lessons was identical in its teaching style, as opposed to the likely variety which might characterize such a span of lessons under typical teaching conditions.

The results of the experiments have at least one implication for the training of teachers. The major finding was that teachers' use of the recitation strategy was more significant than whether they used probing, redirection, or a particular level of higher cognitive questioning. This finding suggests that training teachers in these discrete skill competencies may not be as critical as providing training in a strategy which incorporates the competencies.

CONTRIBUTORS

MEREDITH D. GALL, Associate Professor, College of Education, University of Oregon, Eugene, Oregon 97403.

BEATRICE A. WARD, Associate Laboratory Director for Teacher Education, Far West Laboratory for Educational Research and Development, 1855 Folsom Street, San Francisco, California 94103.

DAVID C. BERLINER, Professor, College of Education, University of Arizona, Tucson, Arizona 85712.

LEONARD S. CAHEN, Senior Program Associate, Far West Laboratory for Educational Research and Development, 1855 Folsom Street, San Francisco, California 94103.

JANET D. ELASHOFF, Research Statistician, Center for Ulcer Research, Wadsworth V. A., Building 115, Room 223, Los Angeles, CA 90073.

PHILIP H. WINNE, Assistant Professor, Simon Fraser University, Faculty of Education, Burnaby, British Columbia, Canada.

GEORGE C. STANTON, College of Education, Stanford University, Stanford, California 94305.

REFERENCE NOTES

[1]BIERLY, M. M., CLARK, C. M., GAGE, N. L., PETERSON, P. L., & WESSITCH, A. Cataloguing teacher training materials in a computerized retrieval system. Paper presented at the annual meeting of the American Educational Research Association, Chicago, 1974.

[2]THOMPSON, G. R., & BOWERS, N. C. Fourth grade achievement as related to creativity, intelligence, and teaching style. Paper presented at the annual meeting of the American Educational Research Association, Chicago, 1968.

[3]WINNE, P. H. Experiments on teachers' use of higher cognitive questions and student achievement. Manuscript submitted for publication, 1977.

REFERENCES

ANDERSON, D. W., COOPER, J. M., DEVAULT, M. V., DICKSON, G. E., JOHNSON, C. E., & WEBER, W. A. *Competency-based teacher education.* Berkeley, Calif.: McCutchan, 1973.

ANDERSON, R. C., & BIDDLE, W. B. On asking people questions about what they are reading. In Gordon Bower (ed.), *Psychology of learning and motivation, Vol. 9.* New York: Academic Press, 1975.

BERLINER, D. C. Impediments to the study of teacher effectiveness. *Journal of Teacher Education,* 1976, *27,* 5-13.

BLOOM, B. S. (ed.). *Taxonomy of educational objectives, Handbook 1: Cognitive domain.* New York: David McKay, 1956.

BUGGEY, L. J. A study of the relationship of classroom questions and social studies achievement of second grade children (Doctoral dissertation, University of Washington, 1971). *Dissertation Abstracts International,* 1972, *32,* 2543-A. (University Microfilm No. 71-28385.)

DUNKIN, M. J., & BIDDLE, B. J. *The study of teaching.* New York: Holt, Rinehart, & Winston, 1974.

ELASHOFF, J. D. Analysis of covariance: A delicate instrument. *American Educational Research Journal,* 1969, *6,* 383-401.

GAGE, N. L., & WINNE, P. H. Performance-based teacher education. In K. Ryan (ed.), *Teacher education,* 74th yearbook of the National Society for the Study of Education (Part II). Chicago: University of Chicago Press, 1975.

HEATH, R. W., & NIELSON, M. A. The research basis for performance-based teacher education. *Review of Educational Research,* 1977, *44,* 463-484.

OSGOOD, C. E., SUCI, G. J., & TANNENBAUM, P. H. *The measurement of meaning.* Urbana: University of Illinois, 1957.

PECKHAM, P. D., GLASS, G. V., & HOPKINS, K. D. The experimental unit in statistical analysis. *The Journal of Special Education,* 1969, *3,* 337-349.

ROSENSHINE, B. *Teaching behaviors and student achievement.* London: National Foundation for Educational Research in England and Wales, 1971.

ROSENSHINE, B., & FURST, N. F. Research on teacher performance criteria. In B. O. Smith (ed.), *Research in teacher education: A symposium.* Englewood Cliffs, N.J.: Prentice-Hall, 1971.

RYAN, F. L. Differentiated effects of levels of questioning on student achievement. *The Journal of Experimental Education,* 1973, *41,* 63-67.

SANDERS, N. M. *Classroom questions: What kinds?* New York: Harper and Row, 1966.

SAVAGE, T. V. A study of the relationship of classroom questions and social studies achievement of fifth grade children (Doctoral dissertation, University of Washington, 1972). *Dissertation Abstracts International,* 1972, *33,* 2245-A. (University Microfilms No. 72-28661.)

SOAR, R. S. *An integrative approach to classroom learning.* Philadelphia: Temple University, 1966. (ERIC Document Reproduction Service No. ED 033 479.)

SPAULDING, R. L. *Achievement, creativity, and self-concept correlates of teacher-pupil transactions in elementary schools* (U.S. Office of Education Cooperative Research Project No. 1352). Hempstead, N.Y.: Hofstra University, 1965.

TABA, H., LEVINE, S., & ELZEY, F. F. *Thinking in elementary school children* (U.S. Office of Education Cooperative Research Project No. 1574). San Francisco, Calif.: San Francisco State College, 1964.

TABA, H. *Thinking strategies and cognitive functioning in elementary school children* (U.S. Office of Education Cooperative Research Project No. 2404). San Francisco, Calif.: San Francisco State College, 1966.

WRIGHT, C. J., & NUTHALL, G. Relationships between teacher behaviors and pupil achievement in three elementary science lessons. *American Educational Research Journal,* 1970, *7,* 477-493.

Section VIII
Quasi-Experimental Methods in Educational Research

Quasi-Experiments: The Case of Interrupted Time Series

Gene V Glass
Arizona State University

Experimental research has to do with finding causes. Not all researchers seek to establish causes, but those who do distinguish their activities by calling them "experimental." Just what a "cause" is and how causal relationships are determined is a matter of no small philosophical debate. But we can safely ignore that debate and appeal to your intuitive understanding that renders meaningful to you such utterances as "The nail caused the tire to go flat" or "Access to a car causes teenagers' grades to drop."

If every relationship were causal, the world would be a simple place for experimenters. But most relationships aren't. In schools where teachers make above-average salaries, pupils score above average on achievement tests. But it's not safe to say that increasing teachers' salaries will cause an increase in pupils' achievement. Business executives who take long, expensive vacations make higher salaries than executives who don't. But will taking the summer off and touring Europe increase your salary? Try it and find out.

Relationships: Causal and Otherwise

Ordinary sorts of relationships can fail to be causal relationships for two principal reasons; methodologists have named these reasons (a) the *third-variable problem,* and (b) the *ambiguous-direction-of-influence problem.* The third-variable situation occurs when two things are related because each is causally related to a third variable, not because of any causal link between each other. The teachers' salaries and pupil achievement example is probably an instance of the "third-variable problem." In this case, the third variable might be the wealth of the community; rich communities pay teachers more and have pupils who score higher on achievement tests for a host of reasons connected to family wealth but not to teachers' pay. Teachers are professionals who want to be paid well and deserve to be; but I doubt that, once the negotiations are finished, a teacher tries any harder to teach the pupils because of a few hundred dollars on the salary schedule. So the relationship of teachers' salaries and pupil achievement—a relationship that is an empirical fact, incidentally—is due to common relationships to a third variable, and not to a causal link between them.

The business executive's vacation is an example of ambiguous direction of influence. A travel agent might publish a graph in an advertisement that shows the relationship I mentioned. But the simple fact of the relationship leaves quite ambiguous whether long vacations cause higher salaries (presumably through improving morale and vitality and the like) or higher salaries cause long, expensive vacations. The truth is obvious in this case, and it is quite the opposite of the direction of influence that the travel agents wants people to believe. But many other examples are less clear. Does enhanced motivation cause pupils to learn successfully in school, or is it mainly the other way around: success in learning causes an increase in motivation to learn? The truth is probably some of each in unknown amounts—which goes to show how ill-advised one is to think of each relationship as if it were a causal relationship.

Experimentalists have devised a methodology that lays both of these problems to rest. They contrive two or more sets of circumstances that are alike in all respects except for the phenomenon that is being tested as a possible cause, and then they subsequently observe whether the expected effect ensues. For example, an experimentalist might take a large sample of teachers and their pupils and divide them into two *identical* groups except that one group's teachers receive a $500.00 raise and the other group's do not. Then a year later he or she measures the pupils' achievement to see whether it has been affected. By setting up two identical groups of teachers and their pupils, the experimenter ruled out all possible third variables as explanations of the eventual difference in pupil achievement. Can it be said that an achievement advantage for the pupils of the better paid teachers is not really due to increased pay since the better paid teachers might have had older pupils or smarter pupils or the better paid teachers might have had more experience? In other words, might not there be some third-variable problems here? No, because the teachers and pupils were equivalent in all respects at the beginning of the year. Can it be said that the direction of influence between salaries and achievement is ambiguous in this experiment? No, because the different salaries were set by the experimenters *before* pupil achievement was observed. Hence, the differences in achievement could not have caused the differences in teacher salaries; the only possible direction of influence is the other way around.

This style of experimental thinking has been around for well over 100 years. For many decades it was relatively impractical because it held that the conditions compared in the experiment had to be identical in all respects except for the hypothesized cause; that is, all third variables were to be ruled out by ensuring that they did not vary between the conditions. The problem is that all the possible third variables can't possibly be known and even if they could be, they couldn't possibly be equated. Imagine having to equate the high- and low-paid teachers on their age, sex, height, weight, IQ, experience, nationality, and on and on.

Randomized Experiments

The experimental method received a big boost in the 1920s when a young Englishman named Ronald Fisher devised an ingenious, practical solution to the third-variable problem. Fisher reasoned that if, for example, chance alone was used to determine which teachers in the experiment were paid more and which less, then any of an infinite number of possible third variables would be equated between the two groups—not numerically equal, but equated within the limits of chance, or *randomly equated* as it has come to be known. If a coin flip determines which teachers enter the high-pay group and which the low-pay group, then with respect to any third variable you can imagine (eye color, shoe size, or whatever) the two groups will differ only by chance. Fisher then reasoned as follows: if, after the experiment, the only observed differences between the conditions are no larger than what chance might account for, then those differences might well be due to the chance differences on some third variables. But if the differences are much larger than what chance might produce (e.g., if all of the pupils of well-paid teachers learn much more than the pupils of poorly paid teachers), then chance differences in third variables could not account for this result (differences in teacher pay must be the cause of the large differences in pupil achievement). Because experimenters must calculate the size of differences that chance is likely to produce and compare them with the differences they actually observe, they necessarily become involved with probability theory and its application to statistics.

Fisher's modern experimental methods were applied in agricultural research for 20 years or so before they began to be applied in psychology and eventually in education. In the early 1960s, a psychologist, Donald Campbell, and an educational researcher, Julian Stanley (Campbell & Stanley, 1963), published a paper that was quickly acknowledged to be a classic. They drew important distinctions between experiments of the type Fisher devised and many other designs and methods being employed by researchers with aspirations to experiments but failing to satisfy all of Fisher's conditions. Campbell and Stanley called the experiments that Fisher devised "true experiments." The methods that fell short of satisfying the conditions of true experiments they called "quasi-experiments", quasi meaning seemingly or apparently but not genuinely so.

True experiments satisfy these conditions: the experimenter sets up two or more conditions whose effects are to be evaluated *subsequently;* persons or groups of persons are then assigned strictly at random, that is, by chance, to the conditions; the eventual differences between the conditions on the measure of effect (for example, the pupils' achievement) are compared with differences of chance or random magnitude.

Quasi-Experiments: The Interrupted Time Series

Quasi-experiments cannot be so easily described. There are many varieties of them, and the various species arise from different ways of attempting to control for third variables without actually using random assignment. One of the most promising and frequently used quasi-experimental designs is known as the *interrupted time-series experiment*. It is the subject of the remainder of this paper.

In Figure 1 appears a graph of the number of depressed thoughts (the solid black line) recorded for 49 consecutive days by a mildly depressive young

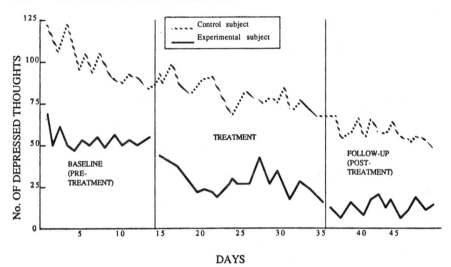

FIGURE 1. *Incidence of depressed thoughts for an experimental subject receiving behavioral therapy and for a control subject.*

woman. On the first day, she counted about 70 depressed thoughts; on the second day, about 55. After 14 days of recording (after the first solid vertical line in Figure 1) the woman was placed on a behavioral modification therapy designed to eliminate depression. The therapy was continued for 21 days and then terminated (at the second vertical line), and the recording of depressed thoughts continued for an additional 14 posttreatment days.

By studying the pattern of the graph, paying particular attention to what happens to the series precisely at the point of shifting from no-treatment to treatment or vice versa, we hope to learn something about the effect of the therapy on depressed thoughts. In general terms, the therapy is called a *treatment* or an *intervention* and depressed thoughts are the *outcome* or *dependent variable*.

You might often find that a time-series experiment is a workable alternative when the conditions of a true experiment can't be met; for example, when you have only one or two units (persons or classrooms) instead of a substantial number, or when different units can't be treated in different ways (methods A and B) at the same time. But the time-series experiment imposes its own requirements, the foremost of which is that it sometimes requires that data be recorded for many consecutive points in time before and after a treatment is introduced. How many is "many"? We'll return to this important question later.

Another set of circumstances in which one might use a time-series experiment to assess the effect of a treatment is with data archives and naturally occurring interventions. In this case, the intervention is made by someone other than the researcher and it is not normally made for experimental purposes—although the researcher makes use of it for causal analysis. The data to evaluate the impact of the intervention come from archives: collections of data gathered routinely across time for administrative purposes. An example of this type of *archival time-series experiment* appears as Figure 2. Here you see a graph of the traffic fatality rate in Great Britain, by month, from 1961 through 1970. The dependent variable is the number of traffic deaths in a month divided by the number of miles driven in Great Britain, in units of 100,000,000. For example, there were about 12 deaths per 100,000,000 miles driven in January 1961; that is, if the total mileage driven in Great Britain in January 1961 was 300,000,000, then there were about $3 \times 12 = 36$ traffic deaths that month. (Incidentally, "miles driven" is estimated from gas tax revenues, assuming some reasonable average figure for mileage per gallon.) In October 1967, the British Road Safety Act of 1967 instituted a variety of measures designed to reduce traffic accidents, foremost among which was setting up road blocks and administering breath tests to discover drunken drivers. This intervention is indicated by the vertical line in Figure 2.

The simple logic of the time-series experiment is this: if the graph of the dependent variable shows an abrupt shift in level or direction precisely at the point of intervention, then the intervention is a cause of the effect on the dependent variable. In the two examples presented thus far, the particular causal questions are these: "Did the behavioral psychotherapy reduce the rate of depressed thoughts?" and "Did the British Road Safety Act of 1967 reduce the traffic fatality rate?"

The effect of an intervention on an outcome variable can assume a variety of forms. Some of these are depicted in Figure 3. The possibilities sketched in Figure 3 are pretty obvious and there's not much to be said about them with the exception of one important point: the causal argument is stronger to the extent that the experimenter correctly anticipates the precise form of the inter-

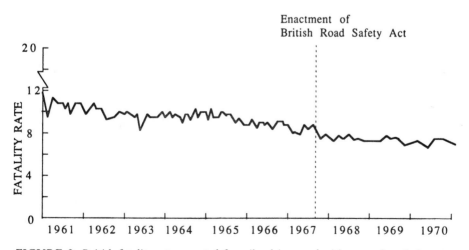

FIGURE 2. *British fatality rate corrected for miles driven and with seasonal variations removed.* (Source: Ross, 1973)

vention effect. Having detailed expectations about how the graph should change in response to an intervention is the best protection against deluding oneself and being led astray by extraneous influences and chance occurrences. For example, suppose that a highway safety law required a car tire safety check and replacement of worn tires. Because not all tires would have worn treads at the moment the law was enacted, and because perhaps 10% of the worn tires might be detected and replaced monthly for about the first year, an intervention effect like that in case E in Figure 3 might be anticipated. If an abrupt level change—case A—were observed in the data instead, the chain of causal reasoning from tire inspection to reduced accidents would be weakened, even though the possibility of an effect due to some unknown cause remained strong.

Carefully spelled-out expectations for the form of an effect are crucial where

A. Abrupt change in level

B. Delayed change in level

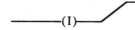

C. Temporary change in level

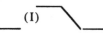

D. Decaying change in level

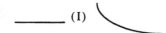

E. Abrupt change in direction

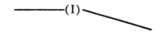

F. Delayed change in direction

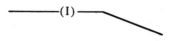

G. Temporary change in direction

H. Accelerated change in direction

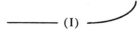

I. "Evolutionary operations" effect

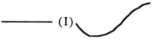

J. Change in variability

FIGURE 3. *Varieties of intervention effects in the time-series experiment.* [(I) denotes the time at which an intervention is introduced.]

delayed effects might exist (for example, cases B and F in Figure 3). Delayed effects occur frequently and are perfectly plausible. For example, the Mental Health Act of 1965 authorized construction of community mental health centers that couldn't possibly have begun to function significantly before 1967. An experimenter who does not have definite expectations about the form of an effect may interpret as an effect every little ephemeral and irrelevant jump or wiggle in the curve. Figure 4 is a graph of the Dow-Jones Industrial Average for the 1960s. It's amusing to speculate about each twist and turn and what loosed the bulls and the bears, but without some clear expectations, scanning the peaks and valleys is an undisciplined game.

Graphs of time-series data can change level and direction for many reasons, some related to the intervention and others not. Separating potential reasons for effects into those essentially related to the intervention and those only accidentally related is the principal task in analyzing time-series experiments. You might recognize the time-series experimental design as an extension in both directions (the past and the future) of the old and disreputable pretest-posttest experiment. In the pretest-posttest design, a group of persons is observed, a treatment is applied to them, and then they are observed a second time. An increase (or a decrease) of the group average from the first observation to the second is taken to be the effect of the independent variable (the treatment) on the dependent variable that was observed. The pretest-posttest design has such a bad reputation because so many influences other than the treatment can account for a change in scores from pre to post. The person or persons in the experiment could grow tired, smarter, or less cooperative from the single premeasure to the postmeasure. Likewise, two less-than-identical tests might be given before and after, or the experimental units could have been chosen because they fell so far from the average on the pretest thus greatly increasing the odds of their regression (i.e., movement) toward the mean of the posttest. Each of these influences can cause increases or decreases in scores that are confounded with whatever effects the intervention or treatment might have. The pretest-posttest design deserves its bad press.

The time-series experiment adds many preintervention and postintervention observations and thus permits separating real intervention effects from other long-term trends in a time series. Consider Figure 1 again. The series of depressed thoughts for the control subject shows a gradual, regular decline from Day 1 to Day 49. The course that the graph follows shows no abrupt shifts at those points in time when the experimental subject, represented by the solid black line, is put on treatment and taken off. There is no evidence of an intervention effect on the control subject's graph, as there ought not to be, since this subject was given no therapy but merely recorded the rate of depressed thoughts for 49 days. But notice how, if a single premeasure had been taken on the control subject around Day 5 and a single postmeasure around Day 25, it would have appeared as though this subject had experienced a sizable reduction in depressed thoughts due to treatment. To be sure, the control subject's graph shows a decline across time, but the decline could be due to many extraneous

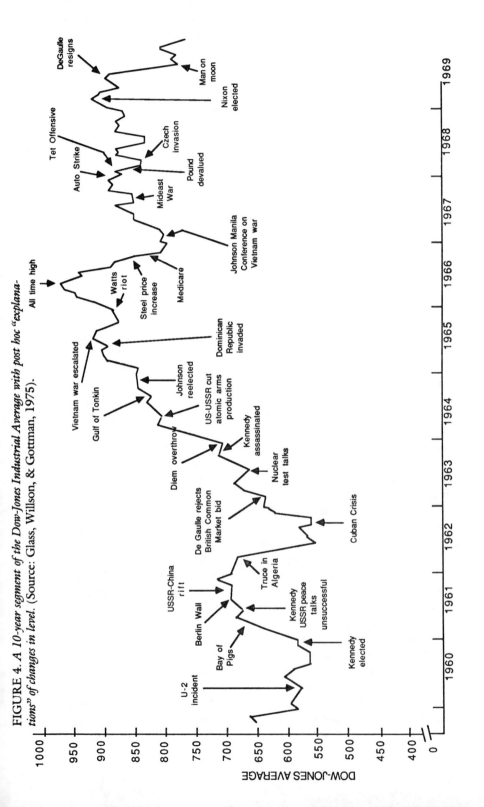

FIGURE 4. A 10-year segment of the Dow-Jones Industrial Average with post hoc "explanations" of changes in level. (Source: Glass, Willson, & Gottman, 1975).

factors, including becoming bored counting depressed thoughts, a shifting standard of what constitutes a depressed thought, hormonal changes, and the like.

There are many different ways to arrange experimental units and to plan the intervention of one or several treatments into series. Some ways may be cheaper or safer than others, depending on many circumstances of particular applications. In Figure 5, several possible alternative time-series designs are sketched. They are special-purpose designs, each created for reasons of economy or validity. For example, Design A uses one person or a single, undifferentiated group of persons, but evaluates the effect of more than one intervention. The Os in the diagram stand for observations or measurements; they are taken repeatedly across time (from left to right) in the diagram. The Is stand for interventions, that is, the introduction of a treatment. The "1" and the "2" are added to the I's in Design A to indicate that two different treatments were introduced into the series.

Time-series experiments differ in important ways depending on whether the "experimental unit" is a single person or a group of persons. And if the unit is a large group of persons, one can either measure each person in the group at each point in time or subsample different portions of the group at different

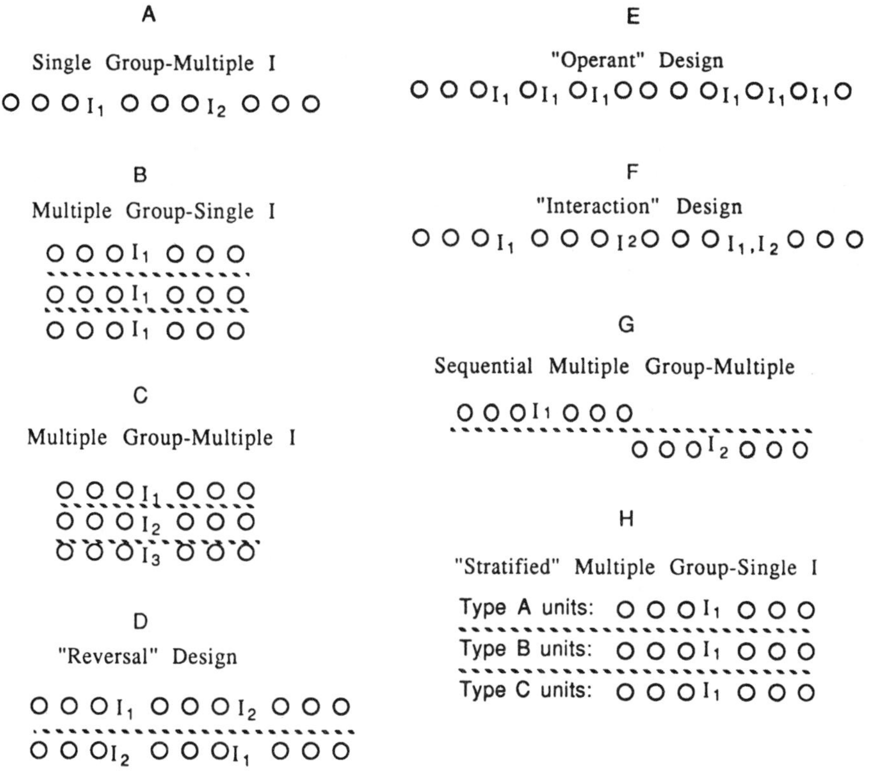

FIGURE 5. *Variations on the basic time-series experimental design.* (O represents an observation or measurement of the dependent variable; I represents an intervention.)

times. For example, in Figure 6 appear the results of a time-series experiment on the effects of Outward Bound—a wilderness camping experience—on participants' self-confidence. Several hundred participants were available for study, but it would have been unnecessary and too costly to give the self-confidence questionnaire to each subject during each of the 45 weeks of the study. But by randomly sampling a new group of 20 persons each week from the beginning to the end, no participant was burdened by the testing and yet an accurate picture was obtained of the group's response to treatment.

There are two suggestions that are most important for preventing misinterpretations of time-series experiments and for getting the most out of them. The first has to do with statistical analysis and distinguishing the ordinary gyrations of a series from the genuine effects of an intervention. The second suggestion deals with exploring in large data banks, and classifying and subdividing the collection of data so that hidden effects can emerge.

Statistics for Time-Series Experiments

Consider the statistical analysis question first. The graph of a real time series will show a good deal of fluctuation quite apart from any effect an intervention might have on it. Consider, for example, the graph of the series in Figure 7, where the number of anxious thoughts of a neurotic patient is recorded for 10 days before psychotherapy and for 21 days during therapy. I showed the graph in Figure 7 to 13 researchers and asked them to judge whether the drop in the curve at the point of intervention was significant; i.e., whether it was so large as to lead them to believe that the introduction of therapy actually reduced anxious thoughts, or whether the roughly 7-point drop at the intervention point was merely a random fluctuation, unaccountable in terms of the intervention, like the 9-point increase between days 5 and 6 or the more than 9-point rise between Days 29 and 30. Of the 13 researchers who studied the graph, 5 judged the intervention to be effective and 8 judged it ineffective. Statistical analysis by jury in this instance proved inconclusive.

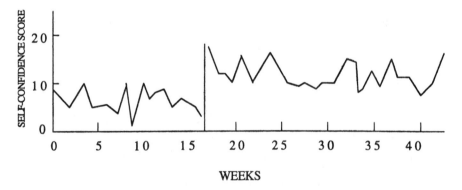

FIGURE 6. *Self-confidence scores of a large group of participants before and after an Outward Bound wilderness experience.* (Source: Smith et al., 1976).

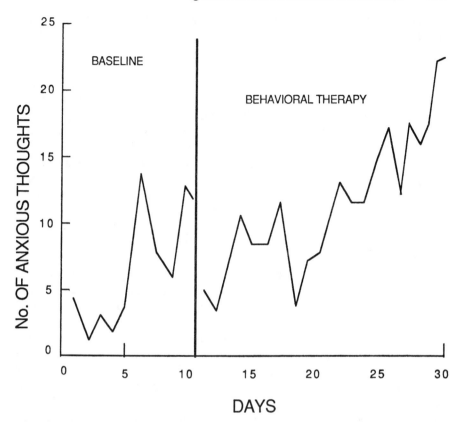

FIGURE 7. *Incidence of anxious thoughts for a single subject before and during behavioral therapy* (after Komechak, 1974).

A key distinction has to be drawn between two types of series: those that are *stationary* and those that are *nonstationary*. The distinction makes all the difference in the world when it comes to inspecting graphs and analyzing whether or not an intervention had an effect. The difference between stationary and nonstationary time series is the difference between graphs that fluctuate around some fixed levels across time and graphs that wander about, changing their level and region haphazardly. The graph of British traffic fatalities in Figure 2 is reasonably stationary, with most of the preintervention observations contained in a region between 8 and 11. The graph of the Dow-Jones average (Figure 4) is decidedly nonstationary. It hovers in the 600 to 700 region for the first 3 years, then rises to the 800 region and beyond for the next 7 years. The time series in Figure 6 is stationary, on the other hand.

It is far easier to detect an intervention effect in a stationary process than in a nonstationary one. Intervention effects are seen as displacements of the curve, and as you can see, nonstationary processes are, by definition, curves that are subject to displacements of level and slope at random points in time. The trick with nonstationary time series is to distinguish the random displacements from the one true deterministic displacement caused by the intervention. And that's not easy.

If a process is basically nonstationary, you need to establish that fact and, furthermore, be able to estimate the degree of nonstationarity before you can decide how much displacement of the curve precisely at the point of intervention is convincing evidence of an effect. How can one establish the fact and character of nonstationarity? By patiently watching the series for a long time before intervening. This is why the researchers who looked at Figure 7 and tried to guess whether the intervention was really effective or not, did such a bad job. The preintervention period, the "baseline" if you will, simply wasn't long enough to establish the character of the process; i.e., it wasn't long enough to give one a good idea of how the series should behave in the absence of any intervention. The circumstances in Figure 2 are quite different. The British fatality rate can be expected to be about 8 to 10 after mid-1967 as it was for several months before.

Once again, the statistician must act as a messenger of the doleful news: *the single most important thing to remember about time-series experiments is that they require long baseline periods for establishing whether the process is stationary or nonstationary.*

How long is "long"? Once again, the statistician must, in honesty, give a vague answer where a precise one is expected. It's difficult to say exactly how long a baseline must be for a time-series experiment to be safe. The answer depends in part on how much one knows in advance about the process being studied. If a researcher has studied extensively a particular phenomenon—like "out-of-seat time" for pupils in a classroom—and has never seen much nonstationarity, it's conceivable that a satisfactory baseline can be established in relatively short order in a time-series experiment, a dozen or so points in time, say. But when a series is quite nonstationary, 40 or 50 baseline time points may be needed before the process is sufficiently understood that one would attempt to assess the effects of an intervention.

Let me hazard a generalization that admits many exceptions. We have found that time-series of observations of a single individual are often stationary, particularly if you discard the first few points during which the subject may be acclimating to the equipment or observation procedures. On the other hand, time-series based on large groups of persons—like classrooms, cities, or the population of an entire nation—are often nonstationary. I hasten to point out that this generalization isn't always true even in the examples presented here.

To prevent being accused of evading the question of how many data points are needed in a time-series experiment, I want to indicate in very general terms how satisfied a statistician would be, working with series of different lengths. No statistician I know would insist on more than 100 points in time, but some of the more rigid ones might not accept fewer. Fifty time points (25 pre and 25 post) is a good round number, provided you make a definite hypothesis about the form of the intervention effect and stick with it; that is, provided you don't succumb to the temptation of fishing around in the data after you see it and taking second and third guesses at the form of the intervention effect. Fifteen preintervention points is certainly cutting things as thin as they'll go, and even then so short a baseline is only safe if you know a lot in advance about the probable statistical character of the series. If you're held to under 10 preintervention points, then you shouldn't be performing a time-series experiment unless you have an intervention so potent that it will work huge effects—in which case you'll probably know it without an experiment. If you attempt time-series experiments with too short baselines you're likely to end up with data like those in Figure 8. There the incidence of child molestation is graphed for a 12-year period around the enactment of three regulations that made pornography easily available to adults. The time series is simply too short to permit any kind of conclusion.

One final statistical point bears mentioning. Time series nearly always evidence a form of statistical correlation that is quite unlike what we are accustomed to in working with random samples. For many reasons, today's score is

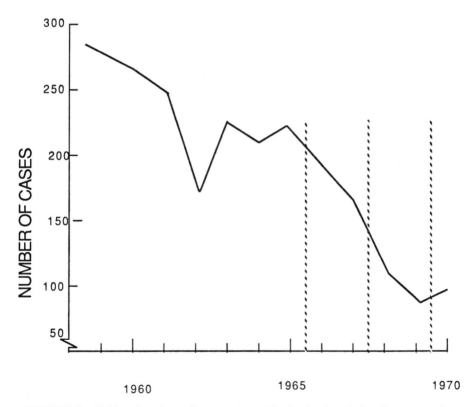

FIGURE 8. *Child molestation (offenses against girls) in the city of Copenhagen.* (Broken vertical lines represent successive liberalizations of Danish pornography laws.) (Source: Kutchinsky, 1973).

more highly correlated with either yesterday's or tomorrow's score than it is with either the score from a week ago or a week hence. This condition of correlation within the series wreaks havoc with ordinary statistical techniques; it's about the only violation of standard statistical assumptions (normality, equal variance, and independence) that is worth worrying about. The proper means are known of taking account of this form of correlation, but the methods are complex—by elementary textbook standards. At the end of this paper, I've given references in which you can pursue these more technical questions on your own.

Investigation and Detective Work

And now for suggestions about getting the most out of a time-series experiment. In some time-series experiments, it frequently happens that subsections of a large data pool reveal intervention effects that aren't apparent in the complete body of data. Consider the data in Figure 2, for example. If there is any effect of the British Road Safety Act of 1967 on the traffic fatality rate, it certainly isn't very apparent in the graph in Figure 2. But look at the graph in Figure 9 to see what happened when the fatalities on weekend nights were singled out of the total body of data. There we see a huge, more than 50%, reduction in fatalities coincident with the implementation of the Road Safety Act in October 1967. We can move from the equivocal results of Figure 2 to the clear certainty of Figure 9, merely by separating the larger body of data.

Why is the effect so apparent in Figure 9 when it was barely discernible (or indeed, not discernible at all) in Figure 2? As was mentioned earlier, an essential

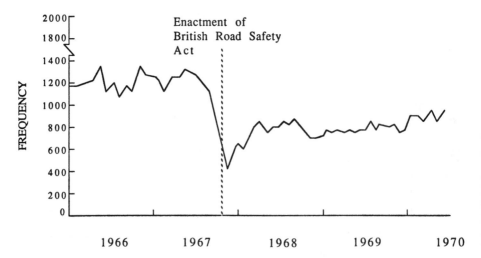

FIGURE 9. *Fatalities for Friday nights, 10:00 p.m. to midnight; Saturday mornings, midnight to 4:00 a.m.; Saturday nights, 10:00 p.m. to midnight; and Sunday mornings, midnight to 4:00 a.m.; corrected for weekend days per month, seasonal variations removed.* (Broken vertical line represents implementation of the Road Safety Act.) Source: Ross, Campbell, & Glass, 1970)

feature of the Road Safety Act was a program of roadblocks where drivers were tested for blood alcohol level. And what time is better for finding drunks on the road than weekend nights? The picture is completed in Figure 10 when one inspects the fatalities curve for the hours commuting to and from work in the morning and late afternoon when there are few drunken drivers. Sorting the data in Figure 2 into two different series in Figures 9 and 10 not only has revealed the intervention effect, but has illuminated the whole question of how the Road Safety Act worked its effect.

Opponents of the anti-drunk-driver features of the Road Safety Act argued that other features of the law were actually responsible for the decrease in fatalities: for example, the construction of more and better traffic signals, a tire inspection program, and a reduction in the numbers of motorcycles and mopeds on the road. The pattern of the time series in Figures 9 and 10 refutes these counterclaims, as each of the counterclaims would lead one to expect an effect that was initially small then grew, and was of equal size for commuting hours and weekend nights.

Consider Figure 11 as a final example where the answers aren't so clear. The figure is a graph of the enrollment of the Denver Public Schools from 1928 to 1975, and the experimental question concerns forced racial integration and "white flight." In 1969, in the Federal District court, Judge Doyle rendered a decision in the Keys vs. Denver Public Schools case that represented the first forced integration decision in a major northern city. The question is, "Was there a resulting flight of white families to the suburbs to escape racially integrated schools?"

FIGURE 10. *Fatalities for Mondays through Fridays, 8:00 a.m. to 10:00 a.m. and 4:00 p.m. to 5:00 p.m., corrected for weekdays per month, seasonal variation removed.* (Broken vertical line represents implementation of the Road Safety Act.) Source: Ross, Campbell, & Glass, 1970)

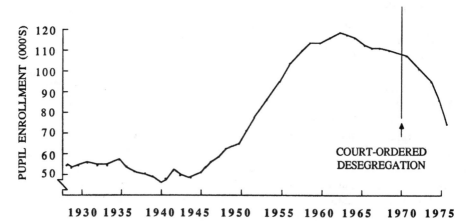

FIGURE 11. *Enrollment of Denver public schools from 1928 to 1975.*

The total enrollment of the Denver Public Schools dropped from 1970 on, but it had been dropping ever since 1960. The question is whether the enrollment dropped faster after 1969 than before, and it appears to, but the situation is hardly unequivocal. The enrollment grew as fast during the 1950s as it fell in the early 1970s, and no one implicated racial strife or harmony in the earlier acceleration. Moreover, the national birthrate was falling sharply in the late 1960s, exactly 5 years ahead of what looks like a sharp decline in Denver School enrollment in the 1970s; and for all that Judge Doyle's decision might have done, it is stretching things to believe that it could have affected the birthrate 5 years before it was handed down.

The Denver case in Figure 11 has to remain uncertain. But I suspect that it could be resolved fairly conclusively by breaking down and plotting in several alternative ways the total enrollment series in Figure 11. Breaking the enrollment data down by grade might cast a little light on things. If it's really white flight that is causing the decline, one might expect a larger decline at the elementary grades than at the secondary grades, particularly grades 11 and 12 where parents would likely decide to stick it out for the short run. If enrollment data existed separately for different ethnic groups, these time series would provide a very revealing test. If they showed roughly equal declines across all ethnic groups, the "white flight" hypothesis would suffer a major setback. Data on enrollment that could be separated by individual school, neighborhood, or census tract would be exceptionally valuable. These various units could be ranked prior to looking at the data on their susceptibility to white flight. Such a ranking could be based on variables like "pre-1969 ethnic mixture," "percentage of change in ethnic mixture of the school under the desegregation plan," or "mobility of families based on percentage of housing values mortgaged or amount of disposable income." If the large enrollment declines fell in the highly susceptible regions, the pattern would constitute some degree of support for the white flight hypothesis.

All in all, time-series experiments require little more than generous baselines, good graphing skills, and a lot of practical savvy about where to look for the hiding effects. At their best, they are almost as much fun as detective work—fictional detective work, that is.

References

Campbell, D. T., & Stanley, J. C. (1963). Experimental and quasi-experimental designs for research on teaching. In N. L. Gage (Ed.), *Handbook of research on teaching*. Chicago: Rand McNally.

Glass, G. V, Willson, V. L., & Gottman, J. M. (1975). *Design and analysis of time-series experiments*. Boulder, CO: Colorado Associated University Press.

Komechak, M. G. (1974). *Thought detection as a precipitator of anxiety responses*. Doctoral dissertation, North Texas State University.

Kutchinsky, B. (1973). The effect of easy availability of pornography on the incidence of sex crimes: The Danish experience. *Journal of Social Issues, 29*, 163–181.

Ross, H. L. (1973). Law, science, and accidents: The British Road Safety Act of 1967. *Journal of Legal Studies, 2*, 1–78.

Ross, H. L., Campbell, D. T., & Glass, G. V (1970). Determining the social effects of a legal reform. In S. S. Nagel (Ed.), *Law and social change* (pp. 15–32). Beverly Hills, CA: Sage.

Smith, M. L., et al. (1976). Evaluation of the effects of Outward Bound. In G. V Glass (Ed.), *Evaluation studies review annual: Vol. 1* (Chapter 19). Beverly Hills, CA: Sage.

Suggestions for Further Reading

Time-Series Experiment Design

The following references deal with general questions of the design of time-series experiments and their application to specific fields of study.

Campbell, D. T. (1969). From description to experimentation: Interpreting trends as quasi-experiments. In C. W. Harris (Ed.), *Problems in measuring change* (pp. 212–242). Madison: University of Wisconsin Press.

Campbell, D. T. (1969). Reforms as experiments. *American Psychologist, 24,* 409–429.

Campbell, D. T., & Stanley, J. C. (1966). *Experimental and quasi-experimental designs for research.* Chicago: Rand McNally.

Cook, T. D., & Campbell, D. T. (1979). *Quasi-experimentation: Design and analysis issues for field settings.* Chicago: Rand McNally.

Glass, G. V, Willson, V. L., & Gottman, J. M. (1975). *Design and analysis of time-series experiments.* Boulder, CO: Colorado Associated University Press.

Gottman, J. M. (1973). N-of-one and N-of-two research in psychotherapy. *Psychological Bulletin, 80,* 93–105.

Gottman, J. M., & Lieblum, S. R. (1974). *How to do psychotherapy and how to evaluate it.* New York: Holt, Rinehart & Winston.

Kratochwill, T. R. (Ed.). (1979). *Strategies to evaluate change in single subject research.* New York: Academic Press.

Thoresen, C. E., & Anton, J. L. (1974). Intensive experimental research in counseling. *Journal of Counseling Psychology, 21,* 553–559.

Analysis of Time-Series Experiments

The following references deal with problems in the inferential statistical analysis of time-series experiments. Unfortunately, they are not simple. Each requires some background in statistics and a good deal of dedication to extracting its message.

Bower, C. P., Padia, W. L., & Glass, G. V (1974). *TMS: Two FORTRAN IV programs for analysis of time-series experiments.* Boulder, CO: Laboratory of Educational Research, University of Colorado.   A manual for a computer program based on the analysis procedures derived in Glass, Willson, & Gottman (1975).

Box, G. E. P., & Jenkins, G. M. (1970). *Time-series analysis: Forecasting and control.* San Francisco: Holden-Day.   The seminal work on the "non-spectral" representation of time-series processes. No attention given to the intervention problem, but the bases for solving it are found here. Heavy going.

Box, G. E. P., & Tiao, G. C. (1965). A change in level of non-stationary time-series. *Biometrika, 52,* 181–192.   The first rigorous treatment of the intervention problem. Provides the accepted solution for the most commonly encountered nonstationary process.

Box, G. E. P., & Tiao, G. C. (1975). Intervention analysis with applications to economic and environmental problems. *Journal of the American Statistical Association, 70*, 70–79.   A modern treatment of the problem that the same authors solved in 1965. The new solution is mathematically more unified and elegant, but practically it will lead to virtually the same results as the earlier solution.

Glass, G. V, Wilson, V. L., & Gottman, J. M. (1975). *Design and analysis of time-series experiments*. Boulder, CO: Colorado Associated University Press.   Presents a solution to the intervention analysis problem in the general case.

Gottman, J. M., & Glass, G. V (1979). Analysis of the interrupted time-series experiment. In T. R. Kratochwill (Ed.), *Strategies to evaluate change in single subject research*. New York: Academic Press.   Further applications of the techniques derived in Glass, Willson, and Gottman (1975).

McDowall, D., McCleary, R., Meidinger, E. E., & Hay, R. A. (1980). *Interrupted time series analysis*. Beverly Hills, CA: SAGE.

Study Questions

1. What is one basic difference between experimental and nonexperimental research?

2. Describe two problems that interfere with causal interpretation of the relationship between two variables.

3. Describe the major difference between experimental and quasi-experimental research designs.

4. Why might a researcher choose to use an interrupted time-series design instead of a true experimental design?

5. If a researcher is to identify the effect of an intervention using an interrupted time-series design, what two conditions must be satisfied?

6. Try to think of some readily available data that could be analyzed using an interrupted time-series design. What kinds of educational data are routinely collected by most school systems or colleges, year after year?

7. Is there any way to rule out the potential effects of all third variables?

8. How do researchers identify or demonstrate the effects of experimental interventions when they analyze data from time-series experiments?

9. How do carefully delineated hypotheses help a researcher to demonstrate the effect of an intervention in a time-series design?

10. What is the difference between stationary and nonstationary time series?

11. Can standard statistical procedures typically be used when analyzing data from time-series experiments? Why or why not?

12. How do long baselines of data aid in interpreting the results of time-series experiments?

13. If a school system abandoned ability grouping in April and a long-standing time-series on average reading achievement increased sharply from the previous June to the following June, could the change be used as evidence of the causal effect of the policy shift? Would the evidence be strong and convincing? What additional data might be required?

14. Why is it frequently useful to develop separate time series for subgroups of large populations? Give an example to illustrate your reasoning.

Readings

Introduction
An Application of Time-Series Models to an Educational Research Study

Richard M. Jaeger

These two readings illustrate an application of the time-series analysis procedures described in the preceding paper by Glass. Both readings were selected by Gene V Glass. The first, by Mayer and Kozlow (1980), illustrates the use of what Glass (Figure 5) called the "multiple-group, single-intervention design." The researchers examine changes in the average achievement of two eighth-grade classes on a science concepts test, as a result of instruction on a science concept called "crustal evolution." The second reading, by Willson (1982), contains a reanalysis of the Mayer and Kozlow data. Willson uses some sophisticated statistical analysis procedures that were specially developed for the examination of data collected in time series. In addition, the Willson reading provides an illuminating discussion on the kinds of models that can be used to describe expected patterns of student achievement that might result from the use of an instructional treatment.

There are several reasons that these articles were selected to illustrate the use of time-series models in educational research. First, they illustrate an objective that is common in educational research studies—trying to determine the effects of an instructional treatment. Second, they are clearly written and, with the exception of the "Analysis" section of Willson's reading, avoid the use of complicated technical vocabulary. In other words, you should find these readings understandable even if your education in statistics is limited. Finally, these readings will add to your understanding of the practical application of time-series methods, since they show you how a real time-series study is designed, and how the results of such a study can be interpreted.

The Mayer and Kozlow Reading

In reading Mayer and Kozlow (1980), you should pay particular attention to the research questions the authors attempted to investigate. First, you must realize that observation in elementary or secondary school classrooms is both intrusive and time consuming. Whether a data collector merely sits in the back of a classroom and records what takes place, or asks students to provide specific information, the act of data collection is very likely to interfere with the principal instructional purpose of the class. In time-series research, data must be collected on a regular basis—such as daily or weekly—over an extended period of time. The danger of intrusion is thus far greater than would be the case if a more traditional research design were used, for example, one that required collection of data only twice (just prior to an intervention and just following an intervention). So one objective of the Mayer and Kozlow research was to determine whether a time-series study could be conducted in a typical classroom setting without upsetting instruction or taking too much class time.

Second, Mayer and Kozlow wanted to investigate the kinds of learning patterns a time-series study would show, and, in particular, to determine whether students' average achievement would increase during instruction and decrease (through forgetting) once instruction had ended. Note that Mayer and Kozlow had specific expectations about the pattern and shape of their time series, assuming their intervention was effective. They expected what Glass (Figure 3) termed "an abrupt change in direction" when their intervention was introduced and when it was removed.

Figures 1 and 2 in the Mayer and Kozlow reading illustrate the actual patterns of average student achievement they observed in two classrooms. When you study these figures, you should consider the question of whether these time series are stationary or nonstationary. Do you think that data have been collected at enough time points to tell? Just by looking at the figures, would you conclude that students' average achievement increased during instruction and then decreased after instruction stopped?

You might be tempted to conclude that Figure 1, which shows data for Class A, is more convincing than Figure 2, which shows data for Class B. Note that students' average achievement scores appear to vary more from day to day in Class B than in Class A, thus making it more difficult to identify a pattern. In Class B, students answered different achievement test items from one day to the next, and these items differed in their difficulty. In Class A, most of the same test items were used each day, although a given student answered different test items. Thus the pattern of achievement scores shown for Class B must be attributed, in part, to differences in the tests used each day, as well as to changes in students' actual learning. This third variable was not well controlled in Class B, and thus it muddies the interpretation of the time series.

Mayer and Kozlow used very simple, but intuitively appropriate, statistical analyses in trying to interpret the results of their time-series research. As shown in their Table I, they correlated students' average scores on the achievement test with the sequence numbers of the days on which they collected data. That is, they paired students' average achievement on Day 1 with the number 1, students' average achievement on Day 2 with the number 2, etc. For students in each class, they computed one correlation coefficient for Days 1 through 8 (the baseline period), another correlation coefficient for Days 9 through 18 (the intervention period), and a third correlation coefficient for Days 19 through 26 (the follow-up period). If the patterns of students' achievement scores followed their expectations, Mayer and Kozlow reasoned that the baseline correlations would be close to zero, that the intervention-period correlations would be positive (since they expected students to show increasing achievement as they were exposed to more instruction), and that correlations from the follow-up period would be negative (since they expected students to forget more of what they had learned as the time following instruction increased). Think about these expectations as you review the data in Table I, to see what really happened.

Notice that students' average achievement in Class A increased during the two days immediately following the end of instruction (Figure 1). In Class B, students' average achievement dropped a little on the day immediately following instruction, and then increased on the second day. Mayer and Kozlow interpreted these patterns as a "momentum effect," thus suggesting that students' cumulative learning continued to build for a couple of days after instruction ended, as a result of their having "put it all together" or having become enthusiastic about the instructional material. Table II contains the results of data analyses that reflect this supposition. When you read this section of Mayer and Kozlow, think about what Glass said in his paper concerning after-the-fact interpretations of time series. Do you think the "momentum effect" is a plausible explanation? What do you think of an interpretation that is based on only two data points?

In his paper, Glass told you a lot about the promises and pitfalls of time-series research designs. When you consider fundamental issues concerning the Mayer and Kozlow reading—Did they achieve their research objectives? Do you agree with their conclusions?—think about Glass's advice concerning the data requirements of stationary and nonstationary time series, the importance of specifying the time series' expected response to intervention, and the likely influence of third variables.

The Willson Reading

You should approach the Willson (1982) reading with the objectives of learning a bit more about the methodology of time-series research and trying to understand Willson's reanalysis of the Mayer and Kozlow data.

In his Figure 1, Willson illustrates two time-series patterns that might result from an instructional intervention, and two time-series patterns that might model students' forgetting after instruction has ended. His "Increasing Ramp Function" (1a) and "Declining Ramp Function" (1c) correspond to Mayer and Kozlow's expectations concerning the general patterns of their time series.

Willson notes the importance of having an observation for *every* time period (e.g., day or week) in a time series, and gives advice on how to estimate missing data, in case some days or weeks have been omitted. You should realize that having complete data is far more important if sophisticated statistical procedures are going to be used for analysis than if the time series is to be analyzed solely by inspecting a graph. Thus the two data points that are missing in the

Mayer and Kozlow data (Friday of the second week during the baseline period and Monday of the third week during the intervention period) are far more troublesome for Willson's analysis than for Mayer and Kozlow's.

You might find the Willson's "Analysis" section to be hard reading. He uses many statistical terms such as "parametric," "nonparametric," "frequency domain," "time domain," and probably worst of all, "autoregressive integrated moving average model (ARIMA)." Although this section would be a good bit clearer to you if you knew the definitions of these terms, you can get the general idea even if you know none of them.

Willson has assumed that the data collected by Mayer and Kozlow fit a specific statistical model, and has analyzed their data as though his assumptions were correct. Assuming a specific model is always a more powerful approach to data analysis than is the alternative, and it is a particularly useful procedure when the assumptions can be validated. Willson assumed that the data collected by Mayer and Kozlow for each class during the baseline and intervention periods would satisfy a statistical equation that, if graphed, would look like the "Ramp Function" of Figure 1a. He also assumed that the data collected during the baseline and forgetting periods, if analyzed together, would look like the "Declining Ramp Function" of Figure 1c. He further assumed that the differences between students' actual average achievement scores, and the average achievement scores predicted by these models, would be related to each other on successive days. By using statistical procedures that are consistent with these assumptions (called autoregression analysis), Willson was able to show that the Mayer and Kozlow data fit his models. When he conducted his analyses of the data for Class A, Willson decided that the extremely high average achievement score earned by students on the first day of the baseline period was the result of factors that were unrelated to the rest of the time series. In other words, he decided that the first day's data produced an "oddball score" that would best be ignored. Screening data for outlying and seemingly uninterpretable scores prior to analysis is in the best traditions of statistical practice, and can often save researchers from totally misleading interpretations of results.

Although based on more powerful statistical procedures, Willson's conclusions are quite similar to those of Mayer and Kozlow. In both classes, the "Ramp Function" (Figure 1c) appears to provide a good description of students' average achievement during the intervention period. However, substantial loss of achievement during the follow-up period was not confirmed for either class.

This summary and interpretation of the Willson reading has been provided as an aid to your understanding of the original. Now that you've read the summary, the reading should be far easier to comprehend. By approaching the reading with the summary in mind, you should learn some important new concepts and some fundamental terms in the language of time-series research.

AN EVALUATION OF A TIME–SERIES SINGLE–SUBJECT DESIGN USED IN AN INTENSIVE STUDY OF CONCEPT UNDERSTANDING

VICTOR J. MAYER

The Ohio State University

M. JAMES KOZLOW

University of British Columbia, Vancouver

Introduction

Time-series single-subject designs for use in intensive studies in learning were introduced in a report of an investigation by Mayer and Lewis (1979). That report includes a rationale for use of such designs in science education studies. It also describes an evaluation of the use of time-series single-subject designs in an intensive testing situation. The dependent variable used was student attitude toward the science class and the independent variable, teaching methods. The major conclusions were that a five-item semantic differential could be developed to be reliable when used in the design, and that the design could produce valid information on variation in student attitudes due to instructional methodologies. The relative success of this first full-scale effort to use the design in a classroom situation encouraged the first author to modify the design for measuring concept learning as well as attitudes.

The study reported here is the development and evaluation of an intensive single-subject time-series design for use in studying learning of concepts. It focuses on answering two questions: (1) Can procedures for measuring concept learning on a daily basis be devised that will interfere little with the normal classroom routine and take a minimum of time away from instruction? (2) Can such procedures yield valid information on the learning of a science concept? To answer these questions an intensive descriptive study was designed to investigate learning of the concept of crustal evolution.

Procedures

The two subjects chosen for the study were two eighth-grade earth-science classes in a junior high school situated in a central Ohio suburban community. The students were from families representing a broad range of socioeconomic backgrounds. The two classes were taught by the same teacher, the science department chairman. He normally maintained a very informal classroom with almost all instruction of a student-centered, small group, laboratory, or activity-oriented nature.

A multiple-group single-intervention design was adapted from that defined by Glass, Willson and Gottman (1975; pp. 39–41):

$$\text{Class A} \ldots O_5 \ O_6 \ O_7 \ O_8 \ O_9 \ I \ O_{10} \ldots I \ O_{17} \ O_{18} \ O_{19} \ O_{20} \ O_{21} \ldots$$
$$\text{Class B} \ldots O_5 \ O_6 \ O_7 \ O_8 \ O_9 \ I \ O_{10} \ldots I \ O_{17} \ O_{18} \ O_{19} \ O_{20} \ O_{21} \ldots$$

©1980 by the National Association for Research in Science Teaching

Published by John Wiley & Sons

0022-4308/80/0017-0455$01.00

Daily observations (0) were made in each of the subjects (Class A and Class B) for a period of 26 days. The intervention (I) stage, days 9 to 18, consisted of instruction using a 10-day unit on crustal evolution. The eight days prior to the intervention constituted the baseline stage, which was established to identify any systematic variation in student knowledge of the concept of crustal evolution. The eight days following the end of the intervention constituted the followup stage.

In designing the procedure for the collection of data on changes in understanding of the concept of crustal evolution, multiple-choice items were chosen. According to Ebel (1972; pp. 187–188), they are the most highly regarded and widely used form of objective testing. He states that they are adaptable to the measurement of most important educational outcomes including knowledge, understanding, and judgment, the expected levels of learning science concepts. Experience with the use of multiple-choice items also indicated that students were able to respond to them rapidly. Two approaches for collecting data were developed using multiple-choice items. The first required all students to respond to the same three items on a given day, with different three-item tests given on successive days. The advantages over the second method were that it was much simpler and less time-consuming to develop the instrument. And, since all students took the same test on the same day, their scores could be compared. The second method required students to respond to one item, with every student getting a different item on a given day. Using this method, the effects of any inherent differences in the difficulty of items upon the data could be minimized. Also, it would take the least student time for completion.

The concept of crustal evolution was chosen for instruction during the intervention; this was the independent variable. It was appropriate for the earth science classes involved in the investigation and yet the concept was relatively unfamiliar to students in those classes. Three broad objectives were defined, encompassing crustal evolution. Each of these was further subdivided into two to four specific objectives for the purpose of developing an instructional unit and test items.

An attempt was then made to generate an item universe, that is, all of the items possible that would measure understanding of the concept, the dependent variable. Three individuals, a graduate student in earth science education, a teacher teaching eighth-grade earth-science, and the first author, independently developed as many items as possible relating to the specific and general objectives. The resulting items were examined for duplication, consistency with objectives, wording, and structure. An item pool of 48 items was the result.

A unit was developed concurrent with the development of the item pool. The objectives were used to identify appropriate teaching materials for 10 days of instruction. They were grouped such that a two- or three-day instructional sequence focused on a single group of objectives. Instruction was carefully structured through the use of student guides to activities and discussions and teachers guides.

When the unit was completed it was carefully compared with the item pool to ensure content validity. The unit was then piloted with four eighth-grade earth-science classes. The item pool was randomly divided into two parts. Each part was given to two of the classes (about 50 students) as a posttest of the unit. The unit was redesigned as a result of teacher feedback. The item pool was extensively modified from item-analysis information. Some items were deleted and others were revised. Additional items were developed through word substitution in existing items. An effort was also made to insure that there was an equal number of items relating to each of the three broad unit objectives. The final item pool consisted of 54 items.

The two approaches described earlier were used to obtain daily measures of student understanding of crustal evolution. Class A responded to the *one-item instrument,* which consisted of a single item for each student, randomly drawn from the item pool. Each student was assigned a different item on a given day. A new random assignment of items was made each day and no student was given the same item more than once throughout the 26 days of data collection. Class B responded to the *three-item instrument*, in which one item was drawn randomly from items representing each of the three unit objectives. Every student was given the same three-item test on a given day and different tests were given on successive days.

Two forms of a *crustal evolution posttest*, to be administered at the end of the intervention, were generated from the item pool. Each form consisted of 32 items, including 10 items that were common to both forms. The 10 common items were randomly selected from the complete pool and the remaining items were then randomly assigned to alternate forms one item at a time. The KR 20 reliabilities were Form 1 (Class A), .77 and Form 2 (Class B), .71.

An individual from the research project staff observed both classes every day during the intervention. Information was recorded on the concurrent use of the unit in the two classes and on the time taken for the administration of the data-collecting instruments.

Analysis and Interpretation of Data

Were procedures for measuring concept learning developed that interfered little with normal classroom routine and that took a minimum of class time? This, of necessity, is a judgmental question. However, the log of classroom observations indicated that the one-item procedure took an average of less than two minutes of class time to administer and the three-item instrument only slightly longer. Once the teacher grew accustomed to administering the instruments, it became a part of the daily classroom routine, and therefore, resulted in minimum disruption.

Did the data collecting result in valid data? To determine this a form of concurrent validity was used. Any standard psychology text illustrates learning curves where the amount of information learned increases over the period of time during which instruction takes place. After cessation of instruction, the curve drifts downward due to forgetting. If the data collection techniques are valid, similar patterns should be noted—during intervention, a growth in learning, and during the followup, a downward drift in the learning curve. The data obtained from the daily administration of the multiple-choice instruments were analyzed to answer this question.

Data for those students who had missed three or more days of intervention were omitted from the analysis, leaving data for 19 students in Class A and for 21 students in Class B. The total enrollments in Classes A and B were 24 and 25 respectively.

The data were reduced to a single score for each class for each day. For Class A, which received the one-item tests, the number of students who responded correctly to their item was divided by the total number of students present. For Class B, which received the three-item tests, the student scores were first converted to a proportion by dividing the number correct by three and then the class mean was computed. The class scores for each day are plotted in Figure 1 for Class A and in Figure 2 for Class B. A visual examination of the two graphs reveals a positive trend during the intervention and a negative trend during the followup. The very high score on day 1 in Class A is very puzzling and thus far unexplained. Although not repeated with Class B, the first-day score in that class is also higher than would be anticipated.

To determine the significance of these patterns, correlation coefficients between day and class score were calculated for each of the three stages of data collection in each class. The means, standard deviations, and correlations for each stage for each class are included in Table I.

During baseline, Class A had a negative though not significant correlation of scores with

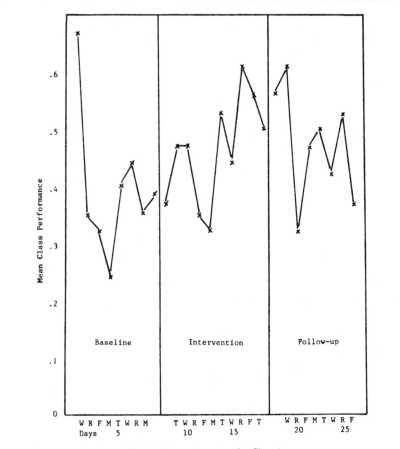

Fig. 1. Data on learning for Class A.

time, whereas Class B has a positive correlation significant at the .1 level. If the first-day scores are eliminated, both baselines have positive but not significant correlations with time. In both classes, there was a significant ($p \leqslant .05$) positive correlation of class score with time during the intervention stage, indicating an increased understanding of crustal evolution. Neither correlation during the followup stage was significant.

The data for Class A are those one might expect to reflect a typical learning curve. The data in the baseline do not exhibit any pattern or trend. The intervention data show a gradual positive and significant drift, and the followup data exhibit a gradual decline. This pattern demonstrated the validity of the one-item technique for obtaining data on knowledge acquisition using the intensive time-series design.

The data for Class B, however, though exhibiting the expected pattern during the intervention stage, do not for the other two. The baseline data have a positive, significant ($p \leqslant 0.1$) drift and there is an absence of drift in the followup data.

In order to investigate the possibility that daily fluctuations in performance may have been partially due to differences in the difficulty levels of the test items, the mean difficulty of all items used each day was calculated. Item difficulty indexes were obtained from the results of the crustal evolution posttests which were given at the end of the intervention stage. Since both classes did not respond to all items and since the two classes did not perform at the same level (Class A, $\bar{X} = 6.11$; Class B, $\bar{X} = 4.67$) on the 10 common items, it was necessary to make an adjustment for some items. The arbitrary decision was made to use Class B performance as the standard of item difficulty. The observed difficulty levels for the 32 items on the Class B form were used as difficulty indexes for these items. An adjustment was made to the 22 items which were on the Class A form but not on the Class B form. The relative performance of the two classes on the 10 common items was used to make the adjustment. The mean difficulty of these 10 items was .61 for Class A and .47 for Class B. The difference (.14) was substracted from the difficulty levels of the 22 items which were on the Class A form only, to get an estimate of what the difficulty levels for these items might have been if they had been given to Class B.

These difficulty indexes were used to calculate the mean difficulties of all items used each day with each class.

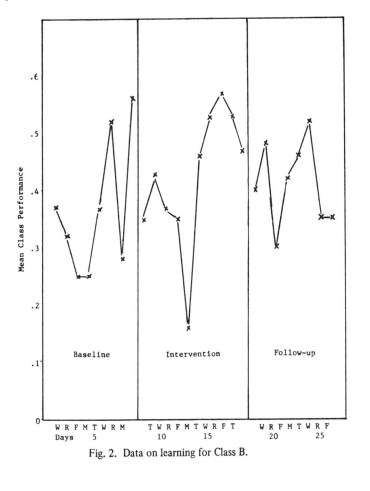

Fig. 2. Data on learning for Class B.

TABLE I

Correlations (r), Means ($\bar{x}$), and Standard Deviations (σ) for the Three Stages

Stage (days)	Class A			Class B		
	BL (8)	IN (10)	FU (8)	BL (8)	IN (10)	FU (8)
r (p<)	-.33(0.21)	.58(0.04)	-.47(0.15)	.51(0.10)	.55(0.05)	-.12(0.39)
$\bar{x}$	.40	.46	.47	.37	.42	.41
σ	.13	.09	.10	.12	.12	.07

One possible reason for the differences in the obtained learning curves for the two classes is that the daily fluctuations in mean item difficulty are more pronounced for Class B than for Class A. The mean difficulties for Class A range from .43 to .56, but for Class B they range from .30 to .66. The positive trend during the baseline stage for Class B could be due to the fact that the items used toward the end of this stage tended to be less difficult than those used at the beginning. The absence of a negative trend during the followup stage for Class B could be due to this same effect. Only 18 three-item tests were generated. The tests given during the followup stage were the same as those given during the baseline stage. This fluctuation of difficulty level from day to day is a serious limitation to the use of the three-item instrument for data collection.

The relatively high means during the first two days of the followup in both classes seem to indicate the occurrence of some type of "momentum effect" with the classes continuing to increase their knowledge about the topic after instruction in crustal evolution had ended. To determine the likelihood of a "momentum effect," the first two days of the followup were added to the intervention data for both classes. Table II summarizes the correlations and means. For Class A, the positive correlation for intervention plus two days was much higher than for the intervention alone and the negative trend for the followup minus two days was not as pronounced as it was for the eight days of followup. This would support some type of "momentum effect" occurring in the learning of concepts. The absence of these shifts in Class B could be due to the large fluctuations in item difficulty from day to day.

Could familiarization of students with the items account for the apparent learning curve? An examination of student data for Class A indicated that no student received the same item twice. In Class B, students did receive the same items in the baseline and followup

TABLE II

Correlations (r), Means ($\bar{x}$) and Standard Deviations (σ)
of Days 9-20 and 21-26

Days	Class A		Class B	
	9-20	21-26	9-20	21-26
r (p <)	0.71(.005)	0.23(0.33)	0.46(.07)	0.07(0.45)
$\bar{x}$	0.48	0.44	0.43	0.40
σ	0.10	0.09	0.11	0.08

EVALUATION OF TIME-SERIES DESIGN

stages. Students apparently did not learn the items, however, since Class B exhibited a greater decline in performance than Class A during the followup stage. It might be possible for item familiarity to result from discussion about items among class members. Since the items were not used for grading purposes, however, the major motivation for this would not be present. Also, neither the teacher nor the classroom observers noticed the occurrence of any discussions of items during the class period. It is possible that such discussions occurred after class, but this was fully 45 minutes after the items had been seen by the students. It seems most likely then that the curve represented by the data are indeed learning curves and not the result of item familiarization.

Conclusions

The results of this study demonstrate that a data-collecting procedure can be developed for measuring concept understanding in an intensive single-subject time-series design. The procedure took a minimum of class time, resulted in little disturbance of the usual class routine, and provided valid measurement of learning of the concept of crustal evolution. The results indicate that the one-item data collection procedure is more valid than the three-item procedure. The main problem with the three-item procedure is the large fluctuation in difficulty level of items from day to day.

References

Disinger, J. F., & Mayer, V. J. Student development in junior high school science. *Journal of Research in Science Teaching*, 1974, **11**, 149-155.

Ebel, R. L. *Essentials in educational measurement.* Englewood Cliffs, N.J.: Prentice-Hall, 1972.

Glass, G. V., Willson, V. L., & Gottman, J. M. *Design and analysis of time-series experiments.* Boulder, Colo.: Colorado Associated University Press, 1975.

Mayer, V. J., & Lewis, D. K. An evaluation of the use of a time-series single-subject design. *Journal of Research in Science Teaching*, 1979, **16**, 137-144.

Manuscript accepted November 20, 1979

MORE ON TIME SERIES DESIGNS:
A REANALYSIS OF MAYER AND KOZLOW'S DATA

VICTOR L. WILLSON

College of Education, Texas A&M University,
College Station, Texas 77843

Abstract

A recent article by Mayer and Kozlow introduces a time series experiment to science education researchers. This article examines in greater detail design considerations and re-analyzes their data using time series analysis.

The first applications of time series experimental methodology to science education research were reported by Mayer and Lewis (1979) and by Mayer and Kozlow (1980). This article discusses Mayer and Kozlow's work and presents a reanalysis of their data which is intended to be heuristic, not critical. (All data were supplied by Dr. Mayer and permission was granted to use the data.) Both design and analysis will be examined. It is important to distinguish time series experimental design from time series analysis. The former, as presented by Campbell and Stanley (1966) and detailed by Glass, Willson, and Gottman (1975), is concerned with structuring treatment conditions and observations over time to make causal inferences. Time series analysis is a set of statistical techniques from which an appropriate technique can be selected to analyze collected data in the framework of a time series design. Just as data from in a randomized experiment might be analyzed using a one-way analysis of variance or a Kruskal- Wallis *H*-test, data from a time series design may be subjected to several alternative analysis techniques.

Design Considerations

The design employed by Mayer and Kozlow is a multiple-group single intervention design with baseline, treatment period, and post-treatment follow-up. This design is eminently practical for school settings and can be set up and conducted easily by the classroom teacher. The independent variable is an indicator variable time series consisting typically of the value zero for each observation (daily in Mayer and Kozlow) during baseilne and nonzero during treatment. The values during treatment depend on the nature of the treatment. In the typical educational setting, knowledge gained through a curriculum is expected to follow an upward trend. In Figure 1 are various time series that might model educational treatments. The simplest are the ramp function in which knowledge is gained at a constant rate [Fig. 1(a)] and the step function [Fig. 1(b)] in which knowledge is gained in a short period (in a day, perhaps) and is maintained at a constant level. Forgetting during a post-treatment

© 1982 by the National Association for Research in Science Teaching
Published by John Wiley & Sons, Inc.   CCC 0022-4308/82/070571-05$01.50

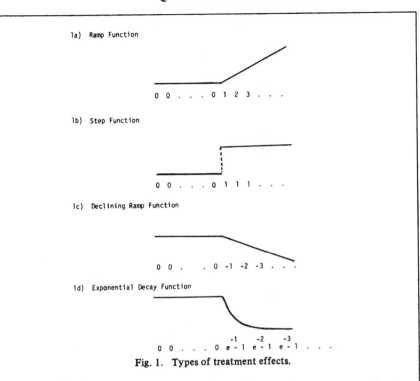

1a) Ramp Function

0 0 . . . 0 1 2 3 . . .

1b) Step Function

0 0 . . . 0 1 1 1 . . .

1c) Declining Ramp Function

0 0 .   . 0 -1 -2 -3 . . .

1d) Exponential Decay Function

0 0 . . . 0 e-1 e-1 e-1 . . .

Fig. 1.   Types of treatment effects.

period can be modeled by a declining ramp function [Fig. 1(c)], a downward step function, or an exponential decay [Fig. 1(d)] which is suggested by the psychological literature (Kintsch, 1970). More sophisticated learning curves employing logarithms or exponents can also be easily constructed. The dependent variable in a science education time series experiment is likely to be a cognitive or attitude measure. The dependent variable for time series analysis must be an interval or ratio score measured at approximately equal intervals (daily, weekly, etc.). When data "holes" occur, such as a holiday, the best procedure is to forecast a score for that time from the remaining data. Data points before and after the hole can be analyzed independently, each providing an estimate. These estimates are then weighted and averaged to produce the final estimate. Only data in a given treatment condition should be used to avoid confounding of treatment condition with the estimate. It is necessary to use a full data set since the statistical structure of time series analysis requires regular measurements, and parameters are conceived and estimated under this assumption. As long as the number of holes is small in relation to the total number of observations (perhaps less than 5%), no problem is likely to occur in this data estimation.

A practical need to maintain regularity in data points occurs when there is a recurrent, or seasonal effect: For example, in daily measurement of pupils it is not uncommon to have a correlation between scores five days apart, assuming five observations per week (weekends do not exist in education), which reflects activities, attitudes, and learning interests that vary during the week. It means that Mondays are more similar to each other than to any other days; the same is true for each other day. Removing even one day from such a series destroys this regularity and introduces spurious correlation between data at other intervals. In Mayer and Kozlow's data, two days were missing and should be estimated.

The construction of the dependent variable tests in science education was discussed well by Mayer and Kozlow. Since the use of the same tests or items on a daily basis is ruled out by memory effects, the use of item sampling is needed. Cooney and Willson (Note 1) presented a method to solve this problem: the application of matrix sampling of test items and students. In this solution not all children need to be tested each day (or whatever period is being used). Mayer and Kozlow chose to test each child each day with one item (class A) or three items (Class B) working from a fifty-four-item pool. An alternative is to allocate students and items randomly using a matrix sample. For example, using Mayer and Kozlow's classes, each class of about twenty-five students would be randomly split each week into five groups of five students. The pool of fifty-four items would be reduced to fifty and randomly split into five subtests. One group of students each day would receive a subtest for the five-day school week. The next week, items and students would be rerandomized until the testing period of six weeks was over. Cooney and Willson (Note 1) showed that this procedure produces a virtually identical time series to that which would have been produced if all students took each item each day.

Item difficulty variance can be controlled either by stratifying the item pool or by allowing items to vary randomly across the matrix sample. While the latter will increase error variance, it will be cheaper and simpler if attention is paid to the item generation. Thus, poor items are removed before conduct of the experiment, as was done in Mayer and Kozlow's study.

Attitude items may be similarly treated, but there should be greater concern for homogeneity or factorial simplicity of the pool of items. Use of Thurstone-scaled statements may have a real advantage since the matrix sample may be stratified by range of scale values.

Ratings by observers, performance counts, or sociometric measures may also be used in a time series design. One caveat about counts is that currently used time series analysis techniques do not work well with rare frequency distributions, so dependent variables which are expected to be constant much of the time are not compatible with time series analysis. Other techniques based on the Poisson distribution may eventually be refined for use with time series data.

Analysis

Time series analysis techniques can be classified first as parametric or nonparametric. Since little has been published on nonparametric techniques, only parametric techniques will be discussed further. With these techniques data may be described in a time domain or frequency domain. Frequency domain models are based on spectral analysis, which typically requires 100 or more observations, making spectral analysis inappropriate for Mayer and Kozlow's study. Time domain models for time series analysis have been treated in a general case, called the autoregressive integrated moving average (ARIMA) model, by Box and Jenkins (1976). Other treatments of the ARIMA model have been given by Glass, Willson, and Gottman (1975) and McCleary and Hay (1980).

In this section, a reanalysis of Mayer and Kozlow's (1980) knowledge data collected on two classes over a 26-day period is presented. Their treatment was a junior high unit on crustal evolution presented to two classes. The program used is PROC AUTOREG of the Statistical Analysis System (Barr et al., 1979). The SAS procedure does not handle the entire ARIMA class of time series models (see Glass et al., 1975) but proved adequate for Mayer and Kozlow's data.

The Mayer and Kozlow (1980) study was analyzed using a regression model relating daily achievement to treatment condition (baseline or treatment) and forgetting condition (baseline or forgetting). The treatment condition was assumed to produce a ramp function for learning [Fig. 1(a)] and the forgetting condition a declining ramp function. In addition, error in the regression model was assumed to follow the form of a simple ARIMA process, an autoregressive process of order 1. This means that the errors are treated as if correlated, each with its successor. The need to account for such correlation has been detailed in Glass et al. (1975) and mainly concerns obtaining correct denominators for tests of hypothesis of the regression weights for the treatments.

A check on the adequacy of the autoregressive model for errors is conducted through examination of residuals of fit to the regression model, which form a new time series. If the model is correct, the residual time series should consist of random, uncorrelated scores. A time series analysis of these scores assumes a zero mean and no correlation between any score and any successors beyond that likely by chance.

The analysis discussed above was applied to Mayer and Kozlow's (1980) data. Several details must be discussed before results are given, however. In their class A data, the first data point is greater than any other and quite extreme, as it was over four standard deviations from the mean (see Mayer & Kozlow, 1980, p. 458). It was considered an outlier in this analysis and discarded as completely atypical. Consequently, one might apply windsorized t-distributions to all that follows (Winer, 1971, pp. 51-53). This would reduce degrees of freedom by 2. For this analysis, it was assumed that the series for class A began one day later than that in Mayer and Kozlow (1980).

A second point is that significance tests in an experiment such as this should be directional. That is, the slope of the ramp function for treatment is expected to rise, not fall, so that the alternative hypothesis to no change is a significant, positive slope. Similarly, only a negative forgetting curve slope is tested. This greatly increases the power for the tests, which is important when there are few data points, as in the Mayer and Kozlow study.

Results

In class A in Mayer and Kozlow's study (1980), each student got one item of the crustal evolution item pool each day and the gain in knowledge from beginning of treatment to end has a significant slope ($t = 1.959$, $df = 22$), at $p < 0.01$, while the slope for forgetting, although in a downward direction, was not significant ($t = 1.163$, $df = 22$). The estimate of pretreatment test knowledge was about 41%, with a 0.7% average gain per day.

For class B, which received three item tests each day from the item pool, the treatment gain was significant at $p < 0.10$ ($t = 1.35$, $df = 22$) with an average daily gain of 0.6% and the forgetting slope parameter was nonsignificant ($t = 0.20$, $df = 22$). The pretreatment knowledge on the test items averaged 38%, not significantly different from the other class. There was greater variability in the difficulty of items used in class B (Mayer & Kozlow, 1980, p. 460) than in class A. This is expected to produce greater daily variation and will reduce the power of detect effects, which apparently occurred with the class B data.

This analysis generally supports the analysis performed by Mayer and Kozlow but puts the results on a somewhat firmer statistical footing. Mayer and Kozlow chose to examine correlation coefficients (standardized slopes) for the three intervention conditions. In general, it is hazardous to do this since any statistical comparison of the slopes depends on the degree of correlatedness of the residuals, as noted earlier. In this particular study, the autoregressive parameters were nonsignificant (class A, $t = 0.68$, $df = 24$; class B, $t = -0.65$, $df = 25$), and the residuals were uncorrelated. This means that ordinary least squares regression was used to analyze the data. It is never safe to assume, however, that this condition holds. Glass et al. (1975), for example, reported that over three-quarters of a sample of 100 behavioral time series they examined required time series analyses because of autocorrelation of some form.

Discussion

This article is designed to further familiarize science education researchers with the utility of time series designs and to present an example of formal analysis. It has not been presented as a primer on time series design or analysis. Glass et al. (1975), Cook and Campbell (1979), or McCleary and Hay (1980) should be studied for that purpose. Time series experimental design can be readily mastered by a careful reader. Time series analysis is quite complex in the general case and requires grounding in statistics. It is further complicated by the lack of easily accessible software. Major statistical packages are adding time series analysis programs, and this restriction will soon be lifted. Analysis will then be simpler. It is well to remember in this field that analysis should be as simple as possible, but no simpler, else it becomes simpleminded.

Acknowledgment

Thanks are given to Dr. V. J. Mayer for his assistance in providing the data and in explaining their collection and layout.

Reference Note

1: Cooney, J., & Willson, V. L. The use of time series designs and multiple matrix sampling as evaluation tools. Paper presented at AERA Annual Meeting, Boston, April 10, 1980.

References

Barr, A. J., Goodnight, J. H., Sall, J. P., Blair, W. M., & Chilko, D. M. *Statistical analysis system user's guide 1979 edition.* Raleigh, NC: ASA Institute, Inc., 1979.

Box, G. E. P., & Jenkins, G. M. *Time-series analysis: Forcasting and control.* San Francisco: Holden-Day, 1976.

Campbell, D. T., & Stanley, J. C. *Experimental and quasi-experimental designs and research.* Chicago: Rand-McNally, 1966.

Glass, G. V., Willson, V. L., & Gottman, J. M. *Design and analysis of time series experiments.* Colorado Associated University Press, 1975.

Kintsch, W. *Learning, memory, and cognitive processes.* New York: Wiley, 1970.

Mayer, V. J., & Lewis, D. K. An evaluation of the use of a time-series single-subject design. *Journal of Research in Science Teaching,* 1979, **16**, 137–144.

Mayer, V. J., & Kozlow, M. J. An evaluation of a time-series single-subject design used in an intensive study of concept understanding. *Journal of Research in Science Teaching,* 1980, **17**, 455–461.

McCleary, R., & Hay, R. A., Jr. *Applied time series analysis.* Beverly Hills, CA: Sage Publications, 1980.

Winer, B. J. *Statistical principles in experimental design.* New York: McGraw-Hill, 1971.

Manuscript accepted April 21, 1982

American Educational Research Association

MEMBERSHIP APPLICATION

Mail this form with your check to: AERA
P.O. Box 19700
Washington, DC 20036

Please type
all information   Name:

☐ New
☐ Renewal

Last   First   Middle Initial

Mailing Address:

City   State   Zip or foreign postal code

Type of Membership Requested

	1 Year	2 Year
[ ] Voting	$45 00	$ 85 00
[ ] Family	$68 00	$128 00
[ ] Student	$20 00	—
[ ] Associate	$45 00	$ 85 00
[ ] International Affiliate	$45 00	$ 85 00

If you reside outside the United States, please add $5 00 per year to dues for postage and handling ($10 00 for 2 years)

Publications

In addition to the *Educational Researcher* and the *Annual Meeting Program*, I wish to receive as part of my membership dues the following two publications

[ ] *American Educational Research Journal* (quarterly)
[ ] *Review of Educational Research* (quarterly)
[ ] *Journal of Educational Statistics* (quarterly)
[ ] *Educational Evaluation and Policy Analysis* (quarterly)
[ ] *Review of Research in Education* (annual, casebound)

In addition to these two, I wish to subscribe at the special member rate of $12 each a year to the following

[ ] *American Educational Research Journal*
[ ] *Review of Educational Research*
[ ] *Journal of Educational Statistics*
[ ] *Educational Evaluation and Policy Analysis*
[ ] *Review of Research in Education*

Divisional Membership Requested

One divisional membership (two for husband and wife members) is included in membership dues Additional divisional affiliations are $1 00 each per year ($2 00 each for 2 years)

[ ] A:	Administration
[ ] B:	Curriculum Studies
[ ] C	Instruction and Learning
[ ] D:	Measurement and Research Methodology
[ ] E	Counseling and Human Development
[ ] F	History and Historiography
[ ] G	Social Context of Education
[ ] H:	School Evaluation and Program Development
[ ] I:	Education in the Professions
[ ] J	Postsecondary Education
[ ] K	Teaching and Teacher Education

Applicant's
Signature:

Student Membership

Proof of graduate student status or the endorsement of a voting member who is a faculty member at the student's institution is required

Signature of
Endorser

New Member
Sponsor

Address

City   State   Zip

Payment Enclosed

Membership dues	$
International postage & handing*	
Additional divisional affiliations*	
Additional subscriptions*	
Total	$

*For 2-year memberships, double the fees (international postage and handling—$10 00, additional subscriptions—$24 00, additional divisional affiliations—$2 00 each)

For Office Only

Member Number   Member Type

Date Pd

AM   YS   Exp   Source
☐   ☐ ☐   ☐   ☐ ☐

Dues include a subscription to *Educational Researcher* (valued at $10 00) and two additional publications valued at $12 00 each